PRINCIPLES OF CORPORATE
INSOLVENCY LAW

by

Roy Goode

THOMSON

SWEET & MAXWELL

First edition 1990
Second edition 1997

Published in 2005 by
Sweet & Maxwell Limited of
100 Avenue Road London NW3 3PF
http:/www.sweetandmaxwell.co.uk
Typeset by LBJ Typesetting Ltd
Printed in England by Athenaeum Press Ltd, Gateshead

A CIP catalogue record for this book is available from the British Library

ISBN 0421 930209

For Catherine to whom I owe so much

Preface

When I first introduced what was then a half course on corporate insolvency law at Queen Mary College over 20 years ago it was in the hope rather than the expectation that the students would find the subject as exciting as I did. I was agreeably surprised to find that they appeared to enjoy it, and as the course developed the class size steadily grew. The subject is now firmly established in the academic postgraduate curriculum and is currently taught at a number of law schools, including Oxford.

Part of the fascination of corporate insolvency lies in the fact that it is inseparable from the general law of property and obligations. Since the starting position of insolvency law is respect for pre-insolvency entitlements, the subject cannot be understood without a good grasp of the general law, particularly the law relating to property, trusts, equity and security interests; and in all of these fields the law is in a state of flux. Thus in insolvency cases the courts are periodically exercised by that most fundamental of questions: what is property? It is not possible to avoid all the minutiae of this complex subject, but for students there is a particular interest in the clash of opposing principles and policies, which not infrequently arouse fierce discussion in the classroom. And that is as it should be. An essential part of postgraduate education lies in the cut and thrust of debate in seminars and the development of an awareness of the complexities and contradictions of the law. One of the aims of this book is to convey the intellectual excitement of the subject and the opportunities it offers for enriching the student's knowledge of the general law and the difficulties confronting the law in striking a fair balance between competing interests.

This has been a period of intensive legislative and judicial activity. The Insolvency Act 2000 was swiftly followed by the Enterprise Act 2000, which largely abolished new administrative receiverships, replacing them with administration, in respect of which both the principal Insolvency Act and the Insolvency Rules were entirely recast. The Act also introduced provisions requiring a prescribed part of floating charge assets to be surrendered for the benefit of ordinary unsecured creditors. These provisions are not free from ambiguity and it remains to be seen how they will be interpreted. A new section 1A of the Insolvency Act enables directors of a small eligible company to obtain a moratorium, but the process, set out in a new Schedule A1 of some 45 paragraphs, is so tortuous that it is hard to see why insolvency practitioners would want to make use of it.

To read the amended Insolvency Act 1986 it no longer suffices to be a lawyer; it is necessary to become a physical geographer in order to find one's way around provisions which are randomly dispersed among the body of the Act, the bizarrely numbered Schedules A1 and B1 and the Insolvency Rules, with seemingly no logic in the distribution nor any conception that it might be useful if all the provisions dealing with the same subject were brought together in clearly stated requirements. So if one reads paragraph 23 of Schedule B1 dealing with restrictions on the power of directors or the company to appoint an administrator there is neither an explicit statement nor the slightest hint of any requirement that the company must be unable or likely to become unable to pay its debts. Indeed, there is no provision anywhere in the Act that says this is a condition of such an appointment. It comes in by inference as a matter to be included in the statutory declaration under paragraph 27(2). And those who enjoy finding their way round mazes might give Hampton Court a miss and try their hands at tracking down the meaning of "hire-purchase agreement" in paragraph 43(3). All that is required is perseverance and a passion for concentric circles.

Many other important legislative changes have taken place or are impending. They include the settlement finality Directive and the financial collateral Directive, providing significant immunities from insolvency law for market and exchange contracts; the EC Insolvency Regulation, replacing in almost identical form the ill-fated European Insolvency Convention, which had foundered on the twin rocks of John Major's refusal of co-operation with Europe because of the row over British beef and a desire not to prejudice the UK's sovereignty over Gibraltar; and the UNCITRAL Model Law on Cross-Border Insolvency, which it is planned to bring into force in the UK on April Fool's day 2006.

The courts, too, have been hard at work, with a cornucopia of cases covering everything from disclaimer of waste licences to voidable transactions, from wrongful trading and the disqualification of directors to the provision of assistance to foreign courts and the extent of jurisdiction over oversea companies, and from receivership and administration to a company voluntary arrangement for the Dean and Chapter of Bradford Cathedral— the first ecclesiastical feat of its kind and, sad to say, the last as a perceived loophole in the system was closed. The Insolvency Regulation has also attracted its fair share of case law, mainly focused on the identification of the debtor company's centre of main interests (COMI) but also addressing difficult issues relating to the time when proceedings are deemed to have been opened and the effect of a change of the COMI before the hearing of a winding-up petition.

As an indication of the speed of development, the decision of Peter Smith J. in *Krasner v McMath* on the insolvency super-priority of protective awards and claims for payment in lieu of notice was handed down on July 25, 2005 only to be overruled by the Court of Appeal in *Re Ferrotech* on August 9! Through the good offices of Ruth Pedley, of CMS Cameron McKenna, I was just in time to include a reference to both of these unreported cases.

All these developments, coupled with a range of new ideas, have necessitated a substantial amount of rewriting. The treatment of assets comprising the company's property has been substantially expanded; the chapter on administration has been completely rewritten and considerably enlarged; the analysis of vulnerable transactions has been refined in the light of major decisions of the House of Lords and lower courts. There is a new chapter on the Insolvency Regulation, which deals with the applicable law, jurisdiction, recognition and enforcement in relation to intra-Community insolvencies and raises complex issues as to determination of the applicable law and its relationship to the *lex concursus*. A number of these have not yet come before English courts but I have sought wherever possible to offer an analysis which combines reasonable textual interpretation with an approach that leads to a sensible outcome. The concluding chapter, on international insolvency, has been substantially rewritten to reflect modern theories of jurisdiction and to provide a treatment of the UNCITRAL Model Law. With the needs of the practitioner in mind I have also included a set of appendices of primary materials, including the text of the Insolvency Regulation, the amending Regulation of April 12, 2005, the invaluable Virgós-Schmit Report on the European Insolvency Convention from which the Regulation is derived and which is essential to an understanding of the Regulation, and the UNCITRAL Model Law.

With all this legislative and judicial activity going on, I find myself increasingly in sympathy with Baron Bramwell who, on being told that the line he was proposing to take in a case was at complete variance with one of his own earlier decisions, replied: "The matter does not appear to me now as it appears to have appeared to me then."

In writing this, my final edition, I have received valuable assistance both from the writings of other scholars, here and abroad, and more directly from a number of people whom I consulted. They are identified in a separate page of acknowledgments. To all of them I am greatly indebted. I should like to say in conclusion, as so often in the past, that this new edition could not have been written without the constant support of my wife Catherine, who has shown extraordinary tolerance towards this obsessive author and made no protest when almost every living room in our small house was taken up with manuscript, proofs, books and other writing paraphernalia. But this is the last new edition to come from my pen. It is time to make way for younger and more vigorous scholars who will bring new ideas to a subject which I hope they will find as absorbing as I have over the past 20 years.

Roy Goode

Oxford

August 12, 2005.

Acknowledgements

AN EXPRESSION OF THANKS

Every author is, of course, in debt to those who have gone before him or her in the field. They are too numerous to mention individually here, but references to their works are to be found throughout the book.

I should like to express my deep appreciation to my friend and colleague Professor Dan Prentice, of Pembroke College, Oxford, who took on the burdensome task of reading the entire manuscript as well as a substantial proportion of the proofs and saved me from a number of egregious errors. Thanks are also due to Robert Stevens, of Lady Margaret Hall, for a number of perceptive comments, and to Nicholas Anson, a postgraduate student on the BCL course, who raised several interesting issues and also alerted me to some recent Australian decisions, as did Oren Bigos, of Mallesons, Melbourne, Australia, himself a former BCL student, who had previously assisted me with proof reading of my book on commercial law. Other Oxford colleagues to whom I owe thanks are Professor Andrew Burrows, who alerted me to relevant literature on insolvency and restitution, and Louise Gullifer, who pressed me hard on the meaning of the statutory provisions relating to the prescribed part and did much to clarify my thinking.

I owe a particular debt to Vanessa Mak, a doctoral student in Oxford, for her Herculean labours both in literature searches and in meticulous proof-reading. Friends and colleagues in the practicing profession have also been particularly helpful. Ruth Pedley organised a lunch-time meeting with the insolvency partners of her firm CMS Cameron MCKenna to discuss my draft chapter on administration, and from them I received a number of valuable insights that would otherwise have eluded me. A particular word of appreciation is due to Ashley Smith, who went through the chapter with a fine toothcomb and alerted me to a number of errors and omissions which I hope I have succeeded in rectifying. A similar service was provided by the insolvency partners of Slaughter and May, through the good offices of Sarah Paterson, in relation to the chapters on the European Insolvency Regulation and international insolvency.

I am indebted also to Stephen Leinster, of the DTI Insolvency Service, who masterminded the passage of the insolvency provisions of the Enterprise Act 2002, and whose encyclopaedic knowledge of the legislation proved immensely helpful. To Dr Rizwaan Mokal, of University College London, himself the author of a new and important book on the theory of corporate insolvency law, I should like to express my thanks for a number of perceptive comments and for letting me have advance sight of his book, to which I have made several references. Professor Ian Fletcher, one of the world's leading experts on international insolvency, gave me the benefit of his knowledge on aspects of the Insolvency Regulation and advance sight of the second edition of his work on international insolvency. I have also continued to draw on the immense knowledge of Professor Jay Westbrook, of the University of Texas Austin, who is ever available to solve a knotty problem. Professor Herbert Kronke, Secretary General of UNIDROIT, also gave me some helpful thoughts concerning the Insolvency Regulation, while Professor Alex Flessner gave me an update on the German decisions in the *Eurofood* litigation.

Finally, I should like to express my warm thanks to the Sweet and Maxwell team: Eleanor Norton, the publishing editor, Claire Patient, the editor, and Brenda Nicholls, the Production Controller, and to Amjed Ghafoor, who prepared the tables, Robert Spicer, who prepared the index, and Laurie Burgess, of LBJ Typesetting, who typeset the work.

Preface to the Second Edition

In the first edition of this book I sought to lay out the fundamental principles of corporate insolvency law and to demonstrate that it is not simply a collection of rules but possesses a structure and concepts a knowledge of which is essential to a true understanding of the subject. So much has happened over the past seven years, and so many new ideas have surfaced, that this new edition is almost a new book. I have rewritten and reorganised most of the original text, and substantially expanded both the general theoretical treatment and the analysis of particular issues and statutory provisions.

There are four entirely new chapters. The first, dealing with the philosophical foundations of corporate insolvency law, examines the different perceptions of the role of corporate insolvency law and the interests which it is designed to protect. There is a new chapter on the winding-up process which focuses on the principles governing entitlement to a winding-up order: *locus standi*, the existence of grounds for winding-up and a material interest in the order being made. The third new chapter briefly examines the complex but extremely important subject of set-off and netting. Decisions of the House of Lords and Court of Appeal have radically changed the perception of rights of set-off on insolvency. Also dealt with are arrangements for the pre-insolvency netting of obligations by novations, close-outs and payment netting. The fourth new chapter gives a brief treatment of some of the key issues arising in cross-border insolvency and the various steps taken by legislation, conventions and judicial co-operation to bring about orderly cross-border reorganisations and arrangements.

In preparing this new edition I owe a particular debt of gratitude to my friend and colleague Dan Prentice, with whom I share a postgraduate course on corporate insolvency law and whose meticulous reading of the typescript and detailed comments saved me from a number of errors. I am also indebted to my friend Nick Segal, of Allen & Overy, who performed a like service and who has been so generous in imparting the fruits of his long experience. The students themselves have provided a rich harvest of ideas which I have sought to capture before they were lost to an ever-fading memory. I should also like to express my thanks to the Society of Practitioners of Insolvency and its form President, Gordon Stewart, for kindly supplying me with copies of the Society's annual surveys and other material; to the Department of Trade and Industry for statistical information and copies of annual reports on companies; to Jane Whitfield, one of my postgraduate students at Oxford, for her very effective research assistance over the Long Vacation in searches in legal literature on insolvency; and to Sweet and Maxwell for piloting through this new edition so smoothly. Finally, a word of gratitude to that long line of corporate debtors without whom this book could never have been written.

This new edition is dedicated to my wife Catherine. For nearly 33 years, despite all the pressures of her own demanding work, she has given me unstinting encouragement and support and has borne with good humour and grace the rigours of marriage to an absent-minded academic who at certain critical points in the process of authorship has engulfed our small home with law reports, textbooks and manuscripts. My debt to her is immeasurable.

St. John's College,   Roy Goode
Oxford,
July 9, 1997.

Preface to the First Edition

Corporate insolvency law is a subject of peculiar fascination; one, indeed, of which universities in this country are in the course of acquiring practical experience! Part of its intellectual interest lies in its close relationship to company law and to the law relating to security interests in personal property, which come together in that most brilliant of equity's creations, the floating charge. But for the scholar it possesses the additional attraction of encompassing a wide range of complex, not to say controversial, policy issues which are only now beginning to receive in this country the attention the deserve.

This book had its origins in my Commercial Law Lectures 1989, a set of five lectures on corporate insolvency law delivered at the Centre for Commercial Law Studies, Queen Mary College, in January and February 1989. In addition to substantially revising and expanding these I have added four more topics, resulting in a work of nine chapters and 219 pages of text.

My principal objective in this book, as in others in the same series, has been to concentrate on fundamentals: to stand back from the minutiae of the statutory provisions governing the insolvency of companies and to identify the concepts and principles of corporate insolvency law, showing how these both implement and modify the general law relating to property and obligations. This is an unusual approach but I make no apology for it, because I firmly believe that corporate insolvency law cannot be adequately comprehended without a grasp of the basic principles of property and contract law and of equitable obligation. Also central to corporate insolvency law is the principle of *pari passu* distribution, which can itself be understood only if one has a clear perception of the concept of *value* and of what constitutes an unjust enrichment of a particular creditor or other party at the expense of the general body of creditors. In concentrating on fundamental principles I have sought to provide for insolvency practitioners, academic lawyers and students in this country and in other parts of the Commonwealth a framework of the kind that Professor Thomas H. Jackson of Harvard University has furnished for American practitioners and scholars in his outstanding work *The Logic and Limits of Bankruptcy Law* published in 1986.

But this book is not concerned solely with general principle; it also examines the provisions of the Insolvency Act 1986 and related legislation and case law with what I hope is sufficient analytical rigour and detail to be of assistance in the resolution of everyday problems confronting the insolvency practitioner, and to provide a reliable guide to those intending to move into this field. Particular attention has been devoted to three topics: vulnerable transactions (transactions at an undervalue, preferences, etc.), which will continue to play a prominent role in corporate insolvency; receivership and the new administration order procedure; and improper trading, with particular reference to wrongful trading and the duties and liabilities of directors. The current legislation is still very young, so that we are all feeling our way and it will be many years before certain key problems are fully worked out by the courts and by writers in the field.

I should like to express my particular indebtedness to John Gibson of Price Waterhouse for his invaluable assistance in providing information and in commenting in detail on the manuscript; to Nick Segal of Allen and Overy for a like service and for a number of helpful ideas; to Neil Cooper of Robson Rhodes for material supplied; to Mark Homan, also of Price Waterhouse, for supplying me with a copy of his admirable survey on the administration order procedure to which I have made numerous references in the text; and to my brother-in-law Philip Rueff, a member of the Bar, for bringing to my attention some cases in the criminal law which I would otherwise have overlooked. Finally, I should like to express once again my thanks to Sweet & Maxwell, for guiding this new creation safely to publication, replete with tables and index.

The law is stated on the basis of information available to me at November 24, 1989.

St. John's College   Roy Goode
Oxford,
January 1990.

Contents

Sources of Definitions

A finding aid to selected defined terms relating to corporate insolvency

Abbreviations

CA   = Companies Act 1985

CA 1989   = Companies Act 1989

CCA   = Consumer Credit Act 1974

CCDA   = Company Directors Disqualification Act 1986

FMIR 1996   = Financial Markets and Insolvency Regulations 1996

FMISFR   = Financial Markets and Insolvency (Settlement Finality) Regulations 1999

IA   = Insolvency Act 1986

IR   = Insolvency Rules 1986

Note: the sources listed below are confined to companies and to statutory provisions relating to England and Wales. They do not include sources of definitions relating to bankruptcy or to provisions confined to Scotland. The provisions relating to administration are those contained in Sch.B1 to the Insolvency Act 1986, which take effect under the revised s.8 of the Act and, with certain exceptions, replace the original Part II of the Act.

"Acquired property"	IA Sch.B1, para.70(3)
"Administration order"	IA Sch.B1, para.10
"Administrative receiver"	IA ss.29(2), 251, 388(4), Sch.11 para.1(2); CDDA s.22(3); CA 1989 s.190(1)
"Administrator"	IA Sch.B1, paras 1(1), 75(5), 111(1)
"Associate"	IA ss.249, 435, 436
"Business"	IA s.436
"Become insolvent"	CDDA ss.6(2), 7, 9(2), Sch.1.
"Beginning of the moratorium"	IA Sch.A1, paras 1, 8(1)
"Capital market arrangement"	IA s.72B(2), Sch.2A, para.1
"Capital market investment"	IA s.72B(2), Sch.2A, paras 2, 3

"Centre of main interests"	IR, r.13.13(8); EC Regulation, Preamble, para.13
"Chattel leasing agreement"	IA s.251
"Collateral security"	IA Sch.A1, para.23(6); FMISFR reg.2(1)
"Collateral security charge"	IA s.72F(c), Sch.A1, para.23(6); FMISFR, reg.2(1)
"Commencement of winding up"	IA ss.86, 129
"Company"	CA ss.705, 735; IA ss.111(4)(a), 216(8), 217(6), 388(4), 435(11); CDDA s.22(2).
"Conditional sale agreement"	IA s.436; CCA s.189(1)
"Connected with a company"	IA s.249
"Creditors"	IR rr.4.44, 11.1(2)(b)
"Debt"	IR r.13.12
"Director"	CA s.741; IA ss.214(7), 251; CDDA ss.6(3), 7, 22(4)
"The EC Regulation"	IA s.436
"Enters into a transaction with a person at an undervalue"	IA ss.238(4), 423
"Extortionate" (credit transaction)	IA s.244(3)
"Fixed security"	IA s.71
"Financed project"	IA s.72E(2)(a)
"Floating charge"	IA s.251, Sch.B1, para.111(1)
"Give a preference"	IA s.239(4)
"Goes into insolvent liquidation"	IA ss.214(6), 216(7)
"Goes into liquidation"	IA s.247(2); CDDA s.22(3)
"Hire-purchase agreement"	IA s.436; CCA s.189(1); IA Sch.B1, para.111(1) CCA s.189(1)
"In administration"	IA Sch.B1, paras 1(2)(a), 111(1)
"Insolvency"	IA s.247(1); CDDA s.22(3)
"Insolvent winding up"	IR rr.4.151(a), 4.173(2)
"Involved in the management of a company"	IA s.217(4)

"Liability"   IA s.382(4); IR r.13.12(4)

"Main proceedings"   IR r.13.13(10)

"Market contract"   CA 1989 s.155

"Market charge"   IA s.72F(a); CA 1989 s.173(1),(4)

"Market value"   IA Sch.B1, para.111(1)

"Moratorium"   IA s.1A, Sch.A1, para.1

"Mutual dealings"   IR, r.2.85(2)

"Office holder"   IA ss.233(1), 234(1), 235(1), 238(1), 246(1); CDDA s.7(3)

"Onerous property"   IA s.178(3)

"Onset of insolvency"   IA ss.240(3), 245(5)

"Person connected with a company"   IA s.249

"Person with control"   IA s.435(10)

"Preference"   IA s.239(4)

"Preferential creditor"   IA ss.4(7), 258(7), 386(1)

"Preferential debt"   IA ss.4(7), 386, Sch.6

"Project company"   IA ss.72C(3), 72D(2)(d), Sch.2A, paras 7(1), (2)

"Property"   IA s.436; IR r.7.21(3)

"Property of the company"   IA s.42(2)(b)

"Prove"   IR r.4.73

"Public-private partnership project"   IA s.2C(2)

"Purpose of administration"   IA Sch.B1, para 111(1)

"Qualifying floating charge"   IA Sch.B1, para.14(2)

"Receiver"   IA s.251

"Relevant date"   IA s.387

"Relevant time"   IA ss.240, 245(3),(4)

"Retention of title agreement"   IA s.251

"Secured creditor"   IA s.248(a)

"Security"   IA ss.248(b), 425(4)

"Shadow director"   CA s.741; IA s.251; CDDA s.22(5)

"Solvent winding up"	IR rr.4.151(b), 4.173(2)
"Step-in rights"	IA ss.72C(3), 72D(2)(c), Sch.2A, para.6
"System charge"	IA s.72F(b); FMIR 1996, reg.2(1)
"Transaction"	IA s.436
"Transaction at an undervalue"	IA s.238(4)
"Unable to pay its debts"	IA ss.8, 123, 222, 223, 224
"Voluntary arrangement"	IA s.1(1).
"Writing"	IA Sch.B1, para.111(2)

By IA s.251 any expression for whose interpretation provision is made by CA

Part XXVI, other than an expression defined earlier in s.251, is to be construed in accordance with that provision.

For more comprehensive tables of sources, see *Sealy & Milman*: *Annotated Guide to the Insolvency Legislation* (8th edition), Appendices I and II.

Table of UK Statutes

Paragraph references in **bold** indicate where text of legislation is reproduced

Table of Foreign Legislation

Table of Statutory Instruments

Table of European and International Treaties and Conventions

Table of European Directives

Table of European Regulations

Table of Uniform Rules

Table of UK Cases

Table of Foreign Cases

Australia

Ireland

New Zealand

Singapore

United States of America

Chapter 1

The History and Framework of Corporate Insolvency Law

1. INTRODUCTION

Nature of the subject

This book is devoted to the subject of corporate insolvency law: the law **1–01** relating to the insolvency of companies. Historically this developed separately from the law relating to the insolvency of individuals.[1] In consequence, whereas in American law the term "bankruptcy" in the sense of a legally declared state of insolvency applies alike to individuals and corporations, English insolvency law possesses no such generic term. Individuals become bankrupt, or go into bankruptcy; companies go into liquidation, or winding-up (the terms are synonymous).

When a company becomes insolvent, many questions may arise. Is it capable of being rehabilitated or at least got into better shape before liquidation? If it does go into liquidation, what assets in its possession are to be considered available for distribution among its creditors, who are to be treated as creditors and how are the various classes of claim to be ranked? In what circumstances will transactions entered into by a company before winding-up be rendered void or liable to be set aside, and how should recoveries be dealt with? What duties are owed by the directors of an insolvent company to the company itself and its creditors, and what sanctions may be imposed for breaches of those duties? Finally, what are the qualifications for acting as an insolvency practitioner and what duties and liabilities are imposed upon those who so act? All these issues, and others besides, fall within the province of corporate insolvency law and will be examined in the ensuing pages. This book is primarily concerned with

---

[1] See below, paras 1–05 *et seq.*

1

corporate insolvency law and policy as these currently exist (albeit with critical comment at appropriate places) rather than with normative theories of corporate insolvency law which have over recent years engaged the interest of scholars.[2] There has been a wealth of valuable literature from American scholars in particular,[3] and more recently from academics in England and elsewhere, who have sought to identify from a law and economics perspective the rational goals of a modern insolvency law. These call for a different kind of book.[4] An outline of some of these theories, and the extent to which the objectives they identify are reflected in English corporate insolvency law, will be given in the next chapter.

The role of credit

1–02   Insolvency is the inability to pay one's debts. It therefore necessarily arises from the extension of credit, for without credit there can be no debt. A world without credit is impossible to imagine. Credit—that is, contractual deferment of debt—has existed from the earliest times, well before the advent of banking institutions. A huge amount of credit is extended every year by suppliers, banks and other financial institutions and by investors in the financial markets. Credit facilitates the smooth running and expansion of business and, in good trading conditions, gives a company leverage to increase its profits by undertaking more business than would be possible if it were restricted to using its own funds. The higher the degree of leverage (or "gearing")—*i.e.* the ratio of borrowed funds to shareholders' funds—the greater the profits, so long as trading income exceeds the cost of servicing the borrowings. The converse, of course, is that where the volume of trading declines or trading otherwise becomes unprofitable the obligation to continue servicing the debts accentuates the losses and may precipitate the collapse of the company.

Credit takes two distinct forms: loan credit, in which money is advanced on terms of repayment; and sale credit, in which goods, services or other things are supplied on the basis of payment at a later date, whether in a single sum or by instalments.[5] Sale credit does not in law constitute the

---

[2] One American scholar has classified bankruptcy scholarship as observational (objectively describing existing law and policy), normative (the values that courts and legislatures should seek to achieve in bankruptcy), standard reform (how the law can best achieve its existing objectives) and critical reform (what purposes the law should seek to achieve and how best it could achieve them). See Donald R. Korobkin, "The Role of Normative Theory in Bankruptcy Debates" 82 Iowa L. Rev. 75 (1996).

[3] See paras 2–03 *et seq.*

[4] See, for example, Rizwaan Jameel Mokal, *Corporate Insolvency Law: Theory and Application* (2005); Vanessa Finch, *Corporate Insolvency Law: Perspectives and Principles* (2002).

[5] From an economic perspective finance leasing is equated with conditional sale, and assets subject to a finance lease are required to be shown as an asset in the books of the lessee, not the lessor. See Statements of Accounting Practice, SSAP 21: *Accounting for Leases and Hire Purchase Contracts* and Roy Goode, *Commercial Law* (3rd ed., 2004), pp.721–723.

lending of money, it is simply the contractual deferment of a price obligation. It enables a company to obtain goods or services in advance of payment but does not, of course, give it the free funds it needs to conduct its business. For that purpose the company must look to other sources, in particular, share capital (equity) contributed by its members and borrowings from lenders (debt).

For the purpose of insolvency law there is a vitally important difference between equity and debt. Shareholders are not creditors. Unlike creditors they have no claim to payment from the company except when a dividend is declared or there is a surplus of assets over liabilities on the winding-up of the company. In general, creditors are entitled to be paid ahead of shareholders in the event of a company going into liquidation; only when creditors have been paid in full (which is rarely the case) do shareholders come in to participate in the surplus remaining.[6] Neither group is homogeneous. The ranking of creditors among themselves may be influenced by the grant of security or by subordination techniques,[7] in addition to which insolvency law itself distinguishes between different categories of creditor in the priority stakes; and shares may be ordinary, preferred or deferred, depending on the terms of issue.

Security and quasi-security

A financially strong company will often be able to obtain credit simply on the strength of its undertaking to pay without providing any security. But banks and other lenders frequently feel the need to buttress this undertaking with security in order to ensure that if by mischance the borrower company does become insolvent they will be able to jump ahead of other creditors. Security may be real or personal. Real security is security in an asset or pool of assets and typically takes the form of a mortgage or charge covering specific assets or a class of existing and future assets.[8] Personal security consists of the reinforcement of the debtor company's undertaking by that of a third party, usually in the form of a guarantee of the debt, or by a stronger undertaking by the debtor himself, for example, in a negotiable instrument, claims on which are less easily resisted than those based on the underlying transaction.

Real security in the true sense involves the grant of rights by the debtor company in an asset which it owns or in which it has an interest. But there are other types of transaction which fulfil the function of security but do not involve the grant of such rights. Notable among these is the supply of goods on terms that ownership is not to pass to the buyer until payment. Just as a

1–03

---

[6] Insolvency Act 1986, ss.107, 154.
[7] See below, para.7–08.
[8] See Roy Goode, *Legal Problems of Credit and Security* (3rd ed., 2003). Chap.1.

sale on credit is not in law a loan, so also the retention of title under a sale contract does not constitute a security interest in law, for the debtor is not granting rights over its own asset but merely agreeing that it will not acquire ownership until payment of the price. Other quasi-security devices include sale and repurchase, finance leasing, contractual set-off and the imposition of conditions on the right to withdraw a deposit.[9]

Security and quasi-security play a crucial part in expanding the availability of credit. But in insolvency they also have implications for the general body of creditors, for their effect is to reduce the pool of assets available for the general body of creditors. This is a point to which we shall return later when considering the extent to which corporate insolvency law has a redistributive role.[10]

However, it would be a mistake to assume that the sole purpose of security is to give the secured creditor priority in a winding-up. Security fulfils a number of other functions which are of considerable importance. One of these, particularly in the case of global security under a combined fixed and floating charge, is to provide the secured creditor with a significant degree of control both in relation to the company's conduct and in relation to that of unsecured creditors, who have little incentive to pursue individual enforcement measures when control of most of the assets is vested in a single lender.[11] Another is to enhance the secured creditor's risk-weighted capital for capital adequacy purposes.[12]

The collective nature of the corporate insolvency regime

1–04   When a debtor, whether a private individual, a sole trader, a partnership firm or a company, fails to pay a debt on its due date, the creditor is entitled to avail himself of all the rights and remedies given to him by his contract and by law. Such rights and remedies are of two kinds. First, there are those exercisable by self-help. They include, in given conditions, the creditor's right to accelerate the debtor's liability, to withhold his own performance under the contract or to terminate the contract by reason of the default; the right to enforce—by possession, sale, the appointment of a receiver or otherwise—a security interest, reservation of title or other real right in an asset held by the debtor; the right to forfeit a lease or to distrain against the debtor's goods for rent; and the right to set off the debt against

---

[9] See Roy Goode, *Commercial Law*, pp.605 *et seq.*

[10] See below, paras 2–03 *et seq.*

[11] This is borne out by a study by Julian R. Franks and Oren Sussman, "Financial Distress and Bank Restructuring of Small-to-Medium Size UK Companies" (Centre for Economic Policy Research, Discussion Paper No. 3915, May 2003, noting (at p.4) that "once the liquidation rights are concentrated, the incentives for trade creditors to precipitate bankruptcy are limited."

[12] See generally Roy Goode, *Legal Problems of Credit and Security*, paras 1–01—1–02.

a countervailing money obligation owed by the creditor to the debtor. Secondly, there are judicial (or curial) rights and remedies, including the institution of proceedings against the debtor for payment, delivery, possession, foreclosure or sale, and the enforcement of an ensuing judgment by one or more processes of judicial execution against the debtor's income or assets or enforcement of an order for specific delivery or possession of an asset belonging to the creditor himself.

A creditor who holds a security interest or other real right in an asset owned or possessed by the debtor may proceed to realise that right and to take what is due to him from the proceeds in priority to all other creditors except for those having a stronger claim than he to the asset. A creditor having no right *in rem* in any asset held by the debtor may nevertheless exercise any other form of self-help open to him, such as acceleration of the debt and/or set-off. Failing this the only remaining method open to him of exacting payment, short of a threat of insolvency proceedings, is to obtain and enforce a judgment against the debtor. But other creditors may be pursuing the same course, in which case he will find himself in competition, with the race going to the swiftest. The individual debtor faces the bleak prospect of having all his assets seized, except for the modest value of items exempt from execution, and of having all his income diverted to his creditors to the extent that this exceeds what the court considers it necessary for him to live on. The corporate debtor is in even worse case, for none of its property or income is exempt from execution.

The primary purpose of insolvency law[13] is to replace the free-for-all attendant upon the pursuit of individual claims by different creditors with a statutory regime in which creditors' rights and remedies are suspended, wholly or in part, and a mechanism is provided for the orderly collection and realisation of assets and the distribution of the net realisations of the assets among creditors in accordance with the statutory scheme of distribution.[14] English insolvency law distinguishes individual debtors (including sole traders and partnerships) from corporate debtors. Although there is no longer a separate statute for bankruptcy, and what is now the Insolvency Act 1986 reduces the differences between the rules and procedures governing the insolvency of individuals from those applicable to the insolvency of companies, the regimes remain distinct.[15]

As stated earlier, this book is confined to the principles of insolvency law relating to companies, a subject of peculiar fascination because it involves

---

[13] This term is used in a broad sense to cover both collective procedures initiated by the debtor or creditors following on the debtor's default (in particular, administration, bankruptcy and winding up) and administrative receivership resulting from the steps taken by an individual secured creditor holding a floating charge embracing (with any fixed security) substantially the whole of the debtor company's assets. For a more detailed summary of the objectives of *corporate* insolvency law see below, and for the particular purposes and principles of administrative receivership see Chap.9.

[14] This is the theme of Chap.2.

[15] For some of the major differences between bankruptcy and winding up see below, para.1–24.

an examination not only of complex statutory provisions but also of fundamental questions concerning the distinction between real and personal rights and the extent to which creditors have a legally protectable interest in the proper application of a company's assets. It is impossible to understand corporate insolvency law without a true perception of the principles of the general law of property and obligations and the interrelationship of these and the insolvency legislation.

2. HISTORY AND SOURCES

The early history of insolvency law[16]

1–05   The law governing the insolvency of individuals has its roots in the earliest days of the common law, when there was no collective procedure for the administration of an insolvent's estate and a disappointed creditor could seize the effects of his debtor and, at a later date, his person also.[17] Though the mediaeval law merchant recognised the institution of bankruptcy,[18] borrowed from the *cessio bonorum* of Roman law, bankruptcy law in the modern sense of an official procedure for the collection and realisation of a debtor's estate for distribution among his creditors generally was first introduced in 1542 by a statute of Henry VIII,[19] which after a thunderous preamble denouncing debtors acting in fraud of their creditors, directed that the bodies of the offenders and all their assets be taken by the requisite authorities and the assets sold to pay their creditors "a portion, rate and rate alike, according to the quantity of their debts". Thus was introduced the principle of *pari passu* distribution, which is still the central principle of distribution of an insolvent's free estate. Numerous bankruptcy statutes followed. But in contrast to modern bankruptcy law their aim was penal rather than rehabilitative. The Fraudulent Conveyances Act 1571 outlawed transfers made with intent to delay or defraud creditors. This Elizabethan statute was later held by Lord Mansfield effective to avoid not only fraudulent conveyances but also fraudulent preferences,[20] which defeated

---

[16] V. Markham Lester, *Victorian Insolvency* (1995); the Cork Report (below, n.36), Chap.2; Ian F. Fletcher *The Law of Insolvency* (3rd ed., 2002), pp.6 *et seq.*; Andrew Keay, *McPherson's Law of Company Liquidation* (2001), paras 1.21 *et seq.*

[17] Edward Cooke, *Debtor and Creditor* (Butterworth, 1829).

[18] Indeed the word "bankrupt" itself is said to be derived from the practice at mediaeval fairs of breaking the bench *(banca)* of an insolvent merchant found to have acted dishonestly, thus signifying that he was no longer considered worthy to participate as a member of the mercantile community.

[19] Statute of Bankrupts, 34 & 35 Hen. VIII, c.4.

[20] That is, preferences of one creditor over others made voluntarily rather than under compulsion of proceedings or threats. The precursor of the modern legislation specifically rendering eve of bankruptcy preferences voidable was the Bankruptcy Act 1869, s.92. For the current law relating to voidable preferences, see para.11–69.

6

the law by usurping the function of the authorities and defeated the equality intended by the law.[21] As the list of bankruptcy offences grew, so did the severity of the laws increase.[22] Not until 1705 was legislation introduced for the relief of bankrupts through the concept of discharge from debts for those who co-operated with their creditors.[23] For centuries the bankruptcy legislation was confined to traders, on the theory that while traders might become insolvent through accident or misfortune, such as loss of a ship, the insolvency of a private individual was almost invariably due to his or her profligacy. So there were two systems in place, bankruptcy for traders and "insolvency" for non-traders. Insolvents who were not traders continued to suffer the rigours of individual action under the common law—most notably, imprisonment for a debt and all too often death through disease or starvation—though statutes were enacted for the relief of debtors and Lord Redesdale's Act of 1813[24] established a Court for the Relief of Insolvent Debtors.[25]

It was only with the enactment of the Bankruptcy Act 1861 that the distinction between traders and non-traders was abolished.[26] That Act was later replaced by a series of bankruptcy statutes culminating in the Bankruptcy Act 1914, which codified bankruptcy law and remained in force until 1986, when it was repealed by the Insolvency Act 1985. Mr Markham Lester has recorded the huge importance attached to insolvency law in Victorian England, with numerous reports of royal commissions and parliamentary select committees, the introduction of nearly 100 bills between 1831 and 1914, and a government bureaucracy and budget which dwarfed those of the Home Office.[27] Noteworthy was the Bankruptcy Act 1869, which in s.32 established the first general statutory regime for preferential debts in bankruptcy, covering within defined limits local rates, taxes and wages or salary of clerks, servants, labourers or workers in the employ of the bankrupt,[28] a regime carried over with additions and variations to subsequent bankruptcy legislation.

The Bankruptcy Acts never applied to companies. The birth of corporate insolvency law goes back no further than 1844, when Parliament enacted the Joint Stock Companies Act 1844, the first general Act to provide for the incorporation of a company as a distinct legal entity, albeit with unlimited

---

[21] *Alderson v Temple* (1768) 96 E.R. 384.
[22] See Roy Goode. *Commercial Law*, p.827.
[23] Bankruptcy Act 1705, 4 & 5 Anne, c.17.
[24] 53 Geo III, c.24.
[25] See V. Markham Lester, *Victorian Insolvency*, Chap.3.
[26] Bankruptcy Act 1861, s.69.
[27] V. Markham Lester, *Victorian Insolvency*, pp.2, 4–5.
[28] As regards taxes payable to the Crown, these in any event had priority under the Crown prerogative. Earlier statutes had empowered the court or, under some statutes, the bankruptcy commissioners to allow certain payments to employees and apprentices, but this was a matter of discretion, not of right.

liability for its members.[29] This was followed by the Joint Stock Companies Winding-Up Act 1844, which enabled a company to be made bankrupt in the same way as an individual,[30] and the Joint Stock Companies Winding-Up Acts 1848 and 1849, conferring general winding-up jurisdiction on the Court of Chancery, a jurisdiction overlapping that of the Bankruptcy Court until the passing of the Joint Stock Companies Act 1856 and the Joint Stock Companies Winding Up (Amendment) Act 1857, which left the Court of Chancery with exclusive jurisdiction and thus formally separated bankruptcy and winding up procedure.[31]

But corporate insolvency law initially piggy-backed on bankruptcy law and did not assume a truly distinctive status until the advent of limited liability for members of a company with the enactment of the Limited Liability Act 1855; and the first modern company law statute was the Companies Act 1862, which contained detailed winding up provisions, including a provision for *pari passu* distribution.[32] Section 10 of the Judicature Act 1875 was designed, among other things, to align rules as to proof of debt in company liquidations with those applicable to bankruptcies, but its scope was a matter of controversy and it was not until 1901 that it was finally established by the Court of Appeal that the bankruptcy priority rules were carried over into winding-up.[33] By then, legislation had expressly established categories of preferential debt for winding-up as well as bankruptcy,[34] and from that time until 1986 corporate insolvency law was to remain governed primarily by successive Companies Acts[35]—which incorporated by reference the provisions of the various Bankruptcy Acts

---

[29] Prior to the Joint Stock Companies Winding-Up Act 1844 a company could be incorporated only by charter from the Crown or by special Act of Parliament, which might or might leave the members of the company liable for its debts.

[30] s.1.

[31] See L.C.B. Gower, *Principles of Modern Company Law* (6th ed., 1997), Chap.2 and literature there cited (much of the historical treatment has been omitted from the 7th ed.); Lester, *op. cit.* Chap.6.

[32] Companies Act 1862, s.111, which, however, was confined to voluntary winding-up. It appears to have been assumed that the court would exercise its powers to produce a similar result. From the outset of the companies legislation the expenses of the winding-up, including the liquidator's remuneration, were made payable in priority to the claims of other creditors (see the Joint Stock Companies Act 1856, s.104, which again was confined to voluntary winding-up, and the Companies Acts 1862, ss.110 and 44 and Companies Act 1883, s.6, which were not so confined), a rule which pertains to this day.

[33] *Re Whitaker, Whitaker v Palmer* [1901] 1 Ch. 9, a decision about a deceased person's insolvent estate, but the section applied equally to winding-up of a company. However, the provisions of the Bankruptcy Act 1883 abrogating the Crown's right to priority were held inapplicable to a company liquidation (*Re Oriental Bank Corp.* (1884) 28 Ch.D. 643) and the right was not fully abolished until 2003 (Enterprise Act 2002, s.251).

[34] Companies Act 1883, ss.4–6; Preferential Payments in Bankruptcy Acts 1888 (which applied both to bankruptcy and to winding-up) and 1897. The last of these also provided that claims secured by a floating charge were subordinated to preferential debts. The provision to this effect in the 1897 Act was considered by the House of Lords in *Buchler v Talbot* [2004] A.C. 298 to be of crucial relevance to the understanding of the modern law.

[35] The principal enactments being the Acts of 1908, 1929, 1948 and 1985.

relating to provable debts and to fraudulent preferences—the last of these being the present Companies Act 1985.

The Insolvency Acts 1985 and 1986 and the Company Directors Disqualification Act 1986

Following the recommendations of the Insolvency Law Review Committee **1–06** under the chairmanship of Sir Kenneth Cork,[36] the Insolvency Act 1985 made substantial changes to insolvency provisions of the Companies Act 1985. On the very day the Insolvency Act 1985 came into force[37] it was replaced by the Insolvency Act 1986, a consolidating enactment which repealed and re-enacted the Insolvency Act 1985 and the insolvency provisions of the Companies Act 1985 other than those relating to the disqualification of directors and a few other provisions noted below. The Insolvency Act 1986 was later amended by the Insolvency Act 1994 in order to resolve problems relating to the personal liability of administrators and administrative receivers,[38] and further amended by the Insolvency (No.2) Act 1994 to remove uncertainty concerning the impact of orders under ss.238, 239 and 241 of the 1986 Act[39] on *bona fide* purchasers. The disqualification provisions of the Companies Act and the Insolvency Act 1985 were themselves repealed and re-enacted in a separate consolidation, the Company Directors Disqualification Act 1986.

The Companies Act 1989

Part VII of the Companies Act 1989 contains a set of provisions to modify **1–07** the general law of insolvency so as to exempt contracts and arrangements in the financial markets from various rules of insolvency law and substitute for these the rules of the relevant exchange or clearing house. Several statutory instruments have been made pursuant to Part VII.[40] The purpose is to ensure the stability of the financial markets which might otherwise be threatened if market contracts and arrangements were to be invalidated on the insolvency of a major player.

The Financial Services and Markets Act 2000

Part XXIV of the Financial Services and Markets Act 2000 empowers the **1–08** Financial Services Authority, which oversees the financial markets, to participate in proceedings relating to voluntary arrangements, receivership

---

[36] *Insolvency Law and Practice*, Report of the Review Committee (Cmnd. 8558, 1982).
[37] December 29, 1986.
[38] See below paras 9–49 *et seq.*, 10–93 *et seq.*
[39] Involving the reversal of the effect of transactions at an undervalue and preferences. See below.
[40] See below, paras 1–28 *et seq.*

and voluntary and compulsory winding-up of a company that is an authorised person under s.31 of the Act.

The Insolvency Act 2000 and the Enterprise Act 2002

1–09   The Insolvency Act 1986 was further amended by the Insolvency Act 2000, which introduced into the 1986 Act new provisions on voluntary arrangements and moratoria and amended the provisions of the Company Directors Disqualification Act 1986 on the disqualification of directors. Of much greater import, however, were the insolvency provisions of the Enterprise Act 2002, of which the most significant were those that, with certain exceptions, abolished the long-established institution of administrative receivership. This is not a collective insolvency procedure, rather a debt enforcement remedy available to a creditor holding a floating charge which, with any fixed charges, covers the whole or substantially the whole of the debtor company's property.[41] The remedy is a powerful one, enabling the creditor to appoint an administrative receiver to take control of the company and its assets, largely displacing the directors, and to continue trading as deemed agent of the company, sell off the business or individual assets or hive them down to a new debt-free company which can then be sold off. There had long been disquiet over the power held by such a creditor, the making of what were sometimes seen to be precipitate appointments at almost no notice and, where the creditor was over-secured (as was not uncommon) the lack of incentive to ensure that the costs of the receivership were kept down and the assets realised at the best price. Moreover the receiver's primary duty (apart from discharging preferential debts from floating charge assets) was to its appointing creditor, not to the general body of creditors. A further cause for concern was the ability of the creditor to block an administration—a collective procedure designed for the benefit of the creditors generally—by appointing an administrative receiver before the making of an administration order; and although in many cases the creditor was content to allow an administration this was not always the case and its ability to block it was perceived as inimical to the rescue culture which had begun to be promoted during the 1990s.[42] The Insolvency Act 1986 had introduced a system of company voluntary arrangements, but it proved to be a rather ineffective mechanism for corporate rescue, largely because it did not in itself trigger a moratorium, which could only be brought about through administration.

---

[41] See para.1–23, and Chap.9.
[42] See Vanessa Finch, *Corporate Insolvency Law*, Chaps. 6 and 7 and, for a comprehensive review of the legal aspects as at 1995, David Brown, *Corporate Rescue* (1996). For further discussion of the rescue culture, see para.1–21.

Following a series of studies[43] and a flurry of government papers[44] the decision was taken that in principle all insolvency proceedings should be collective in character. To that end the Enterprise Act 2002 introduced into the Insolvency Act 1986 a provision prohibiting, with certain exceptions, the appointment of an administrative receiver by the holder of a floating charge created on or after September 15, 2003. Instead, the chargee will be able to appoint an administrator, but the making of distributions to the chargee is not a legitimate objective if it is reasonably practicable to achieve either of the two prior-ranking objectives (rescue of the company as a going concern and achieving a better result for creditors as a whole than on an immediate winding up). The Act also provided that in an insolvency proceeding a prescribed part of the assets subject to a floating charge should be made available for the satisfaction of unsecured debts. The effect is to reduce the advantages of a floating charge. The Act also abolishes Crown preference.

The overall effect of the changes introduced by the Enterprise Act is to strengthen the position of ordinary unsecured creditors and to transfer management control of the insolvent company's business and assets from the secured creditor and its administrative receiver to the insolvency administrator, a trend observable in other jurisdictions that have moved away from the practice of piecemeal realisation of assets to reorganisation of the company and its business.[45]

The European dimension

Though the European Community has not yet assumed general compe-   **1–10**
tence in the field of substantive insolvency law, there are several Community instruments which affect English insolvency law, jurisdiction and procedure and which, so far as not directly applicable, have been implemented in the United Kingdom by subordinate legislation under the European Communities Act 1972. Some of these are specific to particular types of organisation. For example, the 2000 Banking Directive[46] contains provisions to require the authorisation of banks and other deposit-taking

---

[43] See, for example, P. Aghion, O. Hart and J. Moore, 'A Proposal for Bankruptcy Reform in the UK' (1993) 9 I.L. & P. 103; 'Insolvency Reform in the UK: A Revised Proposal' (1995) 11 I.L. & P. 67.

[44] DTI, *Productivity and Enterprise—Insolvency: A Second Chance* (Cm 5234, 2001); DTI/Treasury *A Review of Company Rescue and Business Reconstruction Mechanisms: Report by the Review Group* (2000); DTI Insolvency Service, *Company Voluntary Arrangements and Administration Orders: A Consultative Document* (1993); *Revised Proposals for a New Company Voluntary Arrangement Procedure* (1995).

[45] For a recent perceptive analysis of this trend, with references to the shift in the UK approach, see Jay Lawrence Westbrook, "The Control of Wealth in Bankruptcy" 82 Texas L. Rev. 795, 805 (2004).

[46] Directive of the European Parliament and the Council of March 20, 2000 on the taking up and pursuit of the business of credit institutions (2000/12/EC, OJ L126, 26.5.00, p.1).

credit institutions and to ensure their solvency, while their reorganisation and winding-up are governed by the 2001 Banking Winding-Up Directive.[47] Similarly, there has been a series of directives on insurance, followed by the 2001 Insurance Winding Up Directive.[48] Special protection against rules of insolvency law has been given to the financial markets by the Settlement Finality Directive and the Financial Collateral Directive.[49] But what potentially affects insolvent companies generally is the 2000 EC Insolvency Regulation,[50] containing detailed provisions on jurisdiction to open insolvency proceedings in a Member State, main, territorial and secondary proceedings, the right of a liquidator in the main proceedings to request the opening of and to participate in secondary proceedings, the applicable law and rules of recognition of foreign insolvency proceedings.[51]

International insolvency

1–11 There has also been much activity in relaton to cross-border insolvency at the international level. This is discussed in Chapter 14.

The sources of corporate insolvency law

(1) The common law

1–12 Though the greater part of corporate insolvency law is statutory, there are certain regimes governed wholly or partly by common law principles and by the inherent jurisdiction of the court. Until the passing of what is now the Insolvency Act 1986 the law relating to the receivership of companies was almost entirely based on contract and on rules developed by the courts, and though the powers and principal obligations of administrative receivers[52] are now codified in the Insolvency Act 1986 much of receivership law continues to be based on common law principles. Arrangements and compromises concluded between a company and its creditors by contract or by informal agreement remain wholly outside the purview of legislation except so far as they involve dispositions and other dealings which are void or voidable under the Insolvency Act. By contrast, winding up is almost exclusively governed by the Act and subordinate legislation. Yet even

---

[47] European Parliament and Council Directive of April 4, 2001 on the reorganisation and winding up of credit institutions (2001/24/EC, OJ L125, 5.5.2001, p.15).
[48] Council Directive of March 19, 2001 on the reorganisation and winding-up of insurance undertakings (2001/17/EC, OJ L110, 20. 4. 2001, p.28).
[49] See below, paras 1–32 *et seq.*
[50] Council Regulation of 29 May 2000 on insolvency proceedings (1346/2000/EC, OJ L160, 30.06.2000, p.1).
[51] See Chap.14.
[52] See below, paras 9–47 *et seq.*

winding up is influenced by the creative power of the courts. The principle of *pari passu* distribution of assets among ordinary unsecured creditors, which under the Bankruptcy Act 1914 was encapsulated in precisely 11 words[53] and is now relegated to subordinate legislation,[54] has been developed by the courts into a fundamental concept of insolvency law having the most profound repercussions on the validity of pre-liquidation contracts and dispositions entered into between the company and its creditors and between creditors *inter se.*[55] Moreover the statutory provisions delimiting the assets available for distribution predicate that unless otherwise provided the attachment, perfection and priority of security interests and other real rights are to be determined by the general law applicable to transactions outside winding up,[56] the bulk of which is non-statutory. Finally, the court's inherent jurisdiction over its own officers enables it to deny to a liquidator appointed by the court rights and remedies to which he is on the face of it entitled by law where the exercise of those rights or remedies would in the opinion of the court be unfair or inequitable.[57]

(2) Primary legislation

There are two principal statutes dealing with corporate insolvency.   **1–13**

(a) Companies Act 1985

Though most of the provisions of this Act relating to insolvency have   **1–14**
been repealed and re-enacted in the Insolvency Act, a few remain. They
are ss.196,[58] 425–427[59] and 458.[60]

(b) Insolvency Acts 1986, 1994 and 2000

The Insolvency Act 1986, as amended by the Insolvency Act 1994, the   **1–15**
Insolvency (No.2) Act 1994, the Insolvency Act 2000 and the Enterprise
Act 2002, is the main enactment dealing with corporate insolvency. It
also covers personal bankruptcy. There are also a few free-standing
provisions in the amending legislation, *e.g.* s.14 of the Insolvency Act
2000 empowering the Secretary of State to make regulations implementing the UNCITRAL Model Law on Cross-Border Insolvency.

---

[53] Bankruptcy Act 1914 s.33(7), incorporated into companies winding up by the Companies Act 1985, s.612 (now repealed).
[54] Insolvency Rules 1986, r.4.181.
[55] See below, paras 3–10, 7–01.
[56] See below, para.6–01.
[57] This is commonly known as the Rule in *Ex p. James*, having been formulated (though not for the first time) in the Court of Appeal decision in *Re Condon Ex p. James* (1874) L.R. 9 Ch. 609. It is rarely invoked successfully and is general considered the last resort for a party who has no other reasonable grounds for challenging a liquidator's decision.
[58] Dealing with payments of debts out of assets subject to a floating charge.
[59] Concerning arrangements with creditors.
[60] Dealing with fraudulent trading.

In addition, major dispensations from the rules of insolvency law, mostly implementing Community legislation, have been given by and under the Companies Act 1989 in respect of market charges and market contracts,[61] fixed and floating charges securing money market (currency exchange) contracts[62] and systems-charges taken by settlement banks to secure obligations arising from dealings in uncertificated securities[63] and financial collateral arrangements.[64] There are also provisions in Part XII of the Employment Rights Act 1996[65] which entitle an employee, on the insolvency of his or her employer,[66] to obtain from the Secretary of State payment from the National Insurance Fund of any redundancy payment, arrears of pay, amounts awarded for unfair dismissal, and certain other payments, within the limits laid down by the legislation. The Secretary of State then acquires the rights of the employee, including any preferential status of the debts paid.[67] Finally, reference has been made to the powers of intervention in insolvency conferred on the Financial Services Authority by Part XXIV of the Financial Services and Markets Act 2000.

The Company Directors Disqualification Act 1986,[68] to which reference has been made earlier, gathers together the statutory provisions on disqualification of directors previously dispersed over the Companies Act 1985 and the Insolvency Act 1985. However, though s.6 of the Company Directors Disqualification Act imposes on the court a duty to disqualify directors of an insolvent company who it is satisfied are unfit to be concerned in the management of a company, the Act is directed primarily at improper conduct on the part of directors rather than on insolvency as such. It is therefore considered only briefly in Chapter 12.

(3) Subordinate legislation

1–16 Apart from the implementation of EC insolvency legislation there are numerous statutory instruments relating to corporate insolvency, the most important of these being the Insolvency Rules 1986,[69] Part II of which,

---

[61] Companies Act 1989, Part VII; Financial Markets and Insolvency Regulations 1991 (SI 1991/880).

[62] Financial Markets and Insolvency (Money Market) Regulations 1995 (SI 1995/2049).

[63] Financial Markets and Insolvency Regulations 1996 (SI 1996/1469). Both these regulations and those referred to in n.34 above amend Part VII of the Companies Act 1989 pursuant to the powers conferred by Part VII itself.

[64] Financial Collateral Arrangements (No. 2) Regulations 2003 (SI 2003/3226). See further paras 1–34 *et seq.* as to these exemptions under Part VII of the Companies Act 1989.

[65] Formerly Part VII of the Employment Protection (Consolidation) Act 1978.

[66] As to what constitutes insolvency for this purpose see below, para.4–11; and as to the relationship between the provisions of the Employment Rights Act 1996 and those of the Insolvency Act 1986 relating to preferential debts, see below, paras 2–11, 7–28.

[67] Employment Rights Act 1996, s.189(1), (2).

[68] As amended by the Companies Act 1989, the Insolvency Act 2000, the Financial Services and Markets Act 2000 (Consequential Amendments and Repeals) Order 2000 (SI 2000/3649), the Enterprise Act 2002 and sundry other legislation peripheral to insolvency.

[69] SI 1986/1925 as amended. For details of the various amending instruments and the dates these became operative, General note to the Insolvency Rules 1986, in *Sealy & Milman: Annotated Guide to the Insolvency Legislation* (8th ed. 2005).

dealing with administration, was entirely replaced in 2003, subject to transitional provisions.

(4) European Community legislation

The various EC directives mentioned earlier have been implemented by statutory instrument. By contrast the 2000 EC Insolvency Regulation has direct effect, and implementing legislation is neither required nor permissible.

1–17

Defects in the legislative structure and arrangement

It has to be said that the structure of English insolvency legislation does not display a particularly rational structure or scheme of arrangement.[70] One might, for example, have expected a relatively simple division between the Insolvency Act and the Insolvency Rules in which the former was directed to substantive rights and the latter to procedural requirements. Instead, we find a number of provisions of the Insolvency Act that are given over to procedural matters, such as the summoning of meetings and the contents of reports, whilst important substantive rights, such as what debts are provable, set-off in winding up[71] and the priority rules for the payment of liquidation expenses are relegated to the Insolvency Rules.

1–18

The ordering of subjects within the Rules themselves is also mildly eccentric. For example, Chapter 9 in Part 4 deals with proof of debts but we have to trawl through to Part 12, "Miscellaneous and General", to discover the answer to the vital question what debts are provable. Overall, the Insolvency Act and the Insolvency Rules have become a legislative morass through which even the experienced practitioner cannot pick his way without difficulty. Part II of the Act is now to be found in two versions, the original version covering administrations where the petition was presented prior to September 15, 2003 and comprising ss.8 to 27, and the new version, for other administrations, in Sch.B1, which takes effect pursuant to a second s.8! Similarly, there are two versions of Part 2 of the Insolvency Rules.[72] Even the numbering of the schedules is eccentric, with Sch.1 being bizarrely preceded by Schs.1A and 1B.[73] Definitions are dispersed through

---

[70] What is critcised here is the drafting, not the Parliamentary draftsmen, who faced an immense task and frequently had to work under the extreme pressures of the Parliamentary timetable.

[71] But not in bankruptcy, where it is dealt with in the Act itself (s.323), a further illustration of the lack of coherence in the statutory framework.

[72] Both sets of provisions of the Act and rules are helpfully set out by Professors Len Sealy and David Milman in *Sealy & Milman: Annotated Guide to the Insolvency Legislation* (8th ed.), together with explanatory notes.

[73] It has to be conceded that this is not without precedent. The late Desmond Heap once wrote a book on betterment levy in which chapter 1 was preceded by chapter 1A. His explanation was that chapter 1A contained matters normally to be found in a preface but in his experience most people did not read the preface!

the Act, the same term is sometimes defined in different ways, several definitions refer to definitions in other legislation[74] and language that was perfectly comprehensible in earlier legislation has been perversely displaced by language that involves the provision of a definition quite at odds with the normal meaning of the term defined.[75] On even the simplest questions the reader is likely to find himself having to shuttle constantly between the body of the Act, Sch.B1 and the Insolvency Rules. Finally, instead of following the golden rule that wherever possible all provisions dealing with the same issue should be dealt with in the same place the draftsman has adopted the pervasive practice of appearing to do this and then catching the reader out by additional and related provisions elsewhere.[76] A complete rearrangement of the Act and Rules, with substantive rules in the Act, procedural provisions in the Rules, the avoidance of duplication of numbering, and a better organisation of the definitions and substantive provisions, is long overdue.[77]

3. THE INSTITUTIONAL SETTING

1–19   The institutional framework within which corporate insolvency law operates is as follows. The *Secretary of State for Trade and Industry* is given extensive powers to make orders and regulations under the Insolvency Act, and is also given a *locus standi* in certain cases to apply for the winding up of a company. Ministerial responsibility for policy matters relating to corporate insolvency falls within the province of the *Department of Trade and Industry*. Responsibility for the development and implementation of policy and of

---

[74] For an extreme case of definitional complexity, see para.10–59, n.66, describing the path that has to be followed to determine the meaning of "hire-purchase agreement" in Sch.B1, para.43(3).

[75] For example, s.15(4), dealing with the effect of disposal by the administrator of property subject to a floating charge, provided that the charge should have the same priority in respect of any property of the company directly or indirectly representing the property disposed of as he would have had in respect of the property subject to the charge—in other words, the priority in the original property carries through to its product or proceeds. In Sch.B1, para.70(2) the reference is to "the same priority in respect of after-acquired property", which does not convey the same idea at all, since after-acquired property may have no connection with what was originally disposed of, and it takes a definition in para.70(3) to get us back on track.

[76] For example, para.99(3) and (4) of Sch.B1 deals with the priority of the administrator's remuneration and expenses *vis-à-vis* other claims, but to find the order of priority of the expenses themselves it is necessary to turn to r.2.67(1) of the Insolvency Rules.

[77] Mr Francis Bennion Q.C., a former Parliamentary draftsman who was famous for his original thinking and techniques in relation to legislative drafting, was a keen advocate of a process of restatement of statutes after they had completed the Parliamentary process. But if this is to work then it is necessary to avoid undoing it with fresh legislation in the old style, a fact which appears to have eluded successive administrations in relation to the simplification of tax law.

securing compliance with the insolvency legislation has been delegated to *The Insolvency Service*, an Executive Agency of the DTI.[78] This operates under the direction of the Inspector General and Agency Chief Executive and contains a large number of official receivers and examiners in London and the provinces. The Insolvency Service is organised into two main branches; the Official Receivers, operating from local offices across England and Wales, and Head Quarters which is divided into a number of Directorates located in London, Birmingham, Manchester, Watford, Leeds and Edinburgh. The Service has six principal functions: to preserve and protect the assets and carry out the initial stages in the administration of compulsory liquidations (the Official Receivers Section); Official Receivers have a duty to investigate the causes of failure and where necessary report on the conduct of directors of insolvent companies with a view to disqualification (Enforcement Directorate) and/or reporting facts regarding alleged criminal offences to the relevant prosecuting authority—the DTI (Enforcement Directorate) the Enforcement Directorate also act on reports submitted by insolvency practitioners; to act as liquidator of last resort, *i.e.* where no outside liquidator can be found who is willing and able to act (the Official Receivers Section); to authorise and regulate insolvency practitioners (the Insolvency Practitioners Unit) who are not authorised as members of one of the *Recognised Professional Bodies*; to formulate policy and advise Ministers (the Policy Unit); and to operate the Insolvency Services account (Banking Unit).

The *Insolvency Rules Committee* is an advisory non-departmental public body which advises the Lord Chancellor on proposed amendments to the Insolvency Rules. The *Insolvency Practices Council* examines ethical and professional standards in the insolvency profession and puts proposals to the professional bodies. It works in close co-operation with the *Joint Insolvency Committee*, a major forum for discussion of insolvency issues and professional ethics and standards which has representatives from the Insolvency Service and the professional bodies. The *Association of Business Recovery Professionals* (formerly the Society of Practitioners in Insolvency), operating under the brand name *R3*, prepares *Statements of Insolvency Practice* for the Joint Insolvency Committee, and if they are approved they are then adopted by each of the Recognised Professional Bodies.

The organisation of corporate insolvency and insolvency procedures is the task of the *insolvency practitioner*, who is usually either an accountant or a solicitor.[79] A person acts as an insolvency practitioner in relation to a company by acting as its liquidator, administrator, administrative receiver or supervisor under a voluntary arrangement.[80] It is an offence to act as an

---

[78] For a detailed description, see Totty and Moss, *Insolvency*, Vol.2, Chap.34, and the Executive Agency's *A Guide to the Insolvency Service*.

[79] By far the greatest number of insolvency practitioners are accountants. For a detailed treatment, see Totty and Moss, *op. cit.*, Vol.1. Pt.A.

[80] Insolvency Act 1986, s.388(1).

insolvency practitioner without being qualified to do so[81] by authorisation from a recognised professional body[82] of which he or she is a member or from "the competent authority", *i.e.* the Secretary of State or a person or body designated by the Secretary of State.[83] Authorisation will only be given to those who are renewing an existing authorisation or have passed the qualifying Joint Insolvency Examination set by the *Joint Insolvency Examination Board.* An appeal against refusal or withdrawal of authorisation by the competent body lies to the *Insolvency Practitioners Tribunal.* But the tribunal has no jurisdiction to entertain appeals against decisions by the recognised professional bodies, which have established their own internal appeal procedures. Monitoring includes regular visits to offices. Also relevant in this context are the rules of the different Recognised Professional Bodies regulating the conduct of practice in general and of insolvency practitioners in particular. Each of these has its own monitoring unit.

Prominent at the international level is the International Federation of Insolvency Professionals (INSOL International), a worldwide federation of national associations of insolvency professionals, which among other things assists in the development of cross-border insolvency policies, participates in government, NGO and intergovernmental advisory groups and implements research into international insolvency issues. Widely used by practitioners is its set of principles for multi-creditor workouts for debtors in financial difficulties.[84]

4. THE VARIOUS INSOLVENCY REGIMES

1–20 It will facilitate an understanding of the purposes of corporate insolvency law, and the methods by which these purposes are sought to be achieved, if we first outline the different types of insolvency proceeding. Each of these will be examined in more detail in later chapters. There are five distinct legal regimes for handling the insolvency of a company, namely:

(1) Administration.

(2) Administrative receivership.

(3) Winding up (liquidation).

---

[81] *ibid.*, s.389(1).

[82] *i.e.* the accountants' and solicitors' professional bodies and the Insolvency Practitioners Association.

[83] Insolvency Act 1986, s.392(2). See the Insolvency Practitioners Regulations 2005, SI 2005/524.

[84] *Statement of Principles for a Global Approach to Multi-Creditor Workouts* (October 2000). See below, para.10–135.

(4) Statutory compromises, compositions and arrangements with creditors.

(5) Reorganisations ("workouts") which are arranged contractually outside the framework of corporate insolvency law.

Each of these has its own distinctive purposes and principles. But the usual outcome, sooner or later, is winding up and subsequent dissolution of the company. In the case of a company in administration, winding up ensues because the administrator's efforts to restore the company to profitable trading or to bring about a voluntary arrangement involving all the creditors have failed. In the case of a company in receivership the administrative receiver either disposes of the company's assets on a break-up basis, where he sees no prospect of restoring it to profitability prior to sale, or manages the company to the point where it can be sold off as a going concern and then effects the sale, typically through hive down of the business to a specially formed subsidiary which is then sold as a company with assets but no liabilities. The purchase price is channelled back to the debtor company and utilised in discharge of the receiver's remuneration and expenses and payment of preferential debts and sums due to the receiver's debenture holder. In most cases the company remains insolvent and a voluntary or compulsory winding up ensues.

Corporate Insolvencies in England and Wales: 1998 to 2004

Type of insolvency	1998	1999	2000	2001	2002	2003	2004
Liquidations							
Total	13,203	14,280	14,317	14,972	16,305	14,184	12,192
Compulsory Liquidations	5,216	5,209	4,925	4,675	6,230	5,234	4,584
Creditors Voluntary Liquidations	7,987	9,071	9,392	10,297	10,075	8,950	7,608
Proceedings related to insolvency							
Receiverships	1,713	1,618	1,595	1,914	1,541	1,261	864
Administrator appointments	338	440	438	698	643	479	1
Voluntary arrangements	470	475	557	597	651	726	597
Arrangements in Administration (Enterprise Act 2002)						247	457

Source: DTI Statistics Directorate

The relative use of these four insolvency procedures is shown in the table above, subject to the caveat that some companies may have been involved in more than one procedure. The figures for administrator appointments relate to court-appointed administrators (the only method of appojntment prior to September 15, 2003) and the drop in administrator appointments to a single case in 2004 reflects the changes made by the Enterprise Act 2002 in providing for out-of-court appointments, which will be the normal method and are shown under the label "Arrangements in Administration (Enterprise Act 2002)", of which there were 457 in 2004. What is noticeable is the decline in the number of administrative receiverships even before these were abolished and, with the coming into force of the changes made by the Enterprise Act 2002, the gradual replacement of CVAs by arrange- ments in administration, as can be seen from the above table.

Administration

1–21   Though winding up is the fate of most insolvent companies, it is not every insolvency that leads to liquidation. Indeed, with the introduction of the company voluntary arrangement (within or outside the administration procedure) and the use of non-statutory bank-led workouts, facilitated by the London Approach and the INSOL International Statement of Principles for a Global Approach to Multi-Creditor Workouts[85] there is increasing scope for business rescues through restructuring and reorganisa- tion where the enterprise is fundamentally sound and has good prospects of being restored to profitability. The so-called "rescue culture" has developed significantly in recent years. Prior to the changes effected by the Insolvency Act 2000 and the Enterprise Act 2002 it had been increasingly been recognised that:

". . . the corporate rescue and reorganization procedures in England are inadequate and, as a consequence, many companies which are capable of being saved are forced into liquidation with loss to creditors. The goal of promoting rehabilitation and rescue is not being adequately served by the existing procedures."[86]

The administration procedure was first introduced by the Insolvency Act 1985, following a recommendation of the Cork Committee.[87] The Insol- vency Act 2000 introduced a limited moratorium for company voluntary

---

[85] See below, para.10–135.
[86] Nick Segal, "An Overview of Recent Developments and Future Prospects in the United Kingdom" in *Current Developments in International and Comparative Corporate Insolvency Law* (ed. Jacob S. Ziegel, 1994), at p.12. For a valuable comparative UK-US study of the political and social dynamics of corporate insolvency law, see Bruce G. Carruthers & Terence C. Halliday, *Rescuing Business* (1998).
[87] *Insolvency Law and Practice*, Chap.9.

arrangements relating to small companies. Of much greater significance was the Enterprise Act 2002, which greatly enhanced the administration procedure, first, by enabling companies to go into administration without a court order; secondly by abolishing administrative receivership (with certain important exceptions), thereby removing a debenture holder's power to block an administration with its attendant freeze on the exercise of remedies; and thirdly by precluding an administrator from having as his objective distribution to secured or preferential creditors except where he thinks it is not reasonably practicable to achieve either of the higher-ranking objectives specified in the legislation, namely rescuing the company as a going concern or achieving a better result than would be achieved on putting it into liquidation without first being in administration.[88] The primary purpose of these changes was to ensure the collective nature of all insolvency proceedings and to promote the rescue culture. There are special administration regimes for water and sewerage undertakers, protected railway companies, air traffic service companies, public-private partnership companies and building societies. These are excluded from the regime embodied in the new Part II of Sch.B1 to the Insolvency Act 1986.[89]

Administration has some affinities with the American Chapter 11[90] and involves the appointment by the court of an administrator to manage the company for the benefit of creditors generally with a view to securing one of three objectives,[91] arranged in a descending order of priority, namely:

> "(a) rescuing the company as a going concern, or
> (b) achieving a better result for the company's creditors as a whole than would be likely if the company were wound up (without first being in administration), or
> (c) realising property in order to make a distribution to one or more secured or preferential creditors."

1–22 The administration procedure is designed to fill a gap which previously existed in corporate insolvency law, in that there was no mechanism by which a company could be put under outside management for the benefit of unsecured creditors and of the company itself, and no effective step that could be taken to safeguard the company and its assets from precipitate action by creditors—*e.g.* levy of execution, enforcement of security, putting of the company into winding up—while steps were taken to put the company back on its feet and/or organise an arrangement with creditors.

Prior to the Enterprise Act 2002 administration required a court order. This came to be seen as introducing unnecessary delay and expense, and as

---

[88] Insolvency Act 1986, Sch.B1, para.3(4). See Chap.10.
[89] Enterprise Act 2002, s.249.
[90] See below, para.10–21.
[91] Insolvency Act 1986, Sch.B1, para.3(1). The formulation of these is not quite the same as in the original legislation.

the result of amendments introduced by that Act an administrator can be appointed by the holder of a qualifying floating charge or by the company or its directors by giving the specified period of notice of intention to make the appointment and, when this has expired, by filing with the court a notice of appointment and other prescribed documents.[92] This is likely to be the normal mode of appointment. But it remains open to interested parties to apply to the court for an administration order.[93]

The powers of the administrator are very similar to those of the administrative receiver but his role is a very different one, since he is concerned with the interests of creditors generally, not of a particular secured creditor, though his powers of distribution are more limited than those of a liquidator[94] and he must perform his functions with the objective selected in accordance with the Act.[95] Moreover, administration has a unique effect in imposing a total freeze on the enforcement of security rights and rights of repossession, the levy of distress, the institution or continuance of legal proceedings and even the winding up of the company, during the currency of the administration, except with the permission of the court or the consent of the administrator. No other type of insolvency proceeding has this effect, and it is undoubtedly a factor which contributed to the willingness of debenture holders, in certain cases, to allow the appointment of an administrator despite having the legal power to block it by appointing an administrative receiver,[96] a power which remains in those cases where it is still possible to appoint an administrative receiver.

Administrative receivership

1–23   Although the Enterprise Act 2002 largely abolished the institution of administrative receivership, this continues to be available under charges made before September 15, 2003 and also under charges made after that date in respect of a number of categories of charge exempted from the statutory provisions. Accordingly the law governing administrative receivership is likely to remain of importance for the foreseeable future.

The term "administrative receiver" is that used by the Insolvency Act 1986 to describe one whose previous formal appellation was receiver and manager, usually abbreviated to "receiver". An administrative receiver is a receiver appointed under a debenture secured by a floating charge covering (with any fixed security that may have been taken by the debenture holder) the whole or substantially the whole of the company's assets.[97] The primary

---

[92] Insolvency Act 1986, Sch.B1, paras 14–31.
[93] *ibid.*, paras 11–13, 35–39.
[94] See below, para.10–81.
[95] Insolvency Act 1986, Sch.B1, para.3(1).
[96] See para.9–26.
[97] Insolvency Act 1986, s.29(2), and see below, para.9–05.

function of the administrative receiver is to take control of the company's assets and effect such dispositions as will result in payment of the amount due under the debenture, after allowing for the administrative receiver's remuneration and expenses and any sums payable to preferential creditors. At one time the normal practice of receivers was to dispose of assets on a break-up basis and hand back what was left of the company to its directors. But the modern receiver tends to take a broader view of his responsibilities and, though putting the interests of his debenture holder first, also has regard to the interests of the creditors generally and of employees.[98] If the business is inherently sound and capable of being restored to profitability the receiver may find that he will secure a better return by continuing to trade with a view to disposing of the business as a going concern. Hence the conferment upon him of the widest management powers by the typical debenture, these now being enshrined in the Insolvency Act itself. The global nature of the debenture holder's security is made an essential ingredient of the statutory definition because without this the administrative receiver would be unable effectively to exercise the management powers conferred upon him.

Administrative receivership is to be distinguished from receivership *simpliciter*, that is, receivership of a particular asset or assets given in security pursuant to powers contained in the debenture and the Law of Property Act 1925. The function of the Law of Property Act receiver is much more limited. His task is to collect in income and apply it to keep down outgoings and mortgage interest. He has no statutory or implied power to dispose of the charged asset for the purpose of satisfying the debt. His security is specific, not global, he has no management powers and he has no involvement in the collective interest of the general body of creditors. Hence this form of receivership is not an insolvency proceeding, merely a method by which a secured creditor enforces his security.

In a sense this is true also of administrative receivership. In principle, the administrative receiver is concerned solely to protect the interests of his debenture holder, retiring from the scene once the debt due to the latter has been satisfied. In practice, as indicated above, the administrative receiver does take into account the interests of other creditors. Moreover, the all-embracing nature of the security has an impact on unsecured creditors, giving administrative receivership the colour of a collective proceeding; and because of this, modern insolvency law tends to treat administrative receivership as an insolvency regime, as by imposing on the administrative receiver the duty to pay preferential creditors out of the proceeds of property subject to a floating charge,[99] to file a report with the

---

[98] But he owes no direct duty to creditors (other than preferential creditors) or employees, though creditors are indirectly protected by the duty which the receiver owes to the company and which is enforceable by a liquidator.

[99] See below, para.9–63.

Companies Registrar, to report to all creditors and summon a meeting to present his report,[1] to liaise with any creditors' committee appointed to assist him, to render accounts not only to the company but to the Companies Registrar and members of the creditors' committee, and to assume personal responsibility for the salaries and wages of employees whose contracts of employment he adopts.[2] Hence although in concept administrative receivership is not a true insolvency proceeding, merely a method by which the debenture holder can enforce his security, it has many of the incidents of an insolvency regime and is treated as such by the Insolvency Act and by insolvency practitioners.

Winding up

1–24 Winding up, or liquidation, is a collective insolvency process leading to the end of the company's existence (dissolution). The principal role of the liquidator is to collect in and realise the assets, ascertain claims, investigate the causes of failure and, after covering the expenses of the liquidation, to distribute the net proceeds by way of dividend to creditors in the order of priority laid down by the Insolvency Act and the Insolvency Rules. When all this has been done, investigations concluded and reports made, the company is dissolved pursuant to the provisions of the Companies Act[3] and its legal life comes to an end.[4] In contrast to an administrative receiver or administrator, a liquidator has no power to carry on the business of the purpose except so far as may be necessary for its beneficial winding up.[5]

There are now three modes of winding up of an insolvent company,[6] namely a creditors' voluntary winding up, a compulsory winding up and a winding-up through administration. A creditors' voluntary winding up is not, as one might think, a winding up effected by the creditors themselves but results from a resolution of the members to put the company into voluntary winding up by reason of insolvency. This form of liquidation is termed a creditors' winding up because the control of the liquidation is primarily in the hands of the creditors rather than the court. Both the company and the creditors have a right to nominate the liquidator, but in the case of a difference the creditors' nomination prevails unless the court otherwise orders.[7] A compulsory winding up is a winding up by order of the

---

[1] See below para.9–22.
[2] See below paras 9–53 *et seq.*
[3] Companies Act 1985, ss.201–205.
[4] Subject to the power of the court to restore it on application under s.651 of the Companies Act 1985. See n.11, below.
[5] Insolvency Act 1986, Sch.4, para.5.
[6] Formerly there was a third, namely winding up under the supervision of the court (*i.e.* a creditors' voluntary winding up continued under the court's supervision) but this was abolished by the Insolvency Act 1985.
[7] Insolvency Act 1986, s.100.

court made upon a winding up petition presented, in the case of insolvency, by the company, the directors or one or more creditors.[8] A compulsory winding up is more formal and more closely controlled by the court, and the official receiver becomes the liquidator unless and until an outside liquidator is appointed.[9] A company which is in voluntary liquidation may be put into compulsory winding up on a petition presented for that purpose, and if an order is made the winding up thereafter continues as a compulsory winding up. A winding-up through administration is an exit from administration effected by registration of an administrator's notice, producing a deemed creditors' voluntary winding-up, or a court order not involving any petition.

Winding up has much in common with bankruptcy. Under both regimes an insolvency practitioner is appointed—a liquidator of a company, a trustee of a bankrupt—to collect in and realise the insolvent's estate and to distribute dividends according to a statutory order of priority. The two regimes have common underlying principles as to proof and priority of debts and the avoidance of transactions as preferences and transactions at a undervalue.[10] But whereas the ultimate objective of the bankruptcy process is the discharge of the bankrupt from his liabilities, so that he can begin again with a clean slate, free from the burden of his debts, and thus rehabilitate himself into the community, the ultimate fate of a company in winding up is not discharge but legal death through statutory dissolution.[11]

Compromises, compositions and arrangements with creditors, moratoria

A company unable to pay its debts as they are due may be able to reach an **1–25** agreement with its creditors for the satisfaction of their claims otherwise than by payment in full. Such an agreement may be made either within or outside of a statutory framework.[12] There are many different forms of agreement and these possess a bewildering variety of names: composition, compounding, compromise, arrangement, scheme of arrangement,

---

[8] *ibid.*, s.124. Most petitions are presented by creditors. As to the legitimacy of using a winding-up petition as a debt collection device, see para.5–10.

[9] *ibid.*, s.136(2).

[10] The word "avoidance" is here used in a loose sense. Technically the transactions remain valid but the court is given power to reverse their effect and restore the position to what it would have been if they had not been entered into. See below, para.11–02.

[11] Insolvency Act 1986, ss.201–205; Insolvency Rules 1986, r.84 (which enables a company in administration and without assets to move directly to dissolution without first being put into winding-up). However, the court may restore the corpse to life by declaring the company's dissolution void on application by the liquidator or any person appearing to the court to be interested (Companies Act 1985, s.651). The usual ground for exercising this power is that fresh assets have been discovered (*e.g.* insurance policies) which the company needs to be able to collect and distribute.

[12] For an early instructive and practical analysis, see J.R. Lingard, *Corporate Rescues and Insolvencies* (2nd ed., 1989), Chap.5. Non-statutory workouts are discussed below.

voluntary arrangement, moratorium, reorganisation, reconstruction, work-out.[13] In statutory provisions these tend to be used in pairs, but without consistency of terminology. Thus s.425 of the Companies Act 1985 refers to "compromise or arrangement" whilst s.1 of the Insolvency Act 1986 speaks of "composition in satisfaction of its debts or a scheme of arrangement of its affairs", both of these being then brought under the single rubric "voluntary arrangement." A *composition* is an agreement by which creditors accept, in a single sum or by instalments, an amount less than that which is due to them. It involves no transfer of assets or change of any kind in the structure of the company or the rights of its members *inter se* or *vis-à-vis* creditors. Debts which become the subject of a composition are said to be *compounded*, so that composition and compounding are synonymous. An arrangement cannot be a composition if no payment will be received by preferential and unsecured creditors,[14] but this does not prevent it from being a voluntary arrangement so long as such creditors retain rights after the end of any moratorium and accordingly do not suffer a confiscation or appropriation.[15] A *compromise* is an agreement in settlement of a claim which is in doubt, dispute or difficulty of enforcement.[16] The term would seem to cover agreements between a company and its creditors which cannot be enforced in full[17] because of the company's insolvency. *"Arrangement"* (which is synonymous with "scheme of arrangement") has a very wide meaning,[18] embracing such diverse schemes as conversion of debt into equity, subordination of secured or unsecured debt, conversion of secured into unsecured claims and vice versa, increase or reduction of share capital and other forms of reconstruction and amalgamation.[19] Though typically it involves agreement with a number of creditors, it has been held that even an agreement with a single creditor may constitute an arrangement.[20] But both "compromise" and "arrangement" imply an element of give and take and do not cover a situation in which rights are surrendered or extinguished with no countervailing benefit.[21] This does not, of course, mean that creditors who collectively agree to accept less than what is due to them are not concluding a compromise or arrangement, for each creditor benefits

---

[13] And in the case of an individual insolvent, an assignment (to trustees) for the benefit of his creditors.

[14] See below.

[15] *IRC v Adam & Partners Ltd* [2001] 1 B.C.L.C. 222, distinguishing *Re NFU Development Trust Ltd* [1973] 1 All E.R. 135.

[16] *Mercantile Investment & General Trust Co v International Co of Mexico* [1893] 1 Ch. 484n, at 491n, cited in *Re Guardian Assurance Co* [1917] 1 Ch. 431, *per* Younger J. at 443, whose decision was reversed by the Court of Appeal on a different point.

[17] In the words of Younger J. (*ibid.*), "to the uttermost farthing of the rights of the claimant".

[18] *Re Savoy Hotel Ltd* [1981] 3 All E.R. 646, *per* Nourse L.J. at 652; *Re Calgary & Edmonton Land Co Ltd* [1975] 1 All E.R. 1046 at 1054.

[19] For the meaning of "reconstruction", see below, para.1–25.

[20] *Taurusbuild Ltd v Svensak Handelsbanken* unreported, December 16, 1994, CA.

[21] *Re NFU Development Trust Ltd* [1973] 1 All E.R. 135 at 140, *per* Brightman J.; *Re Savoy Hotel Ltd*, above, at 652.

from the partial surrender of rights by the others. *Voluntary arrangement* is the term used in s.1(1) of the Insolvency Act to cover both compositions and schemes of arrangement to which Part I of the Act applies.[22] Other terms which deserve mention are: moratorium, reorganisation, reconstruction and restructuring (or workout). A *moratorium*, is a freeze on the exercise of creditors' rights agreed among the creditors (in which case it may also constitute a voluntary arrangement[23]) or imposed by the Insolvency Act as the result of proceedings for administration. A moratorium arranged by agreement differs from other forms of agreement with creditors in that it does not by itself operate to reduce the debts, merely to defer payment or postpone collection. *"Reorganisation"* is not a term of art but generally denotes any method by which the capital of a company is restructured and typically involves the formation of one or more new companies and, in the case of an insolvent company, a moratorium and various other elements.[24] A *reconstruction* is a form of reorganisation by which the business of a company is transferred to a new company in consideration of the issue of shares in the new company to the members of the old company in exchange for their shares in the latter. A scheme is not a reconstruction unless the business carried on by the new company is substantially the same as that carried on by the old company and the corporators of the old and new company are substantially the same.[25] A *restructuring*, or *workout*, is a reorganisation which is effected by agreement among creditors rather than as an arrangement under the Insolvency Act or the Companies Act, though the terms of the workout may provide for an insolvency proceeding such as winding up or for the distribution of assets to follow the rules of distribution in winding-up.

Modes of arrangement and compromise

Arrangements and compromises may be concluded in one of five ways: **1–26**

(1) As a compromise or arrangement under s.425 of the Companies Act.

(2) As a company voluntary arrangement ("CVA") under Part I of the Insolvency Act.

(3) As an arrangement by way of reconstruction pursuant to s.110 of the Insolvency Act.

---

[22] The heading of Part I of the Act refers to "Company Voluntary Arrangements", commonly abbreviated to "CVA." Only arrangements within Part I of the Act are CVAs.

[23] *IRC v Adam & Partners Ltd*, above, n.15.

[24] For the elements of a typical reorganisation plan in a company voluntary arrangement, see below, para.10–22.

[25] *Re Mytravel Group plc* [2004] All E.R. (D) 385; *Re South African Supply & Cold Storage Co* [1904] 2 Ch. 268.

(4)   As a compromise or arrangement by a liquidator under the Insolvency Act, ss.165–167 and Sch.4, para.2.

(5)   As a non-statutory arrangement or compromise concluded by contract or informal arrangement ("restructuring" or "workout").

Section 425 of the Companies Act, which can be invoked whether or not the company is in liquidation, involves obtaining the sanction of the court to a scheme approved by the requisite majority of creditors of each class at separately convened meetings ordered by the court, is best avoided wherever possible. The procedure is cumbersome and most things that can be done under s.425 can be more simply and expeditiously achieved by a CVA under Part I of the Insolvency Act, particularly since this can (and often will) be effected in the course of administration of the company under an administration order, where the administrator has the benefit of a statutory freeze on the enforcement of creditors' rights. There is, however, one great advantage enjoyed by the s.425 procedure over a CVA, in that once the scheme under s.425 has been approved all creditors are bound,[26] whereas a CVA binds only those creditors who in accordance with the rules had notice of and were entitled to vote at the meeting approving the arrangement.[27] So s.425, despite its drawbacks, continues to be used in a number of cases. Where the compromise or arrangement has been proposed for the purposes of or in connection with a scheme for reconstruction of any company or companies or any amalgamation the court is given specific powers when sanctioning the compromise or arrangement.[28]

Section 110 deals with a specific form of arrangement by which the liquidator in a voluntary winding up may, with the sanction of the court or the liquidation committee, dispose of the company's business to another company in exchange for shares, policies or other like interests in the transferee company. Sections 165–167 and Sch.4 to the Insolvency Act deal with the liquidator's power to make compromises or arrangements with creditors, subject to his obtaining the requisite sanction. It has been held that this procedure is not appropriate as a means of distributing assets otherwise than in accordance with creditors' strict legal rights, since the procedure lacks the safeguards for prospective dissentient creditors provided by s.425.[29] Compromises and arrangements under ss.165–167 and Sch.4 are quite distinct from CVAs, which are governed by Part I of the Insolvency Act 1986 and Part I of the Insolvency Rules 1986 and may be made even if the company is not in liquidation or administration. By contrast, arrangements under ss.165–167 and para.2 of Sch.4 are confined

---

[26] *British & Commonwealth Holdings plc v Barclays Bank plc* [1995] B.C.C. 19, affirmed [1995] B.C.C. 1059.

[27] Insolvency Act 1986, s.5(2)(b).

[28] Companies Act 1985, s.427. As to what constitutes reconstruction, see above, para.1–25.

[29] *Re Trix Ltd* [1970] 3 All E.R. 397.

to companies in liquidation and may be sanctioned either by the liquidation committee or by the court. The provisions relating to such arrangements are of long standing.[30] They are particularly useful in cases where it is impracticable to convene meetings of creditors.[31]

Finally, if the creditors are willing a scheme of arrangement, including a reconstruction, can be effected by a workout outside the statutory provisions altogether, by contract or, in some cases, informal arrangement. The workout has several advantages; it avoids the formality, expense and delay of the statutory modes of arrangement, is much more flexible and generally leaves a greater degree of control with the management. In addition, it may enable the company to avoid an event of default under its loan agreements, and the fact that it is being supported by its major creditors helps to reduce in some measure the effect of the damage to its reputation of becoming insolvent.[32] The success of a workout does, however, depend on the co-operation of all the creditors, which may be difficult to achieve unless they constitute a relatively homogeneous group, such as a syndicate of banks. Nevertheless, a study conducted by Professors Julian Franks and Oren Sussman a few years ago, based on the private records of three clearing banks, revealed a surprisingly high percentage of rescues based on informal work-outs.

1–27

> "Our first finding is that there exists an elaborate rescue process outside formal procedures. About 75% of firms emerge from rescue and avoid formal insolvency procedures altogether (after 7.5 months, on average). Either they are turned-around or they repay their debt by finding alternative banking sources. The remaining 25% of cases enter some form of insolvency procedure, usually administrative receivership or winding up i.e. liquidation. Turnarounds are often accompanied by management changes, asset sales, and new finance or directors' guarantees. There is evidence that these changes significantly influence the bank's response and the likelihood of a successful outcome."[33]

5. EXEMPTIONS FROM RULES OF INSOLVENCY LAW

In order to safeguard the securities markets against the invalidation of dealings in securities, netting arrangements and rules of recognised exchanges and clearing houses governing these matters, under rules of

1–28

---

[30] They go back to s.159 of the Companies Act 1862.

[31] See, for example, *Re Bank of Credit and Commerce International SA (No.3)* [1993] B.C.L.C. 1490.

[32] See generally Totty and Moss, *Insolvency*, Chap.H19.

[33] *The Cycle of Corporate Distress, Rescue and Dissolution: A Study of Small and Medium Sized UK Companies* (2000), p.3.

insolvency law which could adversely affect the efficient functioning of the market and thereby produce systemic risk, wide-ranging provisions have been introduced both by Part VII of the Companies Act 1989, supplemented by subordinate legislation, and by EC Directives designed to insulate such transactions from such insolvency law rules and, in the case of transactions covered by Part VII, to replace them with the approved rules of the exchange or clearing house in question. Under Part VII, these exemptions apply to market contracts, market charges, money market contracts, money market charges and system charges. The Directives are concerned with securing settlement finality and the protection of dealings in financial collateral and related close-out arrangements by requiring Member States to ensure that dealings and arrangements of the kind specified in the directives are not invalidated by rules of insolvency law. There are also special rules governing the winding-up of credit institutions, including EEA credit institutions,[34] and insurance companies.[35] These modify the general rules of corporate insolvency law in a number of important respects. They are not dealt with in the present work.

Market contracts

1–29   A market contract is a contract connected with a recognised investment exchange or recognised clearing house which is entered into by a member or designated non-member of the exchange, or by the exchange itself in connection with the provision of clearing services.[36] Market contracts and the settlement rules of a recognised investment exchange or a recognised clearing house relating to the settlement of market contracts are not to be regarded as invalid at law on the ground of inconsistency with the law relating to the distribution of the assets of a person on winding-up, and similar provisions apply to money market contracts, market charges and system charges.[37] The proceedings of the exchange or clearing house are to take precedence over insolvency procedures.[38] The broad effect is to substitute the approved rules of the exchange or clearing house for the

---

[34] Credit Institutions (Reorganisation and Winding up) Regulations 2004 (SI 2004/1045), implementing the EC directive on the reorganisation and winding up of credit institutions (2001/24/EC dated April 4, 2001, OJ L125, 5.5.2001, p.15).

[35] Financial Services and Markets Act 2000, ss.376–379; Insurers (Reorganisation and Winding Up) Regulations 2004 (SI 2004/353); Insurers (Winding Up) Rules 2001 (SI 2001/3635). These implement the EC directive on the reorganisation and winding-up of insurance undertakings (2001/17/EC dated March 19, 2001, OJ L110, 20.4.2001, p.28).

[36] Companies Act 1989, s.155.

[37] Companies Act 1989, Part VII, as modified by the Financial Markets and Insolvency Regulations 1991 (SI 1991/880), as amended; Financial Markets and Insolvency (Money Markets) Regulations 1995 (SI 1995/2049); Financial Markets and Insolvency Regulations 1996 (SI 1996/1469).

[38] Companies Act 1989, s.159.

insolvency distribution rules, thus in effect creating a self-contained mini-insolvency distribution system for such contracts and charges. The requirements for recognition of an investment exchange or clearing house under the Financial Services Act 1986 include those set out in Sch.21 to the Companies Act 1989,[39] which oblige UK investment exchanges and UK clearing houses to have rules enabling action to be taken in the event of a member's default. The rules must provide for the rights and liabilities of a defaulter,[40] and in particular must provide for sums payable by or to the defaulter in respect of different contracts to be aggregated or set-off so as to produce a net sum,[41] and, in the case of a clearing house for that sum, if payable by the defaulter to the clearing house, to be set off against any property provided by the defaulter as cover for margin, and if payable by the clearing house to the defaulter to be aggregated with any property provided by the defaulter as cover for margin.[42]

Market charges

A market charge means a charge, whether fixed or floating, granted in favour of (*inter alios*) a recognised investment exchange for the purpose of securing debts or liabilities arising in connection with the settlement of market contracts or in favour of a recognised clearing house for the purpose of securing debts or liabilities arising in connection with their ensuring the performance of market contracts.[43]   **1–30**

Money market contracts and charges and systems charges

Part VII of the Companies Act 1989 was extended to money market contracts and money market charges[44] by the Financial Markets and Insolvency (Money Market) Regulations 1995[45] and, within stated limits, to system charges,[46] that is, charges in favour of a settlement bank for the purpose of securing debts or liabilities arising from various types of transfer or transfer agreement relating to uncertificated securities.[47]   **1–31**

---

[39] Companies Act 1989, s.156(1).
[40] These include, in the case of a clearing house, rights and liabilities arising in respect of the effecting by the clearing house of offsetting contracts ("corresponding contracts"), a form of close-out mentioned below, para.8–12. See Companies Act 1989, Sch.21, para.10.
[41] *ibid.*, Sch.21, paras 2(1), (2), 9(1), (2).
[42] *ibid.*, Sch.21, paras 1(4), 9(2).
[43] *ibid.*, s.173. Charges on land are excluded (Financial Markets and Insolvency Regulations 1991 (SI 1991/880), reg.8).
[44] A money market charge is a charge, whether fixed or floating, given in favour of a listed person to secure debts or liabilities arising in connection with the settlement of money market contracts or related contracts (Financial Markets and Insolvency (Money Market) Regulations 1995 (SI 1995/2049).
[45] SI 1995/2049. The regulations were made pursuant to s.171 of the Companies Act 1989.
[46] Financial Markets and Insolvency Regulations 1996 (SI 1996/1469).
[47] *ibid.*, regs.2(1), 3(2).

Settlement finality in dealings in financial collateral

1–32　Two EC Directives have been issued designed to remove from attack under insolvency law netting and close-out arrangements under the rules of designated systems[48] and, more broadly, contractual arrangements to similar effect relating to financial collateral.[49] The European Community has long been concerned to limit systemic risk[50] to ensure both the efficiency and the stability of dealings among participants in recognised clearing and settlement systems. Hence the two Directives in question, the 1998 settlement finality Directive[51] and the 2002 Directive on financial collateral arrangements.[52] The latter in particular is designed to override rules of national law that impair the legal efficacy of financial collateral arrangements and provision within or outside insolvency.

(1) The Settlement Finality Directive

1–33　The effect of the Directive and implementing regulations is largely to remove from attack under general insolvency law the rules of a designated settlement system, and transactions (including the realisation of collateral security) effected in connection with participation in such a system. Thus system rules governing default arrangements, in particular, arrangements for netting and the closing out of open positions,[53] and the application or transfer of collateral security,[54] are to be respected notwithstanding any rules of insolvency law which might otherwise invalidate them. Thus the restrictions imposed by paras 43(2) and 44(5) of Sch.B1 to the Insolvency Act 1986 on the enforcement of security while an administration is current or pending or the order is in force do not apply in relation to a collateral security charge,[55] and s.127 of the Act (which invalidates dispositions made after the commencement of a winding up unless approved by the court) does not apply to a disposition of property as the result of which it becomes subject to a collateral security charge.[56] Of some importance also is the

---

[48] Directive on settlement finality in payment and securities systems, 98/26/EC dated May 19, 1998, implemented in the UK by what are now the Financial Markets and Services (Settlement Finality) Regulations 2001, SI 2001/1349.

[49] Directive on financial collateral arrangements. 2002/47/EC, implemented in the UK by the Financial Collateral Arrangements (No.2) Regulations 2003, SI 2003/3226.

[50] The risk that the failure of one major participant will have a domino effect on the system as a whole.

[51] See above, n.48. The regulations were amended by SI 2001/997 but for technical reasons revoked immediately on the date of entry into force by SI 2001/1349.

[52] See above, n.49.

[53] See paras 8–08 *et seq.*

[54] Including security provided under a charge or repurchase or similar agreement for the purpose of securing rights and obligations potentially arising in connection with the system.

[55] Financial Markets and Insolvency (Settlement Finality) Regulations 1999, SI 1999/2979, reg.19(1).

[56] *ibid.*, reg.19(3).

conflict of laws rule embodied in Art.9(2) of the Directive[57] which provides that where securities are provided as collateral to a (system) participant and/or central bank of a Member State and their right with respect to the securities is legally recorded in a register, account or centralised deposit system located in a Member State, the rights of holders of the collateral are to be determined by the law of that Member State. One effect of this is that rights in relation to securities held through an account with a securities intermediary in a Member State it is the PRIMA law[58] that applies.

The Settlement Finality Directive will require some revision in the light of Art.4 of the 2002 Hague Convention on indirectly held securities.[59]

(2) The Directive on financial collateral arrangements

The 2002 Directive on financial collateral arrangements is altogether **1–34** broader and more ambitious in scope. Its purpose is to facilitate the provision of financial collateral under bilateral transactions, and thereby promote not only the stability of the market but also its efficiency, by requiring Member States to disapply rules of law and statutory provisions that would otherwise invalidate financial collateral arrangements and provision, whether before insolvency (as by rendering void transactions not carried out or perfected in conformity with prescribed formalities) or on insolvency. The Directive covers both directly held and indirectly held securities. Regrettably an understanding of the Directive is somewhat impeded by technical defects, linguistic problems in the English text and the practice of placing in the Preamble substantive rules of interpretation which should be in the text,[60] coupled with a measure of duplication of provisions[61] and inconsistency of terminology.[62] Nevertheless the Directive is to be warmly welcomed as a great step forward in ensuring the legal stability of financial collateral arrangements and provision. We shall note only those provisions relevant to insolvency.

---

[57] Implemented in the UK by reg.23 of the Financial Markets and Insolvency (Settlement Finality) Regulations 1999. It is likely that Art.9(2) will be modified in the light of the 2002 Hague Convention on the law applicable to certain rights held with an intermediary.

[58] The place of the intermediary approach.

[59] See the Explanatory Report on the Convention (rapporteurs: Roy Goode, Hideki Kanda, Karl Kreuzer, assisted by Christophe Bernasconi).

[60] For example, Art.3(1) can be fully understood only by reference to paras (9) and (10) of the Preamble. See below, para.1–37.

[61] *e.g.* Art.3(2) repeats the substance of Art.1(5).

[62] *e.g.* in relation to the expression of formal requirements. See below. Some of these defects have been overcome in the Financial Collateral Arrangements (No. 2) Regulations 2003 (SI 2003/3226) which implement the Directive. However, in a fascinating High Court judgment Mr Peter Prescott Q.C., dealing with an issue concerning registered designs, held that the statutory instrument implementing the relevant directive went beyond what the directive required and was thus *ultra vires* in that it fell outside the rule-making power conferred by s.2(2) of the European Communities Act 1972. This raises the question whether the financial collateral regulations are vulnerable to attack as extending the immunities conferred by the regulations to entities not covered by the directive.

(a) Scope of the Directive

1–35   The Directive covers financial collateral in the form of cash or financial instruments.[63] It distinguishes between arrangements for the provision of collateral and its actual provision. The Directive applies only when the collateral has actually been provided and only where the provision is evidenced in writing[64] and the collateral arrangement (*i.e.* agreement) is evidenced in writing or in a legally equivalent manner.[65] Moreover, though this will be found only in the Preamble,[66] financial collateral is to be considered "provided" only where there is some form of disposession, by which is meant that the collateral is delivered, transferred, held, registered or otherwise designated so as to be in the possession or under the control of the collateral taker or of a person acting on his behalf.[67] In short, the security interest must be not only created but perfected by possession or control. Until then, the Directive has no application and the efficacy of the security interest is left to national law. All the methods of possession or control referred to represent methods of perfection available under existing English law.

(b) Categories of financial collateral arrangement

1–36   Financial collateral arrangements are divided into two categories, title transfer financial collateral arrangements and security ("book-entry") financial collateral arrangements. The former are arrangements, including repurchase agreements, under which full ownership is transferred to the collateral taker.[68] This reflects the securities industry's usage in treating title transfer as a form of collateral even though in English law an outright transfer does not constitute a security interest.[69] Security financial collateral arrangements ought logically to have been defined as arrangements for the provision of security not involving the transfer of

---

[63] Art.1(4)(a). "Financial instruments" are defined in Art.2(1)(e) and cover virtually all forms of instrument issued on a market. See SI 2003/3226, reg.3.

[64] This requires that the financial collateral be identifiable, which in the case of book-entry securities or cash is satisfied by crediting to an account.

[65] The Directive uses the phrase "can be evidenced in writing", which is a somewhat unusual way of saying that it *is* evidenced in writing. This does not mean the agreement must be *in* writing, merely that if it is made orally or inferred from conduct there must be written evidence of it. It is not clear why the phrase "or in a legally equivalent manner" appears in reference to arrangements for the provision of collateral but not in relation to the provision itself, nor what the phrase adds, given that by Art.2(3) "writing" includes recording by electronic means and any other durable medium."

[66] Para.(10).

[67] Para.(9). The same paragraph (reflected in SI 2003/3226, reg.3) makes it clear that this requirement is not to exclude techniques for the substitution of collateral or withdrawal of excess collateral by the collateral provider. See further below.

[68] Some countries do not recognise the grant of security by title transfer. Art.6 requires Member States to ensure that a title transfer financial collateral arrangement can take effect in accordance with its terms.

[69] See below, para.7–14.

full ownership. Unfortunately they are instead defined as arrangements for the provision of security where full ownership of the collateral remains with the collateral provider. Literally construed, this would exclude the transfer of ownership by way of security, *i.e.* in English law terms a mortgage, which would thus fall outside the Directive altogether. Plainly this is not intended, and the definition of "security interest" in the UK financial colateral regulations covers mortgages.

In the case of direct holdings outright title transfer is by entry on the share register; in the case of indirect, or book-entry, holdings title transfer presumably includes not only transfer by novation, that is, transfer to the collateral taker's account, but also assignment. As stated above, title transfer arrangements do not include mortgages, which transfer only security ownership, not full ownership, but do include outright sale and repurchase agreements which are intended to fulfil a security function even if not, under English law, constituting security agreements.[70] Security financial collateral arrangements are, in English law terms, arrangements which create charges or, in the case of bearer securities, pledges, and must also be taken to include mortgages even though on a literal construction these fall outside the definition. However, floating charges would appear to be outside the scope of the Directive, at least until crystallisation, since the requisite element of transfer of control to the creditor is lacking.[71]

(c) Reduction of formalities

One of the main purposes of the Directive is to reduce the requirements for attachment and perfection of a security interest in financial collateral to a minimum. Article 3, of which the first paragraph is expressed in very wide terms, provides as follows: **1–37**

"1. Member States shall not require that the creation, validity, perfection, enforceability or admissibility in evidence of a financial collateral arrangement or the provision of financial collateral under a financial collateral arrangement be dependent on the performance of any formal act.

2. Paragraph 1 is without prejudice to the application of this Directive to financial collateral only once it has been provided and if that provision can be evidenced in writing and where the financial collateral arrangement can be evidenced in writing or in a legally equivalent manner."

Article 3(1) states the basic principle that no formal act is necessary for the creation, validity, etc. of a financial collateral arrangement or the

---

[70] See below, para.7–14.
[71] Joanna Benjamin and Madeleine Yates, *The Law of Global Custody* (2nd ed., 2002), para.4.45.

provision of financial collateral. This, however, is subject to Art.3(2), which would have been clearer if it had said simply that Art.3(1) takes effect subject to the provisions of Art.1(5). These, as stated above, make the application of the Directive dependent on the provision of collateral. What Art.3(2) fails to state is that in order for the collateral to be considered as "provided", the collateral taker's interest must be perfected by some form of "dispossession" of the debtor if the Directive is to apply. The effect would seem to be that, notwithstanding Art.3(1), national law continues to apply to the creation and validity of security interests but that once perfected by possession or control by the collateral taker the provision of financial collateral must be recognised even if not created in the manner prescribed by national law. For interests not so perfected it remains open to the collateral taker to perfect by any other means available under national law, *e.g.* registration.

Article 3(1) must also be read in conjunction with the Preamble, which in effect states[72] that Member States may continue to require the creation or transfer of a security interest in financial collateral to be effected by acts such as endorsement of instruments to order[73] and registration of transfers of directly held securities, which for the purposes of the Directive are not formal acts, but that there should be no formalities for the attachment or perfection of transfers of or security interests in indirectly held (book-entry) securities. As to these it will no longer be open to a Member State to require that a document be executed in any particular form or in a particular manner, that the date of its execution or the amount of the relevant financial obligations be evidenced in any manner or that perfection of a security interest be dependent on registration in a public register, filing with or notification to a public officer, or advertisement. In fact there are currently no formal requirements under English law for the *attachment* of a security interest in registered securities, and formal perfection requirements in the shape of registration in the Companies Registry apply only to floating charges, charges on book debts and charges to secure any issue of debentures. Floating charges are thought to be outside the scope of the Directive,[74] but in any event these requirements were abolished when the UK implemented the Directive, thereby eliminating, for registration purposes, the risk of recharacterisation of a purported fixed security as a floating charge or of a sale and repurchase as a registrable security transaction.

---

[72] Paras (9) and (10).

[73] It is not clear how the requirement that the provision of collateral (as opposed to arrangements for such provision) be evidenced in writing is to be applied in the case of bearer securities, which by nature are transferred by delivery.

[74] See above, para.1–36.

(d) Enforcement

Member States are required to ensure that on the occurrence of an enforcement event[75] the collateral taker has available to a range of enforcement measures, subject to the parties' agreement. **1–38**

(e) Protection from insolvency avoidance

Articles 7 and 8 are designed to protect the provision of financial collateral against avoidance for insolvency. Article 7 requires Member States to ensure that a close-out netting provision can take effect in accordance with its terms notwithstanding the commencement or continuation of winding-up proceedings or reorganisation measures and other specified events. One effect of this provision is to preserve the validity of close-out netting provisions expressed to be triggered by the commencement of a winding-up. Article 8 of the Directive requires Member States to ensure that financial collateral arrangements are protected from avoidance under various rules of insolvency law. In particular, Article 8 precludes avoidance on the sole basis that the financial collateral arrangement has come into existence, or the financial collateral has been provided, within a prescribed period prior to, and defined by reference to, the commencement of winding-up proceedings. Another precludes avoidance of transactions involving the provision of top-up collateral solely on the ground that the top-up was provided on the day of commencement of the winding-up proceedings or after the relevant financial obligations had been incurred. Part 3 of the financial collateral regulations implements all these provisions. **1–39**

EEA credit institutions

There are special rules restricting the institution of winding-up proceedings or the undertaking of reorganisational measures against an EEA[76] credit institution.[77] **1–40**

---

[75] Defined by Art.2(1)(l) as an event of default or any similar event agreed between the parties on the occurrence of which, under the terms of a collateral financial arrangement or by operation of law, the collateral taker is entitled to realise or appropriate financial collateral or a close-out netting comes into force. Again, the drafting is a little strange, for read literally it does not cover a right of realisation given by law unless the relevant event is one agreed between the parties! This comes from the misplacing of the phrase "or by operation of law", which should have been inserted after "parties." It is thought that Art.2(1)(l) is to be interpreted as if drafted in this way.

[76] European Economic Area.

[77] Credit Institution (Reorganisation and Winding Up) Regulations 2004 (SI 2004/1045). See further below, para.13–01.

Chapter 2

The Philosophical Foundations of Corporate Insolvency Law

1. INTRODUCTION

Corporate insolvency law has four overriding objectives: to restore the debtor company to profitable trading where this is practicable; to maximise the return to creditors as a whole where the company itself cannot be saved; to establish a fair and equitable system for the ranking of claims and the distribution of assets among creditors,[1] involving a limited redistribution of rights; and to provide a mechanism by which the causes of failure can be identified and those guilty of mismanagement brought to book and, where appropriate, deprived of the right to be involved in the management of other companies.[2] To facilitate achievement of these objectives insolvency law provides a battery of legal and administrative instruments and institutional structures.

2–01

The instruments by which the above objectives are achieved include the placement of the company and its assets under the control of an external manager,[3] with wide powers of investigation and management, including disposal or closing down of the business; the suspension of rights of individual pursuit of claims and their replacement by a collective debt collection process, followed by distribution of net realisations according to a statutory system of priorities; the avoidance of transactions entered into by

---

[1] The phrase "distribution among creditors" is here used as a shorthand to denote the distribution of realisations of assets. On the winding up of an insolvent company assets are rarely distributed *in specie*; they are sold and the net proceeds used to pay cash dividends to creditors.

[2] See also the Report of the Insolvency Law Review Committee, *Insolvency Law and Practice*, paras 191–199.

[3] Alternatively, continuance of the existing management under the supervision of the court and creditors, as in the case of a reorganisation under Chapter 11 of the American Bankrupty Code, where the debtor-in-possession has the powers of a bankruptcy trustee.

the company which are improper or which it would otherwise be unfair to allow to stand, and the recovery of misapplied assets; the imposition of civil and criminal sanctions, including disqualification, for improper conduct on the part of the directors; and qualification requirements for insolvency practitioners designed to ensure their integrity and competence. Insolvency law also provides for the ultimate death of a company in winding-up by a procedure for dissolution.

Despite this battery of instruments an insolvent company has essentially only two options: to trade out of its difficulties, usually after a process of reorganisation, and to go into liquidation. Administration is usually an interim procedure which may be a route to either process, though it is now possible for a company to move directly from administration to dissolution without first being reorganised or going into winding-up.[4]

The philosophy underpinning English corporate insolvency law is much harder to state since it has never been very clearly articulated. Questions such as the legitimate province of corporate insolvency law and the social and economic policy basis for its ordering of entitlements, which have long been the subject of debate and controversy in the United States, for long lay dormant in this country, and only recently have they begun to attract the attention of scholars. For ease of exposition I shall begin with the particular—the objectives and instruments of corporate insolvency law—before going on to discuss the broader issues of policy which inform, or should inform, legislative and judicial decisions in this field.

2. THE PHILOSOPHY OF CORPORATE INSOLVENCY LAW

2–02   The failure of a corporate enterprise potentially affects a wide range of interests. Those most immediately concerned are, of course, creditors, management, other employees and shareholders. But the failure may have wider repercussions. It may force customers and suppliers into insolvency; it may, in causing job losses, tear the heart out of the local community; in the case of a major bank or industrial company it may even affect the national economy, for example by undermining confidence or by removing a key player from the export market. The community at large may also have an interest in the continued performance of the company's obligations in public law, for example, in the clean-up of environmental pollution caused by the company's activities. So when a company becomes insolvent there are stark choices to be faced: should the sole or primary concern be to maximise returns to creditors? or should it be to preserve the company and/ or its business, even if this can only be done at some expense to creditors'

---

[4] See above, para.10–103.

rights? Is the primary concern the protection of private rights or of public interests?

It will be apparent, therefore, that there are serious questions to be addressed as to the legitimate province of corporate insolvency law and as to its philosophical foundations. Given the pragmatic way in which English law in general has developed it is perhaps unsurprising, but nevertheless disconcerting, to discover the lack of a clearly articulated philosophy of law in this field. Scholars in North America have long been interested in the bankruptcy process,[5] and have devoted much time and effort to policy issues and theoretical constructs, if rather less to empirical research, though this has always been at a much greater level than in other jurisdictions and is beginning to become prominent.[6] More recently academics and insolvency practitioners in the United Kingdom have begun not merely to identify the need for more information about insolvency and the impact of insolvency law—on which there is a serious dearth of hard data—and to explore policy issues and undertake or commission research designed to cast light on the effectiveness of the legal regime governing individual and corporate insolvency, but also to concern themselves with normative theories of insolvency law.[7] Space does not permit more than a brief examination of these issues, on which there is now an enormous amount of literature, particularly in North America. But it is worth reminding the reader that normative theories of bankruptcy law are not concerned with the existing state of the law or with its current objectives; rather they are directed to the question what those objectives should be and how best they may be achieved.[8]

(i) The province of corporate insolvency law

To what extent should bankruptcy affect pre-bankruptcy entitlements?

How should we mark out the territory that should be occupied by corporate insolvency law? What is its legitimate province? This question has been much debated among scholars in the United States as to the function of corporate insolvency law. They divide into broadly two camps: the proceduralists, whose position is that the primary function of bankruptcy law is

2–03

---

[5] In this context "bankruptcy" includes the liquidation of companies.

[6] See below, para.2–03, text and n.15.

[7] See, for example, Rizwaan Jameel Mokal, *Corporate Insolvency Law: Theory and Application* (2005); Vanessa Finch, *Corporate Insolvency Law* (2002).

[8] There are scholars who distrust the value of normative theories, arguing that what matters is the reality of bankruptcy law and policy. For a discussion of the issue see Donald R. Korobkin, "The Role of Normative Theory in Bankruptcy Debates" 82 Iowa L. Rev. 75. See below, para.2–03.

to respect pre-bankruptcy entitlements and to organise a collective procedure to that end; and the "traditionalists", whose position, reflecting existing bankruptcy policy, is that bankruptcy law has a wider role to play and a wider range of interests to accommodate.[9]

Professors Baird, Jackson and Scott are leading proponents of the view that it is not for insolvency law to concern itself with employment protection or with wider community interests, or to reorder substantive rights acquired under pre-bankruptcy law. Their thesis is that whatever rights and privileges may be conferred in other areas of law, insolvency law has one overriding goal: to allocate the common pool of assets in such a way as to maximise benefits for creditors as a whole.[10] The attainment of this goal is threatened whenever individual creditors take unilateral action to fish in the common pool of assets without regard to the interests of other fishers. Therefore insolvency law must impose a collective procedure for the taking of fish. Two other principles must be strictly observed if the aim of collective asset maximisation is to be fulfilled. First, there must be rigid adherence to the absolute priority rule, *i.e.* that shareholders receive nothing until creditors have been paid in full.[11] Secondly, insolvency law must respect the pre-bankruptcy ordering of entitlements. It is the function of insolvency law to translate pre-bankruptcy assets and liabilities into the bankruptcy forum with minimal dislocation.[12] Among the reasons advanced for this view are (1) that the redistribution of rights on insolvency would create a perverse incentive for a particular creditor who would be advantaged by the change to go for an insolvency proceeding even if this would not be in the general interest of the creditors and (2) that insolvency law should distribute assets according to a scheme for which creditors lacking prior knowledge of how they would fare in relation to other creditors in the event of the debtor's insolvency could have been expected to bargain *ex ante* in order to maximise the collective value of the proceedings, and they would have seen this as best achieved, as regards unsecured creditors, by an offer of *pari passu* distribution and, as regards secured creditors, by an assurance that their priority would be maintained and their participation in the collective process compensated so as not to affect the net value of their pre-bankruptcy entitlements, *i.e.* there would be no transfer of net value

---

[9] For an overview by an English scholar of some of the principal theories advanced, see Vanessa Finch, *Corporate Insolvency Law: Perspectives and Principles*, Chap.2.

[10] See Thomas H. Jackson, "Bankruptcy, nonbankruptcy and the creditors' bargain" 91 Yale L.J. 857 (1982); Jackson, *The Logic and Limits of Bankruptcy Law*, Baird and Jackson, "Corporate Reorganizations and the Treatment of Diverse Ownership Interests: A Comment on Adequate Protection of Secured Creditors," 51 Univ. of Chicago Law Rev. 97 (1984); Jackson and Scott, "On the Nature of Bankruptcy: an Essay on Bankruptcy Sharing and the Creditors' Bargain" 75 Virginia Law Rev. 155 (1989).

[11] See Baird and Jackson, "Bargaining after the Fall and the Contours of the Absolute Priority Rule" 55 Univ. of Chicago Law Rev. 738 (1988).

[12] Jackson, "Translating assets and liabilities to the bankruptcy forum", 14 *Journal of Legal Studies* 73 (1985).

from them to unsecured creditors. It follows that rehabilitation of the debtor's business is not a legitimate objective of bankruptcy law except to the extent that it is designed to maximize recoveries for existing entitlement holders.

These basic propositions, which have been developed into very elegant and sophisticated theories of bankruptcy law based on the concept of the creditors' bargain, have not passed unchallenged. Powerful attacks have been launched both on the notion that the sole purpose of insolvency proceedings is to maximise returns to creditors and on the assertion that it is not the function of bankruptcy law to alter relative pre-bankruptcy entitlements.[13] Professor Elizabeth Warren has argued convincingly that there are other interests to consider apart from those of creditors, and that to concentrate so exclusively on maximising returns to creditors is a dangerous over-simplification of the nature and purpose of the bankruptcy process.[14] She has also joined with Professor Jay Westbrook in a trenchant criticism of the use of theoretical constructs to reach policy conclusions without any attempt being made to verify by empirical evidence the premises upon which they are based.[15]

The elegance and conceptual clarity of the theories advanced by Jackson **2–04** and his colleagues have greatly illumined our understanding of the functions of corporate insolvency law. But there is force too in the criticisms that have been made. In postulating that insolvency law should respect the bargain that actual creditors in their own best interests would have reached *ex ante* as to how the debtor's assets should be distributed in the event of its insolvency, the creditors' bargain theory and similar contractarian theories[16] based on a hypothetical agreement among creditors take it as axiomatic that only those with consensual claims against the debtor's assets at the time of opening of the insolvency proceedings (compendiously described as "owners") qualify for consideration as parties to the hypothetical bargain. The holders of non-consensual interests, such as tort creditors, employees in regard to job preservation claims, local suppliers as regards the impact on their business of failure of the insolvent firm and the local community at large when a major employer ceases trading, might deserve distributions of the assets in bankruptcy but this would be conceptually different in character from distributions based on the *ex ante* bargain.[17] Thus bankruptcy law is essentially procedural in character; its role is not to affect pre-

---

[13] See Elizabeth Warren, "Bankruptcy Policy" 54 Univ. of Chicago Law Rev. 775 (1987).

[14] *Loc. cit.*, above, n.13, at pp.800 *et seq.*

[15] Warren and Westbrook, "Searching for Reorganization Realities," 72 Wash. Univ. L.Q. 1257 (1994).

[16] Not to be confused with contractualism, which is concerned with control of the bankruptcy process rather than the ordering of priorities. See below, para.2–08.

[17] Jackson and Scott, "On the Nature of Bankruptcy: An Essay on Bankruptcy Sharing and the Creditors' Bargain", n.10 above, at 177, disclaiming any intent to assess the normative value of distributions to non-consensual interests. For a criticism of the exclusion of non-consensual creditors from representation in the hypothetical creditors' bargain, see Donald R. Korobkin, "Contractarianism and the Normative Foundations of Bankruptcy Law" 71 Tex. L. Rev. 541, 554–555 (1993).

bankruptcy the substance of entitlements but rather to organise a collective regime designed to ensure the preservation of those entitlements to the maximum extent possible.[18] Only to this extent is the rehabilitation of an insolvent business a legitimate function of bankruptcy law.[19]

But there are values to be protected that go beyond the interests of those with accrued rights at the commencement of the insolvency process. One of these is the investigation of the conduct of the directors with a view to sanctions for improper trading and disqualification so as to protect the public against future misconduct, a course of action available in England through the winding-up process even where the company has no assets at all.[20] Another is the interest of shareholders in the preservation of their future expectations. A third is the interest of the workforce in preserving its investment of labour, expertise and loyalty to the enterprise and a fourth that of the community at large, for example, in the continuance of the business[21] or the payment of clean-up costs of pollution.[22] To focus so exclusively on maximising returns to creditors is to ignore the fact that there may be different ways of protecting creditors, some of which will also benefit other interests, such as those of employees, shareholders and the local community, and in so doing may even advance creditors' interests.

The answer Professors Baird and Jackson give to all this is that if interests other than those of common pool creditors are to be protected, this should be done outside bankruptcy law and the protection should not be exclusive to bankruptcy but should be slotted into the scheme of relative non-bankruptcy entitlements. So if it is desired to give special rights to employees or tort claimants, that should be done through labour law or tort law and in the latter case should be a protection equally available against closure of a business outside bankruptcy. It is then for bankruptcy law to respect the special non-bankruptcy entitlement given by labour law or tort law,[23] rather than itself to create a new entitlement in the bankruptcy.

2–05   The argument is neat but ultimately unpersuasive, for it overlooks the fact that certain problems confronting claimants outside the common pool creditors arise specifically because of the company's insolvency and for no other reason. For example, in England labour law already gives rights and

---

[18] For a developed treatment of the procedural theory of bankruptcy law, see Charles W. Mooney, Jr., "A Normative Theory of Bankruptcy Law: Bankruptcy As (Is) Civil Procedure" 61 Wash. & Lee L. Rev. 931. See also Douglas G. Baird, "Bankruptcy's Uncontested Axioms" 108 Yale L.J. 573.

[19] Thus stopping an insolvent company from closing a plant which it would be entitled to close outside bankruptcy is not legitimate: Mooney, n.18 above, at pp.957–958.

[20] See below, para.5–14.

[21] For a discussion of this communitarian approach, see Karen Gross, "Taking Community Interests into Account in Bankruptcy, 72 Wash. Univ. L.Q. 1031 (1994). The communitarian approach has been criticised for its indeterminacy and the wide range of interests that would have to be considered.

[22] See below, para.2–12.

[23] See Jackson, *The Logic and Limits of Bankruptcy Law*, pp.31–32; Baird, "Loss Distribution, Forum Shopping and Bankruptcy: a Reply to Warren", 54 Univ. of Chicago Law Rev. 815.

remedies to employees who are wrongfully or unfairly dismissed or are made redundant. But in the pursuit of these remedies against a solvent company the former employees are not competing with other creditors, for there are by definition enough assets to meet all claims. It is only on insolvency that the ranking of unsecured claims arises. There is thus no scope for the *general law* to prescribe priority for employees or tort claimants. Such a priority rule would make no sense except in the context of bankruptcy, when there is not enough to go round. Moreover, to treat bankruptcy law as confined to creditors confronting the common pool problem is surely to prejudge the very question in issue. It is also wholly inconsistent with insolvency laws around the world, all of which include provisions for claimants outside the common pool creditors.[24] Again, the event most likely to attract the need for investigation of a company's affairs and disqualification of its directors is the company's insolvency; and it is exclusively in the context of insolvency that the need arises to provide for the making of orders against directors guilty of fraudulent or wrongful trading requiring them to contribute to the shortfall of net assets.

If it is conceived to be beneficial to bring all creditors within a collective proceeding for the common benefit of creditors, rather than allow each creditor to pursue his or her own self-serving interests, why should it not be equally beneficial to require creditors as a class to co-operate as part of a wider class of beneficiaries that would include employees and shareholders as regards interests and expectations beyond their pre-bankruptcy entitlements? There was a time in England when the receiver and manager (now termed the administrative receiver) appointed by a debenture holder would see his task as being to move in, sell up and get out. If the business could be sold on a break-up basis to produce enough to cover the debt due to the debenture holder, why invest effort in keeping the business going? Nowadays receivers take an altogether broader view of their role. If there are alternative courses of action, one of which will benefit creditors only, and another which, with a little delay, will confer benefits on employees and shareholders without significant detriment to the creditors, then why should it not be a legitimate function of insolvency law to have regard to those wider interests? They may be subordinate to those of creditors, but that is not a ground for denying that they have their own place in the scheme of things. This theme has been repeated again and again in statements of national policy concerning the role of insolvency law.

"We believe that the aims of a good modern insolvency law are . . .

    (i) to recognise that the effects of insolvency are not limited to the private interests of the insolvent and his creditors, but that other interests of society or other groups in society are vitally affected

---

[24] For the current position under English law, see below, para.2–09.

by the insolvency and its outcome, and to ensure that these public interests are recognised and safeguarded;

(j) to provide means for the preservation of viable commercial enterprises capable of making a useful contribution to the economic life of the country . . ."[25]

"The fundamental purpose of reorganization is to prevent a debtor from going into liquidation, with an attendant loss of jobs and possible misuse of economic resources."[26]

2–06 It is also quite clear that insolvency law has at least some redistributional role to play, for every legal system has developed rules under which some categories of unsecured claim (for example, government taxes and unpaid wages) are accorded preferential status, and may even trump certain forms of security interest,[27] while other categories are ranked below the general body of creditors.[28] Moreover, the concept of the creditors' bargain is fraught with difficulty. Though the creditors' bargain is based on the concept of what real-world parties will do, the parties presented are not in truth real-world parties at all—for example, those examined in a major market survey—but rather imaginary characters invested with the qualities that the scholars would attribute to real persons. But what is the source of identification of these qualities and how do we know that they have any relationship with the qualities of actual creditors? Since in practice creditors do not act collectively in taking credit decisions we have no idea how they would proceed, or what range of factors they would take into consideration, if they were to come together before taking their credit decisions. Secondly, the models that have been constructed postulate that each creditor would be in a position to gauge with reasonable accuracy the relative risks and benefits of individual versus collective action and would thus be guided to a rational outcome. But since no creditor can be sure, in the absence of agreement, what other creditors will do, such a risk assessment is impossible and any creditors' bargain reached on the basis of it cannot in reality be more than a gamble for each creditor—possibly an inspired gamble, in some cases, but a gamble all the same. It is hard to see

---

[25] Report of the (Cork) Review Committee, *Insolvency Law and Practice*, para.198. See also paras 235–240 making the same point in relation to individual bankruptcy.

[26] *NLRB v Bildisco & Bildisco*, 465 US 513, 528 (1983), citing views expressed by Congress, HR Rep. No.95–595, p.220 (1977). See further Dal Pont and Griggs, "A Principled Justified for Business Rescue Laws: A Comparative Perspective (Part I)" (1995) 4 I.I.R. 189.

[27] For example, in England charges which as created were floating charges are subordinate to the claims of preferential creditors (see para.7–40), in addition to which a percentage of net assets subject to a floating charge has to be surrendered to form a fund for unsecured creditors (see para.6–31).

[28] For an argument that large creditors, who are better able to withstand the impact of the debtor's insolvency than small creditors, should suffer some diminution in their distributional rights in favour of small creditors, see Karen Gross, *Failure and Forgiveness* (1997), Chap.10.

how such a notional bargain could form the basis of a rational system of insolvency law. Moreover, if one could imagine a situation in what all creditors, secured and unsecured, *were* to come together to decide what was to happen in the event of disaster, would it not be likely that unsecured trade suppliers, on having brought home to them as a group the relative vulnerability of their position, would insist on a slice of the corporate cake as a condition of their co-operation?

This, indeed, is the central problem of law and economics theories of insolvency, that they begin with untested hypotheses of creditor behaviour which, by the end of the argument, have become imperceptibly converted into findings of fact and are thus made the basis for firm conclusions and policy recommendations. A simple example will suffice. It is assumed as an article of faith that a creditor taking security will charge a lower rate of interest than one who lends on an unsecured basis.

"Secured creditors, for example, would have paid for their priority position by accepting a lower rate of return and, should therefore be allowed to retain the benefits of their initial bargain by receiving an equivalent value for their collateral in bankruptcy. Unsecured creditors, on the other hand, would have obtained a higher interest rate by forgoing security and, in so doing, would have assumed a greater risk that their claims would not be fully satisfied upon default and subsequent bankruptcy. The participants in the bankruptcy bargain could thus be expected to honor this relationship by maintaining the secured creditors' non-bankruptcy entitlements and by preventing redistribution in bankruptcy from secured creditors to unsecured creditors and the debtor."[29]

But in many cases this is simply not how lending works. Banks charge what they consider the market will bear. A bank does not quote a lower rate of interest *because* it is secured; it takes security because of a perceived risk of non-payment and may charge a *higher* rate because of the risk. Similarly, the mere fact that a loan is unsecured does not necessarily mean that the bank will charge a higher rate. Indeed, as regards blue-chip borrowers one could stand the argument on its head and note that with the intense competition for their business among banks they would be well placed to refuse to give security at all, and this same bargaining power would enable them to negotiate the most favourable lending rates.

Similarly, a strict adherence to the absolute priority rule could deprive creditors of the co-operation from shareholders which in some reorganisations has been shown to be essential to the success of the plan. If shareholders are to be persuaded not to obstruct a reorganisation considered desirable by creditors, they too will expect a slice of the pie, though

2–07

---

[29] Jackson and Scott, *loc. cit.*, above, n.10, p.161.

experience has shown that their ability to negotiate this is extremely limited in the case of failure of a large public corporation where management decides to co-operate with the creditors and abandon the shareholders.[30] With a view to meeting considerations of this kind the creditors' bargain theory was reconstructed to hypothesise that creditors would not necessarily bargain for total priority and that what should be predicated is an *ex ante* bargain based on an assumed willingness by all creditors to bear in some degree the risk of an exogenous, or externally imposed, disaster, as opposed to one caused by internal management.[31] Dr Rizwaan Mokal, who is also critical of the creditors' bargain model on a number of counts, has advanced an alternative theory which he terms the authentic consent model.[32] This model, which extends participation to parties other than creditors, is based on the concept of "dramatic ignorance" in which the parties to the creditors' bargain are ignorant not only of insolvency outcomes and of how other creditors would behave but also of their own attributes, such as whether they are voluntary or involuntary creditors, whether they are in a dominant or subordinate position, so that the assumption to be made is that all parties are free and equal and enter into a bargain that is fair and just.

The problem confronting those who have to consider to what extent the different variants of the creditors' bargain theory should influence bankruptcy policy is that most of them assume an original position in which the various players and the bargain they make act in an economically rational manner according to a single set of criteria. This may be an elegant model but has no necessary connection with fact. Human beings and even corporations are usually actuated by wider considerations than pure economic rationality. Moreover, the factors that enter into a rational decision are often much more diverse than those on which economic reasoning is based, so diverse indeed that it is hard to see how any single set of *ex ante* assumptions can be expected to match the complex realities of business life or to accommodate the many categories of decision maker and the variety of circumstances in which their decisions may have to be made. This is not to decry the value of normative theories, simply to note the danger of equating models with fact in reaching policy conclusions.

A leading international insolvency specialist has also attacked the creditors' bargain theory as based on a central assumption of a common pool of assets to which creditors would *ex ante* wish to have recourse.

"This central assumption is not in accord with basic economic facts and legal structures. There is no common pool of assets to which creditors

---

[30] I am indebted to Professor Jay Westbrook for this insight.
[31] See Robert E. Scott, "A Relational Theory of Secured Financing," 86 Col. L. Rev. 901; Jackson and Scott, above, n.10.
[32] Rizwaan Jameel Mokal, "The Authentic Consent Model: Contractarianism, Creditors' Bargain, and Corporate Liquidation", (2001) 21 Legal Studies 400; and see now Mokal, *Corporate Insolvency: Theory and Application*.

wish to have and could have a claim before bankruptcy. Credit, unless it is secured by specific pieces of property, is normally extended with the expectation that not only payment of interest but also repayment of capital will come from the debtor's income, not from a sale of fixed assets. The debtor's income is normally produced not by the assets themselves, but rather by the activities of the debtor which only partly consist in using the assets. This means that, if the debtor is (or has) an enterprise, income is produced by the organizational set-up consisting of owners, managers, employees, and a functioning network of relations with the outside world, particularly with customers, suppliers, and, under modern conditions, with various government agencies; and it is the expected stream of income produced by the ongoing enterprise that allows for the normally peaceful coexistence of creditors with claims of different maturities."[33]

Who should control the bankruptcy?

Leading American scholars have pointed out that earlier debates on the theory of bankruptcy concentrated heavily on priority issues and tended to neglect the central question of control of the bankruptcy assets.[34] But only recently has attention focused on the relevance to control of the distinction between cases where there is a dominant security interest and those where security interests are diffused among a number of creditors none of whom is dominant.[35] This is a crucial consideration in considering whether as a matter of policy insolvency proceedings should fall within the public domain or whether on the other hand the State should permit parties to contract out of bankruptcy rules and adopt their own arrangements, leaving public control as the default situation where no relevant contracts are in place. In America contractualism has secured powerful support[36] and equally powerful opposition.[37] One of the major problems is that in any

2–08

---

[33] Axel Flessner, "Philosophies of Business Bankruptcy Law: An International Overview," in Jacob S. Ziegel (ed.), *Current Developments in International and Comparative Corporate Insolvency Law* 19 at 25–26.

[34] Jay Lawrence Westbrook, "The Control of Wealth in Bankruptcy", 2004 Texas L. Rev. 795 (2004); Douglas G. Baird and Robert K. Rasmussen, "Control Rights, Priority Rights, and the Conceptual Foundations of Corporate Reorganizations", 87 Virginia L. Rev. 921 (2001). Ronald J. Mann, "Strategy and Force in the Liquidation of Secured Debts", 96 Mich. L. Rev. 159 (1997); Robert K. Rasmussen, "Debtor's Choice: A Menu Approach to Corporate Insolvency", 71 Texas L. Rev. 51 (1992).

[35] Westbrook, above n.34.

[36] Alan Schwartz, "A Contract Theory Approach to Business Bankruptcy", 107 Yale L.J. 1807 (1998); Ramussen, above, n.34.

[37] Lynn M. LoPucki, "The Case for Cooperative Territoriality in International Bankruptcy", 98 Mich. L. Rev. 2216 and "Contract Bankruptcy: A Reply to Alan Schwartz", 109 Yale L.J. 317 ((1999); Westbrook, above, n.34.

given case there are likely to be numerous contracts made at different times, on different terms and in different circumstances, and even if there were statutory provision for public notice of agreements that would not, in relation to any one agreement, assist those who became creditors prior to that agreement. Professor Jay Westbrook has effectively demonstrated that contractualism cannot function effectively unless there is a creditor holding a dominant security interest, without which "the contractualist proposals are crippled by intractable problems."[38] But control of the bankruptcy process by a dominant secured creditor is incompatible with the concept of neutral management and can lead to a failure to realise full value for the assets for the benefit of other creditors. Indeed, as Professor Westbrook points out, it was just such a consideration that led the United Kingdom largely to abandon the institution of administrative receivership, which did indeed operate in large degree as a privately contracted ordering of the business and assets of an insolvent company.[39] A novel approach, which certainly has the merit of giving advance notice of the applicable rules while avoiding the problem of multiplicity of contracts and contract choices, is the so-called "menu" approach advocated by Professor Robert Rasmussen which would allow an enterprise, upon its formation, to select from a statutory menu of options the particular bankruptcy regime that would apply in the event of its becoming insolvent.[40] This certainly solves the notice problem but commits the enterprise and other interested parties to a pre-determined bankruptcy regime which may in the event turn out to be quite unsuited to the maximisation of returns to creditors.[41]

Social and economic policy

2–09   What is clear from any comparative survey is that the role of corporate insolvency law cannot be constructed in the abstract, and that the extent to which the law of a particular country adheres to or deviates from the principle of collective maximisation of returns for creditors in an insolvency is directly related to its pre-insolvency social and economic policy.[42] Civil

---

[38] Westbrook, above, n.34 at 831.

[39] This is because by definition an administrative receiver was one appointed by the holder of a floating charge which, with other charges, covered the whole or substantially the whole of the debtor company's assets. The result was that there were few, if any, free assets available to unsecured creditors outside liquidation or to the liquidator himself prior to discharge of the receivership by collection of sums sufficient to pay off the appointing creditor's claims and, from the proceeds of assets subject to a floating charge, preferential debts. Thus if receivership was followed by liquidation the liquidator had to remain on the sidelines while the receiver was in office, and the appointment of a receiver was usually a bar to the making of an administration order. See below, paras 9–26 *et seq.*

[40] Robert K. Rasmussen, "Debtor's Choice: A Menu Approach to Corporate Bankruptcy" 71 Texas L. Rev. 51 (1992).

[41] See to the same effect Jay Westbrook "The Control of Wealth in Bankruptcy" (2004) 22 Texas L. Rev. 795, 832.

[42] See in particular Jose M. Garrido, "The Distributional Question in Insolvency: Comparative Aspects" (1995) 4 I.I.R. 25.

law jurisdictions tend to be more debtor-oriented than common law jurisdictions and to place greater emphasis on workers' rights and the importance of preserving the enterprise. This is particularly true of France,[43] which has a long tradition of government paternalism, coupled with strong judicial control over debt collection activity. English law stands at the opposite end of the spectrum, with an extremely liberal attitude towards creditors' rights, self-help and the use of contractual remedies, coupled with a steady erosion of workers' rights and immunities. American law is also strongly pro-creditor, though imposing more restrictions than English law on enforcement both within and outside bankruptcy. There is no doubt that English corporate insolvency places a heavy emphasis on creditors' rights and adopts as a general principle respect for the pre-liquidation ordering of entitlements. Indeed, the approach of the Cork Committee on the former point was quite uncompromising:

"In the case of an insolvent company, society has no interest in the preservation or rehabilitation of the company as such, though it may have a legitimate concern in the preservation of the commercial enterprise."[44]

But this approach is changing. Moreover, English law, like other legal systems, does recognise certain types of claim as justifying a priority in bankruptcy that they would not otherwise enjoy. Thus within defined limits the claims of employees rank ahead of other unsecured creditors, reflecting the fact that they lack the opportunities open to other creditors to limit their risk and typically have no source of income other than their wages. The same was true of government taxes, but persistent criticism of Crown preference led to its abolition.[45]

The implications of the rescue culture

Reference has already been made to the growth of the rescue culture and the increasing attention paid to the rehabilitation of the business. The corporate reorganisation which this typically entails cannot readily be achieved without some interference with pre-existing entitlements. So far as possible the UK legislation seeks to avoid a significant diminution in a creditor's substantive rights. Rather it aims to restrict their enforcement, as by imposing a temporary freeze on remedial measures or by requiring the creditor to accept a monetary equivalent rather than enforcement *in specie*.

2–10

---

[43] See Axel Flessner, "Philosophies of Business Bankruptcy Law: An International Overview" in *Current Developments in International and Comparative Corporate Insolvency Law* (ed. Jacob S. Ziegel), p.22.

[44] See n.25 above, *Insolvency Law and Practice*, para.193. See further below, para.10–26.

[45] See below para.7–27.

So rights to non-monetary performance of a contract which the liquidator declines to have performed by the company are converted into a right to prove for damages for the loss suffered through non-performance; the initiation of administration, in or out of court, imposes a freeze on most forms of enforcement, a freeze which continues during the currency of the administration[46]; and the administrator of a company is in certain conditions given power to dispose of charged assets free from the security interest[47]; But in certain cases there is a positive disturbance of the relative entitlements that existed before bankruptcy. For example, even a crystallised floating charge is subordinate to the claims of unsecured preferential creditors.[48] A still more significant interference with pre-bankruptcy entitlements is the obligatory surrender of a percentage of assets subject to a floating charge so as to make these available to unsecured creditors.[49]

So the redistribution of pre-liquidation rights does feature, albeit in a limited way, in corporate insolvency law. On the other hand, its primary concern has to be with the disposal or closing down of the company's business and the collection and distribution of net realisations. It is not equipped, except in a very small degree, to address wider economic or social problems, such as the maintenance of employment or the protection of the environment. These can only be tackled by measures outside the purview of insolvency law, for example, employment legislation and environmental regulation, to which reference will be made shortly. Moreover, it may be found necessary not merely to leave these larger issues to be dealt with outside corporate insolvency law but positively to subordinate insolvency law to economic interests that are considered to require a higher priority. Striking in this respect is the almost total exclusion from rules of insolvency law of market contracts, market charges and financial collateral,[50] an exclusion dictated by the desire not to jeopardise the dominance of the City of London as a financial centre by exposing normal market operations and dealings in uncertificated securities to a challenge under insolvency law.

Insolvency law and employment

2–11   There is an almost inevitable tension between creditors' rights on insolvency and those of the company's employees. Where the business is viable and the failure is due to short-term problems or mismanagement the insolvency practitioner will usually wish to maintain a substantial part of the

---

[46] Insolvency Act 1986, Sch.B1, paras 42, 43. See below, paras 10–47 *et seq.*
[47] Insolvency Act 1986, s.70(1). See below, paras 10–78, 10–79.
[48] See below, para.7–46.
[49] See below, para.6–31.
[50] See above, paras 1–29 *et seq.*

workforce,[51] and if the business is sold off or is hived down to a newly-formed subsidiary the employees may be able to treat their contracts of employment as transferred to the new owner of the business under the Transfer of Undertakings (Protection of Employment) Regulations 1981.[52] But whether with or without such a transfer, employees of an insolvent company face the prospect of redundancy, particularly where the insolvency practitioner considers that the company is substantially over-staffed or where the business is disposed of and merged with that of another company which sees the opportunity to make efficiency savings. Whilst employees clearly have a legitimate interest in the outcome of their employer's insolvency, it would obviously be unrealistic to impose on the insolvency practitioner a duty to protect that interest by keeping them in employment where this would damage the company's economic prospects. Quite apart from the duties he owes to existing creditors, the insolvency practitioner will be guilty of fraudulent trading if he allows the company to incur new debts when there is no real prospect that these will be paid when due or reasonably soon thereafter,[53] and may incur a liability for wrongful trading if the company goes into insolvent liquidation and he has failed to take proper steps to minimise loss to creditors.[54]

So other ways have to be found of giving help to employees of an insolvent company. These are provided partly by employment law, partly by insolvency law and partly by the law governing occupational pensions. Employment law gives a measure of protection through statutory provisions as to the transfer of undertakings,[55] and entitlements to arrears of pay,

---

[51] The importance insolvency practitioners attach to job preservation is shown by the change of name of the leading association of insolvency professionals from SPI (Society of Insolvency Practitioners) to R3 (the Association of Business Recovery Professionals).

[52] SI 1981/794. The extent to which the TUPE obligations imposed on a purchaser are inimical to the rescue culture is an open question. There is clear evidence that in some cases it makes it impossible to find a buyer for the company's business. On the other hand, where this is not the case, jobs are preserved instead of being lost. The Department of Trade and Industry was sufficiently concerned about the possible effect of TUPE to put forward proposals in 2001 to exclude it in the case of insolvent companies. However, any exemptions have to operate within the framework of EC law. Article 5 of the amended EC directive on the safeguarding of employees' rights on the transfer of undertaking (Council Directive 2001/23/EC of March 12, 2001) permits the exclusion of the transferor's pre-existing debts to the extent that employees are protected as to these as far as provided by EC law (in the UK by the various statutory schemes), and employers and employee representatives may, exceptionally, agree on changes to the terms and conditions of employment so far as permitted by national law and with a view to ensuring the survival of the business and thereby preserving jobs. Regulations 8 and 9 of the draft Transfer of Undertakings (Protection of Employment) Regulations 2005 issued in March 2005 (URN 05/926) embody both options. Regulation 10 excludes liability of the transferor for pension entitlements, leaving the transferred employees to their rights against the transferee under the Pensions Act 2004 as regards pre-transfer entitlements. For a detailed analysis of the present position see John Armour and Simon Deakin, "Insolvency, Employment Protection and Corporate Restructuring: the Effects of TUPE", Centre for Business Research, University of Cambridge, CBR Working Paper No.204, (2002).

[53] See below, para.12–19.

[54] See below, paras 12–25 *et seq.*

[55] Above, para.2–11.

redundancy payments and compensation for unfair dismissal, all backed by the National Insurance Fund.[56] Under the Insolvency Act 1986 a claim for arrears of pay is preferential, within defined limits.[57] Broadly speaking, these measures do no more than protect in insolvency, and then only to a limited degree, rights the employee would have had against the employer outside winding-up. Under ss.257 and 258 of the Pensions Act 2004 the transferee is required to ensure that transferred employees are, or are eligible to be, active members of the transferor's occupational pension scheme.

Insolvency law and the environment

2–12   We have noted instances where English corporate insolvency law departs from the general principle that relative entitlements acquired before winding-up should be respected. These departures are all concerned with the adjustment of private rights. Altogether more dramatic, though in a restricted area, is the potential impact of public law, and in particular the prospect that an insolvency practitioner might be obliged, under pain of criminal sanctions against the company, to utilise the debtor company's assets to meet the cost of remedying environmental pollution caused by the company's activities, pursuant to a clean-up order under the Environmental Protection Act 1990.[58] This could completely wipe out the assets that would otherwise have been available to meet creditors' claims. The issue has been litigated in several North American cases and has featured in England in relation to a liquidator's right to disclaim a waste management licence as onerous property, thereby bringing an end to the company's duties as licensee.[59] It is not without interest that in *Re Mineral Resources Ltd*,[60] another case concerning disclaimer of a waste management licence, Neuberger J. held that the interests of the community in a healthy environment should prevail over the fair and orderly winding-up of companies, so that the principle of "polluter pays" in the Environmental Protection Act 1990 took precedence over the distribution rules in the Insolvency Act 1986, with the result that though the waste management licence was property it was not property of a kind that could be disclaimed; and he reached this conclusion in full agreement with counsel that the effect would be to make clean-up costs an expense of the liquidation payable in priority to the claims of unsecured creditors. This aspect of the judge's decision was later overruled by the Court of Appeal in *Re Celtic Extraction Ltd*[61] on the ground

---

[56] See generally Totty and Moss, *Insolvency*, Chap.28.
[57] See below, para.7–27.
[58] Sections 26(1), 82(2). See Totty and Moss, *op cit.*, Chap.H1, and below, paras 7–30 *et seq.*
[59] In *Re Celtic Extraction Ltd* [2001] Ch. 475; *Environment Agency v Hillridge* [2004] 2 B.C.L.C. 358. See below, para.7–30.
[60] *Re Mineral Resources Ltd, Environment Agency v Stout* [1999] 1 All E.R. 746.
[61] [2001] Ch. 475.

that an important aspect of implementation of the oft-repeated public policy requirement that the property of unsecured insolvents should be divided equally amongst unsecured creditors was the power of disclaimer, without which the available assets would be appropriated to the claims of future or prospective creditors, so that such a power should not be regarded as overridden unless statute so provided. Nevertheless the *Mineral Resources* case and the discussion of it in *Re Celtic Extraction Ltd* provide a vivid illustration of the way in which the interests of the community may come into consideration as of a higher order than those of unsecured creditors.

(ii) The recognition and ordering of creditors' rights

Who are to be considered creditors?

It would be possible to take a very restricted view of creditor status and to confine creditors for insolvency purposes to those whose claims were in existence and had already matured at the time of winding-up. Indeed, one could go further and exclude the holders of non-consensual claims, such as claims in tort, from the insolvency process. Such an approach, however, would be grossly unfair both to unsecured creditors holding unmatured claims and to tort creditors. In relation to the former it would discriminate against long-term lenders and make them bear the primary loss burden despite their contribution to the company, which arguably is even more important than that of short-term suppliers of credit. In consequence it would discourage long-term loan capital and be likely to lead to precipitate contractual debt acceleration in the event of default. Holders of existing but unmatured debts thus qualify for inclusion in the distribution stakes.[62] So too do contingent creditors,[63] so long as their claims are not so shadowy as to be incapable of valuation. Similarly, to exclude tort claimants would be to debar those who are sharing with contract creditors in a common disaster. Claims for unliquidated damages in contract have always been allowed; similar claims in tort were at one time not provable unless reduced to liquidated sums by judgment or agreement, supposedly because of the much greater difficulty of valuing them than unliquidated claims in contract, but the distinction, criticised by the Cork Committee, has been abandoned.[64]

So in deciding who qualifies for admission to the insolvency process no distinction is made between voluntary (consensual) and involuntary (non-

2–13

---

[62] See further below, para.7–32.
[63] Insolvency Rules 1986, rr.4.86. 12.3(1).
[64] Insolvency Rules 1986, rr 12.3(1), 13.12.

consensual) claimants. The objection to the admissibility of unliquidated tort claims was on the ground of the perceived difficulty of valuation, not their involuntary character. Indeed, some would argue that involuntary creditors should enjoy a higher status in the priority ranking than voluntary creditors, because they did not intend to assume a risk but had it thrust upon them. A similar argument could be made for Crown preference in relation to taxes and duties. But English insolvency law has not followed this path; on the contrary, Crown preference was initially restricted under the Insolvency Act 1986[65] and subsequently abolished by the Enterprise Act 2002,[66] while tort claimants rank with other unsecured creditors. The distinction between voluntary and involuntary creditors is in any event less clear than might be supposed. Many debtors delay payment and take credit which was never offered, and many creditors, faced with competition in the market, have little choice but to allow credit to be taken, with or without their prior agreement. So the distinction is not so much between voluntary and involuntary credit as between having and not having a real choice whether to allow the debt to be incurred in the first place.

Priority entitlements and their impact on the insolvency regime

2–14   It is a fundamental principle of insolvency law, and one which has many aspects,[67] that the debtor's assets are to be distributed *pari passu*. In the language of the Act of 1542, the proceeds of realisations were to be distributed among creditors "rate and rate alike, according to the quantity of their debts." However, we have already remarked that the expenses of the liquidation have to be deducted in computing the net realisations available for distribution and that no dividends can be paid to ordinary unsecured creditors until the preferential debts have been paid in full. Moreover, with some exceptions it is only those assets in which the company has a beneficial interest that are available to its creditors. So property held by the company as bailee or trustee does not form part of the common pool, nor do goods in the possession of the company under a contract of sale reserving title until payment, if payment has not been completed. Again, property beneficially owned by the company but over which it has given security rights constitutes an asset only to the extent of the company's equity of redemption, measured by the difference between the value of the asset and the amount of the secured indebtedness. Similarly, the liquidator takes control of the company's assets subject to equities, such as rights of set-off and rescission of contracts. All these illustrations of the rule that only assets of the company are available for

---

[65] See below, para.7–27.
[66] Enterprise Act 2002, s.251, amending Sch.6 to the Insolvency Act 1986.
[67] See below, paras 7–02 *et seq.*

distribution are manifestations of the broader principle, previously discussed, that corporate insolvency law respects pre-liquidation rights, and in particular property rights and equities.

When bankruptcy was first introduced, property and trust law were much less developed than they are today. Trusts were largely confined to land, debts were not considered assignable, the common law drew a clear distinction between transfers of property and uncompleted agreements for transfer, and non-possessory security over goods was almost invariably considered fraudulent.[68] But since the sixteenth century there has been an explosive growth in the concept of ownership and other real rights (rights *in rem*). The maxim that equity treats as done that which ought to be done, so that an agreement for a mortgage is treated in equity as a completed mortgage, is now so taken for granted that we no longer realise what an enormous step this was, one which largely obliterated the distinction between a *ius in re* and a *ius ad rem*, between a right *in* an asset and a personal right *to* an asset.[69] Thus evolved the concept, remarkable to the eyes of civilians, of an informal security able to be created by pure agreement without any act of conveyance and, in the case of goods, without even the requirement of writing.

Nor was this all. Recognition of the non-possessory security interest in existing personal property was rapidly followed by its extension in equity to future property and, in the case of companies, to global security capable of covering all classes of asset, present and future, to secure all forms of existing and future obligation. The peak of sophistication was reached with the development of the floating charge, a security in a shifting fund of assets from time to time held by the company and given under an agreement which left the company free to dispose of the assets in the ordinary course of business but in certain eventualities, including those specified by contract between the parties, became converted into a full-blooded specific security. **2–15**

Even now we have not exhausted the range of real rights available to the creditor. A profusion of quasi-security devices developed. The retention of title under contracts of sale and hire-purchase agreements, blessed by the courts as falling outside the legal regime governing usury and bills of sale, grew in popularity and became extended to cover products and proceeds and to secure not only the price of the particular goods but all current-account indebtedness. Netting arrangements between parties engaged in mutual dealings became ever more sophisticated.[70] The so-called "flawed asset" was conjured up by ingenious practitioners.[71] It has even been held,

---

[68] *Twyne's Case* (1602) 3 Co. Rep. 80b.
[69] See R. M. Goode, "Ownership and Obligation in Commercial Transactions" (1987) 103 L.Q.R. 433.
[70] See below, Chap.8.
[71] Roy Goode, *Commercial Law* (3rd ed.) p.612.

by-passing theoretical objections, that a bank can take a charge over its own customer's credit balance.[72] Meanwhile equity lawyers had developed the resulting trust, where money paid or property transferred for a purpose which had failed was held to be impressed with a trust in favour of the payer or transferor; and more recently the constructive trust has been forged into a restitutionary proprietary weapon of enormous power which shows few signs of abating.

The result of all these developments has been disastrous for the ordinary unsecured creditor. Every new property right, every added security interest, every proprietary restitutionary remedy, every equity, has eroded his or her stake in the insolvency process. Add to this the categories of debt still enjoying preferential status[73] and it can readily be seen that the lot of the general body of creditors is a very unhappy one. The *pari passu* rule remains the guiding principle of distribution in English winding-up but the free assets available to meet ordinary unsecured claims are in the typical case so small that there is little on which the principle can bite.[74] Thus in those cases where the insolvency estate is swollen by recoveries in respect of void or voidable transactions it is likely to be the preferential creditors who are the main beneficiaries.

The justification for protecting ownership and security rights

2–16   It is now far too late to turn back the clock and unwind equitable security interests, equities and resulting and constructive trusts, though not too late to change our insolvency law and bring the more extended forms of constructive trust into the ambit of our rules on preferences and transactions at an undervalue or subject them to the exercise of judicial discretion which would take account of the existing or potential interests of unsecured creditors.[75] But if we leave on one side the more doubtful (in policy terms) extensions of equitable proprietary rights, we can see that the protection of ownership and security interests rests on sound principles. Rights of ownership should in principle be respected, for if they are not upheld on insolvency the distinction between property and obligation becomes largely meaningless.[76] The same is true of security interests. To

---

[72] *Re Bank of Credit and Commerce International S.A. (No.8)* [1998] A.C. 214.

[73] See Roy Goode, *Commercial Law*, pp.837–838 and below, para.7–27.

[74] See below, para.7–04.

[75] See Roy Goode, "Property and Unjust Enrichment" in *Essays on the Law of Restitution* (ed. Andrew Burrows), Chap.9.

[76] However, ownership has not always been fully protected in English bankruptcy law. Section 38 of the Bankruptcy Act 1914 embodied a concept of reputed ownership by which goods in the possession of the bankrupt under such circumstances as to make him the reputed owner were brought within the bankrupt's estate. The concept was not formally abolished until the repeal of the Act by the Insolvency Act 1985, by which time it had anyway become largely a dead letter.

deny recognition of the secured creditor's real rights upon the debtor's insolvency would be to use the very event against which the security interest was designed to give protection as the ground for its destruction. The economic justification for upholding security rights was well put by Professors Jackson and Kronman in a much-cited article published 26 years ago:

". . . if the law denied debtors the power to prefer some creditors over others through a system of security agreements, a similar network of priority relationships could be expected to emerge by consensual arrangement between creditors. Permitting debtors to encumber their assets achieves the same result, but in a simpler and more economic fashion. If a debtor has more than two or three creditors, free-rider and holdout difficulties are likely to plague any attempt on the part of creditors to work out a set of priority relationships among themselves. These transaction costs can be avoided by allowing the debtor himself to prefer one creditor over another. The rule permitting debtors to encumber their assets by private agreement is therefore justifiable as a cost-saving device that makes it easier and cheaper for the debtor's creditors to do what they would do in any case."[77]

In policy terms, the secured creditor is accorded priority because he bargained for it; other creditors who chose to lend unsecured cannot complain of their subordinated position.[78] If I may be allowed the indulgence of quoting from an earlier paper of my own on the subject:

"The bargain element is widely accepted as a proper ground for giving the secured creditor priority so long as the grant of security does not involve an unfair preference and other creditors have notice of the security interest, so that they are not misled into thinking that the assets comprising the security are the unincumbered property of the debtor. The battle rages over three crucial questions: in what circumstances should new value be required as a condition of making a security interest effective against other creditors? where it is to be required, what should suffice to constitute new value? and what classes of creditor should be entitled to complain of want of value or absence of notice?"[79]

I shall explore these issues later in relation to the avoidance of transactions on winding-up or administration.[80]

---

[77] "Secured Financing and Priorities Among Creditors", 88 Yale L.J. 1143 (1979).
[78] See R. M. Goode, "Is the Law Too Favourable to Secured Creditors?" (1983–84) 8 Can. Bus. L.J. 53 at p.57.
[79] (1983–84) 8 Can. Bus. L.J. 53 at pp.57–58.
[80] Below, Chap.11.

3. THE OBJECTIVES OF ENGLISH CORPORATE INSOLVENCY LAW

2–17   The principles of English corporate insolvency law will be examined in the next chapter. At this stage we would simply note certain basic features of corporate insolvency law and establish what it is it trying to do.

As with other insolvency laws English insolvency law addresses two central questions, priority and control. These questions need to be kept separate. Priority is concerned with the order of distribution of assets as a matter of substantive law. Control is essentially procedural and is designed to safeguard the assets by placing them in the hands of a manager acting for the benefit of the creditors at large, individual actions and enforcement measures being stayed. Such control would be necessary whatever the priority rules.

The priority of claims is largely based on pre-insolvency entitlements, but our insolvency law does possess limited redistributional aspects, particularly in relation to floating charges.[81] Before the abolition (with some exceptions) of administrative receivership it could fairly be said that English law adopted a contractual approach to control, allowing the holders of global security through fixed and floating charges to displace the management of the debtor company by appointing an administrator receiver, whose control of all the assets largely inhibited action by other creditors and left a liquidator waiting on the sidelines until completion of the receivership. That has now changed and our insolvency law has moved away from contractualism to neutral management through an administrator or liquidator, whose appointment imposes an automatic stay on the enforcement of individual claims.

As in other jurisdictions, English law offers two alternative routes for an insolvent company: reorganisation on the one hand and liquidation and distribution of the assets on the other. Administration is an interim procedure which is a prelude to one or other of these or, if they are not achievable, to realisation for the benefit of a secured creditor having a fixed and floating charge over all or substantially all of the company's property.

With these preliminary remarks we can turn to the particular objectives of corporate insolvency law.

Restoring the company to profitable trading

2–18   This objective is realised in only a small percentage of cases, usually as the result of a CVA (whether as part of or without an administration), the appointment of an administrative receiver or a contractually agreed reorganisation ("workout") which may take a variety of forms, including

---

[81] See para.6–31.

conversion of debt into equity, so that the loans to the company are extinguished and the quondam lenders become shareholders.[82] Sometimes an administrator or administrative receiver is able to restore the company to profitable trading and hand back control to the directors. But the most common outcome of insolvency proceedings, of whatever kind, is cessation or disposal of the company's business and the winding-up of the company. The primary concern of administrators and administrative receivers is to safeguard the business and its assets for the benefit of creditors rather than to keep the company in being as a viable trading entity.[83] In most cases this is achieved by getting the business into a position where it can be sold on a going concern basis, after which the company usually ends up in liquidation.

Maximising returns to creditors

This objective has two distinct aspects. First, it reflects the fundamental **2–19** assumption underlying insolvency law that the interests of individual creditors, and in particular their rights to collect in the debts due to them by one or other of the methods of enforcing payment of judgment debts, must give way to the collective interest of the general body of creditors. The free-for-all in which the race goes to the swiftest and individual assets of the company are picked off one by one in the process of execution is seen as inimical to the efficient organisation of the company's affairs for the benefit of creditors as a whole. This is considered best achieved through a collective debt collection procedure involving the ascertainment of the company's liabilities, the collection and realisation of its assets and the distribution of the proceeds by way of dividend among creditors in the statutory order of priority. Whether in any given case a particular creditor does better by pursuing an individual remedy or seeking a collective proceeding through winding-up or administration will, of course, depend on the action taken by other creditors, and in particular on the order in which executions against assets of the company are effected and whether the execution process will be frustrated before completion by the company's being put into winding-up, administration or administrative receivership. The various perceptions of the individual creditors as to the possible outcomes of individual versus collective action provide a typical example of the prisoner's dilemma in game theory.[84] Secondly, the interests of creditors are in principle to be given precedence over all other interests. So in a winding-up only a very a limited measure of statutory support is given to

---

[82] See further below, para.10–122.
[83] See below, paras 9–04, 10–26.
[84] Where the question whether a prisoner is released or serves a term of imprisonment and, if so, the length of that term, is made to depend on whether both prisoners confess, one only confesses or both refuse to confess, and neither prisoner knows the intentions of the other.

employees,[85] whilst in an administration the interests of shareholders, employees and the wider community come low down on the priority list of most administrators.

Providing a fair and equitable system for the ranking of claims

2–20   Equally important in any statutory insolvency regime are the rules governing the ranking of creditors' claims and the distribution of dividends. Since the ranking of claims has no significance for the general body of creditors except in the context of an entitlement to dividend, and since dividends are distributed only in a winding-up, it follows that the statutory rules of priority are in general confined to winding-up and have no function in other insolvency proceedings. To this rule there is one exception. The holder of a debenture secured by a floating charge is postponed to preferential creditors as regards any property comprised in the charge of which he takes possession[86] or which comes into the hands of a receiver he appoints.[87] As will be seen, English corporate insolvency law adopts the general principle that pre-liquidation rights are to be respected but also plays a limited redistributive role through rules of subordination and avoidance.[88]

Identifying the causes of the company's failure and imposing sanctions for culpable management by its directors and officers

2–21   The insolvency of a company causes loss to its creditors and hardship to its employees, many of whom are likely to lose their jobs. Moreover the government has a particular interest in the insolvency of a company for it is very often a creditor for unpaid taxes, in addition to which the National Insurance Fund will be exposed to wage-related and redundancy claims by dismissed employees. Accordingly insolvency legislation provides for the investigation by the liquidator into the causes of failure, the imposition of criminal and/or civil liability on anyone concerned in the management of the company who has been guilty of culpable acts or omissions causing loss to creditors[89] and the disqualification for a specified period of those considered unfit to be directors from participating in the future management of a company.

In theory, therefore, there is adequate machinery to deal with delinquent directors. Unhappily in practice the position is rather different. The task of

---

[85] See above, para.2–11, below, paras 7–27 *et seq.*
[86] Companies Act 1985, s.196.
[87] Insolvency Act 1985, s.40.
[88] See below, para.3–02.
[89] See Chap.12 as to civil sanctions imposed by the Insolvency Act 1986 for fraudulent and wrongful trading. Criminal penalties for fraudulent trading are prescribed by s.458 of the Companies Act 1985.

bringing an offender to book is expensive, time-consuming and uncertain in result. In criminal proceedings for fraudulent trading the prosecution has a heavy burden of proof, the trial is by jury, which has to be taken through often complicated accounts, records and evidence going back over a substantial period, the recollections of witnesses tend to become blurred with the lengthy passage of time that usually passes before the case comes to trial and the defendant has every chance of being acquitted. In the result, no more than a handful of prosecutions for fraudulent trading are brought every year. Wrongful trading is much easier to establish, since the proceedings are civil, not criminal, so that the standard of proof is less onerous, and in any event it is open to the defendant to show that he took every reasonable step to avoid loss to creditors.[90] But civil proceedings also involve substantial expense and creditors are extremely reluctant to throw good money after bad unless they can be satisfied that there is a strong case and that the defendant is worth powder and shot. So whilst the pursuit of wrongdoers is in theory a central plank of insolvency law policy, in practice investigations are likely to be limited, and matters taken no further than a report by the office holder, unless there is compelling prima facie evidence of wrongdoing causing substantial loss and of the defendant's ability to meet any order made against him for payment of contribution to the company's assets.

There is, however, an encouraging increase in the numbers of proceedings leading to disqualification, following on a decision by the Insolvency Service to pursue a more aggressive policy in having unfit directors disqualified. For this purpose winding-up orders can be made, and have been sought, even where the company has no assets.[91]

4. THE INSTRUMENTS OF CORPORATE INSOLVENCY LAW

Placement of the company and its assets under external management

Though directors of a company which is subject to an insolvent proceeding **2–22** retain vestigial powers, they are for the most part displaced by the administrator, administrative receiver or liquidator. English corporate insolvency law is firmly attached to the notion that if a company fails it is necessary to bring in outside management in the form of an individual who is now required to be a qualified insolvency practitioner. The concept of the debtor in possession which is embodied in Chapter 11 of the American Bankruptcy Code[92] and under which the existing management is left in

---

[90] See below, paras 12–36 *et seq.*
[91] Insolvency Act 1986, s.25(1); *Bell Group Finance (Ply) Lid (in liquidation) v Bell Group (U.K.) Holdings Ltd* [1996] B.C.C. 505.
[92] See below, para.10–21.

office, subject to the superintendence of the court and the creditors, has never been adopted in English law. Individual directors may be retained to assist the insolvency practitioner, with whom they have a statutory duty to co-operate, but it is he who performs the management functions previously undertaken by the board.

Administrators and administrative receivers (where the latter can still be validly appointed) are given the widest possible powers of management by the Insolvency Act 1986.[93] These include the power to collect in the company's assets, dispose of assets, carry on or close down the business,[94] establish subsidiaries and transfer the whole or any part of the business and property to subsidiaries, bring proceedings and make arrangements and compromises on behalf of the company and petition for the winding-up of the company.

The powers of liquidators are somewhat more restricted, reflecting the fact that the aim of liquidation is not rehabilitation but disposal of the business and assets and distribution of the net realisations. Thus a liquidator may carry on the company's business only so far as may be necessary for the beneficial winding-up of the company and then only with the sanction of the court in the case of a compulsory winding-up.[95] Some of the other powers are exercisable only with the sanction of the court or the liquidation committee.[96]

Substitution of collective action for individual rights of pursuit

2–23   Inherent in the winding-up process, and also a crucial element in the administration procedure, is the freeze on the pursuit of individual debt enforcement remedies against the company in favour of collective action by the creditors as a whole through the medium of the liquidator in a winding-up or the administrator in an administration. If individual creditors were left free to pursue their rights and to enforce judgments by execution against the company's assets these would quickly disappear, destroying the business enterprise and frustrating the purpose of the particular insolvency proceeding. Hence the legislative provisions by which the rights of individual pursuit are suspended and the liquidator in a winding-up is made responsible for determining the existence and quantum of the company's liabilities and distributing the net proceeds of realisations of assets among creditors in the form of dividends proportionate to their admitted claims,[97] while the role of

---

[93] Sch.B1 para.59, s.42 and Sch.1.
[94] An administrator will usually need the approval of the creditors for the closing down of the business, since this is a major step the need for which may well demonstrate that the administration is unlikely to achieve its purpose.
[95] Insolvency Act 1986, Sch.4, Pt II.
[96] *ibid.*, ss.165, 167, and Sch.4, Pt I.
[97] Known technically as proofs of debt.

the administrator in an administration is to lay proposals before the creditors for the achievement of the purpose or purposes for which the administration order was made. These proposals may include the distribution of assets among creditors under a CVA or a voluntary winding-up.

However, not all types of insolvency proceeding involve the suspension of rights and remedies, and those that do are not applicable to all forms of right or remedy. Thus winding-up converts creditors' rights of action into rights of proof in competition with other creditors but does not affect the enforcement of security interests or other real rights. By contrast, administration[98] freezes the enforcement of both real rights and judicial remedies, including winding-up, but does not bar other forms of self-help such as equitable or contractual set-off. Neither of these two proceedings interferes with any contractual right to accelerate the debtor company's liability or to terminate a contract for default in payment. Administrative receivership, where available, does not in theory affect the enforcement of the rights of individual creditors at all, but in practice it contributes powerfully to the orderly management of the company's affairs since all the assets are subject to the debenture holder's security and are taken into the possession or control of the administrative receiver, so that any judgment taken by an unsecured creditor is likely to prove a *brutum fulmen*, and his only effective weapon is to put the company into liquidation.

Statutory distribution scheme

Though winding-up is no longer the only insolvency regime which is concerned with distributions among the general body of creditors, it remains the paradigm case. For this purpose the Insolvency Act and Insolvency Rules lay down a detailed system of priorities for dealing with claims. These fall into four groups. Arranged in descending order of priority they are: the expenses of the liquidation, which are paid, not proved; preferential debts, which rank at the head of provable debts; ordinary unsecured debts; and deferred debts, which come at the end of the line. The expenses of the liquidation have to be met in the prescribed order of priority. By contrast creditors in each of the remaining three categories are not prioritised and rank *pari passu* among themselves. Secured creditors and the holders of other real rights *(e.g.* suppliers of goods under reservation of title) are not affected by the priority rules, and can resort to the assets in which the security or other rights subsist in disregard of other creditors, except that a charge which as created was a floating charge is subordinate to the claims of preferential creditors and surrender of the prescribed part. The policy underlying the statutory distribution scheme has been discussed earlier.[99]

2–24

---

[98] And to a somewhat less extent, initation of the administration process.
[99] See above, paras 2–03, 2–09.

Avoidance of transactions and recovery of misapplied assets

2–25   A major instrument of corporate insolvency law is the set of statutory provisions under which transactions entered into by the company that were improper or unfair to the general body of creditors or that it would otherwise be unfair to allow to stand are made void or their effect liable to be reversed on an application to the court by the office-holder. In principle, the assets of a company available to the general body of creditors upon a liquidation or for the purposes of an administration order are those owned by the company when it goes into winding-up or administration. But those assets may have been depleted by dispositions and transactions which unfairly favour a creditor of the company at the expense of the general body of creditors—as by giving him a preference or other benefit at a time when the company was unable to pay its debts—or which were not registered in conformity with statutory requirements, thus potentially misleading creditors into believing that the company was still the owner of the assets transferred by it under the disposition. In some cases the transaction is made totally void; in other cases, though the transaction remains valid, its effect may be reversed so as to restore the *status quo*.[1] There is also a summary remedy against delinquent officers for the recovery of assets misappropriated or otherwise acquired by misfeasance.[2] It does not always follow that recoveries of assets by the liquidator under these statutory provisions will ensure for the benefit of the general body of creditors; in certain cases they will be treated as part of the company's general assets so as to be picked up by a prior assignment or charge or by an after-acquired property clause in a debenture.[3]

Sanctioning of delinquent directors

2–26   Directors of an insolvent company are also exposed to criminal proceedings if guilty of fraudulent trading and can be required to contribute to the assets of the company in civil proceedings for fraudulent or wrongful trading.[4] They may also, in appropriate cases, be disqualified from acting as directors or being otherwise concerned in the management of companies for a specified period.[5]

Statutory authorisation of insolvency practitioners

2–27   Prior to the Insolvency Act 1985 any individual who was not an undischarged bankrupt could practise as an insolvency practitioner, without being required to have either a professional qualification or prior experience. The Cork Committee considered that one of the aims of a good

---

[1] See below, para.3–10 and Chap.11.
[2] Insolvency Act 1986, s.212. See below, para.12–12.
[3] See below, para.11–138.
[4] See below, paras 12–16, 12–22.
[5] See below, paras 12–48 *et seq.*

modern insolvency law was "to ensure that the processes of realisation and distribution are administered in an honest and competent manner"[6] and recommended that insolvency practitioners be required to have a professional qualification and to have been in general practice for five years before acting as an insolvency practitioner.[7] That recommendation has been implemented in modified form by requiring insolvency practitioners to be qualified by authorisation from a recognised professional body, the Secretary of State or a competent authority designated by the Secretary of State.[8] There are also rules imposing statutory obligations on insolvency practitioners in the handling of money they receive and in relation to their functions as office-holders.

Dissolution of a company in winding-up

Sooner or later, most insolvent companies end up in liquidation, voluntary or compulsory. The final act in the drama is to terminate the company's existence by having it dissolved and struck off the register of companies. Dissolution after winding-up may occur in one of two ways. The first is where the carrying out of the winding-up would serve no useful purpose because the realisable assets are insufficient to cover the costs and the affairs of the company do not require further investigations. In such a case the official receiver, if he is the liquidator of the company, may apply for its early dissolution.[9] The second occurs where the winding-up has been completed and the liquidator has vacated office.[10] In addition, there is now provision for dissolution of a company in administration where the administrator thinks that the company has no property which might permit a distribution to its creditors and sends notice to that effect to the registrar of companies.[11]

2–28

---

[6] *Loc. cit.*, para.198(g).
[7] *Loc cit.*, para.758.
[8] Insolvency Act 1986 ss.230(2), 390–392; Insolvency Practitioners (Recognised Professional Bodies) Order 1986 (SI 1986/1764).
[9] Insolvency Act 1986, s.262.
[10] *ibid.*, s.205.
[11] *ibid.*, Sch.B1, para.84. As to revival of a dissolved company, see above, para.1–25, n.11.

Chapter 3

The Principles of Corporate Insolvency Law

Though the Insolvency Act 1986, with its 496 sections and 18 schedules, **3–01** obviously embodies the heart of corporate insolvency law, so that there is a natural temptation to commence any study of the subject by plunging straight into s.1 of the Act and working through the various statutory provisions in sequence, the Act itself is not the best starting point. One cannot understand corporate insolvency law without a thorough grasp of the fundamental principles underpinning the legislation. These are not brought together in the Act, nor, indeed, are they readily extracted from it. This is because corporate insolvency law for the most part recognises and adopts rights conferred by the general law and by contract. If, for example, we want to know the rights of a secured creditor when the debtor company goes into liquidation we must first ascertain what rights he acquired before the winding-up. Only then can we assess, in the light of the statutory provisions, the legal impact of winding-up on the continued existence and enforceability of those rights. So also with rights under a contract. First, we must determine their scope under the general law; then we have to consider how far those rights are affected by the winding-up. An examination of the statutory provisions is thus the last part of the analysis, not the first; and it is the interplay between the general law and the particular principles and rules of insolvency legislation that should engage our special attention. This interplay is reflected in a number of basic principles of corporate insolvency law, and it is to these that I now turn. For convenience of exposition I shall take winding-up as the paradigm, though for the most part the principles apply equally to administration.

First principle: corporate insolvency law recognises rights accrued under the general law prior to liquidation

This principle is of cardinal importance. Its effect is that relative entitle- **3–02** ments created before liquidation are preserved, so that insolvency law will in general respect the priority of proprietary over personal claims (and thus of secured over unsecured claims), the subjection of the company's proprietary or contractual rights to countervailing equities, such as rights of rescission or set-off,[1] the priority or subordination attached to securities by the terms of their issue and agreements between creditors for the subordination of secured or unsecured debt. In line with this principle, the general rule is that liquidation does not of itself terminate contracts or extinguish rights, though it does inhibit the pursuit of remedies. So the starting position of insolvency law is that rights accrued prior to the insolvency proceeding will be respected. To this principle there are important exceptions, and it is these which give the transactional side of corporate insolvency law its distinctive character. Most of the remaining principles are particular aspects of this first principle.

Second principle: only the assets of the debtor company are available for its creditors

3–03   This principle follows from the first. It is not the function of corporate insolvency to confiscate for the benefit of creditors assets in the company's possession or control which belong to others. Only that which is the property of the company at the time of liquidation or comes into its hands thereafter is available for its creditors. So assets held by the company on trust do not form part of its estate, nor do goods supplied to it under reservation of title. Similarly, assets over which the company has given security are not available to the creditors except to the extent of the company's equity of redemption. Again, there are exceptions to the principle. The assets available for creditors may be swelled by the statutory avoidance or reversal of pre-liquidation transfers and transactions, *e.g.* as transactions at an undervalue, preferences and floating charges which are void for want of registration or because they were given by an insolvent company for past consideration.[2] Transfers made after the commencement

---

[1] In English insolvency proceedings, what constitutes an equity is governed by English law even if the asset in question is situated abroad or the transaction is otherwise governed by foreign law, and that equity will be enforced by an English court even if not recognised by the *lex rei sitae*. In *Re Scheibler, Ex p. Holthausen* (1874) 9 Ch. App. 722, a firm of merchants, following negotiations for a line of credit with the appellants which were opened when the parties were in Prussia, deposited by way of security the title deeds to a house in Shanghai to cover their liabilities on bills of exchange and then became bankrupt. The Court of Appeal held that the contract was governed by English law under which the deposit created a valid security interest binding on the trustee but that even if it had been governed by German law the contract was personally binding on those who signed the agreement to deposit the title deeds, and who signed it as a personal contract, and was therefore binding on the trustee. A similar decision was given by Luxmoore J. in *Anchor Line (Henderson Bros) Ltd* [1937] Ch. 483, citing *British South Africa Co v De Beers Consolidated Mines Ltd* [1910] 1 Ch. 354, *per* Swinfen Eady J. at 387. In this respect English insolvency law may have the unusual effect of expanding pre-insolvency entitlements under the applicable foreign law.

[2] See below, Chap.11.

of the winding-up are also void unless sanctioned by the court,[3] and since the winding-up of a company not already in voluntary liquidation is deemed to relate back to the presentation of the petition,[4] assets of which the company had ceased to be the owner by the time of the winding-up order may be brought back into its estate. In addition, a percentage in value of assets subject to a floating charge has to be surrendered to form a fund available to unsecured creditors.[5]

As a corollary of the rule that only the company's assets are available for its creditors, the liquidator has no power *as liquidator* to sell assets not beneficially owned by the company or subject to a security interest, though if the company is a trustee with management powers under an active trust the liquidator may, with the consent of the beneficiaries or under an order of the court, manage the trust property on behalf of the beneficiaries and realise trust assets as part of that management. Where the liquidator does so, his remuneration and expenses for so doing cannot be treated as expenses of the liquidation, being for the benefit of the trust beneficiaries rather than the company, and must be borne by the trust assets.[6] Conversely, any portion of the liquidator's work and expenses not attributable to the trust property ought in principle to be borne by the general creditors out of the company's free assets.[7] Nevertheless the courts have in some cases been prepared to allow these to be taken, wholly or in part, from the trust assets,[8] though it is thought this should be done only in exceptional cases, as where there the trust assets form part of a commingled fund and it is difficult to distinguish between trust assets and assets beneficially owned by the company. In cases involving a commingled fund where the task of establishing each individual's beneficial entitlement would be complex and expensive the courts have generally refused to apply the rule in *Clayton's Case*[9] and have directed that the fund, so far as comprising trust assets, be distributed among the beneficiaries *pro rata*.[10] Where the assets consisted

---

[3] Insolvency Act 1986, s.127 below, paras 11–124 *et seq.*

[4] Insolvency Act 1986, s.127. See below, para.5–15.

[5] Insolvency Act 1986, s.176A; Insolvency Act 1986 (Prescribed Part) Order 2003, SI 2003/2097. See below, para.6–31.

[6] *Re Berkeley Applegate (Investment Consultants) Ltd (No.3)* (1989) 5 B.C.C. 803, *per* Peter Gibson J. at 805; *Re French Caledonia Travel Service Pty Ltd* (2003) 204 A.L.R. 353 (NSW Supreme Court). Despite this, in *Re G.P. Stores Ltd*, unreported July 29, 2004, HH Judge Weeks QC ordered costs of the liquidator attributable in part to charged assets to be paid in the first instance out of the free assets of the company. See Claire Sharp, Insolvency Intelligence, January 2005, p.8.

[7] *Re French Caledonia Travel Service Pty Ltd*, above, n.6.

[8] See, for example, *Re London Local Residential Ltd* [2004] 2 B.C.L.C. 72. The basis of this decision by Evans-Lombe J. is unclear, since his conclusion seems inconsistent with his earlier reasoning rejecting the deductibility of all the liquidator's heads of expense not attributable to the administration of property allegedly held on trust.

[9] *Devaynes v Noble, Clayton's Case* (1816) 1 Mer. 572, under which payments in a current account are allocated on the basis of first in, first out.

[10] *Barlow Clowes International Ltd v Vaughan* [1992] B.C.L.C. 910; *Re Eastern Capital Futures Ltd* [1989] B.C.L.C. 371; *Re French Caledonia Travel Service Pty Ltd*, above, n.6.

partly of trust assets and partly of the company's own assets, Morritt J. ordered that the trust moneys be notionally aggregated with the company's assets and that there should be paid from the trust assets the proportion of the liquidator's total remuneration which the trust assets bore to the aggregate fund.[11]

Third principle: security interests and other real rights created prior to the insolvency proceeding are unaffected by the winding up

3–04 This principle follows from the first two. In general, a creditor holding a security interest or other real right is unaffected by winding-up and may proceed to realise his security or assert other rights of property as if the company were not in liquidation. So firmly is this principle applied that where the instrument of charge provides for security in after-acquired property the secured creditor can assert rights even over moneys or other assets falling in after the commencement of the winding-up[12] provided that the consideration for these was already executed before that time, as opposed to being furnished by the liquidator himself, *e.g.* by performance of a contract entered into by the company.[13]

Fourth principle: the liquidator takes the assets subject to all limitations and defences

3–05 In asserting rights in the name of the company[14] the liquidator stands in no better position than the company itself; he takes them as they stand, warts and all.[15] So where the company is a party to a contract, the other party

---

[11] *Re Eastern Capital Futures Ltd*, above, n.10.

[12] *Re Reis* [1904] 2 K.B. 769; *Re Lind* [1915] 2 Ch. 345. See Roy Goode, *Legal Problems of Credit and Security* (3rd ed.), paras 2–13, 2–14.

[13] *Re Collins* [1925] Ch. 556. Where moneys come into the hands of the liquidator as the result of his procuring performance of the company's contract these do not fall within the after-acquired property clause because they are at no time money of which the company is beneficial owner, but on the contrary from the moment of their receipt become subject to the so-called statutory trust for creditors upon which a company in liquidation is considered to hold its free assets. See *Ayerst (Inspector of Taxes) v C. & K. Construction Ltd* [1976] A.C. 167, and cases there cited, which embody the fifth principle referred to below. The trust is a trust for purposes, not for persons. See below, para.3–08.

[14] Unlike a trustee in bankruptcy, in whom the bankrupt's estate vests immediately on his appointment taking effect (Insolvency Act 1986, s.306(1)), a liquidator does not acquire title to the assets of the company in liquidation unless this is vested in him by order of the court under s.145 of the Insolvency Act, a procedure rarely found necessary. What the liquidator acquires is control of the assets and the right to collect them in.

[15] But the liquidator may by statute be able to assert *defences* which the company itself could not have raised prior to liquidation, *e.g.* that a security interest asserted by a creditor is void for want of registration or that a transaction relied on in proceedings against the company should be set aside as a transaction at an undervalue or a preference. Such defences will be discussed in detail in Chap.11.

remains entitled to raise any defences that could have been raised prior to the winding up and to exercise any rights of termination given by the contract.[16] The same is true of equities. In general, an equity, that is, a person's right to impeach or qualify a transaction by which another party acquires an interest in an asset, survives the other party's liquidation. An equity is not in itself an interest in property, nor on the other hand is it a mere right *in personam*; rather, it is an inherent limitation of the interest that has been acquired. A typical equity is a right to rescind a contract by reason of some external vitiating factor such as fraud, misrepresentation or undue influence. This right of defeasance constitutes an inherent qualification of the contract rights. So where a party is induced by the company's fraud or misrepresentation to enter into a contract for the sale of goods or the transfer of other property to the company he does not lose his right to rescind merely by reason of the winding up.[17] The right of rescission can be a very useful remedy for an unpaid seller who was induced to sell by fraud or misrepresentation (*e.g.* the furnishing of a cheque which the buyer company knew would be dishonoured), since ownership in the asset transferred revests in him upon rescission, whereas if he had asserted his right to the price under the contract of sale he would have had to prove in competition with other creditors. Other types of equity are the right to apply for rectification of the contract or to have it set aside for mistake or breach of fiduciary duty; and the right of the holder of a crystallised floating charge to assert priority over a subsequent incumbrancer who took his security interest while the prior charge was still floating but with notice of a negative pledge clause in the charge.[18]

These equities likewise survive the liquidation of the company against whom they are asserted. The pre-liquidation right of set-off is also an equity, but by exception to the general rule it is not exercisable against a party which has gone into liquidation, being displaced by the insolvency rules of set-off.[19]

A case which is difficult to reconcile with the principle that the liquidator takes subject to equities is the majority decision of the House of Lords in *British Eagle*,[20] a controversial decision discussed in a later chapter.[21]

---

[16] This would seem to include a contract term designating the event of liquidation itself as a ground of termination though it is arguable that this runs counter to the principle of *pari passu* distribution. See below, para.7–11.

[17] *Re Eastgate* [1905] 1 K.B. 465; *Tilley v Bowman Ltd* [1910] 1 K.B. 745.

[18] See Roy Goode, *Legal Problems of Credit and Security*, para.5–40.

[19] Roy Goode, *op.cit.*, paras 7–75 *et seq*; Philip Wood, *English and International Set-Off* (1989), Chap.7. The insolvency rule of set-off applicable to a company in liquidation is embodied in the Insolvency Rules 1986, r.4.90.

[20] *British Eagle International Air Lines Ltd v Compagnie Nationale Air France* [1975] 2 All E.R. 390.

[21] See below, para.8–14.

Fifth principle: the pursuit of personal rights against the company is converted into a right to prove for a dividend in the liquidation

3–06   It is upon liquidation that the distinction between real and personal rights against a company becomes of crucial importance. So long as the company is solvent it matters little in financial terms whether the claimant has a mere personal right to payment of a debt or damages or a proprietary interest in an asset from which he can obtain satisfaction of what is owed to him, for he can obtain a judgment on his personal claim and enforce it against any or all of the debtor company's assets or income so far as not subject to a prior interest in favour of a third party. But when the company becomes insolvent, so that there are insufficient assets to go round, the creditor with real rights in an asset *(e.g.* a seller of goods under reservation of title, a mortgagee or chargee of property) can remove it from the maw of the general creditors, whereas the creditor with a purely personal right, though not deprived of the right itself, loses the ability to engage in individual pursuit of satisfaction and is required to lodge his claim with the liquidator in what is called a proof of debt and participate with other unsecured creditors in such *pari passu* distributions of dividend as the liquidator is able to make from realisation of the company's assets after allowing for the expenses of the liquidation and the claims of preferential creditors.

Sixth principle: on liquidation the company ceases to be the beneficial owner of its assets

3–07   Though winding up does not of itself divest the company of legal title to its assets, it ceases to be the beneficial owner and holds the assets on trust to apply them in discharge of the company's liabilities in accordance with the statutory scheme of distribution.[22] Accordingly the assets can no longer be used or realised by the company for its own benefit. Moreover, the fact that the company loses beneficial ownership on winding up may have important tax consequences.[23] A different approach has recently been taken by the High Court of Australia in *Commissioner of Taxation v Linter Textiles Australia Ltd*,[24] Kirby J. dissenting. In the majority view it is not correct to say that the company's beneficial ownership ceases on its going into liquidation. Rather the position is that the company holds its property beneficially but subject to the statutory scheme of liquidation under which

---

[22] *Re Albert Life Assurance Co, The Delhi Bank's Case* (1871) 15 Sol. Jo. 923; *Re Oriental Inland Steam Co* (1874) 9 Ch. App. 557; *Ayerst (Inspector of Taxes) v C. & K. (Construction) Ltd* [1976] A.C. 167. As to the special nature of the trust, see the seventh principle below.

[23] See, for example, *Pritchard v M H. Builders (Wilmslow) Ltd* [1969] 2 All E.R. 670; *Ayerst (Inspector of Taxes) v C. & K. Construction Ltd*, above, n.22.

[24] April 26, 2005.

the liquidator is to pay creditors and distribute any surplus among members.[25] In a strong dissenting judgment Kirby J. pointed out that the English decisions to the effect that the company lost beneficial ownership were not an attempt to import all the features of trust law into the defined statutory relationships following a company liquidation. Rather they were drawing an analogy to explain the construction and operation of the relevant statute. Noting that the decision in *Ayerst* was consistent with the approach taken by courts of New Zealand, Ireland and Hong Kong, Kirby J. said:

"I can see no reason of legal authority, principle or policy to justify this Court's taking a different course from that adopted by the unanimous opinion of the House of Lords on a precisely identical point of revenue law . . . There is no reason why we should take such a course. There are many reasons why we should not."[26]

The trust concept features in a number of other winding-up situations. Sums recovered by the liquidator in respect of wrongful trading, trans-actions at an undervalue and preferences are not considered to be assets of the company but are held by the liquidator for the benefit of creditors in accordance with the statutory order of priority.[27] They are therefore not susceptible to capture by a secured creditor under an after-acquired property clause.[28] Sums paid and property transferred to the supervisor under a company voluntary arrangement are held on trust for the CVA creditor, a trust which survives any subsequent winding-up of the company unless the CVA itself otherwise provides.[29] Such trust may also arise at an earlier stage if the terms of the proposal or the CVA itself indicate an intention to create a trust.[30] In *Re UCT (UK) Ltd*[31] Arden J. acceded to an application by administrators to release them while at the same time authorising them to retain in a designated trust account sums to meet the claims of creditors who would be preferential creditors in a compulsory winding-up in order to facilitate a voluntary winding-up and thereby avoid the additional costs of a compulsory liquidation.

---

[25] Approving a passage from *Ford and Austin's Principles of Corporations Law* (7th ed., 1995) at p.1013.
[26] At para.245.
[27] See below, paras 12–40 *et seq.*, 12–46.
[28] See below, para.6–30.
[29] See below, para.10–130.
[30] See below, para.10–130.
[31] [2001] B.C.C. 734.

Seventh principle: no creditor has any interest *in specie* in the company's assets or realisations

3–08   The statutory trust upon which the company in winding up holds the assets and realisations[32] is not of a kind which confers on the creditors beneficial co-ownership or, indeed, a proprietary interest of any kind.[33] Their rights are limited to invoking the protection of the court to ensure that the liquidator fulfils his statutory duties.[34] Their position is analogous to that of residuary legatees in an unadministered estate.[35] They have a right to compel performance of the executor's duties but no interest in the assets comprising the estate until completion of the administration, during which time beneficial ownership of the assets is in suspense.[36] The company thus holds the assets for statutory purposes, not for persons. Even the declaration of a dividend confers no right on the creditors to sue for the dividend; all they can do is to make an application to the court for an order requiring the liquidator to perform his duties.[37] These principles apply to preferential and ordinary creditors alike. So while preferential creditors can apply to the court to restrain a distribution which ignores their statutory priority, they have no proprietary interest in the assets or realisations as such and no absolute right to prevent the liquidator from incurring expenditure in the pursuit of legal proceedings for the benefit of creditors generally, even if there are sufficient assets to pay the preferential creditors without any recoveries from the proceedings, so that these will be of no benefit to the preferential creditors. The liquidator's duties are owed to the creditors as a whole, and the expenses of the liquidation (including legal costs) are payable out of the assets, not provable as debts, and thus rank ahead of preferential claims. The preferential creditors would have to satisfy the court that in the particular circumstances it was just to restrain the liquidator from pursuing the proceedings.

Eighth principle: liquidation accelerates creditors' rights to payment

3–09   When a company goes into liquidation its liability for payment of unmatured debts becomes notionally accelerated[38] to the extent that it has already been earned by performance. This results from the fact that a

---

[32] See above.

[33] *Ayerst (Inspector of Taxes) v C. & K. Construction Ltd*, above; *Buchler v Talbot* [2004] 2 A.C. 298, *per* Lord Hoffmann at para.28.

[34] *Buchler v Talbot*, n.33 above; *Calgary and Edmonton Land Co Ltd v Dobinson* [1974] Ch. 102.

[35] *ibid.*

[36] *Commissioner of Stamp Duties v Livingston* [1965] A.C. 694.

[37] *Prout v Gregory* (1889) 24 Q.B.D. 281; *Spence v Coleman* [1901] 2 K.B. 199.

[38] It may also, of course, become contractually accelerated. For the effect of acceleration clauses in a winding up, see below, para.7–09.

creditor has an immediate right of proof not only for debts already due to him but for those payable in the future or on a contingency.[39] Debts payable in the future are provable in full but if not due at the date of a dividend distribution are discounted for the purpose of computing the dividend,[40] whilst contingent debts are valued.[41] However, a claim qualifies as a debt for this purpose only to the extent that it has been earned, in the sense that the consideration for it is executed. For example, the principle of acceleration applies to a loan made before winding-up but maturing three years later, and to the future instalments payable at the time of winding-up in respect of the price of goods already delivered, for in both cases the consideration furnished by the creditor is executed. By contrast, a lessor cannot claim to accelerate the future rentals payable under a lease upon the winding-up of the lessee because these have not yet been earned; his remedy, if the liquidator retains possession for the benefit of the winding-up, is to recover each amount of rent as it falls due as an expense of the liquidation,[42] or if it does not so continue, then to prove for each amount of rent as it falls due,[43] or alternatively, if the lease comes to an end through forfeiture by the lessor or disclaimer by the liquidator, to prove for the loss of the future rentals as unliquidated damages.[44]

Ninth principle: unsecured creditors rank *pari passu*

As mentioned earlier,[45] the *pari passu* principle is one of the most fundamental principles of corporate insolvency law.[46] All unsecured creditors are required to share and share alike in a common pool of assets and realisations. This principle, formerly confined to winding-up, now applies also to administrations in which a distribution is made.[47] Agreements and transfers designed to favour a particular creditor by removing from the pool   **3–10**

---

[39] Insolvency Rules 1986, rr.4.94, 12.3(1).

[40] Insolvency Rules 1986, r.11.13.

[41] *ibid.*, r.4.86(1).

[42] *Christopher Moran Holdings Ltd v Bairstow* [2000] 2 A.C. 172 (on appeal from *Re Park Air Services plc* [1997] 1 W.L.R. 1376), per Lord Millett at p.187; *Re ABC Coupler & Engineering Ltd (No.3)* [1970] 1 W.L.R. 702; *Re Oak Pits Colliery Co* (1882) 21 Ch. D. 322; *Re New Oriental Bank Corp (No.2)* [1895] 1 Ch. 753; *Re Lundy Granite Co* (1871) LR 6 Ch. 462, *per* Sir W.M. James L.J. at 466. The principle was extended to dilapidations in *Re Levi & Co* [1919] 1 Ch. 416. See further below, para.7–33.

[43] *ibid.* This is not an exception to the rule that post-liquidation debts are not provable; the rent accruing due after the time of commencement of the winding-up is already a future debt at that time.

[44] See below, para.7–33.

[45] Above, para.2–14.

[46] Insolvency Act 1986, s.107 (voluntary winding-up); Insolvency Rules 1986, r.4.181 (compulsory winding-up). For a detailed discussion, see Michael Bridge, "Collectivity, Management of Estates and the *Pari Passu* Rule in Winding-up" in *Vulnerable Transactions in Corporate Insolvency* (ed. John Armour and Howard Bennett 2003), Chap.1.

[47] Insolvency Rules 1986, r.2.69.

upon liquidation assets which would otherwise be available to the general body of creditors are in principle null and void. Moreover, transfers and transactions made by an insolvent company in the run-up to liquidation[48] which unfairly benefit one creditor at the expense of others are liable to be struck down by the Insolvency Act as transactions at an undervalue or preferences,[49] since these too are conceived as contravening the principle of *pari passu* distribution. The principle has many facets which I shall discuss in detail, together with the exceptions to the principle in a later chapter.[50]

It has been objected with some vigour that the *pari passu* principle is not a central principle of insolvency law at all.[51] Two grounds have been advanced for this contention. First, unsecured creditors usually receive little, if anything, by way of dividend. This is true, but the reason is not the lack of centrality of the *pari passu* principle, which has been adopted in every substantive insolvency enactment since the time of Henry VIII, but the fact that by its nature it applies only to the free assets of the company, and with the development of a huge range of security interests, trusts, reservation of title and other real rights, as well as various equities,[52] the amount of free assets in relation to unsecured claims is usually relatively small. There is only one significant exception to the *pari passu* rule, namely the existence of a category of preferential debts. But these were always a tiny percentage of unsecured claims and are now even smaller with the disappearance of Crown preferential rights. Moreover, within each of the four classes of debt—liquidation expenses, preferential debts, ordinary debts and deferred debts—only the first is subject to a priority ordering. Debts within each of the other three classes rank *pari passu* among themselves; and of these the ordinary unsecured debts are far and away the largest class. It is therefore undeniable that the *pari passu* principle of distribution is the primary principle. What should not be inferred from this, however, is that ordinary unsecured creditors derive much benefit from it. Secondly, it is argued that what the law disallows is not evasion of the *pari passu* principle as such but rather attempts to by-pass the collective mechanism which an insolvency proceeding is designed to produce. If one takes references to the *pari passu* principle literally, there is force in this criticism in that evasion of the principle of collectivity, which is essentially procedural in character, would be outlawed whatever the order of distribution of assets under substantive insolvency law. In other words, what the courts are concerned to do is to bar devices that would by-pass the collective regime, with its restraints on individual enforcement, and allow an individual creditor to evade the statutory order of distribution, whatever

---

[48] The run-up period varies from six months to three years, depending on the circumstances.
[49] See below, paras 11–12 *et seq.*
[50] See below, paras 7–01 *et seq.*
[51] Rizwaan Jameel Mokal, "Priority as Pathology: The *Pari Passu* Myth" [2001] C.L.J. 581.
[52] See below, paras 7–27 *et seq.*

that might be. Yet the fact that *pari passu* distribution is the general principle and the importance of its observance have been stressed in countless decisions by eminent judges[53] as well as by innumerable writers, including scholars from overseas describing their own insolvency laws. Is it, then, the case that all of these have been guilty of a "misunderstanding of the nature of the liquidation regime"[54]? Clearly not; they have simply invoked the *pari passu* rule as a form of shorthand to describe what is in fact the general statutory rule of distribution, and it is in that sense that is referred to in the analysis of the rule which follows later.[55]

Tenth principle: members of a company are not as such liable for its debts

It is a well-established principle of English company law, particularly **3–11** relevant to insolvency, that where a body is created with corporate personality, contracts entered into in the name of that body are its contracts, not those of its members, and liabilities incurred under such contracts are the liabilities of the body corporate, for which the members do not have even a secondary liability unless otherwise provided by statute. In contrast to the position in Continental law and Scots law, a partnership firm is not considered by English law to have separate legal personality; the partnership is merely a business association of individual partners, who are jointly and severally liable for debts incurred in the name of the firm.[56] Under English law the separation of the body corporate from its members and their insulation from liability are a necessary concomitant of corporate personality. This principle was reaffirmed by the Court of Appeal in its rulings in the International Tin Council litigation[57] and applies also to limited liability partnerships.[58] There was a brief period in the history of English law in which creditors had a direct right of action against members of a defaulting company, but such a right has been unknown to English law

---

[53] See, for example, *Buchler v Talbot* [2004] 2 A.C. 298, *per* Lord Nicholls at para.32; *Wight v Eckhardt Marine GmbH* [2004] 1 A.C. 147, *per* Lord Hoffmann at paras 28–32; *Re Celtic Extraction Ltd* [2001] Ch. 475, *per* Morritt L.J. at para.42; *Re Bank of Credit and Commerce International SA (No 8)* [1998] A.C. 214, *per* Lord Hoffmann at paras 5, 9; *Charter Reinsurance Co v Fagan* [1997] A.C. 313, *per* Mance J. at 351; *Re J. Leslie Engineers Co Ltd* [1976] 2 All E.R. 85, *per* Oliver J. at 95; *Re Dynamics Corp of America* [1976] 2 All E.R. 669, *per* Oliver J. at 675; *Re Harrington Motor Co Ex p. Chaplin* [1928] Ch. 105, *per* Atkin L.J. at 122.

[54] Mokal, above, n.51, at 591.

[55] See below, para.7–02.

[56] However, partnerships may now be formed with limited liability under the Limited Liability Partnerships Act 2000.

[57] *Maclaine Watson & Co Ltd v Department of Trade and Industry* [1988] 3 All E.R. 257.

[58] Limited Liability Partnerships Act 2000, s.1(2). Such partnerships are not discussed further in the present work.

since 1855.[59] The principle applies as much to the one-man company[60] as to others[61]; and in the celebrated decision in *Salomon v Salomon & Co*[62] the House of Lords saw nothing objectionable in the sole shareholder holding a debenture over the company's assets to secure payment to him of the price of the business he had sold to the company, thus enabling him as a secured creditor to obtain priority over unsecured creditors when the company became insolvent. The principle that members of a company are not liable for its debts applies not only to companies controlled by individual members but to wholly owned subsidiaries of other companies. So in general a parent company is not liable for the debts of its wholly-owned subsidiary, nor does it incur a liability merely because it exercises overall control of the subsidiary through a group structure, management and financial control, though if it interferes in day-to-day management it could be held a shadow director.[63]

Members of a company will, of course, incur a liability where the company is registered, or re-registered, as an unlimited company, and may also do so where the company acts as their agent or where they undertake a collateral liability, *e.g.* under a guarantee or other contract. Moreover, there are special situations in which the court is willing to pierce the corporate veil, as where the company has been created and used as an engine of fraud[64]; but such cases are exceptional, and it is extremely difficult to persuade an English court to look behind the veil of incorporation. Finally, though a European Economic Interest Grouping created under EEC

---

[59] As explained earlier (above, para.1–05) the first general statute providing for incorporation was the Joint Stock Companies Act 1844, under which the company had legal personality but its members remained liable for its debts. That was changed by the Limited Liability Act 1855. Since that time members of a company have never been *directly* liable as such to creditors. However, upon winding-up members of a limited liability company are liable to contribute to the assets of the company to the amount unpaid on their shares or, in the case of a company incorporated by guarantee, the amount they undertook to contribute to the assets of the company in the event of its being wound up, and members of an unlimited company are liable to contribute to the assets without limitation in whatever amount is needed to cover the company's debts and the expenses of winding up. See Companies Act 1985, s.1(2); Insolvency Act 1986, s.74.

[60] Until relatively recently there was no such thing, strictly speaking, as a one-man company, since every company was required to have at least two members (Companies Act 1985, ss.1(1), 24). Since there was nothing to prevent the second member from holding one share as trustee/nominee of the first, the requirement was rather pointless and has now been abolished as regards companies limited by shares or guarantee (Companies Act 1985, s.24, as amended by the Companies (Single Member Private Limited Companies) Regulations 1992 (SI 1992/1699), introduced pursuant to the 12th Company Law Directive No.89/667 on single-member private limited-liability companies (OJ L393, dated December 30, 1989, p.40).

[61] *Salomon v Salomon & Co* [1897] A.C. 22.

[62] [1897] A.C. 22.

[63] See below, para.12–03.

[64] *Gilford Motor Co v Horne* [1933] Ch. 935. See generally L.C.B. Gower, *Principles of Modern Company Law* (7th ed., 2003), Chap.8.

regulations[65] and registered in this country has legal personality[66] its members are jointly and severally liable for its debts without limit of liability.[67]

---

[65] Council Regulation No.2137/85 July 25, 1985 on the European Economic Interest Grouping (EEIG). The regulation has direct effect under Community law but various matters were left to national law and are provided for by the European Economic Interest Grouping Regulations 1989 (SI 1989/638).

[66] European Economic Interest Grouping Regulations 1989 (SI 1989/638), reg.3.

[67] Council Regulation No.2137/85, Art.24(1).

Chapter 4

The Concept of Corporate Insolvency

1. GENERAL PRINCIPLES

The legal significance of insolvency

A company is insolvent when it is unable to pay its debts. The concept is **4–01**
simple enough but as we shall see there is more than one test of inability to
pay debts and in marginal cases it may be far from easy to determine
whether the test is satisfied as at the relevant time. Insolvency as such is not
a condition to which legal consequences attach. These occur only after
there has been some formal proceeding, such as winding-up or the
appointment of an administrator or administrative receiver.[1] Thus it is
neither a criminal offence nor a civil wrong for a company to become
insolvent or even to trade while insolvent.[2] It is only if the company
becomes subject to a formal insolvency proceeding and improper trading is
established that the question of civil or criminal liability can arise.[3] Again,
insolvency does not *per se* prevent creditors from taking steps to enforce
payment; indeed, the strong support given by English law to individual
initiative means that almost always the race goes to the swiftest. Further,
payments and transfers of property made by an insolvent company are not
on that account alone rendered void or voidable, even if the fact that the
company is insolvent is known to the payee or transferee; a formal
insolvency proceeding is necessary. But the advent of insolvency may affect
transactions previously conducted.[4]

Insolvency legislation confines the terms "insolvency" and "insolvent" to
a formal insolvency proceeding.[5] When referring to a *state of insolvency* it

---

[1] See below Chaps 5, 9 and 10.
[2] Indeed, the premature cessation of trading may be wrongful. See below, para.12–39.
[3] See Chap.12.
[4] See below and Chap.11.
[5] See, for example, the Insolvency Act 1986, ss.240(3). 247(1); Company Directors Disqualification Act 1986, s.6(2).

83

does not use this term but embodies the concept in the phrase "unable to pay its debts."[6] What is a debt for this purpose[7] depends on the particular test of insolvency that is being applied. As we shall see, in determining whether a company can pay its debts as they fall due the word "debt" is strictly confined.[8] By contrast, the balance sheet test of insolvency, where this is applicable, requires assets to be measured not against debts but against "liabilities", an altogether wider expression.[9]

The relevance of a company's inability to pay its debts

4–02 It is with the advent of a formal insolvency proceeding that the company's inability to pay its debts becomes material. This is true not only where the state of insolvency exists at the time of the proceedings in question but where it existed at some earlier time. Thus a winding-up or administration gives retroactive legal significance to an earlier state of insolvency which at the time it first arose had no impact in law. Inability to pay debts is the fundamental concept on which all insolvency law is based.

(1) Inability to pay debts is a ground for winding-up.[10]

(2) If a company goes into insolvent liquidation[11] its directors will in certain circumstances incur a liability for fraudulent trading[12] or wrongful trading.[13]

(3) Transfers at an undervalue and preferences may be set aside if made when the company is unable to pay its debts and it subsequently goes into administration or liquidation.[14]

(4) A floating charge given otherwise than for a specified form of new value by a company unable to pay its debts may be void if the company subsequently goes into liquidation or administration.[15]

---

[6] See, for example, the Insolvency Act 1986, ss.123, 222–224, Sch.B1, para.11(a).

[7] As to the various meanings of "debt" for the purposes of admissibility of claims to proof, see below, paras 7–32 *et seq.*

[8] See below, para.4–17.

[9] See below, paras 4–25, 4–26.

[10] Insolvency Act 1986, s.122(1)(f). Section 122 sets out eight other grounds on which a company may be wound up.

[11] Defined by the Insolvency Act 1986, ss.214(6) and 216(7) in terms embodying one of the two principal tests of insolvency, namely insufficiency of assets to meet liabilities.

[12] Insolvency Act 1986, s.213.

[13] *ibid.*, s.214.

[14] *ibid.*, ss.238–242. See paras 11–12 *et seq.* For a detailed discussion of the concept of insolvency in this context from the perspective of Australian law, see Andrew R. Keay, "The Insolvency Factor in the Avoidance of Antecedent Transactions in Corporate Liquidations" (1995) 21 Monash Univ. L. Rev. 305.

[15] Insolvency Act 1986, s.245. See para.11–110.

(5) An administration order can be made against a company only if it is or is likely to become unable to pay its debts,[16] except where the application for administration is made by the holder of a qualifying floating charge.[17]

(6) A person who is or has been a director of a company which has at any time become insolvent may have a disqualification order made against him where the conditions of s.6(1) of the Company Directors Disqualification Act 1986 are satisfied.

The tests of inability to pay debts

The Insolvency Act 1986 and related legislation prescribe a bewildering **4–03** variety of tests for determining whether a company is to be deemed insolvent for the purpose of the relevant statutory provisions. The reasons for selecting different tests for different provisions have never been clearly articulated. In some cases these differences would seem to have resulted from the piecemeal development of corporate insolvency prior to the Insolvency Act 1985, though for the most part they are not too difficult to justify.[18] These various tests are set out in s.123(1) and (2) of the Insolvency Act 1986:

"123(1) **Inability to pay debts** A company is deemed unable to pay its debts—

(a) if a creditor (by assignment or otherwise) to whom the company is indebted in a sum exceeding £750 then due has served on the company, by leaving it at the company's registered office, a written demand (in the prescribed form) requiring the company to pay the sum so due and the company has for 3 weeks thereafter neglected to pay the sum or to secure or compound for it to the reasonable satisfaction of the creditor, or

(b) if, in England and Wales, execution or other process issued on a judgment, decree or order of any court in favour of a creditor of the company is returned unsatisfied in whole or in part, or

(c) *[provision for Scotland]*, or

(d) *[provision for Northern Ireland]*, or

(e) if is proved to the satisfaction of the court that the company is unable to pay its debts as they fall due.

(2) **Proof that assets less than liabilities** A company is also deemed unable to pay its debts if it is proved to the satisfaction of the court

---

[16] *ibid.*, Sch.B1, para.11(a). It also necessary to show that the administration order is likely to achieve the purpose of the administration (para.11(b)).

[17] *ibid.*, Sch.B1, para.35(2)(a).

[18] See generally below, paras 4–07 *et seq.*

that the value of the company's assets is less than the amount of its liabilities, taking into account its contingent and prospective liabilities."

These various tests fall broadly into two groups. The first group, embodied in paragraphs (a) and (b) of s.123 of the Insolvency Act 1986, consists of two very specific and readily ascertainable facts deemed to establish inability to pay debts, namely failure to meet a statutory demand for payment of a debt in excess of £750 within three weeks and the return of an execution unsatisfied in whole or in part. The second group, contained in s.123(l)(e) and (2), consists of more general criteria of inability to pay debts and divides into the two primary tests described below.[19]

The two primary tests

4–04   The two primary tests of inability to pay debts are the cash flow test (inability to pay debts as they fall due) and the balance sheet test (shortfall of assets in relation to liabilities).[20] The cash flow test, where it applies, is always that formulated by s.123(l)(e) of the Insolvency Act. By contrast the formulation of the balance sheet test varies from one statutory provision to another but the effect in all cases appears to be the same.[21] For most purposes it is the present inability to pay debts that is the crucial factor. However, a company is permitted to go into a members' voluntary winding-up if the directors make a declaration that in their view the company will be able to pay its debts in full, with interest, within a period not exceeding 12 months.[22]

The statutory expression of the distinction between the cash flow test and the balance sheet test is of quite recent origin. Section 80(4) of the Companies Act 1862 embodied a single general formulation, namely that a company was to be deemed insolvent "whenever it is proved to the satisfaction of the court that the company is unable to pay its debts". This formulation, which contrasted sharply with that applicable to bankruptcy,[23]

---

[19] There are no comparable provisions in relation to bankruptcy, where inability to pay is established by the specific tests laid down in s.268 of the Insolvency Act.

[20] Insolvency Act 1986, s.123(l)(e), 123(2).

[21] See below, paras 4–24, 4–34.

[22] See below, para.4–12.

[23] The Bankruptcy Acts never used a general test of insolvency as a basis for making a debtor bankrupt; this could be done only by proof that the debtor had committed one or more acts of bankruptcy. But payments and transfers by the debtor could be set aside as fraudulent preferences if made within a designated period prior to the petition on which the adjudication order was made by a debtor "unable to pay his debts as they become due from his own money," and prior to the Insolvency Act 1985 bankruptcy rules of preference were applicable in the winding-up of companies. See, for example, *Re Washington Diamond Mining Co* [1893] 3 Ch. 95.

was held to exclude contingent and prospective liabilities when applying the balance sheet test,[24] a deficiency remedied by the Companies Act 1907, s.28 of which required the court to take account of contingent and prospective liabilities. This was carried over into successive Companies Acts up to and including the 1985 Act.[25] The present division into inability to pay debts as they fall due and insufficiency of assets in relation to liabilities was first introduced by the short-lived Insolvency Act 1985 in its amendment of s.518 of the Companies Act 1985, replaced by the present s.123(l)(e) and (2). These changes in the statutory formulations since the Act of 1862 need to be borne in mind when referring to earlier case law on the meaning of inability to pay debts. There is in fact a remarkable dearth of English authority on the meaning and content of the two primary tests.[26] This stands in striking contrast to Australian corporate insolvency law, which throughout the present century has built up a substantial doctrine of case law on the cash flow and balance sheet tests[27] to which appropriate references will be made in the ensuing passages.

(1) Cash flow

Under the cash flow, or commercial insolvency, test, which will be **4-05** examined in more detail later in this chapter,[28] a company is insolvent when it is unable to pay its debts as they fall due. For this purpose the fact that its assets exceed its liabilities is irrelevant; if it cannot pay its way in the conduct of its business it is insolvent, for there is no reason why creditors should be expected to wait while the company realises assets some of which may not be held in readily liquidated form.

Despite a number of theoretical problems which have not been fully resolved in English insolvency law,[29] the cash flow test is relatively easy to apply in practice, for the court looks at what the company is actually doing; if it is not in fact paying its debts as they fall due (ignoring cases where there is a bona fide dispute as to the indebtedness) it is assumed to be insolvent.[30] A company which cannot meet its debts as they fall due is

---

[24] *Re European Life Assurance Society* (1869) L.R. 9 Eq. 122. Consideration of such liabilities does not, of course, arise in relation to the cash flow test, where the question is whether the company is able to pay its debts as they fall due. See below, para.4–15.

[25] Companies (Consolidation) Act 1908, s.130(iv); Companies Act 1929, s.169; Companies Act 1948, s.223(d); Companies Act 1985, s.518.

[26] As was noted by Nicholls L.J. in *Byblos Bank SAL v Al-Khudhairy* (1986) 2 B.C.C. 99, 549 at 99, 563, where he observed that only three decisions had been found relevant to the point he had to decide.

[27] For a detailed survey see Andrew R. Keay, *McPherson's Law of Company Liquidation*, paras 3.23 *et seq*, 11.21 *et seq.*, and "The Insolvency Factor in the Avoidance of Antecedent Transactions in Corporate Liquidations" (1995) 21 Monash Univ. L. Rev. 305.

[28] Below, paras 4–15 *et seq.*

[29] See below, para.4–15.

[30] See below, para.4–23.

considered insolvent for the purpose of grounding a winding-up order or administration order or vitiating a transaction under ss.238, 239 or 245 of the Act.[31] But the cash flow test has no relevance to the determination of insolvency for the purposes of the wrongful trading provisions of the Insolvency Act[32] or for the purposes of s.6 of the Company Directors Disqualification Act 1986[33] or Part XII of the Employment Rights Act 1996.[34]

(2) Balance sheet

4–06   The alternative primary test of insolvency is the balance sheet (or asset) test—*i.e.* the company's assets are insufficient to discharge its liabilities. The idea underlying this test, which is discussed in greater detail later,[35] is that it is not sufficient for the company to be able to meet its current obligations if its total liabilities can ultimately be met only by the realisation of its assets and these are insufficient for the purpose. If the cash flow test were the only relevant test then current and short-term creditors would in effect be paid at the expense of creditors to whom liabilities were incurred after the company had reached the point of no return because of an incurable deficiency in its assets.

In the typical case there is no real doubt as to the inadequacy of the company's assets. But in marginal situations it may be very difficult to decide whether the balance sheet test of insolvency is satisfied. This is because the valuation of assets (and, where these are required to be taken into account, of contingent liabilities) is not an exact science but to a considerable extent a matter of judgment as to the amount a willing buyer would pay in the market when dealing with a willing seller. One has only to see the sometimes huge disparity between the estimate put on a work of art by a leading auction house and the actual sale price at auction to realise how difficult it is to give an accurate valuation of assets not having an established market price. Moreover, there is a close link between cash flow insolvency and balance sheet insolvency in that where a company is a going concern and its business can be sold as such with its assets in use in the business, those assets will usually have a substantially higher value than if disposed of on a break-up basis, divorced from their previous business activity. So a company which is commercially solvent has a much greater chance of satisfying the balance sheet test of solvency than one which is unable to pay its debts as they fall due.

---

[31] Relating respectively to transactions at an undervalue, preferences and floating charges given otherwise than for specified forms of new value.
[32] See below, para.4–31.
[33] See below, para.4–10.
[34] See below, para.4–11.
[35] Below, paras 4–24 *et seq.*

The balance sheet test is one of the tests prescribed for the purpose of grounds for winding up, administration or the avoidance of transactions at an undervalue,[36] preferences[37] and floating charges given otherwise than for a prescribed form of new value,[38] and the disqualification of directors under s.6 of the Company Directors Disqualification Act 1986,[39] and is the sole test for the purpose of identifying an insolvent liquidation under the provisions relating to wrongful trading.[40] It does not, however, feature in the insolvency provisions of the Employment Rights Act 1996.[41] The reason for the exclusive use of the balance sheet test in the wrongful trading provisions is that there is no reason to impose liability of the delinquent directors to contribute to the assets of the company except where the assets are insufficient to meet the liabilities and the expenses of winding-up.

Other tests of inability to pay debts

Both the cash flow test and the balance sheet test suffer the disadvantage **4–07** that they require evidence and an analysis of the debtor company's position which may take time to organise and may be the subject of dispute. There are various situations in which the legislature perceived a need to establish insolvency by reference to some irrefutable and easily established external fact or event, either as an alternative to the other two tests or in replacement of them.

(1) Under the Insolvency Act 1986

It will be recalled that, in addition to the cash flow and balance sheet tests **4–08** in s.123(1)(e) and (2) of the Insolvency Act, s.123(1) prescribes two very specific means of showing a company's inability to pay its debts, namely if:

(a) it neglects to pay, secure or compound to the reasonable satisfaction of the creditor a debt exceeding £750 within three weeks of a written demand in the prescribed form[42]; or

(b) execution or other process on a judgment against the company is returned unsatisfied, wholly or in part.[43]

---

[36] See below, para.11–12.
[37] See below, para.11–69.
[38] See below, para.11–108.
[39] See below, para.12–58.
[40] See below, paras 12–22, 12–28.
[41] See below, para.4–11.
[42] See further below, para.5–09.
[43] Separate and more limited provisions are contained in ss.222–224 in relation to unregistered companies.

The same rules apply for the purpose of grounding an administration order except that the court may also make an administration order if the company, though currently able to pay its debts, is likely to become unable to do so,[44] for example where it is likely to begin or to continue trading at a loss without recovery prospects.[45]

A separate ground for a winding-up order is that it is just and equitable that the company be wound up.[46] This ground is also available to actual and prospective creditors.[47]

4–09   Though s.123 is primarily designed to complement the provisions of s.122(1)(f) making inability to pay debts a ground for winding up by the court, the tests of insolvency laid down in s.123 have a much wider application. In determining whether a company was insolvent at a particular time for the purpose of the provisions relating to transactions at an undervalue,[48] preferences[49] and floating charges given for past value[50] the company is to be deemed insolvent if at the relevant time it was unable to pay its debts within the meaning of s.123 of the Insolvency Act (*i.e.* within any of the tests for winding up purposes as set out above) or became unable to do so in consequence of the transaction at an undervalue or preference or (in the case of the floating charge) the transaction under which it was created.[51]

It is not hard to see why it was felt that there was a need for alternative and more specific tests of insolvency for the purpose of a winding-up or administration order. To establish that a company is insolvent, and was already insolvent at an earlier point in time, is much easier for a person already in the saddle as liquidator, administrator or administrative receiver than it is for a party seeking a winding-up or administration order, who at that stage has no access to the company's records and no right to interrogate its officers. This lack of information could deprive unpaid creditors of speedy recourse to winding-up or administration and in so doing inhibit efforts to protect the company's business and assets through the expeditious appointment of a liquidator or administrator. Hence to facilitate the proof of insolvency for the purpose of winding-up or administration proceedings the Insolvency Act (continuing, as regards winding-up, the rules originally prescribed by the Companies Acts) permits

---

[44] Insolvency Act 1986, Sch.B1, para.11(a).
[45] See further para.10–43.
[46] Insolvency Act 1986, s.122(1)(g).
[47] *Re a Company (No.003028 of 1987)* (1987) 3 B.C.C. 575.
[48] See para.11–12.
[49] See para.11–69.
[50] See para.11–108.
[51] Insolvency Act 1986, ss.240(2), 245(4). Inability to pay debts is presumed, unless the contrary is shown, in relation to any transaction at an undervalue which is entered into by the company with a person who is connected with the company (s.240(2)), *i.e.* is a director or shadow director of the company, an associate of such a director or shadow director or an associate of the company (s.249).

alternative methods of satisfying the court that a company is unable to pay its debts and ought to be placed in liquidation or administration. Despite this, the statutory notice procedure is not the preferred option for creditors, who in the case of an undisputed debt will either institute proceedings to obtain a quick judgment[52] in the hope that if the debtor does not pay, execution against its assets will produce payment without bringing the house down[53] or present a winding-up petition immediately based on s.123(1)(e) because they do not wish to be constrained by the three-week period allowed to the debtor company and hope that the threat of winding-up will induce payment.[54]

Somewhat different considerations apply to the avoidance of trans-actions. These can be invoked only where the company is already in liquidation or administration, so that there is not the same need for speedy determination as there is in the case of a petition for winding-up or administration. But the alternative tests of insolvency—failure to meet a statutory demand and an unsatisfied execution against the company—avoid the necessity for expensive and time-consuming investigations by the liquidator or administrator into the company's state of solvency at the time of transactions, which may have taken place up to three years[55] before the winding up or administration order.

(2) Under the Company Directors Disqualification Act 1986

For the purpose of the provisions relating to the disqualification of a director, a company becomes insolvent if it goes into liquidation at a time when its assets are insufficient for the payment of its debts and other liabilities and the expenses of winding up, or an administration order is made or an administrative receiver appointed.[56] Though the occurrence of either of the last two of these events does not necessarily indicate insolvency, the fact that it proved necessary to place the company under external management is a sufficient justification for deeming a state of insolvency to have existed.

4–10

---

[52] In default of appearance or by way of summary judgment on the ground that the defendant has no arguable defence.

[53] The success of this does, of course, depend on the extent to which other creditors are ahead in the execution stakes.

[54] It is established law that in the case of a debt which cannot reasonably be disputed the presentation of a winding-up petition with the object of collecting payment rather than having the company wound up is perfectly legitimate. See para.4–23.

[55] In the case of the provisions relating to the reopening of extortionate credit transactions (Insolvency Act 1986, s.244(2)). In other cases the relevant periods are shorter except for transactions defrauding creditors, where there is no time limit.

[56] Company Directors Disqualification Act 1986, s.6(2).

(3) Under the Employment Rights Act 1996

4–11   Finally, for the purpose of the provisions of the Employment Rights Act 1996 entitling an employee to payments from the National Insurance Fund[57] upon the employer's insolvency and termination of the employment, an employer is considered to have become insolvent when (a) a winding up order or an administration order has been made, or a resolution for voluntary winding up has been passed,[58] with respect to the company, (b) a receiver or manager of the company's undertaking has been duly appointed, or possession has been taken by or on behalf of the holders of any debentures secured by a floating charge, of any property of the company comprised in or subject to the charge, or (c) a voluntary arrangement proposed in the case of the company for the purposes of Part I of the Insolvency Act 1986 has been approved under that Part of the Act.[59] It will be seen that in this case neither the cash flow test nor the balance sheet test comes into consideration. Presumably this reflects a concern to ensure that claims on the National Insurance Fund are triggered only by a readily ascertainable external event not involving questions of judgement or valuation.

Declaration of solvency for members' voluntary winding up

4–12   A somewhat different approach to the concept of insolvency is adopted by s.89 of the Insolvency Act relating to members' voluntary winding up. This requires the directors to make and file a statutory declaration of solvency, but in contrast to the requirement set by the cash flow test it is not necessary for the declaration to state that the company is currently able to pay its existing debts or that its assets are sufficient to cover its liabilities. It suffices for the declaration to state that the directors have formed the opinion that the company will be able to pay its debts in full, together with interest at the official rate (as defined in s.251) within such period, not exceeding 12 months from the commencement of the winding up, as may be specified in the declaration.[60] It is thus technically possible for the directors properly to file a declaration of solvency and put the company into a members' voluntary winding-up even though it is unable to pay its debts both on a cash flow basis and on a balance sheet basis. In practice, it is highly unlikely that a declaration could properly be made in the case of a

---

[57] For arrears of pay, holiday pay, compensation for unfair dismissal, and the like.
[58] This is not confined to insolvent liquidation but applies equally to a members' voluntary winding up.
[59] Employment Rights Act 1996, s.183(3). However, a compromise or arrangement under s.425 of the Companies Act 1985 is not specified as an event by which the employer is deemed to be insolvent.
[60] Insolvency Act 1986, s.89(1).

company with both a deficiency of assets and an inability to pay its debts as they fell due, for a reasonable forecast of an ability to pay debts in full in 12 months would almost invariably enable the company to obtain temporary accommodation to pay its current debts as they fell due.

The time at which inability to pay debts is relevant

At what time must the company be unable to pay its debts in order to attract the statutory provisions? This varies with the provision in question. The relevant time is:

4–13

(1) for the purpose of the provisions relating to the making of a winding-up or administration order, on the hearing of the petition on which the order is to be made[61];

(2) for the purpose of the provisions relating to wrongful trading, when the company goes into liquidation[62];

(3) for the purpose of the provisions relating to avoidance of transactions at an undervalue and preferences, when the transaction is made or the preference given[63];

(4) for the purpose of the provisions relating to avoidance of a floating charge given for past value, when the charge is created[64];

(5) for the purpose of the provisions relating to the disqualification of a director, any time while he was a director or any subsequent time.[65]

It will thus be seen that the question of a company's insolvency may arise prospectively or retrospectively. In assessing a company's financial position for the purpose of the avoidance of antecedent transactions the court has "the inestimable benefit of the wisdom of hindsight".[66] By contrast, where the question is whether a winding-up order should be made on the ground of the company's inability to pay its debts as they fall due such inability must be determined not only as at the date of the hearing of the petition by reference to debts then payable but also as at some near future time by reference to those which will be payable at that time.[67] Hence although the time as at which the company's inability to pay its debts must be tested is very precisely identified, this does not mean that the court is required to

---

[61] *ibid.*, s.122(1)(f), Sch.B1, para.11(b).
[62] *ibid.*, s.247(2).
[63] *ibid.*, ss.238(2), 239(2), as qualified by s.240.
[64] *ibid.*, s.245.
[65] Company Directors Disqualification Act 1986, s.6(1)(a).
[66] *Lewis v Doran* (2004) 208 A.L.R. 385, *per* Palmer, J., at para.108.
[67] *ibid.*, at para.107; and see below, para.4–16.

treat the company's business as frozen at that very time. On the contrary, both of the primary tests involve an element of projection, the cash flow test because the court looks to see not merely whether at the time of the enquiry the company is unable to pay debts then due but whether its position as seen at that time is such that it will be unable to pay its debts becoming due in the near future at the time those fall due,[68] and the balance sheet test because in most cases the court is required to take into account prospective and contingent liabilities.[69]

Inability to pay debts is not the sole criterion for the exercise of the court's powers

4–14 In the discussion that follows it should be borne in mind that a conclusion that the relevant test of inability to pay debts is satisfied merely establishes the statutory ground for the requisite order, it does not necessarily entitle the petitioner to ask for the order as of right. In the first place, a creditor must show a tangible interest in the making of the order.[70] It is not enough that the company is technically insolvent, as many are when starting to trade with the aid of a bank loan repayable on demand. Secondly, the making of an administration or winding up order is within the discretion of the court, as also is an order setting aside a vulnerable transaction or directing a contribution to the assets of the company by reason of wrongful trading and an order for disqualification of a director. Accordingly factors which do not as a matter of law enter into the determination of a state of insolvency—*e.g.* the prospect of additional finance for a company with a deficiency of assets—may nevertheless be relevant when the judge comes to consider whether to exercise his discretion.[71] However, the discretion must be exercised in accordance with settled principles and there is a presumption that a creditor in respect of an undisputed debt is entitled to a winding-up order *ex debito justitiae*.[72]

With these preliminary observations I turn to consider in more detail the various statutory formulations of the cash flow and balance sheet tests of insolvency and to explore some of the more intricate problems awaiting judicial decision.

---

[68] See below, para.4–16.
[69] See below, paras 4–28 *et seq.*
[70] See below, paras 5–07, 5–08.
[71] *Byblos Bank SAL v Al-Khudhairy* (1986) 2 B.C.C. 99, 549, *per* Nicholls L.J. at 99, 562.
[72] See below, para.5–07.

2. THE CASH FLOW TEST[73]

The test restated

The root statutory provision, from which all the other provisions adopting **4–15** the cash flow test are derived, is s.123(1)(e) of the Insolvency Act, by which a company is deemed unable to pay its debts:

> "if it is proved to the satisfaction of the court that the company is unable to pay its debts as they fall due."

This formulation is deceptive in its simplicity. It raises a number of questions which have not been fully explored in English cases. What is the meaning of "debts"? To what extent, if at all, may or should the court look at debts becoming payable in the future? Are debts to be included which, though legally due, are not the subject of any current demand for payment? Is ability to pay to be determined exclusively by reference to the company's own money or can the prospect of raising funds through borrowing or the disposal of assets be taken into account? Must it be shown that the company is able to pay its debts exactly on the due date or is some margin of tolerance to be allowed?

The element of futurity

In answering these questions the court looks at the company's financial **4–16** position taken as a whole. In *Quick v Stoland Pty Ltd*[74] Emmett J., discussing the comparable concept of insolvency under s.95A of the Australian Corporations Law, put the matter in the following way:

> "In order to determine whether the company was solvent at a given time, it would be relevant to consider the following matters:
> —All of the company's debts as at that time in order to determine when those debts were and payable.
> —All of the assets of the company as at that time in order to determine the extent to which those assets were liquid or were realisable within a timeframe that would allow each of the debts to be paid as and when it became payable.
> —The company's business as at that time in order to determine its expected net cash flow from the business by deducting from projected future sales the cash expenses which would be necessary to generate those sales.

---

[73] See also Andrew R. Keay, *McPherson's Law of Company Liquidation*, paras 3.23 *et seq.*
[74] (1998) 29 A.C.S.R. 130 (Federal Court of Australia).

—Arrangements between the company and prospective lenders, such as its bankers and shareholders, in order to determine whether any shortfall in liquid and realisable assets and cash flow could be made up by borrowings which would be repayable at a time later than the debts."

Moreover, the court adopts a commercial, rather than a technical, view of insolvency.[75] So while the phrase "is unable" might at first sight be thought to refer to the inability at the relevant time[76] to pay debts which have then fallen due, its conjunction with the phrase "as they fall due" indicates a continuous succession of debts rather than a calculation of debts existing on any particular day.[77] The essential question is whether the company's financial position is such that it can continue in business and still pay its way. The court therefore has to consider whether any liquidity problem the company may have is purely temporary and can be cured in the reasonably near future.

> "The conclusion of insolvency ought to be clear from a consideration of the debtor's financial position in its entirety and generally speaking ought not to be drawn simply from evidence of a temporary lack of liquidity. It is the debtor's inability, utilizing such cash resources as he has or can command through the use of his assets, to meet his debts as they fall due which indicates insolvency."[78]

For this purpose the court will have regard not only to debts due and payable at the date for assessment, "due and payable" being construed in a commercial rather than a legal sense,[79] but also to claims falling due in the near future, and to the likely availability of funds to meet such future claims and the company's existing debts.[80] In determining this question regard must be had to the company's total financial position. We shall now examine these questions in more detail.

Only debts are to be taken into account

4–17   A debt is a liquidated claim, that is, a claim for an amount which is ascertained or can be readily and without difficulty ascertained,[81] as by mere calculation or the taking of an account.[82] It is to be distinguished from

---

[75] *Sandell v Porter* (1966) 115 C.L.R. 666; *Iso Lilodw' Aliphumeleli Pty Ltd v Commissioner of Taxation* (2002) 42 A.C.S.R. 561.

[76] As to which see above, para.4–13.

[77] *Bank of Australasia v Hall* (1907) 4 C.L.R. 1514 at 1528. discussing the meaning of the comparable phrase "as they become due" in the Australian legislation. See Keay, *op. cit.*, para.11.21.

[78] *Sandell v Porter* (1966) 115 C.L.R. 666, *per* Barwick C.J. at 670–671.

[79] See below, para.4–21.

[80] *ibid.*, n.75; *Expo International Ltd v Chant* [1979] 2 N.S.W.L.R. 820; *Lewis v Doran*, above, n.66, at para.107.

[81] *Stooke v Taylor* (1880) 5 Q.B.D. 565 at 575, *per* Cockburn L.J.

[82] See *O'Driscoll v Manchester Insurance Committee* [1915] 3 K.B. 499.

an unliquidated claim, *e.g.* for damages for breach of contract or tort, which involves questions of liability and assessment. So if B Ltd buys goods from S and the price has become payable, that constitutes a debt which is to be taken into account in deciding whether B Ltd is able to pay its debts as they fall due. But if the price is payable only after delivery and B wrongfully refuses to accept the goods, S's claim is for unliquidated damages for breach of contract and cannot be taken into account under s.123(l)(e), for it involves questions of evidence and valuation.[83]

Only due debts are to be taken into account

The word "due" is capable of being used in both a narrow sense and a **4–18** broad sense. In its narrow sense it denotes a debt which is both existing and immediately payable; in its broad sense it embraces *debitum in praesenti, solvendum in futuro*, that is, an existing indebtedness which has not yet matured. For the purpose of the cash flow test only those liabilities which viewed at the relevant time constitute existing debts presently payable may be considered. In principle existing debts payable in the future,[84] prospective debts and contingent liabilities,[85] and prospective liabilities,[86] must all be ignored. However, it is important to bear in mind the point made earlier, that in looking at the state of the company's affairs the court does not confine itself to the way matters stand on the date of assessment but looks at what is likely to happen in the near future. So although debts payable in the future and contingent debts have to be excluded in determining whether, *at the date of the hearing*, the company is able to discharge debts then due and payable, the court also has to consider whether, in relation to debts which will become due and payable in the near future, the company will be able to pay those debts at the time when payment has to be made. In other words, the date of the hearing is not the only temporal point. Where the court is satisfied that debts which at the date of the hearing have not then become payable or are only contingent will at a later point in the not too distant future become existing debts presently payable and that at that point the company will be unable to pay them, the cash flow test of insolvency is satisfied.

Example 1

The hearing of a winding up petition takes place on May 1. The **4–19** company's liability to its bank for repayment of a loan matures on May 20. In deciding whether on May 1, the company is able to pay its debts as

---

[83] It follows that the wide definition of "debt" in r.13.12 of the Insolvency Rules 1986 is not applicable for the purpose of the cash flow test in s.123(1)(e), though it is for the purpose of the balance sheet test in s.123(2) (see para.4–26). See further below.

[84] *Re Bryant Investment Co Ltd* (1974) 2 All E.R. 683.

[85] See below, para.4–28.

[86] See below, para.4–29.

they fall due the court will consider, among other things, whether the company will be in a position to repay the loan on May 20.

Example 2

4–20 A payment by the company to one of its creditors is being attacked as a preference, and the question for decision is whether at the time of the payment the company was unable to pay its debts as they fell due. At that time the company had a contingent liability as surety under a guarantee. Payment was due from the principal debtor four weeks later and the principal debtor had already convened a meeting to pass a resolution for voluntary winding up by reason of its insolvency. It would have been clear at the time of the alleged preference that the contingent liability would shortly mature into an existing liability. The court can therefore properly take that liability into account in considering whether at the time of the payment in question the company was able to pay its debts as they fell due.

Only debts of which current repayment is required are to be considered

4–21 In deciding whether a company is able to pay debts becoming payable in the future the court will take a commercial view of when payment is required, and will have regard to the fact that it is quite normal for debtors to make, and for creditors to accept, late payment.[87] So even if payment cannot be made on the exact date due, it suffices that it can be made within the period that a creditor would consider acceptable, for which purpose the court will have regard to any indulgence customarily granted by that creditor.[88] By the same token, even debts which are technically due are to be ignored where there is no current indication that the creditors concerned are requiring repayment.[89] If the position were otherwise most banks would be insolvent, for banks operate on the basis that only a relatively small proportion of their depositors will demand repayment at any one time. Where a company arranges an overdraft facility with its bank this is likely, whether as an express or an implied term of the banker-customer contract, to be repayable on demand. But neither party contemplates that such demand will be made so long as the company is continuing to operate as a going concern and the bank is content to allow the relationship to continue. In most cases the overdraft facility will be renewed from year to year and

---

[87] *Iso Lilodw' Aliphumeleli Pty Ltd v Commissioner of Taxation* (2002) 42 A.C.S.R. 561.
[88] See below, para.4–21.
[89] *Re Capital Annuities Ltd* [1978] 3 All E.R. 704, *per* Slade J. at 718. This case is notable for the fact that the company went into winding-up on its own petition and was anxious for the court to declare it insolvent, a declaration the court found unable to make on the available evidence!

continue indefinitely. Accordingly unless the bank has either demanded immediate repayment or is likely to do so in the immediate future the overdraft should be ignored in deciding whether the company is able to pay its debts as they fall due. The same applies to debts due to trade creditors who, by way of indulgence and without contractual commitment to do so, customarily allow a period of trade credit as regards the debts in question.[90]

Again, where a winding-up order was made against a company and creditors of the company in respect of debts payable on demand were related entities of the company and were controlled by the same person controlling the company, and that person had intimated his concern to save the company from liquidation, the court directed that the winding-up should be terminated if each of the creditors gave a written undertaking not to make demand for payment and the controller gave a written undertaking not to procure or permit a breach of the creditors' undertakings.[91]

Insufficiency of liquid assets does not necessarily indicate inability to pay

A company is not necessarily insolvent on the cash flow test simply because   **4–22** it does not have sufficient ready cash to meet its debts as they fall due. It suffices that it can raise the funds needed within the required time, for example by borrowing them[92] or by disposing of liquid assets. But if the borrowing is to be short-term and it is clear that it will not able to be repaid when due then all the company is doing is substituting a prospective creditor who will not be paid for an existing creditor, and the existence of the borrowing ability will not affect its insolvent status. Again, if the asset that is to be disposed of to pay the current debts is essential to the continuance of the company's business as a going concern, the prospective proceeds cannot be taken into account.[93]

---

[90] *Sycotex Pty Ltd v Baseter* (1993) 13 A.C.S.R. 766, *per* Gummow J. at 775, applied in *Sutherland v Eurolinx Pty Ltd* (2001) 37 A.C.S.R. 477. In *Southern Cross Interiors Pty Ltd v Deputy Commissioner of Taxation* [2001] N.S.W.S.C. 621 the New South Wales Supreme Court held that the court will assume that a debt is payable at the time stipulated in the contract unless this presumption is displaced by proof of an express or implied agreement between the parties, a course of conduct sufficient to ground an estoppel or a well-established course of conduct in the industry as to payment other than as stipulated in the contract.

[91] *Brolrik Pty Ltd v Sambah Holdings Pty Ltd* (2002) 40 A.C.S.R. 361.

[92] *Re a Company (No.006794 of 1983)* [1986] B.C.L.C. 261, where the evidence was that the company kept itself going by borrowing from associated companies and other sources. The Australian cases generally disregarded unsecured borrowing as a resource, but that was because the Australian legislation required companies to be able to make payment from their own moneys. This is no longer the case. See the Corporations Act 2001, s.95A. There has never been such a requirement in English corporate insolvency law.

[93] *Re Timbatec Pty Ltd* (1974) 24 F.L.R. 30.

Default in payment is sufficient evidence of inability to pay

4–23   Where a company defaults in payment of an undisputed debt after demand has been made, that is sufficient evidence that it is unable to pay its debts as they fall due,[94] and if it persists in its failure to pay it will be taken to be unable to pay its debts even if in fact it appears to be solvent.[95] This salutary rule, which applies on the failure to pay even a single debt,[96] reflects the view that a company which is able to pay an undisputed debt and chooses not to do so has only itself to blame if the inference is drawn that it is not able to pay. The decision of Harman J. in *Cornhill Insurance plc v Improvement Services Ltd*[97] provides a graphic illustration. In that case, the defendants made a claim on the plaintiffs under an insurance policy covering damage by fire, and agreement was reached between the defendants' solicitors and the plaintiffs' loss adjusters for payment of a total of £1,154. Despite repeated demands by the defendants' solicitors the agreed sum was not paid and eventually the defendants' solicitors threatened to present a winding-up petition. The plaintiffs, a large and prosperous insurance company, applied for an injunction to restrain the presentation of the petition on the ground that it was a public company carrying on a substantial business with huge assets and there was absolutely no evidence that it was insolvent, so that the presentation of a petition would be an abuse of the process of the court. An *ex parte* injunction was granted, but Harman J. refused to continue it on the substantive hearing, holding that in the circumstances the defendants were entitled to present a petition.

> "This is a case of a rich company which could pay an undoubted debt and has chosen—I think I must use that word—not to do so from June 12, to today. In my view in such circumstances the creditor was entitled to (a) threaten to and (b) in fact if it chooses present a winding up petition . . ."[98]

In *Cornhill* the debt was undisputed. What if there is a *bona fide* dispute as to the debt in that the alleged debtor honestly believes that it is not liable? This is not a sufficient answer to the petition; it is necessary for the respondent to go further and show substantial grounds for disputing liability. Thus in *Taylors Industrial Flooring Ltd v M. & H. Plant Hire (Manchester) Ltd*[99] the Court of Appeal held that in the absence of evidence

---

[94] *Re Globe New Patent Iron & Steel Co* (1875) L.R. 20 Eq. 337; *Mann v Goldstein* [1968] 2 All E.R. 769, *per* Ungoed-Thomas J. at 773; *Cornhill Insurance plc v Improvement Services Ltd* [1986] 1 W.L.R. 114.
[95] *Mann v Goldstein*, above; *Cornhill Insurance plc v Improvement Services Ltd*, above, n.94.
[96] *Cornhill Insurance plc v Improvement Services Ltd*, above, n.94.
[97] Above, n.94.
[98] Above, n.94, at 118. The debt was later paid.
[99] [1990] B.C.L.C. 216.

of grounds for dispute of the debt a creditor was perfectly entitled to proceed with the presentation of a winding-up petition on the ground of presumed insolvency without the need to serve a statutory demand under s.123(1)(a). Only if there was a *bona fide* dispute on substantial grounds would the presentation of a petition be an abuse of the process of the court.[1] A mere honest belief by the debtor that it was not liable would not be sufficient if there was no substantial ground of defence. Accordingly the only course open to a solvent debtor against whom a winding-up petition is presented is to pay the debt before the hearing, though it would then be open to any supporting creditors to apply to be substituted for the petitioner.[2] The presentation of a winding-up petition is thus a perfectly legitimate debt collection device; it is not an objection that the creditor's motive is to obtain payment of the debt rather than a winding-up order.

3. THE BALANCE SHEET TEST: GENERAL CONSIDERATIONS

The basic test

Under the balance sheet test a company is insolvent if its assets are insufficient to meet its liabilities. However the insolvency legislation adopts two different formulations of the test, though their effect would seem to be the same. Section 123(2) specifically requires account to be taken of contingent and prospective liabilities.[3] This definition therefore provides an applicable test of insolvency for the purposes of winding-up and of all other provisions applying s.123, namely those relating to administration[4] and the avoidance of transactions.[5] Section 241(b), in defining insolvent liquidation, speaks of "debts and other liabilities and the expenses of winding up." This formulation is adopted *verbatim* in s.6(2) of the Company Directors Disqualification Act 1986. We shall begin with the test laid down in s.123 and then go on to consider whether s.241(b) is different in substance.

4–24

The balance sheet test in section 123(2)

Section 123(2) provides as follows:

4–25

"A company is also deemed unable to pay its debts if it is proved to the satisfaction of the court that the value of the company's assets is less than

---

[1] See para.5–08.
[2] See para.5–11.
[3] For the history of this formulation, see above, para.4–04.
[4] Insolvency Act 1986, Sch.B1, para.11(a).
[5] *ibid.*, ss.238, 239, 245.

the amount of its liabilities, taking into account its contingent and prospective liabilities."

Thus in contrast to the cash flow basis, which is concerned with the payment of debts as they fall due, the balance sheet basis embodied in s.123(1) requires account to be taken of liabilities, including contingent and prospective liabilities. "Liabilities" is a much broader term than "debts."[6] It embraces all forms of liability, whether liquidated or unliquidated and whether arising in contract or in tort or by way of restitution or for damages for breach of statutory duty. It would also seem to encompass contingent and prospective liabilities,[7] but to put the matter beyond doubt s.123(2) expressly covers these.

"Debt" and "liability"

4–26   Rule 13.12 is of some importance in the application of the above definition for the purposes of the balance sheet test of insolvency in winding-up.

> #### "13.12 "Debt", "liability" (winding-up)
>
> (1) "Debt", in relation to the winding-up of a company, means (subject to the next paragraph) any of the following:
>
>> (a) any debt or liability to which the company is subject at the date on which it goes into liquidation;
>> (b) any debt or liability to which the company may become subject after that date by reason of any obligation incurred before that date; and
>> (c) any interest provable as mentioned in Rule 4.93(1).
>
> (2) In determining, for the purposes of any provision of the Act or the Rules about winding-up, whether any liability in tort is a debt provable in the winding-up, the company is deemed to become subject to that liability by reason of an obligation incurred at the time when the cause of action accrued.
>
> (3) For the purposes of references in any provision of the Act or the Rules about winding-up to a debt or liability, it is immaterial whether the debt or liability is present or future, whether it is certain

---

[6] See, for example, *Re a Debtor (No.17 of 1966)* [1967] Ch. 590, where Goff, J., applying the decision in *Re European Life Assurance Co* (1869) L.R. 9 Eq. 122, held that for the purpose of s.6 of the Bankruptcy Act 1914, which referred only to the debtor's inability to pay his "debts", future liabilities could not be taken into account, and dismissed the bankruptcy petition. However, r.13.12(1) of the Insolvency Rules 1986 defines debt in terms which include a future liability. See below.

[7] Indeed, r.13.12(3) of the Insolvency Rules expressly so provides.

or contingent, or whether its amount is fixed or liquidated, or is capable of being ascertained by fixed rules or as a matter of opinion; and references in any such provision to owing a debt are to be construed accordingly.

(4) In any provision of the Act or the Rules about winding-up, except in so far as the context otherwise requires, 'liability' means (subject to paragraph (3) above) a liability to pay money or money's worth, including any liability under an enactment, any liability for breach of trust, any liability in contract, tort or bailment, and any liability arising out of an obligation to make restitution.

(5) This Rule shall apply where a company is in administration and shall be read as if references to winding-up were a reference to administration."

Except in relation to the cash flow test, for which purpose "debt" has a narrower meaning,[8] these definitions are relevant to all statutory provisions relating to winding-up and proof of debt, and they have been successfully invoked as showing that a creditor has a *locus standi* to present a winding-up petition even if the amount of the relevant debt is unascertained, as where it is a liability for untaxed costs.[9] However, they do not exhaustively convey the concept of a liability, particularly in regard to executory contracts and loss and expenditure not arising from a purely legal obligation, nor do they deal with what constitutes an asset. Accordingly these concepts must now be examined. We may note in passing that while r.13.12(2) is confined to debts arising from liability in tort, it is a general principle that only debts in existence at the time of commencement of the winding-up are provable, though it is not necessary that they shall have become payable by that time.[10]

Legal form and economic substance

The question what constitutes an asset is discussed in Chapter 6. At this point we should note that there is a difference between the legal and the accounting conceptions of assets and liabilities. Both law and accountancy distinguish between capital transactions, in which an asset is acquired for a price, and revenue transactions, in which rent is paid for the use of another's assets, or some other revenue expenditure is incurred. But while the general law and tax law concentrate on the location of title,[11] accounting

4–27

---

[8] See above para.4–17.
[9] *Tottenham Hotspur plc v Edennote plc* [1995] 1 B.C.L.C. 65.
[10] See below, para.7–32.
[11] However, in tax law this point has become blurred by the practice of the Inland Revenue, upheld in *Gallagher v Jones* [1994] Ch. 107, in requiring that rentals should be spread not as provided by the lease but in accordance with generally accepted principles of commercial accounting, and in particular those embodied in SSAP 21. See generally David Wainman, *Leasing* (2nd ed. 1995), paras 2.09 *et seq.*

standards focus on economic substance. For example, in law, ownership of an asset held by a company as buyer under a contract reserving title to the seller until payment remains with the seller until payment has been completed, whilst for accounting purposes it is treated as the asset of the buyer. Similarly, the law does not distinguish finance leases from operating leases; both are contracts of hire and in neither case is the lessee treated as owner. But modern accounting rules distinguish a finance lease from an operating lease.[12] A finance lease is one that transfers substantially all the risks and rewards of ownership of an asset to the lessee; an operating lease is one in which such risks and rewards are retained by the lessor.[13] For accounting purposes a finance lease is treated very much as if it were a purchase financed by a loan. The lessee's balance sheet will show the leased item as an asset (which will be depreciated annually) capitalised as the present value of the minimum rentals, while the capital element of the total future rentals outstanding at year-end will be shown as a liability.[14] Accordingly for the purpose of the balance sheet test both entries are relevant in computing the relationship between the debtor company's assets and its liabilities. By contrast, an item comprised in an operating lease will not feature as an asset in the lessee's balance sheet, and payments due under the lease after the end of the accounting period will not appear as liabilities.[15]

Again, while the definition of "debt or liability" in r.13.12 of the Insolvency Rules 1986 is broad, covering contingent liabilities and unliquidated claims, the accounting concept of a liability is broader still and includes projected losses and expenditure which are not obligatory in law but are commercially unavoidable.

These differences between the legal and accounting concepts of what constitutes an asset and what constitutes a liability do not normally matter for the purpose of the balance sheet test of insolvency so long as the company is able to maintain the payments needed to preserve its right to retain assets which in law do not belong to it. In such a situation the crucial factor in applying the balance sheet test is not the status of an individual balance sheet item but the net asset or net liability position. For this purpose it is usually immaterial whether an item for which future payments

---

[12] See SSAP 21 and Roy Goode, *Commercial Law* (3rd ed.), pp.721 *et seq*. Though SSAP 21 is primarily concerned with equipment leasing (and it is in this context that the terms "finance lease" and "operating lease" are normally used), it is equally applicable to leases of buildings. See, for example, para.56.

[13] See SSAP 21, paras 6–8, 15, 17.

[14] In the lessor's balance sheet the asset that will be recorded is not the item itself but the net investment value, represented in the first year by the difference between its cost and the capital element of lease payments attributable to that year and in each subsequent year by the previous year's net investment value less the capital element of lease payments attributable to the subsequent year in question.

[15] This analysis is also relevant to the question whether liability for future rent under a lease is a provable debt. See below, para.7–33.

have to be made by the company is shown as an asset, and the future payments as a capitalised liability, in the company's balance sheet or is treated as still the property of the other party, in which case the company's balance sheet will not record either an asset or a liability in respect of the transaction. The net effect will in many cases be broadly the same. However, if the company is not in a position to keep up its payments under a conditional sale or hire-purchase agreement or finance lease then it faces the prospect of loss of the equipment without a corresponding reduction in its liability, for the other party will have a claim for damages based on the discounted value of the lost value rentals. In that situation it is the legal rather than the accounting treatment that will give a better picture of the company's net asset position.

In most cases, therefore, the court is likely to follow generally accepted accounting principles in deciding what constitutes a balance sheet asset or liability, but may decline to do so where for any reason it considers this would be inappropriate. The discussion which follows should be read with this caveat in mind.

Contingent and prospective liabilities

(1) Contingent liabilities

A contingent event is one which may or may not occur. But to say that a **4–28** contingent liability is a liability which may or may not be incurred is to spread the net far too wide, for the number of contingencies as thus defined is infinite. Is it to be said, for example, that because I may decide at some future date to buy goods and incur a liability for the price I have a contingent liability? Clearly not. No one can tell what transactions I may decide to enter into in the future or on what terms. To give the phrase "contingent liability" any meaning we must restrict it to a liability or other loss which arises out of an existing legal obligation or state of affairs but which is dependent on the happening of an event that may or may not occur. Many of the cases have stressed the need for the liability to arise out of an existing obligation.[16] Examples are the liability of a surety, which is created by the guarantee but arises only on default by the principal debtor; of a drawer or indorser of a bill of exchange, which is created by signature of the bill but comes into existence only if the acceptor as the party primarily liable fails to pay; of an insurer under a policy of indemnity insurance, which is created by issue of the policy but depends on the

---

[16] See *Winter v I.R.C.* [1961] 3 All E.R. 855, *per* Lord Hodson at 864; *Re William Hockley Ltd* [1962] 2 All E.R. 111, *per* Pennycuick J. at 113; *Stonegate Securities Ltd v Gregory* [1980] 1 Ch. 576, *per* Buckley L.J. at 579 (". . . a creditor in respect of a debt which only becomes due in an event which may or may not occur").

occurrence of the event against which cover is given; of a defendant or prospective defendant in a claim for negligence which may or may not succeed. However, it is not every contingent liability that springs from an existing legal obligation. In *Re Sutherland deceased*[17] a majority of the House of Lords considered that to require an existing legal obligation was to take too narrow a view of what constitutes a contingent liability. It is true that this was a tax case, not a decision on insolvency legislation, but what it does show is that in considering whether there is a contingent liability the court has regard to the existing commercial situation, not merely an existing legal obligation. In this regard assistance can be derived from Financial Reporting Standard 12, which defines a contingent liability as:

- a possible obligation that arises from past events and whose existence will be confirmed only by the occurrence or non-occurrence of one or more uncertain future events not wholly within the entity's control; or

- a present obligation that arises from past events but is not recognised because:

  o it is not probable that a transfer of economic benefits will be required to settle the obligation; or
  o the amount of the obligation cannot be measured with sufficient reliability.[18]

It will be seen that in this definition the reference is to "past events" rather than legal obligations. Of course, accounting definitions do not necessarily correspond to legal definitions. But as has rightly been pointed out, the term "contingent liabilities" is ultimately not a term of art and its precise meaning will depend on its context.[19] The court is thus entitled to have regard to commercial realities. In *Re Sutherland* the factual situation was the near-certainty that ships would be sold, producing a balance charge for tax purposes. An example in terms of an existing commercial situation is the projected expenditure to be incurred if a product has to be recalled in order to remedy as a matter of goodwill defects for which the company has no legal liability, past experience having shown that such a recall is likely to be needed at least once during the course of a year. By contrast, the potential liability of a litigant to have an order for costs made against him is

---

[17] *Re Sutherland deceased, Winter v I.R.C.* [1963] A.C. 235.
[18] FRS 12, *Provisions, Contingent Liabilities and Contingent Assets* (replacing SSAP 18, *Accounting for Contingencies*). Contingencies are distinguished from provisions, that is, liabilities which are bound to arise in the nature but where the timing and amount are uncertain. See also below, para.4–34, as to accounting standards. For a detailed discussion of contingent and prospective creditors see Lee Berg Tat, "Claiming a pound of flesh as a contingent or prospective creditor or under the [Singapore] Companies Act" [1993] Singapore L.J. 144.
[19] *County Bookshops Ltd v Grove* [2003] 1 B.C.L.C. 479.

too uncertain and too much in the discretion of the court to rank as a contingent liability.[20]

(2) Prospective liabilities

The phrase "prospective liability" is neither a legal nor an accounting term **4–29** of art. It has been judicially defined as "a debt which will certainly become due in the future, either on some date which has already been determined or on some date determinable by reference to future events."[21] In two other cases it has been described in argument as an unmatured liability which will inevitably ripen into a debt with the passage of time.[22] Such a definition encompasses all forms of *debitum in praesenti, solvendum in futuro*[23] including an indisputable claim for unliquidated damages which remains only to be quantified and will result in a debt for more than a nominal amount.[24] "Prospective liability" thus embraces both future debts, in the sense of liquidated sums due, and unliquidated claims. Examples are liability on an unmatured bill of exchange,[25] a liability payment for work in progress that has been carried out but not yet quantified, and the prospective liability of a building owner under a completed building contract where the sum payable depends not only on completion of the contract works but on adjustments to be made in respect of prime cost sums, provisions, variations and the like. Also included is the capital value of the future rentals payable by a lessee under a finance lease.[26] Where it is necessary to establish inability to pay debts for the purpose of winding-up, the projected expenses of winding-up must, it is thought, be taken into account as a prospective liability, for it is inevitable that such expenses will be incurred. It is curious, however, that while specific reference is made to the expenses of winding-up in the definition of insolvent liquidation in s.214

---

[20] *Glenister v Rowe* [2000] Ch. 76.
[21] *Stonegate Securities Ltd v Gregory*, above, *per* Buckley L.J. at 579.
[22] See, for example, the arguments of counsel *in Re British Equitable Bond and Mortgage Corp Ltd* [1910] 1 Ch. 574 at 576; *Re A Company (No.001573 of 1983)* (1983) 1 B.C.C. 98,937, at 98,939.
[23] Though it is not relevant to the present discussion we may note at this point that other parts of the insolvency legislation speak not of "prospective" debts but of "future" debts. For example, r.13.12(3) of the Insolvency Rules 1986, which provides that for the purposes of references in any provision of the Act or Rules about winding up to a debt or liability it is immaterial whether the debtor or liability is present or future, certain or contingent. Given that "debt" is defined in r.13.12(1) as a debt or liability to which the company is subject at the date on which it goes into liquidation or any debt or liability to which it may become subject by reason of any obligation incurred before that date, it is evident that in the phrase "present or future" the word "present" denotes an existing debt that has become payable while the word "future" means an existing debt that has not yet become payable, in other words, a class of prospective debt, the other class being an unliquidated claim.
[24] *Re Dollar Land Holdings Ltd* [1994] B.C.L.C. 404.
[25] *Re A Company (No.001573 of 1983)*, above, n.22.
[26] See below, para.7–33.

relating to wrongful trading[27] and of an insolvent company in s.6 of the Company Directors Disqualification Act 1986,[28] there is no mention of it in s.123(2), perhaps because it was thought otiose in view of the reference to contingent and prospective liabilities. Similarly, where for the purpose of obtaining an administration order[29] it is necessary to show that the company is or is likely to become unable to pay its debts[30] the projected costs of the administration should be included as prospective liabilities.

The balance sheet test as a ground for an administration order

4–30   An administrator can now be appointed out of court, in which event it is not necessary that the company be insolvent or even likely to become insolvent. But where the company or its directors apply for an administration order the court has to be satisfied either that the company is unable to pay its debts—the test here being the same as for a winding up order—or that it is likely to become unable to do so.[31] Where the cash flow test is relied on—*i.e.* where the contention is that the company is likely to be unable to pay its debts as they fall due—it would seem that this is not confined to the prospect of the company being unable at a future time to pay debts existing at the date of the administration order but extends to the likelihood of its inability to pay future debts. If this be right, the test is satisfied by showing that the company, though currently paying its own way, is likely to trade at a loss in the future and to be unable to pay its future debts as these arise. The meaning of "likely" in what was s.8(1)(a) of the Insolvency Act and is now para.11(a) of Sch.B1 has not been considered but the same word featured in the old s.8(1)(b) ("likely to achieve one or more of the purposes mentioned below"),[32] where its meaning gave rise to a difference of judicial opinion. In *Re Consumer & Industrial Press Ltd*[33] Peter Gibson J. held that "likely" meant more probably than not, *i.e.* a more than 50 per cent chance. But in *Re Harris Simons Construction Ltd*[34] Hoffmann J. considered it sufficient that there was a real prospect of achievement of the purpose or purposes for which the order was sought, even if that prospect was more modest than a 50 per cent chance. However, as stated above these were decisions on section 8(1)(b), whereas we are here concerned with the successor to section 8(1)(a); and Hoffmann J. himself placed

---

[27] Insolvency Act 1986, s.214(6).
[28] Company Directors Disqualification Act 1986, s.6(2).
[29] As opposed to an out-of-court administration.
[30] Insolvency Act 1986, Sch.B1, para.11(a).
[31] Insolvency Act 1986, s.8(1).
[32] See now Insolvency Act 1986, Sch.B1, para.11(b): ". . . reasonably likely to achieve the purpose of the administration".
[33] (1988) 4 B.C.C. 68.
[34] (1988) 5 B.C.C. 11.

reliance on a difference in the wording of the two paragraphs, pointing out that under paragraph (b) it was sufficient that the court "considers" that the making of the order would be likely to achieve one or more of the purposes, etc., whereas in paragraph (a) the court has to be "satisfied" that the company is or is likely to become unable to pay its debts. In the view of Hoffmann J. this change of language was deliberate and was intended to indicate that a lower threshold of persuasion was required for paragraph (b) than for paragraph (a). That view was adopted in *Re Primlaks (UK) Ltd*,[35] where Vinelott J. held that in para.(a) the question was whether it was "probable" that the company would go into liquidation, whereas in para.(b) the test was whether there was a real prospect of achievement of one or more of the stated purposes. Given the distinction drawn by Hoffmann J. between para.(a) and para.(b) of the old s.8 and the fact that sub-para.(a) of para.11 of Sch.B1 corresponds to the old s.8(1)(a) it would seem necessary for the applicant for an administration order to show that it is more likely than not that the company will be unable to pay its debts.

The balance sheet test as a ground for a contribution order for wrongful trading

As previously stated, in determining whether a company has gone into insolvent liquidation for the purposes of an order under s.214 of the Insolvency Act requiring a director involved in wrongful trading to contribute to the assets of the company, the test is that the assets are insufficient for the payment of its debts and other liabilities and the expenses of winding up. Though s.214(6), in contrast to s.123(2), does not expressly refer to contingent or prospective liabilities, the word "liabilities" on its own would seem sufficient to cover these.[36]

4–31

The balance sheet test as a ground of avoidance of transactions

For the purpose of the provisions of the Insolvency Act 1986 relating to transactions at an undervalue made, preferences given and floating charges created by an insolvent company, the test is whether the company was unable to pay its debts within the meaning of s.123 of the Act or became unable to do so in consequence of the transaction or preference sought to be avoided.

4–32

The balance sheet test as a ground of disqualification of directors

For a company that has not gone into administration or administrative receivership the balance test is applied in the same terms as for wrongful trading.

4–33

---

[35] [1989] B.C.L.C. 734. See also *Cream Holdings Ltd v Banerjee* [2003] Ch. 650, a case not concerned with insolvency, where Simon Brown L.J. observed (at 662) that it was not disputed that the word "likely" was capable of a range of definitions.
[36] See above, para.4–26.

4. THE BALANCE SHEET TEST: COMPUTATION OF ASSETS AND LIABILITIES

Problems of valuation

4–34   As previously stated, the valuation of assets is not an exact science, and the same is true of the estimation of contingent liabilities. The purpose of accounts is to furnish a true and fair view of a company's financial position and of profit or loss for the accounting period. Accounts must be prepared in conformity with legislation, and subject to this they are also expected either to conform to guidelines laid down by the accountancy professional bodies or to disclose and explain significant departures from such guidelines. Numerous Statements of Standard Accounting Practice (SSAPs) were issued by the Accounting Standards Committee covering such diverse matters as stock and work in progress,[37] accounting for depreciation,[38] accounting for post-balance sheet events,[39] accounting for contingencies,[40] foreign currency translation[41] accounting for leases and hire-purchase contracts[42] and accounting for goodwill.[43] The Committee's successor, the Accounting Standards Board (ASB), has adopted many of the SSAPs while amending or withdrawing others and has issued its own standards, Financial Reporting Standards (FRS). These include cash flow statements,[44] accounting for subsidiary undertakings,[45] tangible fixed assets,[46] goodwill and intangible assets,[47] and provisions, contingent liabilities and contingent assets.[48] The adopted SSAPs and the FRSs together constitute the statements of standard accounting practice and these are recognised for the purposes of the Companies Act 1985.[49]

The accounting standards are not intended to be rigid rules; they may and should be departed from where this is necessary in order to give a true and fair view of a company's financial affairs. There are a number of issues of accounting practice which are regarded as unsettled, even controversial, and the published standards themselves recognise that there are areas of particular difficulty in which valuation is very much a matter of informed

---

[37] SSAP 9.
[38] SSAP 12, prospectively replaced by FRS 15.
[39] SSAP 17.
[40] SSAP 18, since replaced by FRS 12.
[41] SSAP 20.
[42] SSAP 21.
[43] SSAP 22, as amended by FRS 6 and 7.
[44] FRS 1.
[45] FRS 2.
[46] FRS 15.
[47] FRS 10.
[48] FRS 12.
[49] Companies Act 1985, s.256, pursuant to which the ASB has been prescribed as the issuing body by the Accounting Standards (Prescribed Body) Regulations 1990 (SI 1990/1667).

judgment. Much of the problem centres on the extent to which accounts for the period under consideration should reflect costs incurred or to be incurred and revenue received or to be received in the previous or subsequent accounting period. Particularly difficult is the valuation of stock and work in progress, on which there are widely differing approaches. The crux of the problem was succinctly stated in a written opinion of counsel obtained by the Accounting Standards Committee on the meaning of "true and fair" with particular reference to accounting standards[50]:

". . . it is first necessary to examine the nature of the 'true and fair view' concept as used in the Companies Act. It is an abstraction or philosophical concept expressed in simple English. The law uses many similar concepts, of which 'reasonable care' is perhaps the most familiar example. It is a common feature of such concepts that there is seldom any difficulty in understanding what they mean but frequent controversy over their application to particular facts. One reason for this phenomenon is that because such concepts represent a very high level of abstraction which has to be applied to an infinite number of concrete facts, there can never be a sharply defined line between, for example, what is reasonable care and what is not. There will always be a penumbral area in which views may differ . . . The issue of an SSAP has the effect . . . of creating a *prima facie* presumption that accounts which do not comply are not true and fair. This presumption is then strengthened or weakened by the extent to which the SSAP is actually accepted and applied."

In most cases there is little or no doubt as to a company's insolvency, but in marginal situations the basis of valuation and the assessment of values upon that basis can be crucial. Here lie the seeds of a potentially difficult problem. For the purposes of insolvency legislation the court has to be able to decide whether on a balance of probabilities a particular company is or was at a particular time unable to pay its debts. Different accountants may have different views on the proper approach to a particular valuation; and in relation to the valuation of particular assets professional valuers may place widely differing values on the same asset. Audited accounts are the accounts of the company, not of the auditors.[51] It is not for the company's auditors to force their own views on the company; where there are different and equally legitimate approaches to a particular valuation of an asset or estimation of a liability, the company is free to select whichever of these it

---

[50] This extract is taken from one of two joint Opinions given by Leonard Hoffmann Q.C. (now Lord Hoffman) and Mary Arden in 1983 and 1984 and was subsequently updated by Mary Arden Q.C. (now Arden L.J.) in an Opinion given in 1993, which does not, however, affect the substance of the quoted extract.

[51] A fact which directors of companies in financial difficulties conveniently forget when suing their auditors for negligence!

regards as the most appropriate to its business, the overriding requirement being that the accounts must give a true and fair view. Moreover, as stated earlier, balance sheets are historical documents and values stated in them are not necessarily those current at the time the valuation has to be made and may anyway be valuations at historic cost rather than current value.

4–35   It is thus perfectly possible to envisage a situation in which the application of the balance sheet test shows on one reasonable view that the company is solvent and on another, equally reasonable, view that it is insolvent. Given such a conflict, how should the court deal with the matter? In general, it is for the party asserting a state of insolvency to prove it, not for the other party to refute it. It is thus for the applicant to show that on the balance of probabilities the company was insolvent at the relevant time.[52] In many cases this will become apparent with the benefit of hindsight. For example, it is unlikely that a liquidator will institute proceedings for wrongful trading, or apply to set aside voidable trans-actions, until the liquidation is sufficiently advanced for him to have a reasonable knowledge of the relevant facts, by which time the actual amounts realised on disposal of assets will furnish an additional guide to their value at the relevant date. But this is not, of course, the case where proof of insolvency is the threshold which has to be passed at the outset, as where a creditor petitions for winding up on the ground of insolvency. Here the court has to do the best it can on the evidence available at the time and must weigh conflicting valuations and decide on the balance of probabilities whether the company is able to pay its debts.

Moreover, great care must be taken not to rely too heavily on hindsight. The crucial question is the value of assets and liabilities at the relevant date, not their value at a later date. The latter may be a guide to the former, but this is not necessarily the case. Assets may rise or fall in value because of events occurring after the relevant date. It is necessary to be particularly cautious in applying hindsight to cases involving personal liability, *e.g.* for wrongful trading, or the setting aside of a transaction, *e.g.* as a transaction at an undervalue or preference. Business life is neither static nor certain. Information has constantly to be updated, predictions made about a range of uncertain events, snap judgments formed, rapid decisions taken and adaptations continually made in the light of shifts in customer demand, tax changes, industrial action, political events, inter-national relations, and the like. Just as it is all too easy for historians to pick their way leisurely across the battlefields of Waterloo identifying Napoleon's errors in the tranquillity of academic research, unhindered by all the confusions engendered by blazing guns, cavalry charges, mud, darkness, uncertainty as to the current arrivals or dispositions of troops and

---

[52] However, where a company enters into a transaction at an undervalue with a person connected with the company, its inability to pay its debts at that time is presumed unless the contrary is shown (Insolvency Act 1986, s.240(2)).

ignorance of the intentions of the enemy, so also a professional acquainted with subsequent events in a company's life is all too readily beguiled into the view that he would have done things differently, that what is now apparent was obvious from the start.

It is submitted that where the question is whether a director of a company ought to have concluded that there was no reasonable prospect of the company avoiding insolvent liquidation,[53] the director's reliance on a reasonable accounting view that if the company did go into liquidation its assets would be sufficient in value to cover its liabilities and the expenses of winding up should suffice to render him or her immune from liability, even if in the event the assets realise a much lower figure than estimated, with the result that at the time of liquidation the company in fact has an asset deficiency.

Assets that can be taken into account

In principle, only the assets of the company at the relevant time[54] can be included; the prospect of receiving further injections of cash or other assets cannot be taken into account.[55] These are in general what are referred to in accounting standards as contingent assets[56] However, it is necessary to distinguish prospective assets unconnected with future or contingent liabilities from prospective assets that will arise from the incurring of future or contingent liabilities and thus go to the estimation of the latter. For example, in estimating the contingent liability of a surety it must, it is thought, be legitimate to set against this the value of any security held by the creditor to whose rights the surety would be surrogated on paying off the debt. This is not to bring speculative new assets into account but rather to set a net figure on the contingent liability after taking into account countervailing assets that the discharge of the liability can reasonably be expected to produce.   **4–36**

Valuation of assets: break-up basis or going concern basis?

Whether assets should be valued on a break-up basis or a going concern basis depends on the circumstances. In principle, this should turn on whether, as seen at the relevant time,[57] the business will be continued as a   **4–37**

---

[53] A question which arises in proceedings for wrongful trading under s.214 of the Insolvency Act 1986.

[54] As to the relevant time, see above, para.4–13.

[55] *Byblos Bank SAL v Al-Khudhairy* (1986) 2 B.C.C. 99, 549.

[56] That is, a possible asset arising from past events whose existence will be confirmed only on the occurrence of one or more uncertain future events not wholly within the entity's control" (FRS 12, para.2).

[57] *i.e.* the time as at which the company's solvency falls to be tested.

going concern. If so, the assets should be valued on a going concern basis, which is likely to give them a substantially higher value than on a break-up basis. One of the accounting principles laid down in the Companies Act 1985 is that a company is presumed to be carrying on business as a going concern.[58] The only accounting standard relevant to the going concern basis is SSAP 2:

". . . the enterprise will continue in operational existence for the foreseeable future. This means in particular that the profit and loss account and balance sheet assume no intention or necessity to liquidate or curtail significantly the scale of operations."[59]

This has been interpreted by a Statement of Auditing Standards (SAS) issued by the Auditing Practices Board as meaning that in financial statements prepared on a going concern basis:

(a) assets are recognised and measured on the basis that the entity expects to recover (through use or realisation) the recorded amounts in the normal course of business, and

(b) liabilities are recognised and measured on the basis that they will be discharged in the normal course of business.[60]

Suppose that in the event the business cannot be sold on a going concern basis. Should this affect the relevant date of valuation of the assets? In answering this question it is helpful to apply by analogy the guidance given by FRS 21, *Events After the Balance Sheet Date*.[61] FRS 21, like its predecessor SSAP 17, distinguishes "adjusting events" from "non-adjusting events." Adjusting events are defined by para.3(a) as "those that provide evidence of conditions that existed at the balance sheet date," and under para.8 they require adjustment of amounts recognised in the entity's financial statements. Among the examples given in para.9 are: the settlement after the balance sheet date of a court case that confirms that the entity had a present obligation at the balance sheet date; the receipt of information after the balance sheet date indicating that an asset was impaired at the balance sheet date; the bankruptcy of a customer after the balance sheet date; the sale of inventories after the balance sheet date which gives evidence at the balance sheet date; and the discovery of fraud

---

[58] Companies Act 1985, Sch.4, para.10.

[59] SSAP 2, para.14.

[60] SAS 130, para.5.

[61] This FRS, which embodies International Accounting Standard 10 (revised 2003), replaces SSAP 17, *Accounting for Post Balance Sheet Events*. Events after the balance sheet date are defined as "those events, favourable or unfavourable, that occur between the balance sheet date and the date when the financial statements are authorised for issue" (para.3).

or errors that show that the financial statements are incorrect. Of particular relevance also is the direction in para.14 not to prepare financial statements on a going concern basis if management determines after the balance sheet date that it intends to liquidate the entity or to cease trading or that it has no realistic alternative but to do so. In effect, therefore, such a determination by the management is an adjusting event. Though the concept of adjusting events has not so far featured expressly in any reported case it is reflected in two decisions to the effect that in considering whether there has been a transaction at an undervalue the court may have regard to post-transaction events in order to determine the value as at the time of the transaction.[64]

By contrast non-adjusting events are defined by para.3(b) as those that are indicative of conditions that arose after the balance sheet date and therefore do not allow of changes in amounts in financial statements.[65] An example given is a decline in the value of market investments between the balance sheet date and the date the financial statements are authorised for issue.[66] Again, one of the decisions referred to above, though not referring in terms to non-adjusting events, offers further examples that would fall within this category, namely the sale of a lottery ticket which subsequently produces a large win, the sale or purchase of quoted shares before the disclosure of market sensitive information, the sale of land with hope value which is subsequently realised or the sale of residential property the value of which goes up in line with the market.[67] In all these cases the subsequent event is no evidence at all of the value of what was sold at the time of the transaction, it is an unconnected post-transaction condition.[68]

The same criteria can be applied to determine whether an event occurring after the relevant date for determining inability to pay debts should affect a valuation made as at that date. On this basis an actual or impending cessation of trading after the relevant date could normally be expected to result in a retrospective revaluation of the assets as at the relevant date for the purpose of the balance sheet test of insolvency.

Liabilities to be taken into account

As previously stated, the liabilities to be taken into account in applying the balance sheet test vary with the applicable statutory provision. The legislation employs two distinct formulations:

4–38

---

[64] *Phillips v Brewin Dolphin Bell Lawrie Ltd* [2001] 1 W.L.R. 143; *Re Thoars deceased, Reid v Ramlort Ltd* [2003] 1 B.C.L.C. 499.

[65] FRS 21, para.10.

[66] *ibid.*, para.11. However, material non-adjusting events may require disclosure (para.21).

[67] *Re Thoars deceased*, n.64 above.

[68] See also *Joiner v George* [2003] B.C.C. 298 (in valuing shares it was not legitimate to trade results after the valuation date for those actually known before the valuation date).

(1) All liabilities, taking into account contingent and prospective liabilities

4-39   This is the formulation used in the provisions relating to winding up,[69] administration[70] and the avoidance of vulnerable transactions.[71] It would also appear to include the expenses of a winding up in determining inability to pay debts for the purpose of a winding-up order or the disqualification of a director and the expenses of an administration for the purpose of showing jurisdiction to make an administration order.[72]

(2) Debts and other liabilities and the expenses of winding up

4-40   This formulation is adopted in the provisions relating to wrongful trading[73] and the disqualification of directors.[74] It appears to include contingent or prospective liabilities[75] and thus to have the same meaning as in (1) above, except, of course, that the former will not cover liquidation expenses where no liquidation is involved.

Estimation of liabilities

4-41   Just as problems may arise in the valuation of assets, so also there may be difficulties in the estimation of liabilities. This is particularly likely to be the case as regards unqualified existing liabilities, contingent liabilities and the expenses of liquidation. In the case of existing liabilities which are as yet unquantified, the uncertainty is merely as to the amount, not as to the existence of the liability. A good example is liability incurred to a supplier of services for the value of work in progress, which is as difficult to estimate for the purpose of quantifying liability as it is to value as an asset and will in many cases depend on whether the work is ultimately completed. Another example is the expenses of liquidation. Who can predict what these will be? They depend on a whole variety of factors, *e.g.* whether and to what extent the liquidator will have to take professional advice, whether he will be involved in litigation, how long and complex his investigation into the company's affairs will be. These are matters which are incapable of estimation in any real sense, but the legislation requires the attempt to be made.

   In the case of a contingent liability the difficulty is greater still, since the prospects of the contingency occurring may range from almost zero to a

---

[69] Insolvency Act 1986, s.123(2).
[70] *ibid.*, s.123(2).
[71] *ibid.*, ss.240(2), 245(4), applying s.123.
[72] See above, para.4–29.
[73] Insolvency Act 1986, s.214(6).
[74] Company Directors Disqualification Act 1986, s.6(2).
[75] *ibid.*, s.6(2).

near certainty. Accountancy practice was formerly of limited value in this context, because contingent liabilities were required to be accrued in financial statements only where it was probable that a future event could confirm a loss which could be estimated with reasonable accuracy.[76] In other cases, a contingent liability was merely disclosed by way of a note on the accounts,[77] unless it was so remote that disclosure could be misleading.[78] But the Companies Act 1985 now appears to override the "reasonable accuracy" qualification and to require a contingent liability to be shown if it is "likely" to arise during the financial year to which the accounts relate or a previous financial year.[79] Where a contingent liability is capable of valuation it should presumably be valued on the same basis as if it were being admitted to proof by the liquidator as a claim by the creditor. This does not carry us much further, since the amount for which contingent claims are admitted to proof in a winding up is usually settled by negotiation. The assessment of contingent claims and liabilities is, of course, the particular province of the actuary, but again actuarial practice is of limited relevance, because actuaries base their assessments not on individual cases but on the total of the relevant population, whereas the question with which we are concerned is the valuation of a particular contingent liability incurred by a particular company.

There is no great difficulty in valuing many contingent liabilities. For example, if at the relevant date the company is drawer or indorser of a bill of exchange, or a surety under a guarantee, and the party primarily liable has convened a meeting for the purpose of going into insolvent voluntary winding up with no prospect of paying a dividend, the contingent liability will be little less than the face value of the bill or debt. At the other end of the scale, where the party primarily liable is financially strong or the creditor already holds massive security from the debtor, the contingent liability can be treated as so remote that it need not be given any value. The problem case is the contingency which is not so remote that it can be ignored nor so imminent that it is almost bound to happen. Different approaches are possible. One is to say that if there is a more than even chance of the contingency occurring, the liability should be taken as the present value of the contingent liability, *e.g.* the amount of a guaranteed debt discounted to take account of its futurity. On this approach, a contingent liability with an 80 per cent chance of accrual, though discounted for futurity would not be discounted for the 20 per cent chance that it would not accrue, whilst a liability with a 50 per cent chance of accrual would be disregarded altogether. An alternative approach is to value the contingent liability at the percentage of likelihood of its occurrence, so that if the likelihood were 80 per cent the liability would be taken

---

[76] SSAP 18, para.3.
[77] *ibid.*, para.5.
[78] *ibid.*, para.8.
[79] Companies Act 1985, Sch.4, para.12(b).

in at the present value of 80 per cent of the full liability, whilst a contingent liability with a 10 per cent chance of accrual would be estimated at the present value of 10 per cent of the full liability. Neither of these approaches seems fully satisfactory. The first seems to set the threshold of likelihood too high, while the second is contrary to prevailing practice, which is to value the contingency in full (less any discount for futurity) if it will probably occur and is capable of valuation and disregard it altogether in other cases. It is thought that the question to be asked is whether there is a real prospect that the contingency will occur, in which case it should be brought in at its present value without further discount for the possibility that it may not accrue.

Chapter 5

The Winding-Up Process: An Outline

We have seen earlier[1] that the winding-up of a company is a prelude to its ultimate demise. We also noted that the winding-up of an insolvent company may take one of two forms, a creditors' voluntary winding-up and a compulsory (*i.e.* court-ordered) winding-up. Insolvency practitioners tend to favour voluntary winding-up in order to avoid the need to utilise the Insolvency Services Account, which is obligatory in compulsory winding-up and has the disadvantage that while the rate of interest it pays has moved nearer towards market rates a substantial *ad valorem* fee is charged in connection with the operation of the account. From the perspective of the insolvency practitioner both forms of winding-up now suffer a disadvantage by comparison with administration in that, following the ruling of the House of Lords in *Buchler v Talbot*,[2] the expenses of the winding-up come after the claims of a creditor secured by a floating charge instead of having priority over such claims, as had previously been thought to be the case, whereas the expenses of administration rank ahead of floating charge claims.[3] This has helped to fuel the controversy over the decision, which, however, is plainly correct.[4]

5–01

The purpose of the present chapter is to depict the winding-up process in outline and to focus on a few key issues that arise in connection with the initiation and effect of that process, with particular emphasis on compulsory winding-up. There are now three kinds of winding-up in insolvency, a creditors' voluntary winding-up, a compulsory winding-up by court order and a winding-up through administration. Only the second of these may be used for the winding-up of foreign companies.[5]

---

[1] See above, para.1–24.
[2] [2002] 2 A.C. 298. See below, para.7–40.
[3] Insolvency Act 1986, s.175(2)(b) as applied by Sch.B1, para.65(2).
[4] See below, para.7–40.
[5] Insolvency Act 1986, s.221(4).

1. THE LIQUIDATOR AND HIS ROLE

5–02   The liquidator is an authorised insolvency practitioner whose primary function is to get in the assets, realise them and distribute the net realisations according to a statutory order of priority, paying any surplus to the person entitled. He may carry on the company's business but only so far as may be necessary for its beneficial winding-up.[6] Part of the liquidator's job is also to investigate the causes of failure and to take appropriate steps to bring to book any delinquent directors. The liquidator may be appointed by the creditors, the company, the court or, on the application of the official receiver when acting as liquidator and desiring a private liquidator to be appointed in his place, the Secretary of State.[7] In a compulsory winding-up the liquidator is an officer of the court.[8] As such he is required to act with scrupulous fairness and impartiality, [9] avoiding "dirty tricks" that might be open to an ordinary person,[10] and his status as an officer of the court is relevant to the propriety of contracts he enters into.[11] While the liquidator is responsible for taking custody of the company's assets, they do not automatically vest in him,[12] though where the company is in compulsory winding-up the liquidator can apply to the court for a vesting order.[13] The court cannot refuse to make a winding-up order on the ground that the company's assets are fully mortgaged or that it has no assets,[14] but where the company is in administrative receivership or administration, so that all its assets are under the control of the administrative receiver or administrator, the liquidator must perforce wait on the sidelines as regards his distribution role until completion of the receivership or administration, after which he will take over whatever assets, if any, remain.

The liquidator is not a trustee for creditors but rather an agent for the company with statutory duties which may be enforced by application to the

---

[6] *ibid.*, Sch.4, Pt II, para.5. Where the company is in compulsory winding-up this power may be exercised only with the sanction of the court or liquidation committee (s.167(1)(a)). See below, para.5–05.

[7] *ibid.*, s.137. The usual practice, however, is to convene a meeting of creditors and contributories to choose another liquidator under s.136(4) of the Insolvency Act.

[8] *Re Oasis Merchandising Ltd* [1998] Ch. 170, *per* Peter Gibson L.J. at 186; *Re T.H. Knitwear (Wholesale) Ltd* [1988] Ch. 275, *per* Slade L.J. at 280; *Re International Tin Council* [1987] Ch. 419, *per* Millett J. at 446.

[9] *Re Contract Corp, Gooch's Case* (1872) L.R. 7 Ch. App. 207, *per* Sir W.M. James L.J. at 213; *Ex p. James, re Condon* (1873–74) L.R. 9 Ch. App. 609.

[10] *R. v Tower Hamlets L.B.C., Ex p. Chetnik Ltd* [1988] A.C. 858, *per* Lord Bridge at 874–875, invoking the rule laid down long ago in *Ex p. James* (1874) L.R. 9 Ch. App. 609 in relation to trustees in bankruptcy.

[11] *Re Oasis Merchandising Ltd* [1998] Ch. 170 (in which the liquidator entered into an agreement held to be champertous).

[12] In this respect a liquidator differs from a trustee in bankruptcy, in whom the bankrupt's estate vests immediately on the trustee's appointment without the need for any conveyance, assignment or transfer (Insolvency Act 1986, s.306(1)).

[13] Insolvency Act 1986, s.145(1).

[14] *ibid.*, s.125(1).

court.[15] He does not in general owe any duty to an individual creditor. There are, however, exceptions. The liquidator may incur a liability to an individual creditor for loss caused by fraud or other personal misconduct[16]; such as breach of fiduciary duty or misfeasance,[17] or for breach of contract,[18] or for negligently distributing the company's assets without taking account of a debt which has been or should have been admitted to proof,[19] but in this last case only where the company has been dissolved, so that the creditor is deprived of his ordinary remedy of application to the court.[20]

On behalf of the creditors the liquidator can bring proceedings in the name of the company in respect of causes of action vested in the company but he has no *locus standi* to pursue claims vested in persons *qua* creditors. So if, for example, a company establishes a subsidiary to carry on the business of deposit-taking and the parent runs the subsidiary as its *alter ego*, effectively depriving the subsidiary's directors of any management function and using the subsidiary as a façade through which deposited funds are transferred to the parent, then if in consequence the subsidiary is driven into insolvent liquidation, the liquidator may be able to pursue a claim in the name of the subsidiary against its parent but has no standing to assert claims on behalf of the subsidiary's depositors, who must pursue their own proceedings.[21]

2. CREDITORS' VOLUNTARY WINDING-UP

As mentioned before, a creditors' voluntary winding-up is effected by a **5–03** resolution of the *members*, not the creditors, but once in place operates under the control of the creditors. In the case of a public company it is necessary to convene a meeting to pass an extraordinary resolution to wind up the company on the ground that it cannot by reason of its liabilities

---

[15] *Knowles v Scott* [1891] 1 Ch. 717; *Leon v York-O-Matic Ltd* [1966] 1 W.L.R. 1450.

[16] *Knowles v Scott*, above.

[17] *ibid.*; *Kyrris v Oldham* [2004] 1 B.C.L.C. 305.

[18] The firm employing the individual liquidator may also be liable as a contracting party where it undertakes to appoint one its employees as liquidator and procure him or her to do a proper job (*A & J Fabrications (Batley) Ltd v Grant Thornton* [1999] B.C.C. 807).

[19] *James Smith & Sons (Norwood) Ltd v Goodman* [1936] Ch. 216; *Pulsford v Devenish* [1903] 2 Ch. 625.

[20] *Kyrris v Oldham*, above, a decision on the duties of an administrator, but the principle is the same. Where the company has not been dissolved the liquidator cannot be sued for a dividend even if this has been declared; his remedy is to apply to the court in the winding-up for an order directing the liquidator to perform his statutory duty of distribution (*Spence v Coleman* [1901] 2 K.B. 199, and see above, para.3–06).

[21] This may be one of those exceptional cases where the court will be willing to pierce the corporate veil and hold the parent company liable to the depositors. See, for example, *Jones v Lipman* [1962] 1 W.L.R. 832.

continue its business.[22] Not less than 14 days' notice must be given[23] and the resolution must be passed by a majority of not less than three-quarters of members entitled to vote and voting in person or by proxy.[24] In the case of a private company the resolution may be passed without a meeting or prior notice by resolution in writing of all the members who would be entitled to attend and vote at such a meeting.[25] The company is required to convene a meeting of creditors for a day no later than the fourteenth day after that fixed for the company meeting, at least seven days' notice being given and advertised.[26] In practice the creditors' meeting is usually held after and on the same day as the company meeting. It is presided over by a director of the company appointed for that purpose by the directors, who must lay a statement of affairs before the creditors' meeting showing particulars of the company's assets, debts and liabilities, the names and addresses of the company's creditors and any securities held by them.[27] The creditors and the company may (and almost invariably do) nominate a liquidator at their respective meetings,[28] the creditors' nomination (if any) prevailing unless the court orders otherwise.[29] A liquidator nominated by the company before the holding of a meeting of creditors may not exercise the powers conferred by s.165 of the Insolvency Act until that meeting.[30]

The notice convening a meeting of creditors must specify the date by which creditors must lodge any proxies necessary to entitle them to vote at the meeting.[31] If the proxy is not lodged in due time, the proxy-holder

---

[22] Insolvency Act 1986, s.84(1)(c). It is also possible for a company to go into voluntary winding-up by special resolution under s.84(1)(b) but there is no advantage in so doing, because the majority required is the same as for an extraordinary resolution and it is necessary to give 21 days' notice rather than 14 days, though this period can be shortened if the requisite majority so agree (s.378(3)). Winding-up through administration is a distinctive procedure discussed in para.10–104.

[23] Companies Act 1985, s.369(1)(b). But the meeting may be called upon short notice if so agreed by the requisite majority (s.369(3), (4)).

[24] *ibid.*, s.378(1).

[25] *ibid.*, s.381A(1). There may be cases in which it is desirable for a voluntary winding-up to follow immediately on discharge of an administration, with no interval between the two, in order to ensure that the onset of insolvency for the purposes of the statutory provisions relating to transactions at an undervalue and preferences commenced on the date of the administration order rather than the date of the winding-up, but this cannot be achieved by a resolution conditional on the termination of the administration. See below, para.10–104.

[26] Insolvency Act 1986, s.98(1).

[27] *ibid.*, s.99.

[28] If the company defers the appointment of a liquidator the directors are disabled from continuing to exercise their powers except on an order of the court or to comply with the obligation to convene a creditors' meeting or to dispose of perishable goods or protect the company's assets (Insolvency Act 1986, s.114).

[29] Insolvency Act 1986, s.100.

[30] *ibid.*, s.166(2), a provision designed to overcome the effect of the decision in *Re Centrebind Ltd* [1967] 1 W.L.R. 377 by which a company that deferred calling a meeting of creditors (albeit in breach of the statutory requirements) could get its liquidator in place exercising his statutory powers before the creditors had had an opportunity to make their own nomination.

[31] Insolvency Rules 1986, r.4.51.

cannot vote. However, it is often overlooked that a company need not act by proxy but can appear and vote by its duly authorised representative.[32] The difference between a proxy-holder and a representative is that the former is "another person" authorised to speak and vote as the company's representative[33] whereas a representative is treated as the personification of the company itself. The representative must be authorised by resolution of the directors,[34] a sealed or certified copy of which must be produced to the chairman of the creditors' meeting[35] but need not be lodged before the meeting. At any subsequent meeting a creditor can vote only if, in addition to any necessary proxy, it has also duly lodged a proof of debt which has been admitted by the chairman under r.4.70 of the Insolvency Rules.[36] The chairman is likely to reject a proof where the creditor has not obtained judgment and the debt is genuinely disputed by the company, and in that event the creditor cannot vote at the meeting.

The effect of a creditors' voluntary winding-up differs in a number of respects from that of a compulsory winding-up. Whereas in a compulsory winding-up the winding-up order operates to terminate the director's powers and dismiss them from office,[37] on a voluntary liquidation the powers of the directors come to an end only on the appointment of the liquidator,[38] though between the time of passing of the resolution for voluntary winding-up and the appointment of the liquidator these powers are severely restricted.[39] The liquidation is primarily under the control of the creditors rather than of the court and the liquidator can exercise without sanction certain powers which in a compulsory winding-up would require the sanction of the court or the liquidation committee.[40] There is no equivalent to the retrospective effect of a winding-up order;[41] the winding-up commences on the passing of the resolution to wind up.[42] In consequence, there is also no equivalent of s.127 of the Act, which invalidates dispositions of the company's property between winding-up petition and order unless sanctioned by the court.[43] Whereas a winding-up order

---

[32] Companies Act 1985, s.375(1)(b).

[33] Insolvency Rules 1986, r.8.1(1).

[34] *ibid.*

[35] *ibid.*, r.8.7.

[36] Insolvency Rules 1986, r.4.67(1).

[37] See below.

[38] Insolvency Act 1986, s.103, which, however, allows the liquidation committee or, if none, the creditors to sanction their continuance.

[39] *ibid.*, s.114(2). See n.28 above.

[40] That is, the power to bring or defend proceedings in the name and on behalf of the company and to carry on the business of the company so far as may be necessary for its beneficial winding-up (Insolvency Act 1986, ss.165 and 167 and Sch.4, paras 4 and 5).

[41] See below, para.5–15.

[42] Insolvency Act 1986, s.86. There is now a procedure by which the court can be asked to confirm the winding-up (Insolvency Rules 1986, rr.7.62, 7.63), but this is purely to bring the proceedings within the ambit of the European Insolvency Regulation. See below, para.13–11.

[43] See below, para.11–125.

automatically stays all proceedings against the company except by leave of the court,[44] there is no automatic stay in the case of a voluntary winding-up. It is for the liquidator to apply for a stay,[45] which will normally be granted as a matter of course if the plaintiff's claim is admitted, but not if it is disputed.[46]

5–04 But much of the procedure is common to the two forms of winding-up. The liquidator in a voluntary winding-up, as in a compulsory winding-up, will admit or reject proofs of debt[47] convene meetings of creditors as necessary, report on the conduct of the liquidation from time to time, collect in and realise the assets and make interim and final distributions of dividend to creditors whose proofs have been lodged and accepted. A creditor who fails to lodge a proof prior to a dividend distribution cannot disturb that distribution but upon lodging his proof and having it accepted is entitled to payment of the dividend he would have received ahead of other creditors before any subsequent distribution is made.[48] When the winding-up is completed, the liquidator convenes final meetings of the company and creditors, and subsequently gives notice to the registrar of companies that the meetings have been held and of the decisions (if any) taken at them, upon which he is released.[49] The company is dissolved automatically three months after registration of the liquidator's notice.[50]

The liquidator is entitled to remuneration, fixed either (a) as a percentage of the value of the assets realised or distributed or of the one value and the other in combination or (b) by reference to the time properly given, the remuneration and any percentage being fixed either by the liquidation committee or, if there is none, by a resolution of a meeting of creditors.[51] The liquidator's remuneration and expenses together constitute expenses of the liquidation payable ahead of the claims of creditors and ranking towards the end of the list of priorities for payment of liquidation expenses.[52]

3. COMPULSORY WINDING-UP[53]

Procedural outline

5–05 Proceedings for compulsory winding-up are initiated by petition issued by a creditor or other person having an appropriate *locus standi*.[54] The petition must be served on the company and other parties specified in the

---

[44] Insolvency Act 1986, s.130(2).
[45] Under s.112 of the Act. The application is made in the action sought to be stayed, not in the liquidation.
[46] *Currie v Consolidated Kent Collieries Corp Ltd* [1906] 1 K.B. 134.
[47] As to proofs of debt generally, see below, paras 7–31 *et seq.*
[48] Insolvency Rules 1986, r.4.182(2).
[49] Insolvency Act 1986, ss.171(6), 173(2)(e)(ii).
[50] *ibid.*, s.205(2).
[51] Insolvency Rules 1986, r.4.127.
[52] Insolvency Rules 1986, r.4.218.
[53] See Fidelis Oditah, "Winding up recalcitrant debtors" [1995] L.M.C.L.Q. 107.
[54] See below, para.5–08.

Insolvency Rules[55] and must be advertised as prescribed by the Rules.[56] Various other procedural requirements have to be fulfilled prior to the hearing. These too are set out in the Rules. On the hearing the court may in its discretion make a number of different orders.[57] If the court makes a winding-up order the official receiver becomes liquidator automatically unless and until another liquidator is appointed.[58] Any such liquidator must be an authorised insolvency practitioner. The official receiver may summon meetings of the creditors and contributories for the purpose of choosing another person as liquidator.[59] At such meetings the nomination (if any) of the creditors prevails unless the court otherwise orders.[60] In practice an outside liquidator will not accept an appointment unless he or she is satisfied that there are at least enough assets to cover the costs and expenses of winding-up, including the liquidator's remuneration. In such cases the official receiver will continue in office as liquidator.[61]

The official receiver will normally require the company to furnish a statement of affairs in the prescribed form,[62] showing the company's assets, debts and liabilities, names and addresses of its creditors and details of any securities they hold. The official receiver will convene a first meeting of creditors, notice being given to each creditor and contributory as well as being advertised. If an outside liquidator is to be appointed, it is usually at this meeting that the requisite resolution will be passed.

The various stages in the administration of the liquidation broadly follow the same pattern as for a creditors' voluntary winding-up, though there are numerous differences, some of the more important of which have been set out above.

With these preliminary remarks we can go on to consider certain features of compulsory winding-up deserving particular attention.

Grounds for compulsory winding-up of insolvent company

The primary ground for the winding-up of an insolvent company[63] is that it is unable to pay its debts.[64] Winding-up petitions commonly add as a separate ground that it is just and equitable that the company be wound   **5–06**

---

[55] Insolvency Rules 1986, rr.4.8–4.10.
[56] *ibid.*, r.4.11.
[57] See below, para.5–14.
[58] Insolvency Act 1986, s.136(2).
[59] Insolvency Act 1986, s.136(4). Alternatively the official receiver may apply to the Secretary of State to appoint a liquidator in his place, though the Secretary of State may decline to do so (s.137(1), (3)).
[60] *ibid.*, s.139(4).
[61] The fact that all the assets are mortgaged up to the hilt or that there are no assets at all is not a ground for refusing a winding-up order (Insolvency Act 1986, s.125(1)); there may well be matters to be investigated.
[62] Insolvency Act 1986, s.131(1).
[63] Insolvency is only one ground of compulsory winding-up. Others are set out in the Insolvency Act 1986, s.122(1)(a)–(e). In addition, a winding-up petition may be presented by

up.[65] A winding-up order may be made even where the company is already in voluntary winding-up.[66] The principles governing the exercise of the court's discretion are well set out in the judgment of Lawrence Collins J. in *Re Zirceram Ltd*[67] The usual ground of application is that the voluntary winding-up is not being properly conducted or that, even if it is, the circumstances call for the more rigorous investigation of the company's affairs afforded by a compulsory winding-up and one which is not only independent but seen to be independent. The general principle that a creditor has a prima facie right to a winding-up order applies here too, but the court will have regard not only to the quantity and quality of the petitioning creditor's claim but also to the wishes of a majority of creditors; if they desire the voluntary winding-up to continue that will be an important factor in the court's decision.[68]

What must be shown

5–07   To obtain a winding-up order on the grounds of insolvency a petitioner must show:

(1)   that grounds exist for the making of the order under section 122 of the Insolvency Act, the usual grounds being that the company is unable to pay its debts and that it is just and equitable for it to be wound up;

(2)   that he has a statutory *locus standi* to present the petition; and

(3)   that he has a legitimate interest in the making of a winding-up order.

If these requirements are satisfied then *prima facie* the petitioner is entitled to a winding-up order *ex debito justitiae* and the onus is then on those who oppose the petition to show why a winding-up order should not be made.

---

the Secretary of State on the grounds of public interest (Insolvency Act 1986, s.124A). Sometimes such petitions are insolvency-related, as in *Re Rodencroft Ltd* [2004] B.C.C. 631, where the ground of the application by the Secretary of State for a winding-up order against three companies, which they did not contest, was that they were being used as vehicles for fraud, namely the extraction of assets from them before the advent of formal insolvency proceedings. A winding-up order may also be sought by a member of a company as an alternative to an order for relief under s.459 of the Companies Act 1985 (unfairly prejudicial conduct of company's affairs), but this should not be done as a matter of course (Practice Direction: Applications under the Companies Act 1985 and the Insurance Companies Act 1982 [1999] B.C.C. 741, *Sealy & Milman: Annotated Guide to the Insolvency Legislation*, Appendix V).

[64] Insolvency Act 1986, s.122(l)(f).

[65] *ibid.*, s.122(l)(g).

[66] *ibid.*, s.116.

[67] [2000] 1 B.C.L.C. 751, paras 24 *et seq.*

[68] *Re Gordon & Breach Science Publishers Ltd* [1995] 2 B.C.L.C. 189.

Admittedly it has been said on more than one occasion that the winding-up procedure in the Companies Court cannot properly be used for the purpose of debt collection.

". . . it is trite law that the Companies Court is not, and should not be used as (despite the methods in fact often adopted) a debt-collecting court. The proper remedy for debt collecting is an execution upon a judgment, a distress, a garnishee order, or some such procedure."[69]

However, if this statement means that it is somehow improper for a creditor to resort to winding-up instead of execution in the hope of inducing the company to pay the debt, then it surely goes too far. Very often this is precisely the reason why the petition is launched, and the courts have emphasised that it is improper only where the purpose is to put pressure on the company to pay a sum that is not due or exceeds what is due.[70] But it is thought that Harman J. was intending to do no more than emphasise the undoubted principle that liquidation is a collective debt enforcement procedure[71] and that a winding-up petition is in the nature of the exercise of a class right, so that the interests of other creditors have to be considered.[72] A creditor who does not wish to be constrained by this principle should resort to execution, a process in which the interests of other creditors do not normally feature except in terms of priority by time of execution.

It is an abuse of the process of the court to make a statutory demand or present a winding-up petition based on a claim to which there is a triable defence.[73] There are several reasons for this. The presentation of a winding-up petition is a serious matter, affecting the reputation of the company and its management and potentially paralysing the company's business. In the first place, the Companies Court is not an appropriate forum for the determination of disputed claims.[74]

---

[69] *Re A Company* [1983] 1 B.C.L.C. 492 *per* Harman J. at 495.

[70] See *Re a Company (No 006273 of 1992)* [1993] B.C.L.C. 131, *per* Millett J. at 132, and above, para.4–23.

[71] *Re Lines Bros Ltd* [1983] Ch. 1, *per* Brightman L.J. at 20.

[72] See to the same effect Oditah, *loc. cit.*, at 111.

[73] In *Re a Company (No.0012209 of 1991)* [1992] 1 W.L.R. 351. See also the cases cited in n.74 below. Where the statutory demand is open to attack on this ground the company's remedy is to ask for an order restraining the presentation of the petition.

[74] *Stonegate Securities Ltd v Gregory* [1980] Ch. 576, *per* Buckley L.J. at 579–580; *Re Bayoil SA* [1999] 1 W.L.R. 147; *Montgomery v Wanda Modes Ltd* [2002] 1 B.C.L.C. 289. However, "it is equally important to emphasise that a judge, whether sitting in the Companies Court or elsewhere, should be astute to ensure that, however complicated and extensive the evidence might appear to be, the very extensiveness and complexity is not being invoked to mask the fact that there is, on proper analysis, no arguable defence to a claim, whether on the facts or the law" (*Re Richbell Strategic Holdings Ltd* [1997] 2 B.C.L.C. 429, *per* Neuberger J. at 434, after which comment the judge then examined the evidence in considerable detail before concluding that the petitioner was not a creditor entitled to present a petition).

"The reason for the practice [of requiring disputes to be determined elsewhere] has been essentially pragmatic. The vast majority of petitions to wind up a company are creditors' petitions. The Companies Court procedure on such petitions is ill-equipped to deal with the resolution of disputes of fact. There are no pleadings, there is no discovery and there is no oral evidence normally tolerated on such petitions, even though no doubt pleadings and discovery could be ordered and oral evidence received, and the Companies Court like any other court is perfectly capable of determining such disputes."[75]

5–08   Secondly, if the alleged debt is disputed on substantial grounds the petitioner cannot establish a *locus standi* as a creditor[76] or, in the absence of other factors, show that he has a legitimate interest in having the company wound up.[77] In that connection a debt is *bona fide* in dispute not only where the existence of the debt itself is challenged on substantial grounds but also where, though the debt is undisputed, there is a *bona fide* defence of set-off going to the whole of the debt, or the whole of it above £750,[78] thus affecting the petitioner's *locus standi* as a creditor.[79] Moreover, though a mere cross-claim not pleaded or effective as a set-off does not in law operate in reduction or discharge of the debt owed to the petitioning creditor, yet if it appears to be based on substantial grounds it will normally justify the court in staying or dismissing a petition if it has been presented or restraining its presentation if it has not.[80] But the evidence in support of the cross-claim must show that it is a solid cross-claim.[81] Moreover, the requirement of mutuality must be satisfied. So a statutory demand made against the company by a party claiming in one right cannot be impeached by a cross-demand by the company against that party claiming in another right.[82]

Despite the well-established principle that an alleged debt which is disputed on substantial grounds cannot properly found a statutory demand

---

[75] *Alipour v Ary* [1997] 1 W.L.R. 534, *per* Peter Gibson L.J. at 541. However, the court may allow the petition to proceed where the petitioner would have no other remedy if it were dismissed, and this was the course taken in *Alipour v Ary*.

[76] See below para.5–10.

[77] See below para.5–11.

[78] *McDonald's Restaurants Ltd v Urbandivide Co Ltd* [1994] 1 B.C.L.C. 306.

[79] *Re Ringinfo Ltd* [2002] 1 B.C.L.C. 210, *per* Pumfrey J. at 219.

[80] *ibid.*; *Montgomery v Wanda Modes Ltd* [2002] 2 B.C.L.C. 289 (where it was also held that a cross-claim could be neutralised by a reverse cross-claim if, though not currently a debt, it would assuredly become one); *Re Bayoil SA* [1999] 1 All E.R. 374, disapproving the approach taken in *Re FSA Business Software Ltd* [1990] B.C.L.C. 825); *Re LHF Wools Ltd* [1970] Ch. 27. Where the petition has not yet been presented but a statutory demand has been made, the company can seek an order restraining presentation of the petition For a case where the court made a winding-up order despite the existence of a cross-claim, see *Re FSA Business Software Ltd*, above.

[81] *Greenacre Publishing Group v The Manson Group* [2000] B.C.C. 11.

[82] *Hurst v Bennett* [2001] 2 B.C.L.C. 290.

or a winding-up petition there has been a steady stream of cases involving disputed debts, set-offs and cross-claims,[83] which may indicate a willingness on the part of some petitioners or intending petitioners to chance their arm in the hope of obtaining a winding-up order or at least flushing out the basis of an alleged set-off or cross-claim and the evidence for it before a trial in the appropriate forum.

The statutory grounds for winding-up

A petition by a creditor will be based primarily on para.(f) of s.122(1) of the **5–09** Insolvency Act, namely the inability of the company to pay its debts, though it is customary to reinforce this by reference to the "just and equitable" ground under para.(g). A contributory, in those infrequent cases where he can show a tangible interest,[84] will usually rely on para.(g).

As stated earlier,[85] there are four ways of showing inability to pay debts: neglect to comply with a statutory demand under s.123(1)(a); return of an execution or other process, issued on a judgment or order in favour of a creditor, unsatisfied in whole or in part; proof to the satisfaction of the court that the company is unable to pay its debts as they fall due; and proof to the satisfaction of the court that the value of the company's assets is less than the amount of its liabilities, taking into account its contingent and prospective liabilities. The second of these is self-explanatory, and the third and fourth have been examined in detail in the previous chapter.[86] It will, however, be necessary to say something about the first.

There is nothing in the Act which in terms requires either of the first two grounds to relate to the debt of the petitioning creditor, so that for the purpose of s.122(1)(f) the petitioner would seem to be able to invoke non-compliance with a statutory demand, or non-satisfaction of an execution, issued by another creditor. However, it still would be necessary for him to show some interest of his own, *e.g.* that he has called for payment of his debt and the company has failed to pay it.[87]

A considerable amount of case law has developed around the statutory demand ground and its relationship to other grounds of winding-up. The first point to note is that the inability of the company to pay its debts as they fall due may be invoked by any creditor without the need to make a statutory demand or even to institute proceedings for recovery of the debt. Indeed, the Court of Appeal has emphasised the practical reasons why "the

---

[83] See *Alexander Sheridan Ltd v Beaujersey Ltd* [2004] EWHC 2072; *Re UK (Aid) Ltd*, *GlaxoSmithKline Export Ltd v UK (Aid) Ltd* [2003] B.C.L.C. 351; and the cases cited above, nn.78–82.
[84] See below, para.5–11.
[85] See above, paras 4–07, 4–08.
[86] See above, paras 4–04 *et seq.*
[87] See below, para.5–11.

vast majority of creditors who seek to petition for the winding-up of companies do not serve statutory demands," namely that the assets may be dissipated during the three weeks that have to elapse before a petition can be issued based on the demand.[88] It suffices that the creditor has called for payment and that payment has not been made. Secondly, the fact that the statutory demand is for substantially more than the sum indisputably due does not vitiate it if the amount undisputed exceeds £750.[89] But if there is no such undisputed amount, non-compliance with the statutory demand cannot be used to found a petition, for what is required is "neglect" to pay, that is, a failure to pay a demand without reasonable excuse.[90] Moreover, as stated earlier, it is an abuse of process to serve a statutory demand for a debt which is *bona fide* disputed or for an excessive amount with a view to putting pressure on the company to pay more than is due from it.[91] Thirdly, the fact that the statutory demand is sent to the company by post instead of being left at its registered office as required by s.123(l)(a) does not invalidate it where it is not disputed that the demand was in fact received at the registered office.[92]

Who can present a petition

5–10 Under s.124 of the Insolvency Act 1986 a winding-up petition may be presented by:

(1) the company;

(2) the directors of the company;

(3) any creditor or creditors (including any contingent or prospective creditor);

(4) any contributory or contributories;

(5) a liquidator or temporary administrator appointed in main proceedings opened in another EC Member State pursuant to art.3(1) of the EC Insolvency Regulation who wishes to open secondary proceedings in the United Kingdom pursuant to art.29(3) of the regulation;[93]

---

[88] *Taylors Industrial Flooring Ltd v M. & H. Plant Hire (Manchester) Ltd* [1990] B.C.L.C. 216, *per* Dillon L.J. at 219.

[89] *Re A Company (No.008122 of 1980), Ex p. Trans Continental Insurance Services Ltd* [1990] B.C.L.C. 697.

[90] *Re London and Paris Banking Corp* (1875) 19 Eq. 444.

[91] See above, para.5–07.

[92] *Re A Company (No.008790 of 1990)* [1991] B.C.L.C. 561.

[93] Council Regulation of May 29, 2000 on insolvency proceedings (1346/2000/EC, OJ L160, 30.6.2000, p.1). The term "liquidator" is here used in the extended sense indicated in art.2(b) and Annex C of the Regulation, as meaning any person or body whose function is

(6)   the clerk of a magistrates' court in exercise of the power conferred by s.87A of the Magistrates' Courts Act 1980 (relating to the enforcement of fines imposed on companies); or

(7)   all or any of those parties together or separately.

However, the list in s.124(1) is not exhaustive, since there are statutory provisions elsewhere (including, surprisingly, the Insolvency Act itself) which add additional categories of petitioner. These are:

(8)   the Secretary of State[94];

(9) and (10) an administrator or administrative receiver[95];

(11)   the supervisor of a voluntary arrangement[96];

(12)   the Financial Services Authority, as regards authorised persons as defined by s.32 of the Financial Services and Markets Act 2000.[97]

Where directors of a company present a petition they must do so as a board, not individually. Accordingly either all the directors must join in the petition or it must be presented by one or more directors pursuant to a unanimous or majority resolution of the board.[98]

A creditor may present a petition whether he is an existing creditor whose debts have already become payable or a prospective or contingent creditor. An existing creditor is entitled to petition even if fully secured,[99] though his views are likely to be given less weight than those of unsecured creditors.[1] Prospective and contingent creditors can rely on all the grounds open to existing creditors, including the "just and equitable" ground in para.(g) of s.122.[2] But whereas the interest of an existing creditor is in most

---

to administer or liquidate assets of which the debtor has been divested or to supervise the administration of his affairs. In the case of main proceedings opened in another Member State it denotes any of the officials listed in Annex C in relation to that State. Where the main proceedings are opened in the United Kingdom (which is not the situation discussed here) then for the purpose of the liquidator's powers under the regulation, including the power to open secondary proceedings in another Member State, "liquidator" means a liquidator, a supervisor of a voluntary arrangement, an administrator or an Official Receiver.

[94] Insolvency Act 1986, s.124A.

[95] *ibid.*, Sch.B1, para.21.

[96] Insolvency Act 1986, s.7(4)(b).

[97] Financial Services and Markets Act 2000, s.367, replacing s.92 of the Banking Act 1987, which latter Act was repealed by the Financial Services and Markets (Consequential Amendments and Repeals) Order 2001 (SI 2001/3649), art.3(1)(d).

[98] *Re Instrumentation Electrical Services Ltd* [1988] B.C.L.C. 550; *Re Equiticorp International plc* [1989] B.C.L.C. 597 (a decision on a petition for an administration order, but the principle is the same).

[99] *Re Portsmouth Borough (Kingston, Fratton and Southsea) Tramways Co* [1892] 2 Ch. 362; *Moor v Anglo-Italian Bank* (1879) 10 Ch.D. 681.

[1] See below, para.5–13.

[2] *Re A Company (No.003028 of 1987)* [1985] B.C.L.C. 282. A creditor for untaxed costs has *locus standi (Tottenham Hotspur v Edennote)* [1995] 1 B.C.L.C. 65.

cases self-evident, a prospective or contingent creditor may need to demonstrate a sufficient interest in the making of a winding-up order.[3] A person claiming to be a creditor on a debt which is *bona fide* disputed, that is, disputed on substantial grounds,[4] does not constitute a creditor at all for the purpose of the statutory provisions[5] and the company may apply to have his petition struck out as an abuse of the process of the court without waiting for the substantive hearing,[6] even if at such hearing there might be creditors with undisputed claims who could ordinarily ask to be substituted.[7] If the petition has not yet been presented or advertised, the alternative course is to grant an injunction to restrain presentation or advertisement.[8] But neither of these courses will be taken where the debt is only partially disputed,[9] so long as the amount not in dispute is at least equal to that required for a statutory demand, currently a sum exceeding £750,[10] or where the creditor has a good arguable case and would suffer injustice or loss of a remedy (*e.g.* through removal of assets from the jurisdiction) if the petition were not to be allowed to proceed.[11]

Section 124 of the Act restricts the circumstances in which a contributory can petition for winding-up.[12] More significant in practice than these restrictions is the rule that a contributory must show that he has a tangible interest in the outcome of the liquidation.[13]

Legitimate interest

5–11   It has been said on many occasions, particularly by Harman J., that winding-up proceedings do not constitute a *lis* between the petitioner and the company but are in the nature of an exercise of class rights by a member of the class.[14] A winding-up petition is not simply a means of enforcing a debt, it is also designed to protect the debtor company from harassment and other creditors from piecemeal realisation and unequal

---

[3] See below, and Lee Berg Tat, above para.4–28, n.18.

[4] *Mann v Goldstein* [1968] 2 All E.R. 769, *per* Ungoed-Thomas J. at 775; *Re Welsh Brick Industries Ltd* [1946] 2 All E.R. 197 at 198; *Re A Company (No.001946 of 1990) Ex p. Fin Soft Holding S.A.* [1991] B.C.L.C. 737.

[5] See above, para.5–08.

[6] *Re A Company (No.0012209 of 1991)* [1992] B.C.L.C. 865.

[7] *Re CPBD (No.001889 of 1975)* [1975] C.L.Y. 322.

[8] *Stonegate Securities Ltd v Gregory* [1980] Ch. 576.

[9] *Re Tweeds Garage Ltd* [1962] Ch. 406; *Re A Company (No.008122 of 1989, Ex p. Trans Continental Insurance Services Ltd* [1990] B.C.L.C. 697.

[10] See above.

[11] *Re Claybridge Shipping Co Ltd* [1981] Com L.R. 107; and see *Re a Company (No.002180)* [1996] 2 B.C.L.C. 409.

[12] See below, para.5–11.

[13] See below, para.5–11.

[14] See, for example, *Re A Company* [1983] B.C.L.C. 492, citing *Re Crigglestone Coal Co* [1906] 2 Ch. 327; *Re Pleatfine Ltd* [1983] B.C.L.C. 88.

distribution and to substitute a system of *pari passu* distribution for individual enforcement.[15] The petitioner must therefore show that he has a legitimate current interest in the winding-up of the company. In the case of a creditor it is sufficient to show that he is currently owed a debt of not less than £750[16] which the company, despite request, has failed to pay. In that situation he is *prima facie* entitled to a winding-up order *ex debito justitiae.*[17] It is irrelevant that he may be motivated by antagonism towards the company or its directors.[18] But if there is a *bona fide* dispute as to the whole of the debt, or the whole of it except for not more than £750, it is an abuse of the winding-up process to present a petition, particularly where the object is to exert pressure on the debtor company to pay more than it owes with a view to avoiding the adverse publicity attending the advertisement of the petition.[19]

The position of the contingent creditor is somewhat different. His interest is not so immediate; indeed, the contingency may never occur. It is therefore necessary to consider the likelihood of this happening and the likely ability of the company, if it did happen, to be able to pay its debts at that time as they fell due. The matter was put in the following way by Scott J. in *Re A Company (No.003028 of 1987)*[20]:

"Current inability on the part of a company to pay its debts would not necessarily entitle a contingent creditor to succeed in a winding-up petition. The contingent creditor would, I think, be expected to show, not only and not necessarily a current inability by the company to pay its debts, but rather an inability to pay its debts at the time when the contingent debt became payable. A case of that character would, in my opinion, fall more clearly within para (g) than para (f) of s 122(1)."

This reasoning is not free from difficulty. In the first place, it presupposes that the time when the contingent debt will become payable is known. But it is in the nature of a contingent debt that the event on which it becomes payable is uncertain; that, indeed, is what distinguishes a contingent debt from a prospective debt. We must therefore assume that the learned judge

---

[15] *Re International Tin Council* [1987] Ch. 419, *per* Millett J. at 456. This is one of the reasons why the court will rarely, if ever, entertain separate petitions by different creditors. The petitioner is considered to represent the class, and other creditors who wish to take part should do so by way of support for the petition. If the petitioning creditor abandons his petition (*e.g.* because his debt is paid) another creditor may apply to be substituted. Under s.130(4) of the Insolvency Act a winding-up order operates in favour of all the creditors and all contributories of the company as if made on the joint petition of a creditor and a contributory.

[16] Section 123(1) itself prescribes this minimum only for the statutory demand, but the courts have usually applied it by analogy to other grounds relied on by a petitioning creditor.

[17] *Re A Company (No.0010382 of 1992) Ex p. Computer Partnership Ltd* [1993] B.C.L.C. 597.

[18] *Bryanston Finance Ltd v De Vries (No.2)* [1976] Ch. 63.

[19] See above, para.5–07.

[20] [1988] B.C.L.C. 282 at 294.

intended to refer to the time when the contingent debt *was likely* to become payable. It is true that there are cases in which it can be confidently predicted that the contingency will occur and will do in the immediate future,[21] but there are other situations where this will not be so. Indeed, that was the position in the case cited above, where everything turned on whether the creditor would win an action in the Queen's Bench Division that would enable him to claim that repayment of the loan had been triggered. Secondly, given that what has to be shown is the projected inability of the company to pay its debts as they fall due it is far from clear why para.(g) is more appropriate than para.(f). The typical case where the "just and equitable" ground might be invoked as an independent ground is where the contingent creditor is also a shareholder and complains that he is being prejudiced by oppression or mismanagement; but that complaint would be made *qua* shareholder, not *qua* creditor. Nevertheless, the decision does underline the fact that the interest of a contingent creditor is more tenuous than that of an actual creditor.

Presumably the company's present inability to pay its debts as they fall due is also insufficient for a prospective creditor, and if he is relying on s.122(l)(f) he will have to show that the company will be unable to pay its debts as they fall due at the time when his debt becomes payable. It would also seem, by parity of reasoning, that a prospective or contingent creditor cannot rely on a present deficiency of assets under s.122(2) and again has to look to the situation as it will be when his debt matures or is likely to mature. The essential point is that the company's state of insolvency does not entitle anyone to obtain a winding-up order; the petitioner must be someone who has both a *locus standi* and a sufficient current interest in an order being made.

A contributory, in addition meeting the requirements of s.124, must show that he has a "tangible interest"[22] in a winding-up order, that is, a prospect that there will be a surplus in which his share, even if small in absolute terms, is appreciable in relation to the size of his shareholding.[23]

Advertisement

5–12   Unless the court otherwise directs, the petition must be advertised once in the Gazette or, if that is not reasonably practicable, in a specified newspaper, not less than seven business days before the day appointed for the hearing and, if the petitioner is not the company, not less than seven business days after service of the petition on the company.[24] Though the

---

[21] See above, para.4–18.
[22] *Re Rica Cold Washing Co* (1879) 11 Ch.D. 36, *per* Jessel M.R. at 43.
[23] *Bryanston Finance Ltd v De Vries (No.2)* [1976] Ch. 63.
[24] Insolvency Rules 1986, r.4.11.

court has power to dispense with advertisement this will be exercised only in exceptional circumstances, for advertisement serves the dual purpose of enabling creditors and other interested parties to attend and bring before the court material relevant to the question of whether a winding-up order should be made and giving notice to the public of the presentation of the petition, information to which they are in principle entitled.[25] But the court will restrain advertisement in appropriate cases, as where the presentation of the petition is an abuse of the process of the court because, for example, the debt is bona fide disputed on substantial grounds.[26]

The substantive hearing

The existence of grounds for winding-up, *locus standi* and a sufficient interest in the petitioner are all threshold questions which can either be left to be dealt with at the substantive hearing or raised at an earlier stage by way of an application to strike out the petition. In the latter case the court's task is to decide whether the petition fails *in limine* or can proceed to a substantive hearing. Decisions on how to balance opposing views on whether a winding-up order should be made are matters to be dealt with at the substantive hearing. If the petition is unopposed a winding-up order will usually be made as a matter of course. But if for other purposes it is desired to obtain a definitive ruling that the company is insolvent appropriate evidence will have to be called, and if this is insufficient the petition will be dismissed even if the company is as anxious as the petitioner for a winding-up order to be made and, indeed, if the company itself is the petitioner.[27]

5–13

A creditor to whom a debt is currently owed is *prima facie* entitled to a winding-up order *ex debito justiae*,[28] but the court may decline to make an order if it is opposed by the majority of creditors.[29] In that connection the court will have regard not only to the number of opposing creditors but to the value of the debts owed to them and to the quality of the creditors.[30] So if they are independent creditors who, though a minority in number, represent a substantial majority in value their wishes are likely to be heeded. The court will to a considerable extent discount creditors who are connected with the company,[31] *e.g.* who are directors or shareholders, and will also give less weight to creditors who are fully secured and thus have

---

[25] *Applied Data Base Ltd v Secretary of State for Trade and Industry* [1995] 1 B.C.L.C. 272.
[26] See above, para.5–07.
[27] See *Re Capital Annuities Ltd* [1979] 1 W.L.R. 170, a decision on s.50 of the Insurance Companies Act 1974. See also above, para.4–21, n.89.
[28] See above, para.5–07.
[29] Contributories also have the right to be heard in opposition. See, for example, *Re Rodencroft Ltd* [2004] B.C.C. 631.
[30] *Re Lowestoft Traffic Services Ltd* [1986] B.C.L.C. 81.
[31] *Re Lowestoft Traffic Services Ltd* [1986] B.C.L.C. 81.

only a limited interest in the liquidation. Where the company has a cross-claim against the petitioning creditor that is a matter which the court can take into account in exercising its discretion whether to make a winding-up order.[32]

Members of the company presenting a petition as contributories on the ground that it is just and equitable for the company to be wound up are entitled to a winding-up order if the court is of the opinion that the petitioners are entitled to relief either by winding-up or by some other means, that in the absence of any other remedy it would be just and equitable to wind up the company and that there is no other remedy available to the petitioners which it would be unreasonable of them not to pursue.[33]

Orders that can be made at the hearing

5–14 At the hearing of the petition the court may dismiss it, adjourn it conditionally or unconditionally or make an interim order or any other it thinks fit, but it cannot refuse to make an order only on the ground that the assets have been fully mortgaged or that the company has no assets.[34] A winding-up order cannot be made during the interim moratorium imposed when the company is about to be put into administration[35] or during the currency of an administration,[36] and where an administration order is made any winding-up petition must be dismissed.[37]

Commencement of winding-up

5–15 Upon a winding-up order being made the winding-up is deemed to commence at the time of presentation of the petition unless a resolution for voluntary winding-up had been passed prior to the petition being presented, in which case the winding-up is deemed to have commenced at the time of passing of the resolution.[38] The retrospective effect of the winding-up order may have important consequences, *e.g.* in relation to dispositions made by the company[39] and the provisions of the Insolvency Act relating to transactions at an undervalue and preferences.[40]

---

[32] See cases cited in para.5–08, n.80, above.
[33] Insolvency Act 1986, s.125(2). See *Vujnovich v Vujnovich* [1990] B.C.L.C. 227.
[34] *ibid.*, s.125(1).
[35] *ibid.*, Sch.B1, para.44. See below, paras 10–67 *et seq.*
[36] *ibid.*, para.42.
[37] *ibid.*, para.40(1)(a).
[38] Insolvency Act 1986, s.129.
[39] See Insolvency Act 1986, s.127, and below, paras 11–126 *et seq.*
[40] See below, paras 11–12 *et seq.*, 11–69 *et seq.*

Effect of winding-up order

On the making of a winding-up order no action may be proceeded with or commenced against the company except by leave of the court and subject to such terms as the court may impose and control of the assets[41] passes to the official receiver as the initial liquidator. The winding-up order terminates the powers of the directors[42] and operates as notice discharging employees except where the business is continued for the beneficial winding-up of the company, the liquidator indicates that he would like them to remain in employment and they agree to do so.[43] Neither a declaration of insolvency nor winding-up itself constitutes a repudiation of other types of contract except where the circumstances show that the company is unable or unwilling to continue performance.[44]

5–16

4. WINDING-UP THROUGH ADMINISTRATION

The third form of winding-up, introduced by the Enterprise Act 2002, is as an exit route from administration.[45]

5–17

---

[41] But not title to them unless a vesting order is made under s.145 of the Insolvency Act.
[42] *Measures Bros. Ltd v Measures* [1910] 2 Ch. 248.
[43] *Re Oriental Bank Corp, Macdowell's Case* (1886) 32 Ch.D. 366.
[44] *Mess v Duffus & Co* (1901) 6 Com. Cas. 165; *Re Phoenix Bessemer Steel Co, Ex p. Carnforth Haematite Iron Co* (1876) 4 Ch.D. 108. For a useful recent analysis, see Meng Seng Wee, "Insolvency and the Survival of Contracts" [2005] J.B.L. 494.
[45] See para.10-103.

Chapter 6

Winding-up: Assets Available for Distribution

Introduction

The fundamental principles governing the distribution of assets on the **6–01**
winding-up of a company were outlined in Chapter 3. It is worth restating
three of these at the outset. First, only the assets of the company at the
time it goes into liquidation or accruing to it subsequently are available for
its creditors. As we shall see, this principle—which among other things
excludes property so far as held by the company on trust or subject to a
security interest or as buyer under a conditional sale agreement[1]—is subject
to important exceptions. Secondly, what constitutes an asset of the company
is to be determined primarily by the general principles of property and
contract law applicable to solvent parties. It is for this reason that
insolvency law cannot be properly understood without a thorough grasp of
the general law. There are, it is true, certain rules of pre-insolvency law
which are modified by insolvency legislation, but the starting point in each
case is the determination of the assets of the company in accordance with
the general law and the principle referred to earlier that, at least as a
starting position, insolvency law respects pre-insolvency entitlements.[2]
Thirdly, a distinction is to be drawn between assets coming to the company
after the commencement of winding-up which do not result from any
activity of the liquidator and recoveries by the liquidator through performance of a contract or as the result of proceedings for fraudulent or
wrongful trading and the like. The former are susceptible to capture under
an after-acquired property clause in a mortgage or charge, while the latter
are statutory recoveries which the liquidator holds for the benefit of the
general body of creditors, not in right of the company. They are thus not to

---

[1] See below, paras 6–34 *et seq.*
[2] See above, paras 3–02 *et seq.*

be equated with free assets of the company which it was capable of giving in security as after-acquired property, but are held on trust for the general body of creditors.[3]

1. DELINEATION OF THE PROPERTY OF THE COMPANY

6–02 There are various reasons why it may be necessary to know whether a right or facility constitutes property for the purpose of insolvency law. The first is that in general it is only assets beneficially owned by the company that are distributable among creditors. The second is that contractual provisions by which, on the insolvency of a company, it is to be divested of property that has been transferred to it outright are void under insolvency law. The third is that the liquidator is entitled to disclaim onerous property, for which purpose it may be necessary to determine whether what is in issue is property before turning to the question whether it is onerous property. Finally, the concept of property of the company may be relevant for the purpose of determining whether, after the presentation of a winding-up petition, there has been a disposition of the company's property in contravention of s.127 of the Insolvency Act 1986,[4] an issue examined in several cases in relation to an overdraft maintained by the company with its bank.[5]

What constitutes property?

6–03 Section 107 of the Insolvency Act 1986, embodying the general principle of *pari passu* distribution, provides as follows:

> "Subject to the provisions of this Act as to preferential payments, the company's property in a voluntary winding-up shall on the winding-up be applied in satisfaction of the company's liabilities pari passu and, subject to that application, shall (unless the articles otherwise provide) be distributed among the members according to their rights and interests in the company."

Though there is no exactly comparable provision for compulsory winding-up, the same rules apply.[6] So all the assets of the company constitute its estate available for distribution in accordance with the statutory order of

---

[3] As to the nature of the trust, see above, para.3–07.
[4] See below, paras 11–124 *et seq.*
[5] See below, paras 11–129 *et seq.*
[6] Insolvency Rules 1986, r.4.181(1).

priority. But what is meant by "the company's property"? Section 436 indicates that this is to have the widest meaning, stating that in the Act, except in so far as the context otherwise requires:

> " 'property' includes money, goods, things in action, land and every description of property wherever situated and also obligations and every description of interest, whether present or future or vested or contingent, arising out of, or incidental to, property."

Like most definitions this one is not free from difficulty. For one thing, it is circular, "property" being defined as including "every description of property". Moreover, the reference to "obligations" is a little strange, since obligations owed *by* the company are liabilities, not assets, while obligations owed *to* the company (which is evidently what is meant) are already encompassed within the phrase "things in action". But as we shall see, the concept of property is notoriously difficult[7] and depends on the context in which it is invoked,[8] so that we cannot fairly criticise the draftsman for giving us a self-referential definition. What is clear is, first, that "for something to qualify as 'property', it must involve some element of benefit or entitlement for the person holding it"[9] and, secondly, that the concept of property is not exhausted by the division into choses in possession and choses in action. Intangible rights which are not enforceable by action may nevertheless have value and be transferable, for example, transferable quotas and licences, which fall within the definition of property even though they are not enforceable by action and thus are not choses in action.[10]

The assets of a company in liquidation, like those of a solvent company, are not confined to physical things or to things which are fully owned by the company. Any beneficial interest held by the company, whether in tangible or intangible property and whether full or limited, indefeasible or defeasible, present, future or contingent, held absolutely or held by way of security, constitutes an asset. Thus the company's assets may include freehold or leasehold property, goods owned by the company, possession of goods under a lease or hire-purchase agreement, negotiable instruments held by the company, insurance policies, intellectual property rights, contract, tort and restitution claims, options, quotas and licences and

---

[7] For a detailed treatment, see J.E. Penner, *The Idea of Property in Law* (1997), particularly Chaps 5 and 6. For a classification of property, see also Kevin Gray, 'Property in Thin Air' [1991] C.L.J 252, and other materials cited by L.S. Sealy and R.J.A. Hooley, *Commercial Law: Text, Cases and Materials* (3rd ed. 2003), pp.61 *et seq.*

[8] *Nokes v Doncaster Amalgamated Collieries Ltd* [1940] A.C. 1014, *per* Lord Porter at 1051.

[9] *Re SSSL Realisations (2002) Ltd* [2005] 1 B.C.L.C. 1, *per* Lloyd J at para.60.

[10] *Attorney-General of Hong Kong v Nai-Keung* [1987] 1 W.L.R. 1339; and see below, para.6–07.

security interests in tangible or intangible property owned by another.[11] A claim under the Third Parties (Rights against Insurers) Act 1930[12] has also been held to constitute property.[13] Pure contract rights not associated with tangible or intangible property are also property in themselves. This may seem strange, for is it not the case that property is to be distinguished from obligation and that a contract right as such creates a purely personal obligation which can only become property in the relations between a party to the contract and a third party acquiring an interest in the contract rights, such as an assignee? The answer is that in the context of winding-up the liquidator holds the contract not for the company itself but on a statutory "trust" for the creditors,[14] who thus occupy the position of third parties. Thus from the perspective of the liquidator and creditors a contract right is undoubtedly a species of property and indeed may be an asset of great value even if not conferring a right to another form of property. Examples are the rights of a concessionaire under a distribution agreement, the right to give or refuse consent to an act which the other party may wish to perform, the right to carry out work and earn substantial sums under a profitable building contract.

6–04   All this seems quite clear cut. However, various types of interest raise difficulties. This is particularly true of non-transferable (or non-assignable) rights, limited interests and defeasible interests. Then there are rights which will accrue to the company only on the discharge of obligations, as in the case of executory contracts. Further, assets in the possession of the company may turn out to belong to others, for example, through reservation of title under a sale agreement or through some form of trust, and questions may arise as to whether the fruits of liability insurance form part of the company's estate or belong to the party to whom the liability was incurred.

Finally, the property of the company is not limited to assets in which it has an interest at the time of commencement of the winding-up. Other assets may fall into the estate later, whether by virtue of rights granted prior to the winding-up or because of the liquidator's own activities, in addition to which the estate may be swelled by recoveries from directors and other parties against whom the liquidator or the company has rights of action

---

[11] The main division is between tangibles and intangibles, but intangibles themselves can be subdivided into documentary intangibles, such as negotiable instruments, documents of title to goods, bearer securities, which embody rights so as to make these transferable by delivery of the document with any necessary indorsement, and pure (or non-documentary) intangibles, which are not so embodied, such as ordinary contract rights, insurance policies, intellectual property rights, debts not represented by a negotiable instrument and registered securities. See generally Roy Goode, *Commercial Law* (3rd ed.), pp.29, 47 *et seq*. In many respects documentary intangibles are treated in law in the same way as tangibles, for example in their susceptibility to claims for conversion.

[12] See below, para.6–18.

[13] *Re Compania Merabello San Nicholas SA* [1973] Ch. 75.

[14] See above, para.3–07.

under the Insolvency Act or by the obligatory surrender to the liquidator of a percentage of assets comprised in a floating charge. However, there is a distinction between assets vested in the company at the time of winding-up and assets which are only recoverable by the liquidator subsequently in exercise of his statutory powers. The latter are not "the company's property" within the meaning of the Insolvency Act 1986[15] and are thus not susceptible to capture by a secured creditor under an after-acquired property clause.[16]

But we still need to have a clearer idea of the concept of property. The badges of a property right were set out by Lord Wilberforce in *National Provincial Bank Ltd v Hastings Car Mart Ltd*[17] in the following terms[18]:

> "Before a right or an interest can be admitted into the category of property, or of a right affecting property, it must be definable, identifiable by third parties, capable in its nature of assumption by third parties, and have some degree of permanence or stability."

The third of these elements, transferability, has also been emphasised in other cases.[19] One may add that the right should also possess value,[20] that is, value capable of being realised by transfer[21] independently of any asset to which the right is annexed.[22]

Non-transferable rights

There are various kinds of right that are expressed to be non-transferable or are transferable only with the consent of another or in restricted conditions. These include contract rights which by the terms of the contract

6–05

---

[15] Sch.4, para.6.

[16] *Re Oasis Merchandising Ltd* [1988] Ch. 170; and see below, para.6–30.

[17] [1965] A.C. 1175 at pp.1247–1248.

[18] At pp.1247–1248.

[19] *Attorney-General of Hong Kong v Nai-Keung* [1987] 1 W.L.R. 1339; *Re Celtic Extraction Ltd* [2001] Ch. 475, *per* Morritt L.J. at para.33; and see n.21 below.

[20] *Re Celtic Extraction Ltd, per* Morritt L.J. at para.33.

[21] The word "transfer" is here used broadly to denote any mechanism by which a benefit previously enjoyed by one person may be made available to another in his place. In private law rights may be transferred by assignment or by novation, the latter involving the replacement of the original oblige by a new oblige with the consent of the obligor. As shown below, there may be other mechanisms by which benefits may be transferred, particularly in relation to statutory licences and quotas.

[22] This point is particularly relevant in relation to licences and quotas. See below, para.6–07. The ability to exclude others from access to a resource has been said to be much closer to the core of property than the conventional legal emphasis on the assignability or enforceability of benefits (Kevin Gray, "Property in Thin Air" [1991] C.L.J. 252 at pp.294–295, citing *Victoria Park Racing and Recreation Grounds Co Ltd v Taylor* (1937) 58 C.L.R. 479). See also James Penner, *The Idea of Property in Law*, Chap.4, emphasising the significance of the right of exclusion. Excludability is undoubtedly an element in the concept of property, but in the context of insolvency law, at any rate, it is hard to see how a right which is not transferable as a thing possessing independent value can constitute property, though it may well enhance the value of an asset to which it is annexed, in which case it is unnecessary to treat it as property at all. See below, para.6–09.

are not assignable, or are not assignable by one party without the other's consent[23]; various kinds of statutory licence; quotas issued by a government department or statutory authority; and membership of a club or exchange.[24] Since one of the badges of a property right is transferability, the question arises whether a right expressed to be a non-transferable right can be a species of property at all. The answer to this question appears to depend on whether the right has a separate, realisable value in the hands of the company in liquidation as opposed to being merely a factor which enhances the value of something else but is incapable of being separately enjoyed and disposed of. Where the asset is truly non-transferable in the sense that it is by its nature personal to the holder and cannot be separately disposed of at all by the company, at law or in equity, either by assignment or by novation or by some other mechanism having a similar effect,[25] then it is not property for the purposes of the Insolvency Act. We shall consider four categories of case: the assignment or trust of contract rights which are expressed by the terms of the contract to be non-assignable; the transfer of licences and quotas which are capable of being separately transferred, albeit sometimes not without difficulty; the assignment of rights of pre-emption; and truly non-transferable rights.

(1) Assignment or trust of contract rights expressed to be non-assignable

6–06 It is not uncommon for a contract to contain a provision prohibiting a party from assigning its rights under the contract. There are several legitimate commercial reasons for such a stipulation. The debtor[26] may have a good working relationship with its creditor and may not wish to find itself dealing with a new party who is less accommodating. The debtor may also not wish to risk overlooking a notice of assignment and, having mistakenly paid the original creditor, finding itself compelled to make a second payment, to the assignee. Moreover, where the debtor is engaged in continuing mutual dealings with the original creditor it will not want to have its right of set-off brought to an end as regards cross-claims arising after its receipt of notice of assignment.[27] Does this mean that an assignment to the debtor company in breach of a no-assignment clause is wholly ineffective? This was the view of Croom-Johnson J. in *Helstan Securities Ltd v Hertfordshire County*

---

[23] There are also rules of public policy restricting assignment. For example, the assignment of a bare right of action constitutes champerty and is void. See Roy Goode, *Legal Problems of Credit and Security* (3rd ed.), para.3–39, and the standard works on contract law.

[24] *Money Markets International Stockbrokers Ltd v London Stock Exchange Ltd* [2002] 1 W.L.R. 1150; *Bombay Official Assignee v Shroff* (1932) 48 T.L.R. 443. See below, para.7–13.

[25] *e.g.* a system under which a licence is surrendered and then re-granted to a different person. See below.

[26] For convenience the term "debtor" is used to include any form of obligor, whether the performance owed is the payment of money or otherwise.

[27] See Roy Goode, *Legal Problems of Credit and Security* (3rd ed.), paras 3–40, 7–66.

Council,[28] but his ruling went further than was necessary for the decision. Certainly the debtor is entitled to insist that it will not deal with anyone other than the original creditor and that it does not recognise the title of the assignee. But it is quite another thing to say that as between assignor and assignee the assignment has no proprietary effects. The debtor generally has no legitimate interest in controlling the assignor's power of alienation and it is strongly arguable that a restriction on alienation is contrary to public policy.[29] Where what is assigned is a debt, the effect of the assignment in breach of a no-assignment clause is to create a trust of the debt in favour of the assignee, who, being unable to collect the debt from the debtor, will usually be content to treat the assignment as relating to the collected proceeds in the hands of the assignor. But where the rights assigned are not monetary in character, the assignee may have a legitimate interest, as beneficiary of a trust of the contract right itself, in enforcing the trust so as to preclude the assignor from appropriating the contract rights for his own benefit. On this basis it has been held that there is no reason why contracts assigned to a partnership should not form part of the partnership assets even if, as between the assignor and its counter-party, the contracts were not assignable.[30]

It will now be evident that non-assignable contract rights do not, on closer examination, contravene the general requirement of transferability, for while they are not transferable at law so as to be enforceable against the assignor's counterparty they are assignable in equity so as to produce proprietary effects in the relationship between the assignor and the assignee.

(2) Statutory licences and quotas

In several cases the courts have had to consider the status of licences and quotas as a species of property. In a case concerning a waste management licence granted under the Environmental Protection Act 1990 to a company which later went into liquidation the Court of Appeal held that the licence, which was not transferable by the holder but could, by surrender and re-grant, be transferred by the Environment Agency on application and had value, constituted property and was capable of being "onerous property" so as to enable the liquidator to disclaim it under s.436 of the Insolvency Act 1986.[31] Similarly, a milk quota, which gave a milk producer exemption from

6–07

---

[28] [1978] 3 All E.R. 262.
[29] See R. M. Goode, "Inalienable Rights?" (1979) 42 M.L.R. 553, to which extensive supportive references were made by Lord Browne-Wilkinson in *Linden Gardens Ltd v Lenesta Sludge Disposals Ltd* [1994] 1 A.C. 85.
[30] See *Don King Productions Inc v Warren & Co* [1999] 2 All E.R. 218, applied in *Swift v Dairywise Farms Ltd (No. 1)* [2000] 1 W.L.R. 1177; *Re Turcan* (1888) 40 Ch.D. 5; Roy Goode, *Legal Problems of Credit and Security* (3rd ed.), para.3–42.
[31] *Re Celtic Extraction Ltd* [2001] Ch. 475, applying *National Provincial Bank Ltd v Hastings Car Mart Ltd* [1965] A.C. 1175 and *Attorney-General of Hong Kong v Nai-Keung* [1987] 1 W.L.R. 1339 and, in relation to the power of disclaimer, overruling *Re Mineral Resources Ltd, Environment Agency v Stout* [1999] 1 All E.R. 746.

a levy that would otherwise be payable but which had to follow the land to which it was attached and could not be dealt with independently, was nevertheless held, on the evidence before the court, to be an independent asset having a distinct economic value capable of being realised by contractual devices based on the principle of a composite holding.[32] Accordingly it constituted property within the definition of s.436 of the Insolvency Act and was held on trust for the company so as to entitle the liquidators to require an accounting of the proceeds of sale of the quota. However, not all statutory licences are property; the relevant statute may itself preclude this. So s.36 of the Coal Industry Act 1994 provides that a licence under that Act is not to be treated as property for the purposes of the Insolvency Act 1986.

(3) Assignable rights of pre-exemption

6–08   An assignable right of pre-emption constitutes property even though the grantor of the right may never decide to sell the asset to which the right relates. Unless and until he so decides, the right is contingent. Nevertheless it is has value, for the grantor is bound not to offer the asset to anyone other than the grantee of the pre-emption right without first offering it to the grantee and if the grantor breaches that obligation he may incur a liability in damages to the grantee.[33]

(4) Truly non-transferable rights

6–09   We are left with rights which are not transferable either at law or in equity. Non-transferable rights are of different kinds. In his book *The Idea of Property in Law*, Dr James Penner draws a useful distinction between restrictions on the scope of property rights which are not intended to strike at the property-like character of the right and those that are.[34] Applied to the question of alienability, one can distinguish a thing which is not transferable, in law or in equity, because it is personal to the holder and thus is not property, from a thing which is not by its nature personal to the holder but which legislation has ordained is not to be sold, *e.g.* a stock of cancerous substances. Though not generally saleable in its existing form[35] this is undoubtedly property, because the rights in it are not personal to the holder; the prohibition on sale is not intended to deprive the substances of

---

[32] *Swift v Dairywise Farms Ltd* [2000] 1 W.L.R. 1177.
[33] *Dear v Reeves* [2002] Ch. 1.
[34] At pp.100–101.
[35] It might, of course, be saleable if treated or have a value for the purposes of chemical research.

their property character but rather to safeguard the public from harm. *A fortiori* a statutory provision which does not directly prohibit assignment of contractual rights but merely requires a prohibition against assignment to be included in the contract and attaches certain adverse consequences for failure to do so does not deprive the rights of their character as property.[36] But a right which is purely personal to the company and is incapable of being disposed of as a separate asset does not constitute property for the purposes of the Insolvency Act so as to form part of the company's estate. It was on this ground that in *City of London Corp v Bown*[37] Dillon L.J. held that a secure periodic tenancy, being personal to the tenant and incapable of realisation for the benefit of creditors by his trustee in bankruptcy, did not form part of the bankrupt's estate for the purpose of s.306 of the Insolvency Act.

We need, however, to be clear that the fact that a right personal to the company and not transferable is not property does not mean it contributes no value, merely that it has no independent value capable of being separately realised so as to qualify it for the status of an independent asset. But it may well enhance the value of an asset. Suppose, for example, that a retailing company holds a licence under the Consumer Credit Act 1974 to carry on a consumer credit business, so that its customers can buy on credit, and after carrying on the business for some time goes into insolvent liquidation. The licence does not come to an end[38] but it is not assignable.[39] So while it adds value to the company's overall business, part of which could not lawfully be carried on without the licence, it has no independent value and cannot be transferred. Accordingly it does not constitute property of the company. But this is not a problem, for there is no reason why it needs to be treated as a separate asset; it suffices that it adds to the value of the business. One can think of other examples, such as non-transferable membership of an exchange carrying with it a proportionate interest in the assets of the exchange on its being wound up and non-transferable tax losses which can be set against future profits of the company.

Moreover, a right which, though in itself transferable, is inseparably annexed to personal status and cannot be transferred so as to produce value for the company is not a free-standing asset that can be treated as part of the company's estate. It is necessary to emphasise that what we are concerned with is not whether an asset is capable of transfer by someone but whether it is transferable so as to produce value for the company. For example, if a company that is a member of an exchange holds shares for which it cannot receive any consideration on transfer and which on the

---

[36] *Re Landau* [1998] Ch. 223 (statutory provisions requiring pension trust deeds to include a no-assignment clause).
[37] (1990) 60 P. & C.R. 42.
[38] Goode, *Consumer Credit Law and Practice*, para.[27.212].
[39] Consumer Credit Act 1974, s.22(2).

cessation of membership by reason of the company's insolvency have to be surrendered to the exchange without consideration, and are then transferable by the exchange to other members for value, the shares do not constitute a free-standing asset of the company, nor do they constitute value in its hands for the purpose of the rule against divestment on insolvency.[40]

Factors limiting the interest held

6–10   An item of tangible or intangible property held by the company is an asset of the company only to the extent of its interest in it. The strength and quantum of that interest may be limited or extinguished by external vitiating factors or by the terms on which the interest is held. As we shall see, in relation to the latter the law draws a sharp distinction between contractual provisions which limit the quantum or duration of an interest, to which effect will be given, and provisions for the divestiture, on the company's insolvency, of ownership of assets previously transferred to it,[41] which are void as contravening the *pari passu* principle and may also be void on the separate ground of repugnancy.[42] The factors which may qualify in an asset fall broadly into four groups:

(1) Factors which prevent the interest taking effect or render it voidable or terminable

6–11   The company's rights under a contract, including a contract pursuant to which it has acquired or is to acquire land or goods, may be subject to some unfulfilled condition precedent[43] or some equity rendering it vulnerable to avoidance *ab initio, e.g.* by way of rescission for fraud, misrepresentation or undue influence. Alternatively the contract, though not voidable, may be subject to a right of termination by the other party, *e.g.* for default in payment or other breach or on the occurrence of some non-promissory condition subsequent. The liquidator takes control of assets, including contract rights, in the condition in which he finds them, warts and all. He acts in right of and in the name of the company, and an asset of the company which before liquidation was conditional, defeasible or determinable does not cease to be so by reason of the liquidation.[44] So, for example,

---

[40] *Money Markets International Stockbrokers Ltd v London Stock Exchange Ltd* [2002] 1 W.L.R. 1150. See below, para.7–13.

[41] See below, para.7–11.

[42] See below, para.7–14.

[43] For example, a contract of sale of land may be subject to a condition that it is not to take effect unless the purchaser obtains planning permission for development of the land within a specified period.

[44] However, the majority decision of the House of Lords in *British Eagle International Airlines Ltd v Compagnie Nationale Air France* [1975] 1 W.L.R. 758 appears to be a deviation from this principle. See para.8–14. Special rules apply in relation to market contracts (above, para.1–29) and financial collateral (above, para.1–32).

the right of the other party to rescind a contract for misrepresentation and thereby reacquire property transferred under it or to terminate the contract for breach and recover possession of any property leased under it remains unaffected by the company's winding-up,[45] though the liquidator may be able to invoke the court's equitable jurisdiction to grant relief against forfeiture.[46]

The principle that the liquidator takes subject to equities is not always easy to reconcile with the countervailing principle that a contractual provision is invalid to the extent that its application after the commencement of a winding-up would deprive the company in liquidation of an asset that would otherwise be available to creditors, thereby contravening the principle of *pari passu* distribution. An example is the provision in a construction contract empowering or requiring the employer to pay a sub-contractor direct in stated events, such as the main contractor's default in payment to the sub-contractor of sums due under the sub-contract. If the employer has become entitled or obliged to make such payment before the main contractor goes into liquidation but has not actually done so, can it still pay the sub-contractor after the winding-up has commenced?[47] In early cases in which an affirmative answer was given to this question the issue of conformity with the insolvency principle of *pari passu* distribution was not raised. In *Re Wilkinson, Ex p. Fowler*,[48] the contract empowered the employer's engineer, if he considered the main contractor to be guilty of undue delay in paying the sub-contractor, to order payment by the employer to the sub-contractor direct. The main contractor became insolvent and the question arose whether that revoked the engineer's authority to make such an order. Bigham J. held that it did not; the authority was irrevocable and was not affected by the bankruptcy. The question of compatibility with insolvency law was not raised, so that the case is not an authority on that point. The decision was followed in *Re Tout and Finch Ltd*[49], which was decided in favour of the sub-contractor on the additional ground that under the main contract the contractor's entitlement to retention moneys in the hands of the employer was expressed to be fiduciary as trustee for the sub-contractor. This was held to constitute an equitable assignment of the retention moneys by the main contractor. Again, no reference was made to insolvency law.

---

[45] *Re Eastgate* [1905] 1 K.B. 465; *Tilley v Bowman Ltd* [1910] 1 K.B. 745. Both of these involved a sale of goods induced by the fraud of the bankrupt buyer, and it was held that the trustee in bankruptcy took subject to the seller's right to disaffirm the contract. See also below, para.7–11.

[46] *Transag Haulage Ltd v DAF Finance plc* [1994] 2 B.C.L.C. 88.

[47] For an instructive discussion of this issue, see Michael Bridge, "Collectivity, Management of Estates and the *Pari Passu* Rule in Winding-Up" in Armour and Bennett, *op. cit.*, at paras 1.49 *et seq.*

[48] [1905] 2 K.B. 713.

[49] [1954] 1 W.L.R. 178.

The effect of these and similar decisions, except so far as based on trust or assignment, was undermined by the controversial decision of the House of Lords in the *British Eagle* case,[50] in which a multilateral netting arrangement was held to contravene the *pari passu* principle and the majority of their Lordships rejected the argument that the liquidator could not invoke the rights under the contract entered into by the parties without being bound by the agreed machinery for payment through the netting arrangement. There has been one decision since *British Eagle* in which the validity of a direct payment clause was upheld,[51] *British Eagle* being distinguished on the ground that in that case the effect of the payment arrangement was to divest the company in liquidation of an asset, namely the debt owed to it, whereas the effect of the direct payment clause was to qualify the company's entitlement to payment as main contract and render it subject to reduction in favour of the sub-contractor. But in a series of subsequent decisions by appeal courts in different common law jurisdictions[52] the earlier cases have been distinguished on one ground or another and the direct payment clause has been held ineffective in the main contractor's insolvency as contrary to the *pari passu* rule. The effect of the cases is that in the absence of a trust or equitable assignment a mere contractual provision for payment direct to the sub-contractor is not considered to affect the status of the employer's debt as an asset of the company in liquidation or lead to its being characterised as a flawed asset[53] or one to be equated with a voidable interest but is simply a provision for divestment of an asset which belongs absolutely to the company.

The position where the company is assignee of a contract under an assignment made in breach of a provision prohibiting assignment has already been discussed.[54]

(2) Factors which limit the measure or quantum of the asset

6–12   Such limitations take various forms. First, there are interests in tangible or intangible property which fall short of full ownership. They include the interest of the company as lessee, mortgagor (the interest is limited to the equity of redemption[55]), mortgagee (the interest is limited to a security

[50] *British Eagle International Airlines Ltd v Compagnie Nationale Air France* [1975] 2 W.L.R. 758, discussed below, para.8–12.
[51] *Glow Heating Ltd v Eastern Health Board* [1988] I.R. 110.
[52] *B. Mullan & Sons Contractors Ltd v Ross* (1996) 54 Con. L.R. 163 (Northern Ireland Court of Appeal); *Hitachi Plant Engineering & Construction Ltd v Eltraco International Pte Ltd* [2003] 4 S.L.R. 384 (Singapore Court of Appeal); *Attorney-General v McMillan & Lockwood Ltd* [1991] 1 N.Z.L.R. 53 (New Zealand Court of Appeal).
[53] See below, para.7–16, and Roy Goode, *Legal Problems of Credit and Security* (3rd ed.), para.1–21.
[54] Above, para.6–06.
[55] *Re Pyle Works Ltd* (1890) 44 Ch.D. 534, *per* Cotton L.J. at pp.577–578.

interest) and bailee, *e.g.* under a pledge, lease or hire-purchase agreement. Secondly, there are pure contract rights which are limited in time and come to an end on expiry of the stated period. Thirdly, there are interests shared with others, as where the company holds property as joint tenant or tenant in common. Such shared interests can arise by contract or involuntarily, as in the case of a product produced by a person's wrongful commingling of materials owned by the company with those of the commingler or a third party. Fourthly, there are contractual rights to money which by the terms of the contract are measured by reference to an ultimate credit balance resulting from mutual dealings between the parties. Examples are the right to a balance on a current account, where the debits and credits form a blended fund and the company has no right to any particular credit item, merely to the credit balance (if any) ultimately struck; and the right of the company as dealer in futures, options and foreign currency to such credit balance (if any) in its favour as results from the netting out of the sums payable by and to the company under separate contracts.

The feature which is common to all these rights and interests is that they are limited not by their defeasibility or subjection to countervailing obligations or cross-claims but by the inherent limits to their quantum which are imposed by the factors in question.[56] The distinction is of considerable significance in corporate insolvency law, for there may be circumstances in which a countervailing obligation or right of set-off cannot be asserted against a claim by the liquidator in the name of the company, so that the debtor must pay the company in full and prove in the winding-up for his cross-claim, whereas the liquidator cannot disregard or strike down an inherent limitation on the quantum of the company's asset. A good illustration is furnished by the decision of Millett J. in *Re Charge Card Services Ltd*.[57] In that case the company in liquidation had sold receivables to a factor pursuant to a factoring agreement by the terms of which the company's account with the factor was to be credited with the purchase price of receivables and debited with discounting charges, administration charges and sums payable to the factor under indemnity and recourse provisions. The factor was given the right to retain against any credit balance sums prospectively chargeable to the company as a debit to its account. The company through its liquidator challenged the factor's right of retention in respect of sums not falling to be debited until after the company had gone into voluntary liquidation, asserting that such retention constituted a registrable and unregistered charge on book debts, or alternatively an impermissible set-off of a contingent claim. Millett J. held

---

[56] An old illustration from the law of real property is the distinction between a determinable fee and a fee simple upon condition. The former is an inherent limit on the quantum of the estate, the latter a defeasance of an unlimited estate. See Megarry and Wade, *The Law of Real Property* (6th ed. 2000), paras 3–062 *et seq.*

[57] [1986] 3 All E.R. 289.

that the retention was not a matter of charge or set-off but of account. The company's entitlement was not to the purchase price of a receivable as such but to the ultimate balance on the account after allowing for debits and retentions. The company's claim accordingly failed.

However, it is not always easy to distinguish a contractual limitation on the quantum of an asset from a contractual provision which removes the asset from the general body of creditors. Particular problems have arisen in relation to the netting-out of obligations in a clearing system, an arrangement giving rise to an acute division of opinion in the House of Lords in the *British Eagle* case[58] as to whether the effect of netting arrangements was that a participant's entitlement at one time was only to a net credit (if any) in its favour resulting from the clearing, or whether on the other hand the clearing house arrangements resulted in an impermissible cutting down on liquidation of the debt vested in the company against its counterparty, to the advantage of other participants in the clearing rather than the general body of creditors. We shall return to this issue in a subsequent chapter.[59]

(3) Factors which subject the asset to a countervailing liability or obligation

6–13   The right comprising the asset may be linked to a correlative liability or obligation in such a way that the company cannot enforce the right unless it is willing to discharge the liability or perform the correlative obligation. This position is not altered by the winding-up of the company. So the liquidator cannot compel the other party to a contract which is still executory at the time of winding-up to perform his outstanding obligations unless the liquidator is willing and able to procure the company to perform its own outstanding obligations.[60] Similarly, where prior to the winding-up cash was deposited by the company with a bank on terms that it was to be withdrawable only on discharge of liabilities of the company or a third party to the bank, the liquidator can compel release of the deposit only by procuring the performance of the stipulated condition.[61]

(4) Set-off

6–14   Set-off is an equity which entitles a party, in given conditions, to set off one monetary claim (or a claim reducible to money) against another so as to reduce or extinguish his liability. This is not, strictly speaking, a pre-

---

[58] *British Eagle International Airlines Ltd v Compagnie International Air France* [1975] 2 W.L.R. 758.
[59] See below, Chap.8.
[60] See further on executory contracts the discussion at paras 6–16 *et seq.*
[61] Such a deposit is commonly known as a "flawed asset." See Roy Goode, *Commercial Law* (3rd ed.), p.612.

liquidation equity to which the liquidator takes subject, for the various rights of set-off available under the general law prior to liquidation[62] are automatically displaced by the statutory right of set-off given by the insolvency legislation.[63] This, however, is not dissimilar, the legislation providing that where before the winding-up there have been mutual credits, mutual debts or other mutual dealings between the company and another party, debts owed by the company to the other party are required to be set off against debts owed by him to the company and only the balance (if any) is payable to the liquidator.[64]

Executed contracts

An executed contract is one which has been wholly performed by one party,[65] leaving outstanding only the unperformed obligations of the other party. In contrast to the position with executory contracts,[66] where performance outstanding on one side can only be compelled if the other party is willing and able to give its own counter-performance and the liquidator may decline to perform and, indeed, may disclaim the contract if it is unprofitable,[67] the question of future non-performance and disclaimer cannot arise in relation to executed contracts. The company is entitled to recover or retain all benefits already received under an executed contract without having to perform its obligations. So where a company which is a party to a contract goes into liquidation, then if it is the other party who has fully performed the company is entitled to retain the benefit of his performance and the other party is left to prove for a dividend in the winding-up, whilst if it is the company which has fully performed the liquidator can enforce the other party's outstanding obligations in the usual way. For example, A sells goods to B Company, which goes into liquidation after acquiring ownership and possession but without having paid the price. B Company can retain the goods, leaving A to prove as an unsecured creditor. Is this unfair to A? No, because he neither reserved title until payment nor bargained for any form of security, so he took his chance with other creditors and he ought not to be placed in a better position than he was in prior to the winding-up.[68] Or take the converse case. A buys goods from B Company and pays the price but B Company goes into liquidation

6–15

---

[62] See Chap.8.
[63] See below, paras 8–16 *et seq.*
[64] Insolvency Rules 1986, r.4.90.
[65] Excluding aspects of non-performance which would not justify the other party in terminating the contract or withholding his own performance. See the discussion of executory contracts, below.
[66] See below para.6–16.
[67] See below, paras 6–20 *et seq.*
[68] See R. M. Goode, "Ownership and Obligation in Commercial Transactions," (1987) 103 L.Q.R. 433 at 430.

without having dispatched or delivered the goods. B Company can retain the price, leaving A to prove lodge a proof for either a sum equal to the price, as money paid on a total failure of consideration, or a sum equal to the value of the undelivered goods as damages for breach of contract. This is no more unfair than in the previous example. A parted with his money freely; he takes his chance with other unsecured creditors.[69] If it were A who had been the defaulting party there is again no problem; the liquidator of B Company simply sues A in the usual way. We can thus see that the benefits received by the company under an executed contract constitute an unencumbered asset, as opposed to an asset commingled with a liability.

Executory contracts

6–16   The position is very different in the case of an executory contract. Such a contract is traditionally defined in English textbooks as a contract in which obligations remain to be performed on both sides. A distinguished American commercial lawyer, Professor Vern Countryman, has provided us with a more sophisticated definition which has been accepted as the classic test of an executory contract for the purpose of American bankruptcy law. According to this definition an executory contract is:

> "a contract under which the obligations of both the bankrupt and the other party to the contract are so far unperformed that the failure of either to complete performance would constitute a material breach excusing the performance of the other."[70]

The essential point of an executory contract as thus defined is that each party's right to future performance is linked to and dependent upon that party's own willingness and ability to perform. As another leading authority, Professor Thomas H. Jackson, has aptly put it:

> "Fundamentally, executory contracts ... are nothing more than mixed assets and liabilities arising out of the same transaction."[71]

We have seen earlier that factors which operate to subject an asset of the company to a correlative obligation or liability remain unaffected by

---

[69] A similar view was expressed by the Insolvency Law Review Committee in its Report *Insolvency Law and Practice* (Cmnd. 8558. 1982), para.1052.

[70] "Executory Contracts in Bankruptcy: Part I", 58 Minn. L. Rev. 439, 460 (1973).

[71] *The Logic and Limits of Bankruptcy Law*, p.106. Executory contracts have given rise to remarkably little case law or discussion in England, no doubt because English law has no equivalent to Chap.11 of the United States Federal Bankruptcy Code, where the characterisation of the contract and its consequences have generated a considerable volume of doctrine and jurisprudence. See Jay L. Westbrook, "A Functional Analysis of Executory Contracts" 74 Minn. L. Rev. 227 (1989) for a detailed analysis.

liquidation. If the liquidator wishes to secure performance by the other party of obligations to be performed in the future, he must procure the company to carry out its own future obligations. But unless the other party has acquired proprietary rights under the contract[72] the liquidator is not obliged to procure performance by the company. He can either disclaim the contract if it is unprofitable[73] or simply decline to procure its performance by the company, in which case the other party can exercise any right he may have to terminate the contract for non-performance.[74] In either case the contract comes to an end and the solvent party is left to prove for damages for the loss resulting from the company's breach of contract, against which the company can set off the value of the other party's future performance of which it has been deprived. The result is that the respective values of the two outstanding performances are netted out and the balance is admitted to proof against the company or payable to the company, as the case may be.[75] The position is, of course, different if the contract continues in force, for as we have seen the winding-up does not produce an acceleration of liability in the case of executory contracts.[76] Where the liquidator accepts the benefit of continued performance by the solvent party, the liability of the company in respect of that performance is an expense of the liquidation.[77]

Will the court order specific performance by the company of an **6–17** unperformed obligation to deliver goods under a contract of sale or to convey property which prior to liquidation the company had contracted to sell? The crucial point to bear in mind here is the distinction between real rights and personal rights on liquidation. A party having a real right against the company continues free to assert it; a person having a mere personal claim cannot demand that it be met from the company's general assets, for this would be to offend against the *pari passu* principle by giving the claimant preferential treatment over other unsecured creditors. So the question to be answered in each case is whether the claimant's right to the goods or the property is proprietary or personal. In the case of a contract for the sale of land, the buyer becomes the owner in equity upon exchange of contracts, subject to payment of the price. So the buyer can obtain specific performance of such a contract if he is willing to tender the price.[78]

---

[72] See below.

[73] Insolvency Act 1986, s.178(3). See below, paras 6–16 *et seq.*

[74] Alternatively he can apply for rescission of the contract under s.186 of the Act and prove for any damages that may be awarded.

[75] Where the continuance of the contract does not require active future performance by the creditor, *e.g.* in the case of equipment leased to the company and in its possession, that part of the money obligation which accrues under the contract up to the time of proof or earlier termination or rescission of the contract is provable as a debt, not as damages.

[76] See above, para.3–09; below, para.7–32.

[77] See below, para.7–23.

[78] *Pearce v Bastable's Trustee in Bankruptcy* [1901] 2 Ch. 122; *Re Bastable, Ex p. Trustee* [1901] 2 K.B. 518. The liquidator cannot disclaim the contract in such a case *(ibid.)*. By contrast the court will not normally order specific performance of a contract entered into by the company in liquidation to *purchase* the property (*Holloway v York* (1877) 25 W.R. 627).

On the other hand, goods sold under a contract of sale are considered not to vest in equity in the buyer on the conclusion of the contract. This is because the Sale of Goods Act 1979 is regarded as constituting a complete code for the transfer of property under a contract of sale, assuming that the parties themselves have not expressly created a trust or equitable interest. The buyer obtains the property in the goods at the time when the parties intend it to pass,[79] subject to the goods being identified or ascertained.[80] Until then the buyer has no real rights of any kind, merely a contractual right to transfer of the property and delivery of the goods. So a buyer who has paid the price before ownership or possession have been transferred to him cannot expect to salvage his position by obtaining an order for specific performance against his seller, for since he has no proprietary interest in the goods the effect of an order for specific performance would be to remove an asset from the general body of creditors for no corresponding benefit and give the buyer preferential treatment in breach of the *pari passu* rule.

Suppose now that it is the company which has contracted to buy the property or the goods. In the case of the property the company becomes owner in equity upon exchange of contracts, but its ownership remains incomplete and inchoate until it has paid the price,[81] without which the liquidator cannot compel execution of the conveyance. In the case of a contract for the sale of goods, the company has no interest in the goods at all prior to transfer of the legal title, for the reason given above, and if the liquidator, wishes to obtain delivery he must tender the price.[82] The net effect is therefore the same in the two transactions.

Indemnities and insurance contracts

6–18   A company incurs a liability to one party in respect of which it is entitled to an indemnity from another party. The company becomes insolvent. Does the first party acquire direct rights against the indemnifier? In principle, no. There is no privity of contract between the first party and the indemnifier;[83] the contract or indemnity concluded between the insolvent company and the indemnifier is *res inter alios acta* so far as the third party is concerned, and confers no rights on him. Suppose the liquidator actually collects payment from the indemnifier to cover the amount of the third party's claim. Does not this entitle the third party to treat the sum recovered as

---

[79] Sale of Goods Act 1979, s.17.
[80] *ibid.*, s.16.
[81] See *Shaw v Foster* (1872) L.R. 5 H.L. 321; *Lysaght v Edwards* (1876) 2 Ch.D. 499; *Rayner v Preston* (1881) 18 Ch.D. 1, *per* James L.J. at 13; and R. M. Goode. "Ownership and Obligation in Commercial Transactions" (1987) 103 L.Q.R. 433 at 437, text and n.6.
[82] Sale of Goods Act 1979, s.28.
[83] *Re Harrington Motor Co Ltd* [1928] 1 Ch. 105.

belonging to him in equity? Again, the answer in principle is no, and for the same reason. If a company chooses to insure itself against liability that is entirely its own affair. It owed the third party no duty to insure against the liability to him in the first place; it owes no duty to pay the insured claim out of the insurance proceeds; if solvent, it could equally well do so from its other assets, and the position does not change by reason of the winding-up.[84] The sum recovered under the indemnity does not belong to the claimant, it is an asset of the estate which enures for the benefit of the general body of creditors, of which the claimant is one.[85] This common law principle applies to indemnities in general and insurance contracts in particular. But the Third Parties (Rights against Insurers) Act 1930 provides a statutory exception to what was felt to have been a harsh rule. The effect of that Act in relation to a company in winding-up is that where the company has incurred a liability to a third party against which it is insured under a contract of insurance, then upon the winding-up the company's rights against the insurer vest in the third party.[86] However, there are several potential problems facing a claimant. First, the right of indemnity to which the third party succeeds does not arise until the existence and amount of the insured's liability to the third party have been established by a judgment, arbitral award or agreement. If the insured company has been dissolved without its liability being thus established, there is no right of indemnity to which the third party can succeed.[87] The only remedy then open to the third party is to apply to the court under s.651 of the Companies Act 1985 to declare the dissolution void.[88] Secondly, if the policy requires that the insured "pay to be paid," *i.e.* that the insured shall first pay out the claim against it before it can recoup itself from the insurer, then if the insured goes into liquidation without having paid the claim there is again no right of indemnity capable of being transferred to the third party.[89] Thirdly, in order for the statutory provisions to operate the company must still have a claim under the insurance contract at the time it goes into winding-up. If before that date the claim has been paid, the policy is exhausted as regards that claim, the statutory provisions do not apply and the amount received forms part of the company's general assets.

---

[84] *ibid.*

[85] *ibid.*

[86] Third Parties (Rights against Insurers) Act 1930, s.1(1), subsequently extended by s.149 of the Road Traffic Act 1972. See Malcolm Clarke, *Law of Insurance* (4th ed. 2002), *MacGillivray & Parkington on Insurance Law* (10th ed. 2003), paras 28–11 *et seq.*, 2071 *et seq*; Raoul Colinvaux, *The Law of Insurance* (7th ed. 1997), paras 19–20 *et seq.*, 20–21 *et seq.*

[87] *Bradley v Eagle Star Insurance Co Ltd* [1989] B.C.L.C. 469 (Lord Templeman dissenting); *Post Office v Norwich Fire Insurance Society Ltd* [1967] 2 Q.B. 363.

[88] Such an application must ordinarily be made within two years of the date of dissolution. In the *Eagle Star* case (above, n.87) that period had already expired, so that there was no way of resuscitating the company.

[89] *The Fanti* and *The Padre Island* [1991] 2 A.C. 1.

Liabilities

6–19   That a liability is not an asset may seem too obvious to need stating. Despite this it has been suggested in some cases that where a company draws cheques on an account in overdraft after the presentation of a winding-up petition disposes of property for the purpose of s.127 of the Insolvency Act 1986. It now seems to be settled that in general this is not the case, though there are situations in which an increase in an overdraft erodes what is an asset of the company, as where the overdraft is secured on assets not already fully charged.[90]

2. DISCLAIMER OF ONEROUS PROPERTY[91]

Nature and purpose of disclaimer

6–20   A liquidator's disclaimer is a unilateral repudiation of a contract entered into by the company before winding-up and is designed to bring the contract to an end so as to obviate the need for future performance. The purpose of the disclaimer provisions is twofold: first, to allow the liquidator (whether in a solvent or a solvent liquidation) to complete the administration of the liquidation without being held up by continuing obligations on the company under unprofitable contracts,[92] or continued ownership and possession of assets which are of no value to the estate; and, secondly, in an insolvent liquidation to avoid the continuance of liabilities in respect of onerous property which would be payable as expenses of the liquidation, to the detriment of unsecured creditors. It should be borne in mind that liquidation does not of itself bring a contract to an end, nor is it necessarily a ground for the solvent party to terminate the contract. The liquidator is not obliged to procure the company to continue performance if he considers this would not benefit the company, but neither (apart from the disclaimer provisions) can he compel the other party to treat the contract as at end. It is precisely to resolve such a stalemate, which could inhibit completion of the winding-up, that the law gives the liquidator the right to terminate the contract unilaterally by disclaimer where it is unprofitable.

The power of disclaimer

6–21   The liquidator's ability to repudiate the company's obligations under a contract by the simple device of not performing them is buttressed by wide statutory powers to disclaim onerous property.[93] It is no longer necessary to

---

[90] See below, paras 11–129 *et seq.*
[91] See Totty and Moss, *Insolvency*, Chap.H7.
[92] *ibid.*, para.H7–01.
[93] Insolvency Act 1986, ss.178–182. What constitutes property has been discussed earlier. It will be recalled that a waste management licence held by the company in liquidation is property and can be disclaimed as onerous property by the liquidator. See above, para.6–07.

obtain leave of the court as it was under earlier legislation. A party aggrieved by the disclaimer can apply to the court to reverse the liquidator's decision[94] but the court will not interfere unless the liquidator's action was in bad faith or perverse.[95]

The liquidator cannot disclaim an executed contract,[96] nor are his powers of disclaimer exercisable in respect of a market contract or a contract effected by the exchange or clearing house for the purpose of realising property provided as margin in relation to market contracts,[97] a transfer order or a contract for the purpose of realising security under the settlement finality regulations,[98] or, where a collateral-provider or a collateral-taker within the financial collateral regulations is being wound up, to any financial collateral arrangement within those regulations;[99] and in these cases it is irrelevant whether the contract is executed or executory.

What constitutes onerous property

Onerous property is defined as (a) any unprofitable contract, and (b) any **6–22** other property of the company which is unsaleable or is not readily saleable or is such that it may give rise to a liability to pay money or to perform any other onerous act.[1] In *Transmetro Corp Ltd v Real Investments Pty Ltd*[2] Chesterman J. in the Supreme Court of Queensland set out an instructive summary of the principles to be extracted from prior authority to determine whether a contract was unprofitable:

"A contract is unprofitable for the purposes of section 568 if it imposes on the company continuing financial obligations which may be regarded as detrimental to the creditors, which presumably means that the contract confers no sufficient reciprocal benefit.

Before a contract may be unprofitable for the purposes of the section it must give rise to prospective liabilities.

---

[94] Insolvency Act 1986, s.168(5).
[95] *Re Hans Place Ltd* [1993] B.C.L.C. 768.
[96] This is because if the company has fully performed it has no prospective liabilities, so that the contract is not onerous (see para.6–22) which if it is the solvent party that has fully performed it is entitled to lodge a proof for its claim.
[97] Companies Act 1989, s.164(1). "Market contract" is defined by s.155 of the Act and denotes a contract connected with a recognised investment exchange or recognised clearing house (s.155(1)).
[98] Financial Markets and Insolvency (Settlement Finality) Regulations 1999 (SI 1999/2979), reg.16(1).
[99] Financial Collateral Arrangements (No.2) Regulations 2003 (SI 2003/3226), reg.10(4).
[1] Insolvency Act 1986, s.178(3), which reversed the effect of the decision *Re Potters Oils Ltd (No.1)* [1985] B.C.L.C. 203 that a worthless asset could not be disclaimed if its retention did not bind the possessor to the performance of an onerous act but would merely cost money to remove.
[2] (1999) 17 A.C.L.C. 1314 at para.21.

Contracts which will delay the winding-up of the company's affairs because they are to be performed over a substantial period of time and will involve expenditure that may not be recovered are unprofitable.

No case has decided that a contract is unprofitable merely because it is financially disadvantageous. The cases focus on the nature and cause of the disadvantage.

A contract is not unprofitable merely because the company could have made, or could make, a better bargain."

This summary has been adopted in Australia by Santow J. in *Global Television Pty Ltd v Sportsvision Australia Pty Ltd*[3] and in England by Lloyd J. in *Re SSSL Realisations (2002) Ltd*.[4] It relates exclusively to limb (a) of the definition of onerous property. An example of property within limb (b) is a waste management licence, the continuance of which would involve the liquidator utilising the company's assets to fulfil the conditions of the licence, including the carrying out of any necessary remedial works to remove pollution.[5]

Effect of disclaimer

6–23   The effect of a disclaimer is to determine, as from the date of the disclaimer, the rights, interests and liabilities of the company in or in respect of the property disclaimed.[6] It should be emphasised that the liquidator is not entitled to use his power of disclaimer to disturb accrued rights and liabilities.[7] So he cannot disclaim executed contracts,[8] and he has no right to disclaim a contract entered into by the company to sell land, for this would be to deprive the buyer of his equitable ownership[9]; nor can he disclaim the expired term of a lease, for this is no longer the property of the company.[10] Similarly, the disclaimer of an executory contract has no effect on rights and liabilities already accrued. It does not result in rescission of the contract *ab initio* but operates only to terminate the contract as to liabilities accruing after the time of the disclaimer. By the same token disclaimer does not affect transfers of property to the company. For example, if the company has bought property which proves to be unsaleable, a disclaimer by the liquidator does not terminate or rescind the sale

---

[3] (2000) 35 A.C.S.R. 484, a decision of the Supreme Court of New South Wales.
[4] [2005] 1 B.C.L.C. 1 at paras 64–66.
[5] *Re Celtic Extraction Ltd* [2001] Ch. 475, in which it was conceded that if the licence constituted property, as the Court of Appeal found (see above), then it was onerous property.
[6] Insolvency Act 1986, s.178(4).
[7] *Capital Prime plc v Worthgate Ltd* [2000] 1 B.C.L.C. 647.
[8] See above, n.96.
[9] See above, para.6–17, text and n.78.
[10] *Re No.1 London Ltd* (1991) B.C.C. 118.

contract so as to revest the property in the vendor; its sole effect, in the absence of any other interest in the property, is to vest ownership in the Crown as *bona vacantia*.[11]

The statutory provisions have been construed in a restrictive sense as terminating the company's interest only to the extent necessary to release the company and its property from liability.[12] In the case of a lease the route to this result is sometimes complex. Happily the complexities have been unravelled by the illuminating speech of Lord Nicholls in *Hindcastle Ltd v Barbara Attenborough Association Ltd*.[13] Lord Nicholls, after exploring the history of the disclaimer provisions, pointed out that the purpose of these is to facilitate the administration of the winding-up by freeing the company in liquidation from all liability under the lease. In consequence the lease is deemed to be extinguished as between lessor and lessee, and if they are the only parties then the lease does indeed come to an end and the lessor's reversion is accelerated. But where there are other parties the lease is deemed to continue in force so far as they are concerned, subject only to the qualification that there can be no claim against the lessee. So if a guarantee has been given in respect of the lessee's obligations, the surety remains liable on the notionally preserved lease, and in lieu of his extinguished indemnity can, on discharging his liability to the lessor,[14] prove for the amount he has paid and can also seek an order vesting the lease in him,[15] whilst if a sub-lease has been granted the position of the sub-lessee continues as if the lease were still in force but without rights of action against the lessee. The effect would seem to be the same as if the sub-lessee had become a direct tenant of the lessor on the terms of the sub-lease. If the company is the assignee of a lease, the disclaimer extinguishes its liability on the lease but does not affect the liability of the assignor.[16]

Remedy of party aggrieved by disclaimer

Any person suffering loss or damage in consequence of the operation of the disclaimer is deemed to be a creditor of the company and may prove for the loss or damage in the winding-up.[17] Where the property disclaimed is an

6–24

---

[11] For another example of vesting in the Crown as *bona vacantia*, see *Environment Agency v Hillridge* [2004] 2 B.C.L.C. 358.

[12] *Hindcastle Ltd v Barbara Attenborough Association Ltd* [1988] 1 All E.R. 737; *Warnford Investments Ltd v Duckworth* [1978] 2 All E.R. 517; *Hill v East and West India Dock Co* (1884) 9 App. Cas. 448.

[13] [1997] A.C. 70, overruling *Stacey v Hill* [1901] Q.B. 660.

[14] Until then he is barred from proving by the rule against double proof (see below, para.7–35). This is consistent with s.178(6), by which a person suffering loss in consequence of an operation of the disclaimer can prove to the extent of the loss. A surety does not suffer a loss until he has made payment to the creditor.

[15] Under s.181(2) of the Insolvency Act.

[16] *Warnford Investments Ltd v Duckworth*, above.

[17] Insolvency Act 1986, s.178(6).

unprofitable contract, the disclaimer operates to terminate the contract, and the other party becomes entitled to prove in the winding-up for his loss,[18] which in principle should be calculated on the basis of an accepted repudiation.[19] No time limit is laid down for exercise of the power of disclaimer, so that in the case of a contract the liquidator is in principle free to continue the contract for so long as he is willing and then disclaim it as being unprofitable. However, he loses his right to disclaim if he fails to give notice of disclaimer within 28 days, or such longer period as the court may allow, after service of a notice on him by the other party requiring him to decide whether he will disclaim or not.[20] Loss of the right to disclaim does not mean that the liquidator comes under an obligation to procure continued performance of the contract by the company; its sole effect is that the liquidator loses the right to terminate the contract unilaterally by notice,[21] thus enabling the other party to elect to hold the contract open for future performance. If the liquidator chooses to allow the company to default on its obligations, the contract nevertheless continues in force unless and until the other party exercises a right to treat it as repudiated under general principles of contract law or obtains an order for rescission of the contract, which may be made on such terms as to payment by or to either party of damages for the non-performance of the contract, or otherwise as the court thinks just.[22] Where the contract is of a continuing character, the liquidator fails to disclaim and the other party is able to proceed with performance without the liquidator's co-operation, as where the company holds goods under a leasing agreement or has agreed to pay for advertising services provided by the creditor,[23] that party would seem entitled to prove for each sum payable under the contract as it falls due.

3. SWELLING THE ASSETS AVAILABLE TO CREDITORS

Post-liquidation receipts and recoveries

6–25   The assets coming under the control of the liquidator at the time of winding-up may be augmented subsequently in various ways. The question then arises whether these represent an addition to the company's general

---

[18] *ibid.*, s.178(4).

[19] *Christopher Moran Holdings Ltd v Bairstow* [2000] A.C. 172, reversing the decision of the Court of Appeal sub nom. *Re Park Air Services plc* [1997] 1 W.L.R. 1376. See further below, para.7–33.

[20] Insolvency Act 1986, s.178(5).

[21] *Re Sneezum Ex p. Davis* (1876) 3 Ch.D. 463; *Stead, Hazel & Co v Cooper* [1933] 1 K.B. 840.

[22] Insolvency Act 1986, s.186(1). Where damages are awarded to the party contracting with the company he may prove for these as a debt in the winding-up (s.186(2)). The effect of continuance of the contract on the computation of the sum for which the aggrieved party can prove is discussed in relation to the liabilities of the company at para.7–32.

[23] See, for example, the decision of the House of Lords in *White & Carter (Councils) Ltd v McGregor* [1962] A.C. 413.

assets so as to make them susceptible to capture by a prior assignment or charge, including a fixed or floating charge covering after-acquired property, or whether they are to be treated as held by the liquidator for the benefit of the general body of creditors. Six classes of case in particular deserve attention:

(1) Sums earned on completion of performance by the liquidator

The law distinguishes sums already earned by the company by performance   **6–26**
of its part of the contract prior to winding-up from sums becoming due to the company after winding-up which come into existence only because of the liquidator's voluntary decision to perform. In the former case, the debts arise under an executed contract and are assets of the company which are caught by the assignment or by the after-acquired property clause in the debenture, as the case may be; in the latter, the contract is still executory at the time of winding-up and payment of the debts becomes due through the liquidator's action in adopting the contract and carrying it through to completion. Such debts thus enure for the benefit of the general body of creditors in the winding-up and are not picked up by the assignment or the after-acquired property clause.[24]

The underlying idea is very reasonable. The liquidator has used the money and other resources of the company to carry out the contract; therefore the fruits of performance should belong to the general body of creditors free from the prior interest. In effect, this equates the company in liquidation with the holder of a purchase-money interest who, under the general law, usually enjoys priority over an earlier security interest covering after-acquired property.[25] However, in both the bankruptcy cases in which this principle was applied[26] part of the work necessary to earn payment had been carried out before the bankruptcy; nevertheless the whole of the debt was held to vest in the company free from the prior interest. In neither case does it appear to have been argued that the sum paid to discharge the debt should be divided between the assignee or chargee and the trustee in bankruptcy according to the respective values of the pre-bankruptcy and post-bankruptcy performances. This seems harsh. Suppose that prior to the liquidation the company has performed 90 per cent of the contract assigned or charged, leaving the liquidator only the remaining 10 per cent to complete. Is it reasonable that the entire payment received as consideration for the completed contract should be held for the benefit of the general body of creditors free from the assignment or charge? Would it not be

---

[24] *Re Collins* [1925] Ch. 556; *Wilmot v Alton* [1897] 1 Q.B. 17.
[25] See *Abbey National Building Society v Cann* [1991] 1 A.C. 56 and Roy Goode, *Commercial Law* (3rd ed.). pp.670–671.
[26] See n.24 above.

fairer to allow 10 per cent to be so held and to treat the remaining 90 per cent as caught by the assignment or charge?

(2) Falling in of contingent or reversionary assets

6–27 After the date of the winding-up contingent assets may become actual assets because of the occurrence of the contingency (as where a purchase of property to the company is made conditional on planning permission, which is subsequently granted, for development of the property) and assets not vested in possession may fall into possession, as where a lease granted by the company comes to an end or a prior interest held by another person is discharged. In principle, these form an addition to the company's general assets and are therefore capable of being captured by a prior assignment or charge.

(3) Exercise of a remedy vested in the company before winding-up

6–28 Where a purported contract entered into by the company before winding-up is void, *e.g.* for want of *consensus ad idem*, any property supposedly transferred under it will remain vested in the company. If the company was the transferee, it will have no interest in the property but may have a proprietary claim to any money paid which is still identifiable in the hands of the payee. Where the contract is not void but voidable at the company's instance, *e.g.* for misrepresentation by the other party, the liquidator is entitled to avoid it in the company's name. Where the assets of the company have been misappropriated by its officers, the liquidator can institute misfeasance proceedings in much the same way as the company could have done, except that on liquidation a summary remedy becomes available.[27] In all these cases the recovered assets form part of the general assets of the company and enure for the benefit of an assignee or chargee under an assignment or charge covering assets of the description in question.

(4) Avoidance of a transaction, or reversal of its effect, under the Insolvency Act

6–29 The Insolvency Act contains eight different sets of provisions by which a transaction entered into by the company before winding-up may be avoided, or its effect reversed or ameliorated, because of its impropriety or unfairness to other creditors.[28] In those cases where the transaction is

---

[27] See Insolvency Act 1986, s.212. See below, para.12–12.
[28] For the application or recoveries, see below, para.11–138.

rendered totally void the assets will be susceptible to capture by a prior assignment or charge. In other cases they will enure for the benefit of the general body of creditors except as regards an asset in which the assignee or chargee had a pre-existing interest which was not overreached by the transaction. These statutory provisions are examined in detail in Chapter 11.

(5) Contribution orders for fraudulent and wrongful trading

In the winding-up of a company a director guilty of fraudulent trading[29] or wrongful trading[30] may be ordered to make such contribution (if any) to the company's assets as the court thinks proper.[31] In bringing contribution proceedings the liquidator acts on behalf of the general body of creditors, not in right of the company, so that recoveries are not caught by a prior assignment or charge,[32] nor are they assignable by the liquidator, any purported assignment being champertous.[33]

6–30

(6) Ring-fenced fund from assets subject to a floating charge: the prescribed part

Although debts secured by floating charges have been subordinate to preferential claims for well over a century, the holder of the charge has until recently been entitled to assert its charge in full against ordinary unsecured creditors. In its review of insolvency law the Cork Committee had recommended that 10 per cent of the net proceeds of assets subject to a floating charge should be required to be surrendered to constitute a fund

6–31

---

[29] Insolvency Act 1986, s.213. See below, paras 12–04, 12–16.

[30] *ibid.*, s.214 See below, para.12–22.

[31] *ibid.*, ss.213(2), 214(l). See below, para.12–44.

[32] See below, para.12–46.

[33] *Re Oasis Merchandising Services Ltd* [1998] Ch. 170. For a criticism of the decision as conceptually flawed, see John Armour and Adrian Walters, "Funding Liquidation: A Functional View" (2006) 122 L.Q.R. (publication pending), who pose the question how such recoveries could be administered by the liquidator in pursuance of his statutory duty if they were not assets of the company. The question is a fair one, for there is a long line of authority that such statutory recoveries are held by the liquidator on trust for the general body of creditors, not for the company itself. See, for example, *Re Yagerphone Ltd* [1935] Ch. 392, *per* Bennett J.; *N.W. Robbie & Co Ltd v Witney Warehouse Co Ltd* [1963] 1 W.L.R. 1324, *per* Russell L.J. at 1338. However, though the statutory recoveries are not the property of the company, the liquidator has by necessary implication a power and duty to distribute them among the creditors, for whose benefit the right of recovery was given.

available to ordinary unsecured creditors.[34] This recommendation[35] was not adopted by the government of the day but two decades later finally surfaced in revised form in the new s.176A of the Insolvency Act 1986. Under s.176A where assets are subject to a floating charge created on or after September 15, 2003[36] the liquidator[37] must make a prescribed part of the company's net property available for the satisfaction of unsecured debts and must not distribute that part to the proprietor of a floating charge except in so far as it exceeds the amount required for the satisfaction of unsecured debts. A company's net property is defined as the amount of its property which would, but for the section, be available for the satisfaction of claims of holders of debentures secured by, or holders of any, floating charge created by the company.[38] Since preferential debts have priority over claims secured by a floating charge,[39] it follows that where the company's free assets are insufficient to cover the preferential debts the unpaid balance of these must be met from the floating charge assets before any distribution can be made under the section, so that preferential creditors, having already been provided for, do not participate in the distribution.

Example

6–32   The company's free assets have a net value of £50,000, it also has property worth £100,000 which is subject to a floating charge to secure £90,000 of debt. The preferential debts are £70,000 and ordinary unsecured debts £40,000. Section 176A will apply as follows:

Free assets: £50,000
Preferential debts: £70,000
Shortfall: £20,000 to be met from property proceeds
Company's net property   £80,000

---

[34] *Insolvency Law and Practice: Report of the Review Committee* (Cmnd. 8558, 1982), paras 1538 *et seq*. The holder of the floating charge would not itself be entitled to participate in the 10% fund without surrendering his charge *in toto* but the percentage payable to unsecured creditors would be capped to prevent their percentage of debts received exceeding that of the debenture holder (para.1539).

[35] The origin of which is not generally known-even to members of the Insolvency Law Review Committee! It was the present writer who, while serving on the Legal Panel set up by the Committee, suggested it to a member of the Committee, as a means of taking the heat off the floating charge, while passing the time in conversation on the train home after cerebral stimulation in the shape of a couple of pints of beer at St. Pancras Station. It was somewhat to the writer's astonishment that this idea featured as a recommendation in the Committee's report six months later!

[36] The section does not apply to a floating charge created before September 15, 2003 (Insolvency Act 1986, s.176A(9); Insolvency Act 1986 (Prescribed Part) Order 2003 (SI 2003/2097), art.1).

[37] The section also applies to administrators and receivers in that they must set aside the prescribed part. However, except where an administrator or receiver has power to make a distribution he must hand over the prescribed party to the liquidator to distribute.

[38] Insolvency Act 1986, s.176A(6).

[39] *ibid.*, s.175(2)(a).

The prescribed percentage is then applied to the sum of £80,000 producing £19,000 for unsecured creditors as set out below. The section does not apply (a) where the company's net property is less than the prescribed minimum *and* the liquidator thinks that the cost of making a distribution to unsecured creditors would be disproportionate to the benefits[40]; (b) if and in so far as it is disapplied by a CVA under Part I of the Insolvency Act 1986 or a compromise or arrangement under s.425 of the Companies Act 1985[41]; or (c) the court so orders on the application of the liquidator, administrator or receiver on the ground that the cost of making a distribution to unsecured creditors would be disproportionate to the benefits.[42]

The relevant percentage is that fixed by the Insolvency Act 1986 (Prescribed Part) Order 2003[43] and is as follows:

> Where the company's net property does not exceed £10,000 in value: 50%
>
> Where the company's net property exceeds £10,000 in value then:
>
> 50% of the first £10,000 in value; and
> 20% of the excess;
>
> but with a maximum prescribed part of £600,000.

The minimum value of the company's net property is £10,000, so that if the actual value of the assets subject to the floating charge is below this figure the section will not apply if in the view of the liquidator the cost of making a distribution would be disproportionate to the benefits, whereas if the liquidator is not of that view then 50 per cent of the value will have to be made available from the assets subject to the floating charge. Contrary to the recommendation of the Cork Committee there is no provision capping the distribution so as to ensure that unsecured creditors receive no greater percentage than the debenture holder. In the example given above, the value of the company's net property is £80,000, and the sum to be handed over for the unsecured creditors is £5,000 + £14,000 = £19,000, leaving a balance for the holder of the floating charge of £61,000, so that the chargee suffers a loss of £29,000.

The prescribed part has been calculated so as to offset the gain to the holder of a floating charge resulting from the abolition of Crown preference. Since debts secured by the floating charge will no longer be subordinate to claims of the Crown (*e.g.* for unpaid taxes) the provisions relating to the prescribed part are designed to maintain neutrality for the

---

[40] *ibid.*, s.176A(3).
[41] *ibid.*, s.176A(4).
[42] *ibid.*, s.176A(5).
[43] SI 2003/2097.

holder of a floating charge, leaving it neither better nor worse off than before Crown preference was abolished, while at the same time increasing the return to unsecured creditors.

The prescribed percentage in value is to be made available to unsecured creditors, not to the company itself, which means that it is treated in the same way as recoveries for fraudulent or wrongful trading and is not part of the company's estate so as to be susceptible to capture by an after-acquired property clause in a security agreement.

6–33 So long as the floating charge is in existence and unsecured creditors have not been fully paid the holder is not entitled to participate in the prescribed part. In the unlikely event that unsecured creditors receive 100p in the pound the holder of the floating charge is entitled to the return of the prescribed part or such balance as remains after the liquidator has taken what is necessary to complete the payment to unsecured creditors. Moreover, there is nothing to prevent the chargee from giving up his security and proving as an unsecured creditor.[44] So much is clear. However, there remain a number of questions for which the wording of s.176A is less felicitous.

(i)   Can the holder of the floating charge participate in the prescribed part in relation to a separate debt owed to him which is not secured by the floating charge? It is thought that he can, since the purpose of s.176A is to preclude the chargee from entitlement to a share in the prescribed part in respect of debts secured by the charge.

(ii)   If there are two floating charges, can the holder of one participate in the prescribed part given up by the other? It would seem not. In the first place, s.176A(2)(b) states that the liquidator shall not distribute the prescribed part to the proprietor of "a" floating charge. If it had been intended to restrict that provision to the holder of the particular floating charge from whose security the prescribed part comes s.176A(2)(b) would surely have said so. Secondly, in the typical case most if not all of the assets covered by one floating charge will also be covered by the other, so that to allow one holder to participate in the other's surrendered prescribed part would be to give him through the back door an interest in the same fund that he could not obtain directly as the party surrendering that fund.

(iii)   What happens if there are two floating charges and the floating charge that has priority exhausts the charged assets? If, as has been suggested above, the existence of the subordinate charge precludes the holder from participating in the prescribed part surrendered by the senior floating chargee, the sensible course is for the holder of the junior charge to surrender it, since it is valueless anyway, and come in as an unsecured creditor.

---

[44] Which in at least one case may be to his advantage. See, (iii) below.

(iv) If the holder of the floating charge realises his security before the prescribed part has been distributed, can he then participate as an unsecured creditor for any balance owed to him? Again, it is thought that the answer is no. To allow the chargee to come in at this stage *qua* unsecured creditor would be to upset the neutrality which s.176A is designed to provide. Moreover, the section could not be made to work in that situation, for it envisages a distribution to the holder of the floating charge after unsecured creditors have been fully paid, whereas if the chargee shares the prescribed part *pari passu* with other creditors this could never happen. Finally, it would be odd if the floating chargee's position depended on whether, at the time of distribution of the prescribed part, he had or had not realised his security.

4. ASSETS BELONGING TO THIRD PARTIES

Assets held by the company but belonging solely to third parties under transactions which are not subject to avoidance or capture pursuant to the statutory provisions referred to above are not available for the company's creditors. This applies both to assets which never belonged to the company and to those in which the company had an interest that has come to an end, for example, leases or rental agreements that have expired, contracts that have been terminated. Three cases are deserving of particular mention, namely assets held by the company on trust, assets subject to a security interest and goods in the possession of the company as buyer under a contract reserving title to the seller until payment.[45]

6–34

Assets held on trust

(1) Trust assets do not form part of the estate

Where the company holds an asset on trust for a third party, this does not form part of its estate so as to be available for creditors. Trust property is excluded whether the trust is express,[46] implied,[47] constructive or resulting.[48]

6–35

---

[45] For an instructive analysis of a broad range of issues encompassing the second and third of these issues, see William Goodhart and Gareth Jones, "The Infiltration of Equitable Doctrine into English Commercial Law" (1980) 43 M.L.R. 489.

[46] *Re English & American Insurance Co Ltd* [1994] 1 B.C.L.C. 649; *Re Kayford Ltd* [1975] 1 All E.R. 604.

[47] *Re Fleet Disposals Ltd* [1995] B.C.L.C. 345; *Re C.A. Pacific Finance Ltd* [2000] 1 B.C.L.C. 494.

[48] *Barclays Bank Ltd v Quistclose Investments Ltd* [1970] A.C. 567.

Thus if money is lent to a company for a specific purpose which is frustrated by the advent of winding-up, there is a resulting trust in favour of the lender[49]; if a bank by mistake makes a payment twice over to another bank on behalf of a customer and the payee bank goes into liquidation, the mistaken payment can be recovered as money impressed with a constructive trust[50]; if money paid by a mail order customer in advance when ordering goods is, on the advice of accountants concerned about the financial position of the company, paid into a trust account to be released only on delivery of the goods, and the company goes into liquidation, money held in the account for customers to whom goods had not been delivered is held on trust for them and does not form part of the company's general assets.[51] Where the assets administered by the liquidator include assets held by the company as trustee, the costs attributable to the administration of those assets should be borne by the trust fund, not by the company's own assets.[52]

(2) Assets which cease to be trust assets

6–36   Assets initially subject to a trust may cease to be so as the result of authorised dealings by the trustee. Thus in the case of a trading trust established by a trust instrument which authorises the trustees to carry on trade for the benefit of the beneficiaries any disposition of a trust asset, whether absolutely or by way of security, falling within the actual or apparent authority of the trustees binds the beneficiaries, so that the asset is lost to the trust fund (in the case of an absolute disposition) or held by the trustees subject to the security interest (in the case of a disposition by way of security), and any proceeds of the disposition received by the trustees

---

[49] *Barclays Bank Ltd v Quistclose Investments Ltd above* (loan for the purpose of paying a dividend to shareholders); *Carreras Rothmans Ltd v Freeman Mathews Treasure Ltd* [1985] 1 All E.R. 155 (payments to advertising agency by client for sole purpose of discharging the agency's obligations to media creditors); *Re EVTR Ltd* [1987] B.C.C. 389 (payment to be used for purchase of equipment). As to the first of these cases, see Sir Peter Millett, "The Quistclose Trust: Who Can Enforce It?" (1985) 101 L.Q.R. 264.

[50] *Chase Manhatten Bank NA v Israel-British Bank (London) Ltd* [1979] 3 All E.R. 1025. But the authority of this decision has been weakened by the criticism made by Lord Browne-Wilkinson in *Westdeutsche Landesbank Girozentrale v Islington London Borough Council* [1996] A.C. 669 at 715.

[51] *Re Kayford Ltd* [1975] 1 W.L.R. 279. The decision is controversial but in my view correct. There has been much debate about protection for the prepaying buyer. See, for example, Thomas H. Jackson and Anthony T. Kronman, "A Plea for the Financing Buyer", 85 Yale L.J. 1 (1975); Aleck Dadson, "A Fresh Plea for the Financing Buyer" (1985–86) 11 C.B.L.J. 171; Martin Boodman, "The Prepaying Buyer: Another Perspective" (1986) 11 C.B.L.J. 257; Office of Fair Trading, *The Protection of Consumer Prepayments: A Discussion Paper* (1984); Ogus and Rowley, *Prepayments and Insolvency* (OFT Occasional Paper, 1984). For a good discussion incorporating selected materials see Graham Moffat. *Trusts Law: Text and Materials* (3rd ed. 1999), pp.586–592. Under s.20A of the Sale of Goods Act 1979 prepaying buyers of an unidentified part of a bulk now acquire a proportionate interest in the bulk pending delivery.

[52] See above, para.3–03.

will become part of the trust fund in place of the original asset. This point was well brought out in the *Space Investments* case,[53] where the settlement deed authorised the trustee bank (*inter alia*) to open and maintain savings or current accounts with any bank, including itself. The bank accordingly placed trust moneys on deposit with itself and subsequently went into insolvent liquidation. On an application to the Supreme Court of the Bahamas to determine the question whether the trust creditors ranked in priority to the general creditors the trial judge ruled in favour of the trust creditors, and this decision was upheld by the Court of Appeal of the Bahamas but reversed on further appeal to the Privy Council. It was held by the Privy Council that since the deposit of trust funds with the bank was authorised by the settlement and under well-established principles of banking law became the general moneys of the bank, whose obligations were those of a debtor, not a trustee, the beneficiaries ranked *pari passu* with other unsecured creditors and did not enjoy any special status or priority. The funds in question ceased to be impressed with a trust as soon as they were deposited.

(3) Trust of money presupposes an identifiable fund

A trust can exist only in relation to an identifiable asset or fund; a purely **6–37** personal monetary obligation does not create a trust. The point is an elementary one but is sometimes overlooked because the parties are misled by a conventional label attached to a particular form of money obligation. The typical case is the so-called retention fund provided by standard term building contracts under which the employer retains a small percentage of each progress payment as a safeguard against non-completion and defects and undertakes to hold the retention moneys on trust for the contractor. If the employer goes into liquidation after completion of the works the contractor may demand release of the "fund" as money held on trust for the contractor. But in reality there is no fund; all that the employer has done is to deduct the contractually agreed percentage from payments he would otherwise have made. In other words, the employer has not created a fund at all but merely withheld payment, so that there is no trust asset to which the contractor can have recourse.[54] The effect of the contractual provision is to impose on the employer a personal obligation to appropriate and set aside as a trust fund the amount of retention moneys withheld[55] and the court will usually grant a mandatory injunction to require such fund to

---

[53] *Space Investments Ltd v Canadian Imperial Bank of Commerce Trust Co (Bahamas) Ltd* [1986] 3 All E.R. 75.
[54] *Re Jartay Developments Ltd* (1983) 22 Build. L.R. 134; *MacJordan Construction Ltd v Bookmount Erostin Ltd* [1992] B.C.L.C. 350.
[55] *Rayack Construction v Lampeter Meat Co Ltd* (1979) 12 Build. L.R. 30.

be established in order to protect the contractor against the employer's insolvency.[56] But a mere obligation to establish the fund does not suffice, for until the obligation has been performed there is no *res* to which the trust can attach, and the court will not grant a mandatory injunction after the employer has gone into liquidation.[57]

Assets subject to a security interest

6–38 Assets do not belong to the company to the extent that they are subject to a mortgage or other security interest; all the company has is the equity of redemption.[58]

Goods supplied under reservation of title

6–39 Where goods are supplied to a company under a contract of sale which reserves title to the seller until payment and the company goes into liquidation before it has paid the full price, the goods remain the property of the seller unless and until the liquidator completes payment; and if he fails to do so the seller may repossess the goods. Contracts of sale often seek to extend reservation of title in one or more of three ways. The first is by using it to secure not only the price of the particular goods sold but other obligations of the buyer under prior or subsequent contracts. This has been upheld as a perfectly legitimate term of a sale contract by which the parties exercise their freedom to agree upon the conditions on which the property is to pass.[59] A second method is to extend the retention of title to proceeds of authorised resales. In the *Romalpa* case[60] it was held by the Court of Appeal, affirming the decision of the trial judge, that a reservation of title clause may also be validly extended to cover the proceeds of sale of goods sold by the buyer with the seller's authority and as his agent. However, relying on the fact that certain crucial concessions were made in that case courts in subsequent cases have been able to distinguish *Romalpa* virtually out of existence, and a retention of title to proceeds will almost invariably be struck down as a charge on book debts which is void for want of registration under s.395 of the Companies Act 1985.[61] In a third type of

---

[56] *ibid., Concorde Construction Co Ltd v Colgan Ltd* (1984) 29 Build. L.R. 120.

[57] *Re Jartay Developments Ltd* (1983) 22 Build: L.R. 134.

[58] *Re Pyle Works Ltd* (1890) 44 Ch.D. 534, *per* Cotton L.J. at pp.577–578.

[59] *Armour v Thyssen Edelstahlwerke A.G.* [1991] 2 A.C. 339; *Clough Mill Ltd v Martin* [1984] 3 All E.R. 982.

[60] *Aluminium Industrie vaassen BV v Romalpa Aluminium Ltd* [1976] 1 Lloyd's Rep. 443.

[61] See, for example. *E. Pfeiffer-Weineinkauf GmbH v Arbuthnot Factors Ltd* [1988] 1 W.L.R. 150; *Compaq Computers Ltd v Abercorn Group Ltd* [1992] B.C.C. 484; *Modelboard Ltd v Outer Box Ltd (in liquidation)* [1993] B.C.L.C. 623.

extension the reservation of title clause is made to cover products resulting from the commingling of the goods with other goods. Usually this too will be struck down as an unregistered charge,[62] since title cannot be reserved to that which the seller never owned.[63]

5. EFFECT OF DISSOLUTION OF COMPANY

When a company is dissolved, its legal existence comes to an end, and any undistributed assets, together with any assets thereafter coming into the hands of the company, pass to the Crown as *bona vacantia*,[64] though application may be made to the court to restore the company to the register[65] so as to enable the assets to be collected and distributed.   **6–40**

---

[62] Registrable under s.396(1)(c) of the Companies Act 1985 as a charge which, if executed by an individual, would have been registrable as a bill of sale.
[63] *Clough Milt Ltd v Martin*, above; *Re Peachdart Ltd* [1984] 1 Ch. 131.
[64] Companies Act 1985, s.654.
[65] *ibid.*, s.651.

Chapter 7

The Proof, Valuation and Ranking of Claims in Winding-Up

Introduction

In Chapter 6 we defined and described the assets of the company available   7–01
for distribution to its creditors. The present chapter looks at the liabilities
side of the company's balance sheet and discusses the treatment of claims
in the winding-up and the order of distribution of assets among the
competing creditors.[1]

1. THE PARI PASSU PRINCIPLE OF DISTRIBUTION

The principle stated

The most fundamental principle of insolvency law is that of *pari passu*   7–02
distribution, all creditors participating in the common pool in proportion to
the size of their admitted claims. In the case of voluntary winding-up this
principle is expressed in the Insolvency Act itself.

> "Subject to the provisions of this Act as to preferential payments, the
> company's property in a voluntary winding up shall on the winding up be
> applied in satisfaction of the company's liabilities *pari passu* . . ."[2]

In the case of compulsory winding-up the principle is found in the
Insolvency Rules.

---

[1] The phrase "distribution of assets" does not mean distribution *in specie* but is the
conventional shorthand for distribution by way of dividend of the net proceeds resulting
from dispositions of the assets by the liquidator.
[2] Insolvency Act 1986, s.107.

"Debts other than preferential debts rank equally between themselves in the winding up."[3]

A similar principle applies in administration,[4] though its application is more limited. It is this principle of rateable distribution which marks off the rights of creditors in a winding-up from their pre-liquidation entitlements. Prior to winding-up[5] each creditor is free to pursue whatever enforcement measures are open to him. Where self-help (*e.g.* by repossession of goods, realisation of security or exercise of a right of set-off) is not available the creditor must have recourse to legal process and, if the debtor company fails to satisfy a judgment voluntarily, enforce the judgment by execution against the company's assets or income. The rule here, in the absence of an insolvency proceeding, is that the race goes to the swiftest. The creditor initiating the earliest execution has first bite at the cherry and whatever is left is available for the next in line. A creditor who leaves it too late finds he has a *brutum fulmen*—there is a judgment in his favour but no assets against which to enforce it. Liquidation puts an end to the race. The principle first come first served gives way to that of orderly realisation of assets by the liquidator for the benefit of all unsecured creditors and distribution of the net proceeds *pari passu*. The *pari passu* principle is all-pervasive. Its broad effect is to strike down all agreements which have as their object or result the unfair preference of a particular creditor by removal from the estate on winding-up of an asset that would otherwise have been available for the general body of creditors.[6] The principle is buttressed by related rules on preference by which pre-liquidation payments and transfers made in the run-up to winding-up may be avoided.[7]

Pari passu principle is primarily relevant to winding-up

7–03 Since the *pari passu* principle is concerned to ensure an equitable distribution of the company's estate among its creditors, its application as a mandatory rule is largely confined to liquidation, for this is the only collective insolvency process which has as its primary objective the distribution of assets among the general body of creditors in accordance with a statutory *pari passu* rule that cannot be excluded by contract.[8] It is true that an administrator can now make distributions with leave of the court under

---

[3] Insolvency Rules 1986, r.4.181(1).
[4] *ibid.*, r.2.69. See below, para.10–81.
[5] Or administration. See Chap.10.
[6] It is true that the approach would be the same whatever the distribution rule. But as pointed out earlier (above, para.3–10) the reference to the *pari passu* principle in this context is simply shorthand to describe what is in fact the central rule of distribution.
[7] See below, Chap.11.
[8] See below, para.7–06.

Sch.B1 to the Insolvency Act 1986,[9] and that the Insolvency Rules apply the *pari passu* principle to administration,[10] but in practice most distributions are likely to be made pursuant to a company voluntary arrangement under Part I of the Insolvency Act or a compromise or arrangement under s.425 of the Companies Act 1985 and will be governed by the terms of those arrangements, which have to be approved by the requisite majority of creditors, rather than by any *a priori* rule of distribution. For the same reason the *pari passu* principle has no necessary application to informal work-outs. No doubt in the great majority of these cases a distribution to ordinary unsecured creditors will be expected to follow the order of priorities that would apply in a winding-up, but there is no rule of law precluding creditors from approving an arrangement on a different basis.[11] Moreover, in many cases there will be no free assets to distribute.

The *pari passu* principle does not in any event apply to administrative receivership, for this is not a true collective insolvency proceeding[12] and if the receiver, after meeting out of floating charge assets payments to preferential creditors, the costs of preserving and realising the assets, his other expenses and remuneration and the claims of his debenture holders, has a surplus, his duty is to pass it to any subsequent secured creditor or, if none, then to the company; he has no general power of distribution.

The *pari passu* rule: its significance in practice

I have described the *pari passu* principle of distribution as fundamental and all-pervasive. This, at least, is the theory of insolvency law. In practice, as was pointed put by the Cork Committee many years ago,[13] a rateable distribution among creditors is rarely achieved. There are three main reasons for this.   **7–04**

First, the principle is in general confined to assets of the company and does not affect creditors having rights *in rem*. These include secured creditors, who under the liberal regime allowed by English law can take security for present and future indebtedness over future as well as present assets, including fixed charges over future debts and floating charges over all assets; suppliers of goods under contracts which reserve title until payment, a technique now in widespread use; and third parties for whom the company holds assets on trust or who have proprietary tracing rights in

---

[9] Insolvency act 1986, Sch.B1, para.65.
[10] Insolvency Rules 1986, r.2.69.
[11] Section 4 of the Insolvency Act 1986 precludes approval of a proposed CVA which would affect the enforcement rights of a secured creditor or the priority of a preferential debt but leaves the creditors free to agree on a distribution among unsecured creditors otherwise than on a *pari passu* basis.
[12] See para.1–23.
[13] *Insolvency Law and Practice* (Cmnd. 8558), para.1396.

equity to assets in the possession or under the control of the company. The effect of these rights *in rem* is substantially to reduce the corpus of assets available for unsecured creditors.

Secondly, the liquidator takes the assets subject to equities affecting them, such as a right to avoid a transaction for misrepresentation or undue influence.

Thirdly, huge chunks of what free assets remain have to be applied to meet claims ranking in priority to those of the ordinary unsecured creditor. These embrace (a) expenses of the liquidation, which are "pre-preferential" liabilities payable in full (rather than having to be proved) and include the liquidator's expenses and remuneration, which can be substantial; and (b) various claims of employees.[14] When all these have been satisfied, the dividend produced by what is left is often pitifully small.[15] The effect is largely to frustrate a primary objective of the insolvency process and to deprive the general body of creditors of any significant interest in the winding-up process.[16] Yet the *pari passu* principle retains some practical importance, if only in a negative sense, in that it may have the effect of invalidating pre-liquidation transactions by which a creditor hopes to secure an advantage over his competitors, and where it does have this effect it may result in an expansion of the assets available for distribution.[17] It is thus necessary to examine the scope of the principle in some detail.

Debts covered by the *pari passu* principle

7–05   The *pari passu* principle applies only (a) to provable debts payable to the general body of creditors,[18] and (b) within each separate class of preferential, ordinary and deferred creditors.[19]

The *pari passu* rule may not be excluded by contract

7–06   A contractual provision purporting to exclude the principle of *pari passu* distribution, whether in bankruptcy or in winding-up, is void.

> "... a man is not allowed, by stipulation with a creditor, to provide for a different distribution of his effects in the event of bankruptcy from that which the law provides."[20]

---

[14] See below, para.7–27.

[15] Though it may be somewhat enhanced by recoveries in respect of void or voidable transactions (below, Chap.11) and under the new provisions requiring a percentage of the net realisations of assets subject to a floating charge to be surrendered for the benefit of unsecured creditors (see below, para.6–31).

[16] A point I developed more fully in "The Death of Insolvency Law" (1980) 3 Co. Law. 123.

[17] See below, paras 7–14 *et seq.*

[18] See below, para.7–32.

[19] See below, para.7–42.

[20] *Ex p. Mackay* (1873) 8 Ch. App. 643, *per* James L.J. at 647.

". . . a person cannot make it a part of his contract that, in the event of his bankruptcy, he is then to get some additional advantage which prevents the property being distributed under the bankruptcy laws."[21]

But as we shall see the *pari passu* principle, broad though it is, does admit of some exceptions.[22]

2. IMPACT OF THE PARI PASSU *PRINCIPLE*

Arrangements which do not offend against the *pari passu* principle

We shall come to the exceptions to the *pari passu* principle a little later.[23]   **7–07**
At this point it is worth noting the various types of arrangement which are not considered to offend against the principle of *pari passu* distribution at all. These include subordination agreements, provisions for acceleration of liability on winding-up, determinable interests in the sense of interests which automatically come to an end on the expiry of a given period or the occurrence of a specified event, limited interests and contract rights terminable by a party on notice, pre-emption provisions in articles of association of a company providing for the compulsory transfer at a reasonable price of the shares of any member that goes into liquidation or bankruptcy, and rules of an exchange by which members who hold shares in the exchange by virtue of their membership cannot receive consideration for any transfer and have to surrender the shares on cessation of member-ship on account of insolvency or for any other reason.. These cases apart, it is probably not possible to set out an exhaustive statement of the circumstances in which a provision for termination of an interest on insolvency is void.

> ". . . it is not possible to discern a coherent rule, or even an entirely coherent set of rules, to enable one to assess in any particular case whether such a provision (a 'deprivation provision') falls foul of the principle . . . and perhaps not surprisingly, it is not entirely easy to reconcile the conclusions, and indeed the reasoning, in some of the cases."[24]

With this caveat, we can turn to the established exceptions to the rule of invalidity.

---

[21] *Ex p. Mackay* (1873) 8 Ch. App. 643, *per* Mellish L.J. at 648.
[22] See below, paras 7–19 *et seq.*
[23] Below, para.7–19.
[24] *Money Markets Ltd v London Stock Exchange Ltd* [2002] 1 W.L.R. 1150, *per* Neuberger J. at para.117.

Subordination agreements[25]

7–08   Though in general creditors are free to agree among themselves that the secured or unsecured claim of one of them shall be subordinated to the claims of the others, there was until relatively recently concern that in the event of winding-up a subordination agreement might be held void as running counter to the mandatory provisions of the insolvency legislation. This was thought to be a possible consequence of the decision of the House of Lords in *National Westminster Bank Ltd v Halesowen Presswork and Assemblies Ltd*[26] to the effect that rules for the administration of assets in winding-up embody not merely private rights which creditors are free to vary or waive but rules of public policy for the orderly administration of estates. In the *Halesowen* case it was held that a debtor could not contract out his statutory set-off. There was a fear that, by parity of reasoning, a creditor could not subordinate his claim in winding-up to a claim of equal rank, for this would (so it was argued) infringe the *pari passu* rule in much the same way as the IATA clearing house arrangement was held to do by a majority decision of the House of Lords in the *British Eagle* case.[27] Conflicting decisions had been given in other parts of the Commonwealth, some courts holding that a subordination agreement contravened the mandatory rules of insolvency law,[28] while others considered that such an agreement had no effect on other creditors and was unobjectionable.[29]

In England there are now two decisions in favour of the validity of subordination agreements. In the first, *Re Maxwell Communications Corp (No.2)*,[30] Vinelott J., after reviewing all the relevant authorities, concluded that the principle laid down in *Halesowen* applied only to those rules the infringement of which would give one creditor an advantage denied to other creditors. A subordination agreement would not have this effect.[31] To deny such an agreement validity could have the most serious consequences, particularly in view of the widespread recognition of the efficacy of such agreements in insolvency in foreign jurisdictions and of the fact that in many cases a company could not continue to trade and obtain credit unless some of its creditors, which might include the company's parent, were willing to subordinate their indebtedness. In the second case, *Re SSSL Realisations (2002) Ltd*,[32] Lloyd J. held that the validity of a subordination

---

[25] See generally Philip R. Wood, *The Law of Subordinated Debt*; E. Ferran, *Company Law and Corporate Finance*, Chap.16.
[26] [1972] A.C. 785, Lord Cross of Chelsea dissenting.
[27] *British Eagle International Airlines Ltd v Compagnie Nationale Air France* [1975] 2 All E.R. 390.
[28] See, for example, *Re Orion Sound Ltd* (1979) 2 N.Z.L.R. 574.
[29] See, for example, *Horne v Chester & Fein Property Developments Pty Ltd* (1987) 11 A.C.L.R. 485.
[30] [1994] 1 B.C.L.C. 1.
[31] On the contrary, it could have precisely the opposite effect of benefiting all the ordinary unsecured creditors, not merely the creditor in whose favour the subordination was agreed.
[32] [2005] 1 B.C.L.C. 1.

agreement was not affected by the fact that the subordinated creditor was also in insolvent liquidation. To these considerations one might add that the Insolvency Rules expressly recognise the right of a creditor to assign his right of dividend to another creditor,[33] which would typically occur in cases where the first creditor had agreed to be subordinated to the second. It would therefore be strange if the subordination agreement pursuant to which such an assignment was made were to be held invalid.

Provisions for acceleration of liability on winding-up

In the case of an executed-contract, winding-up automatically accelerates the debt,[34] subject to a statutory discount to allow for the acceleration when a dividend distribution comes to be made.[35] But to cover cases where the contract is still executory at the time of winding-up, so that the liquidator has the option to adopt it, the other party may seek to provide in the contract for acceleration of the company's liability in the event of its going into liquidation. In this case the acceleration clause would appear to be of no effect, for if the liquidator were to adopt the contract he would have to use the company's assets to make payment before the company had received the benefit against which the payment was to have been made, whilst if he did not adopt it the other party would be in the position of being able to prove for a supposed debt in respect of which payment had not been earned. This conclusion is reinforced by r.4.92 of the Insolvency Rules, under which a creditor may prove for rent and other payments of a periodical nature only so far as due and unpaid up to the date the company went into liquidation.[36]

7–09

Interests limited by reference to solvency

Where an interest is granted which by its terms is not absolute but is limited in time so as to come to an end when the company goes into winding-up, it is not considered to offend against any principle of insolvency law, for the interest was never the outright property of the company. This distinction between a "determinable interest" and an outright transfer with a provision for divestment on winding-up is a very fine one and has been strongly

7–10

---

[33] Insolvency Rules 1986, r.11.11(1), which requires a liquidator who receives notice of the assignment to pay the dividend to the assignee.

[34] See above, para.3–09.

[35] Insolvency Rules 1986, r.11.13(2).

[36] If the lease or contract under which the rent or other periodical sum is payable continues in force, so that the company receives the *quid pro quo* for the payment, the creditor can adjust his proof so as to claim for each further sum as it falls due. See above, para.6–16, below para.7–32.

criticised but represents the present law. It is discussed a little later in the context of provisions for divestment of ownership on winding-up.[37]

Provision for termination on winding-up of interest limited by reference to factors other than insolvency

7–11   This category differs from that just considered in that the interest granted is by its nature limited in time irrespective of the question of solvency, as in the case of a lease. However, the same considerations apply. English law distinguishes sharply between agreements by which a party who has transferred an *absolute* interest in an asset to another is given the right to *recapture* the asset on the transferee's insolvency and agreements entitling a party to *terminate* a *limited* interest conferred on another, or a contract with another not creating any interest, if that other becomes insolvent. Agreements of the former kind are considered to remove from the debtor's estate property which should be available for the general body of creditors[38]; agreements of the latter kind simply define bankruptcy or liquidation as the event on which the interest that has been granted ends or becomes terminable. Where the termination of a limited interest is automatic there is no removal of an asset from the estate, because the former asset no longer exists; where the termination is at the discretion of the grantor of the interest then the terminability of the interest is an inherent qualification of its quantum which binds the trustee or liquidator and creditors as it binds the bankrupt or company in liquidation. *A fortiori* termination of a contract conferring purely personal rights is not considered a breach of the *pari passu* principle.

It is generally assumed that a provision for forfeiture of a lease on winding-up appears not to contravene the *pari passu* principle, since it is merely a qualification of the lessee's estate,[39] of the same kind as that discussed above. The validity of such forfeiture clauses seems to be assumed by s.146(9) and (10) of the Law of Property Act 1925, which deal with relief against forfeiture in cases where bankruptcy of the lessee is a condition of the forfeiture.[40] So the lessee's liquidator takes the lease as he finds it; forfeiture is not conceptually a divestment of an asset vested in the lessee but rather an event which marks the end of the duration of the lessee's estate.

It is generally assumed that a similar principle applies to provisions for the termination of a lease or hiring of chattels, or, indeed, of any kind of agreement, upon the bankruptcy or liquidation of a party. It is true that the

---

[37] See below, para.7–14.
[38] See below, para.7–16.
[39] *Doe d. Hunter v Galliers* (1787) 2 Term Rep. 133.
[40] They also apply even where the lease is expressly drawn as a determinable interest ending on a breach of covenant by the lessee (Law of Property Act 1925, s.146(7)).

doctrine of estates does not apply to chattels; nevertheless the concept of a terminable interest is equally capable of application to limited possessory interests in chattels and, indeed, to pure contract rights.

There is, however, an unreported county court decision in which a provision for termination of a hire-purchase agreement on bankruptcy was held void as depriving the estate of an asset, contrary to bankruptcy law.[41] In policy terms there is much to be said for the approach adopted in that case and, indeed, for its extension to the termination of pure contract rights. The distinction between recapture of an asset transferred outright and termination of a limited interest is redolent of the highly artificial distinction referred to later[42] between a determinable fee and a fee simple upon a condition. The effect of a termination provision is that a lease or contract right which immediately prior to liquidation constituted an asset of the company is removed from the reach of the general body of creditors so that in form and in substance, the termination operates as a forfeiture.[43] Moreover, the extinction of a lease expands the lessor's interest in the leased property, converting it from a reversionary interest encumbered by the lease into an unencumbered interest in possession, so that in substance, if not in law, there is a transfer of an asset from the company's estate to that of the lessor. In the case of a contract not relating to property of any kind it is nevertheless the case that the contract right itself is an asset whose termination reduces the estate of the company and frees the other party from the burden of the contract. American bankruptcy law roundly declares *ipso facto* termination clauses ineffective, however they are formulated.[44] This is a sound rule and one which English law could sensibly follow. The solvent party's default remedies in the event of breach by the company remain exercisable in just the same way against the liquidator as against the company itself and there seems no good reason why the advent of winding-up should by itself confer a windfall on the solvent party at the expense of creditors.[45]

It is, indeed, a matter for some astonishment that the validity of contractual provisions for termination of rights on winding-up has yet to be authoritatively determined.

Pre-emption provisions in articles of association

The common pre-emption provision in articles of association of a company **7–12** requiring a member to transfer its shares on becoming bankrupt or going into liquidation is not open to attack on the ground of repugnancy or

---

[41] *Re Piggin, Dicker v Lombank Ltd* (1962) 112 L.J. 424.
[42] See below, para.7–14.
[43] As is shown by the fact that in *Transag Haulage Ltd v DAF Finance plc* [1994] B.C.C. 356 the court exercised its equitable discretion to grant relief against forfeiture in relation to a hire-purchase agreement which had come to an end pursuant to a provision of the agreement making it terminable on the appointment of a receiver.
[44] Bankruptcy Code, s.541(c)(1). At common law the principle was confined to leases.
[45] There are, however, necessary exceptions to be made in relation to market contracts. As to the special treatment of these, see paras 1–29 *et seq.*

inconsistency with insolvency law so long as the provision applies to all members and the price is either fair or, where the restrictions on transfer make it impossible to establish a market value, is not shown to be less than the price that would have been obtained without the insolvency.[46]

Provision for termination on winding-up of interest annexed to membership status

7–13   The typical case concerns the rules of an exchange by which the holding of shares in the exchange is dependent on membership and the member is not entitled to receive any consideration on transfer of the shares and must surrender them without consideration on cessation of membership on winding-up or bankruptcy or for any other reason. Such a provision is valid in that the interest is inseparable from membership and has no value capable of being realised by the company.[47] The decision of Neuberger J. in *Money Markets International Stockholders Ltd v London Stock Exchange Ltd*[48] provides a good illustration.

> The claimant, a member firm of the London Stock Exchange, held in that capacity a single 'B' share in the Exchange carrying with it voting rights and a proportionate interest in the assets held by the Exchange in the event of its being wound up. Under the rules of the Exchange 'B' shares could only be transferred to and held by member firms, no consideration could be paid or given for any transfer and the directors could direct a member firm to dispose of all or any of its 'B' shares. If a 'B' shareholder ceased to be a member or became bankrupt or if a disposal was directed, the shareholder was bound to transfer its shares to other members without consideration, and they were entitled and obliged so to acquire them, when called upon by the directors to do so. Following its failure to honour stock exchange contracts the claimant ceased to be a member and went into voluntary liquidation. Each 'B' share then had a value of £2.8 million. The claimant instituted proceedings for an order for reinstatement and as member or alternatively compensation for the loss of its 'B' share on the ground that the divestiture removed an asset from the reach of its creditors, contrary to a basic principle of insolvency law. *Held*: though the effect of the provision for transfer was indeed to divest the claimant of an interest in property that would otherwise be available to creditors it did not contravene any rule of insolvency law, for the

---

[46] *Borland's Trustee v Steel Bros & Co* [1901] 1 Ch. 279. See generally as to such pre-emption clauses *Gore-Browne on Companies*, para.23[4].

[47] The fact that it has value in the hands of the exchange and may be sold to other members is irrelevant; what matters is value realisable in the hands of the company.

[48] [2002] 1 W.L.R. 1150, applying *Bombay Official Assignee v Shroff* (1932) 48 T.L.R. 443.

property right was never independently transferable but was ancillary to membership, could not be transferred for consideration and came to an end when the claimant's membership, which was dependent on the personal attributes and acceptability of a particular individual, was validly and reasonably terminated for dishonour of its financial obligations.

In the course of his judgment Neuberger J. engaged in an extensive review of the rule invalidating deprivation of an asset on insolvency and the exceptions to it. The judgment is interesting not only for its acceptance of the defendant's central argument but also for its rejection of some of the other arguments that had been advanced against the application of the no-deprivation rule. In particular, Neuberger J. did not consider it relevant that the forfeiture provisions also applied in specified non-insolvency events or that it was not made with the intention of disadvantaging creditors on an insolvency, and he also did not accept the argument that it was an inherent feature of the share that it could be taken away, in other words, it was a "flawed asset",[49] for that would be to emasculate the no-deprivation principle and would also be inconsistent with the repugnancy rule.

It is important to note that, because members of the exchange were precluded by the rules from receiving consideration for a transfer of shares even while solvent, the rule requiring surrender of the shares to the exchange for no consideration in the event of a person ceasing to be a member on insolvency did not deprive that person of any benefit it would have enjoyed prior to insolvency. There was thus no divestment of value offending against any rule of insolvency law. Hence the case is to be distinguished from *Borland's Trustee v Steel Bros & Co Ltd*,[50] where the shares were not an incident to membership of anything except the company itself and were transferable for value, so that the articles of association imposing an obligation of transfer on a member's insolvency would have been struck down if they had required a compulsory sale for no consideration, thus depriving the estate of an asset which had transferable value before the insolvency.

Agreements which normally do or may contravene the *pari passu* principle

Provision for divestment of ownership on winding-up

The transfer of property in an asset to a company upon the condition that the asset is to revest in the transferor if the company goes into liquidation is void on at least two counts.[51] First, the provisions for revesting will be

7–14

---

[49] Fidelis Oditah, "Assets and the Treatment of Claims in Insolvency", (1992) 108 L.Q.R. 459 at 474.
[50] [1901] 1 Ch. 279. See above, para.7–12.
[51] It may also be vulnerable under the rule against perpetuities.

rejected as void for repugnancy, being inconsistent with the outright transfer of ownership.[52] Secondly, they run counter to the principle of insolvency law, on which the *pari passu* rule is based, that property cannot be transferred to a person on terms that it will not be available to his creditors, for this would be inconsistent with the mode of application of the tranferee's assets prescribed by law.[53] Forfeiture clauses of this kind are used in a variety of contexts[54] and will almost invariably be struck down except where the asset in question has no value.[55] On the other hand, there is no objection to a disposition by which property is transferred to the company for an interest coming to an end on winding-up, for insolvency law continues to distinguish between a determinable interest and an absolute interest which is made defeasible on insolvency by a condition subsequent.[56] The distinction is a fine one but has long been established in property and trust law.[57] A determinable interest is an interest the quantum of which is limited by the stipulated event, so that the occurrence of that event marks the end of the duration of the interest, whereas a defeasible interest is one which is granted outright and then forfeited.[58] So a transfer of property to a company until it goes into liquidation is a disposition for a potentially limited period and the advent of liquidation marks the natural end of the company's interest, so that there is no longer an asset to which the divestiture rule can apply, whereas an outright transfer with a proviso for retransfer if the company goes into liquidation is a forfeiture, a defeasance of an outright interest by reason of a condition subsequent, and as such is void as repugnant to insolvency law.[59]

This distinction between a determinable interest and an interest forfeitable on a condition subsequent has rightly been characterised in an Irish

---

[52] The root decision on conditions repugnant to legally prescribed methods of devolution is *Holmes v Godson* (1856) 8 De G. M. & G. 152. See to the same effect *Metcalfe v Metcalfe* (1889) 43 Ch.D. 633; *Re Ashton, Ballard v Ashton* [1920] 2 Ch. 481; *Ex p. Mackay* (1873) 8 Ch App. 643; *Re Machu* (1882) 21 Ch.D. 838. The last case involved a disposition by will but the principle applies with equal force to other dispositions.

[53] *Ex p. Mackay* (1873) L.R. 8 Ch. App. 643; *Ex p. Jay, Re Harrison* (1880) 14 Ch.D. 19; *Caboche v Ramsay* (1993) 119 A.L.R. 215.

[54] See below and Gerard McCormack, *Proprietary Claims and Insolvency* (1997), pp.25–28.

[55] *Money Markets International Stockbrokers Ltd v London Stock Exchange Ltd* [2002] 1 W.L.R. 1150.

[56] *Whitmore v Mason* (1861) 2 J. & H. 204, *per* Lord Hatherley at p.210; *Ex p. Barter* (1884) 26 Ch.D. 510, *per* Fry L.J. at pp.519–520; *Re Scientific Investment Pension Plan Trusts* [1999] Ch. 53.

[57] *Whitmore v Mason*, above. n.56; *Ex p. Barter*, above, n.56. The distinction forms the basis of the protective trust, a well-established device for ensuring that an individual can have property conferred upon him without risking its forfeiture to creditors on bankruptcy, the determinable interest giving way on bankruptcy to a discretionary trust. See Moffat and Chesterman. *op. cit.*, pp.211 *et seq.* and literature there cited.

[58] See Megarry and Wade, *The Law of Real Property* (6th ed.), paras 3–062 *et seq.*

[59] It may be noted that the grantor of the interest, though able to make it determinable upon the bankruptcy of another, has never been allowed to make it determinable on his own bankruptcy. See note to *Wilson v Greenwood* (1818) 1 Swans. 471 at 481, approved by Lord Hatherley in *Whitmore v Mason* (1861) 2 John & H. 204 at 210.

decision as "little short of disgraceful to our jurisprudence" when applied to "a rule professedly founded on considerations of public policy,"[60] a view endorsed in *Re Sharp's Settlement Trusts*[61] by Pennycuick J., who nevertheless concluded that it was well established and had to be accepted so far as comprehensible.

The other cases considered below are all variations of the divestment principle.

Vesting clauses in building contracts

A provision in a building contract vesting the builder's materials in the building owner upon the builder's liquidation contravenes the *pari passu* principle since it operates to divest the estate of an asset belonging to the estate at the time of liquidation.[62] The position is otherwise where the right of forfeiture arises prior to winding-up.[63]   **7–15**

Direct payment clauses in building contracts

Building contracts commonly provided that in the event of a main contractor's insolvency the employer should be entitled to utilise sums that would otherwise be payable to the main contractor to make direct payment to sub-contractors of sums due to them from the main contractor. Since the majority decision of the House of Lords in *British Eagle International Airlines Ltd v Cie Nationale Air France*[64] such provisions have come under attack as procuring payment to the sub-contractor out of funds that should have been available to the general body of creditors, thus contravening the principle of *pari passu* distribution.[65] The first question to consider is whether the funds would, indeed, have been available to creditors. It seems clear that where payment to the sub-contractor was to be made from retention funds held for the benefit of the main contractor there could be no infringement of the *pari passu* rule to the extent that prior to liquidation   **7–16**

---

[60] *Re King's Trust* (1892) 29 L.R. Ir 401, *per* Porter M.R. at 410.
[61] [1972] 3 W.L.R. 765.
[62] *Re Harrison Ex p. Jay* (1880) 14 Ch.D. 19. Whether a vesting clause does have this effect is a question of construction. The common provision by which plant and materials brought on to the site "shall be deemed to become the property of the employer" on the contractor's insolvency does not necessarily mean that ownership is in fact to pass and may signify merely that the employer is to have the right to use the plant and materials as if it were the employer. For a relatively recent example, see *Re Cosslett Contractors Ltd* [1998] Ch. 495.
[63] *Re Garrud, Ex p. Newitt* (1880) 16 Ch.D. 522.
[64] [1975] 2 W.L.R. 758. See also paras 6–11, 8–12.
[65] For a general discussion, see Michael G. Bridge, "Collectivity, Management of Estates and the *Pari Passu* Rule in Winding-up" in *Vulnerable Transactions in Corporate Insolvency* (ed. John Armour and Howard Bennett), pp.26 *et seq.*

the main contractor had ceased to have an interest in the retention fund, because it had mortgaged such interest[66] or had agreed to hold it on trust for the sub-contractor.[67] More difficult is the case where the right to payment under the main contract remains vested in the main contractor but the contract provides that the employer may withhold payment until all sub-contractors have been paid sums that have become payable to them under their sub-contracts. Such was the position in *Attorney-General v McMillan & Lockwood Ltd*,[68] which produced a division of opinion in the New Zealand Court of Appeal. The majority view was that upon the main contractor going into liquidation the continued application of the provision as to withholding of payment was barred by the *pari passu* rule. The minority view, as expressed by Williamson J., was that the liquidator could not stand in any better position than the company had before it went into winding-up and was therefore not entitled to disregard the withholding clause.[69] Williamson J. considered that it was necessary to balance the various public policy considerations, and this led him to the conclusion that it would not be contrary to public policy for the withholding clause to continue to operate after the company had gone into liquidation. This difference of view corresponds precisely to that which featured in *British Eagle*, discussed earlier,[70] the majority decision of the New Zealand Court of Appeal following the majority decision of the House of Lords in *British Eagle*.

Provision for security or increased security on winding-up

7–17   An agreement that on liquidation an unsecured debt shall become secured on part of the company's assets or that the amount already secured on those assets shall increase clearly contravenes the *pari passu* principle, since it diminishes the estate at the time of liquidation.[71]

Sale with provision for retransfer on winding-up

7–18   Where a person sells goods on credit to a company under a contract which provides for retransfer to the seller if the company goes into liquidation without having completed payment, the provision is void, for its effect is to deprive the estate of an asset owned by the company at the time it goes into liquidation.[72]

---

[66] *Drew & Co v Josolyne* (1887) 18 Q.B.D. 590.
[67] *Re Tout & Finch Ltd* [1954] 1 W.L.R. 178. See further para.6–11.
[68] [1991] 1 N.Z.L.R. 53.
[69] For an English decision to the same effect see *Re Wilkinson* [1905] 2 K.B. 713.
[70] Above, para.6–11, below, para.8–14.
[71] *Ex p. Mackay* (1873) 8 Ch. App. 643.
[72] *Holroyd v Gwynne* (1809) 2 Taunt. 176.

3. EXCEPTIONS TO THE PARI PASSU PRINCIPLE

The *pari passu* principle, though of fundamental importance, is not   **7–19**
absolute. For reasons of policy insolvency law provides certain deviations.
But before considering these I should like to mention cases which are often
advanced as exceptions to the *pari passu* principle but which in reality
involve an entirely different principle.

False exceptions to the *pari passu* principle

The principle of *pari passu* distribution of assets does not apply to the rights   **7–20**
of secured creditors, suppliers of goods under agreements reserving title or
creditors for whom the company holds assets on trust.[73] This, however, is
not because these are exceptions to the rule but because such assets do not
belong to the company[74] and thus do not fall to be distributed among
creditors on any basis.

True exceptions to the *pari passu* principle

There are a number of true exceptions to the *pari passu* principle. They fall   **7–21**
broadly into four categories: rights which are analogous to security, such as
set-off; claims enjoying a super-priority, in that they are payable in full
instead of being provable for dividend, such as liquidation expenses and
possibly environmental clean-up costs resulting from post-liquidation
remedial works; claims which in the distribution of dividend are given
preferential treatment over ordinary unsecured debts, such as various kinds
of claim by employees; and claims which are deferred, ranking below those
of the general body of creditors. These departures from the *pari passu*
principle are based on a combination of history, policy and pragmatism and
reflect a wide range of considerations: the protection of legitimate expectations, such as set-off; the need to obtain the continuing supply of goods and
services, or the continuance of a lease of premises, for the beneficial
winding-up of the business (thus necessitating the payment in full of debts
arising under post-liquidation contracts and sometimes debts payable under

---

[73] There is said to be one case in which moneys held on trust are subject to a right of set-off,
namely where the solvent creditor holds property of the company with authority, still
current at the time of winding-up, to convert it into money; but this appears not to be a true
exception, but rather to turn on an implied agreement that the solvent party is to be a
debtor, not a trustee. See below para.8–27.
[74] In the case of assets subject to a security interest, the assets do not belong to the company
to the extent of the security interest but the company does, of course, have an equity of
redemption.

pre-liquidation contracts); the desire to provide safeguards for those who have not voluntarily assumed a risk and are ill-equipped to provide for it, such as employees; and conversely the wish to subordinate the claims of those who are expected to bear a higher risk than the general body of creditors, such as shareholders and those who while engaged in the management of the company were guilty of improper conduct to the detriment of creditors.

(1) Set-off

7–22   Where, before the company goes into liquidation, there have been mutual credits, mutual debits or other mutual dealings between the company and any creditor of the company proving or claiming to prove in the liquidation, an account is to be taken of what is due from each party to the other in respect of the mutual dealings, and the sums due from one party are to be set off against the other, only the balance being provable in the liquidation or (as the case may be) paid to the liquidator.[75] Set-off on insolvency represents a major incursion into the *pari passu* principle, for its effect is that a creditor who owes money to the company on a separate account may resort to self-help by setting off the debt due to him against his own indebtedness to the company, thus ensuing payment of his claim *pro tanto* ahead of other creditors.[76] The policy justification for allowing set-off is that each of the two parties engaged in mutual dealings extends credit in reliance on his ability to take what is due to him out of what he owes, without which he would not have extended credit in the first place. So insolvency set-off responds to the principle of respecting legitimate expectations.

On winding-up the insolvency set-off rules displace other forms of set-off, including contractual set-off, not previously exercised. But set-offs implemented before winding-up remain effective, and parties to mutual dealings frequently seek to reduce insolvency risk by netting agreements which reduce their mutual obligations to a single balance of indebtedness. The subject of set-off and netting is of great importance and not inconsiderable complexity and is dealt with in the next chapter.

(2) Liquidation expenses generally

7–23   The expenses properly incurred in the winding-up, including the remuneration of the liquidator, are payable out of the assets in priority to all other claims.[77] Liquidation expenses are paid, not proved; that is to say, the

---

[75] Insolvency Rules 1986, r.4.90(1), (3), (8). To the extent that the balance payable to the liquidator results from a contingent or prospective debt it is to be paid only when the debt has become due (r.4.90(8)). See below, para.8–39.

[76] It is also possible to regard set-off as a false exception to the *pari passu* principle in that it constitutes an equity qualifying the claim of the company in liquidation, so that only what is left after allowing for the set-off represents an asset available for distribution among the general body of creditors.

[77] Insolvency Act 1986, ss.115 (voluntary winding-up), 175(2)(a) (compulsory winding-up).

liquidator discharges such expenses in full from the assets as payment accrues due, instead of the post-liquidation creditors having to prove for a dividend in competition with other creditors.[78]

The order in which liquidation expenses are to be paid is prescribed by r.4.218 of the Insolvency Rules 1986 but may be adjusted by the court under s.156 of the Act. But apart from adjusting the order of priority the court has no discretion as to the categories of expense that are payable as expenses of the liquidation and is bound to treat as liquidation expenses all the expenses listed in r.4.218.[79] Thus the rule is mandatory and is not governed by the *Lundy Granite* principle[80] applicable to continuing obligations under a pre-liquidation contract by which such obligations may be paid as expenses of the liquidation if, but only if, the liquidator chooses to adopt the contract for the benefit of the winding-up.[81]

Not infrequently it is necessary for a liquidator to institute proceedings, either in the name of the company for some cause of action vested in the company, such as a claim against a director for breach of fiduciary duty or against a third party for breach of contract, or in his own name, for proceedings which he alone can bring, for example, against directors for a contribution order for fraudulent or wrongful trading under s.213 or 214 of the Insolvency Act 1986. In a compulsory winding-up such sanctions have always needed the sanction of the court.[82] By contrast, in a voluntary winding-up the liquidator could bring such proceedings without the sanction either of the court or of the liquidation committee, and this applied to proceedings under ss.213 and 214 as well as to proceedings in the name of the company. One of the concerns of the liquidator, whether in a voluntary or a compulsory winding-up, was how to cover the costs of the litigation. The liquidator would naturally wish to have his costs covered in full, whilst creditors would be concerned to ensure that assets available for distribution would not be frittered away in legal costs in pursuing claims that might be unsuccessful or, even if successful, did not lead to recovery from the defendant. Preferential creditors, in particular, would not wish the liquidator to utilise assets sufficient to pay their claims in full to pursue litigation which could be of no benefit to them, only to ordinary unsecured creditors. In such a case their own recourse was, and remains, to apply to the court for an order to safeguard their position. But in general a liquidator was entitled to be indemnified from the free assets of the company, including any sums recovered in the litigation, in respect of costs properly incurred by

---

[78] See further below, para.7–32.
[79] *Re Toshoku Finance UK plc* [2002] 1 W.L.R. 671, overruling the decision in *Re Kentish Homes Ltd* [1993] B.C.L.C. 1375 and approving the decision in *Re Mesco Properties Ltd* [1980] 1 W.L.R. 96.
[80] So termed after the decision of the Court of Appeal in *Re Lundy Granite Co Ex p. Heavan* (1871) L.R. 6 Ch. App. 462. See below.
[81] *Re Lundy Granite Co Ex p. Heavan* (1871) L.R. 6 Ch. App. 462; and see below.
[82] See now Insolvency Act 1986, Sch.4, Part II.

him. However, this was not the case as regards costs incurred in pursuing claims for fraudulent or wrongful trading, and this for two reasons. First, such costs were not considered to be expenses of the liquidation at all, for recoveries under ss.214 (wrongful trading) and 239 (preference) were not assets of the company but were held on trust for unsecured creditors, so that the costs were not incurred in getting in any of the assets of the company within the old r.4.218(1)(a), nor were they "necessary disbursements" within r.4.218(1)(m). The same would have been true of costs incurred in connection with the pursuit of claims under ss.213 (fraudulent trading) and 238 (transactions at an undervalue). Secondly, if the claim was unsuccessful it could not be said that the costs were incurred in getting in assets of the company. Thirdly, even if such costs had qualified as expenses of the liquidation the liquidator could not as of right take them out of the sums recovered, since these were not the property of the company, and his entitlement to recoupment was available only out of the company's assets.[83] The court had a discretion to allow recoupment but would not do so if the facts did not warrant exercise of such discretion or there was insufficient information before the court to enable it to do so.[84]

The position has been somewhat alleviated by changes to r.4.218(1)(a) of the Insolvency Rules 1986, which expressly cover the costs incurred by the liquidator in conducting or defending legal proceedings.[85] This amendment removes the first two obstacles referred to above but unfortunately fails to address the third, namely that recoveries for wrongful trading and preferences are not the property of the company. It is hard to see why the courts have had such difficulty in allowing recoupment. It is well established that where a liquidator incurs expense in preserving or realising assets for the benefit of a third party, for example, where he sells assets subject to a security interest, the costs are to be recouped from the proceeds recovered for the benefit of that party.[86] There seems no reason not to apply the same principle to recoveries under ss.213 and 214. It seems strange that the sum available to creditors for such recoveries should not be net of expenses incurred in procuring them. The principle that the cost of realisations are deductible from the proceeds of the property realised was applied in *Re Berkeley Applegate (Investment Consultants) Ltd*[87] and has recently been

---

[83] *Lewis v Inland Revenue Commissioners* [2001] 3 All E.R. 499 (also *sub nom. Re Floor Fourteen Ltd, Lewis v IRC*); *Re M.C. Bacon Ltd (No.2)* [1991] Ch. 127; *Mond v Hammond Suddards* [2000] Ch. 40. In *Re Exchange Travel Holdings Ltd (No.3)* [1997] 2 B.C.L.C. 579, the Court of Appeal had reached the opposite conclusion but commented that the point had not received the depth of argument its importance warranted, and that it was not necessary to reach any final conclusion on it. This enabled the Court of Appeal in *Lewis v Inland Revenue Commissioners* to prefer the decisions in the other cases cited above.
[84] *Lewis v Inland Revenue Commissioners*, n.83, above.
[85] Insolvency Rules 1986, r.4.218(1)(a)(i). It may be noted that proceedings for statutory recoveries now require sanction in all cases (Insolvency Act 1986, Sch.4, para.3A).
[86] See above, para.6–35.
[87] [1989] Ch. 32.

restated (albeit *en passant* in the course of a speech dealing with a different issue) by Lord Nicholls in *Buchler v Talbot*.[88] There is thus powerful support for the argument that this should follow as a matter of course in relation to the deduction from recoveries under ss.213 and 214 of costs properly incurred in obtaining such recoveries. That, of course, does not resolve the problem in cases where the liquidator's claim is unsuccessful. Here he has to ask the court to exercise its discretion to allow recoupment from the free assets of the company, and he is well advised to seek this in advance of the proceedings.[89]

(3) Post-liquidation creditors: new contracts

The liquidator of a company cannot simply procure an instantaneous cessation of activity. He may need to continue trading so far as may be necessary for the beneficial winding-up of the company,[90] and in any event it will be necessary for a limited period to retain some staff, procure the continuance of supplies of goods and service and enter into new contracts. These are all activities conducted for the benefit of the existing creditors, but it is obvious that the liquidator cannot expect fresh goods and services to be supplied for nothing; there is no reason why parties to post-liquidation transactions should be expected to subsidise existing creditors and if asked to do so they would simply decline to do business. It follows that post-liquidation creditors have to be treated differently from pre-liquidation creditors. In doing business with them the liquidator has perforce to engage the assets of the company. This is achieved by classifying his obligations under post-liquidation transactions as expenses of the liquidation, which as stated above are payable out of the assets rather than being provable and ranking ahead of the claims of preferential and other unsecured creditors.[91]

7–24

---

[88] [2004] 2 A.C. 298 at para.63.

[89] For a detailed discussion, see Richard Gregorian and Daniel Butler, "Liquidators; litigation expenses, funding arrangements and the amendment to rule 4.218" ((2004) I.L. & P. 151).

[90] A power he may exercise without sanction in the case of a voluntary winding-up and with the sanction of the court in the case of a compulsory winding-up (Insolvency Act 1986, s.167(1)(a) and Sch.4, Pt II, para.5).

[91] This is provided directly in the case of voluntary winding-up by s.115 of the Insolvency Act 1986 and indirectly in the case of both forms of winding-up by r.4.180(1) of the Insolvency Rules 1986, which imposes on the liquidator the duty to distribute dividends "subject to the retention of such sums as may be necessary for the expenses of the winding up." Rule 12.2 lists the items that are to be regarded as expenses of the winding-up and r.4.218 sets out the order of priority in which expenses of the winding-up are to be paid, subject to the court's powers under s.156 of the Act and r.4.219 of the Insolvency Rules.

(4) Post-liquidation claims accruing under pre-liquidation contracts

7–25 The principle is thus plain enough: the expenses of the liquidation, including the claims of post-liquidation creditors,[92] are paid in full in priority to other debts, the claims of preferential creditors are then met, and it is only the pool of assets remaining after these claims have been paid that is available for the general body of ordinary unsecured creditors. More difficulty is caused by the continuance in force of contracts and leases made by the company before liquidation and not repudiated by the liquidator upon liquidation. Liabilities accrued under such contracts or leases before the winding-up are, of course, caught by the *pari passu* principle and enjoy no priority. But what is the position where the contract or lease imposes continuing obligations, *e.g.* for payment of rent for equipment or premises, sums accruing due under building contracts not completed at the time of liquidation. Here the *Lundy Granite* principle is relevant, raising the question whether (and if so, when) the liquidator merely continues in passive possession of the land or goods without disclaiming the transaction or whether he actively adopts the transaction, in the sense that he takes it over for the benefit or convenience of the winding-up, for example to run the business or with a view to disposing of it. In the former case the post-liquidation rent is merely a provable debt[93]; in the latter, it is payable as an expense of the liquidation so far as accruing after the liquidator's adoption of the contract but provable, not payable, so far as accruing before that adoption.[94] The treatment of a post-liquidation liability under a pre-liquidation contract is a judge-made exception to the general rule that only claims arising under post-liquidation contracts can be treated as expenses of the liquidation. It is based on the need to avoid a liquidator being able to use leased premises or other assets for nothing, to the detriment of the lessor,[95] and is a concept now implicitly embodied in r.4.218(1)(a) and possibly other sub-rules as well.[96]

(5) Payments of pre-liquidation debts to preserve assets or avoid other loss

7–26 Though pre-liquidation debts are in general provable, not payable, there may be cases in which the liquidator finds it necessary to pay such debts in order to preserve the assets or otherwise avoid loss to the estate. In these

---

[92] For a discussion of the position in relation to environmental clean-up liability, see below, para.7–30.

[93] The lessor cannot, however, prove for rent before it falls due, because until then it has not been earned. The principle applies to all executory contracts. See below, paras 7–32, 7–33.

[94] *Re ABC Coupler and Engineering Co Ltd (No.3)* [1970] 1 All E.R. 657; *Re Downer Enterprises Ltd* [1974] 2 All E.R. 1074; *Re Oak Pits Colliery Co* (1882) 21 Ch.D. 322; *Re National Arms & Ammunition Co* (1885) 28 Ch. D. 474; *Re Lundy Granite Co, Ex p. Heavan*, n.80 above.

[95] The authorities are extensively reviewed in *Re ABC Coupler and Engineering Co Ltd (No 3)*, n.94 above.

[96] *Re Toshoku Finance UK plc* [2002] 1 W.L.R. 671, *per* Lord Hoffmann at para.38.

cases he is entitled to recoup himself from the assets in respect of such payments as costs of the liquidation. Typical cases are payments to avoid forfeiture of a lease, distress or termination of a contract. Until recently liquidators also found themselves compelled to pay the pre-liquidation claims of public utilities, such as suppliers of electricity, gas, water and telephone services, in order to avoid the disconnection of supplies. The pressure thus exerted by monopoly suppliers to obtain payment ahead of other creditors despite being unsecured and non-preferential attracted severe criticism from the Cork Committee,[97] and as a result of the Committee's recommendations such suppliers are now prohibited from making payment of outstanding pre-liquidation charges a condition of the continuance of supply.[98]

(6) Claims which by statute are given priority

These fall into two groups. First, there are the expenses of the liquidation, which come ahead of all other claims and among themselves rank in the order of priority, prescribed by r.4.218 of the Insolvency Rules.[99] They have been discussed earlier in relation to post-liquidation creditors.[1] Their payment is mandatory and is not dependent on the question whether they benefit the estate, as it would be under the *Lundy Granite* principle in relation to continuing liabilities under pre-liquidation contracts.[2] Secondly, there are preferential debts, listed in Sch.6 to the Insolvency Act. In contrast to liquidation expenses, preferential debts rank *pari passu* among themselves.[3] Though the priority of preferential debts has to be respected by liquidators and administrators, this applies only in relation to the company's assets, not assets contributed by a third party such as a purchaser of the insolvent company.[4]

7–27

Preferential debts were formerly of two kinds: sums payable to the Crown, *e.g.* for taxes, and sums due to employees. Crown preference was strongly criticised by the Cork Committee as causing hardship to the general body of creditors while producing benefits insignificant in terms of total government receipts,[5] though the Committee did accept that there was

---

[97] *Insolvency Law and Practice* (Cmnd. 8558, 1982), Chap.33.
[98] Insolvency Act 1986, s.233. They are, however, entitled to make the liquidator's personal guarantee of payment a condition of future supply (s.233(2)(a)).
[99] As amended by the Insolvency (Amendment) Rules 1995.
[1] See above, para.7–24.
[2] *Re Toshoku Finance UK plc* [2002] 1 W.L.R. 671. See below.
[3] It seems that, apart from classical Roman law, English insolvency law is unique in not ranking preferential debts *inter se*. See the interesting comparative survey by José M. Garrido, "The Distributional Question in Insolvency: Comparative Aspects" (1995) 4 I.I.R. 25 at 50.
[4] *IRC v Wimbledon Football Club Ltd* [2005] B.C.L.C. 66.
[5] Insolvency Law Review Committee, *Insolvency Law and Practice* (Cmnd. 8558, 1982), paras 1409 *et seq.*

a case for retaining Crown preference for collected taxes, that is, taxes collected by the taxpayer for the Crown by invoice (as in the case of value added tax) or deduction (as in the case of PAYE and national insurance contributions), on the basis that in substance, though not in law, these were trust moneys for which the debtor company was to be accountable as a tax collector rather than pay as a taxpayer,[6] as opposed to assessed taxes, such as income tax and corporation tax. The government accepted this view, and the legislation was changed to abolish the Crown's preferential status as regards assessed taxes by omitting these from Sch.6 to the Insolvency Act 1986. With the enactment of the Enterprise Act 2002[7] the Crown's preferential status was abolished altogether, so that even collected taxes are no longer preferential, leaving only the claims of employees as preferential debts. However, the Crown's right of subrogation to preferential debts of employees paid from the National Insurance Fund remains.[8] The abolition of Crown preference, which in the absence of other measures would have increased the amount of assets available to the holder of a floating charge, was counter-balanced by provisions requiring a percentage of assets subject to a floating charge to be surrendered for the benefit of unsecured creditors, the percentage being fixed at a figure roughly comparable to the benefit conferred on the holder of a floating charge by no longer being subordinate to Crown claims for unpaid taxes and the like.[9]

In relation to employees, the Cork Committee, rejecting the submission of the Trades Union Congress that all debts due to employees in respect of wages or salaries should be preferential without any limitation in amount or extent, noted that there had been substantial improvements in the position of wage earners through the introduction of unemployment pay, earnings-related benefits, severance and redundancy payments and other social security benefits, coupled with the ability, under the Employment Protection Acts, to obtain immediate payment of claims out of what was then the Redundancy Fund.[10] The Committee therefore contended itself with recommending that the financial hardship to employees through the insolvency of the employer should in future be dealt with under the employment protection legislation through its provisions for claims on the Redundancy Fund, not by overlapping provisions of the insolvency code, and that the existing financial and other limits should be reconsidered and, where lower, brought into line with what was then provided under preferential debt provisions contained in what was then s.319 of the Companies Act 1948.[11] This recommendation to eliminate the preferential

---

[6] Cmnd. 8558, 1982, para.1418.

[7] Section 251, which provided that the relevant paragraphs of Sch.6 to the Insolvency Act should cease to have effect.

[8] See below, para.7–28.

[9] See above, para.6–31.

[10] Cmnd. 8558, 1982, paras 1428–1430. The fund is now the National Insurance Fund.

[11] *Insolvency Law and Practice*, paras 1432–1433.

status of employees under insolvency law and ensure that at least equivalent claims could be made on the Redundancy Fund instead was not adopted. Though both the previous statutes have been repealed the general position remains broadly what it was before.

The employee has preferential status within defined limits under Sch.6 to the Insolvency Act 1986 and has a parallel right to make a claim on the National Insurance Fund. However, the latter right is more restricted in scope than under the Insolvency Act. To the extent that recoveries from the National Insurance Fund do not exhaust his rights as a preferential creditor under the 1986 Act the employee can rely on his preferential status and then prove as an ordinary unsecured creditor for any balance. Where the Secretary of State makes a payment from the National Insurance Fund he is subrogated to the rights of the employee in the winding-up and to the extent that such payment is in respect of a debt that is preferential under the Insolvency Act he stands in the shoes of the employee as a preferential creditor.[12] This runs counter to the recommendations of the Cork Report,[13] but the reason given—"it is thought desirable that more funds should be left for the unsecured creditors"—is unconvincing, since there seems no reason why the general body of creditors, who would have been subordinated to claims of the employees themselves, should find themselves in a better position because such claims have been met by the Crown.

7-28

The preferential rights of employees fall into two broad categories. The first consist of any sum owed by the insolvent employer in respect of unpaid employer's and employees' contributions to an occupational pension scheme where these fall within Sch.4 to the Pension Schemes Act 1993[14] (as amended by s.90 of the Pensions Act 1995).[15] These rights are now buttressed by the Pension Protection Fund established under the Pensions Act 2004[16] and by the duty of the Board of the Fund to assume responsibility for the pension scheme in certain conditions.[17] The second category of employees' preferential rights consists of unpaid remuneration, holiday remuneration and related employment rights.[18] Crucial to the determination of preferential debts is the concept of the relevant date, which features in several paragraphs of Sch.6 to the Insolvency Act and is defined in s.387. Four types of event are capable of providing a trigger for preferential status and, in theory at least, this could produce four different relevant dates, necessitating a separate computation of preferential debts as at each such date.[19]

---

[12] Employment Rights Act 1996, s.18; Pension Schemes Act 1993, s.127(3). These are specific examples of a broader right of subrogation to preferential claims. See below.

[13] Above, n.91, para.1343.

[14] Insolvency Act 1986, Sch.6, para.4.

[15] See David Pollard and Isobel Carruthers, "Pensions as a Preferential Debt", *Insolvency Intelligence*, May 2004, 65.

[16] Pensions Act 2004, s.173.

[17] *ibid.*, s.127.

[18] Insolvency Act 1986, Sch.6, para.5.

[19] See below, para.9–64.

Reference has already been made to the Crown's right of subrogation where it meets preferential claims of employees from the National Insurance Fund. A more general provision in Sch.6 to the Insolvency Act gives preferential status to so much of any sum owed in respect of money advanced for the purpose as has been applied for the payment of a debt which, if it had not been paid, would have been a debt falling within paras 9 to 10 of the Schedule, *i.e.* as remuneration or holiday remuneration.[20] The effect is similar to that produced by subrogation of the lender to the employee's preferential rights. In a case on a similar, though not quite identical, provision in Australian legislation it has been held that the preferential wages claim must be shown to have been discharged from the sum lent; it does not suffice that it is discharged from a general fund constituted by an account in which the sum lent was commingled with other moneys so as to make it impossible to identify the loan as the source of payment.[21]

There can be no doubt that employees do deserve special protection. Very often their wages or salaries are their sole source of income. The loss of employment can thus have a devastating effect on them and their families, an effect exacerbated by non-payment of their entitlements by their employer. The relationship between employee and employer is a continuing relationship requiring mutual trust and confidence and it is a relationship in which the employee is very clearly the subordinate. Moreover, without the work of the employees the employer's business would not function and creditors would not get paid. Yet there remains much force in the view of the Cork Committee that other creditors too can find themselves in the position of being involuntary creditors (to which one might add that small trade suppliers, who are often in a very weak bargaining position when dealing with large companies, are contributing value in the same way as employees) and that the right way to protect employees from the effects of their employers' insolvency is through the National Insurance Fund and social security benefits. However, there seems little prospect of any radical change in the system.

(7) Claims which by statute are deferred

7–29   Various categories of deferred debt are prescribed by statute.[22] We need not consider them here except to draw attention to (a) the power of the court, when making a declaration under s.213 or 214 of the Insolvency Act

---

[20] Insolvency Act 1986, Sch.6, para.11.
[21] *Capt'n Snooze Management Pty Ltd v McLellan* [2002] V.S.C. 432.
[22] See Partnership Act 1890, ss.2(3)(d), 3: Companies Act 1985, s.178(3)-(6); Insolvency Act 1986, s.74(2)(f) (see n.74, above); Insolvency Rules 1986, r.12.3(2A). As to deferment of floating charge, see below, para.7–40.

1986,[23] to direct that the whole or any part of any debt owed to him by the company shall rank in priority after all other debts owed by the company and after interest on those debts[24]; (b) the subordination of claims by shareholders or other members of the company which are held in their capacity of members,[25] *e.g.* for unpaid dividend, sums payable on redemption of their shares[26]; and (c) in the case of assets subject to a floating charge created on or after September 15, 2003, the obligatory surrender of a prescribed percentage in value of the net property subject to the floating charge so as to make this available to unsecured creditors.[27]

The subordination of claims of a shareholder in his capacity as such is of long standing and is based on the fact that as a member he has contracted that the company's assets are to be applied in satisfaction of its debts, and it would be inconsistent with that contract to allow him to obtain satisfaction of his claim from those assets while external creditors remain unpaid.[28] So where a person is induced by a misrepresentation of the company to subscribe for shares in it, his claim against the company is subordinated unless he rescinds the contract with the company for the purchase of the shares.[29] But claims which a *transferee* has against the company for a misrepresentation inducing him to buy the transferred shares are not claims vested in him *qua* member and are thus not subordinated.[30] Similarly, a loan by a company to its subsidiary is not subordinated, for the parent

---

[23] Relating respectively to fraudulent trading and wrongful trading by such person.

[24] Insolvency Act 1986. s.215(4). See also s.215(2)(a), which enables the court to impose a statutory charge-back to the company on debts owed by the company to him. See below, para.12–44.

[25] Insolvency Act 1986, s.74(2)(f), which subordinates sums due to a member of a company (in his character of a member) by way of dividends, profits or otherwise, a provision held to be confined to claims linked to membership—for example, sums due on a reduction of capital approved by the court or on an authorised redemption of preference shares—rather than independent contractual claims. For a survey of the relevant authorities see *Soden v British & Commonwealth Holdings plc* [1998] A.C. 298.

[26] See below, n.35.

[27] See above, para.6–31.

[28] *Re Addlestone Linoleum Co* (1887) 37 Ch.D. 191; *Houldsworth v City of Glasgow Bank* (1880) 5 App. Cas. 317; *Webb Distributors (Aust) Pty Ltd v State of Victoria* (1993) 179 C.L.R. 15. This principle seems unaffected by s.111A of the Companies Act 1985, which in providing that membership of a company does not deprive a person of his right to claim damages against the company appears merely to have been intended to confer a right previously unavailable even against a company not in winding-up. See *Re Addlestone Linoleum Co*, above, n.111, *per* Kay J. at pp.199–200.

[29] *ibid.*, n.25. But rescission ceases to be possible once the company is in winding-up (*Re Addlestone Linoleum Co*, above, n.28; *Southern British National Trust Ltd v Pither* (1937) 57 C.L.R. 89, *per* Dixon J. at 113).

[30] *Soden v British & Commonwealth Holdings*, above, n.22; *Re Media World Communications Ltd, Crosbie v Nadoo* [2005] F.C.A. 51 (Finkelstein J., Federal Court of Australia). For a note on the case, which has apparently spread alarm among US investors into Australia, see Oren Bigos, "Are shareholders' claims provable in administration?" (2005) 13 Insol. L.J. 115.

company's claim is as creditor, not as shareholder, and the same applies to directors' remuneration.[31]

It would seem that debts are deferred only if so prescribed by statute. In the United States the courts developed the doctrine of equitable subordination, primarily directed at loans by a parent company to a greatly under-capitalised subsidiary. In general three conditions have to be satisfied in order for the court to apply the doctrine of equitable subordination, namely: (1) the subordinated creditor must have engaged in some type of inequitable conduct, (2) such conduct must have resulted in injury to other creditors or conferred an unfair advantage on the subordinated creditor, and (3) equitable subordination must not be inconsistent with the provisions of the Bankruptcy Act.[32] The doctrine is now incorporated by reference in s.510(c) of the federal Bankruptcy Code.[33] It does not appear to have been applied so far in common law jurisdictions outside the United States, though in *Canada Deposit Insurance Corp v Canadian Commercial Bank (No.3)*[34] the Supreme Court of Canada, while declining to apply the doctrine on the facts of the case before it, was at least prepared to entertain arguments as to its applicability. English law appears not to have evolved any doctrine of equitable subordination, no doubt because the statutory provisions, and in particular those enabling the court to subordinate claims of creditor-directors found guilty of fraudulent or wrongful trading,[35] are thought to give the court all the powers it needs.

Special cases: market contracts; environmental liability

7–30   There are two categories of case which do not fit neatly within the above classification. First, there are special categories of contract related to the operation of financial and money markets, exchanges and clearing houses, which in varying degrees are protected from attack under insolvency law.[36] Secondly, there is the question of clean-up liability under legislation enacted for the protection of the environment.[37] If the company's operations before winding-up have caused damage to the environment, for example, through oil pollution or land contamination, can the relevant regulatory body require the liquidator to apply the assets of the company to remedy the damage in priority to the claims of other creditors? Alternatively, if the regulatory body carries out the remedial works itself, can it

---

[31] *Re Dale and Plant Ltd* (1889) 43 Ch.D. 255; *Soden v British & Commonwealth Holdings plc* [1998] A.C. 298, *per* Lord Browne-Wilkinson at 324.
[32] *Re Mobil Steel Co*, 563 F.2d 692 (5th Cir. 1977).
[33] Jay Lawrence Westbrook and Elizabeth Warren, *The Law of Debtors and Creditors* (4th ed. 2001), pp.716 *et seq.*
[34] (1993) 97 D.L.R. (4th) 385 at 419–422.
[35] Insolvency Act 1986, s.215(4) (see below, para.12–44).
[36] See above, paras 1–29 *et seq.*
[37] Environmental Protection Act 1990; Environment Act 1995. See Totty and Moss, *Insolvency*, Chap.H1.

exercise its statutory right of recoupment from the offending company ahead of the claims of other creditors? Again, if the liquidator, for the purpose of beneficial winding-up, continues operations which cause environmental damage, to what extent are assets of the company that would otherwise be available for creditors required to be utilised to meet a clean-up order or to recompense the relevant body for the cost of remedial works it has itself undertaken? Does a lender face potential liability if it has taken security over the polluting asset?[38] Astonishingly, despite the fact that such issues have long been known in relation to environmental protection legislation both in the United States and in Canada, United Kingdom legislation is entirely silent on these crucial questions.[39] Much depends on how the court decides to characterise the liability. Is it to be equated with an ordinary unsecured debt so as to be provable (or in the case of post-liquidation activity, payable as an expense of the liquidation) or is it to be treated quite separately as a public liability carrying a distinctive priority?

Such cases as there are have examined this question in the context of disclaimer of a waste management licence as onerous property. In two decisions, *Re Celtic Extraction Ltd*[40] and *Minister for the Environment and Local Government v Irish ISPAT Ltd*[41] the latter in Ireland, where the wording of the legislation is somewhat different, it has been held that a waste management licence is property and that there is no reason of public policy why it cannot be disclaimed in the same way as any other onerous property.[42] In the former case it was held that the "polluter pays" principle cannot be applied to cases where the polluter cannot pay so as to preclude disclaimer and thereby require payment to be made by unsecured creditors out of the assets available for distribution to them in priority to their own claims in the liquidation.[43] In the Irish decision it was pointed out that the liquidator holds the assets of the company on trust for creditors, so that the "polluter pays" principle cannot be achieved. Where the liquidator takes over the licence for the benefit of the liquidation then on general principles the cost of fulfilling the conditions of the licence would seem to be an expense of the liquidation, but if the liquidator is simply completing work in progress as liquidator rather than taking over or adopting the licence for the benefit of the liquidation there is no basis for giving the claim for such cost priority and disapplying the normal rule of *pari passu* distribution.[44]

---

[38] Prudent lenders usually undertake a "green audit" with a view to satisfying themselves on this question before making an advance on such property.

[39] It has to be said that UK legislative activity in the field of corporate insolvency law has long been characterised by the failure, when the new legislation is introduced, to take the opportunity to resolve significant and well-known problems arising even under the pre-existing law in the UK itself.

[40] [2001] Ch. 465, overruling in part the decision of Neuberger J. in *Re Mineral Resources Ltd* [1999] 1 All E.R. 746.

[41] July 29, 2004, Carroll J. (Irish High Court).

[42] As to this, see above, para.6–20 *et seq.*

[43] [2001] Ch. 475, *per* Morritt L.J. at para.39.

[44] *Minister for the Environment and Local Government v Irish ISPAT Ltd*, above.

The above cases establish that there is no reason of public policy why a liquidator should not be permitted to disclaim a waste management licence as onerous property and thereby avoid applying the company's assets to the continuing cost of compliance with the environmental requirements. As yet there appear to have been no decisions on the effect of service of a remediation notice where there is no disclaimer. In such a case, although the liquidator incurs no personal liability,[45] he faces the dilemma that either the company fails to comply with the remediation notice, thereby attracting sanctions, or the funds that would otherwise be available to unsecured creditors have to be utilised to meet the costs of compliance. It remains to be seen how the courts will approach this situation.

4. PROOF OF DEBT

The nature of proof

7–31   A creditor wishing to be treated as such for the purpose of voting and dividend is required to submit a formal claim, known as a proof of debt (or proof) to the liquidator.[46] Since dividends are distributed only among those creditors whose proofs have been lodged and admitted,[47] a creditor is not entitled to dividends if his proof has been rejected or to participate in a dividend distribution made, before he has lodged his proof.[48] Nor on lodging his proof can he require prior distributions to be reopened, but he has a prior right to the dividend he lost before any future distributions of dividend are made.[49]

Provable debts

7–32   In general, all claims by creditors are provable against the company, whether they are present or future, certain or contingent, ascertained or sounding only in damages.[50] Under r.13.12(1) "debt" means:

> "(a) any debt or liability to which the company is subject at the date it goes into liquidation;

---

[45] Environmental Protection Act 1990, s.78X(3), (4)(a).
[46] Insolvency Rules 1986, r.4.73. In the case of a voluntary winding-up the liquidator is not obliged to call for proofs to be in writing but usually does so.
[47] Insolvency Rules 1986, r.11.6(1).
[48] In calculating and distributing a dividend the liquidator is required to make provision for certain unproved debts, including disputed proofs and claims (Insolvency Rules 1986, r.4.182(1)).
[49] *ibid.*, r.4.182(2).
[50] *ibid.*, r.12.3(1).

(b) any debt or liability to which the company may become subject after that date by reason of any obligation incurred before that date[51]; and

(c) any interest provable as mentioned in Rule 4.93(1)."

It is immaterial whether the debt or liability is present or future, whether it is certain or contingent, or whether its amount is fixed or liquidated, or is capable of being ascertained by fixed rules or as a matter of opinion.[52] The word "liability" itself is widely defined, covering a liability to pay money or money's worth, any liability under an enactment, any liability for breach of trust, any liability in contract, tort or bailment, and any liability arising out of an obligation to make restitution.[53]

It will be seen that provable debts include those becoming payable after winding-up pursuant to an obligation incurred before winding-up, for example, pre-liquidation debts maturing after liquidation,[54] unliquidated damages in contract or tort,[55] and claims for interest payable in respect of a period up to the date of winding-up or, if the liquidation was immediately preceded by an administration, any period after the date that the company entered administration.[56] Rent and other payments of a periodical nature may be proved so far as due and unpaid up to the date of liquidation or, if the liquidation was immediately preceded by an administration, up to the date that the company entered administration,[57] while further payments accruing due from the company under executory contracts continuing in force will, if constituting expenses of the liquidation, be payable in full from the company's assets or, if not, will be provable, as they fall due.[58]

Debts arising under contracts made after the date of the winding-up are not provable but are payable as expenses of the liquidation in priority to other claims.[59] There are, moreover, certain types of pre-liquidation debt, both under the Insolvency Rules and at common law, for which the creditor cannot prove. Under the Insolvency Rules certain obligations imposed by statute are not provable at all,[60] while others are provable only when the claims of other creditors have been met in full.[61] But nothing in the Rules

---

[51] In determining whether any liability in tort is provable the company is deemed to become subject to it by reason of an obligation incurred when the cause of action accrued (*ibid.*, r.13.12(2)).

[52] *ibid.*, r.13.12(3).

[53] *ibid.*, r.13.12(4).

[54] And see *ibid.*, r.4.94, and below, para.7–33.

[55] Prior to the Insolvency Act 1986 a claim in tort was not provable unless it had become liquidated by judgment or agreement before the winding-up. But see *Re Berkeley Securities (Property) Ltd* [1980] 1 W.L.R. 1589.

[56] *ibid.*, r.4.93 as amended.

[57] *ibid.*, r.4.92 as amended.

[58] See above, para.3–09; below, para.7–33. As to the effect of disclaimer, see above, para.6–23.

[59] See above, para.7–23.

[60] Insolvency Rules 1986, r.12.3(2).

[61] *ibid.*, r.12.3(2A).

prejudices any enactment or rule of law under which a particular kind of debt is not provable, whether on grounds of public policy or otherwise.[62] So debts cannot be proved if they are statute-barred or otherwise unenforceable.[63]

Amount of proof

7–33   Debts incurred prior to the liquidation (or, if the liquidation was immediately preceded by an administration, on the date that the company entered administration) but payable in the future under executed contracts—that is, contracts under which payment has already been earned by performance— are admitted to proof at full value;[64] but where the debt has not become due at the date of declaration of any dividend it is discounted for the purpose of calculating the dividend entitlement.[65] Contingent claims must be estimated and admitted to proof at the estimated amount.[66] The same applies to unliquidated claims for damages.[67] The position is otherwise as regards sums payable in the future under executory contracts, for example, rent accruing due under a lease or payments that will become due under a construction contract yet to be completed. Here the rule is that there can be no proof for a sum that has not been earned by performance—in the case of a lease, by the expiry of the period for which the rent is due,[68] and in the case of a construction contract by performance of the work for which the payment is due.[69] The creditor thus has to prove separately for each sum as it is earned.[70]

Where a lease is disclaimed or otherwise comes to an end, the lessor's claim becomes converted into an immediate right to prove for unliquidated damages based on the present value of the future rentals,[71] credit being

---

[62] *ibid.*, r.12.3(3).

[63] See *Gore-Browne on Companies*, vol.2, para.34.87 and cases there cited.

[64] Insolvency Rules 1986, r.4.94 as amended.

[65] *ibid.*, r.11.13. The formula originally contained in this rule was criticised by Lord Millett in *Christopher Moran Holdings Ltd v Bairstow*, also *sub nom. Re Park Air Services plc* [2000] 2 A.C. 172 at 187–188 on the ground (*inter alia*) that the discount was applied not to the reducing balance but to the original sum outstanding. This has now been corrected in a revised r.11.13 as well as in r.2.105 (administration).

[66] Insolvency Rules 1986, r.4.86.

[67] *ibid.*

[68] *Christopher Moran Holdings Ltd v Bairstow* [2000] 2 A.C. 172 (on appeal from *Re Park Air Services plc* [1997] 1 W.L.R. 1376), *per* Lord Millett at 187; and see above, para.3–09.

[69] Once performance has taken place then as regards the amount earned the creditor can prove immediately even if the amount in question, though due, has not yet become payable, *e.g.* where in a construction contract the requisite architect's certificate has not yet been issued. In such a case the amount due is provable as a future debt.

[70] See para.3–09, above.

[71] *Christopher Moran Holdings Ltd v Bairstow* [2000] A.C. 172, reversing the decision of the Court of Appeal *sub nom. Re Park Air Services plc* [1997] 1 W.L.R. 1376, which had held that the rent was claimable as such, instead of the loss of rent being recoverable as damages, so that no discount was to be deducted—a decision criticised as untenable in the 2nd edition of this book at p.166.

given for the present value of the future rentals that may reasonably be expected from a lease to a new tenant.

No deduction need be made for third party receipts

The creditor can maintain his proof for the full amount of the debt without **7–34** giving credit for sums received from a surety or other third party, whether before or after the winding-up, which are less than the full amount of the debt.[72] For this purpose it makes no difference whether the sum is received by actual payment or through set-off.[73] But where the surety's liability is for a specified part of the debt and he pays that part his liability is extinguished and the creditor must give credit for the payment in his proof.[74] For reasons which are not clear there is a special rule governing negotiable instruments. Where the claim is on a negotiable instrument credit must be given for sums received from a third party before proof,[75] but need not be given for receipts after proof.[76]

No double proof

Only one proof may be lodged for the same debt. So a surety may not prove **7–35** for his right of indemnity against the company as principal debtor until the creditor has received payment in full.[77] Again, however, a surety of a specified part of a debt (as opposed to one who guarantees the whole debt with a limit of liability) is discharged from liability on paying that part and becomes entitled to lodge a proof for the sum paid,[78] with the result that the creditor's proof must be correspondingly reduced.[79]

---

[72] *Ellis v Emmanuel* (1876) 1 Ex.D. 157; *Re Sass* [1896] 2 Q.B. 12. See Roy Goode, *Legal Problems of Credit and Security* (3rd ed.), para.8–18. The position is otherwise in the case of a claim against a solvent debtor and an insolvent surety.

[73] The position is otherwise, of course, where the debtor company is solvent and the surety who has a right of set-off is insolvent, for the set-off in insolvency is mandatory and the payment thereby effected *pro tanto* extinguishes the principal debt. See *M.S. Fashions Ltd v Bank of Credit and Commerce International SA* [1993] Ch. 425 and below, para.8–19.

[74] See *M.S. Fashions Ltd v Bank of Credit and Commerce International SA* [1993] Ch. 425. The surety is also entitled to share rateably with the creditor in securities given and dividends received in respect of the whole debt *(Re Butlers Wharf Ltd* [1995] B.C.C. 717, *Goodwin v Gray* (1874) 22 W.R. 312).

[75] *Re Blackburne* (1892) 9 Morr. 249.

[76] *Re Houlder* [1929] 1 Ch. 205; and see Goode, *op. cit.*, para.8–19.

[77] *Re Fenton* [1931] 1 Ch. 85. For a helpful summary of the rule against double proof see the judgment of Robert Walker J. in *Re Polly Peck International plc, In administration (No.3)* [1996] 1 B.C.L.C. 428, where the learned judge declined to pierce the corporate veil by treating two companies in a group as a single entity so as to preclude a double proof.

[78] *Re Sass*, above, *per* Vaughan Williams J. at 15.

[79] Goode, *op. cit.*, para.8–18.

Secured creditors

7–36 Subject to the special rules concerned floating charges,[80] creditors who are fully secured are largely unaffected by the liquidation process. They can remove their security from the pool and realise it to satisfy what is due to them, accounting to the liquidator for any surplus.[81] Where the company is in compulsory liquidation there are certain restrictions. Though proceedings are not usually needed to enable the creditor to realise his security, yet if for some reason the creditor finds it necessary or desirable to institute proceedings against the company he must first obtain leave of the court.[82] Moreover, since the liquidator in a compulsory winding-up is an officer of the court he cannot be interfered with in the exercise of his functions without leave of the court, so that if he declines to part with possession of the property in which the creditor has his security interest the creditor is not allowed to resort to self-help but must again obtain leave of the court. In practice, leave will almost invariably be granted, for what is involved is not the property of the company but (to the extent of the security interest) the property of the secured creditor. As James L.J. pointed out long ago in *Re David Lloyd & Co*,[83] the legislative provisions requiring leave of the court:

"... were intended, not for the purpose of harassing, or impeding, or injuring third persons, but for the purpose of preserving the limited assets of the company or bankrupt in the best way for distribution among all the persons who have claims upon them ... But that has really nothing to do with the case of a man who for present purposes is to be considered as entirely outside the company, who is merely seeking to enforce a claim, not against the company, but to his own property. The position of a mortgagee under such circumstances is, to my mind, exactly similar to that of a man who said, 'You the company have got property which you have taken from me, you are in possession of my property by way of trespass and I want to get it back again' ... The mortgagee says, 'There is some property upon which I have a certain specific charge, and I want to realise that charge. I have nothing to do with the distribution of your property among your creditors, this is my property.' Why a mortgagee should be prevented from doing that I cannot understand."

A secured creditor has a number of options. He can surrender his security and prove for the full amount of the debt due to him,[84] a procedure rarely

---

[80] See above, para.6–31, below, para.7–39.
[81] For other options open to a secured creditor, see below.
[82] Insolvency Act 1986, s.130(2).
[83] (1877) 6 Ch.D. 339 at 344–345.
[84] Insolvency Rules 1986, r.4.88(2).

used since it rarely has advantage; he can value his security in his proof and prove for the balance of the debt[85]; he can realise his security and, if the proceeds are insufficient to cover the amount due, can prove for any deficiency[86]; and he can simply rest on his security without lodging a proof at all. The secured creditor needs to examine his options carefully. To the extent that he proves for his debt his claim is subject to set-off, whereas if he rests on his security without proving it is not.[87]

The justification for upholding security rights has already been described in an earlier chapter.[88]

Execution creditors

Where a creditor has issued execution against the goods or land of a company or has attached any debt due to it, and the company is subsequently wound up, he is not entitled to retain the benefit of the execution or attachment against the liquidator unless he completed the execution or attachment before the commencement of the winding-up.[89]

7–37

5. RANKING OF CLAIMS

Priority of claims

Most of the priority rules concerning unsecured creditors have already been referred to.[90] As pointed out earlier, secured creditors are not in general involved in the competition except to the extent of any balance remaining due to them after realising their security, for as we have seen assets of the company available for unsecured creditors do not include the interests of third parties. Secured creditors will, of course, be competing among

7–38

---

[85] Curiously, the Insolvency Rules do not expressly provide for the amount provable by a secured creditor who elects to value his security; they merely require the security to be disclosed and valued (r.4.75(1)(b)), provide for the surrender of the security, if not disclosed, unless the court grants relief for inadvertence or honest mistake (r.4.96) and allow the secured creditor, with the agreement of the liquidator or leave of the court, to alter the value put upon the security in his proof (r.4.95). But it is clear that only the balance of the claim above the stated value can be proved; and if the creditor understates this he risks redemption by the liquidator at the value stated (r.4.97(1)).

[86] Insolvency Rules 1986, rr.4.75(1)(g), 4.88. If he proves for the full debt he is deemed to have surrendered his security.

[87] *Re Norman Holding Co Ltd* [1991] 1 W.L.R. 10.

[88] See above, para.2–16.

[89] Insolvency Act 1986, s.183(1), which is qualified by s.183(2). As to what constitutes completion of the execution or attachment see s.183(3). See also Roy Goode, *Legal Problems of Credit and Security* (3rd ed.), paras 5–43—5–46.

[90] Above, paras 7–02, 7–19 *et seq.*

themselves, but assuming that all their interests have been duly perfected insolvency law has nothing to say about this competition, which is governed by the general law.[91]

There are two cases in which a creditor holding a duly perfected security does not enjoy priority. Both of these concern floating charges.[92]

(1) The statutory surrender of the prescribed part

7–39 Under s.176A of the Insolvency Act 1986 a prescribed part of the net property subject to a floating charge[93] and still remaining after any payment to the preferential creditors from the floating charge assets[94] has to be surrendered so as to be available as a ring-fenced fund for unsecured creditors. This provision, which is confined to floating charges created on or after September 15, 2003, has already been discussed.[95]

(2) Postponement to preferential creditors

7–40 Under s.175(2)(b) of the Insolvency Act claims secured by a floating charge[96] are postponed to those of preferential creditors in a winding-up. This provision has its origin in s.2 of the Preferential Payments in Bankruptcy Amendment Act 1897, which was motivated by the sense that floating charges were typically taken over raw materials and manufactured articles that had benefited from the work of employees, who ought therefore to be paid in priority. The policy was stated with great clarity by Mr George Kemp in moving the Second Reading of the Bill in the House of Commons:

> "To make plain the incidence of the order of payment in the case of a company being wound up, he would take the case of a limited company, with, they would suppose, an ordinary share capital of £300,000, debentures to a similar amount, and weekly wages paid of £1,000. They would suppose, too, that there was a mortgage of £10,000 on the lands and buildings of the company. First in order of payment there came this mortage of £10,000. Secondly, came the workpeople with their claims for

---

[91] See Goode, *op. cit.*, Chap.9.
[92] For a summary of the priorities of distribution, see below, para.7–63.
[93] *i.e.* a floating charge created on or after September 15, 2003 (Insolvency Act 1986, s.176A(9); Insolvency Act 1986 (Prescribed Part) Order 2003 (SI 2003/2097), art.1), referred to hereafter as a "new" floating charge, pre-September 15, 2003 charges being labelled "old" floating charges.
[94] See above, para.6–31.
[95] See above, paras 6–31 *et seq.*
[96] That is, a charge which as created was a floating charge (Insolvency Act 1986, ss.40(1), 251), even if it has crystallised before the accrual of the preferential debt.

their wages—if their wages were in arrears, say two weeks, £2,000—as against the debenture holders under a floating charge on the remaining assets of the company; then came the debenture holders, and fourthly came the ordinary shareholders.[97] What was the justice of this? First of all, the mortgagee got his money, because it was on the lands and buildings, which were not in any way affected by, nor did they affect, the work of the workpeople. Secondly, why should the workpeople come in priority to the debenture holders under a floating charge? For the reason that the raw material and the articles partly or wholly manufactured were part of the assets of the debenture holders. This raw material had benefited by the work of the workpeople to the extent of the time for which their wages were in arrear. Therefore it was only right and just that the workpeople should have the benefit of the enhanced value of these articles, which, as the law stood at the present time, would be first claimed by the holders of debentures or debenture stock."[98]

Until recently it had been thought, as the result of the decision of the Court of Appeal in *Re Barleycorn Enterprises Ltd*,[99] that they were also postponed to the expenses of the winding-up, which have priority over preferential debts so far as the assets available for general creditors are insufficient to meet them.[1] However, the decision in *Re Barleycorn* was overruled by the House of Lords in *Buchler v Talbot*,[2] where the House of Lords reviewed the history of the statutory provisions and pointed out that it had never been intended that liquidation expenses should be recoverable from assets not belonging to the company in liquidation. The current statutory provisions were derived from the Preferential Payments in Bankruptcy Act 1888 as extended by the Preferential Payments in Bankruptcy Amendment Act 1897, and these said nothing about liquidation expenses. To the extent that the assets were subject to a floating charge they were not the

---

[97] Ordinary unsecured creditors should, of course, have been mentioned before shareholders; no doubt the omission was an oversight and was in any event not material to the illustration, though they were not material.

[98] H.C.Deb. 10 Feb. 1897, cols.72–73. The reasoning would not, it is true, have applied to raw materials still unprocessed at the time of winding-up, but given what was then perceived to be the fractional amount of unpaid wages as a percentage of the debentures it would no doubt have been unnecessarily pedantic to treat these separately from the manufactured stock.

The reasoning on which the 1897 Act was based offers a solution to the question how preferential claims should be dealt with if the Law Commission's proposals to abolish the floating charge as a distinct form of security and treat it as a fixed charge (*Company Security Interests: A consultative report* (Law Com. Cons. Paper No.176, 2004), paras 2.56 *et seq.*) were to be adopted, namely to subordinate to preferential claims charges (which in the new regime would be fixed charges) over raw materials, stock in trade and receivables, the three significant categories of asset typically covered by a floating charge.

[99] [1970] Ch. 465.

[1] Insolvency Act 1986, s.175(2)(b).

[2] [2004] 2 A.C. 298, reversing the decision of the Court of Appeal *sub nom. Re Leyland Daf Ltd* [2002] 1 B.C.L.C. 571.

company's assets and could not be resorted to for payment of liquidation expenses. Realisation of the assets produced two distinct funds: the proceeds of the free assets and the proceeds of the floating charge. The costs of administering each fund were to be borne by the fund in question. So the costs of preserving or realising assets subject to the floating charge would come out of the floating charge proceeds,[3] whilst the liquidation expenses would come out of the company's free assets.

The decision in *Buchler v Talbot* has generated a great deal of debate and controversy. It has been criticised on policy grounds as producing harsh consequences for liquidators, including the possibly unintended consequence of swelling, at the expense of the liquidator, the amount of floating charge assets a percentage of which has to be surrendered to form a ring-fenced fund for unsecured creditors,[4] and has also been attacked as misconceived in terms of doctrine and principle,[5] but it has been defended with equal vigour as fully consistent with general property law concepts and with the structure of insolvency law,[6] a view endorsed by the present writer. It is true that the decision removes from the reach of the liquidator assets previously available to meet the expenses of the liquidation, and may cause difficulties on that account, but there was never justification for treating assets subject to a floating charge as if they were free assets of the company.

A circularity problem

7–41   Where by virtue of a priority agreement or the impact of a negative pledge clause a floating charge has priority over a subsequent fixed charge, which in turn has priority over preferential debts, a circularity problem arises. The fixed charge, by agreement, is subordinate to the floating charge, which is subordinate to the claims of preferential creditors, which in turn rank behind those of the fixed charge.

The most satisfactory way of resolving this conundrum is to accept the basic premise that preferential creditors should not be given a windfall purely by virtue of a private agreement between the fixed charge and the

---

[3] This would be so whether the realisation was by the chargee or by the liquidator. See *Buchler v Talbot*, n.2 above, *per* Lord Nicholls at para.31, and above, para.3–03.

[4] Vijay SV Selvam, "New order for insolvency distributions: a question of property, not priority", (2004) I.L. & P. 102 at 103–104.

[5] R.J. Mokal, "Liquidation expenses and floating charges—the separate funds fallacy" [2004] L.M.C.L.Q. 387, arguing, among other things, that assets subject to a floating charge remain beneficially owned by the company until the security has been enforced—a difficult argument to sustain without destroying the established concept of a floating charge as an existing security (see Roy Goode, *Legal Problems of Credit and Security* (3rd ed.), paras 4–03 *et seq.*) which thus leaves the company only with an equity of redemption (*Re Pyle Works Ltd* (1890) 44 Ch.D. 534, *per* Cotton L.J. at 577–578).

[6] John Armour and Adrian Walters, "Funding Liquidation: A Functional Law" (2006) 122 L.Q.R. (publication pending).

floating chargee which does not in any way concern other creditors. This windfall can be avoided by treating the floating chargee as subrogated to the rights of the fixed chargee to the extent of the sum secured by the floating charge, so that to that extent the floating chargee obtains priority, over preferential creditors in right of the fixed chargee.[7] Such a solution does justice to everyone. Preferential creditors remain in exactly the same position as they did before and the rights of the parties to the inter-creditor agreement are respected. The correctness of this approach was conceded in *Re Woodroffes (Musical Instruments) Ltd,*[8] but in *Re Portbase Clothing Ltd*[9] Chadwick J. felt unable to adopt it and preferred the decision of Nicholson J. in the Victorian case of *Waters v Widdows,*[10] in which it was held that the fixed chargee, in subordinating his claims to those of the floating chargee, also subordinated them to the preferential debts. In that case this result was said to be dictated by the statutory policy of protecting preferential creditors. It is hard to see why. The purpose of the legislation is to give priority to preferential debts over those secured by a floating charge, not those secured by a fixed charge. The objection of Chadwick J. to the subrogation solution was that it put the floating chargee in the same position as if the fixed chargee had assigned his chargee or declared a trust of the proceeds in favour of the floating chargee. The answer to this is surely that the preferential creditors, who are strangers to the priority agreement, have no right to invoke its terms to gain priority for themselves over a fixed charge to which they would otherwise be subordinate, and that the fixed chargee should thus remain entitled to enforce his charge in priority to the claims of preferential creditors and then hand over the proceeds to the floating chargee to the extent of the amount secured by the floating charge. Applying the principle of subrogation does no more than short-circuit this procedure and allow the floating chargee to enforce the fixed chargee's priority directly and for his own benefit, so achieving the result intended by the priority agreement but without disturbing the position of the preferential creditors.[11]

Summary of priorities

In line with the earlier discussion, fixed security interests and other real rights held by third parties do not need to feature in the ordering of priorities because to the extent that assets held by the company are subject   **7–42**

---

[7] See Roy Goode, *Legal Problems of Credit and Security* (3rd ed.), paras 5–60—6–61 and *Commercial Law* (3rd ed.), pp.671–673.

[8] [1986] Ch. 366.

[9] [1993] Ch. 388.

[10] [1984] V.R. 503.

[11] See also Lightman and Moss, *The Law of Receivers and Administrators of Companies* (3rd ed.), para.11–034, expressing the view that *Portbase* could have undesirable consequences. The circularity problem does not arise in relation to the statutory surrender of the prescribed part of floating charge realisations for the benefit of unsecured creditors, for the prescribed part applies only to the floating charge assets remaining after any payment to preferential creditors, who thus do not participate in it. See above, para.6–11.

to these they do not constitute the property of the company at all and therefore do not compete in the priority stakes.[12] By contrast debts secured by floating charges are, as we have seen, in competition both with preferential creditors and with ordinary unsecured creditors. As regards the latter, it is necessary to distinguish old charges, created prior to September 15, 2003, from new charges, created on or after that date. Where an administrative receiver has been appointed under a floating charge it is his responsibility to respect these and other priorities[13] and to make payments accordingly out of the assets coming into his hands. He must also set aside the prescribed part of any net property subject to a floating charge[14] and pay this and any remaining surplus over to the liquidator,[15] who must distribute it according to the following ranking:

(1) expenses of the liquidation, in the statutory order of priority, subject to adjustment by the court;

(2) preferential debts *pari passu*;

(3) the prescribed part of the net property subject to a floating charge;

(4) ordinary unsecured creditors *pari passu*;

(5) deferred creditors *pari passu*.

---

[12] This is subject to the liquidator's right to look to the proceeds of such assets for recoupment of expenses properly incurred by him in preserving or realising them.
[13] For the order of application of the assets by the receiver, see below, para.9–71.
[14] See above, para.6–31.
[15] The receiver does not himself have a power to distribute the prescribed part. See below, para.9–67.

Chapter 8

Set-Off and Netting

1. THE NATURE AND PURPOSE OF SET-OFF AND NETTING

Set-off

Set-off is the right of a debtor who is owed money by his creditor on **8–01** another account or dealing to secure payment for what is owed to him by setting this off in reduction of his own liability.[1] For example, A sells raw materials to be B to be made up into finished products which B then sells to A. If A owes B £1,000 for products sold and delivered to him but is owed £400 by B for raw materials then in any claim against him A is not obliged to pay B the £1,000 he owes and then sue separately for recovery of the £400 (or if B is in liquidation, prove in the liquidation in competition with other creditors) he is owed but may set off the latter sum against his indebtedness and discharge the debt by paying B (or B's liquidator) the balance of £600.

Set-off is available both outside and within bankruptcy and liquidation. In both cases it provides a speedy remedy to secure payment but the policy reason for providing the remedy depends on the type of set-off involved. Contractual set-off is recognised as an incident of party autonomy in the conclusion of contracts. The banker's right of combination is similar except that it derives from implied rather than express agreement. In the case of

---

[1] See Philip Wood, *English and International Set-Off*, and *Law and Practice of International Finance: Title Finance, Derivatives, Securitsations, Set-Off and Netting* (1995), Part III; Rory Derham, *Set-Off* (3rd ed., 2003); Shelagh McCracken, *Banker's Remedy of Set-Off* (2nd ed., 1998). The leading early works are Richard Babington, *A Treatise on the Law of Set-Off* (1827), Basil Montagu, *Summary of the Law of Set-Off* (2nd ed., 1828) and two American publications, Oliver Barbour, *Treatise on the Law of Set-Off* (1841) and T. W. Waterman, *Treatise on the Law of Set-Off* (2nd ed., 1872). For historical and comparative surveys, see William H. Loyd, *The Development of Set-Off* 64 U.Pa.L.Rev. 541 (1916) and Michael E. Tigar, *Automatic Extinction of Cross-Demands: Compensatio from Rome to California* 53 Cal.L.R. 224 (1965).

independent (or statutory) set-off[2] the remedy is given primarily to avoid circuity of action. By contrast, the policy underlying transaction (or equitable) set-off is that it would be unjust to allow a party to enforce his money claim without giving credit for the cross-claim if so required. Similarly the provision of insolvency set-off reflects the view that where parties have been giving credit to each other in reliance on their ability to secure payment by withholding what is due from them it would be unjust, on the advent of liquidation, to deprive the solvent party of his security by compelling him to pay what he owes in full and be left to prove for his own claim. This has traditionally been the policy justification for what is a clear exception to the *pari passu* principle, in that it allows the solvent party to collect payment ahead of other creditors to the extent of the set-off and thus puts him in a position analogous to that of a secured creditor.[3]

Thus set-off is an essential tool in the hands of a debtor who has a cross-claim against his creditor and is particularly used in banking transactions and in mutual dealings in the financial markets. But in dealings on an organised market the legal protection of netting[4] and set-off has in recent years been seen as fulfilling a much more fundamental need, namely the reduction of systemic risk. Hence the issue of EC Directives and of implementing national legislation designed to ensure that rules of insolvency law do not imperil rights of set-off in market contracts.[5] This special treatment of market and related contracts should be constantly borne in mind as a major qualification of the general principles discussed in the present chapter.

2. TYPES OF SET-OFF

8–02   There are five main types of set-off. The labels traditionally used to describe these are decidedly uninformative, and I have adopted the terminology coined by Mr Wood[6] which is much more meaningful and is already gaining acceptance in the courts. Features common to all forms of set-off other than contractual set-off are that (a) they are confined to situations in which both claim and cross-claim are for money[7] or one party's

---

[2] See below, para.8–03.

[3] Set-off does not in law constitute a form of security, for the debtor who asserts it is not acquiring any rights over an asset of the creditor but simply seeking to reduce or extinguish the claim against him. See below, para.8–24.

[4] See below, para.8–09.

[5] See above, para.1–29; below, para.13–61.

[6] In his superb and massive work *English and International Set-Off*.

[7] It is not clear what policy objection there can be to set-off in respect of non-money fungibles. If each party has a duty to deliver or transfer items of property that are mutually interchangeable, why should not the party with the larger obligation be entitled to deduct what is due to him and deliver or transfer the balance? This can be done by agreement but not, it seems, in the absence of agreement.

claim is to money and the other's is to property which the first party is authorised to dispose of and thus convert into money, and (b) they require mutuality of parties, that is, the claim and cross-claim must be due from the same parties in the same right. The five types of set-off are the following:

(1) Independent set-off

This embraces two distinct forms of set-off. The first is sometimes known as statutory set-off, by which is meant set-off under rules carried over from the former Statutes of Set-Off, or alternatively as legal set-off, by way of contradistinction with equitable set-off. The second is that form of set-off which equity applied by analogy with the Statutes of Set-Off, where all the conditions for statutory set-off were present except that one of the liquidated cross-claims was equitable.[8] The particular characteristics of independent set-off are (a) that it is a purely procedural defence which does not operate to reduce or extinguish the creditor's claim except at the point where judgment is given for the balance and (b) that, in contrast to transaction set-off, it is not necessary that the claim and cross-claim should be connected to each other. It is only in this latter feature that independent set-off has any utility in modern law; in all other respects it is overshadowed by the much broader transaction set-off.

8–03

(2) Transaction set-off

This form of set-off, traditionally labelled equitable set-off, arises where the claim and cross-claim, even if not arising from the same transaction, are so closely connected that it would be inequitable for one claim to be enforced without credit being given for the other. Though transaction set-off was historically seen as a purely procedural remedy,[9] in modern law it is now capable of operating as a substantive defence in those cases where this is not precluded by the nature or terms of a contract between the parties and the set-off is not given by way of analogy to the Statutes of Set-Off.[10] Transaction set-off may validly be excluded by agreement.[11]

8–04

(3) Contractual set-off

Contractual set-off is that for which provision is made by express agreement of the parties. Outside insolvency it is free of several of the limitations governing other forms of set-off. It operates as a substantive defence,

8–05

---

[8] See Roy Goode, *Legal Problems of Credit and Securities* (3rd ed.) paras 7–04, 7–42.

[9] See Goode, *op. cit.* para.7–48.

[10] See *BICC plc v Burndy Corp* [1985] 1 All E.R. 417; *Pacific Rim Investments Pte Ltd v Lam Seng Tiong* [1995] 3 S.L.R. 1; and generally Roy Goode, *Legal Problems of Credit and Security*, paras 7–48 *et seq.*

[11] *Coca-Cola Financial Corp v Finsat International Ltd* [1998] Q.B. 43.

taking effect upon the occurrence of the act or event agreed between the parties.

(4) Current account set-off

8–06   By this is meant the implied contractual right given to bankers operating different current accounts for the same customer to combine them and treat them as one, thus setting off a debit balance on one account against a credit balance on the other. Though current account set-off could be regarded as a form of contractual set-off,[12] the label "contractual set-off" is usually reserved for express contractual provisions by which mutual obligations may be netted out, *i.e.* set off against each other. Current account set-off is a substantive right which when exercised consolidates the different accounts and reduces the customer's monetary position to a single net debit or credit balance. It is not clear what type of act constitutes exercise of the right. The traditional view was that the accounts were to be treated as notionally a single account from the beginning unless otherwise agreed.[13] But it seems more realistic to treat the accounts as distinct until actually combined by notice, book-entry or the initiation of a computer process transferring balances to one account from the other or others, and until then to treat the right of set-off as an unexercised equity.

Since it is now established that foreign currency is to be treated as money, not as a commodity,[14] there seems no reason why a claim in one currency cannot be set off against a claim in another, though at the point when the balance is to be struck it will, of course, be necessary to convert the foreign currency into sterling if payment is to be made in sterling.

(5) Insolvency set-off

8–07   This is the right of set-off given by insolvency law, and as regards companies by rr.2.85 and 4.90 of the Insolvency Rules 1986, dealing respectively with set-off in administration and in liquidation. Insolvency set-off too operates as a result of substantive law. It is automatic and is not dependent on the taking of any procedural steps.

---

[12] This predicates that the accounts are to be treated as separate rather than evidencing a single indebtedness. See below, para.8–06.

[13] See, for example, *Bailey v Finch* (1871) L.R. 7 Q.B. 34, *per* Blackburn J. at 40.

[14] See *Miliangos v George Frank (Textiles) Ltd* [1976] A.C. 443; *The Halcyon The Great* [1975] 1 W.L.R. 515.

3. CONTRACTUAL SET-OFF, NETTING AND THE IMPACT OF INSOLVENCY

Contractual set-off and netting

The simple form of contractual set-off is a clause in a contract providing **8–08** that one party is entitled to set-off against any sums it owes to the other all sums owed to it by the other. This basic form is typically used where it is known in advance that the mutual obligations will be monetary or the various contracts will be unilateral and thus executed from the beginning,[15] so that no special contractual arrangements are required to convert non-monetary obligations (*e.g.* to deliver commodities) into monetary obligations or to cancel executory contracts or close them out by offsetting or reverse transactions. But there are many contractual relationships which are not of this character and require a process that leads, automatically or by unilateral action by one party, to consolidation of the mutual claims into a single net balance. This contractually adopted process is known as netting.

Netting

The terms "netting" and "set-off" are sometimes treated as interchangeable **8–09** but in financial circles netting is used to denote contractual arrangements by which claims of different parties against each other are reduced to a single balance. Moreover, whereas set-off in its legal sense is confined to cases involving money obligations on both sides or claims reducible to money, netting includes, in the commodities, futures and securities markets, delivery obligations as well.

Netting is now defined by statute as:

> "the conversion into one net claim or obligation of different claims or obligations between participants resulting from the issue and receipt of transfer orders between them, whether on a bilateral or multilateral basis and whether through the interposition of a clearing house, central counterparty or settlement agent or otherwise."[16]

Netting can thus be viewed as both the procedure for and the outcome of a contractually completed set-off. It includes such arrangements as bilateral contract consolidation,[17] settlement netting,[18] the conversion of non-

---

[15] Because a unilateral contract is by definition a contract in which only one party makes a promise and the other accepts by performance.

[16] Financial Markets and Insolvency (Settlement Finality) Regulations 1999, SI 1999/2979, reg.2(1).

[17] Otherwise known as netting by novation. As to "close-out" netting, see below, para.8–12.

[18] Also termed payment netting.

monetary into monetary claims through the exercise of a right to cancel or close out transactions, and the adoption of institutional rules governing bilateral and multilateral clearing and settlement or providing for novation of all relevant contracts to a clearing house or central counterparty.[19] The main objectives of netting are to reduce the number of settlements, thus saving costs, and to minimise the risk of a party becoming insolvent. From a market and regulatory perspective netting, particularly multilateral netting, provides a measure of protection against systemic risk and, in so doing, influences capital adequacy requirements.

Netting arrangements are designed to ensure as for as possible either that all set-offs are completed before the relevant date,[20] so that there is no need to resort to insolvency set-off, or that the contractual rights on both sides will have undergone such conversion (if any) as may be necessary to satisfy the requirements of the Insolvency Rules as to mutuality of claims and parties.[21] For this purpose a number of techniques are available which in normal circumstances can be expected to be effective. These include the following:

(1) Novation netting (contractual consolidation)

8–10   Novation netting, or contractual consolidation, involves the amalgamation of two or more executory contracts into a single new contract to be performed at a future time. The characteristic of this form of netting, which distinguishes it from settlement netting, is that the fusion of the claims on both sides into a new claim for a single balance or a single delivery obligation occurs immediately each new contract is concluded,[22] with payment or other performance to be made at a future time agreed between the parties. Thus each new contract is automatically consolidated into the previous contract, so that at any one time only a single performance under a single contract is involved on one side or the other and no question of netting or set-off arises. By contrast, in settlement netting the contracts remain separate until they have been netted out at maturity and the net balance paid or delivery obligation discharged.

Contractual consolidation may be effected by provision for bilateral consolidation of contractual obligations or by clearing house rules providing

---

[19] See below, paras 8–10 *et seq.*

[20] *i.e.* before the winding-up and before the creditor has notice of the creditors' meeting under the Insolvency Act 1986, s.98 or of the winding-up petition, as the case may be.

[21] See below, para.8–24. Netting is also an important technique for reducing the risk of failure of banks and other credit institutions and is recognised as such by an EC Directive 96/10 (OJ L58 dated 3.4.1996, p.17), amending Directive 89/647/EEC as regards recognition of contractual netting by the competent authorities. See below, para.8–15, and Dermot Turing, "Set-Off and Netting: Developments in 1996 Affecting Banks" [1997] 12 J.I.B.L. 155.

[22] Or on the occurrence of such other event as may be agreed between the parties.

for novation of notified contracts to the clearing house. In the former case the contract may provide that in stated eventualities, which could include notice by one party to the other, all outstanding contracts between them shall be consolidated into and replaced by a single contract under which only the net balance is payable. Alternatively, each contract may provide for its automatic consolidation with subsequent contracts as and when these come into existence, so that no set-off situation ever arises. In contractual set-off through clearing house rules, the clearing house becomes substituted as a principal in relation to each of the parties.[23] For example, under the General Regulations of the London Clearing House (LCH), members who are parties to a sale transaction are required to register it with LCH, whereupon the transaction is automatically novated and replaced by two separate transactions in both of which LCH is substituted for one party as the principal, becoming seller to the original buyer and buyer from the original seller. The effect of this system of automatic novation is that payment and delivery obligations become owed by and to LCH. In this way payment rights and obligations arising from all dealings entered into by a particular trader are internalised and consolidated into a single credit or debit balance in the trader's current account with LCH.

Contractual netting does, of course, depend upon the obligations on both sides being of the same kind. It is not possible to net a payment obligation against a delivery obligation or vice versa. So where mutual dealings involve both delivery and payment obligations it is necessary to devise some contractual procedure, such as rescission or close-out, by which one type of obligation is converted to the other.[24] Similarly, while the fact that the claim and cross-claim are in different currencies is no bar to a right of set-off,[25] completion of the set-off requires either that one currency is converted to the other or that both currencies are converted to a third currency at a given rate of exchange.

(2) Settlement (or payment) netting

As mentioned above, whereas contractual consolidation involves the amal- **8–11** gamation of unmatured claims, settlement netting is the process by which matured claims are netted out and paid. It is only the act of payment of the net balance which extinguishes the claims on both sides. Again, settlement netting may be effected either by bilateral arrangements or by multilateral arrangements through a clearing house. In the former case the parties simply agree that when claims on both sides mature those on one side shall

---

[23] See Wood, *English and International Set-Off*, paras 5–127 *et seq.*; Goode, *Commercial Law* (3rd ed.), pp.157, 472.
[24] See below, para.8–12.
[25] See below, para.8–12.

be set off against those on the other and the balance paid. In the case of netting through a clearing house the procedure is that at the end of each clearing (which may be daily or at such other intervals as the clearing house rules prescribe) the position of each clearing house member is netted out in relation to all other clearing house members to produce a "net net" series of balances in which members are either creditors or debtors in relation to the clearing as a whole. Payment is then made by in-house transfers from debtor members to creditor members in the books of the clearing house or of a bank (typically the central bank) where all the clearing house members hold an account. These multilateral netting arrangements have not always proved effective in the event of an insolvency of a clearing house member, but the problem has been considerably alleviated by European Community directives. The impact of insolvency on settlement netting is considered later.[26]

(3) Close-outs

8–12   Insolvency set-off, like other forms of set-off, requires that claim and cross-claim be monetary claims or involve relief based on the non-payment of money. Accordingly it is not possible to set off a money claim against an obligation to deliver or transfer property, tangible or intangible, except where the party invoking the set-off holds the property with instructions or authority to convert it into money and the instructions or authority have not been revoked at the time of liquidation.[27] So in a situation where the claims on one side or both are not to payment of money but to the delivery of assets, such as commodities or securities, it is important to have a mechanism in place by which the delivery obligations are replaced by money obligations prior to the advent of liquidation. There are various "close-out" mechanisms by which this may be achieved: acceleration of performance on both sides and the replacement of a delivery obligation by a payment obligation, the two payment obligations then being netted out; the termination of a delivery obligation and its replacement by a payment obligation, and netting out; or the conclusion of a reverse transaction, so that, for example, a contract to purchase securities is closed out by a countervailing contract to sell them, the parties then settling their mutual obligations by the payment of differences.[28]

Concern as to the efficacy of close-out netting in national legal systems led to the issue of the European Community directives to which reference

---

[26] See below, para.8–14.
[27] See further below, para.8–27 in relation to close-outs and related techniques concerning financial collateral.
[28] See the definition of "close-out netting" in the Financial Collateral Arrangements (No.2) Regulations 2003 (SI 2003/3226), reg.3.

has already been made.[29] These are designed to safeguard close-out netting arrangements from attack under insolvency laws with a view to reducing the systemic risk that would attend the inability of a major player to reduce its exposure by a close-out.

Insolvency displaces other forms of set-off

Netting arrangements work perfectly well as regards transactions where the netting is completed before winding-up. Once a company has gone into liquidation the rules of insolvency set-off, where relevant, come into play and are mandatory,[30] displacing all other forms of set-off not exercised prior to the winding-up. This is of no great significance in relation to independent set-off, transaction set-off and current-account, for in virtually every situation in which these forms of set-off are available there would be an automatic set-off under the rules of insolvency set-off. Indeed, the latter are broader, not only because they are self-executing but also because the principle of insolvency law under which future claims are accelerated and contingent claims are discounted and admitted to proof means that insolvency set-off extends to these claims, which would be outside the scope of the three other forms of set-off just mentioned.[31] But contractual set-off is in a different category, for outside insolvency the parties are free to agree on almost any kind of netting and set-off arrangement they choose. It thus becomes of importance to know whether a contractual set-off has come into effective operation before the winding-up of one of the parties to the mutual dealings. If it has not, two consequences follow. First, the right of set-off ceases to be exercisable. Secondly, if two or more contracts constituting the mutual dealing between the parties are executory the liquidator is free to cherry-pick, requiring performance of the profitable contract while disclaiming or declining to perform the unprofitable contract and leaving the other party to prove in the winding-up without the benefit even of insolvency set-off.[32]

We consider, first, the decidedly adverse impact of general insolvency law on uncompleted multilateral netting arrangements and, secondly, the ameliorating effect of provisions of the Companies Act 1989 relating to the settlement of market contracts and money market and related contracts under the rules of a recognised investment exchange or a recognised clearing house[33] and subsequent European Community Directives and

8–13

---

[29] Above, paras 1–33, 1–34.
[30] See below, para.8–19.
[31] For the discount method, see below, para.8–18.
[32] This is because of the rule that sums earned by the company by post-liquidation activity are not part of its general assets and are thus not susceptible to insolvency set-off of pre-liquidation claims. See above, para.7–24, and below, para.8–26.
[33] See above, paras 1–29 *et seq.*

implementing legislation.[34] The remainder of the chapter is devoted to the rules governing the admissibility of set-off in winding-up or administration.

Effect of insolvency under the general insolvency law

8–14   Once a clearing house member goes into liquidation then as a matter of general insolvency law its claim on other members can no longer be subjected to netting out through the clearing, for the effect of this is to reduce the member's claim against its counterparty by reference to sums due from that member to third parties, in contravention of the mutuality requirement, and to prefer other participants in the clearing to the member's creditors as a whole, contrary to the *pari passu* rule. In other words, an asset of the member, namely its claim against counterparty, is being removed from the general body of creditors and distributed exclusively among the clearing house members. This was the conclusion reached in the controversial decision of the House of Lords in *British Eagle International Air Lines Ltd v Compagnie Nationale Air France*,[35] to which reference has previously been made and which now requires examination in a little more detail.

The International Air Transport Association (IATA) set up a clearing house system by which sums due from member airlines to each other would be netted out each month, remittances being sent by IATA to airlines having a net credit balance and collected from airlines with a net debit balance. British Eagle went into liquidation owing money to a number of airlines but with a claim against Air France which the liquidator sought to recover. Air France pleaded that the liquidator was bound by the IATA system and could collect only from IATA and then only such sum (if any) as was due it after netting out the claims of airlines who were creditors of British Eagle. The liquidator's contention that this contravened the *pari passu* rule, in that it removed from British Eagle's estate for the benefit of other member airlines a sum due from Air France which would otherwise have been an asset available to the general body of creditors of British Eagle, was upheld by the House of Lords by a majority of three to two. It was not suggested that the arrangements were in themselves in any way improper, but in the view of the majority their effect was to give other members of IATA to whom British Eagle owed money a preference over its general creditors. Two of their Lordships[36] dissented on the ground that the arrangements were perfectly proper, were not intended to avoid rules of insolvency law, were to be applied no differently after liquidation than

---

[34] See above, paras 1–32 *et seq.*
[35] [1975] 2 All E.R. 390.
[36] Lord Morris of Borth-y-Guest and Lord Simon of Glaisdale.

before and were as binding on the liquidator as they had been on British Eagle itself.

It is clear that the crucial question in *British Eagle* was whether its claim to payment was against Air France directly, with IATA acting simply as agent in providing a clearing mechanism, or whether on the other hand the claim was simply an item in the computation of British Eagle's net net debit or credit balance with IATA, the latter acting as principal. If, as the majority held, British Eagle's contractual entitlement lay directly against Air France then clearly its subjection to the claims of other clearing house members was an infringement both of the *pari passu* principle and of the requirement of mutuality which precludes the set-off of claims of third parties against the amount due to the company in liquidation. But if, as was the view of the minority, the effect of the clearing house arrangements was that British Eagle's claim was only to such sum as after netting out in the clearing fell to be credited or debited to its account with IATA, then its counterparty for the purpose of computing its claim was IATA, which would clearly be entitled to set off cross-claims vested in it in respect of services supplied to British Eagle by other airlines.

It has to be said that the minority view is much more in keeping with commercial reality (to say nothing of commercial convenience) than that of the majority. Moreover, the decision of the majority is difficult to reconcile with the principle, emphasised by Lords Morris and Simon, that a liquidator stands in the shoes of the company in liquidation and takes each contract as he finds, so that he cannot procure the company to enforce those provisions which are for its benefit without at the same time being bound by the contractual conditions qualifying the company's entitlement.[37] In policy terms a multilateral netting arrangement should not be regarded as offensive to insolvency law if it is intended to operate in the same way outside and inside insolvency, so that it is not a device designed to improve the position of one party by reason of the insolvency of another.

The preservation of netting arrangements under market contracts and EC Directives

Fortunately, in relation to recognised markets and clearing houses the effect of *British Eagle* has been largely negated by special statutory provisions in Part VII of the Companies Act 1989, supplemented by subordinate legislation, designed to safeguard from invalidation under rules of insolvency law market contracts, market charges, money market contracts, money market charges and system charges in favour of settlement banks and by EC Directives and implementing legislation designed to

8–15

---

[37] See above, para.8–14.

preserve the validity of netting arrangements in insolvency in relation to financial collateral in order to reduce systemic risk. These have been outlined earlier. As will have been seen, some of these exemptions from insolvency law are directed to ensuring the validity on insolvency of close-outs and set-off and netting arrangements. The decision in *British Eagle* does not appear to affect the validity of agreements which impose conditions for the repayment of debt, for example "flawed asset" agreements by which a bank takes a cash deposit from a corporate customer on terms that this is not to be withdrawable until the customer and its associated companies have discharged their obligations to the bank. Such an arrangement does not remove the asset from the general body of creditors of the company, it qualifies the claim itself by defining the conditions in which the credit balance is to become repayable, pending which it is held in suspense.[38]

4. INSOLVENCY SET-OFF: GENERAL PRINCIPLES

The right of set-off in insolvency

8–16   The right of set-off in company insolvency is to be found in rr.2.85 and 4.90 of the Insolvency Rules 1986, dealing respectively with set-off in administration where the administrator makes an authorised distribution and set-off in winding-up. The two rules have been substantially revised and expanded to take account of certain criticisms made by the House of Lords in *Re Park Air Services Ltd*[39] and to provide greater detail and clarity and bring the rule on set-off for liquidation into line with the rule in administration. The amendments[40] came into effect on April 1, 2005. Since r.4.90 is somewhat broader, in that distribution is involved in almost every winding-up and all the case law hitherto has concerned set-off in winding-up, we shall focus on r.4.90, and then turn to consider what rules are special to set-off in administration under r.2.85.

Set-off in winding-up

8–17   For ease of reference in examining some of the case law on insolvency set-off we set out the old r.4.90, the main features of which are largely, though not entirely, unchanged.

---

[38] See Roy Goode, *Legal Problems of Credit and Security* (3rd ed.) para.1–21; Philip Wood, *English and International Set-Off*, paras 5–196 *et seq.*
[39] [2002] 2 A.C. 172.
[40] Insolvency (Amendment) Rules 2005 (SI 2005/527).

"Rule 4.90 Mutual credit and set-off

(1) This Rule applies where, before the company goes into liquidation, there have been mutual credits, mutual debts or other mutual dealings between the company and any creditor of the company proving or claiming to prove for a debt in the liquidation.

(2) An account shall be taken of what is due from each party to the other in respect of the mutual dealings, and the sums due from one party shall be set off against the sums due from the other.

(3) Sums due from the company to another party shall not be included in the account taken under paragraph (2) if that other party had notice at the time they became due that a meeting of creditors had been summoned under section 98[41] or (as the case may be) a petition for the winding up of the company was pending.

(4) Only the balance (if any) of the account is provable in the liquidation. Alternatively (as the case may be) the amount shall be paid to the liquidator as part of the assets."[42]

Principles underlying insolvency set-off

As stated above, the wording of r.4.90 has undergone substantial change, **8–18** but the basic idea remains the same. The creditor has a right of set-off against the company only where he is a creditor "proving or claiming to prove for a debt in the liquidation." We shall discuss the meaning of "debt" shortly. It is not necessary that the creditor shall have a lodged a proof; it suffices that he is "claiming to prove", which has been interpreted as meaning that he is entitled to prove.[43] However, though a right to prove is a necessary condition of the creditor's right of set-off, it is not a sufficient condition; it is also necessary to satisfy the requirements of mutuality.[44] Where this is the case an account is to be taken of what is due from each party to the other in respect of the mutual dealings, the sums due from one party are to be set off against the sums due from the other and only the balance owed to the liquidator is provable in the liquidation.[45] The concept of "sum due" has been expanded to reflect the definition of "debt" in r.13.12, though this is not free from criticism.[46] If the balance is in the

---

[41] *i.e.* the meeting of creditors which a company is required to convene when convening its own meeting to pass a resolution to go into a creditors' voluntary winding-up.
[42] *i.e.* if the company's claim against the creditor exceeds the creditor's claim against the company. For the revised r.4.90 see para.8–22.
[43] *Stein v Blake* [1996] A.C. 243, *per* Lord Hoffmann at 253.
[44] See below, paras 8–24 *et seq.*
[45] Insolvency Rules 1986, r.4.90(3), (8).
[46] See below, para.8–27.

liquidator's favour it is payable to him as part of the assets if it has become due and payable, but if the debt owed to the company is only contingent or prospective the balance is to be paid when it has become due and payable.[47]

The revised r.4.90, which is set out a little later, removes much of the doubt and controversy surrounding the original rule, though for a statement of the three basic principles governing the taking of the account we must still turn to two masterly analyses, by Hoffmann L.J. at first instance in *MS Fashions Ltd v Bank of Credit and Commerce International S.A. (No.2)*[48] and Lord Hoffmann (as he had now become) in *Stein v Blake.*[49] In the former he laid out the three principles in the following terms:

"Certain principles as to the application of these provisions have been established by the cases. First, the rule is mandatory ('the mandatory principle'). If there have been mutual dealings before the winding-up order which have given rise to cross-claims, neither party can prove or sue for his full claim. An account must be taken and he must prove or sue (as the case may be) for the balance. Secondly, the account is taken as at the date of the winding-up order ('the retroactivity principle'). This is only one manifestation of a wider principle of insolvency law, namely, that the liquidation and distribution of the assets of the insolvent company are treated as notionally taking place simultaneously on the date of the winding up order: see *In re Dynamics Corporation of America* [1976] 1 W.L.R. 757, 762, *per* Oliver J. Thirdly, in taking the account the court has regard to events which have occurred since the date of the winding up ('the hindsight principle'). The hindsight principle is pervasive in the valuation of claims sand the taking of accounts in bankruptcy and winding up."[50]

In *Stein v Blake*[51] Lord Hoffmann returned to the hindsight principle in the context of contingent claims:

"How does the law deal with the conundrum of having to set off, as of the bankruptcy date, 'sums due' which may not yet be due or which may become owing upon contingencies which have not yet occurred? It employs two techniques. The first is to take into account everything which has actually happened between the bankruptcy date and the moment when it becomes necessary to ascertain what, on that date, was the state of account between the creditor and the bankrupt. If by that time the contingency has occurred and the claim has been quantified,

---

[47] Insolvency Rules 1986, r.4.90(8).
[48] [1993] Ch. 425, affirmed by the Court of Appeal.
[49] [1996] 1 A.C. 243.
[50] *MS Fashions Ltd v Bank of Credit and Commerce International S.A. (No.2)*, above n.48, at 432–433.
[51] Above, n.43.

then that is the amount which is treated as having been due at the bankruptcy date. An example is *Sovereign Life Assurance Co v Dodd* [1892] 2 Q.B. 573, in which the insurance company had lent Mr Dodd £1,170 on the security of his policies. The company was wound up before the policies had matured but Mr Dodd went on paying the premiums until they became payable. The Court of Appeal held that the account required by bankruptcy set-off should set off the full matured value of the policies against the loan.

But the winding up of the estate of a bankrupt or an insolvent company cannot always wait until all possible contingencies have happened and all the actual or potential liabilities which existed at the bankruptcy date have been quantified. Therefore the law adopts a second technique, which is to make an estimation of the value of the claim. Section 322(3) says:

> 'The trustee shall estimate the value of any bankruptcy debt which, by reason of its being subject to any contingency or contingencies or for any other reason, does not bear a certain value.'

This enables the trustee to quantify a creditor's contingent or unascertained claim, for the purposes of set-off or proof, in a way which will enable the trustee safely to distribute the estate, even if subsequent events show that the claim was worth more. There is no similar machinery for quantifying contingent or unascertained claims *against* the creditor, because it would be unfair upon him to have his liability to pay advanced merely because the trustee wants to wind up the bankrupt's estate.[52] The estimation of value applies not only to liquidated claims but also those that are unliquidated—for example, damages for breach of contract—though it has to be said that, in contrast to the rules governing proof of debt, the set-off rules have never explicitly referred to damages or unliquidated claims in describing what falls within the phrase "debt or liability".[53]

The mandatory principle

Insolvency set-off is mandatory and cannot be excluded by agreement of the parties. This was so held by a majority decision of the House of Lords in *National Westminster Bank Ltd v Halesowen Presswork and Assemblies Ltd*[54] The reason given is that the statutory provisions are considered to regulate matters of public interest in the orderly administration of the estate and are not purely a source of private rights enacted for the benefit

8–19

---

[52] On this aspect the law has been changed by the new rr.4.90 and 2.85. See below, para.8–39.
[53] See below, para.8–30.
[54] [19721 A.C. 785, Lord Cross dissenting.

of individual debtors of the estate having cross-claims against it. This majority ruling in *Halesowen*, though consistent with the imperative language of the set-off provision, constitutes an impediment to the reorganisation of companies in financial difficulty, a fact recognised in *Halesowen* but in the majority view requiring legislation to deal with it. The Insolvency Law Review Committee gave much thought to the matter, pointing out that it was a common practice for a company in difficulty, when negotiating a moratorium with its creditors, to agree to open a new bank account with its existing bankers and keep this in credit, the bank for its part undertaking not to set off existing indebtedness, so that the fund would be preserved intact for any liquidator and the bank would not receive a preference. The present law made it necessary for the company to open another account with a different bank.[55] The committee concluded that there was no sound policy for maintaining the prohibition against contracting-out of insolvency set-off and good commercial reasons for reversing it, and they recommended legislation to that effect.[56] No steps have yet been taken to implement this recommendation.

The retroactivity principle

8–20   The effect of this principle is that the account between the company and the creditor asserting a right of set-off is considered to be taken as at the date of winding-up even though it is not taken, and in practice cannot be taken, until a later date. In other words, insolvency set-off is self-executing and, once the facts are known, operates automatically from the point of liquidation without the need for any procedural step.[57] It follows that it is not open to the creditor to assign his claim against the company after the commencement of the winding-up and prior to the taking of the account,[58] for the claim must be treated as *ipso jure* ceasing to exist as a separate claim upon the company going into liquidation, the claim and cross-claim being then automatically combined by force of law to produce a single net debit balance due to or from the creditor. However, this net balance, if in favour of the company, is capable of assignment by the liquidator or, if in favour of the solvent party, by that party, at any time after the company has gone into liquidation, without the need to wait for the taking of accounts.[59] This follows from the fact that the ultimate quantification of claim and cross-claim and the striking of a balance take effect from the date of liquidation.

---

[55] *Insolvency Law and Practice*, (Cmnd. 8558, 1982), para.1341.
[56] Cmnd. 8558, 1982, para.1342.
[57] *Stein v Blake*, above, *per* Lord Hoffman at 254, 255, 258.
[58] This is now expressly provided by r.4.90(2)(d)(i) of the amended Insolvency Rules 1986. See below, para.8–26.
[59] *Stein v Blake*, above, n.43, at 258.

The hindsight principle

This is closely linked to the principle of retroactivity. The court looks at   **8–21**
post-liquidation events to determine the state of account as at the date of
liquidation. It applies in particular to the valuation of claims, whether these
are made by way of set-off or otherwise. Contingent claims which crystallise
into debts after the date of liquidation are brought into account as debts
and may be revalued accordingly[60] with retrospective effect.[61] Similarly,
amounts put in for existing but unliquidated claims may be adjusted if the
claims become liquidated or are able to be more accurately valued in the
light of post-liquidation events.[62] It follows from the hindsight principle, as
well as from the retroactivity principle, that an assignment of the net
balance can be made at any time after the company goes into liquidation,
whether or not the net balance has then been struck.

Conditions of application of insolvency set-off in winding-up

In order for r.4.90 as revised to apply seven conditions must be satisfied: **8–22**

(1)   The claim must be one for which the creditor has proved or is entitled
      to prove.

(2)   There must have been mutual credits, mutual debts or other mutual
      dealings between the parties.

(3)   The company's claim must not have been based on the creditor's
      wrongdoing.

(4)   The mutual dealings must have taken place before the company goes
      into liquidation.

(5)   The claims on both sides much be such as will in their nature
      terminate in debts.

(6)   The claim by the solvent party must be one which would be admissible
      for proof at the time when it becomes necessary to ascertain the state
      of accounts between the company and the solvent party.[63]

---

[60] See Insolvency Rules 1986, r.4.86(1).

[61] Subject only to the qualification that revaluation does not disturb distributions of dividend
already made, though any additional sum payable as the result of it will have priority in any
future distribution.

[62] See further below, para.8–30, as to unliquidated claims.

[63] By this is meant the time when it is necessary for *any* purpose to ascertain the state of
account, not necessarily any single point in time.

(7)   The debt which the solvent party seeks to set off must not be a debt of a category excluded by r.4.90(2).

There was previously a further condition, namely that the company's claim had to have matured by the time it became necessary to ascertain the state of accounts. That condition has now gone. It is open to the company to set off a claim which is still contingent at the time of taking of the account, even though the effect is to accelerate the solvent party's liability to the company to the extent of the set-off.[64]

We shall examine each of the remaining seven conditions in turn.

Claim must be admissible for proof

8–23   Though the fact that the creditor's claim is provable is not a sufficient condition of his right to have it included in the set-off account, it is a necessary condition. A claim which is not provable cannot be asserted by way of set-off.[65] Hence the creditor may not set off a claim which is unenforceable,[66] nor can he assert a claim embodied in a proof which the liquidator has rejected, for this would be to allow him to by-pass the rejection without going through the proper procedure of applying to the court under r.4.83 to reverse the liquidator's decision.[67] Again, a surety who is debarred by the rule against double proof from proving in the principal debtor's winding-up[68] cannot achieve his objective by asserting a set-off.[69]

Mutual credits, mutual debts and other mutual dealings

8–24   In its original form the statutory provision was confined to mutual credits and mutual debts. The phrase "and other mutual dealings" was added by s.39 of the Bankruptcy Act 1869. The word "other", which taken literally would have cut down the previous right of set-off by requiring that the mutual credits and debits should be such as to constitute mutual dealings, has been construed as a linguistic slip,[70] since it is clear that s.39 was

---

[64] Insolvency Rules 1986, r.4.90(4)(b). See below, para.8–39.

[65] *Re Fenton Ex p. Fenton Textile Association Ltd* [1931] 1 Ch. 85; *Re West End Networks Ltd, Secretary of State for Trade and Industry v Frid* [2004] 2 All E.R. 1042. This is implicit in the reference in r.4.90(1) to "any creditor of the company proving or claiming to prove for a debt in the liquidation"; and see *Stein v Blake* [1996] A.C. 243, *per* Lord Hoffmann at 253.

[66] *Pott v Clegg* (1847) 16 M. & W. 321.

[67] *Bank of Credit and Commerce International (Overseas) Ltd v Habib Bank Ltd* [1999] 1 W.L.R. 42.

[68] The rule against double proof precludes a surety who has not paid the debt from lodging a proof in respect of his prospective right of indemnity, for this would lead to a proof for the same debt by two people, the surety and the creditor.

[69] *Re Glen Express Ltd* [2000] B.P.I.R. 456.

[70] Or, as the High Court of Australia put it in *Gye v McIntyre* (1991) 171 C.L.R. 609 at 623, "a linguistic problem".

intended to broaden rather than constrict the right of set-off, and as the High Court of Australia pointed out,[71] "credits" and "debits" will ordinarily represent the outcome of dealings rather than the dealings themselves. This was the approach taken by the House of Lords in *Re West End Networks Ltd, Secretary of State for Trade and Industry v Frid*,[72] where it was held that the word "dealings" should be construed in an extended sense. In particular, it was not confined to consensual dealings but covered the imposition of a statutory obligation analogous to a guarantee and even the commission of a tort. In that case the question was whether a company which had gone into voluntary liquidation was entitled to set off a VAT credit against the Secretary of State's claim by statutory subrogation to the rights of unpaid employees which she had discharged in pursuance of a statutory obligation. It was held that the Secretary of State's statutory liability for the sums due to the employees was analogous to a contract of guarantee and the fact that it was statutory rather than contractual did not change its character as arising from a dealing forming so as to make the claim and cross-claim mutual debts or other mutual dealings susceptible to set-off.[73] As to claims in tort, it is thought that not all tort claims qualify for entry into a set-off account. The particular tort claim the House of Lords had in mind was that which featured in *Gye v McIntyre*,[74] namely a claim for damages for fraudulent misrepresentation inducing a contract. That plainly is a claim arising from a business dealing and one which was held part of mutual dealings between the parties. By contrast a claim against the company in tort for, say, conversion would not be a claim arising from a dealing.[75]

The requirement of mutuality has two facets.[76] First, the respective characters of the claim and the cross-claim must be commensurable. This means that claim and cross-claim must both be monetary claims or claims which a party is entitled to have reduced to money.[77] So a person holding property as bailee or trustee for another cannot set off against his delivery or accounting obligation a money claim against the bailor or beneficiary. This rule is so strictly applied that even if the property held by the trustee is itself a money fund, the trustee is not permitted to set off his personal claim against the beneficiary, and if the beneficiary goes into liquidation the trustee must transfer the fund to the liquidator intact and is left to prove in

---

[71] (1991) 171 C.L.R. 609 at 623.

[72] [2004] 2 All E.R. 1042.

[73] An unusual feature of the case was that the Secretary of State had wanted to treat her claim on this basis and sought to deduct the VAT credit from her proof, and it was the liquidator who rejected the proof on the ground that it should have been for the full amount. It must be rare for a proof to be rejected as being for too low a figure!

[74] Above, n.70.

[75] See the discussion in Derham, *The Law of Set-Off* (3rd ed.), para.8.44, citing the decision of the New South Wales Supreme Court in *Re Leeholme Stud Pty Ltd* [1965] N.S.W.R. 1649.

[76] See Derham, *op. cit.*, above n.1, Chap.7; Roy Goode, *Legal Problems of Credit and Security* (3rd ed.), paras 7–82 *et seq*.

[77] See below.

the liquidation for his cross-claim.[78] Secondly, there must be mutuality of parties, that is, the claim and cross-claim must be between the same parties in the same right. So it is not possible to set off against a claim by the company in liquidation a cross-claim against a third party, even if prior to liquidation there had been a valid contractual set-off along these lines, for on winding-up any contractual set-off, so far as not already exercised, disappears. Again, a claim against the company in liquidation cannot be set off against a claim vested in the company as trustee for a third party. In determining mutuality the court will look at the beneficial ownership of claim and cross-claim rather than the legal title, but will require clear evidence that the beneficial interest is vested in someone other than the party holding the legal title.[79] The Crown is regarded as indivisible, so that a sum due from one department of State can be set off against a sum due to another department.[80]

In general, a person holding bonds through an account with an intermediary cannot assert a set-off against the issuer of the bonds, with whom he has no relationship, his dealings being with his own intermediary. There may, however, be cases in which such a person does acquire a direct claim against the issuer, for example where the terms of the bond issue entitle him to call for delivery of definitive certificates which place him in a direct relationship with the issuer or where, in the case of a permanently immobilised global certificate, he is nevertheless given and exercises a right given by the bond trust deed or a deed poll to call for delivery or transfer of the underlying securities in extreme circumstances, such as the issuer's insolvency.

Company's claim must not have been based on creditor's wrongdoing

8–25   The creditor cannot escape from the consequences of a misfeasance or other wrongdoing for which the company is making a claim by invoking a right of set-off against the claim. So the creditor cannot set off the debt

---

[78] *National Westminster Bank plc v Halesowen Presswork and Assemblies Ltd* [1972] A.C. 785, *per* Lord Kilbrandon at 821; In *Re Mid-Kent Fruit Factory* [1896] 1 Ch. 567. The underlying principle appears to be that money held on trust is held for a particular purpose and cannot be applied for a different purpose, namely towards discharge of a cross-claim, without the consent of the person for whom it is held. Another way of reaching the same result is to say that a contract claim and a trust claim do not constitute mutual dealings. There is authority that the principle does not apply in relation to a money fund held on a bare trust (*Re ILG Travel Ltd* [1995] 2 B.C.L.C. 128), but it is questionable whether this is correct. For an excellent treatment of set-off in relation to trust funds, see S.R. Derham, *Set-Off* (3rd ed.), Chap.10.

[79] *Bank of Credit and Commerce International SA v Prince Fahd Bin Salman Abdul Aziz Al-Saud* [1997] B.C.C. 63.

[80] *Re West End Networks Ltd, Secretary of State for Trade and Industry v Frid*, n.72 above, in which it was held that a VAT credit due from Customs and Excise could be set off against a claim by the Secretary of State for Trade and Industry for the amount paid to employees to whose rights she was subrogated.

owed to him by the company in liquidation against a claim by the company by way of misfeasance proceedings for the recovery of misappropriated funds[81] or for damages for conversion[82] or recovery of a sum paid to him by way of a voidable preference[83] or settlement.[84] Any other conclusion would enable the wrongdoer to benefit from his wrongdoing by recovery through set-off instead of having to prove in the winding-up in competition with other creditors.[85]

The mutual dealings must have preceded the liquidation

This is expressly stated in r.4.90. However, it is not necessary that the **8–26** dealings should have given rise to mutual *debts* prior to the winding-up. It suffices that the mutual dealings have created obligations which give rise to claims that can be set against each other at the time when it becomes necessary to ascertain the state of accounts between the parties.[86] Thus the fact that a claim is still contingent at the time of commencement of the winding-up does not affect its eligibility for set-off if it crystallises into a debt after the winding-up.[87] Of course, the claim must not offend the rule against double proof.[88] So a surety who prior to the winding-up has a contingent right to be indemnified by the debtor if the latter later defaults in payment to the creditor cannot assert the right as a set-off after the debtor's default unless he has paid the debt.[89]

The claims on both sides must be such as will in their nature terminate in debt

Set-off is in principle confined to mutual money obligations, secured or **8–27** unsecured.[90] The solvent party cannot rely on set-off to withhold property of the company in his possession or control, whether as bailee or as bare

---

[81] *Manson v Smith* [1997] 2 B.C.L.C. 161.

[82] *Smith (Administrator of Cosslett (Contractors) Ltd v Bridgend County Borough Council* [2002] 1 A.C. 336.

[83] *Re a Debtor (No.82 of 1926)* [1927] 1 Ch. 410.

[84] *Lister v Hooson* [1908] 1 K.B. 174.

[85] *Manson v Smith*, n.81 above, *per* Millett J. at 165.

[86] *Stein v Blake* [1996] 1 A.C. 243; *Re West End Networks Ltd, Secretary of State v Frid* [2004] 2 All E.R. 1042.

[87] *Re West End Networks Ltd, Secretary of State v Frid*, n.86 above. For detailed comment on the case see Ian Fletcher, "Crown Set-Off and Contingent Liabilities", *Insolvency Intelligence* January 2005, p.6. This was published before the amendment to r.2.85 and needs to be read in that light.

[88] See para.7–35.

[89] *See Re West End Networks Ltd, Secretary of State v Frid*, n.86 above, *per* Lord Hoffmann, paras 16–17.

[90] The fact that one of the debts is secured does not affect the right of the debtor to set off his own cross-claim against it; the effect of this is simply to reduce the amount of the secured

trustee, and in the latter case this applies as much to a money fund held by
the solvent party as bare trustee for the company as it does to tangible
property so held. Accordingly if B, a bailee of goods owned by A Co,
wrongfully sells the goods he cannot set off a debt due to him from the
company against his obligation to account for the proceeds, for the
company's claim to the proceeds is not a mere money claim in debt but a
claim to ownership of the money fund which is enforceable as a proprietary
claim in equity. Additional grounds for refusing a set-off are that a person
cannot take advantage of his own wrong by converting another's property
into money[91] and that a misappropriation is not a dealing.[92]

However, there are at least two apparent exceptions to the rule precluding set-off against property and trust moneys. First, if the property of the
company in liquidation is subject to a lien or other security interest in
favour of the solvent party the security carries through to the proceeds of
sale and may be enforced by retention of the proceeds to the extent of the
amount owing to the secured creditor. This is not a true set-off, merely a
method of enforcing the security interest. Secondly, if property of the
company is held by another with instructions or authority to convert it into
money, then so long as that authority remains unrevoked at the time of
liquidation the other party, on selling the property, can set off against his
liability to account for the proceeds a debt owed to him by the company in
liquidation, even if the sale does not take place until after winding-up,
provided that the proceeds are received by the claimant by the time it
becomes necessary to ascertain the state of accounts between him and the
company. This is the principle established in *Rose v Hart*,[93] which has been
said to constitute an anomalous exception to the rule, that a money claim
may not be set off against a proprietary claim and to the separate mutuality
rule that trust funds are not susceptible to set-off.[94] But this is doubtful. The
essence of the rule in *Rose v Hart* is the provision of mutual credits, the

obligation. See *MS Fashions Ltd v Bank of Credit and Commerce International SA (No.2)*,
above n.48, *per* Dillon L.J. at 446; *Re ILG Travel Ltd* [1996] B.C.C. 21. There is a rather
cryptic observation by Rose L.J. in *Re Bank of Credit and Commerce International SA (No.8)*
[1996] Ch. 245 at 258 that "[I]nsolvency is concerned with the distribution of the debtor's
uncharged assets among his unsecured creditors. Trust property and security stand outside
the scheme of distribution and the scope of insolvency set-off. Set-off ought not to prejudice
the right of a secured creditor to enforce his security in any order he chooses and at a time
of his choice." It is, of course, true that in principle a secured creditor is unaffected by a
bankruptcy or liquidation and need not prove in competition with other creditors. However,
he can enforce his security only for the amount due to him, and to the extent to which his
claim is satisfied by the automatic set-off arising under r.4.90 of the Insolvency Rules there
is no longer a debt to be enforced (the same applies to set-off outside liquidation-see above,
para.8–01).
[91] *Smith v Bridgend County Borough Council* [2002] 1 A.C. 336.
[92] *Manson v Smith* [1997] 2 B.C.L.C. 161, *per* Millett L.J. at 164. Another way of reaching the
same result is to say that a contract claim and a trust claim do not constitute mutual
dealings.
[93] (1818) 8 Taunt. 499.
[94] Derham, *op cit.*, para.10.15.

solvent party extending credit to the company in reliance on his prospective receipt of the proceeds of the company's property for which the company gives credit to him, and that the credits are such "as must in their nature terminate in debts."[95] Hence the true basis of the decision in *Rose v Hart* would seem to be that the person holding the company's property with instructions to convert it into money has implied authority, by virtue of their mutual dealings, to regard himself as a mere debtor for a sum equal to the proceeds, not as a trustee of the proceeds themselves, which he is free to treat as his own moneys.

The significance of the distinction is well established in decisions on reservation of title to goods under contracts of sale which authorise resale by the buyer but impose no express requirement that he is to account for the proceeds of sale. In such cases the court is likely to infer that the buyer is merely to be a debtor for the amount of the proceeds (or of such part of them as is necessary to discharge his price obligation), not a trustee.[96] A similar principle applies where the terms of the agreement between the parties impose on the solvent party a duty to hold the proceeds on trust for the company but entitle him to deduct sums due to him from the company. Such an agreement will be construed as creating a charge on the proceeds, so that the solvent party is not a bare trustee but one whose trust obligation applies only to the balance remaining in his hands after he has deducted from the proceeds the amount due to him.[97] The absence of a duty to keep the proceeds segregated from the solvent party's own moneys is not inconsistent with such a trust.[98] The position is otherwise where the solvent party is a bare trustee of the proceeds and thus has a duty to make them over to the company in liquidation without deduction.[99]

All this presupposes that the disposition of the company's property was **8–28** authorised, for if it was not the person making it can hardly contend that he had authority to treat the proceeds as his own.[1] Moreover, as previously mentioned, a person cannot rely on his own wrongdoing to create a set-off or to serve as a mutual dealing. So if he never had authority to sell in the first place or his authority was revoked prior to the sale he will be a trustee of the entire proceeds and will have no right to set off his cross-claim against his duty to account.[2]

In the light of these considerations the decision of the Court of Appeal in the controversial decision in *Rolls Razor Ltd v Cox*[3] is hard to justify. In that

---

[95] *Rose v Hart* (1818) 8 Taunt. 499, *per* Gibbs C.J. at 506.

[96] *Re Andrabell Ltd* [1984] 3 All E.R. 407; *Hendy Lennox Ltd v Grahame Puttick Ltd* [1984] 2 All E.R. 152. See R. M. Goode, *Proprietary Rights and Insolvency in Sales Transactions* (2nd ed.), pp.99 *et seq.*

[97] *Re ILG Travel Ltd* [1996] B.C.C. 21.

[98] *ibid.*

[99] *ibid.*; *Henry v Hammond* [1913] 2 K.B. 515.

[1] R. M. Goode, *op. cit.*, p.99.

[2] *Rose v Hart* (1818) 8 Taunt. 499; *Eberle's Hotels & Restaurant Co Ltd v Jonas* (1887) 18 Q.B.D. 459.

[3] [1967] 1 All E.R. 397.

case the defendant was a self-employed salesman appointed by the plaintiffs to sell their washing machines in return for commission and was required by the terms of his appointment to hand over the proceeds without deduction. The company also deducted a percentage of each week's commission to form a retention fund to which it could resort if the salesman defaulted in his obligations in regard to machines or proceeds. The company having gone into liquidation, the defendant asserted a lien and a right to set off the commission and retention moneys due to him against the proceeds he had received of two washing machines sold for the company prior to liquidation and the value of (*inter alia*) an unsold table top still in his possession at the time of liquidation and seven tap-adaptors, not for sale, which were used in the demonstration of the machines. The Court of Appeal upheld this contention as regards the goods, and proceeds of goods, held for sale[4] (Winn L.J. dissenting as to the table top) on the ground that while the defendant did not have a lien on the goods, there were mutual credits-by the company to the defendant in respect of the proceeds of sale and by the defendant to the company in respect of the retention fund-so that a right of set-off arose which the company had not been entitled to defeat by purporting to terminate the agent's authority to sell.

The majority decision is hard to justify. In the first place, the table top had not in fact been converted into money even after the winding-up, and in no previous case had a money claim been set off against an obligation to deliver unrealised property. Secondly, the defendant's contention that he was entitled to a lien on the goods was rejected, not merely because he was a mere agent, not a factor, but also because this was inconsistent with the terms of his agreement with the company requiring him to deliver up the goods on termination of the agreement. Surely it was equally inconsistent with the agreement that he should be allowed to sell the goods after termination of his authority and then deduct what was due to him from the proceeds. The decision in *Rose v Hart*[5] was specifically predicated on the assumption that the agent's authority to sell remained unrevoked up to the time of sale, and the same was true of the decision in *Palmer v Day*.[6] Nor could it be said that the defendant's authority to sell was irrevocable because it was coupled with an interest,[7] namely the right to look to the proceeds for payment of his commmission, for this, too, was prohibited by the agreement. Accordingly it could not be said that there were mutual credits, and that being so the defendant's authority to sell had been effectively brought to an end by the company and would in any event have come to an end on the winding-up. The defendant was thus not a mere

---

[4] But not the tap-adaptors held for use only.
[5] (1818) 8 Taunt. 499.
[6] [1895] 2 Q.B. 618.
[7] See *Bowstead and Reynolds on Agency* (17th ed.), paras 10–006 and 10–007.

debtor but a trustee, who ought not to have been allowed to profit from his own act of conversion.[8] It is true that the set-off provisions are mandatory—a point relied on by Lord Denning M.R. to overcome the contract point—but they do not apply at all unless the test of mutuality is satisfied, and this is not the case where the claim on one side is to payment of money and on the other to delivery of property held on trust or to the proceeds of property wrongfully converted. The present position has rightly been described as anomalous[9] and is a good illustration of hard cases making bad law.

Claim by solvent party must be of a kind admissible to proof at the relevant time

The solvent party cannot assert a set-off in respect of a claim which would not be admissible for proof at the time when it becomes necessary to ascertain the state of accounts between the parties. So a claim which is statute-barred cannot be used as a set-off,[10] nor can a claim which is so contingent as to be incapable of estimation by the liquidator.[11] The solvent party cannot avoid this result by deferring the lodging of his proof, for the statutory provisions as to the taking of an account do not depend on the lodging of a proof but apply at any point in time where the occasion arises for the taking of the account.[12] Not all claims eligible for proof are also eligible for set-off. The requirement of mutuality must also be satisfied.[13]

8–29

Unliquidated damages

A claim for unliquidated damages has been admissible for set-off since s.10 of the Judicature Act 1875 imported into winding-up the rules of set-off in bankruptcy,[14] in which set-off had, as previously mentioned, been extended by s.39 of the Bankruptcy Act 1869 to cover mutual dealings and it was this that was held to cover unliquidated claims for damages.[15]

8–30

---

[8] See above, para.8–25.
[9] Wood, *op. cit.*, para.9–304.
[10] *Pott v Clegg* (1847) 16 M. & W. 321.
[11] See Insolvency Rules 1986, rr.4.86, 13.12(3).
[12] *Stein v Blake*, above.
[13] *Bank of Credit and Commerce International S.A. v Prince Fahd Bin Salman Abdul Aziz Al-Saud* [1997] B.C.C. 63.
[14] *Mersey Steel and Iron Co, Ltd v Naylor, Benzon & Co* (1889) 9 App. Cas. 434; *Re Asphaltic Wood Pavement Co, Lee & Chapman's Case* (1885) 30 Ch.D. 216.
[15] *Booth v Hutchinson* (1872) L.R. 15 Eq. 30. Hence it is unnecessary to rely on the new r.4.90, based on the more general r.13.12(3), a rule of long standing which strangely, in contrast to r.12.3(1) relating to provable debts, does not refer specifically to claims for damages or, indeed, unliquidated claims of any kind but states merely that a sum shall be regarded as being due to or from the company "whether . . . its amount is fixed or liquidated, or is capable of being ascertained by fixed rules or as a matter of opinion".

Solvent party's claim must not be excluded by rule 4.90(2)

8–31   Rule 4.90(2) of the revised Insolvency Rules 1986 sets out the various categories of debt that are to be excluded from the concept of mutual credits, mutual debts or other mutual dealings. These are as follows:

(1) Debt arising out of obligation incurred with notice of winding-up meeting or petition

8–32   Debts due from the company in liquidation to another party are not to be included in the account of mutual dealings if they arose out of an obligation incurred at a time when that other party had notice that a meeting of creditors had been convened under s.98 of the Insolvency Act or that a petition for winding-up was pending. It is to be noted that the relevant time is not when the debt became payable but when the obligation which arose from it was incurred. So provided that the solvent party was without notice of the above facts when the debt was contracted, the fact that he later acquires notice before the debt matures does not debar him from having it brought into account.

(2) Debt arising out of obligation incurred with notice of administration application

8–33   A debt is excluded from the set-off account if arising out of an obligation where the liquidation was immediately preceded by an administration and at the time the obligation was incurred the creditor had notice that an application for an administration order was pending or a person had given notice of intention to appoint an administrator.

(3) Debt arising out of obligation incurred during an administration immediately preceding the liquidation

8–34   If the liquidation was immediately preceded by an administration, a debt arising from an obligation incurred during the administration is not eligible for inclusion in the set-off account.

(4) Debt acquired by assignee in certain events

8–35   In general a person owing the company money is entitled to set off against his liability a claim vested in him as assignee. So a debtor to the company can purchase a claim against the company and set this off against the company's claim on him. However, the right of set-off is potentially vulnerable if the assignment is taken at a time when the company is insolvent. Though this is not by itself a bar to inclusion of the assigned debt in the set-off account, the effect of r.4.90 is that the debt cannot be included if it was acquired by the creditor, by assignment or otherwise,[16] pursuant to an agreement between the creditor and any other party:

(i) after the company went into liquidation;

(ii) at a time when the creditor had notice that a meeting of creditors had been summoned under s.98;

(iii) at a time when the creditor had notice that a winding-up petition was pending;

(iv) where the liquidation was immediately preceded by an administration, at a time when the creditor had notice that an application for an administration order was pending or a person had given notice of intention to appoint an administrator;

(v) during an administration which immediately preceded the liquidation.

Position where claim by company is contingent

The set-off rules were formerly incapable of being applied where it was the company liquidation that had the contingent claim. That is no longer the case.[17]   **8–36**

5. INSOLVENCY SET-OFF IN SPECIAL SITUATIONS

(i) Set-off in relation to unmatured or contingent claims under executed contracts

The question addressed here is the extent to which unmatured or contingent claims arising under contracts wholly performed by the claimant may be set off by or against the other party.   **8–37**

Unmatured or contingent claims by the solvent party

The effect of the statutory provisions for the admission to proof of unmatured debts at their face value[18] and of contingent claims at their estimated value is that as from the date of liquidation such claims are   **8–38**

---

[16] For example, by contractual subrogation. But acquisition by legal subrogation, as where the creditor was a surety for the company and has paid the debt due to the creditor, is not barred, for the right of subrogation is not conferred by agreement.

[17] See below, para.8–39.

[18] But discounted for the purpose of dividend distribution (Insolvency Rules 1986, r.11.13(2)).

notionally converted into matured debts and are automatically set off against any matured debts owed by the creditor to the company. This, however, is subject to the rule against double proof which (*inter alia*) precludes a surety from proving or setting off his right of indemnity against the insolvent company until he has paid in full the amount of the guaranteed debt or such separate part of it as he has guaranteed.[19]

Unmatured or contingent claims against the solvent party

8–39   In the converse case where it is the company in liquidation that has the unmatured or contingent claim the position was formerly that the rules set out above did not apply. This was because the liquidator has no right to accelerate the liability of the solvent party; the principle of acceleration applies only to claims *against* the company. Thus the solvent party was entitled to prove for his claim in full without offset of the company's unmatured or contingent claim against him. If the latter claim matured into an immediately payable debt the liquidator could sue for it in the name of the company but the solvent party was entitled to set off against the liquidator the amount of his own cross-claim after giving credit for any dividend received.[20]

These complexities have now been removed as the result of changes to r.4.90, the effect of which is that the liquidator may now set off even future or contingent claims against the solvent party, thus accelerating the solvent party's liability for set-off purposes, but any balance remaining due from the solvent party is to be paid only when it falls due and payable.[21] In other words, the acceleration is limited to what is necessary to exhaust the set-off rights of the company in liquidation.

(ii) Set-off in relation to deposits taken by a bank which becomes insolvent

8–40   The collapse of the Bank of Credit and Commercial International SA gave rise to a number of actions concerning the effect of the insolvency rules where the bank had loaned money to a borrower and taken a security deposit of funds from a third party. In some cases this was underpinned by the third party's personal guarantee, in others it was not. In one case the guarantee contained a "principal debtor" clause which was held to impose on the surety the liability of a principal debtor for repayment. In working

---

[19] See above, para.7–35.
[20] *MS Fashions Ltd v Bank of Credit and Commerce International S.A. (No.2)*, above n.48, at 435.
[21] Insolvency Rules 1986, r.4.90(8).

out the insolvency set-off rules it is necessary to distinguish three situations.[22] The first is where the depositor gives a personal guarantee which contains a principal debtor clause, so that his liability is not merely contingent. The second is where he gives a personal guarantee which does not contain a principal debtor clause and provides for payment on demand, so that his liability is contingent on demand being made. The third is where he gives no personal guarantee at all but merely deposits funds with the creditor as security for the loan to the borrower.

(1) Deposit reinforced by personal guarantee containing a principal debtor clause

In *MS Fashions Ltd v Bank of Credit and Commerce International SA*   **8–41**
(No.2)[23] the issue was concisely presented by Hoffmann L.J. in the following terms:

> "A bank advances money to a company. Repayment is guaranteed by a director who has a deposit account with the bank. As between himself and the bank, the director is expressed to be a principal debtor. On the insolvency of the bank, can the director set off his claim for return of his deposit against his liability to pay the company's debt, so that the debt is wholly or *pro tanto* extinguished? Or can the bank claim the whole debt from the company and leave the director to prove in the liquidation for his deposit?"[24]

Hoffmann L.J. held that as a matter of construction the effect of the principal debtor clause was that the director was not merely making a deposit by way of security but was assuming a personal liability for repayment jointly and severally with the borrower company, or alternatively severally, that such liability was not merely contingent and that accordingly the liquidation of the bank resulted in an automatic set-off of the deposit against the liability, thus *pro tanto* extinguishing the indebtedness of the borrower company. It was therefore not open to the liquidator, as it would have been if there had been no principal debtor clause, to recover from the borrower without giving credit for the deposit, leaving the director to prove as an unsecured creditor for the amount of his deposit released from the charge as the result of the borrower's repayment.

On the finding of a personal guarantee as a matter of construction the result reached was inevitable. However, it has to be said that the evidence

---

[22] For an excellent discussion, see Richard Calnan, "The Insolvent Bank and Security Over Deposits" (1996) JIFBL 185.
[23] [1993] Ch. 425.
[24] *ibid.*, at 430.

for a personal guarantee was decidedly tenuous; and the ruling that the charge itself could be analysed as the creation of a personal liability not exceeding the amount of the deposit[25] is not sustainable, for it imports a personal liability where none is needed except, of course, for the purpose of arriving at the desired result! In *Re Bank of Credit and Commerce International SA (No.8)*[26] the Court of Appeal felt unable to agree with this ruling and Lord Hoffmann himself, in the subsequent appeal to the House of Lords,[27] acknowledged that it produced anomalous results and was based on the peculiar wording of the guarantee.

(2) Deposit reinforced by personal guarantee payable on demand with no principal debtor clause

8–42   In this situation the surety is not a principal debtor and in the absence of demand his liability is merely contingent. As we have seen, a contingent claim *by* the company in liquidation *against* the solvent party was formerly not accelerated by the liquidation, so that unless demand was made, converting the contingent claim into a matured debt, no set-off could be invoked by the liquidator. In consequence the liquidator could avoid the independent set-off by refraining from making the requisite demand, thus maintaining the company's claim in full against the borrower without having to give credit for the sum that would have been treated as received from the surety in a balance of account had the set-off provisions been triggered. Under the revised r.4.90 the solvent party's liability is accelerated to the extent of the company's right of set-off.

(3) Deposit not reinforced by any personal guarantee

8–43   This was the situation in the *BCCI* case mentioned above, where the facts were otherwise very similar to those in *MS Fashions*. Money was deposited with the bank by way of non-recourse collateral security[28] for a loan to the principal debtor. The bank then went into liquidation. The liquidator declined to resort to the security deposit and sought repayment from the principal debtor without giving credit for the deposit, leaving the depositor to prove as an unsecured creditor. The borrower and the depositor contended that credit should be given for the deposit. Among the various

---

[25] *ibid.*, at 431.
[26] [1996] Ch. 245; [1996] B.C.L.C. 204 *sub nom. Morris v Agrichemicals Ltd.* See below, para.8–43.
[27] *Re Bank of Credit and Commerce International SA* [1998] A.C. 214 at 224–225.
[28] It had at one time been thought that this was conceptually impossible, but see now *Re Bank of Credit and Commerce International SA* [1998] A.C. 214, *per* Lord Hoffmann at 226–228 and Roy Goode, *Legal Problems of Credit and Security* (3rd ed.) para.3–12.

grounds advanced were: that the depositor as a non-recourse surety had a right to pay off the debt and to have his deposit utilised for that purpose; that the liquidator's approach would expose the borrower to a double liability, namely to repay the loan and to indemnify the depositor against the loss of his deposit through the bank's insolvency; that the bank's inability to repay the deposit discharged the borrower *pro tanto* from liability by reason of the bank's "loss" of the security in becoming insolvent and its consequent inability to return it; and that the deposit was paid to the bank on trust to be applied for a particular purpose, namely discharge of the principal debt, for which it should be used by the liquidator.

The House of Lords,[29] affirming the decision of the Court of Appeal,[30] had no difficulty in rejecting all these arguments. In the absence of any personal guarantee by the depositor it was not possible to set off the deposit against the loan. The bank owed money to the depositor and the borrower owed money to the bank. The debts were therefore not due from the same parties, so that the mutuality which was essential to avoid a preference over other creditors was lacking. The proposition that the borrower was exposed to double liability was fallacious, since it rested on the assumption that the borrower was obliged to indemnify the depositor against the loss of his deposit, a proposition which was untenable. The surety's only right to indemnity was where he had paid off the principal debt. Nor could the principle relating to loss of securities by the creditor avail the borrower or depositor. The deposit had not been disposed of or the depositor's legal entitlement to repayment impaired; the position was simply that the bank was unable to repay. In any event there was no basis for saying that the loss of a security provided by a surety discharges the principal debtor; at best it would discharge the surety. Finally, there was no evidence to show that the deposit had been impressed with a purpose trust. The bank was a mere debtor.

It was recognised that this result produced the paradox that a surety who gave no personal guarantee was worse off than one who gave a personal guarantee and thus had his liability extinguished by set-off. But that was inevitable if injustice to the general body of creditors was to be avoided. The point here is that what the depositor was seeking to do was to avoid the consequences of the bank's insolvency so far as he was concerned by requiring the bank to utilise the deposit to pay off the debt. But the deposit was an asset of the bank which under the *pari passu* principle should be available for the general body of creditors. In the absence of any trust affecting it the depositor, as an unsecured creditor, had no right to give instructions to the liquidator as to the application of the deposit. By collecting repayment from the borrower the liquidator would cause the debt to be discharged, thus freeing the deposit from the security and entitling

---

[29] Re *Bank of Credit and Commece International SA* [1998] A.C. 214.
[30] [1996] Ch. 245.

the depositor to repayment. In that situation the depositor should stand in the same position as other unsecured creditors.

(iii) Set-off in relation to executory contracts

8–44 It will be evident from the foregoing that where all the relevant contracts are executed and the claims on both sides are for money or are reducible to money insolvency set-off will rarely be a problem in English law. Set-off in relation to existing liquidated claims, even if payable in the future, is straightforward. Unliquidated claims and contingent claims are valued (so far as capable of estimation) and become treated as the equivalent of liquidated claims for purposes of proof and set-off.

The one real danger zone is that occupied by executory contracts.[31] Where the contracts on both sides are still in force and executory at the time of winding-up the solvent party is exposed to the risk of cherry-picking by the liquidator, who may seek to enforce the contract that is profitable to the estate[32] while disclaiming the unprofitable contract[33] and leaving the solvent party to prove in the winding-up for damages. In principle such damages cannot be set off against the solvent party's liability under the other contract because of the principle that post-liquidation receipts derived from the activity of the liquidator and use of the company's resources do not belong to the company in its own right,[34] so that the requisite element of mutuality is lacking.[35] The solution is to provide in each contract that all executory contracts will automatically be terminated, rescinded or closed out by a reverse transaction in the event of either party going into liquidation.

(iv) Preferential debts

8–45 Where the creditor is owed both preferential and non-preferential debts, a set-off available to the company in liquidation for less than the total amount due is not to be applied exclusively to the preferential debts (thus benefiting the estate) or exclusively to the non-preferential debts (thus

---

[31] See above, para.6–16.

[32] Which in principle he can do except where (a) the winding-up of the company can be regarded as a repudiatory breach or (b) the court accedes to an application by the solvent party to rescind the contract under s.186 of the Insolvency Act 1986, which it will normally do only where the two contracts are so connected that it would be inequitable to allow the liquidator to enforce one contract if he is not prepared to procure the company's performance of the other.

[33] Under s.178 of the Act. See above, paras 6–20 *et seq.*

[34] See above, para.7–24.

[35] See Wood, *English and International Set-Off*, paras 5–18, 7–145 *et seq.*, for an exhaustive analysis with reference to typical transactions.

preserving the creditor's priority intact) but is to be applied to the two sets of debt rateably.[36]

(v) Voidable preferences

No question of preference can arise where the creditor collects payment by exercise of right of set-off, for this does not require the consent of the company at all, let alone a desire on its part to improve the creditor's position. Payment by the company into an overdrawn account with its bank is likewise not capable of being a preference where the payment does not exceed the amount of a credit balance held by the company on another account to which the bank could have resorted by way of combination of accounts if the payment in question had not been made, for the effect of the payment is *pro tanto* to reduce the available amount of set-off against the account in credit, so that the position of other creditors is unaffected.

    Where, by virtue of an agreement between a company and its directors, the company has a contractual right to set off against one director's credit balance an amount due from another director, exercise of that right is not a preference of the first director, for it is for the company's benefit, not that of the first director.[37]

8–46

(vi) Specially protected transactions and arrangements

In order to promote market stability and reduce systemic risk, various types of transaction concluded on a market or through a recognised clearing house or settlement system enjoy special protection from insolvency rules. This has been discussed earlier.[38]

8–47

(vii) Foreign currency set-off

For the purpose of proving a debt incurred or payable in a currency other than sterling, the amount of the debt is to be converted into sterling at the official rate of exchange prevailing on the date when the company went into liquidation.[39] This now applies also in relation to set-off under r.4.90 of the Insolvency Rules 1986.[40]

8–48

---

[36] *Re Unit 2 Windows Ltd* [1985] 2 All E.R. 647. This would appear to apply equally to a combination of accounts not effected prior to the winding-up. See Tony Shea, "Statutory Set-Off", [1986] 3 JIFBL 152, 154.

[37] *Re Exchange Travel (Holdings) Ltd (No.3)*. [1996] B.C.L.C. 524.

[38] Above, para.1–23 *et seq.*

[39] Insolvency Rules 1986, r.4.91(1).

[40] *ibid.*, r.4.90(6).

6. SET-OFF IN ADMINISTRATION

8–49   The rules governing insolvency set-off presuppose that the insolvency administrator has power to make distributions and for that purpose admit proofs and apply the relevant rules of insolvency set-off. A liquidator has always been invested with both the power and the duty to distribute; indeed, after collecting in the assets that is his primary function. By contrast the powers of distribution of an administrator were closely circumscribed.[41] So when administration was first introduced there were no rules of set-off in administration. When the Insolvency Act 1986 was amended to modify and simplify the administration procedure and to empower the court to give permission for the administrator to make a distribution[42] the opportunity was taken to amend the Insolvency Rules 1986 by substituting a new Part II, including a new r.2.85 providing for mutual credits and set-offs in administration.[43] This was modelled on rule 4.90 but with important differences in wording which caused concern to insolvency practitioners. Accordingly the Insolvency (Amendment) Rules 2005[44] substituted a new r.2.85 for the existing rule and modified r.4.90 to bring the two rules into alignment.

Since an administrator cannot make a distribution to general creditors without the permission of the court, r.2.95 applies only where the administrator, being authorised to make the distribution in question, has, pursuant to r.2.95, given notice that he proposes to make it.[45] As the result of the alignment of rr.2.85 and 4.90 the regimes applicable to set-off in administration and liquidation are essentially the same, with the substitution of references to (1) administration for references to liquidation, and (2) a winding-up immediately preceding the administration for references to a liquidation which was immediately preceded by an administration.

---

[41] See below, para.10–81.
[42] Sch.B1, para.65(2).
[43] Insolvency (Amendment) Rules 2003 (SI 2003/1730).
[44] SI 2005/527.
[45] Insolvency Rules 1986, r.2.85(1).

Chapter 9

Administrative Receivership

1. THE DEVELOPMENT OF ADMINISTRATIVE RECEIVERSHIP

Old-style receivership: the receiver of income

Historically, receivership is not an insolvency proceeding at all, merely a   **9–01**
method by which a secured creditor can enforce his security. Originally, a
mortgagee whose mortgagor defaulted could apply to the court to appoint a
receiver to collect the rents and profits of the mortgaged property and
apply these to payment of the mortgage interest. Subsequently it was found
more convenient for the appointment to be made by the mortgagor himself
at the request of the mortgagee, thus obviating an application to the court.
Later still, mortgagees began reserving the power to make the appointment
themselves, at the same time providing that the receiver was to be the agent
of the mortgagor, not of the mortgagee. In making the appointment the
mortgagee acted as agent of the mortgagor,[1] a fact which explains the
apparent anomaly of an agency created by an agreement to which the,
agent is not a party.[2] In due course, the power to appoint a receiver of
income was made statutory,[3] though it was the practice to exclude or
expand the statutory provisions relating to the circumstances in which a
receiver could be appointed and his powers on appointment. But the role of
such a receiver was, and remains, a receiver of income.

Modern receivership: the receiver and manager

With the expansion of business and the increased provision of credit to   **9–02**
finance the establishment and operation of the undertaking creditors
became increasingly concerned to secure stronger protection for their

---

[1] *Gaskell v Gosling* [1896] 1 Q.B. 669, per Rigby L.J. at 691. Though Rigby L.J. was a
dissenting minority, his judgment was approved by the House of Lords on appeal, *sub nom.*
Gosling v Gaskell [1897] A.C. 575.
[2] See further para.9–40.
[3] See now Law of Property Act 1925, ss.101(l)(iii). 109.

investment, in particular, by reserving the right to appoint not merely a receiver but a manager of the business, the two offices almost invariably being combined in the same person. In order for the receiver and manager to have effective powers of management it was, of course, necessary to provide the creditor with global security covering the whole or substantially the whole of the company's assets and undertaking. Thus evolved the modern debenture, which typically created a fixed charge over fixed assets and a floating charge over the rest of the company's undertaking, with power to appoint a receiver and manager,[4] having extensive authority to get in the assets, run the company's business and dispose of the assets either piecemeal or as part and parcel of a sale of the business as a going concern. A debenture holder could still apply to the court for the appointment of a receiver, but there was little advantage in so doing, for an application to the court would involve time and expense and the receiver's powers would be circumscribed by the terms of the order and his need to work within a judicial framework, whereas a receiver and manager appointed pursuant to the debenture had all the powers conferred by the debenture and could still be declared to act as agent of the mortgagor.

The introduction of the administration regime

9–03   Administrative receivership is essentially a debt enforcement mechanism for the benefit of the debenture holder who appoints the receiver. Prior to 1986 there was no machinery by which an external manager could be appointed to run the company's business and safeguard the assets for the benefit of the general body of creditors, and the administrative receiver owed no duty to creditors generally. The Insolvency Act 1986, re-enacting the Insolvency Act 1985, created just such machinery in the form of administration.[5] Under this new insolvency regime application could be made to the court to appoint an administrator to take control of the assets and manage the company for the benefit of all the creditors. The administrator was given the same extensive powers as an administrative receiver.[6] An application to the court had the effect of imposing a freeze on the exercise of most remedies, including the enforcement of security, but did not prevent the appointment of an administrative receiver, and if such an appointment were made before the making of an administration order the court was in general precluded from making such an order except with the debenture holder's consent.[7] Thus except where the security was vulnerable the debenture holder could always block administration by appointing an administrative receiver.

---

[4] Thus crystallising the floating charge (see para.9–35).
[5] Insolvency Act 1986, Part II.
[6] Insolvency Act 1986, s.14 and Sch.1.
[7] *ibid.*, s.9(3).

2. THE PARTIAL ABOLITION OF ADMINISTRATIVE RECEIVERSHIP

A review group set up by the Department of Trade and Industry and the **9–04** Treasury published a report in 2000[8] showing that views on the merits of administrative receivership were divided. Most respondents felt that administrative receivership was an integral part of the rescue culture that had been developing and contributed to the rescue and survival of companies, in that the receiver could take rapid and effective action to prevent further deterioration on the business of the company, a sizeable number of businesses were sold off by the receiver on a going concern basis and the costs of initiating the procedure were relatively low.[9] Banks were keen to support the rescue of viable companies but feared that changes to the existing system would reduce their security and their ability to enforce it. On the other hand, others felt that receivership placed too much power in the hands of one creditor and that this could lead to unnecessary business failures, particularly since there was a lack of incentive to consider the interests of other creditors and to maximise the value of the debtor company's estate.[10] Research conducted by Professor Julian Franks and Dr Oren Sussman,[11] based on material provided by three clearing banks, has shown that about 75 per cent of companies emerged from bank supervision and avoided formal insolvency procedures but that during the period in which the company was in intensive care the amount owed to the bank shrank while the amount owed to trade and expense creditors increased. Where a formal insolvency proceeding ensued, the average recovery rates were 77 per cent for the bank, 27 per cent for preferential creditors and virtually nil for unsecured creditors.[12] A subsequent small survey by R3, subsidiary to its main survey for the period January 2002 to June 2003, gives a similar dismal return for ordinary unsecured creditors, at just 5 pence in the pound.[13]

The principal recommendation of the review group was that the power of veto given to the holder of a floating charge to block an administration by appointing an administrative receiver should be abolished.[14] But under the influence of the Treasury, which considered that the whole institution of administrative receivership was inimical to corporate rescue through a collective insolvency proceeding, government thinking hardened. A White Paper published by the Department of Trade and Industry in 2001[15] set out the new thinking.

---

[8] Review of Company and Business Reconstruction Mechanisms (May 2000), para.73.
[9] *ibid.*, para.48.
[10] *ibid.*, para.49.
[11] *The Cycle of Corporate Distress, Rescue and Dissolution: A Study of Small and Medium Size UK Companies* (2000).
[12] *ibid.*, pp.3–4.
[13] R3, Corporate Insolvency in the UK, 12th Survey (July 2004), p.27.
[14] Review of Company and Business Reconstruction Mechanisms, para.73.
[15] Insolvency—A Second Chance (Cm. 5234).

"The Position of Unsecured Creditors

2.2 Throughout this period there has also been widespread concern as to the extent to which administrative receivership as a procedure provides adequate incentives to maximise economic value. There has, equally importantly, been concern about whether it provides an acceptable level of transparency and accountability to the range of stakeholders with an interest in a company's affairs, particularly creditors. For secured lenders, administrative receivership is an important mechanism, not least given that it is one over the inception of which they have complete control. Since 1986, a person acting as an administrative receiver of a company has had to be an authorised insolvency practitioner. There is little doubt that the existence of professional obligations on insolvency practitioners has had a beneficial effect on the way in which they discharge their duties. But the fact remains that, notwithstanding recent case law, an administrative receiver's principal obligation is towards his appointor. At law, they remain substantially unaccountable to any other creditor for the way in which a company's assets are dealt with. There is no equivalent of the duty owed by an administrator in an administration procedure to act in the interests of the creditors as a whole.

2.3 The maximisation of recoveries and the minimisation of costs are areas where the lack of a wider and more general accountability, and with it the absence of properly aligned incentives, can impact very substantially on the interests of unsecured creditors in an administrative receivership. For example, an administrative receiver is entitled to solely consider the interests of his or her appointor when determining the timing of a sale of a business. Where an offer is made which is sufficient to satisfy the secured creditor's claim and the administrative receiver's costs, there would appear to be little incentive for the receiver to delay the sale with a view to obtaining a better offer which might provide some return for unsecured creditors. Furthermore, it should be borne in mind that unsecured creditors have no right to challenge the level of costs in a receivership, even though they have an identifiable financial interest where there are sufficient funds to pay the secured creditor in full. The Insolvency Act 1986 (Sections 46, 48 and 49) did introduce requirements on administrative receivers to notify and report to creditors and provides for the possibility of a committee of creditors being established. But, in practice, very few such committees are appointed. Finally, it seems clear that the increasing importance of the international dimension in insolvency is likely to highlight the poor fit between international law, based on collective procedures, and administrative receivership. Taking all these factors into account, we do not believe that the present framework for administrative receivership provides an adequate basis for accountability or properly aligned incentives in relation to the bulk of cases giving rise to administrative receivership.

The Way Forward

. . .

2.5 The Government's view is that, on the grounds of both equity and efficiency, the time has come to make changes which will tip the balance firmly in favour of collective insolvency proceedings in which all creditors participate, under which a duty is owed to all creditors and in which all creditors may look to an office holder for an account of his dealings with a company's assets. It follows that we believe that administrative receivership should cease to be a major insolvency procedure. We therefore propose to restrict the right to appoint an administrative receiver to the holders of floating charges granted in connection with transactions in the capital markets . . ."

The outcome was a set of provisions in the Enterprise Act 2002 amending the Insolvency Act 1986 in two major respects. First, the new provisions make it easier for a company to go into administration by dispensing with the need for a court order. This was an essential step, because as research had shown a key factor powering many appointments of administrative receivers was speed in the assumption of management control and the collection of assets, and the delay involved in court-appointed administration was considered to place assets at risk.[16] Secondly, they prohibit the appointment of an administrative receiver altogether under a "qualifying floating charge"[17] except where it is a charge created before September 15, 2003 or, if it is a charge created on or after that date, it falls within one of the specified exceptions.[18] Save in these cases the debenture holder's remedy is to appoint an administrator, which is less efficacious in that whilst an administrative receiver's primary task was to safeguard the interests of his debenture holder an administrator is required to give priority to other objectives, where reasonably practicable.[19] There are eight exceptions, which are designed to safeguard large capital market arrangements involving the issue of a capital market investment, public-private partnership projects incorporating step-in rights, utility projects, urban regeneration projects, large-scale project finance incorporating step-in rights,[20] financial market charges, system-charges and collateral security

---

[16] Alan Katz and Michael Mumford, *Comparative Study of Administration and Administrative Receivership as Business Rescue Vehicles* (August 2003), pp.x, 14. See further below, para.10–07.

[17] As defined by the Insolvency Act 1986, Sch.B1, para.14. See below, para.10–10.

[18] Enterprise Act 2002, s.250, inserting s.72A into the Insolvency Act 1986. Section 72A applies in spite of an agreement or instrument which purports to empower a person to appoint an administrative receiver, by whatever name (s.72A(4)(b)).

[19] See below, Chap.10.

[20] See *Feetum v Levy* [2005] 1 All E.R. (D) 198.

charges, registered social landlords and protected railway companies.[21] As regards a regards a floating charge falling within one of these categories or created before September 15, 2003 the holder of the charge remains free to appoint an administrative receiver, and while such a receiver is in office no administrator can be appointed.[22]

3. THE LEGAL NATURE OF ADMINISTRATIVE RECEIVERSHIP[23]

9–05   The term "administrative receiver", first introduced by the Insolvency Act 1985, and carried forward into the Insolvency Act 1986,[24] is simply the statutory label for the individual who was previously termed receiver and manager. Administrative receivership has long been the *de facto* monopoly of the accountancy profession and requires professional skill and judgment of a high order, since it is the task of the administrative receiver, with his team of assistants, to take over the management of the company from the directors, with a view to trading it out of its difficulties,[25] and for that purpose to keep the company afloat, negotiate with banks and other creditors, dispose of unprofitable sectors of the business, eliminate unnecessary expenditure and generate income, so that in due course the business can be sold as a going concern or hived down into a specially formed subsidiary which can be disposed of as a clean company with assets but no liabilities. Only a qualified insolvency practitioner can act as administrative receiver.[26]

As mentioned earlier,[27] administrative receivership is not a true collective insolvency proceeding but remains in principle a method by which a particular debenture holder can enforce his security. But by statute several insolvency features have become attached to administrative receivership, so that it is considered an insolvency proceeding even though the administrative receiver's duty is in principle owed only to his debenture holder,[28] not to the general body of creditors.

---

[21] Insolvency Act 1986, ss.72A–72G and Sch.2A. The exceptions relating to urban regeneration and protected railway companies were inserted by the Insolvency Act 1986 (Amendment)(Administrative Receivership and Urban Regeneration etc) Order 2003 (SI 2003/1832). For the definitions of the various categories, see Insolvency Act 1986, Sch.2A, as amended.

[22] Insolvency Act 1986, Sch.B1, paras 17(b), 25(c). See further below, para.9–12.

[23] See generally *Kerr & Hunter on Receivers and Administrators* (18th ed. 2005); Lightman and Moss, *The Law of Receivers and Administrators of Companies* (3rd ed. 2000); Andrew Keay and Peter Walton, *Insolvency Law: Corporate and Personal* (2003).

[24] See below.

[25] Of course, this is not always possible. Sometimes the administrative receiver has no choice but to close the business down and dispose of the assets at the best price he can get.

[26] See below, para.9–24.

[27] See above, para.1–23.

[28] And, by statute, to preferential creditors as regards assets within the scope of a floating charge. See below, paras 9–63 *et seq.*

The administrative receiver defined

An administrative receiver is defined by s.29(2) of the Insolvency Act 1986 **9–06** in the following terms:

> "(a) a receiver or manager of the whole (or substantially the whole) of a company's property appointed by or on behalf of the holders of any debentures of the company secured by a charge which, as created, was a floating charge, or by such a charge and one or more other securities; or
>
> (b) a person who would be such a receiver but for the appointment of some other person as the receiver of part of the company's property."

Several aspects of this definition require comment.

"The whole or substantially the whole of a company's property"

Four questions arise in relation to this phrase: (1) what does "whole or **9–07** substantially the whole" mean? (2) as at what date is the position to be tested? (3) what is the effect of the prior appointment of a receiver of part of the property? And (4) can an administrative receiver be appointed if another administrative receiver is in post under a different debenture?

(1) "Whole or substantially the whole"

What matters here is not the scope of the debenture under which the **9–08** receiver is appointed but the scope of the appointment. Debentures frequently empower the debenture holder to crystallise a floating charge, and to appoint a receiver, in respect of a specific asset or part only of the assets, since this provides the necessary security over a threatened asset or class of assets without inhibiting the continuance of the rest of the company's business. A receiver so appointed is not an administrative receiver even if the debenture under which he is appointed covers substantially the whole of the assets. It is necessary that his receivership should encompass substantially the whole of the assets. It is thought that this is to be determined by reference to the total value of the company's property, not by reference to the number of items within the scope of the appointment.

(2) As at what date?

It is clear from the wording of s.29(2) that the time when the above **9–09** requirement has to be satisfied is the time of the receiver's appointment. The fact that the company acquires substantial additional assets later which happen to fall outside the scope of the charge, and thus of the appointment, is irrelevant.

(3) Prior receiver of part of property

9–10   Limb (b) of s.29(2) provides that the term "administrative receiver" includes a person who would be a receiver of the whole or substantially the whole of the company's property but for the appointment of some other person as receiver of part of the company's property. For example, another debenture holder may have appointed a Law of Property Act receiver under a fixed charge of a specific property or a receiver under a floating charge limited to a particular class of asset. It is in fact not unusual for floating charges to be taken over a limited class of asset, for example, floating charges taken to secure the financing of stock in trade for brewers or for motor dealers, which are commonly confined to the stock in question. Section 29(2)(b) appears to have been inserted *ex abundante cautela*, for on the view taken here the requirement that the floating charge and any other charges together cover the whole or substantially the whole of the company's property relates only to the relationship between the company and the debenture holder,[29] and is thus not affected by the fact that another receiver holds part of the property.

(4) Another administrative receiver in post

9–11   The view has been expressed that a person cannot be appointed an administrative receiver if another administrative receiver has already been appointed.[30] However, it is necessary to distinguish the appointment of an administrative receiver from his exercise of management functions. It is clear that only one person, or two or more people acting jointly under the same instrument,[31] can perform the functions of an administrative receiver at any one time, but that is not a reason for denying the validity of the second appointment. All that happens is that the second administrative receiver has to wait on the sidelines until the prior administrative receivership has been completed. There is nothing unusual in this kind of situation. It is a common occurrence for a company to go into liquidation while still in administrative receivership. In such a case the liquidator's statutory powers in relation to the control and disposal of the assets and the

---

[29] See below para.9–11.
[30] See Fidelis Oditah, "Lightweight Floating Charges" [1991] J.B.L. 49 at 51 *et seq.*; Marks and Emmett, "Administrative Receivers: Questions of Identity and Double Identity" [1994] J.B.L. 1.
[31] Insolvency Act 1986, s.33(2).

management of the company's business for the purpose of its beneficial winding-up[32] are not exercisable while an administrative receiver is in post, for so long as the debenture holder's security interest in the whole of the assets subsists it has priority over the claims of the general body of creditors whom the liquidator represents. This demonstrates that there is no inherent objection to having two office-holders in post at the same time, though only one of them can exercise *in rem* management powers. As between two administrative receivers priority should in principle be determined by the priority of the respective debentures under which they were appointed;[33] but once the first administrative receiver has effectively entered upon the receivership he can only be displaced by a court order removing the first receiver.[34] While the court may be expected to give due weight to the priority of the competing debentures, the fact that a debenture holder no longer has power to replace its receiver without leave of the court shows that this is not now considered to be a matter exclusively within the private domain, and that the court will have regard to the interests of creditors.[35] Can it be said that the effect of the first security is to prevent the second security from covering the whole or substantially the whole of the company's property? This calls for an emphatically negative response. Notwithstanding the infelicitous wording of s.29(2)(b) it is clear that s.29(2)(a) is concerned solely with relations between the debenture holder and the company and is not addressed to competing security interests. All that is necessary is that, as between the debenture holder and the company, security which includes a floating charge is given over substantially the whole of the company's property. How that security ranks with a similar security given to another creditor is irrelevant. The later interest still covers substantially the whole of the company's property, subject to the prior charge. Put another way, the company's property after giving the first charge over all its property is its equity of redemption, and in charging this

---

[32] *ibid.*, Sch.4.

[33] Where there are two floating charges each of which covers all the assets priority will in principle go to the earlier, even if the later was the first to crystallise, for there is a presumption that the freedom which a floating charge allows to a company to dispose of its assets in the ordinary course of business does not extend to the grant of another floating charge over all the assets. See *Re Benjamin Cope & Sons Ltd* [1914] Ch. 800. The position is otherwise where the subsequent floating charge covers only part of the assets and power to create such charge in priority to the first floating charge was reserved to the company by the first floating charge (*Re Automatic Bottle Makers Ltd* [1926] Ch. 412). However, the distinction drawn in the latter case between a subsequent floating charge covering all the assets and one covering only part of the assets seems unnecessary; the sole question in each case should be whether the terms of the first floating charge permit a subsequent charge to be given ranking in priority to the earlier floating charge.

[34] Insolvency Act 1986, s.45(1).

[35] That some judicial control may be necessary is demonstrated by the facts in *Downsview Nominees Ltd v First City Corp* [1993] A.C. 295, where a debenture holder who appointed a receiver for the sole purpose of preventing enforcement of a subsequent debenture by a receiver previously appointed by the holder of the second debenture was held liable in damages for loss caused. See further below, para.9–33.

to the second debenture holder the company is charging the whole of its remaining property.

This is not a mere technical question. It is important that the law should allow concurrent appointments—even if only one can take effect in possession—for the second chargee needs to be able to ensure that there is no interval between the completion of the first administrative receivership and the appointment of the second administrative receiver during which the latter appointment could be blocked by the making of an administration order. Recognition of the validity of the second appointment *ab initio* ensures a seamless progression from one receivership to the other.

(5) An administrator in post

9–12 By contrast, it is not possible to have a concurrence of administration and administrative receivership. It is a question of who is appointed first. Once a company is in administration an administrative receiver may not be appointed.[36] If, on the other hand, an administrative receiver is in office an administrator may not be appointed by the company or its directors,[37] and an application for an administration order must normally be dismissed unless his appointor consents to it, whether the receiver was appointed before or after the making of the application.[38] Where, however, the court has and exercises power to appoint an administrator any administrative receiver must vacate office.[39]

"Appointed by or on behalf of the holders of any debentures of the company"

9–13 This precludes a receiver appointed by the court from being an administrative receiver, a logical provision, for the powers of a court-appointed receiver are limited by the terms of the order appointing him and this could be incompatible with the powers conferred on administrative receivers by Sch.1 of the Act.

"Secured by a charge which, as created, was a floating charge, or by such charge and one or more other charges"

9–14 Several points arise in connection with this element of the statutory definition.

---

[36] Insolvency Act 1986, Sch.B1, para.43(6A).
[37] *ibid.*, para.25(c).
[38] *ibid.*, Sch.B1, para.39.
[39] *ibid.*, Sch.B1, para.41(1).

(1) Distinction between fixed and floating charge

I have discussed elsewhere the nature of the floating charge and the **9–15** characteristics which distinguish it from a fixed charge.[40] The courts have been much occupied with the distinction in relation to a charge over book debts given in favour of a bank where the charger is required to pay the proceeds into a bank account but is free to draw on the account as and when needed unless the bank intervenes. This was upheld by the Court of Appeal in its controversial decision in *Re New Bullas Trading Ltd*,[41] a decision which the Privy Council declined to follow in *Agnew v Commissioners of Inland Revenue*[42] on the basis that the company's power to utilise the proceeds was inconsistent with the nature of a fixed charge. This is plainly correct. It has been established for well over a century that the mere fact that the chargee has power to intervene is not sufficient to establish the charge as a fixed charge; it is necessary both to introduce and to operate a control mechanism which ensures that the company is not free to deal with the proceeds as its own pending the bank's intervention. The Privy Council decision was followed by the House of Lords in *Re Spectrum Plus Ltd*.[43]

(2) Crystallisation is irrelevant

The fact that the charge under which the receiver is appointed crystallised **9–16** before his appointment, and was therefore no longer floating, is irrelevant. What matters is its character at the time of creation. This is in line with the definition of "floating charge" in s.251 of the Act as a charge which as created was a floating charge.[44]

(3) Residual floating charge suffices

It is not necessary that the floating charge should itself cover the whole or **9–17** substantially the whole of the company's property; it suffices that a floating charge and one or more fixed charges together encompass such property. Because of the advantages of a fixed charge over a floating charge in terms

---

[40] *Commercial Law* (3rd ed.), Chap.25; *Legal Problems of Credit and Security* (3rd ed.), Chap.IV.
[41] [1994] B.C.L.C. 485.
[42] [2001] 2 A.C. 710.
[43] *Re Spectrum Plus Ltd., National Westminster Bank plc v Spectrum Plus Ltd* [2005] All E.R. (D) 368, in which the House of Lords reversed the decision of the Court of Appeal, overruled *Siebe Gorman & Co Ltd v Barclays Bank Ltd* [1979] 2 Lloyd's Rep. 142 and disapproving *Re New Bullas Trading Ltd*, above, n.41 by which the Court of Appeal had rightly regarded itself as bound.
[44] The definition is also relevant (*inter alia*) to the treatment of priorities between preferential debts and those secured by a crystallised floating charge. See below, para.9–63.

of priority over subsequent security interests and the claims of preferential creditors, lenders tend to take fixed security over as many classes of asset as possible, leaving the floating charge to gather up the rest. This is fully compatible with s.29(2). A vestigial ("lightweight") floating charge is all that is needed. But if there is no floating charge at all the receiver will not be an administrative receiver. Accordingly there may be circumstances in which the debenture holder would find it convenient to argue that a charge which is described as a fixed charge is in fact a floating charge—an argument which for other purposes he could be expected strenuously to resist!

Where there are fixed charges as well as a floating charge it is not necessary that all the charges should be comprised in the same debenture. What matters is their aggregate effect.

(4) Susceptibility of future assets to floating charge suffices

9–18   The fact that at the time of the receiver's appointment there are no assets currently within the scope of the floating charge does not prevent the receiver from being an administrative receiver. It suffices that the floating charge has the potential to catch after-acquired property of the company. In *Re Croftbell Ltd*[45] it was conceded that a receiver was not precluded from being an administrative receiver merely because at the time of the debenture the company had no assets (for otherwise the company could not grant a floating charge at the commencement of its business when it had no assets) or all the assets were subject to a fixed charge. But it was contended that if the evidence showed that the company had no intention of entering into trading transactions, so that the floating charge served no purpose but to frustrate the appointment of an administrator by the court,[46] it had to be disregarded. This contention was rejected by Vinelott J., who held that the question whether a debenture holder had power to appoint an administrative receiver could not turn on the company's intentions at the time it executed the debenture, for those intentions might change and future assets might fall within the floating charge.

Appointment under fixed charge

9–19   If a debenture holder has a floating charge and a fixed charge which together encompass substantially the whole of the company's property, is a receiver appointed under the fixed charge an administrative receiver? In an unreported decision by Vinelott J. in *Meadrealm Ltd v Transcontinental*

---

[45] [1990] B.C.L.C. 844.
[46] See Insolvency Act 1986, s.9(3) (now Sch.B1, para.39). See below, para.9–26.

Gulf Construction Ltd[47] this question was answered in the negative; only a receiver appointed under a floating charge could qualify as an administrative receiver. However, the decision is not easy to reconcile with the wording of s.29(2), and would seem to focus on the wrong issue. The crucial question is not the nature of the charge or charge-element under which the receiver is appointed but the property over which he is appointed. A receiver appointed in respect of only part of the assets simply cannot function as an administrative receiver, for he has no *in rem* powers over those assets outside the scope of his appointment and is therefore inhibited from effectively managing the company's business. Hence the requirement that the receiver be appointed in respect of the whole or substantially the whole of the company's property. That is all that s.29(2) requires. If this requirement is satisfied it should not matter under which element of a security package the appointment is made. Indeed, to speak of an appointment "under a fixed charge" is rather misleading, for it confuses the security interest with the instrument by which the security is created and the source of the appointment with the property to which the appointment relates. If a fixed charge covers substantially the whole of the company's property and there is a residual floating charge over the rest, that should suffice. Admittedly the continuance of the company's business could, in theory at least, lead to the acquisition of further substantial assets outside the scope of the floating charge, so that the fixed charge would cease to cover substantially the whole of the company's property, but again that would seem to be irrelevant, for as stated earlier the material time is the time of the receiver's appointment.

The three categories of receiver

With the enactment of what is now the Insolvency Act 1986 there are three categories of receiver:

9–20

(1) The administrative receiver, defined above.

(2) The receiver of income only (*i.e.* the Law of Property Act receiver).

(3) Other types of receiver, that is:

   (a) a receiver of only part of the company's property,[48] whether appointed out of court or by the court;[49]

---

[47] Unreported, November 29, 1991.
[48] Other than a receiver who would be a receiver of the whole but for the appointment of another person as receiver of part and who is thus himself an administrative receiver.
[49] For a case where a receiver of a particular property was appointed by the court on the application of the mortgagee even though there was an administrator in post, see *Sinai Securities Ltd v Hooper* [2004] B.C.C. 973.

(b) an all-assets receiver appointed by the court.

I shall confine myself to the administrative receiver.

Mode of appointment

9–21   A receiver is only an administrative receiver if he is appointed out of court by the debenture holder.

Administrative receiver compared with other types of receiver

9–22   An administrative receiver has a number of characteristics which mark him out from other types of receiver.

(1)   An administrative receiver is deemed to be the company's agent unless and until it goes into liquidation,[50] and the same is true of a Law of Property Act receiver.[51] A receiver appointed by a debenture holder in relation to part only of a company's property is the agent of the debenture holder who appoints him unless the debenture provides otherwise,[52] as it almost invariably will.

(2)   The appointment of an administrative receiver usually prevents the making of an administration order.[53] This is not true of other receivers.

(3)   An administrative receiver is an office-holder for the purpose of the Insolvency Act,[54] with attendant powers, duties and privileges which are not necessarily possessed by other receivers.

(4)   The powers conferred on the administrative receiver by the debenture holder are deemed to include those set out in Schedule 1 to the Insolvency Act; in the case of other receivers, such powers must be conferred by the terms of the debenture itself.

(5)   Only a receiver who is an administrative receiver can apply for an order under section 43 of the Insolvency Act to dispose of property charged to another creditor.

(6)   An administrative receiver is required to obtain a statement of affairs from the officers of the company, and to send a report to the registrar of companies[55]; other types of receiver are merely required to file accounts.

---

[50] Insolvency Act 1986, s.44(1)).
[51] Law of Property Act 1925, s.109(2).
[52] *Re Vimbos Ltd* [1900] 1 Ch. 470; *Deyes v Wood* [1911] 1 K.B. 806.
[53] See below, para.9–26.
[54] Insolvency Act 1986, ss.233(1), 234(1), 238(1), 246(1).
[55] *ibid.*, ss.47, 48.

(7) An administrative receiver may now be removed only by the court[56]; a receiver who is not an administrative receiver may be removed by the debenture holder who appointed him, if the debenture so provides.

(8) An administrative receiver cannot be appointed during the period in which the company is in administration[57]; no such restriction applies to the appointment of other types of receiver, though they would be powerless to act until the administration order had been discharged.[58]

(9) An administrative receiver must vacate office on the making of an administration order[59]; other types of receiver need vacate office only on being required to do so by the administrator.[60]

(10) The acts of an administrative receiver are valid notwithstanding any defect in his appointment[61]; there is no similar rule for ordinary receivers.

These differences reflect the fact that the administrative receiver takes over substantially the whole of the company's assets and manages the business, so that he is treated in much the same way as an office-holder in a collective insolvency proceeding such as administration or liquidation.

The multi-faceted character of administrative receivership

To define an administrative receiver is simple, because the Insolvency Act itself provides us with a definition. It is much more difficult to identify the legal essence of administrative receivership. This is because the administrative receiver has two sets of powers and owes duties to two different parties, in consequence of which he does not fit readily into any identified mould.[62] The first set of powers relates to the possession, management and realisation of the security. These powers are exercised in right of the debenture holder and, being given for the enforcement of the debenture holder's rights in rent, are unaffected by the company's liquidation. The second set of powers, conferred by the company through the execution of the debenture and exercised by the receiver as agent of the company,

9–23

---

[56] *ibid.*, s.45(1). Prior to the Insolvency Act 1985 it was for the debenture holder to remove a receiver and appoint another in his place, if so empowered by the debenture.

[57] *ibid.*, Sch.B1, para.43(6A).

[58] Because of the restrictions imposed on the enforcement of security, the repossession of goods and the commencement or continuance of proceedings (Insolvency Act 1986, Sch.B1, para.43) and the fact that the management of the business is placed under the control of the administrator (*ibid.*, paras 59, 60, 64(1) and Sch.1).

[59] *ibid.*, para.41(1).

[60] *ibid.*, para.41(2). Presumably a court-appointed administrator of all the company's assets remains in office unless and until the court otherwise orders.

[61] *ibid.*, s.232.

[62] See below, para.9–23.

enables him to conclude contracts in the name of the company, thus committing it to further liabilities, and to engage and dismiss staff and generally run the business. The agency powers come to an end on the winding-up of the company except to the extent to which their exercise is ancillary to the enforcement of the security.[63]

In his legal relationships the administrative receiver, like the Roman God Janus, faces two ways. He owes a limited duty of care to the company as its deemed agent[64] and a separate duty of care to the debenture holder who appointed him[65] yet at the same time he possesses a high degree of autonomy. His agency for the company is of a peculiar kind, since it exists primarily for the protection and enhancement of the debenture holder's security. Accordingly the company has no power either to terminate the agency or to control its deemed agent as to the manner in which he performs his duties. Further, his obligations to the company are subordinated to his duties to his debenture holder, so that even if his acts cause damage to the company's interests he incurs no liability so long as what he did was for the proper protection of the debenture holder and he did not needlessly damage the company's business.[66] In addition, his deemed agency for the company largely protects his debenture holder from responsibility for his acts or omissions.[67] On the other hand, he is not at the beck and call of the debenture holder. To the contrary, the debenture holder has no right to give directions to the receiver in the conduct of his receivership; indeed, if the debenture holder does so he risks being held liable for any improper acts or omissions of the receiver, who will then be treated as his agent.[68] The independence of the administrative receiver is reinforced by the fact that he can now only be removed by order of the court.[69] He is also required by statute to ensure that where the free assets of the company are insufficient to pay preferential creditors any shortfall is made good from property subject to a floating charge in priority to the claims of the chargee.[70]

So the administrative receiver is a protean character, changing his colour, shape and function according to circumstances. He can best be described as an independent contractor whose primary responsibility is to protect the interests of his appointor but who also owes a duty to his deemed principal, the company, to refrain from conduct which needlessly damages its business or goodwill, and a separate duty, by statute, to observe the priority given to preferential creditors over claims secured by a floating charge. Since this is

---

[63] See below, para.9–69.
[64] As to the source and extent of this duty, see below, para.9–47.
[65] See below, para.9–47.
[66] See below, para.9–47.
[67] Insolvency Act 1986, s.44(1)(a).
[68] See below, para.9–78.
[69] Insolvency Act 1986, s.45(1).
[70] See para.9–63.

the only kind of receiver I intend to discuss I shall for brevity refer to him hereafter simply as "the receiver." I shall examine a little later the precise nature of the agency power and its relationship with the exercise of security rights on behalf of the debenture holder.[71]

4. APPOINTING THE RECEIVER OUT OF COURT

Who can be appointed

A person can be appoimted a receiver of a company only if qualified to act as an insolvency practitioner in relation to the company.[72] This means that he must be qualified both generally and in relation to the company itself. A qualified insolvency practitioner is a person authorised to act as such by:

9–24

(1)   a recognised professional body; or

(2)   the Secretary of State; or

(3)   a competent authority designated by the Secretary of State.[73]

Only an individual can be a qualified insolvency practitioner.[74] Moreover, a person cannot be appointed who is an undischarged bankrupt, a person subject to a disqualification order under the Company Directors Disqualification Act 1986 or a patient within Part VII of the Mental Health Act 1983.[75] Even if otherwise qualified, an insolvency practitioner cannot act as receiver of a company until he has furnished appropriate security for the proper performance of his functions,[76] as where he is covered by a bond, whether in relation to his practice generally or in relation to a particular receivership.

Grounds for appointment

The Insolvency Act is silent as to the grounds on which a receiver may be appointed out of court. Though a chargee under a charge by deed has certain implied powers under s.101 of the Law of Property Act 1925 to

9–25

---

[71] See para.9–63.
[72] Insolvency Act 1986, s.230(2). But the fact that a receiver is appointed who is not qualified does not affect the validity of his acts (Insolvency Act 1986, s.232).
[73] See the Insolvency Act 1986 ss.390–392 and the Insolvency Practitioners (Recognised Professional Bodies) Order 1986 (SI 1986/1764).
[74] Insolvency Act 1986, s.390(1).
[75] *ibid.*, s.390(4).
[76] *ibid.*, s.390(3).

appoint a receiver of income, the debenture is the sole source of the right to appoint a receiver with management powers.[77] The well drawn debenture should therefore provide for every event on which the appointment of a receiver may be desired. There is no implied power to appoint a receiver merely because the security is in jeopardy.[78] A purported appointment will not, of course, be effective if the debenture under which the appointment is made is invalid. In addition, it is necessary that any conditions for making the appointment which are specified in the debenture are either satisfied at the time of the receiver's acceptance of the appointment[79] or are waived by the directors under the terms of the debenture, failing which the appointment will be a nullity. So an appointment made on the basis of a premature or otherwise invalid demand is of no effect.[80] However, an appointment made on an invalid ground is effective if at the time of the receiver's acceptance of the appointment[81] a valid ground of appointment existed.[82] The appointment:

(1)   may be made despite the filing of an application for an administration order[83];

(2)   may not be made during the currency of an administration order[84];

(3)   if made before such an order, is displaced by the order, upon the making of which the administrative receiver must vacate office[85];

(4)   prevents the making of an administration order except:

    (a)   by the consent of the person by whom or on whose behalf the receiver was appointed; or

    (b)   where, if an administration order were made, any security by virtue of which the receiver was appointed would be liable to be released or discharged as a transaction at an undervalue or a preference or liable to be avoided under s.245 of the Insolvency

---

[77] However, if the company has invited the debenture holder to appoint the receiver in the mistaken belief that the debenture holder has become entitled to make the appointment, it is precluded from saying that the appointment is ineffective, and the receiver is a trespasser, up to the time it discovers the mistake and asks him to withdraw. See below, para.9–29.

[78] *Cryne v Barclays Bank plc* [1987] B.C.L.C. 548. The court has power to appoint a receiver "in all cases in which it appears to the court to be just and convenient to do so" (Supreme Court Act 1981, s.37(1)), and it is a well established ground for appointment that the security is in jeopardy (*ibid.*).

[79] It is this, rather than the time of making the appointment, that is the relevant time (*R.A. Cripps & Son v Wickenden* [1973] 1 W.L.R. 944, *per* Goff J. at 953–954).

[80] See below, para.9–29.

[81] See n.79 above.

[82] See, for example, *Byblos Bank SAL v Al-Khudhairy* [1987] B.C.L.C. 232.

[83] Insolvency Act 1986, Sch.B1, para.39.

[84] *ibid.*, para.43(6A).

[85] *ibid.*, para.41(1).

Act as a floating charge given for past value by an insolvent company.[86]

The phrase "would be liable to be released or discharged" presumably means that the court must be satisfied on the evidence before it, which may well be incomplete, that on a balance of probabilities the conditions in which a court could exercise its powers of release or discharge or in which the floating charge would be rendered void would be fulfilled if an administration order were then made, whether or not the court would be likely to exercise its powers in the particular circumstances. Such a ruling is, of course, operative solely for the purpose of making an administration order and does not constitute a *res judicata* preventing the debenture holder from contending in subsequent proceedings under ss.238–240 or 245 that the debenture is not liable to be avoided under those sections.

Blocking an administration order

The effect of the Insolvency Act is that an administrative receiver and an **9–26** administrator cannot be in post at the same time.[87] The reason for such a rule is obvious; since both are given the widest powers of management but represent different interests, it is not possible for their functions to be exercised concurrently. Subject to the provisions of para.39(1) of Sch.B1 it is the first to be appointed who prevails. A debenture holder whose security is not vulnerable thus has power to block an administration by appointing an administrative receiver, and he may do this at any time prior to the company's entry into administration, whether or not an application for an administration order has been made.[88] It therefore behoves the debenture holder to keep a watchful eye to ensure that he does not overlook such an application. He is helped in this regard by being given two sources of warning that an application has been made, so that he can consider whether to acquiesce in the appointment or to block it by appointing a receiver. First, notice of the application is required to be given to him as soon as reasonably practicable,[89] thus enabling him to intervene and apply to have his own nominee appointed as administrator.[90] Secondly, a copy of the application and of the supporting affidavit and exhibits must be served on

---

[86] *ibid.*, para.39. See generally Chap.11 as to these grounds of avoidance. Potential invalidity of the security for non-registration is not designated as an event enabling an administration order to be made, since this can be cured by registration out of time with leave of the court prior to the initiation of steps for the winding-up of the company. See Companies Act 1985, s.404.

[87] *ibid.*, paras 17(b), 25(c), 39, 41(1), 43(6A).

[88] Insolvency Act 1986, Sch.B1, paras 39(2), 43(6A).

[89] *ibid.*, para.12(2).

[90] *ibid.*, para.36.

him five clear days before the hearing date,[91] though this time may be abridged by the court so far as is consistent with allowing the debenture holder an adequate opportunity to consider whether to exercise his power of appointment before it is suspended.[92] The above requirements appear to be purely directory, so that where the applicant fails to comply with them and in consequence the debenture holder does not learn of the application until after the administration order has been made, this would not appear to invalidate the order. Moreover the unfortunate debenture holder has no *locus standi* to apply for the administration order to be discharged or the administrator replaced. The damage having been done, he must accept with such fortitude as he can command the involuntary loss of his right to appoint a receiver, and appears to have no right to damages or compensation, even assuming he could establish loss.[93]

Conditions of a valid appointment by the debenture holder

9–27　In order for the debenture holder's appointment of a receiver to be valid six conditions must be fulfilled:

(1)　The company is not in administration.[94]

(2)　The security under which the receiver is appointed is valid. The appointment will be void *ab initio* if:

　(a)　the granting of the security was *ultra vires* the company and the debenture holder is not protected by s.35 of the Companies Act 1985[95]; or

　(b)　the company is already in winding-up, or goes into winding-up, and the security was not duly registered[96] or is set aside by the court under s.241 or rendered void by s.245 of the Insolvency Act or as a post-petition disposition not sanctioned by the court.[97]

---

[91] Insolvency Rules 1986, rr.2.6(3), 2.8(1).

[92] *ibid.*, r.12.9; Re *A Company No.00175 of 1987* [1987] 3 B.C.C. 124. In the case of a bank, the address for service is the address of an office where, to the knowledge of the petitioner, the company maintains a bank account or if this is not known the bank's registered office, or if none, then its usual or last known address (Insolvency Rules, r.2.7(4A)). There is no provision in the Act or Rules for advertisement of the petition.

[93] The well-recognised tort of abuse of process does not encompass mere procedural irregularity.

[94] See above para.9–26.

[95] Which provides (*inter alia*) that in favour of a person dealing with the company in good faith, any transaction decided upon by the directors is deemed to be one which it is within the capacity of the company to enter into, and that a party to a transaction so decided on is not bound to enquire as to the capacity of the company to enter into it.

[96] Companies Act 1985, s.395.

[97] Insolvency Act 1986, s.127 (see para.11–125); Re *Goldburg (No.2)* [1912] 1 K.B. 606. which concerned comparable provisions under the then Bankruptcy Act by which the trustee's title to the bankrupt's estate related back to the act of bankruptcy which the adjudication order was made.

If the company is not in winding-up when the receiver is appointed, the fact that the security is potentially void or voidable does not at that time affect the validity of the appointment, but subsequent avoidance of the security nullifies the appointment retrospectively unless, in the case of an order for release or discharge of the security, the court exercises what appears to be a power to set aside the security as from the date of its order, without retrospective effect.[98]

(3) The obligations secured by the debenture arise from a valid contract. Hence a receiver appointed under a valid debenture because of default in payment of sums payable under an invalid guarantee secured by the debenture is not validly appointed.[99]

(4) The power to appoint a receiver has become exercisable under the terms of the debenture.[1]

(5) The appointment has been made by the person[2] and in the manner[3] authorised by the debenture.

(6) The person appointed is qualified to act.[4]

Where these conditions are satisfied the appointment of the receiver will be a valid appointment. Good faith in the making of an appointment does not appear to be a prequisite of its validity, but if an appointment is made in bad faith the debenture holder will be liable for any loss thereby caused to the company.[5] The fact that the company is in liquidation is not a bar to the appointment of a receiver,[6] and it is not necessary to obtain either the consent of the liquidator or the leave of the court to such an appointment. However, as the liquidator is an officer of the court the receiver cannot take possession of any assets within the liquidator's control except with his consent or by leave of the court, to which the receiver is entitled as a matter of right.[7]

The acts of an individual as administrative receiver are valid notwithstanding any defect in his appointment, nomination or qualifications,[8] but the section is confined to defects in form or procedure and cannot be invoked where the receiver has never been validly appointed at all.[9]

---

[98] See below, para.9–31.
[99] *Ford & Carter Ltd v Midland Bank Ltd* (1979) 129 N.L.J. 543.
[1] See above and, in the case of an appointment made after failure to comply with a demand for payment, below, paras 9–26 *et seq.*
[2] *Harris & Lewine Pty Ltd (in liquidation) v Harris & Lewin (Agents)* (1975) A.C.L.C. 28, 279.
[3] *R. Jaffe Ltd (in liquidation) v Jaffe (No.2)* [1932] N.Z.L.R. 195.
[4] Under s.390 of the Insolvency Act 1986, see above, para.9–24.
[5] See below, para.9–47, as to examples of bad faith.
[6] *Re Pound & Hutchins* (1889) 2 Ch.D. 402.
[7] *Re Potters Oils Ltd (No.2)* [1986] 1 W.L.R. 201 at 206; *Re Pound & Hutchins*, above.
[8] Insolvency Act 1986, s.232.
[9] See below, para.9–31.

The demand for payment

9–28   One of the most common grounds on which a receiver is appointed pursuant to powers conferred by the debenture is non-compliance with a demand for payment. An appointment made on the basis of a premature or otherwise invalid demand is of no effect. Two questions then arise: what constitutes a valid demand for payment? And what time must the debenture holder allow the company to satisfy the demand?

The validity of the demand

9–29   On this question the authorities establish the following propositions:

(1)   *Unless otherwise provided by the debenture itself, the demand is valid if calling merely for payment of "all moneys due" without specifying the amount.*[10] The commercial necessity of allowing the creditor to make a general demand in this way without stating the amount due was well put by the High Court of Australia in *Bunbury Foods Pty Ltd v National Bank of Australasia Ltd.*[11]

> ". . . to require the creditor in all cases to specify the amount of the debt may operate to impose an onerous burden upon him. Some accounts may be so complex and so constantly changing that it is difficult at any given time to ascertain or to assert the precise amount that is due and payable. Indeed, the ascertainment of the amount may in some instances require the resolution over time of complex issues of fact and law. Yet, in order to preserve the value to the creditor of his security, he may need to call up the debt as a matter of urgency. It is of some materiality to note that it is not essential to the validity of a notice calling up the debt that it correctly states the amount of the debt. There is little point in requiring that the notice should state the amount if the correctness of the amount is not essential to the validity of the notice. In this situation insistence on the requirement may result in creditors taking insufficient care in stating the amount of the debt, thereby contributing to confusion on the part of debtors."[12]

(2)   *A demand is not normally rendered invalid because it is for more than the amount due.*[13] An understatement of the amount due clearly does not prejudice the debtor company, and this is usually true of an

---

[10] *Bank of Baroda v Panessar* [1987] Ch. 335; *Bunbury Foods Pty Ltd v National Bank of Australasia Ltd* (1984) 51 A.L.R. 509.

[11] (1984) 51 A.L.R. 609.

[12] *ibid.*, at 619.

[13] *ibid.*, and cases there cited.

overstatement, since in most cases the debtor is manifestly unable to pay even the lower, correct, amount. The principle established in relation to the enforcement of mortgages is that the making of an excessive demand by the mortgagee does not dispense with the duty of the mortgagor to tender that which is actually due.[14] However, there may be exceptional cases where this is not so. One possible case is where the debtor company has been led by the creditor to believe that a tender below the excessive amount demanded will be rejected, though even here it might be said that the company should still tender what is actually due. Another is where the company is dependent on the creditor for information as to the amount due—as where it is a surety for future advances from time to time made to the principal debtor—and the company would have been able to pay the sum actually due if it had known what it was but is unable to pay an amount demanded by the creditor which is grossly in excess of the indebtedness.

(3) *A demand is invalid if what is claimed* is *not due at all.*[15] But if the receiver was appointed by the debenture holder at the invitation of the board of the company and that invitation was extended in the mistaken belief that grounds had occurred entitling the debenture holder to make the appointment, the company cannot treat the receiver as a trespasser for the period he is in possession of the assets prior to being required by the company to withdraw after their discovery of the mistake.[16]

(4) *If, following an excessive demand, the company tenders the amount actually due, the subsequent appointment of a receiver will be invalid, since ex hypothesi there is no default.*

(5) *The company is entitled only to such time as is reasonable to implement the mechanics of payment*[17] *but is not entitled to an opportunity to raise the finance required.*[18] In this respect the English rule is stricter than that applied in Australia[19] and Canada.[20] Indeed in Canada there is at least one decision in which it has been held that the duty to give

---

[14] *Campbell v Commercial Banking Co of Sydney* (1879) 40 L.T. 137: *Clyde Properties Ltd v Tasker* [1970] N.Z.L.R. 754.

[15] *Jaffe v Premier Motors Ltd* [1970] N.Z.L.R. 146.

[16] *Ford and Carter Ltd v Midland Bank Ltd*, above, n.99.

[17] How long this is may depend on whether the demand is made during or outside banking hours. See *Sheppard & Cooper Ltd v TSB Bank plc (No.2)* [1996] B.C.C. 965, *per* Blackburne J. at 969.

[18] *Cripps (Pharmaceuticals) Ltd v Wickenden* [1973] 2 All E.R. 606; *Bank of Baroda v Panessar*, above, where in both cases the time elapsing between service of the demand and the appointment of the receiver was approximately one hour and Goff J. in the former case was prepared to accept that even minutes would be sufficient if the company was unable to pay.

[19] See *Bunbury Foods Pty Ltd v National Bank of Australasia Ltd*, above, n.10.

[20] *Ronald Elwyn Lister Ltd v Dunlop Canada Ltd* (1982) 135 D.L.R. (3d) 1.

reasonable notice is not merely a presumptive rule of construction of the security instrument but is founded on the twin concepts of public policy and unconscionability and cannot be waived.[21] It is fair to say that the doctrine of unconscionability has been developed in Australia and Canada into a major instrument for controlling contract terms in a way that goes well beyond English law, which continues to attach great importance to predictability in the legal outcome of commercial disputes.[22]

(6)   *If the debtor company clearly could not have met the demand in any event, the shortness of time between demand and payment is irrelevant.*[23]

(7)   *Where the company is a surety, it is a question of construction whether the debenture holder has to make demand on the principal debtor as well as on the company.*[24]

Conditional appointment

9-30   The debenture holder may appoint the intended receiver in advance under an appointment to take effect after default and demand for payment.[25] Accordingly it is not an objection to the validity of the appointment that the receiver has the instrument in his hands before demand has been made. The common practice of making appointments in this way reflects the perceived need to have the receiver in possession as soon as possible after demand in order to preserve the assets and reduce the risk of their removal.

Effect of defective or invalid appointment

9-31   Under s.232 of the Insolvency Act the acts of an individual as receiver are valid notwithstanding any defect in his appointment, nomination or qualifications. But in relation to the appointment or nomination the section

---

[21] *Waldron v Royal Bank of Canada* [1991] 4 W.W.R. 289 (British Columbia Court of Appeal). Section 244 of the Canadian Bankruptcy and Insolvency Act 1992 now requires the creditor to give the debtor 10 days notice before enforcing the security.

[22] In *Sheppard & Cooper Ltd v TSB Bank plc* [1996] B.C.C. 653 the Court of Appeal hinted that the demand point might need review, recognising its importance in a number of Commonwealth as well as English decisions on it. See the judgment of Sir John Balcombe at 658.

[23] *Cripps (Pharmaceuticals) Ltd v Wickenden*, above; *Bank of Baroda v Panessar*, above; *Sheppard & Cooper Ltd v TSB Bank plc (No.2)* [1996] B.C.C. 965.

[24] See, for example, *DFC Financial Services Ltd v Coffey* [1991] B.C.C. 218, where the Privy Council, taking a different view on the construction point from the Court of Appeal of New Zealand, held that the debenture holder was entitled to proceed directly against the surety as if it was a primary obligor without first making demand on the principal debtor as well.

[25] *Cripps (Pharmaceuticals) Ltd v Wickenden*, above; *Windsor Refrigerator Co v Branch Nominees Ltd* [1961] Ch. 375.

is confined to defects in form or procedure and does not validate acts done by one who was appointed under an invalid security or when the power of appointment had not become exercisable or who has acted without being appointed at all or, when disqualified.[26] In cases outside s.232 a receiver who acts when not validly appointed is liable to the company in damages for trespass or conversion, where the elements of these torts are satisfied,[27] or alternatively as constructive trustee of assets coming into his hands.[28]

The company can ratify a defective or invalid appointment and may be estopped from disputing the validity of the appointment if with knowledge of its invalidity the company proceeds to deal with the-receiver on the footing that he was validly appointed.[29] In the absence of such ratification or estoppel an appointment made before the right to appoint was exercisable is not cured by subsequent accrual of the right to appoint, nor can a second appointment be validly made until the appointor has remedied his wrongdoing by restoring the company to possession of its assets and renewing his demand.[30]

At common law the invalidity of a receiver's appointment does not convert him into the agent of the debenture holder who appointed him,[31] so that the debenture holder is not in principle responsible for the receiver's acts or omissions.[32] However, by s.34 of the Insolvency Act the appointee may now ask the court for an order requiring the debenture holder to indemnify him against any legal liability he has incurred solely by reason of the invalidity of the appointment. In practice, such indemnities are commonly exacted by receivers as a condition of accepting appointment.

Points to check before accepting an appointment

It follows from what has been said above that before accepting appointment as receiver the intended appointee should satisfy himself as far as possible that the security was duly registered and appears otherwise unimpeachable, that the instrument of appointment was signed by those empowered to sign it and that the appointment appears to be valid in other respects, and

9–32

---

[26] *Morris v Kanssen* [1946] A.C. 549, a decision on a comparable provision in the Companies Act 1929, s.143 and Table A.

[27] There cannot be conversion of a chose in action, such as contractual rights (*OBG Ltd v Allan* [2005] All E.R. (D) 134). The claimant may have an action for tortious interference with a contract but that requires an intention to prevent performance (*ibid.*, Mance L.J. dissenting).

[28] *Rolled Steel Products (Holdings) Ltd v British Steel Corp* [1986] Ch. 246.

[29] *Bank of Baroda v Panessar*, above. See also above, para.9–27, as to the effect of inviting the debenture holder to make the appointment in the mistaken belief that the debenture holder had become entitled to do so. A similar estoppel applies where there is acquiescence in the appointment of an administrator. See below, para.10–40.

[30] *Cripps (Pharmaceuticals) Ltd v Wickenden*, above, *per* Goff L.J. at 618.

[31] *Bank of Baroda v Panessar*, above.

[32] *ibid.*

should wherever possible obtain an indemnity against the consequences of an invalid appointment.[33]

Must the debenture holder consider the company's interests when appointing a receiver?

9–33   The debenture holder is entitled to prefer his own interests to those of company in making the appointment, for his position is inherently adverse to that of the company, and it is a general principle of mortgage law that a mortgagee is entitled to subordinate the debtor's interest to his own, so long as he is acting in good faith.[34] Accordingly the debenture holder owes no general duty to the company to refrain from appointing a receiver merely because this would cause damage to the company,[35] unless he acts in bad faith,[36] for example, by appointing a receiver solely for the purpose of disrupting an existing receivership under a subsequent debenture and preventing its enforcement[37] or maliciously with a view to damaging the company or another creditor. He does, however, have a duty not to appoint a person who he has reasonable grounds for believing is incompetent[38] or not qualified to act as an insolvency practitioner. There must, it is thought, be a strong presumption that a person who is legally qualified to act possesses the necessary competence and accordingly that a belief in his competence is reasonable.

When the appointment takes effect

9–34   The appointment is of no effect until is accepted by the appointee before the end of the business day next following that on which the instrument of appointment is received by him or on his behalf, but subject to this it is deemed to be made when the instrument of appointment is so received.[39] It

---

[33] These are not, of course, the only matters he will need to consider. Others include the sufficiency of the assets to meet his remuneration and expenses, the fact that the company is or is likely to go into liquidation (thus bringing an end to the receiver's agency powers) and the adequacy of his own professional expertise. See generally Gordon Stewart, *Administrative Receivers and Administrators* (1987), p.309; Louis G. Doyle, *Administrative Receivership Law and Practice* (1995), Chaps 6 and 7; Stanley Samwell, *Corporate Receiverships* (2nd ed. 1998), pp.56–58.

[34] *Shamji v Johnson Matthey Bankers Ltd* [1991] B.C.L.C. 36; *Cuckmere Brick Co Ltd v Mutual Finance Ltd* [1971] 1 Ch. 949, *per* Salmon L.J. at 965.

[35] *Shamji v Johnson Matthey Bankers Ltd*, above n.34; *Re Potters Oils Ltd (No.2)* [1986] 1 W.L.R. 201.

[36] *ibid.*

[37] *Downsview Nominees Ltd v First City Corp* [1993] A.C. 295.

[38] See *Shamji v Johnson Matthey Bankers Ltd*, above, n34.

[39] Insolvency Act 1986, s.33. To save time the instrument of appointment may be executed in advance of default and given to the intended receiver to become effective by his acceptance of it after demand and default.

is not entirely clear from the statutory provisions whether failure to accept the appointment renders it retrospectively void or merely terminates it on expiry of the time allowed for acceptance. The words "is of no effect" rather than "ceases to have effect" suggest that the latter is the proper interpretation. At first sight the point appears to be relevant to the validity of the appointee's acts in the period between receipt of the instrument of appointment and expiry of the time allowed for his acceptance of it. But this possibility is more apparent than real, because no formality is prescribed for acceptance, which may be in writing, by word of mouth or even by conduct,[40] so that it is difficult to envisage a situation in which the appointee could act as receiver without thereby accepting the appointment and perfecting his status. What is clear is that acceptance of the appointment within the time laid down operates retrospectively to the date of receipt of the instrument of appointment.

5. EFFECT OF THE APPOINTMENT

General effects

The appointment of a receiver: 9–35

(1)   crystallises a floating charge, if this has not already crystallised;

(2)   usually prevents the making of an administration order[41];

(3)   suspends the directors' powers of management as regards assets comprised in the security and the general conduct of the business[42];

(4)   terminates those contracts of employment which are incompatible with the administrative receiver's management powers—a question which depends not so much on the designation of the office held by the employee as on the particular circumstances[43]—but does not affect other contracts of employment[44];

(5)   does not affect the subsistence of other contracts.[45]

---

[40] Acceptance must be confirmed in writing within seven days and the appointment publicised (Insolvency Act 1986, s.46(1); Insolvency Rules 1986, r.3.1). But non-compliance with these formalities does not affect the validity of the appointment.

[41] See below, para.9–26.

[42] See below, paras 9–36 *et seq.*

[43] Contrast *Re Mack Trucks (Britain) Ltd* [1967] 1 All E.R. 977 with *Griffiths v Secretary of State for Social Services* [1974] Q.B. 468.

[44] *Re Foster Clark's Indenture Trusts* [1966] 1 All E.R. 43.

[45] See further paras 9–51 *et seq.*

Impact of the appointment on the powers of directors

(1) In general

9–36   The broad effect of the appointment of a receiver is to divest the directors of the company of their management powers during the currency of the receivership.[46] To this general principle there are at least two, and possibly three, exceptions. First, the directors' powers remain exercisable as regards assets which are outside the scope of the debenture or which the receiver decides to ignore or abandon, *e.g.* the company's right of action against his own debenture holder.[47] Secondly, the directors retain a residue of powers relating to matters which do not entrench on the powers and functions of the receiver, *e.g.* the power to maintain the statutory books and file the statutory returns, to obtain such information and accounts from the receiver as are necessary for that purpose and, it would seem, to ascertain the amount required to redeem the debenture.[48] Thirdly, the directors possibly retain a power to oppose a winding-up petition,[49] despite the fact that the administrative receiver is now given power both to present and to defend such a petition.[50]

(2) Actions against the debenture holder

9–37   Special problems arise where the directors consider that the debenture holder has acted in breach of duty and wish to have proceedings instituted against him. The receiver is then in the invidious position of having to decide whether to sue those who appointed him. Moreover, since any proceedings would have to be brought in the name of the company, not of the receiver, the charged assets would have to be deployed to meet the costs incurred in the litigation, to the detriment of the debenture holder, who might find that if his action succeeded and he recovered costs against the company the payment of these would diminish his security. In effect his own assets would be used to sue him. In *Newhart Developments Ltd v Co-operative Commercial Bank*[51] these difficulties did not arise because the company had been given a full indemnity for its costs by outside sources. Accordingly there could be no possible threat to the assets comprising the

---

[46] *Moss Steamship Co Ltd v Whinney* [1912] A.C. 254, *per* Lord Atkinson at 263; *Re Emmadart Ltd* [1979] Ch. 540, *per* Brightman J. at 547.
[47] *Newhart Developments Ltd v Co-operative Commercial Bank* [1978] Q.B. 814. See further below, para.9–37.
[48] *Gomba Holdings UK Ltd v Homan* [1986] 3 All E.R. 94.
[49] *Re Reprographic Exports (Euromart) Ltd* (1978) 122 S.J. 400.
[50] Insolvency Act 1986, Sch.1, item 2l.
[51] See above, n.47.

security. By contrast no such indemnity was initially given in *Tudor Grange Holdings Ltd v Citibank NA*,[52] and Sir Nicolas Browne-Wilkinson V.C., who entertained grave doubts as to the correctness of the *Newhart* decision while accepting that he was bound by it, held that the absence of an indemnity enabled him to distinguish the case from *Newhart* and that the directors had had no power to institute the proceedings. The Vice-Chancellor would have struck them out on this ground but for the offer of an indemnity during the course of the application to strike out the claim.[53] His view was that a receiver who felt embarrassed by his position could always apply to the court for directions.

In *Newhart* it was contended that any recovery of damages against the debenture holder would produce a circular transfer, because the damages would themselves become subject to the debenture holder's charge. But that does not mean that the proceedings are of no benefit to the company, for as Shaw L.J. pointed out,[54] the recovery goes in or towards discharge of the debt. The argument that the claim against the debenture holder is itself part of the security, so that the receiver is the *dominus* of any such claim, is, of course, correct in that the receiver is the party having the primary right to launch the proceedings in the company's name and to have control of the litigation. But if he chooses to abandon that right (and he is obviously going to be reluctant to bring proceedings against the debenture holder who appointed him) then as pointed out in *Newhart*[55] he cannot at the same time deny the right, and indeed the duty, of the directors to procure the institution of proceedings by the company, for it is only within the scope of the assets covered by the debenture that the receiver has a function to perform. Notwithstanding the misgivings expressed by the Vice-Chancellor in *Tudor Grange*, the approach adopted by the Court of Appeal in *Newhart* is clearly correct. If proceedings can be taken against the debenture holder without risk to the assets the subject of the security but the receiver is unwilling to pursue the claim, then, assuming the claim is arguable and not purely vexatious, why should the receiver be allowed to stifle it? It is true that the receiver can always apply to the court for directions,[56] but he cannot be compelled to do so, and no one else apart from the debenture holder has a *locus standi* to seek directions. In any event, is hard to see what purpose would be served by this procedure. Either the company's claim against the debenture holder is arguable, in which case it should be allowed to proceed to trial, or it is not, in which case the debenture holder can apply to have it struck out as disclosing no cause of action.

---

[52] [1992] Ch. 53.
[53] In the end the claim was struck out on other grounds.
[54] [1978] Q.B. 814 at 820.
[55] By Shaw L.J. at 819.
[56] Under the Insolvency Act 1986, s.35.

(3) Actions against the receiver

9–38   Where the proposed defendant is the receiver himself then plainly it is the company acting through its directors that has the right to institute proceedings.[57] If the position were otherwise the company would in practice be left remediless, and common sense indicates that the company must have a remedy against a receiver who acts improperly.[58]

Termination of the receivership

9–39   If the receivership comes to an end, whether by collection of what is due to the debenture holders and preferential creditors or otherwise, without the company having gone into liquidation, it is the duty of the receiver to hand back control of the company to the directors. This is an infrequent occurrence, since almost invariably a company in receivership goes into liquidation before the receiver is discharged.[59] Where control is restored the directors are entitled to call for delivery up of all books and documents relating to the company's affairs which are the property of the company. Books and documents in the possession of the receiver do not belong to the company merely because they relate to its affairs, for as pointed out earlier the receiver owes duties to his debenture holder as well as to the company and also has working papers of his own. The guiding principle is that documents brought into existence in discharge of the receiver's duty to the debenture holder belong to the debenture holder, those brought into being in discharge of his duty to the company belong to the company, and working papers and other documents intended solely for his own use to enable him to fulfil his duties are the property of the receiver himself.[60]

6. POWERS OF THE RECEIVER

From whom the receiver's powers emanate

9–40   The powers of a receiver appointed out of court emanate, directly or indirectly, from the debtor company. At first sight it seems anomalous that a receiver can be appointed and can exercise powers under a debenture to

---

[57] *Watts v Midland Bank* [1986] B.C.L.C. 15.
[58] *ibid., per* Peter Gibson J. at 21.
[59] For an exception, see *Gomba Holdings UK Ltd v Minories Finance Ltd* [1989] 1 All E.R. 261. See further, below, para.9–69.
[60] *ibid.,* affirming the decision of Hoffman J. [1988] B.C.L.C. 60 and applying, as regards the receiver's working documents, the principle in *Chantrey Martin & Co v Martin* [1953] 2 All E.R. 691.

which he is not a party and by virtue of an appointment by an instrument to which the company is not a party. But the anomaly disappears once it is appreciated that in making the appointment the debenture holder acts as agent of the company.

"Though it was the mortgagee who in fact appointed the receiver, yet in making the appointment the mortgagee acted, and it was the object of the parties that he should act, as agent for the mortgagor. Lord Cranworth, in *Jefferys v Dickson*, stated the doctrine of Courts of Equity on the subject to the effect following. The mortgagee, as agent of the mortgagor, appointed a person to receive the income, with directions to keep down the interest of the mortgage, and to account for the surplus to the mortgagor as his principal. These directions were supposed to emanate, not from the mortgagee but from the mortgagor; and the receiver therefore, in the relation between himself and the mortgagor, stood in the position of a person appointed by an instrument to which the mortgagee was no party . . . Of course the mortgagor cannot of his own will revoke the appointment of a receiver, or that appointment would be useless. For valuable consideration he has committed the management of his property to an attorney whose appointment he cannot interfere with. By degrees this form of appointment of receivers became more complicated, and their powers more extensive; but the doctrine explained by Lord Cranworth in the case cited was consistently adhered to, and it remained true throughout that the receiver's appointment, and all directions and powers given and conferred upon him, were supposed to emanate from the mortgagor, and the mortgagee, though he might be the actual appointor, and might have stipulated for all the powers conferred upon the receiver, was in no other position, so far as responsibility was concerned, than if he had been altogether a stranger to the appointment."[61]

Thus the receiver is notionally appointed by the company through the agency of the debenture holder and his powers derive from the debenture and, being given to secure the rights of the debenture holder, cannot be restricted or revoked except with the debenture holder's consent. It would be possible for the debenture to confer on the debenture holder the right to invest the receiver with powers, or to enlarge his powers, in the instrument of appointment itself, but in practice these are given by the debenture, not by the instrument of appointment under powers conferred by the debenture.

Accordingly the source of the receiver's powers is the debenture under which he is appointed. This is true even of the powers listed in Sch.1 to the

---

[61] *Gaskell v Gosling* [1896] 1 Q.B. 669, *per* Rigby L.J. at 692–693 in a judgment subsequently approved by the House of Lords [1897] A.C. 575.

Insolvency Act, for these are not independent statutory powers but powers deemed by the Act to be included in the debenture except so far as inconsistent with its provisions.[62] The purpose of the Schedule is to avoid the necessity for a long list of powers in the debenture itself; most of the acts the receiver is likely to wish to undertake are listed in the Schedule, which in its 23 items covers virtually every aspect of management of the business and the assets comprised in the security. The receiver thus has all these powers (except as varied or excluded by the debenture) and any additional powers conferred by the express terms of the debenture.

Since the powers listed in Sch.1 are deemed to be derived from the debenture rather than being directly conferred by the statute, it would seem that they are only as effective as they would have been if set out expressly in the debenture. It follows that the receiver cannot rely on such powers to do acts as agent of the company[63] which are *ultra vires* the company.[64] Doubts have been expressed whether the receiver can use the company's seal[65] or call up uncalled capital of the company,[66] these powers being typically vested by the articles of association in the directors or those acting on behalf of the directors. But the difficulty is more apparent than real. All the powers listed in Sch.1 are conferred on the receiver for the purpose of preserving, protecting and realising the security,[67] and may therefore be validly exercised for that purpose, even though the effect is to displace the board's own management powers.[68] This is the effect of the authority conferred by the charge on the debenture holder to appoint the receiver. Alternatively, the company could confer a separate power of attorney on the debenture holder.[69] A separate question is whether the power to call up uncalled capital remains exercisable after the company has gone into liquidation. There seems no reason why it should not be if the security includes uncalled capital.[70]

---

[62] Insolvency Act 1986, s.42(1).

[63] *Aliter*, acts relating to the security, for these represent the exercise on behalf of the debenture holder, of his rights as a secured creditor. See below.

[64] But see above, para.9–27, text and n.95.

[65] Item 8 in the Schedule.

[66] Item 19 in the Schedule.

[67] By s.42(2)(b), in the application of Sch.1 to the administrative receiver of a company references to the property of the company are to the property of which he is, or but for the appointment of some other person as the receiver of part of the company's property, would be the receiver and manager.

[68] A further argument advanced against the administrative receiver's power to use the company's seal is that under the statute it is contractual in character and does not survive the company's liquidation. The Law Commission has expressed the view that this is not the case and that in this respect the power is best seen as statutory. See Law Commission Consultation Paper No.143, 1996, The Execution of Deeds and Documents By or on Behalf of Bodies Corporate, para.8.33.

[69] Law Commission Consultation Paper No.143, 1996, para.8.34. Again, however, doubt has been expressed whether this continues after the liquidation. It was held not to do so in *Barrows v Chief Land Registrar The Times*, October 26, 1977, but the weight of opinion is to the contrary. See the Law Commission's Consultation Paper, above n.68, para.8.38. The Law Commission has recommended that the law be clarified on these various points.

[70] Section 74 of the Insolvency Act makes contributories liable for unpaid capital.

Receiver's powers are ancillary to the debenture holder's security interest

The receiver's ability to exercise full management powers derives not only   **9–41**
from the terms of his appointment, which embody the powers conferred by
the debenture, but from the fact that the debenture holder has a security
interest over the whole or substantially the whole of the company's
property.

Content of the receiver's powers

The receiver has: **9–42**

(1)   all the express powers conferred by the debenture;

(2)   implied authority to do whatever is necessary for, or ordinarily
       incidental to, the effective exercise of his express authority in the
       usual way,[71] except so far as the debenture otherwise provides;

(3)   as implied terms of the debenture, all the powers listed in Sch.1 to the
       Insolvency Act 1986, except in so far as they are inconsistent with any
       provisions of the debenture[72];

(4)   power with leave of the court to dispose of property subject to a prior
       or equal security interest.[73]

Schedule 1 lists 22 specific powers, followed by a general power to do all
other things incidental to the exercise of the specific powers. The latter
include the power to take possession of the property of the company,[74] and
for that purpose to take any expedient proceedings, to sell or otherwise
dispose of the property, to borrow money and grant security, to appoint
professionally qualified advisers, to bring and defend actions, to make any
payment which is necessary or incidental to the performance of his
functions, to carry on the business of the company, establish subsidiaries
and transfer assets to subsidiaries, to make arrangements or compromises
. on behalf of the company and to present or defend a winding-up petition
against the company.

Classification of powers as *in rem* and personal (agency)

The receiver's powers are both *in rem* and personal. His *in rem* powers are   **9–43**
held in right of the debenture holder and derive from the security created
by the debenture. They include the power to collect in the assets comprising

---

[71] *Bowstead and Reynolds on Agency* (18th ed. 2005), Art.27.
[72] Insolvency Act 1986, s.42(1).
[73] *ibid.*, s.43. See below, para.9–65.
[74] *i.e.* the property of which he has been appointed receiver (Insolvency Act 1986, s.42(2)(b)).

the security, to possess, control and use those assets and to deal with and dispose of them, whether by way of sale, lease, charge or otherwise. His personal powers are those vested in him by virtue of his position as deemed agent to manage the company's business. To the extent that the conduct of the business involves dealing with assets comprised in the security the *in rem* powers and the personal powers overlap. But the latter include powers which are purely personal. The distinction between the receiver's *in rem* powers and his purely personal (or agency) powers is that the former, as stated above, relate to the assets of the company comprised in the security whereas the latter relate to everything else, in particular the power to involve the company in further liabilities as its agent. Thus the purely personal powers include the power to make or continue contracts on behalf of the company, to repudiate contacts entered into by the company,[75] to hire and fire staff, to borrow money and grant security, to employ solicitors and accountants to assist him, to pay debts due from the company, to accept and indorse bills of exchange in the company's name, to buy stock and property for the purpose of the business and generally to carry on the business and exercise managerial functions.

The distinction between the *in rem* powers of the receiver and his purely personal powers is of little significance so long as the company is not in winding-up. But once liquidation supervenes the receiver's status as agent of the company comes to an end[76] and his purely personal powers fall away.[77] By contrast his *in rem* powers continue, for liquidation does not affect the enforcement of security interests or of acts taken for the preservation or realisation of security.[78]

Power of sale

9–44   Prior to the winding-up of the company assets forming part of the security may be sold in one of two ways. First, the receiver can exercise his agency powers and sell in the name of the company. If he does this the sale takes effect subject to the debenture under which he was appointed and any other incumbrances, including, those junior to such debenture.[79] This is because a receiver selling in the company's name is exercising the company's power of sale and cannot transfer any greater rights than the company itself could have done if not in receivership. Accordingly if the purchaser is to acquire an unincumbered title it will be necessary for the debenture holder and other incumbrancers either to join in the conveyance to concur in the sale

---

[75] See below, para.9–52.
[76] Insolvency Act 1986, s.44(1)(a).
[77] See para.9–69.
[78] See para.9–69.
[79] *Re The Real Meat Co Ltd* [1996] B.C.C. 254.

free from their interests or to release those interests under deeds of release. Secondly, the debenture holder can sell as mortgagee, and if he wishes can appoint the receiver his agent for that purpose. Such a sale overrides junior security interests, which then attach, in due order of priority, to any surplus proceeds remaining after the mortgagee exercising the power of sale has been paid. This is the form of sale that should be adopted if it is desired that the sale shall override junior security interests; and it is the only form of sale open once the company has gone into liquidation (for winding-up terminates the receiver's agency powers) except where the sale is authorised or ratified by the liquidator. Any sale by the liquidator in the name of the company would, again, take effect subject to the debenture and any other security interests.

Power to dispose of assets subject to a prior or equal security interest

Where, on application by the receiver, the court is satisfied that the **9–45** disposal (with or without other assets) of any property of which he is receiver and which is subject to a security interest of prior or equal ranking would be likely to promote a more advantageous realisation of the company's assets than would otherwise be effected, the court may by order authorise the receiver to dispose of the property as if it were not subject to the security.[80] This provision does not apply to property subject to a security interest ranking after that of the debenture holder,[81] for the obvious reason that it is always open to the debenture holder, either directly or through the receiver as his agent, to sell as mortgagee and thus override subsequent interests without need of a court order.

It is a required condition of any order giving leave to dispose of the property that the net proceeds of sale plus the amount by which those proceeds fall short of the value determined by the court as the net amount which would be realised by sale on the open market by a willing vendor are to be applied in discharging the sums secured by, the displaced security.[82] Accordingly any deficiency comes out of the assets available to the debenture holder and is payable to the secured creditor in priority to the claims of the debenture holder and of preferential and other creditors. It would seem that if the price fixed by the court was too high, this enures for the benefit of the secured creditor unless the court adjusts the figure.[83]

---

[80] Insolvency Act 1986, s.43(1), (2), (7).
[81] *ibid.*, s.43(2).
[82] *ibid.*, s.43(3).
[83] *Quaere* whether it has power to do this after the sale has taken place.

Protection of bona fide third party

9–46   A person dealing with a receiver in good faith and for value is not concerned to enquire whether he is acting within his powers.[84] However, this does not protect a party who deals with a person acting as receiver but never validly appointed.

7. DUTIES AND LIABILITIES OF THE RECEIVER

Nature of duties owed by receiver

9–47   I have already explained that the receiver owes a duty of care to his debenture holder, a limited duty of care to the company and a statutory duty to preferential creditors, as well as an obligation to retain for the benefit of general creditors the prescribed part of the net property subject to a floating charge. He also owes a duty of care to any other party having an interest in the equity of redemption, *e.g.* a subsequent mortgagee, and a duty to a surety to exercise reasonable care in the perfection or realisation of the security in order to protect the surety's right of subrogation, failing which the surety is released from that part of his liability which would have been discharged from the proceeds of the security if reasonable care had been taken and may, if he has made payment under his guarantee, have a positive remedy in damages. The receiver owes no separate duty to ordinary unsecured creditors,[85] nor is it necessary to their interests to impose such a duty, for they are adequately protected by the receiver's duty to the company, a breach of which is actionable at the suit of the liquidator in the name of the company. The receiver will not normally incur any personal liability under environmental law[86] and it is thought that he cannot be required to apply assets subject to the security interest towards the cost of compliance with a remediation notice, though as yet there appear to have been no decisions on the point.[87]

The duty owed by the receiver to the company was at one time considered to be of a quite limited kind,[88] as was shown by the Privy Council in *Downsview Nominees Ltd v First City Corp Ltd*[89] In that case it was held that a receiver owes no duty of care *in tort* for negligence, for to

---

[84] Insolvency Act 1986, s.42(3).
[85] *Lathia v Dronsfield Bros.* [1987] B.C.L.C. 321.
[86] Environmental Protection Act 1990, s.78X(4)(a).
[87] See further above, para.7–30, as to disclaimer of polluted land as onerous property and para.2–12 as to the treatment of clean-up costs in winding-up.
[88] For a penetrating discussion see Alan Berg, "Duties of a Mortgagee and a Receiver" [1993] J.B.L. 213.
[89] [1993] AC. 295.

impose this would be incompatible with his right and duty to act in the best interests of his debenture holder.[90] Certain specific duties are imposed on him in equity,[91] namely (a) to act in good faith and for the purpose of obtaining repayment for his debenture holder and (b) to take proper care to obtain the best price reasonably obtainable when selling the charged assets.[92] These equitable duties broadly parallel those of the mortgagee himself where he does not enter into possession. They are owed not only to the company itself but to subsequent incumbrancers and to sureties. So a receiver who instigates his appointment and exercises his powers not with the *bona fide* intention of securing repayment for his debenture holder but for his own personal advantage and in order to obstruct the work of another receiver appointed under a junior security interest is liable in damages for loss caused to the junior incumbrancer.[93] Two decades before *Downsview* the judgments in the Court of Appeal decision in *Cuckmere Brick Co Ltd v Mutual Finance Ltd*[94] had seemed to suggest a more general duty of care in negligence.[95] But in a subsequent decision of the Court of Appeal reliance on the tort of negligence rather than by reference to duties imposed in equity was deprecated.[96] Moreover, in emphasising the equitable source of the receiver's obligation in *Downsview* Lord Templeman was doing no more than echoing what he himself had earlier said in giving the advice of the Board in the decision of the Privy Council in *China and South Sea Bank Ltd v Tan Soon Gin*.[97]

Although *Downsview* was not received without criticism,[98] it was long thought that it accurately reflected the classical approach of English law towards the duty of mortgagees and their receivers, an approach generally mirrored in Australian and Canadian jurisprudence. But in policy terms the result was seen as profoundly unsatisfactory. At the heart of the problem is

---

[90] One of the more striking aspects of the decision in *Downsview* is that in the Court of Appeal of New Zealand it was accepted without any argument to the contrary by counsel that Gault J. at first instance was correct in basing the existence of the receiver's duties to a subsequent debenture holder on negligence, and neither of the parties challenged those conclusions in their case as presented to the Board. It was the Board itself which took the initiative in selecting an arena not chosen by the parties.

[91] [1993] A.C. 295, *per* Lord Templeman at 317.

[92] See to the same effect *Cuckmere Brick Co Ltd v Mutual Finance Ltd* [1971] Ch. 949. The standard of care required in equity and in tort would appear to be the same. See *Henderson v Merrett Syndicates Ltd* [1995] 2 AC. 145, *per* Lord Browne-Wilkinson at 205; *Bristol and West Building Society v Mothew* [1996] 4 All E.R. 698, *per* Millett L.J. at 711. Breach of the equitable duty is technically visited by an award of equitable compensation rather than damages but this has been declared a historical distinction without a difference (*Bristol and West Building Society Ltd v Mothew*, above, *per* Millett L.J. at 711).

[93] *Downsview Nominees Ltd v First City Corp Ltd*, above n.89.

[94] [1971] Ch. 949.

[95] See in particular the judgment of Salmon L.J. at 966, referring to the "neighbours" test of proximity formulated by Lord Atkin in *Donoghue v Stevenson* [1932] A.C. 562.

[96] By Nourse L.J. in *Parker-Tweedale v Dunbar Bank plc* [1991] Ch. 12 at 18.

[97] [1990] 1 A.C. 536.

[98] See, for example, Lightman and Moss, *The Law of Receivers and Administrators of Companies* (2nd edn.), para.7–13. See now the 3rd edn. at paras 7–019 *et seq.*

the traditional reluctance of equity to impose fetters on mortgagees in the exercise of their powers of sale, coupled with the ambivalent attitude of modern English law towards the expansion of liability in tort for pure economic loss, the boundaries of liability being expanded at one time only to be contracted the next. At one time it was thought that as the result of *Downsview* there were only two duties imposed by equity on the mortgagee or his receiver, namely to act in good faith and to use reasonable care to obtain the best price on a sale, and that so long as he fulfilled them the receiver incurred no liability to the company, subsequent incumbrancers or sureties for loss or damage caused by the exercise of his functions. That view, however, has been shown to be too narrow. Thus while the receiver is under no obligation to carry on or continue the company's business, so long as he does so he must act with due diligence.[99] Perhaps one can extract from this a more general principle that while the receiver's primary duty is to his debenture holder and he is entitled to subordinate the interests of creditors to that duty, yet whatever functions he does choose to perform should be performed with due care and diligence.

9–48   A review of legal policy in this area is now overdue. There is little doubt that the dangers involved in imposing a more generalised duty on receivers and their debenture holders have been exaggerated, whilst insufficient regard has been paid to recurrent criticisms by companies in receivership and junior incumbrancers that their interests are not adequately safe-guarded by the present law relating to sales by mortgagees and receivers. Thus the company is not entitled to complain about the decision of a mortgagee or receiver not to sell or about the timing of any sale, even if it can be demonstrated that the debenture holder would lose nothing, and the company might gain a great deal, from a temporary deferment of the sale.[1] The receiver is under no obligation to improve the mortgaged property or to increase its value, nor is he obliged to pursue, or continue the pursuit of, an application for planning permission to develop the property instead of proceeding with an immediate sale.[2] Moreover, although as we have seen the receiver, while running the company's business, owes a duty to exercise due diligence in so doing,[3] he is entitled, if he so chooses, to decide not to continue the company's business,[4] and to sell a part of the business which would be better kept. It would also seem that he can select a particular asset to realise for the benefit of his debenture holder even though the removal of that asset would damage the company's business and there are other assets to which he could resort and on which the business is less

---

[99] *Medforth v Blake* [2000] Ch. 86. See also *Yorkshire Bank plc v Hall* [1999] 1 W.L.R. 1713.

[1] See *Silven Properties Ltd v Royal Bank of Scotland* [2004] 4 All E.R. 484; *Cuckmere Brick Co Ltd v Mutual Finance Ltd* [1971] Ch. 949, *per* Salmon L.J. at 966; *South Sea Bank Ltd v Tan Soon Gin* [19901 1 A.C. 536.

[2] *Silven Properties Ltd v Royal Bank of Scotland*, above, n.19.

[3] *Medforth v Blake* [2000] Ch. 86.

[4] *Downview Nominees Ltd v First City Corp Ltd* [1993] A.C. 295 at 314.

dependant.[5] One has considerable sympathy with the observation by Sir Donald Nicholls V.C. in *Palk v Mortgage Services Funding plc*[6]:

> "In the exercise of his rights over his security the mortgagee must act fairly towards the mortgagor. His interest in the property has priority over the interest of the mortgagor, and he is entitled to proceed on that footing. He can protect his own interest, but he is not entitled to conduct himself in a way which unfairly prejudices the mortgagor. I have given two examples where the law imposes a duty on the mortgagee when he is exercising his powers: if he lets the property he must obtain a proper market rent and if he sells he must obtain a proper market price.[7] *I confess I have difficulty in seeing why a mortgagee's duties in and about the exercise of his powers of letting and sale should be regarded as narrowly confined to these two duties.*"[8] [emphasis added]

The fact is that English law has not kept pace with developments in legal policy in other major common law jurisdictions. The New Zealand Receiverships Act 1993, while retaining the receiver's overriding obligations to act in good faith and for a proper purpose and to obtain the best price reasonably obtainable when selling, also imposes on him an obligation to exercise his powers with reasonable regard to the interests of unsecured creditors of the debtor company, guarantors and ornery, claiming, an interest, in property, through the debtor.[9] The Canadian Bankruptcy and Insolvency Act requires the receiver to deal with the assets in a commercially reasonable manner.[10] The Australian Corporate Law Reform Act 1992 requires the receiver to exercise the degree of care and diligence that a reasonable person in a like position in a corporation would exercise, in the corporation's circumstances.[11] There is much to be said for a similar change of direction in English receivership law. It is clear that the very limited responsibility of a receiver in the protection of the interests of general creditors was a powerful factor in the government's decision to abolish administrative receivership,[12] with certain exceptions mentioned earlier.

---

[5] But he must act in good faith. See below, para.9–52.
[6] [1993] Ch. 330.
[7] By this the Vice-Chancellor plainly meant that the mortgagee has a duty to take reasonable care to obtain a proper market rent or a proper market price, not a strict duty.
[8] [1993] Ch. 330 at 338.
[9] Section 18.
[10] Section 247.
[11] Section 232(4).
[12] See above, para.9–04.

The receiver's liability on contracts

9–49   Section 44 of the Insolvency Act 1986, as amended by the Insolvency Act 1994, deals with the deemed agency of the receiver prior to winding-up of the company and with his liability in respect of new contracts and contracts of employment which he adopts.

"(1) The administrative receiver of a company—

    (a) is deemed to be the company's agent, unless and until the company goes into liquidation;

    (b) is personally liable on any contract entered into by him in the carrying out of his functions (except in so far as the contract otherwise provides) and, to the extent of any qualifying liability, on any contract of employment adopted by him in the carrying out of those functions; and

    (c) is entitled in respect of that liability to an indemnity out of the assets of the company.

(2) For the purposes of subsection (l)(b) the administrative receiver is not to be taken to have adopted a contract of employment by reason of anything done or omitted to be done within 14 days after his appointment.

(2A) For the purposes of subsection (l)(b), a liability under a contract of employment is a qualifying liability if—

    (a) it is a liability to pay a sum by way of wages or salary or contribution to an occupational pension scheme,

    (b) it is incurred while the administrative receiver is in office, and

    (c) it is in respect of services rendered wholly or partly after the adoption of the contract.

(2B) Where a sum payable in respect of a liability which is a qualifying liability for the purposes of subsection (l)(b) is payable in respect of services rendered partly before and partly after the adoption of the contract, liability under subsection (l)(b) shall only extend to so much of the sum as is payable in respect of services rendered after the adoption of the contract.

[(2C) and (2D) define what constitute wages or salary for the above purposes]

(2E) This section does not limit any right to indemnity which the administrative receiver would have apart from it, nor limit his liability on contracts entered into or adopted without authority, nor confer any right to indemnity in respect of that liability."

Entry into new contracts

Until the company goes into liquidation the receiver is deemed to be its **9–50** agent[13] and as such can commit it to future liabilities by entering into contracts in its name and on its behalf. The receiver is, however, personally liable on any contract he enters into (*i.e.* even in the name of the company) in the carrying out of his functions except so far as the. contract otherwise provides,[14] but is entitled to an indemnity in respect of that liability out of the assets of the company.[15] Though the receiver is personally liable on new contracts entered into on behalf of the company, it is the company, not the receiver, who is party to the contract. Accordingly the receiver's disclaimer of personal liability on a contract is not subject to the Unfair Contract Terms Act 1977.

Continuance of existing contracts other than contracts of employment

The receiver does not incur personal liability, (except in relation to **9–51** contracts of employment[16]) merely because he procures the company to continue or complete, an existing contract.[17] This logically follows from the fact that the receiver is not a party to the contract, merely a receiver and manager of the business, so that in the absence of any statutory provision imposing liability there is no reason why he should be in any different position from that of directors. The position is the same for continuing contracts such as the hire of equipment. If the receiver causes the company to continue a rental agreement and incur further rentals, these are the liability of the company, not of the receiver.[18] The principle of liquidation law that sums accruing due under leases and contracts continued by the liquidator for the beneficial winding-up of the company are payable in full as expenses of the liquidation does not apply to receivership.

> "The reason is not far to seek. The appointment of an administrative receiver does not trigger a statutory prohibition on the lessor or owner of goods such as that found in section 30 in the case of a winding-up order. If the rent or hire is not paid by the administrative receiver the lessor or owner of the goods is at liberty, as much after the appointment of the administrative receiver as before, to exercise the rights and remedies available to him under his lease or hire purchase agreement. Faced with the prospect of proceedings, an administrative receiver may choose to

---

[13] Insolvency Act 1986, s.44(1)(a).
[14] *ibid.*, s.44(1)(b).
[15] *ibid.*, s.44(l)(c). See further para.9–57 as to questions arising in relation to the indemnity.
[16] See below, paras 9–53 *et seq.*
[17] *Re Newdigate Colliery Ltd* [1912] Ch. 468.
[18] *Hay v Swedish & Norwegian Railway Co Ltd* (1892) 8 T.L.R. 775.

pay the rent or hire charges in order to retain the land or goods. But if he decides not to do so, the lessor or owner of the goods has his remedies. There is no occasion, assuming that there is jurisdiction, for the court to intervene and order the administrative receiver to pay these outgoings."[19]

But in appropriate cases the court has power to order expenses incurred by a party in dealing with a receiver to be paid as an expense of the receivership, as where the receiver unsuccessfully brings or defends proceedings in the name of the company and an order for costs is made against the company.[20]

Repudiation of contracts

9–52 Equally the receiver does not in general incur a liability either to the company or to the other party to a contract by repudiating the contract in the name of the company or by failing or refusing to allow the company to perform its part of the contract, and this is so even though the result is to expose the company to termination of the contact and/or a liability in damages.[21] There are several reasons for this. First performance of the company's part of the contract is likely to involve the expenditure of money or the application of assets forming part of the security, and the debenture holder is not obliged to release assets from his security interest but on the contrary is entitled to have his security enforced, and thus stands in a better position than the company itself.[22] Secondly, the power to carry on the company's business is a power conferred on the receiver primarily for the benefit of his debenture holder, so that he must be free to decline to perform contracts, and indeed to shut down entirely an unprofitable part of the company's business, if he considers that this is in the best interests of the business of which he is receiver.[23] All that is required of the receiver is

---

[19] *Re Atlantic Computer Systems plc* [1992] Ch. 505, *per* Nicholls L.J. at pp.524–525, applied in *Brown v City of London Corp* [1996] 1 W.L.R. 1070; *sub nom. Re Sobam BV* [1996] B.C.C. 351.

[20] *Anderson v Hyde* [1996] 2 B.C.L.C. 144, a decision of the Court of Appeal of Northern Ireland; *Bacal Contracting Ltd v Modern Engineering (Bristol) Ltd* [1980] 2 All E.R. 655.

[21] *Re Newdigate Colliery Ltd* [1912] 1 Ch. 468; *Airlines Airspares Ltd v Handley Page Ltd* [1970] Ch. 193; *Re Diesels & Components Pty Ltd* (1985) 9 C.L.R. 269, (1985) B.C.L.C. 314.

[22] *ibid.* See also *Edwin Hill & Partners v First National Finance Corp plc* [1989] BCLC 89, in which it was held that a debenture holder who without appointing a receiver or otherwise enforcing its charge insisted on the company appointing a new and more prestigious firm of architects to supervise a development was not liable to the former architect for wrongful interference with the contract, for it had a right equal or superior to that of the plaintiff and the fact that it brought about the termination of the plaintiffs' engagement through an accommodation with the company, not by enforcement of its security, did not deprive it of legal justification for its actions. In argument it was conceded that the debenture holder could not have been liable if it had interfered with the contract by exercising its power of sale and that the same probably applied if it had appointed a receiver.

[23] *Kernohan Estates Ltd v Boyd* [1967] N.I. 27.

that he act in good faith and without needlessly damaging the company's goodwill.[24] Any duty of care he owes to the company[25] is subordinate to that owed to his debenture holder,[26] and he owes no duty at all to ordinary unsecured creditors.[27] Thirdly, the receiver as deemed agent of the company is entitled to take advantage of the principle, of agency law formulated in *Said v Butt*[28] that an agent acting *bona fide* within the scope of his authority is not liable for inducing a breach of contract by his principal,[29] for he is treated as the principal's *alter ego* and his acts are those of the principal.

The principles underlying the receiver's right to decline to perform the company's contracts have yet to be fully worked out. If the receiver acts wantonly he may incur a liability to the company as its deemed agent for loss caused by his actions and a liability to the third party for procuring a breach of contract. What is less clear is whether, because performance of the contract would involve the application of money or other assets comprising the security, the receiver is justified in preventing performance when the remaining assets provide ample cover and can be realised just as quickly as those which would be used in performing the contract.[30] It would seem that in this regard the receiver's position is not essentially different from that of his debenture holder. In general, a secured creditor may resort to whatever part of his security he chooses, without regard to the interests either of his debtor or of third parties, and his receiver must, it is thought, be in the same position. To put the matter in another way, a person contracting with a company takes the company as he finds it, and cannot complain if the debenture holder or his receiver exercises the rights conferred on them by the company over the assets of the company or negotiates with the company to achieve the same results as would be achieved by exercise of those rights.

The receiver is not, however, entitled to disregard legal or equitable proprietary rights acquired by the other party to the contract. Accordingly he can be ordered to give specific performance of a contract of sale of land entered into by the company,[31] to refrain from assigning an option already assigned by the company in equity to a third party[32] and to respect a lien over goods in favour of the company's agent, even if the goods were not received until after the receiver was appointed and the agent had notice of his appointment.[33]

---

[24] *ibid.*
[25] See above, para.9–47, and, for an instructive discussion, David Milman. "The Receiver as Agent" (1981) 44 M.L.R. 658.
[26] *Re B Johnson & Co (Builders) Ltd* [1955] Ch. 634, *per* Jenkins L.J. at 661.
[27] *Lathia v Dronsfield Bros.* [1987] B.C.L.C. 321.
[28] [1920] 3 K.B. 497.
[29] *Welsh Development Agency v Export Finance Co Ltd* [1992] B.C.L.C. 148.
[30] Other secured creditors may be protected by the doctrine of marshalling.
[31] *Freevale Ltd v Metrostore Holdings Ltd* [1984] Ch. 199.
[32] *Telemetrix plc v Modern Engineers of Bristol (Holdings) plc* [1985] 1 B.C.C. 99, 417.
[33] *Re Diesels & Components Pty Ltd*, above, n.21.

Moreover, in *Land Rover Group Ltd v UPF (UK) Ltd*[34] it was held that while a receiver is in a privileged position in being able to procure the company not to perform a contract, his appointment does not preclude an order for an interim injunction against the company to secure fulfillment of its contractual obligations where this would otherwise be granted. However, that case may have turned on its own special facts and moreover was not a final adjudication, merely an interlocutory proceeding. It is thought that in general a receiver is perfectly entitled to take the position that it will not allow the company's assets to be used, or its own negotiating position in handling a contract undermined, to the possible detriment of the debenture holder.

Adoption of contract of employment

9–53   Under s.44(2)(b) of the Insolvency Act 1986 the receiver is personally liable, to the extent of any qualifying liability, on any contract of employment adopted by him in the carrying out of his functions. For this purpose he is not to be taken to have adopted the contract by virtue of anything done or omitted to be done, within 14 days after his appointment.[35] Section 44 has had a chequered history which it is necessary briefly to describe in order to show how it assumed its present form.

(1) Nicoll v Cutts[36] and the original section 44(2)

9–54   In *Nicoll v Cutts* it had been held that a receiver was not personally liable for salaries or wages payable under contracts of employment in existence at the time of his appointment and continued by him thereafter. This was felt to be unduly harsh on employees retained by the receiver for the purpose of carrying on the business, and during the progress of the Insolvency Bill 1995 opportunity was taken to insert what is now s.44(2)(b) of the 1986 Act. However, there was much uncertainty as to the construction of s.44, in particular as to (a) the meaning of "adopted", (b) the type of conduct constituting adoption, (c) whether it was open to a receiver to stipulate that in keeping on employees he was not adopting their contracts, (d) whether a receiver could adopt part only of a contract, such as the benefits without the burdens, or some liabilities but not others, (e) the extent of the liabilities incurred by the receiver if he did adopt a contract, and (f) whether it was

---

[34] [2003] 2 B.C.L.C. 222.
[35] Insolvency Act 1986, s.44(2).
[36] [1985] B.C.L.C. 322, holding that the appointment of a receiver out of court (unlike an appointment by the court) did not operate to terminate contracts of employment, and that the position of the receiver under such contracts was no different from what it was under other types of continuing contract.

possible to contract out of such liabilities. Similar questions arose in relation to the comparable, but not identical, provisions of s.19(6) of the Insolvency Act relating to the liability of administrators. This led to an unreported decision concerning a company called Specialised Mouldings Ltd and three major sets of proceedings involving three companies, Paramount Airways, which was in administration, and Leyland DAF and Ferranti, both of which were in administrative receivership.

(2) Re Specialised Mouldings Ltd[37]

In this case Harman J. held, on an application for directions under s.35 of **9–55** the Insolvency Act, that a receiver can avoid adopting an employment contract by stipulating expressly that he does not do so. In reliance on this decision it became common practice for a receiver to write to all employees after his appointment to say that their contracts with the company would be continued on the same basis as previously, that the receiver was not adopting the contract and that he assumed no personal liability in relation to the employee's employment. In the first edition of this book I commented as follows:

> "The authority of this decision is somewhat weakened by the fact that the learned judge did not reduce his judgment to writing, and it is submitted that it is wrong. Adoption is not merely a matter of words but of fact. It is difficult to see how a receiver can claim not to have adopted a contract of employment if he allows the contract to remain in force and continues to make use of the employee's services. Such an interpretation drives a coach and horses through section 44(2) and deprives it of any significant meaning."

This passage was later approved by Dillon L.J. in the *Paramount* case,[38] and appears to be consistent with the subsequent ruling of the House of Lords on this aspect of the case.[39]

(3) Powdrill v Watson[40] prior to the House of Lords ruling

In this case two employees of Paramount Airways who had been retained **9–56** by the administrator on terms that they would be paid during the interim period but that the administrators were not adopting their contracts of

---

[37] February 13, 1987, summarised in Gordon Stewart, *Administrative Receivers and Administrators*, p.512.
[38] See n.40 below at para.9–57.
[39] See below.
[40] [1993] B.C.C. 662, affirmed [1994] B.C.C. 172; [1994] 1 All E.R. 513 *sub nom. Re Paramount Airways Ltd (No.3)*.

employment were later made redundant. They petitioned the court under s.27 of the Insolvency Act seeking an order for payment from the assets of pay in lieu of notice and unpaid holiday pay, together with bonuses and compensation for unfair dismissal. The case was decided at first instance by Evans-Lombe J. The first question was what constituted adoption of the contract for the purpose of s.19(6) of the Act. Evans-Lombe J. cited with approval the statement in the first edition of this work that "a receiver adopts a contract through any act or acquiescence (after expiry of the 14–day period) which is indicative of his intention to treat the contract as on foot". Evans-Lombe J. went on to hold that despite the terms of the letter from the administrators the contracts of employment had been adopted, and upheld the claims for pay in lieu of notice and holiday pay but dismissed the remaining claims.[41] That decision was in substance affirmed by the Court of Appeal[42] which held that the contracts of employment were continuing contracts and in adopting them the administrators had adopted them in their entirety.

(4) The Insolvency Act 1994 and Powdrill v Watson in the House of Lords

9–57 The ruling by the Court of Appeal gave rise to consternation on the part of insolvency practitioners, who were worried that they might be exposed to claims by former employees who had not received prior payment out of the assets. This concern was heightened by the fear that when applied to the position of administrative receivers under s.44(2) the decision might be held to expose them to all the liabilities of the employer on the relevant contract, whether incurred, or relating to services performed, before, during or after the termination of the receivership.[43] Accepting that the matter was urgent the government acted with what Lord Browne-Wilkinson was later to describe as "almost unprecedented speed"[44] by introducing the Insolvency Bill 1994, which was passed into legislation barely a month after the Court of Appeal ruling. The Insolvency Act 1994 modified ss.19 and 44 by restricting the priority of claims by employees in an administration, and the personal liability of receivers in an administrative receivership, to "qualifying liabilities", that is, specified wage and wage-related claims incurred during the administration or receivership, and then only to sums payable in respect of services rendered by employees after the adoption of the

---

[41] [1993] B.C.C. 622.

[42] [1994] B.C.C. 172; *sub nom. Powdrill v Watson* [1994] 2 All E.R. 513.

[43] These fears proved to be well-founded, in that Lightman J. gave a ruling precisely to this effect in *Re Leyland DAF Ltd (No.2)* and *Re Ferranti International plc* [1994] B.C.C. 658, two cases which he heard together. The ruling did not apply in relation to administration, since what was then s.19(6) made it clear that the priority given to employees' claims was limited to liabilities incurred during the administrator's period of office.

[44] *Powdrill v Watson* [1995] 2 A.C. 394 at p.443.

contract. However, the government declined to incorporate provisions making the new legislation retrospective, so that serious problems remained. In the end these were largely resolved by the House of Lords, which held[45] that the employees' priority was limited to liabilities under adopted contracts so far as incurred during the period of the administration and did not extend to pre-administration or post-administration liabilities. On the other hand, it was not limited to liabilities incurred in return for services actually provided after adoption of the contract. In this respect the 1994 Act cut down the priority still further.

There remains one point to clarify which was left untouched by the 1994 Act. Precisely what is meant by adoption? It was always clear that it did not mean novation, *i.e.* entry by the receiver into a new contract, for the receiver would be liable under such a contract by virtue of the opening words of s.44(1)(b) and there would have been no need for s.44(1)(b) to make reference to contracts of employment. Nor did adoption require an act by which the receiver made manifest an intention to assume personal liability. Such liability flows from the adoption of the contract, rather than the other way round. What, then, constitutes the act of adoption of an employment contract? Is it sufficient that the administrative receiver takes no positive steps to terminate it? Or is some more positive step required?

It is evident that on this crucial point Lord Browne-Wilkinson had a change of mind during the course of his speech. Starting from the position that "the mere continuation of the employment by the company does not lead inexorably to the conclusion that it has been adopted by the receiver"[46] and that adoption "can only connote some conduct by the administrator or receiver which amounts to an election to treat the continued employment with the company as giving rise to a, separate liability in the administration or receivership"[47] he was in the end reluctantly driven to the conclusion that the contract of employment is inevitably adopted by the receiver unless he terminates or repudiates[48] the contract within 14 days of his appointment.[49]

Conclusions on section 44

We are now in a position to summarise the present state of the law in the light of the decision of the House of Lords in *Powdrill v Watson* and of the amendments to s.44 of the Insolvency Act:

9–58

---

[45] In *Powdrill v Watson* [1995] 2 A.C. 394, in which the House heard consolidated appeals in the *Leyland DAF* and *Ferranti* cases.

[46] [1995] 2 A.C. 394 at 448.

[47] *ibid.*, at 449.

[48] The contract of employment is one of the few contracts that can be brought to an end by a repudiatory act without the need for its acceptance by the other party as terminating the contract. Though this is disputed by some authorities Lord Browne-Wilkinson's speech gives support to the view generally accepted that employment contracts are an exception to the usual rule in contract law.

[49] [1995] 2 A.C. 394 at 450, 452.

(1) By "adoption" of a contract of employment is meant causing or allowing it to continue in force.

(2) The receiver adopts a contract of employment if he does not within 14 days of his appointment[50] either terminate the contract or repudiate it, *e.g.* by refusing to pay wages.

(3) The receiver's liability is confined to wages or salary, holiday pay and other entitlements designated as qualifying liabilities under subss.(2A), (2C) and (2D) of s.44.

(4) The receiver is responsible only for a liability incurred while he is in office, not for liabilities incurred before he accepted his appointment or after his discharge.

(5) He is also not liable for payments in respect of services rendered before his adoption of the contract, and where services are rendered partly before and partly after such adoption then he is liable only to the extent of the services rendered after adoption.

(6) For the purpose of computing the receiver's liability, sums due to the employee are considered to accrue day by day under the Apportionment Act 1870, so that where, for example, a sum in respect of services rendered during the receivership does not become payable until after the receiver has ceased to hold office it will be apportioned and he will be liable only for such part as is deemed to accrue under the Apportionment Act between the commencement of the provision of the services and the ending of the receiver's period of office.

(7) Where the receiver adopts the contract he thereby assumes personal liability upon it and is not entitled to disclaim liability or to select which liabilities he will undertake and which he will not. This is not because the exempting words of s.44(2) are confined to new contracts made by the receiver (for as Lightman J. pointed out in *Leyland DAF* they would be inappropriate in relation to contracts entered into by the company prior to the receivership and to which the receiver was not a party) but because to allow the receiver to exclude liability on contracts he has adopted would be contrary to the policy of the legislation.

Receiver's right to indemnity

9–59 By s.44(1)(c) of the Insolvency Act the receiver is entitled to an indemnity out of the assets of the company in respect of his personal liability on contracts entered into on behalf of the company or contracts of employment adopted by him. But the receiver's power to commit the company to

---

[50] It will be recalled that under s.44(2) of the Insolvency Act the receiver is not to be taken to have adopted a contract of employment by reason of anything done or omitted to be done within 14 days after his appointment.

new contractual liabilities comes to an end on liquidation, when his agency terminates,[51] and if, after liquidation, he enters into new contracts he has no statutory right of indemnity. This seems clear from s.44(3), which provides that s.44 does not limit the receiver's liability on contracts entered into or adopted without authority, nor confer any right of indemnity in respect of that liability. But if the liquidator chooses to accept and retain on behalf of the company the benefit of a post-liquidation contract concluded by the liquidator—*e.g.* by retaining goods purchased in the name of the company after winding-up—then on general restitutionary principles the receiver should be indemnified or reimbursed out of the assets of the company to the extent of any benefit the company has derived from the adopted transaction.

Debentures almost invariably provide for payment of the receiver's remuneration and expenses out of receipts and realisations before these are applied towards discharge of the amount secured by the debenture,[52] and the receiver's entitlement has priority over the claims of the debenture holder and preferential creditors even in the absence of an express provision in the debenture.[53] Such expenses include liabilities incurred by the receiver under contracts entered into by him on behalf of the company. However, the receiver cannot resort to assets of third parties, or to assets of the company which are subject to a security interest ranking in priority to that of his debenture holder.

Leases

The receiver is not liable to the lessor either for rent accrued due prior to **9–60** the time of his appointment or for rent accruing due after his appointment, even if takes actual possession himself.[54] This is because, in contrast to a liquidator, the receiver who takes beneficial occupation does so as manager in right of the debenture holder, not as successor to the business in right of the company. It follows that post-receivership rent is not payable to the lessor as an expense of the receivership in the way that post-liquidation rent would have been payable on a winding-up, for the debt is that of the company but the company's money and other assets are subject to the debenture and there is no reason why the security should be made available to discharge the company's indebtedness.[55] The lessor has his usual battery of remedies against the company for non-payment of the rent, including

---

[51] Insolvency Act 1986, s.44(1)(a).
[52] See, for example, J.R. Lingard, *Bank Security Documents* (3rd ed. 1993), document 1, clause 7.02; document 2, clause 8.02.
[53] *Re Glyncorrwg Colliery Co Ltd* [1926] Ch. 951.
[54] *Hand v Blow* [1901] 2 Ch. 721, distinguishing the Irish decision in *Baife v Blake* (1850) 1 I.R. Ch. Rep. 365; *Consolidated Entertainments Ltd v Taylor* [1937] 4 All E.R. 432.
[55] *Hand v Blow*, above n.54.

forfeiture of the lease, distress and service of a notice under s.6 of the Law of Distress Amendment Act 1908[56] requiring sub-lessees to pay their sub-rents direct to him.[57]

If the company has sub-let the premises, the receiver is entitled to collect the sub-rentals and retain these for the benefit of the debenture holder, and may do so without paying the rent due to the lessor, there being no privity of contract between lessor and sub-lessee and thus no connection between the rent payable under the head lease and, that payable under the sub-lease.[58] The lessor may either forfeit the lease or serve a notice under s.6 of the Law of Distress Amendment Act 1908 on the sub-lessee requiring him to pay the sub-rentals direct to the head lessor to the extent necessary to discharge the head lessee's obligations. Neither the appointment of a receiver nor the crystallisation of a floating charge resulting from such appointment affects the lessor's right to serve a s.6 notice,[59] and even entry into possession by the debenture holder or his receiver does not alter the position.[60] The debenture holder cannot claim a superior title under the rule in *Dearle v Hall* as an equitable assignee who is the first to give notice to the sub-tenants, because s.6 confers on the lessor what is in effect a statutory right to garnishee the rent due from the sub-tenants and any assignee of the lease takes subject to the possibility of this right being exercised, so that the question of competing assignments does not arise.[61]

Rates

9–61   The receiver normally incurs no personal for payment of business rates, even where he takes possession, for his possession is generally as deemed agent of the company, not on his own account.[62] Moreover, even where his deemed agency comes to an end as the result of the company going into liquidation this does not by itself mean that he is in rateable occupation, of the premises, for the company continues to be in possession itself unless there is some act or event by which it is divested of possession.[63]

---

[56] *Quaere* whether the receiver or his debenture holder can serve a declaration of his interest on the lessor under s.1 of the Law of Distress Amendment Act 1908.

[57] See below.

[58] *Hand v Blow*, above n.54.

[59] *Re Offshore Ventilation Ltd* (1989) 5 B.C.C. 160.

[60] *ibid.*

[61] *ibid.*

[62] *Brown v City of London Corp* [1996] 1 W.L.R. 1076: *sub nom. Re Sobam BV* [1996] B.C.C. 351; *Ratford v North Avon District Council* [1986] 3 All E.R. 193; *Rees v Boston Borough Council* [2002] 1 W.L.R. 1304 where the authorities were extensively reviewed by Jonathan Parker L.J. See generally Lightman & Moss, *op. cit.*, Chap.20.

[63] *Re Beck Foods Ltd* [2002] B.P.I.R. 665, applying a series of earlier decisions, including *Re Marriage, Neave & Co* [1896] 2 Ch. 663 and *Ratford v Northavon District Council* [1897] Q.B. 357.

Liability in tort for trespass or conversion

A receiver has to take control of the company's assets as quickly as possible **9–62** after his appointment, in order to preserve the assets and to prevent their disappearance. Within the very limited time available he has little or no opportunity to verify the company's title to assets of which it is in possession, which may well include property belonging to a third party, such as stock or equipment supplied under reservation of title and not fully paid for. At common law a receiver who takes possession of or sells a third party's asset or does some other act inconsistent with that party's right to possession incurs the normal liabilities in tort for trespass or conversion, even if acting in good faith. However, he is now given a measure of protection by the Insolvency Act, which gives him immunity from liability for seizing or disposing of property which is not the property of the company if at the time of the seizure or disposal he believes, and has reasonable grounds for believing, that he is entitled (whether in pursuance of an order of the court or otherwise) to seize or dispose of that property.[64] In such a case he also has a lien on the property, or the proceeds of its sale, for expenses incurred in connection with the seizure or disposal.[65] The statutory provisions are confined to the seizure and sale of tangible property, and do not apply to the collection in of debts due to a third party. But as to these no statutory protection is necessary, for intangibles are not susceptible to a claim for conversion[66] and to the extent that the collection in of the debts induces a breach of contract between the company and the debtors the receiver is entitled to rely on the rule in *Said v Butt* which protects agency against personal liability.[67]

The floating charge and preferential debts

(1) The priority of preferential debts

One of the major weaknesses of a floating charge is that it is subordinated **9–63** to the claims of preferential creditors if, when the company is not in course of being wound up, the debenture holder takes possession of any property comprised in the charge[68] or appoints a receiver[69] or if the debtor company

---

[64] Insolvency Act 1986, s.243(3), (4).
[65] *ibid.*
[66] *OBG Ltd v Allan* [2005] All E.R. (D) 134.
[67] *Welsh Development Agency v Export Finance Co Ltd* [1992] B.C.C. 270; and see above, para.9–52.
[68] Companies Act 1985, s.196(1), (2), as amended by the Insolvency Act 1986, s.439(1) and Sch.13.
[69] Insolvency Act 1986, s.40. This section applies whether or not the receiver is an administrative receiver. Curiously the priority of preferential creditors is not triggered by a sale by the mortgagee without taking possession or appointing a receiver.

goes into winding-up[70] or into administration where the administrator makes a distribution.[71] Until the enactment of the Insolvency Act 1985 (later replaced by the Insolvency Act 1986) a floating charge which crystallised otherwise than by reason of one of the above events took priority over preferential debts arising subsequent to crystallisation, for in relation to these the charge had ceased to be a floating charge[72] and was thus outside the statutory provisions then in force.[73] An astute draftsman could thus pave the way for circumventing the priority of preferential creditors by use of automatic or semi-automatic crystallisation clauses triggered by events other than possession, winding-up or the appointment of a receiver. That was later changed. Both under the Insolvency Act 1986 and the Companies Act 1985 a floating charge means a charge which *as created* was a floating charge.[74] So preferential debts now have priority over a floating charge[75] whether they arise before or after crystallisation, and the assets out of which the preferential claims are to be discharged include not only the free assets of the company but those which are subject to a crystallised floating charge. Moreover—and this was the law even before the legislation change referred to above—assets which come in under the charge after it has crystallised (*e.g.* through the receiver's trading activity) are within the preferential net even though there was never a moment when they were subject to a floating charge, for the statutory provisions catch all

---

[70] *ibid.*, s.175(2)(b), which applies whether the company goes into compulsory or voluntary liquidation. Section 175(2)(b) differs from s.40 of the Insolvency Act 1986 and from s.196 of the Companies Act 1985 in the way that it gives effect to the priority, providing that the preferential debts are to be paid out of the floating charge assets only to the extent that the assets available to general creditors are insufficient for the purpose, whereas the latter statutory provisions provide for payment to preferential creditors in the first instance out of assets subject to the floating charge, the chargee having a right to recoupment from the assets available for payment to general creditors. The distinction is logical in that where the company is in winding-up but not in receivership there is only one fund available for payment to preferential creditors.

[71] Insolvency Act 1986, Sch.B1, para.65(2).

[72] *Re Griffin Hotel Co Ltd* [1941] Ch. 129; *Stein v Saywell* [1969] A.L.R. 481; *Re Christonette International Ltd* [1982] 3 All E.R. 225 (in which the same result was reached by a different route, Vinelott J. holding that assets subject to a crystallised charge were no longer assets of the company for the purpose of the statutory provisions).

[73] *i.e.* the Companies Act 1985, ss.196(1), (2), 614(2), (6), re-enacting the Companies Act 1948, ss.94(1), 319(5).

[74] Insolvency Act 1986, ss.40(1), 251; Companies Act 1985, s.196(1), as amended by Insolvency Act 1986, s.439(1) and Sch.13.

[75] Insolvency Act 1986, ss.40, 175(2). It had previously been thought that since preferential debts have priority over claims secured by a floating charge and liquidation expenses have priority over preferential debts the floating charge claims would likewise be subordinated to liquidation expenses. This had been so held in *Re Barleycorn Enterprises Ltd* [1970] Ch. 465, which, however, did require a considerable judicial exegesis to arrive at this result under the former legislation. But the decision has now been overruled by the House of Lords in *Buchler v Talbot* [2004] 2 A.C. 298, where it was held that there was no basis upon which liquidation expenses could be taken out of a fund which, to the extent of the security interest created by the floating charge, was not the company's property at all. Accordingly floating charge claims have priority over liquidation expenses. See further above, para.7–40.

assets *potentially* within the scope of the floating charge, including those acquired by the company after crystallisation.[76] The only good news for debenture holders is that the range of preferential debts has been significantly reduced, as recommended by the Cork Committee,[77] in that Crown preference, which was removed as regards assessed taxes by what is now the Insolvency Act 1986, has been abolished altogether,[78] leaving only various types of claim by employees.[79] Moreover, as stated above floating charge assets are no longer to be treated as subject to the expenses of the liquidation. Where the assets subject to the floating charge and the company's free assets are insufficient to meet the claims of the preferential creditors in full, these abate rateably.[80]

A receiver appointed under a floating charge at a time when the company is not in winding-up is under a statutory duty to pay preferential creditors out of the assets coming into his hands in priority to the claims of the debenture holder.[81] However, this duty applies only in relation to assets the subject of the floating charge, not those comprised in a fixed charge. Hence if a receiver is appointed under a debenture containing both a fixed and a floating charge, the mere fact that he is appointed under a floating charge does not attract the operation of the statutory provisions to the assets coming into his hands under the fixed charge.[82] Further, if the receiver, on selling the assets the subject of the fixed charge, realises a surplus, that surplus cannot be said to be caught by the floating charge, even if the proceeds are in a form covered by the charge, for *ex hypothesi* the sum realised has been sufficient to discharge the debt due to the debenture holder, so that there is no longer any obligation left to be secured. It follows that the receiver's duty is to hand the surplus back to the company if it is not in liquidation or to the liquidator if it is.[83]

The above statutory provisions give the preferential debts priority only over the claims of the debenture holders under the floating charge; their claims are subordinate to those of the receiver for the costs of preserving and realising the assets and his expenses and remuneration.[84]

---

[76] *Inland Revenue Commissioners v Goldblatt* [1972] 1 Ch. 498.
[77] *Report of the Review Committee on Insolvency Law and Practice* (Cmnd.8558, 1982), para.1450.
[78] Enterprise Act 2002, s.251.
[79] Insolvency Act 1986, Sch.6.
[80] Where the company is in winding-up this is provided expressly by s.175(2)(a) of the Insolvency Act 1986. Where the event triggering the priority of the preferential debts is the taking of possession by the chargee s.196(2) of the Companies Act 1985 does not deal with the point but its predecessor has been held.
[81] Insolvency Act 1986, s.40(2). The relevant date for determining the preferential debts is the date of the appointment of the receiver by debenture holders (s.387(4)(a)). See further Totty and Moss, *Insolvency*, vol.2, para.H2–11.
[82] *Re Lewis Merthyr Consolidated Collieries Ltd* [1929] 1 Ch. 498; *Re G.L. Saunders Ltd* [1986] 1 W.L.R. 215.
[83] *Re G.L. Saunders Ltd*, above n.82.
[84] *Re Glyncorrwg Colliery Co Ltd* [1926] Ch. 951.

(2) Events triggering the priority

9–64   As stated above, any one of four distinct events can trigger the priority of preferential debts over a floating charge and thus establish a priority point at which the preferential debts have to be determined, namely the taking of possession of the security by or on behalf of the chargee,[85] the appointment of a receiver,[86] the winding-up of the debtor company and the making of a distribution by an administrator when the company is in administration. It is theoretically possible for all four events to occur, in which case it may become necessary to determine the preferential debts in existence at four different points in time,[87] though there will usually be an overlap, as where preferential debts existing on the appointment of a receiver are still preferential[88] and unpaid at the time of winding-up. The debenture holder or its receiver is thus well advised to collect the amounts due under a crystallised floating charge while there are still sufficient free assets left to cover the preferential debts.

There is a division of judicial opinion as to whether the appointment of a receiver by the holder of a floating charge subordinates only the appointing chargee to the claims of preferential creditors or all other holders of floating charges. In *Griffiths v Yorkshire Bank plc*,[89] Morritt J. adopted the former construction of s.40 of the Insolvency Act 1986, pointing out that there were various ways in which the holder of a floating charge could enforce his security without taking possession or appointing a receiver, *e.g.* by sale of the asset given in security,[90] while in *Re H. & K. Medway Ltd*[91]

---

[85] A question which never seems to have been discussed is what is meant by "possession". In particular, is the section confined to tangible property? It is thought that it should be construed broadly to cover any kind of asset over which the chargee acquires control equivalent to possession. If the section were confined to tangibles it would exclude the receipt of money credited to the chargee's bank account.

[86] A receiver acts independently of the debenture holder who appointed him and therefore in taking possession does not act "on behalf of" the debenture holder so as to bring s.196 of the Companies Act 1985 into play concurrently with s.40 of the Insolvency Act 1986 (*Re H. & K. Medway Ltd* [1997] 1 W.L.R. 1422).

[87] This depends on the sequence of events. If the company is already in liquidation when possession is taken or the receiver is appointed, neither s.196(2) of the Companies Act 1985 nor s.40(2) of the Insolvency Act 1986 applies, and the relevant date for determining the preferential creditors is the date of winding-up.

[88] This will not necessarily be the case. For example, preferential claims for unpaid wages are limited to (*inter alia*) wages for the four months preceding the relevant date (as defined by the Companies Act 1985, s.196(3) and the Insolvency Act 1986, s.387), so that a claim for unpaid wages which is preferential at the time of appointment of a receiver may no longer be preferential at the time of winding-up.

[89] [1994] 1 W.L.R. 1427.

[90] However, the proceeds of sale would themselves fall within s.40. An argument that might be advanced against this is that at the moment of receipt the proceeds constitute *pro tanto* payment of the debt secured by the charge, so that there is never a time when they represent an asset comprised in the charge. But in *Inland Revenue Commissioners v Goldblatt* [1972] Ch. 498 just such an argument was robustly rejected by Goff J., who, in the context of what

Neuberger J. held that all floating charges became subordinated, not merely the charge held by the creditor appointing the receiver. There are arguments to support either position but on balance those in favour of the latter decision seem preferable.

(4) The effect of successive priority events

The four possible priority events are not mutually exclusive as regards the obligations of the receiver towards the liquidator (for expenses of the liquidation) and preferential creditors, but each set of preferential creditors is entitled to look only to assets remaining within the floating charge. Suppose, for example, that a receiver is appointed, that from the assets in his hands he pays the preferential creditors and makes a partial payment to his debenture holder and that before he has completed his receivership the company goes into liquidation with a new set of preferential creditors. The payments already made to the receivership preferential creditors and the debenture holder cannot be disturbed. But if the receiver is still holding assets subject to the floating charge the liquidator is entitled to resort to these for the liquidation expenses and payment to the liquidation preferential creditors.[92] So assets originally within s.40 of the Insolvency Act 1986 but not resorted to under that section may later fall within s.175(2)(b) of the Act on a winding-up.

9–65

(5) Effect of receiver's failure to pay preferential claims

A receiver who after notice of a preferential claim neglects to satisfy it from assets available and instead applies those assets or their proceeds for other purposes—as by making a payment to the debenture holder or by exhausting the assets in the continuance of the company's business—is liable in damages to the preferential creditor in tort and/or for breach of statutory duty to the extent of the preferential creditor's resulting loss.[93] For this purpose it is immaterial that the debenture holder's debt has been satisfied by payment from the proceeds of assets subject to a fixed charge. The receiver is still responsible for payment of the preferential debts out of moneys coming into his hands from the assets the subject of a floating

9–66

---

was then s.94(1) of the Companies Act 1948 (now s.196 of the Companies Act 1985), considered (at 506) that it would be extraordinary if the statutory provisions were to protect the preferential creditors when the debenture holder took possession as mortgagee and not protect them when the debenture holder took assets in satisfaction of his claim.

[91] Above, n.86.

[92] *Re Leyland Daf Ltd, Buchler v Talbot*, above n.75.

[93] *Westminster City Council v Treby* [1936] 2 All E.R. 21; *IRC v Goldblatt* [1972] 1 Ch. 498; *Woods v Winskill* [1913] 2 Ch. 303; *Westminster Corporation v Haste* [1950] Ch. 442.

charge.[94] The debenture holder who with notice of the preferential claim receives a payment or other benefit from assets which should have been applied in payment of that claim is liable:

(1) direct to the preferential creditor for breach of statutory duty; alternatively for wrongfully procuring and being a party to such breach by the receiver or alternatively as constructive trustee for receiving the money or benefit with notice of the breach[95]; and

(2) to indemnify the receiver in respect of his own liability.[96]

However, the receiver incurs no liability to the company, for he is not the party that has suffered a loss.[97]

The receiver's duty to set aside the prescribed part of floating charge assets

9–67   Reference has already been made to the fact that in insolvency proceedings the prescribed part of the net property subject to a floating charge has to be made available for unsecured creditors.[98] This obligation, to which there are certain exceptions,[99] applies to a receiver as it does to a liquidator and to an administrator making a distribution.[1] The prescribed part may not be distributed to the proprietor of a floating charge except so far as it exceeds the amount required for the satisfaction of unsecured debts.[2] Where the company is in liquidation the receiver should make over the prescribed part to the liquidator rather than paying the unsecured creditors himself, which is not his ordinary function. But if the company is not in liquidation[3] then it is presumably for the receiver to distribute the prescribed part to unsecured creditors, there being no other office-holder in place for that purpose.

Environmental liability

9–68   The position of the administrative receiver in relation to the company's obligations under environmental obligation is unclear. On the one hand he cannot, it is thought, be required to use assets comprised in the security to

---

[94] *Re Pearl Maintenance Services Ltd* [1995] B.C.C. 657.
[95] *IRC v Goldblatt*, above.
[96] *Westminster City Council v Treby*, above. In principle the debenture holder ought to be liable to indemnify the receiver even if taking the payment or benefit without notice of the breach, unless he has changed his position in reliance on the payment or benefit so that it would be inequitable to order him to restore it. See R.M. Goode [1981] J.B.L. 473 at 477.
[97] *Re BHT (UK) Ltd* [2004] 1 B.C.L.C. 568.
[98] See above, para.6–31.
[99] See above, para.6–31.
[1] Insolvency Act 1986, s.176A(1)(d).
[2] *ibid.*
[3] Or in administration where the administrator intends to exercise a power to make a distribution.

pay for remedial works or clean-up costs, for to the extent of the security the assets do not belong to the company.[4] Moreover, he is protected from personal liability.[5] On the other hand, he cannot carry on the business in breach of environmental legislation, and if he were to do so he could incur criminal and other sanctions. The position, then, would appear to be that the receiver has a choice: to carry on the business, with an obligation to use the charged assets to the extent necessary to ensure compliance with the legislation; or to discontinue the business and, if he can, to dispose of it or the assets comprising it. The choice he makes will depend on his judgment as to whether the benefits to his debenture holder from continuing the business sufficiently outweigh the costs of compliance and environmental risks to make it worthwhile to carry on the business.

8. IMPACT OF WINDING-UP ON THE RECEIVERSHIP

Termination of the receiver's agency

As has already been mentioned, the winding-up of the company terminates the receiver's deemed agency for the company,[6] and thus his power to commit the company to future liabilities, *e.g.* under new contracts made in the carrying on of the business. It follows that he has no statutory right to be indemnified from the assets of the company in, respect of those liabilities.[7] But the advent of winding-up does not terminate the receivership,[8] for the receiver remains free to exercise security rights for the benefit of his debenture holder,[9] and for this purpose it is immaterial whether he exercises those rights in the name of the debenture holder as chargee or mortgagee or in the name of the company.[10] In other words, winding-up terminates the receiver's purely personal powers, but not his *in rem* powers.[11] A good illustration is furnished by the decision of Goulding J. in *Sowman v David Samuel Trust Ltd*.[12] In that case:

9–69

> A company in receivership subsequently went into winding-up. The receiver continued to realise the company's assets, including property which had been mortgaged to the company to secure a debt due to it

---

[4] This does of course depend on the wording of the particular statute.
[5] Environment Protection Act 1990, s.78X(4)(a).
[6] Insolvency Act 1986, s.44(1).
[7] See above, para.9–59.
[8] Nor does it prevenl the debenture holder from appointing a receiver if the company goes into liquidation first (*Re Potters Oils Ltd (No.2)* [1986] 1 All E.R. 890).
[9] *Sowman v David Samuel Trust Ltd* [1978] 1 All E.R. 616.
[10] *ibid.*
[11] See above, para.9–43.
[12] See above n.9.

from the mortgagor. By a provision in the debenture pursuant to which the receiver had been appointed the debenture holders were irrevocably appointed the attorneys of the company to execute any deed or instrument in the name of the company and on its behalf which might be necessary for any of the purposes of the security. In the conveyance the sale was expressed to be made by the company as mortgagee, acting by its attorneys the debenture holders, at the request of the receiver and in exercise of the power of sale conferred on the company by the mortgage and by statute. The purchaser having applied for registration as proprietor, the Chief Land Registrar declined to effect the registration in view of doubts as to the continued powers of the receiver after the commencement of the winding-up. In subsequent proceedings the further argument was advanced that the sale of the company's property by the receiver was void under section 227 of the Companies Act 1948 as a post-petition disposition made without leave of the court.

It was held that whilst winding-up terminated the receiver's agency to bind the company personally by acting as its agent, it did not in the least affect the powers conferred on him by the debenture to hold and dispose of the property comprised in the debenture and for that purpose to use the company's name. Those powers, being coupled with an interest, were irrevocable, both at common law and by statute; and for this purpose a power given to the receiver for the purpose of securing a benefit to the debenture holders was as irrevocable as a power given to the debenture holders themselves. Further, the sale did not contravene section 227 because, though made in the company's name, it was a sale of property which did not belong to the company but formed part of the debenture holders' security.

Some months after this decision it was held that winding-up did not affect the receiver's power to convey a legal estate by selling in the company's name pursuant to the power of sale conferred by the debenture.[13]

As pointed out earlier,[14] there are in fact two ways in which the sale may be effected. It may be a sale in the-name of the company acting by its receiver,[15] who affixes the company seal, or it may alternatively be made by the debenture holder (directly or through the receiver as its agent) as mortgagee. The latter method should be adopted where there is a subsequent mortgage which it is desired should be overreached by the sale. But since the receiver's purely personal powers come to an end on liquidation, any new contract which he enters into and which is not within

---

[13] *Barrows v Chief Land Registrar The Times*, October 20, 1977. On a further aspect of this case see above, para.9–69, text and n.9.

[14] See above, para.9–44.

[15] Or acting by the debenture holder pursuant to any power of attorney conferred by the debenture, assuming, if the company is in liquidation, that the power of attorney survives. See above, para.9–43.

any actual or apparent authority conferred on him by the liquidator does not bind the company unless ratified by the liquidator, so that in the absence of such authority or ratification the receiver is personally liable without the benefit of the statutory indemnity.[16] In such a case the sale should be made by the debenture holder as mortgagee.

The fact that the receiver ceases to be the agent of the company does not mean that he becomes the agent of the debenture holder,[17] merely that the receiver acts on his own account and is liable as a principal.[18]

Relationship between receiver and liquidator

Since the receiver has all, or substantially all, of the assets of the company under his control by virtue of the security created by the debenture and retains the power to manage and realise those assets, the liquidator must perforce stand on the sidelines during the receivership, since until then there is no estate for him to administer. But any duties owed by the receiver to the company as its deemed agent may be enforced by the liquidator in the name of the company and the liquidator may also take proceedings against the receiver for misfeasance.[19] The receiver is entitled to retain assets in his hands until his expenses (including any liabilities he has incurred) and remuneration, any sum payable to preferential creditors out of assets subject to a floating charge and the amount due to his debenture holders[20] have been paid. Any surplus remaining, so far as not payable to a subsequent chargee, must be handed over to the liquidator, to whom the receiver also has a duty to render proper accounts of his receipts and payments when so required.[21]

9–70

9. ORDER OF APPLICATION OF REALISATIONS BY RECEIVER

Realisations of assets by the receiver must first be applied in discharge of any security ranking in priority to the charge under which he was appointed. After this it is necessary to distinguish realisations of fixed charges assets from those of floating charges and, in relation to the latter,

9–71

---

[16] See para.9–59 above. If the liquidator accepts the benefit of the contract on behalf of the company the receiver would seem to acquire a restitutionary right of recoupment to the extent of such benefit and the company becomes liable on the contract as an undisclosed principal.

[17] *Gosling v Gaskell* [1897] A.C. 575.

[18] *ibid.*

[19] Insolvency Act 1986, s.212(1)(b).

[20] Including contingent liabilities of the company to the debenture holder where these are secured by the debenture (*Re Rudd & Son Ltd; Re Fosters and Rudd Ltd* (1986) 2 B.C.C. 98).

[21] Insolvency Act 1986, s.41(1).

to distinguish further between floating charges created before September 15, 2003 ("old charges") and those created on or after that date ("new charges").

Realisations of fixed charge assets

9–72 Any priority security interest having been satisfied, the order of application of realisations from fixed charge assets is as follows:

(1) any costs of preserving and realising the assets, whether incurred by the receiver or (if the company is in liquidation) by the liquidator for the benefit of the chargee;

(2) the receiver's costs, remuneration and expenses;

(3) sums due to the chargee;

(4) sums due to any secured creditor ranking after the chargee, or if he has appointed a receiver, then that receiver;

(5) any surplus to the company, payment being made to its liquidator if it is in winding-up.

Realisations of floating charge assets: old charge

9–73 Realisations of assets subject to an old charge are to be applied in the following order:

(1) any costs of preserving and realising the floating charge assets, whether incurred by the receiver or (if the company is in liquidation) by the liquidator for the benefit of the chargee;

(2) the receiver's costs, remuneration and expenses;

(3) preferential debts, so far as the free assets of the company are insufficient to meet them;

(4) sums due to the chargee

(5) sums due to any secured creditor ranking after the chargee or, if he has appointed a receiver, then that receiver;

(6) any surplus to the company, payment being made to its liquidator if it is in winding-up.

Realisations from floating charge assets: new charge

9–74 Realisations of assets subject to a new charge are to be applied in the following order:

(1) any costs of preserving and realising the assets;

(2) the receiver's costs, remuneration and expenses;

(3) preferential debts, so far as the free assets are insufficient to meet them;

(4) the claims of ordinary unsecured creditors as regards the prescribed part of the floating charge assets;

(5) sums due to the chargee;

(6) sums due to any secured creditor ranking after the chargee or, if he has appointed a receiver, that receiver;

(7) any surplus to the company, payment being made to its liquidator if it is in winding-up.

Where a receiver is appointed under a debenture containing both a fixed and a floating charge, preferential creditors have priority only as regards the assets subject to the floating charge, not those comprised in the fixed charge.[22] Where the whole of the assets subject to a floating charge have been utilised towards payment of preferential debts, any surplus remaining from sale of assets subject to the fixed charge must be paid to the company. It is not claimable by preferential creditors as being within the scope of the floating charge, for *ex hypothesi* the debenture has been fully satisfied, so that there is no longer a floating charge in existence capable of attaching to the surplus.[23] Where the company is not in liquidation and no other person has an interest in the property realised or its proceeds, the surplus is payable to the company itself.

Allocation of receivership expenses as between assets subject to a fixed charge and those subject to a floating charge is a matter of some moment, for the greater the proportion of expenses allocated to the floating charge assets the smaller the amount of assets available to preferential creditors in priority to others. To the extent that costs can fairly be attributed to one charge rather than the other they should be allocated to that charge. For example, the cost of realisation of floating charge assets should be charged to those assets, and of realisation of fixed charge assets to the assets within the fixed charge, where such costs are capable of being separately identified. In other cases the fairest solution would seem to be to allocate the cost in the proportion that the net costs of each realisation bear to the total.[24]

10. TERMINATION OF THE RECEIVERSHIP

When the receivership comes to an end

The period of the receiver's office ends on the earliest of the following events:

9–75

---

[22] *Re Lewis Merthyr Consolidated Collieries Ltd* [1929] 1 Ch. 498.
[23] *Re G.L. Saunders Ltd* [1986] 1 W.L.R. 215.
[24] See also Lightman & Moss, *op. cit.*, para.21–055, advocating a rateable allocation.

(1)   his death[25];

(2)   his removal by order of the court[26];

(3)   his resignation[27];

(4)   his ceasing to be qualified as an insolvency practitioner[28];

(5)   his vacation of office on completion of his duties.[29]

Removal of the receiver

9–76   The debenture holder can no longer remove the receiver he has appointed; this can be done only by order of the court.[30]

Mandatory vacation of office

9–77   A receiver must vacate office if he ceases to be qualified to act as an insolvency practitioner in relation to the company.[31] Moreover, once he has realised enough assets to pay off the debenture holder, preferential creditors from the proceeds of assets subject to a floating charge, and other possible claims against him to which he is entitled to an indemnity out of the assets, it is his duty to make the requisite payments and hand back control to the company.[32]

---

[25] This is considered too obvious to require express provisions in the Act or Rules! Where the receiver dies the person appointing him must, forthwith on his becoming aware of the death, give notice as provided by the Insolvency Rules 1986, r.3.34.

[26] Insolvency Act 1986, s.45(1). This is now the only way in which an administrative receiver may be removed; the debenture holder can no longer do so, even if the debenture purports to give him the power of removal.

[27] *ibid.*, s.45(1). But this must be in the prescribed manner, *i.e.* as provided by r.3.33 of the Insolvency Rules 1986.

[28] Despite the wording of s.45(2) of the Insolvency Act, which might be thought to imply that the receiver continues to hold office until he fulfils his duty under that sub-section to vacate it (and see also Insolvency Rules 1986, r.3.35(1)), the joint effect of s.45(2) and ss.389 and 390 would seem to be that a receiver's office comes to an end automatically when he ceases to be qualified to hold it.

[29] Curiously neither the provisions of the Act nor those of the Rules define the moment at which a receiver vacates office; they simply require him to give notice that he has done so (Insolvency Act, s.45(4); Insolvency Rules, r.3.35). It is thought that he vacates offices when he does any act signifying that he regards himself as discharged from office. The giving of notice will typically be such an act.

[30] Insolvency Act 1986, s.45(1).

[31] *ibid.*, s.45(2). See above, para.9–24.

[32] In practice the receiver may be reluctant to do this where a liquidation is pending, and may be able to rely on a *bona fide* uncertainty as to the possible existence of preferential debts or other claims which have not yet been notified to him or adequately quantified.

11. THE POSITION OF THE DEBENTURE HOLDER AFTER APPOINTING A RECEIVER

The receiver as an independent agent

Although the receiver is appointed by the debenture holder, to whom he **9–78** owes a duty of care in the conduct of the receivership, he is his own master in the management of the company's business and the method of carrying out his other duties as receiver. The debenture holder is not entitled to instruct the receiver in the performance of his duties; indeed, it is dangerous to attempt to do so, for the receiver will then become the *de facto* agent of the debenture holder, who will be liable to the company for his negligent acts or omissions,[33] though with a right of indemnity against the receiver.[34]

---

[33] *American Express International Banking Corp v Hurley* [1985] 3 All E.R. 564.
[34] *ibid.*

Chapter 10

Administration and Company Voluntary Arrangements[1]

1. GENESIS OF THE ADMINISTRATION PROCEDURE

The company in trouble

Companies become insolvent for a variety of reasons. Some of the most **10–01** common causes are loss of market share, lack of cash flow and the failure of management to respond to changed circumstances. When a company is insolvent or on the verge of insolvency it has one of three options: to go into immediate liquidation; to seek to trade out of its difficulties; or to secure a standstill by agreement or statutory moratorium with a view to disposing of the business or realising the assets to better advantage than on an immediate winding-up. In the great majority of cases the company will have reached the point of no return, so that there is no alternative to an immediate winding-up. Where there is perceived to be a viable business it may be possible to rescue the company as a going concern by a variety of means. These include negotiating time with the company's creditors outside any formal insolvency proceeding; securing the agreement of creditors to a contractual restructuring, or workout; organising a company voluntary arrangement (CVA) under Part I of the Insolvency Act 1986 or a scheme of

---

[1] See Muir Hunter, *Kerr & Hunter on Receivers and Administrators* (18th ed.); Lightman and Moss, *The Law of Receivers and Administrators of Companies* (3rd ed.); R.J. Mokal, *Corporate Insolvency Law: Theory and Application*, Chap.7; John Armour and R.J. Mokal, "Reforming the governance of corporate rescue: the Enterprise Act 2002" [2005] L.M.C.L.Q. 32; Andrew R. Kay and Peter Walton, *Insolvency Law: Corporate and Personal*, Chap.7; Edward Bailey, *Voluntary Arrangements*. For an earlier comprehensive treatment of this subject, with international comparisons, see David Brown, *Corporate Rescue*. See also Fletcher, Higham and Trower, *The Law and Practice of Corporate Administrations*; Grier and Floyd, *Corporate Recovery: Administrations and Voluntary Arrangements*. For a perceptive critical analysis of the original administration regime, see Prentice, Oditah and Segal, "Administration: The Insolvency Act 1986, Part II" [1994] L.M.C.L.Q. 487.

arrangement under s.425 of the Companies Act 1985, within or outside administration under Part II of the Insolvency Act; or securing a moratorium contractually or through administration with a view to disposing of the business or the assets to better advantage than on an immediate liquidation and then putting the company into a creditors' voluntary winding-up. Much will depend on the nature of the business and of the market in which it operates, the amount of the liabilities and the way these are divided between trade and finance creditors, the willingness of a major finance creditor to inject new funds, and whether the company is of a sufficient size to justify the expense of elaborate arrangements for a restructuring or other arrangement.

So the formal insolvency proceedings available are winding-up,[2] administration, in which the company is placed under the management of an external administrator, supported by a creditors' committee; a CVA and a scheme. These last two may precede, run in parallel with or follow administration. Until recently there was a fifth route, the appointment of an administrative receiver by a debenture holder under a floating charge covering, with any other charges, the whole or substantially the whole of the company's property. But as we have seen, administrative receivership has largely been abolished as regards floating charges made on or after September 15, 2003 and the remedy has been replaced by administration.

The official statistics for 2004 show that while there were 12,192 liquidations in England and Wales there were only 1,601 administrator appointments and 597 voluntary arrangements,[3] and some of these will have been followed by liquidation. This does not mean that administration and voluntary arrangements are failures, merely that the great majority of insolvent companies are beyond remedial measures. But the outcome of administrations where these do take place has frequently been favourable, and this is true to an increasing extent of CVAs conducted within administration. Moreover, the available statistics do not deal with restructurings outside insolvency proceedings.

10–02   With the prohibition on the appointment of administrative receivers under most new floating charges and its replacement by an appointment of an administrator by the holder of the floating charge, or alternatively by the company and its directors, without the need for a court order, the situation is likely to change, and we can expect a substantial increase in the number of administrations, a trend liable to be accelerated by the decision of the House of Lords in *Buchler v Talbot*[4] that liquidation expenses rank after claims secured by a floating charge, whereas in the case of administration the reverse is true[5]; and while administrations will, it is thought, continue to

---

[2] See Chaps 5–7.
[3] DTI Statistics and Analysis Directorate: Insolvency, Statistics Release 6 May 2005.
[4] [2004] 2 A.C. 298.
[5] Insolvency Act 1986, s.175 as applied by Sch.B1, para.65(2).

be small in number compared with the number of liquidations, there is little doubt that there will be a significant shift from the latter to the former[6] and from receivership to administration. Indeed, the trend is already becoming apparent, as can be seen from the following table:

	2002	2003	2004	1st quarter 2005
Receivership appointments	1541	1261	864	114
Administrator appointments (pre-Enterprise Act 2002)	643	497	1	0
Administrator appointments (Enterprise Act 2002)	—	247	1601	489
Compulsory liquidations	6230	5234	4584	1064
Creditors' voluntary liquidations	10075	8950	7608	1835

Source: DTI Statistics and Analysis Directorate: Insolvency, Statistics Release May 6, 2005.

There are, however, situations in which a company's entry into administration presents serious drawbacks. One is that administration would trigger cross-default clauses or contractual provisions for acceleration of liability, termination of the contract or the cessation of intellectual property rights, which the creditor concerned is not willing to waive or for which a waiver cannot be negotiated in the limited time available. Another relates to the potential tax disadvantages arising from the fact that the company's entry into administration triggers the start of a new accounting period with effect from the previous day,[7] and trading losses made in the trading period prior to administration can be set off only against gains on capital assets made during the same period, not against gains made after the company has entered administration.[8] Moreover, corporation tax is chargeable on the profits of the company arising in the administration in its final year[9] and where it is payable on chargeable gains accruing on the realisation of any asset (whether the realisation is effected by the administrator, a secured creditor or a receiver or manager appointed to deal with a security) it constitutes an expense of the administration[10] and is thus payable ahead of the claims of preferential creditors.[11]

---

[6] See Lisa Linklater, "New style administration: a substitute for liquidation?" (2005) 26 Co. Law 129.

[7] Income and Corporation Taxes Act 1988, s.12(7ZA).

[8] This is the combined effect of ss.393A(1)(a) and 12(7ZA) of the Income and Corporation Taxes Act 1988.

[9] Income and Corporation Taxes Act 1988, s.342A(2).

[10] Insolvency Rules 1986, r.2.67(j).

[11] Insolvency Act 1986, s.175 as applied by Sch. B1, para.65(2).

The law prior to the Insolvency Act 1985

10–03   Prior to the Insolvency Act 1985 English insolvency law viewed liquidation as the centrepiece of corporate insolvency law and concerned itself primarily with the disposal of the business, where it could be sold as a going concern, or with individual assets on a break-up basis. The only form of external management available was receivership, which as we have seen from the previous chapter is first and foremost an enforcement weapon for the unpaid debenture holder and is not a proceeding for the benefit of unsecured creditors, though they do derive some incidental benefits from the marshalling of the assets in one hand. All that could be done for unsecured creditors outside winding-up, apart from a contractual arrangement outside the statutory framework, was to seek to conclude a formal scheme of arrangement under s.425 of the Companies Act 1985.

   The procedure under s.425 is complex, costly and slow, and the statutory provisions did not impose any moratorium pending approval of the scheme by the court, so that individual creditors remained free to pursue their claims without regard to the wishes of those supporting the arrangement, a risk that could be avoided only by presenting a winding-up petition and applying to the court for a stay of pending proceedings[12] under s.126 of the Insolvency Act 1986. Negotiations for an informal arrangement did not, of course, have the effect of imposing a compulsory moratorium either, and when concluded such arrangements suffered the additional disadvantage that they did not bind dissentient creditors, who could therefore either scupper the proposed scheme or alternatively demand to be paid off in order to avoid their presenting a winding-up petition. Accordingly where there was no receiver in post to discourage the trigger-happy unsecured creditor a company would all too often be forced to stop trading and go into liquidation.

The growth of the rescue culture

10–04   Though liquidation continues to lie at the heart of corporate insolvency law, there is no doubt that over the past two decades a sea change in attitudes has taken place. The impetus for a new approach came from evidence to the Insolvency Law Review Committee (the Cork Committee) and from the Committee's Report *Insolvency Law and Practice*.[13] The Cork Committee, which devoted a whole chapter to the subject of administration in its Report,[14] drew attention to these problems and proposed a procedure

---

[12] A weakness of s.126 is that it only empowers the court to stay proceedings that are pending; it cannot impose a stay on the institution of proceedings.

[13] Cmnd. 8558, 1982.

[14] *Insolvency Law and Practice*, Chap.9.

by which the court could appoint an administrator to manage the company, with the same powers as a receiver and manager. The grant of an administration order would, so long as the administration continued, have the effect of freezing the enforcement of rights against the company, whether by secured creditors or otherwise, thus facilitating the simpler regime of voluntary arrangements proposed in the Report.

From these proposals, which were implemented in the Insolvency Act 1985 and re-enacted in the Insolvency Act 1986, evolved what has become known as the rescue culture,[15] a philosophy of reorganising companies so as to restore them to profitable trading and enable them to avoid liquidation. The instruments for implementing this philosophy are: the administration procedure, to which this chapter is largely devoted; the CVA under Part I of the Insolvency Act 1986; the long-established, if cumbersome, reorganisation under what is now s.425 of the Companies Act 1985; and the contract-based restructuring, or "workout," an arrangement concluded outside any statutory framework in which the principal creditors get together with view to hammering out a sensible structure of reorganisation. The workout, depending so heavily as it did on the co-operation of the creditor banks, received a much-needed fillip from the moral suasion exercised by the Bank of England, which introduced the London Rules (later renamed the London Approach) designed to secure the co-operation of the banking community in taking a positive approach to the continuance of financial support for distressed companies pending a reorganisation.[16] Much use is also made of the INSOL International *Statement of Principles for a Global Approach to Multi-Creditor Workouts*, particularly in cross-border insolvencies.

While it remains the case that most insolvent companies end up in liquidation, a number of companies whose fate would previously have been liquidation have been saved and nursed back to health; and even where liquidation has ultimately supervened, administrations and workouts have facilitated the sale of the company as a going concern, or a more advantageous realisation of its assets, and a better return for creditors in the winding-up.

---

[15] The phrase has now passed into English jurisprudence. See the speech of Lord Browne-Wilkinson in *Powdrill v Watson* [1995] 2 A.C. 394 at 442, 445, 446.

[16] See below, para.10–135.

2. ADMINISTRATION PRIOR TO THE ENTERPRISE ACT 2002

Purposes of administration

10–05 The function of administration is to place the insolvent company under external management for the benefit of all creditors in order to achieve one or more statutory purposes, which in the original legislation[17] were defined in s.8 of the Insolvency Act 1986 as follows:

> "(a) the survival of the company, and the whole or any part of its undertaking, as a going concern;
>
> (b) the approval of a voluntary arrangement under Part I;
>
> (c) the sanctioning under section 425 of the Companies Act 1985 of a compromise or arrangement between the company and any such persons as are mentioned in that section; and
>
> (d) a more advantageous realisation of the company's assets than would be effected on a winding up."

Though the purposes are now expressed differently, it was and remains the case that administration is not in itself a reorganisation procedure; rather it is a temporary holding mechanism to keep the business afloat under external management until a decision can be taken as to the best exit route, which might or might not be a company voluntary arrangement under the Insolvency Act or a compromise or arrangement under the Companies Act.[18] The unique feature of administration is the automatic moratorium it imposes on the enforcement of remedies even by secured creditors and suppliers of goods under leasing, conditional sale and hire-purchase agreements, whose rights of enforcement of the security or recovery of their property would not be affected by winding-up, while under the original legislation the initiation of an arrangement plan did not of itself trigger a moratorium, and still does not do so except in a limited class of case.[19]

Procedure to place company in administration

10–06 As originally enacted, the Insolvency Act required the presentation of a petition for an administration followed by the making of the order. The effect of both the petition and the order was to impose a moratorium,

---

[17] Contained in Part II of the Insolvency Act 1986, comprising ss.8–27, and supplemented by Part 2 of the Insolvency Rules 1986. These were replaced by Sch.B1 of the Act, inserted by s.248 of the Enterprise Act 2002, and a new Part 2 of the Rules, but continue to apply to administrations based on a petition presented prior to September 15, 2003. The present chapter is confined to the new provisions, apart from occasional references to the original provisions for comparison.

[18] See further below, paras 10–106 *et seq.*

[19] See below, para.10–34.

though it remained open to a debenture holder to appoint an administrative receiver before the hearing of the petition, in which case an administration order could not normally be made[20]; nor could an order be made if the company was in winding-up.[21] In most cases it was necessary for the petitioner not only to depose to his belief that the company was or was likely to become unable to pay its debts and to set out which of the statutory purposes was expected to be achieved by the making of an administration order but also to have his affidavit reinforced by exhibiting a report by an independent person (usually the proposed administrator) giving a picture of the financial position of the company and the statutory purposes that might be achieved by administration.

Weaknesses of the statutory regime

We shall discuss a little later the current purposes of administration and its relationship with the company voluntary arrangement. Suffice it to say at this point that the administration procedure proved less efficacious than had been expected. There were several reasons for this. As has been previously pointed out, administration could usually be blocked by the appointment of an administrative receiver. There were various reasons why in practice debenture holders were often willing to allow an order to be made,[22] but where they chose to appoint an administrative receiver nothing could be done to place the company in administration unless the debenture holder by whom or on whose behalf the receiver was appointed consented to the making of the order or the charge was vulnerable under one or other of ss.238–240 and 245 of the Insolvency Act 1986.[23] The requirement to obtain a court order, the making of which was usually dependent on a detailed report by the proposed administrator, caused significant delay and often substantial expense which was a particular difficulty for small companies. Though it was envisaged that administration would be a short-term procedure no time limit was laid down for the completion of an administration. The administrator generally had no power to make distributions even to preferential creditors without a court order, and the extent of the court's power to make such an order was the subject of conflicting

10–07

---

[20] Insolvency Act 1986, ss.10(2)(b), 9(3). See now Sch.B1, paras 44(7)(c), 39(1).

[21] *ibid.*, s.8(4). See now Sch.B1, para.8(1).

[22] See the second edition of this work at pp.293–294. The research by Katz and Mumford (below, para.10–13, n.55) showed that even before the new regime introduced by the Enterprise Act 2002 had begun to have an impact administrations had reached parity in number with administrative receiverships and that resort by debenture holders to their power of veto was rare, though this may have been because the existence of the power meant that in some cases administration was not considered an option.

[23] Insolvency Act 1986, s.9(3). See now Sch.B1, para.39(1).

decisions.[24] Finally, as stated above, an administration order could not be made if the company was in liquidation.[25]

As mentioned in the previous chapter,[26] a groundswell of complaints about the adverse effects of administrative receivership led, first, to the proposal that the debenture holder's power of veto should be abolished and, secondly, to the more radical proposal, implemented in the Enterprise Act 2002, to abolish administrative receivership altogether as regards appointments under new charges except in defined categories of case where the exigencies of the capital markets or considerations of social policy dictated its retention. The new approach was succinctly set out in the Government's White Paper presaging the insolvency provisions of the Enterprise Act.[27]

3. PRINCIPAL CHANGES INTRODUCED BY THE ENTERPRISE ACT 2002

10–08   It is no exaggeration to say that the Enterprise Act 2002 revolutionised the law governing administrative receivership and administration, inserting a new Chapter IV into Part III of the Insolvency Act 1986. The principal changes introduced by the 2002 Act are the following:

- The abolition of administrative receivership except in specific cases.

- The facility to enter administration without a court order.

- The absence of a requirement to show actual or impending insolvency on an out-of-court appointment by the holder of a qualifying floating charge or on an application by such a holder for an administration order where the court is satisfied he could make an out-of-court appointment.

- The replacement of multi-purpose administration with a regime in which there is only a single purpose, to be selected according to a three-part hierarchy.

- Flexibility in the ordering of entry and exit routes, including the ability to move from winding-up to administration.

---

[24] See, for example, *Re TXU UK Ltd* [2003] 2 B.C.L.C. 341; *Re UCT (UK) Ltd* [2001] 1 B.C.L.C. 443; *Re Powerstore Trading Ltd* [1998] B.C.L.C. 190; *Re WBSL Realisations Ltd* [1995] 2 B.C.L.C. 576.
[25] Insolvency Act 1986, s.8(4). See now Sch.B1, para.8(1).
[26] Above, para.9–06.
[27] DTI, *Productivity and Enterprise: Insolvency—A Second Chance.* See the extract from the White Paper set out above, para.9–04.

- A time limit for completion of an administration.

- Conferment on the administrator of power to make distributions to secured and preferential creditors and, with the permission of the court, to ordinary unsecured creditors.

- The provision of a statutory priority of expenses of the administration, albeit one which the court can vary.

However, the changes do not affect protected railway companies under the Railway Act 1993 or other bodies subject to special administration regimes as listed in s.249(1) of the Enterprise Act 2002. Thus s.59 of the Railways Act 1993 and Sch.6 to that Act prescribe a special regime for protected railway companies[28] in the form of a railway administration order, to which the old Part II of the Insolvency Act 1986 applies with the modifications made by Sch.6 to the 1993 Act.

Abolition of administrative receivership

It is no longer possible for the holder of a qualifying floating charge to appoint an administrative receiver under a qualifying floating charge created on or after September 15, 2003 except in the various categories of case previously described.[29] The abolition of administrative receivership reflects three underlying objectives: transparency, accountability and collectivity.[30] The holder of a qualifying floating charge will no longer be able to appoint an administrative receiver accountable primarily to the chargee and having only a limited reporting duty to other creditors. By way of compensation, the chargee will enjoy a number of privileges not available to others.

10–09

(1) Whilst the company or its directors cannot appoint an administrator where a petition for winding-up has been presented or an administration application has been made and the petition or application has not been disposed of,[31] no such restriction applies to an appointment by the holder of a qualifying floating charge.[32]

(2) If the holder of a qualifying floating charge applies for an administration order under paragraph 35(1)(a) of Sch.B1 to the Insolvency Act and the application includes a statement that it is made in reliance on

---

[28] Of which one was Railtrack plc. See *Winsor v Bloom, re Railtrack plc* [2002] 1 W.L.R. 3002.
[29] Above, para.9–04.
[30] See Steve Leinster, "Policy Aims of the Enterprise Act", *Recovery*, Autumn 2003, 27 at 28.
[31] Insolvency Act 1986, Sch.B1, para.25.
[32] *ibid.*, paras 40(1)(b), 44(7).

that paragraph then by way of exception to the general rule[33] the court may make an administration order whether or not satisfied that the company is or is likely to become insolvent.[34]

(3) If an application is made for the appointment of an administrator by a person who is not the holder of a qualifying floating charge, the latter, having received notice of the application, may either make an appointment under para.14 (giving notice to the court to which the application is made[35]) or intervene to apply to have its nominee appointed, and the court is required to grant such an application unless it thinks it right to refuse to do so because of the particular circumstances of the case.[36]

(4) Where the company is in compulsory winding-up (but not in voluntary winding-up) the chargee may make an administration application, and if this is granted the court is required to discharge the winding-up order.[37]

(5) Finally, the holder of a qualifying floating charge who makes an out-of-court appointment is given the facility of filing a notice of appointment with the court outside court business hours.[38]

But even where the administrator is appointed by or on the nomination of the chargee his primary objective, where reasonably practicable, is to perform his functions not for the benefit of the appointing debenture holder, as was the main function of the administrative receiver, but for the benefit of the creditors generally[39] and he is obliged to attend the initial meeting of creditors and may be required to convene other creditors' meetings[40] and attend meetings of the creditors' committee.[41]

In order for a chargee to be able to appoint an administrator three conditions have to be satisfied: the charge is a qualifying floating charge; the chargee is the holder of a qualifying floating charge; and the power to appoint an administrator has become exercisable under the terms of the charge instrument.

---

[33] *ibid.*, para.11(a).

[34] *ibid.*, para.35(2)(a).

[35] *ibid.*, r.2.18.

[36] *ibid.*, para.36. There is no express provision for replacement of an administrator already appointed by the company or its directors, but the court could exercise its power under para.88 to remove the administrator and then appoint the debenture holder's nominee under para.92.

[37] *ibid.*, para.37.

[38] See below, para.10–40, n.73.

[39] *ibid.*, Sch.B1, para.3(2).

[40] *ibid.*, paras 51, 56.

[41] *ibid.*, para.57.

(1) The charge is a qualifying floating charge

A qualifying floating charge is one created by an instrument which: **10–10**

    (a) states that para.14 of Sch.B1 to the Insolvency Act 1986 applies to the floating charge,

    (b) purports to empower the holder of the floating charge to appoint an administrator of the company, or

    (c) purports to empower the holder of the floating charge to make an appointment which would be the appointment of an administrative receiver within the meaning of s.29(2) of the Insolvency Act.[42]

(2) The chargee is the holder of a qualifying floating charge

For the purposes of para.14(1) a person is the holder of a qualifying **10–11** floating charge in respect of a company's property if he holds one or more debentures of the company secured:

    (a) by a qualifying floating charge which relates to the whole or substantially the whole of the company's property[43];

    (b) by a number of qualifying floating charges which together relate to the whole or substantially the whole of the company's property; or

    (c) by charges and other forms of security which together relate to the whole or substantially the whole of the company's property and at least one of which is a qualifying floating charge.[44]

In sub-paragraph (c), "charge" is used in its narrow sense to denote a mere incumbrance, as opposed to a mortgage, whilst "other forms of security" covers a mortgage, a lien or any other form of security.[45] Since para.14(1) is confined to security for debentures, "charges and other forms of security" is plainly confined to consensual security and does not extend to charges or liens created by statute or other operation of law.

    It should be noted that while in the case of administrative receivership the reference to "the whole or substantially the whole of the company's

---

[42] *ibid.*, para.14(2), omitting para.(d), which relates to Scotland. For a detailed analysis of s.29(2), see above, paras 9–06 *et seq.*

[43] See above, para.9–08.

[44] Insolvency Act 1986, Sch. B1, para.14(3).

[45] See *ibid.*, s.248(b). The only other form of consensual security known to English law is pledge (see Roy Goode, *Legal Problems of Credit and Security* (3rd ed.), paras 1–05, 1–42), but the restrictions on the enforcement of security also apply to non-consensual liens and other rights of detention and retention given by law. See below, para.10–53.

property" refers not to the scope of the debenture but to the property falling within the scope of the receiver's appointment,[46] the same reference in para.14 is to what is secured by the debenture. Literally construed, this would suggest that if the debenture so provides it would be open to the holder of a qualifying floating charge to crystallise the charge as to part only of the assets comprised in it in the same way as was previously open to the appointor of an administrative receiver.[47] It is not clear why the wording of the statutory provision was changed, but it is wholly incompatible with the concept of administration that the chargee should be able to select the assets to which the administration is to apply; indeed, it would be inconsistent with the duty of the administrator to take control of all the property to which he thinks the company is entitled.[48] So while partial crystallisation remains an available technique for other purposes—for example, to enable the chargee to realise a particular asset or assets without paralysing the company's management capability—it cannot be used to restrict the assets to which the administration relates.

(3) The power to appoint an administrator has become exercisable

10–12 It is not sufficient that the chargee is the holder of a qualifying floating charge. The Act further provides that an administrator may not be appointed under para.14 while a floating charge on which the appointment relies is not enforceable.[49] This means not only that the charge must be valid and enforceable in a general sense but also that the chargee has become entitled in particular to enforce the charge by appointing an administrator. A purported appointment made under a qualifying floating charge before the power to make the appointment has become exercisable is a nullity in just the same way as would have been the case upon a premature appointment of an administrative receiver.[50] But the chargee has the right of any other creditor to apply for an administration order[51] and in that case the court may make an order whether or not satisfied that the company is or is likely to become unable to pay its debts so long as it is satisfied that the chargee could make an appointment out of court under para.14.[52]

Even where the above conditions have been satisfied, the holder of a qualifying floating charge may not appoint an administrator if a provisional liquidator of the company has been appointed or an administrative receiver

---

[46] See above, para.9–08.
[47] See Roy Goode, *Legal Problems of Credit and Security* (3rd ed.), para.4–56.
[48] Insolvency Act 1986, Sch.B1, para.67.
[49] *ibid.*, Sch.B1, para.16.
[50] See above, para.9–25.
[51] Insolvency Act 1986, Sch.B1, para.12(1)(c).
[52] *ibid.*, Sch.B1, para.35(2)(a). See further below, para.10–14.

is in office,[53] but this does not preclude the holder from applying for an administration order, though in this case it is necessary to show that the conditions of para.11 of Sch. B1 are satisfied.

Administration without court order

A major impediment to administration, the delay and expense involved in **10–13** obtaining an order for administration, has now been removed. Though specified persons may still apply for an administration order, it is instead open to the holder of a qualifying floating charge or to the company or the directors to appoint an administrator by filing a notice of appointment and other prescribed documents.[54] This will undoubtedly become the normal mode of appointment. One of the principal reasons why banks often appointed administrative receivers instead of allowing an administration was because of the need for the appointee to be able to take control of the assets as a matter of urgency.[55] The steps to be taken to bring about the appointment of an administrator depend on whether he is appointed out of court or by the court.[56] But once the administrator is in post, his powers, duties and liabilities are governed by rules common to the two methods of appointment.

Under the old regime, where a company could be put into administration only by court order, most CVAs were made outside administration on a proposal of the directors, since it took too long and was too expensive to promote a CVA within administration on a proposal of the administrator. The ready availability of out-of-court administration may have the effect of increasing the use of CVAs within administration, thereby securing the benefit of the statutory moratorium which is unavailable for CVAs proposed by the directors of companies which are not small eligible companies.

Out-of-court administration is incompatible with the EC directive on the reorganisation and winding-up of insurance undertakings,[57] so that in relation to these paras 14 and 22 of Sch.B1 to the Insolvency Act 1986 (dealing respectively with the appointment by the holder of a qualifying floating charge and the company or its directors) are disapplied.[58] Other cases in which court-appointed administration is likely to continue to be used are where the holder of a qualifying floating charge is precluded from

---

[53] *ibid.*, Sch.B1, para.17.

[54] *ibid.*, Sch.B1, paras 14, 18(1), 22, 29(1).

[55] Alan Katz and Michael Mumford, *Comparative study of Administration and Administrative Receivership as Business Rescue Vehicles*, para.6.3.2.

[56] See below, paras 10–39, 10–42.

[57] 2001/17/EC dated 19 March 2001 (OJ L110, 20.4.2001, p.28), art.2(c). But as the result of a recent amendment to the Annexes to the EC Insolvency Regulation this is no longer a problem as regards other types of company. See below, para.13–11.

[58] Insurers (Reorganisation and Winding Up) Regulations 2004 (SI 2004/353), reg.52.

making an out-of-court appointment[59] or wishes to block an administration application by the company or its directors[60] or where it is necessary to institute or intervene in proceedings before a foreign court which may be reluctant to recognise the status of an administrator appointed by a chargee rather than by a court.

No requirement of actual or impending insolvency as regards holder of qualifying floating charge

10–14   Under the original statutory provisions the court could not make an administration order unless satisfied that the company was or was likely to become unable to pay its debts within the meaning of s.123 of the Insolvency Act.[61] That remains the case where there is an application for an administration order which is made by a person other than the holder of a qualifying floating charge[62] but there is no such requirement for an out-of-court appointment by the holder of a qualifying floating charge under para.14 of Sch.B1 or on application by a chargee who could make such an appointment.[63] Out-of-court appointments by the company or by directors are governed by para.22, which gives no hint of any requirement that the company is or is likely to become unable to pay its debts. It is only when one reaches para.27(2)(a), which involves a statutory declaration as to the company's inability to pay debts, that it becomes apparent that actual or impending insolvency is by necessary implication a prerequisite to the appointment of an administrator under para.22.

   The ability of the holder of a qualifying floating charge to make an appointment without the need for the company to be insolvent or facing insolvency is a welcome change because it enables steps to be taken to place the company in administration before its financial position has become critical and in this respect follows Chapter 11 of the American Bankruptcy Code.

Replacement of multi-purpose administration with single-purpose administration

10–15   The provisions concerning the purposes of administration have been recast, and differ in important respects from those originally contained in s.8 of the Insolvency Act.[64] In particular, there can only be one stated purpose, to

---

[59] By Insolvency Act 1986, Sch.B1, para.17. See above, para.10–09.
[60] Under *ibid.*, Sch.B1, para.36. See above, para.9–26.
[61] *ibid.*, s.8(1)(a). As to the meaning of s.123, see above, paras 4–24 *et seq*.
[62] *ibid.*, Sch.B1, para.11(a).
[63] *ibid.*, para.35(2)(b).
[64] See below, para.10–28.

be selected according to a three-part hierarchy and to be determined by the administrator's view of what is reasonably practicable and what will achieve the best result for the company's creditors as a whole.[65] The new provisions came into force on September 15, 2003 as regards all administrations other than those in respect of which a petition for an administration order was presented before the above date.[66]

Flexibility in the ordering of entry and exit routes

A key element of the new regime is the flexibility it provides in the selection of routes into and exits from administration. This is discussed later.[67] One of the new features is that although a person may not normally be appointed administrator of a company in winding-up,[68] it is open to the holder of a qualifying floating charge in respect of a company in compulsory liquidation to apply for an administration order, and if this is made then any winding-up order is discharged.[69] In theory, at least, it would be possible for the company to go into liquidation a second time at a later date! A liquidator may apply for an administration order whether the company is in compulsory or in voluntary liquidation.[70] In the latter case the order must provide for the removal of the liquidator from office.[71]

10–16

Time limit for completion of the administration

The Insolvency Act now provides for the automatic ending of an administrator's appointment at the end of one year beginning with the date on which it takes effect.[72] The appointment may, however, be extended by the court for a specified period more than once, or by consent of the requisite creditors[73] once only for a period not exceeding six months, and may be further extended by the court, but not after the administrator's term of office has expired.[74]

10–17

---

[65] See below, para.10–28.

[66] Enterprise Act 2002 (Commencement No.4 and Transitional Provisions and Savings) Order 2003 (SI 2003/2093), art.3(2)).

[67] Below, para.10–103.

[68] Insolvency Act 1986, Sch.B1, para.8(1)(b).

[69] *ibid.*, Sch.B1, para.37, to which para.8(1)(b) is subject.

[70] *ibid.*, Sch.B1, para.38, to which para.8(1)(b) is subject.

[71] Insolvency Rules 1986, r.2.13(a), made pursuant to the Insolvency Act 1986, Sch.B1, para.38(2)(b).

[72] Insolvency Act 1986, Sch.B1, para.76(1).

[73] Namely each secured creditor and unsecured creditors whose debts amount to more than 50% of the company's unsecured debts (*ibid.*, Sch.B1, para.78(1)).

[74] *ibid.*, Sch.B1, paras 76, 77. Note that the extension order itself has to be made before expiry of the administrator's term of office; it is not sufficient that his application for an extension is filed before that time.

Extension of administrator's power of distribution

10–18   This is discussed later in this chapter.[75]

Statutory priority of administration expenses

10–19   We have seen that in a winding-up the expenses of the liquidation are payable in a statutory order of priority, albeit this may be adjusted by the court.[76] Prior to the changes to the Insolvency Rules 1986 as a result of the enactment of the Enterprise Act 2002 there was provision for the administrator's expenses and remuneration to be charged on the property coming into his hands, including property subject to a floating charge, in priority to the claims of the chargee,[77] but there was no statutory order of payment of the expenses and remuneration *inter se*, this being left to the administrator's discretion.[78] That has now changed, and the order of priority of expenses of the administration is set out in rule 2.67 of the Insolvency Rules, subject to the court's powers of adjustment.[79] However, the formulation of the rule is a little confusing. The order of priority is set out in para.(1) of the rule. Paragraphs (2) and (3) empower the court to vary the order of priority where the assets are insufficient to satisfy the liabilities. This seems to imply that the automatic application of the priority list in para.(1) is confined to cases where there is no shortfall in the assets, in which case the list would be entirely unnecessary. That, however, is not what is intended. Paragraph (1) comes into play only in case of an insufficiency of assets.[80] In that situation it will apply automatically unless the court decides to make an order varying it. This mirrors r.4.218. However, it is not clear why in both cases the court's discretion is triggered by an excess of liabilities over assets; one would have thought that the relevant question is whether the available assets are sufficient to enable the *administration expenses* to be paid in full. That, it is thought, is how the courts are in practice likely to apply it.

---

[75] See below, para.10–81.

[76] See above, para.7–40.

[77] Insolvency Act 1986, s.19(4), See now Sch.B1, para.99.

[78] *Re Salmet International Ltd* [2001] B.C.C. 796.

[79] It is necessary to distinguish "expenses of the administration", which covers the entire list, from "expenses properly incurred by the administrator in performing his functions in the administration of the company", which though at the top of the list is presumably to be distinguished from items lower in the list, such as necessary disbursements, which one might ordinarily think of as expenses incurred in the performance of the administrator's functions. The position in relation to legal costs incurred by the administrator in the exercise of his power to bring or defend proceedings (Sch.1, paras 1, 4, 5) is unclear, since r.2.67 does not contain any equivalent to the revised r.4.218(1)(a). Such costs could fall either within sub-para.(a) as expenses properly incurred by the administrator in performing his functions or within sub-para.(f) as necessary disbursements in the course of the administration.

[80] And not always then. See below.

The question to what extent new liabilities incurred by the administrator and liabilities in respect of continuing contracts concluded before the administration constitute expenses of the administration is considered later.[81]

4. NATURE AND PURPOSES OF ADMINISTRATION

Relationship between administration and reorganisation

Administration is commonly described as a reorganisation procedure, but this is not the case. The characteristic of a reorganisation is that the business is preserved, at least initially,[82] and an arrangement concluded with the creditors by which the debts owed by the company are restructured, for example, by rescheduling, by acceptance by creditors of less than the amount due or by conversion of debt into equity, so that creditors become converted into shareholders. Though it is certainly open to the administrator to propose a CVA under Part I of the Insolvency Act 1986[83] or a compromise or arrangement under s.425 of the Companies Act 1985,[84] this does not necessarily involve a reorganisation and where it does the reorganisation itself is carried out through the CVA or the compromise or arrangement under whichever is the applicable procedure, and the main effect of the administration is to impose a moratorium on the enforcement of creditors' rights. In practice, by far the most commonly achieved purpose of administration to date has been a more advantageous realisation of the company's assets than would be effected on a winding-up. This, of course, has nothing to do with reorganisation. It involves restoring the company to a condition in which it can be sold off as a going concern, or if this is not possible, disposing of the assets on terms more advantageous than could be obtained by a liquidator. Once this has occurred then, unless there is a distribution within the administration, liquidation, either voluntary or compulsory, is almost inevitable. Creditors will receive distributions of dividend in the usual way and the company will then be dissolved.[85]

10–20

English corporate rescue compared with reorganisation under Chapter 11

Though administration and an associated CVA have been seen as the English equivalent of a reorganisation under Chapter 11 of the American federal Bankruptcy Code, there are major differences between the two.

10–21

---

[81] Below, para.10–93.
[82] Not infrequently arrangements contemplate, and may even provide for, the ultimate winding-up of the company.
[83] Insolvency Act 1986, s.1(3). As to CVAs, see below, para.10–115.
[84] Companies Act 1985, s.425(1).
[85] For the case where the company can move straight from administration to dissolution see below, para.10–103.

Chapter 11 is devoted specifically to reorganisation and combines an automatic moratorium with a mechanism for the approval of a plan. By contrast, as stated above, administration is not in itself a reorganisation procedure at all, merely a temporary measure which provides a gateway to a variety of alternative exit routes, of which the CVA is only one.[86] Thus whereas under Chapter 11 the moratorium and the reorganisation are the key components of a single process, English insolvency law produces an uneasy split between the moratorium imposed by the administration and the CVA, which does not by itself attract a moratorium at all except in the case of small eligible companies. In a Chapter 11 proceeding the existing management is largely left in place.[87] Indeed, the "debtor in possession" is treated as a distinct legal entity akin to a trustee in bankruptcy. Administration, on the other hand, is predicated on the assumption that where a company becomes insolvent this is usually due to a failure of management and the last people to leave in control are those who were responsible for the company's plight in the first place. Hence the requirement that the administration of the company be placed in the hands of an external manager, a qualified insolvency practitioner (almost invariably an accountant) working in close co-operation with a creditors' committee. A fundamental principle of administration and of the CVA is that the creditors cannot approve proposals which would affect the enforcement rights of secured creditors.[88] There is thus no equivalent to the Chapter 11 "cramdown" by which a plan may be imposed on a class of dissenting creditors, including secured creditors, so long as they receive an equivalence in value.[89] Apart from the moratorium on enforcement of security interests produced by an administration, and the administrator's power to dispose of assets subject to a floating charge, with the chargee's priority attaching to the proceeds,[90] and assets subject to a fixed charge under an order of the court on condition of application towards the sums secured of the net proceeds and such further sum as is necessary to bring these up to market value,[91] the rights of secured creditors are sacrosanct and may not be affected by proposals for a CVA[92] or proposals by an administrator.[93] In an English reorganisation the interests of shareholders are generally regarded as of little or no account; in a reorganisation under Chapter 11 shareholders, too, are considered to have a stake in the outcome.[94]

---

[86] See above, para.10–20.
[87] But see para.10–25 below.
[88] See below, para.10–121.
[89] Bankruptcy Code, s.1129(b)(2).
[90] Insolvency Act 1986, Sch.B1, para.70.
[91] *ibid.*, para.71.
[92] *ibid.*, s.4(3).
[93] *ibid.*, para.73(1)(a).
[94] See below, para.10–26.

Characteristics of administration

The statutory regime for the administration of companies is now contained in the new Part II of the Insolvency Act 1986 and the new Part 2 of the Insolvency Rules 1986. The particular features that characterise the administration procedure are the following:

10–22

(1) Deferment to the interests of secured creditors

The legislation and its interpretation by the courts embody an underlying policy to interfere as little as possible with the rights of secured creditors and holders of other real rights, such as sellers under retention of title and lessors. Thus the court cannot as a rule make an administration order if, in cases where the appointment of an administrative receiver is still permitted,[95] the debenture holder gets in first and appoints an administrative receiver[96]; and the courts are reluctant to refuse leave to secured creditors to enforce their security, and to title-retention sellers and lessors to recover their property, where this might cause them significant loss.[97] A proposal for a CVA, whether made outside or within an administration, may not affect the right of a secured creditor to enforce his security or affect the priority of a preferential creditor except in either case with the creditor's concurrence[98] and an administrator has a general power to make a distribution to secured or preferential creditors without the permission of the court.[99] The deference which English law shows to secured creditors reflects a respect for third-party titles of much the same kind as in a winding-up,[1] though in administration proceedings there is a greater willingness to restrict enforcement of real rights in the interests of creditors as a whole than would be appropriate for a winding-up.

10–23

(2) Preservation of the priority of preferential creditors

Similarly, a proposal for a CVA may not be approved if it disturbs the priority of any preferential debt.[2] However, this applies only to distributions to be made, directly or indirectly, from the company's own funds; it does not preclude distribution to ordinary unsecured creditors from funds supplied by a third party who has no recourse to the company for reimbursement.

10–24

---

[95] See above, para.10–10.
[96] Insolvency Act 1986, Sch.B1, para.17(b). See above, para.9–26.
[97] See below, para.10–54.
[98] Insolvency Act 1986, s.4(3), (4) and Sch.B1, para.73.
[99] *ibid.*, Sch.B1, para.65(1), (3).
[1] See above, paras 3–03, 6–34 *et seq.*
[2] Insolvency Act 1986, s.4(4).

A CVA put forward by the Wimbledon Football Club contained a provision that all Football Creditors (as defined) should be paid 100p in the pound, while preferential creditors, including the Inland Revenue, would be paid only 30p in the pound. However, the Football Creditors were to be paid from the funds provided by the purchaser of the club under the sale agreement *without reducing the price to be paid for the club itself*. It was held that this did not infringe s.4(4)(a) of the Insolvency Act. The position would have been otherwise if the payment had reduced the price, for it would then in substance have come from funds that the company would otherwise have received. Had s.4(4)(a) been infringed the court would have had to revoke the approval of the CVA.[3]

(3) External management

10–25   The placing of the company under external management is, as we have seen,[4] one of the features that distinguishes administration from reorganisation under Chapter 11. However, the circumstances may allow of so-called "light touch" administration where the administrator devolves much of the responsibility for day-to-day running of the business to its existing management, while on the other hand in Chapter 11 proceedings there is a growing trend towards displacement of the existing management and the appointment of a chief restructuring officer or corporate recovery specialist.

(4) Preservation of the business rather than the company

10–26   A further distinction between the United Kingdom administration procedure and Chapter 11 relates to the question whether shareholders are to be considered interested parties so as to have a stake in the reorganisation. The Cork Committee was uncompromising in its view that in terms of social policy administration was about saving the business, not the company.

> "In the case of an insolvent company, society has no interest in the preservation or rehabilitation of the company as such, though it may have a legitimate concern in the preservation of the commercial enterprise."[5]

Ideally, of course, it is desirable to preserve the company as well as the business, so as to preserve the trading relationships and maintain at least part of the workforce. This remains the first objective of administration

---

[3] *IRC v Wimbledon Football Club Ltd* [2005] 1 B.C.L.C. 66.
[4] Above, para.10–21.
[5] *Insolvency Law and Practice*, para.193.

where it is reasonably practicable.[6] In the words of Lord McIntosh when steering the Enterprise Bill through the House of Lords:

"Company rescue is at the heart of the revised administration procedure. We want to make sure that viable companies do not go to the wall unnecessarily. That is why we are restricting administrative receivership and revising administration to focus on rescue and to make it more accessible to companies as well as their creditors. That is not just good for the companies themselves; it is also good for their suppliers, customers and employees.

The emphasis on company rescue will create more incentive for company management to take action promptly and use the administration procedure before the situation becomes terminal. That is why the purpose directs the administrator first to perform his or her functions 'with the objective of rescuing the company'."[7]

But frequently this is not possible, and faced with a choice between keeping the company alive in a damaged and irrecoverable state and disposing of its undertaking insolvency practitioners will follow the latter course in the interests of creditors. It is in keeping with this approach that creditors alone are involved in the approval of proposals by the administrator to achieve the purpose of the administration.[8] There is no provision for any meeting of members to consider the proposals, nor do they have a right to participate as members in the creditors' meeting under para.51 of Sch. B1 to the Act.[9] Their sole remedy, if they object to the proposals, is to apply to the court for an order under para.74 of Sch. B1 of the Act as a class, or part of a class, which will be unfairly harmed by implementation of the proposals.[10] By contrast Chapter 11 reflects the view that shareholders, too, have an interest which, though subordinate to that of creditors, nevertheless has a claim to be considered. In part the differences in approach are based on cultural factors.

"In the U.S. a variety of factors, including a deep emotional commitment to the entrepreneurial ethic, make the owners of the corporation central to a salvage proceeding. In the U.K., the prevailing view seems to be that

---

[6] See below, para.10–29.

[7] *Hansard*, H.L. Deb. 29 July 2002, col. 766.

[8] Insolvency Act 1986, Sch.B1, paras 49 *et seq.*

[9] The position is otherwise in the case of a CVA, where proposals have either to be approved in identical form by separate meetings of creditors and members or have to be approved at the creditors' meeting, with a member having the power to apply to the court if the decision taken at the creditors' meeting differs from that taken at the meeting of members (ss.4A, 5(1)). In the abence of such an application the creditors' decision stands.

[10] The power to make an order affecting proposals approved by creditors is implicit in Insolvency Act 1986, Sch.B1, para.74(6)(c).

the prior owners were the ones whose venality or incompetence created the problem and their interests disappear from moral or legal consideration once a formal proceeding has begun. Americans are much more willing to believe that financial difficulty is the result of external forces and that preservation of the company, not just the business, is a crucial social concern."[11]

In part also the involvement of members of the company in plans under Chapter 11 is a pragmatic response to the perceived need to have their support. An empirical study by Professors LoPucki and Whitford[12] indicated that in the reorganisation of large public corporations creditors, in order to avoid delay in confirmation of the plan and as "the price of peace", were willing to bargain with shareholders to allow them a share in the distribution under the plan. The authors of the study did, however, express some scepticism as to whether concessions made to shareholders were really necessary and how far they would in practice have been able to defeat or delay the plan if they had been excluded. In the United Kingdom too the practice of allowing shareholders a small amount of the equity is not unusual in the large restructurings of listed companies and for similar reasons.

The emphasis placed by insolvency practitioners on rescue of the business rather than of the company itself is sensible, reflecting the fact that it is often more advantageous either to hive down the assets to a new company free from liabilities and then sell the new company—a practice now less common than formerly—or alternatively to dispose of the assets or of the whole undertaking of the company, leaving the company itself to go into liquidation, than it is to preserve the corporate entity. Where this is so, the first of the three statutory objectives cannot be achieved, and it is necessary to resort to the second.[13]

(5) Disposal of the business or assets as the primary objective where rescue of the company not possible

10–27   As previously stated, while the moratorium imposed in administration facilitates CVAs and arrangements under s.425 of the Companies Act, the primary function of administration as a distinct procedure is to rescue the

---

[11] Jay L.Westbrook, "A comparison of bankruptcy reorganisation in the U.S. with administration procedure in the U.K" (1990) I.L. & P. 86 at 88. This remains true of the great majority of Chapter 11 filings, but the position is otherwise in the case of filings by large public corporations, many of which use Chapter 11 merely to sell their assets and divide up the proceeds, with no intention of rescuing the company itself. See Douglas G. Baird & Robert K. Rasmussen, "The End of Bankruptcy" 55 Stan. L. Rev. 751 (2002).

[12] "Bargaining over equity's share in the bankruptcy reorganisation of large, publicly held companies" 139 U. Pa. L. Rev. 125 (1990).

[13] See below, para.10–28.

company as a going concern or, if this is not possible, to dispose of its assets and undertaking, not to reorganise the company by arrangement with its creditors.

Objective of administration and conditions

(1) Replacement of plurality of purposes with a single purpose

Under the old regime, where administration could come about only by court order, an order could be made only in order to achieve one of the three specified statutory objectives[14] and only if the court was satisfied that the company was or was likely to become unable to pay its debts and that the administration order was reasonably likely to achieve the purpose of administration.[15] The new regime, which provides for out-of-court administration, is different in a number of other respects. First, the plurality of purposes has been replaced by a single purpose selected according to a threefold hierarchy. Secondly, the purpose does not have to be identified prior to the company's entry into administration. The rules and forms are predicated on the basis that the court need not concern itself with determination of the appropriate objective because this will be decided by the administrator according to what he thinks is reasonably practicable. So while the statement of the proposed administrator is required to express his opinion that the purpose of administration is likely to be achieved,[16] none of the prescribed documents (application, affidavit or statement) requires that the particular objective the proposed administrator has in mind be identified. Thirdly, the requirement of actual or impending insolvency applies only to administration by court order on the application of the company or the directors or on the application of the holder of a qualifying charge who does not satisfy the court that he could make an out-of-court appointment.

10–28

In a sense the identification of the objective of administration is a second-stage exercise, reached only where the decision has been taken that it is administration that is the insolvency process best suited to the company financial situation.[17] Administration is not an end in itself, merely an interim phase in the life of the company which will either be successful—resulting in restoration of the business to normal trading or the conclusion of a voluntary arrangement or disposal of the business or the assets without liquidation—or unsuccessful, in which case the company will normally go into insolvent liquidation or be "wound up" through administration. The new regime is embodied in para.3 of Sch.B1, which provides as follows:

---

[14] Insolvency Act 1986, Sch.B1, para.3. See below.
[15] *ibid.*, Sch.B1, para.11.
[16] See form 2.2B, prescribed by r.2.3(5) of the Insolvency Rules 1986.
[17] See above, para.10–28.

"Purpose of administration

3 (1) The administrator of a company must perform his functions with the objective of—

    (a) rescuing the company as a going concern, or

    (b) achieving a better result for the company's creditors as a whole than would be likely if the company were wound up (without first being in administration), or

    (c) realising property in order to make a distribution to one or more secured or preferential creditors.

(2) Subject to sub-paragraph (4), the administrator of a company must perform his functions in the interests of the company's creditors as a whole.

(3) The administrator must perform his functions with the objective specified in sub-paragraph (1)(a) unless he thinks either—

    (a) that it is not reasonably practicable to achieve that objective, or

    (b) that the objective specified in sub-paragraph (1)(b) would achieve a better result for the company's creditors as a whole.

(4) The administrator may perform his functions with the objective specified in sub-paragraph (1)(c) only if—

    (a) he thinks that it is not reasonably practicable to achieve either of the objectives specified in sub-paragraph (1)(a) and (b), and

    (b) he does not unnecessarily harm the interests of the creditors of the company as a whole."

It will be seen that the original four purposes, from which it was permissible to select either one purpose or two or more purposes without these having to be prioritised, have been reduced to a single purpose selected according to a given hierarchy.[18] Moreover, the approval of a voluntary arrangement under Part I of the Insolvency Act has sensibly been dispensed with as an objective in itself; instead, the administrator may exercise his power to propose a CVA.[19] Paragraph 3 arranges the objectives in a strict hierarchical order, requiring the administrator to select a single objective only, and to follow the hierarchy. Thus rescue of the company as a going concern is the first priority. It is only if the administrator thinks that it is not

---

[18] "The purpose of administration" is defined in Sch.B1, para.111, as "an objective specified in paragraph 3."
[19] Insolvency Act 1986, s.1(3).

reasonably practicable to achieve that objective, or that he could achieve a better result for the company's creditors as a whole without a rescue, that he is permitted to select objective (b) in the performance of his functions. Last in the priority list is the objective of realising the company's property in order to make a distribution to one or more secured or preferential creditors, an objective that can be pursued only if the administrator thinks that it is not reasonably practicable to achieve either of the higher-ranking objectives, and subject to the proviso that he does not unnecessarily harm the interests of the creditors of the company as a whole.[20]

(2) Rescue of the company and rescue of the business

We have already noted the contrasting attitudes in the United Kingdom and the United States to the preservation of the company as an entity rather than simply its business, with the view of the Cork Committee that there is little interest in preserving the company whilst in America shareholders are seen as continuing to have a stake in the enterprise deserving of at least some recognition.[21] In theory that is the position under the Insolvency Act 1986. Paragraph 3(1)(a) identifies as the top-ranking priority of administration "rescuing the company as a going concern." This is to be compared with the previous formulation in s.8 of the Act, "the survival of the company, and the whole or any part of its undertaking, as a going concern", which in the opinion of Harman J. in *Re Rowbotham Baxter Ltd*[22] did not cover the survival of a hive-down company,[23] as opposed to the debtor company itself. That remains the case under the new wording. As originally presented, the relevant provision of the Enterprise Bill referred only to rescuing the company.[24] The government agreed to clarify th e policy at the committee stage of he Bill in the House of Lords and accepted an amendment at Report to add "as a going concern" in order to make it clear that the primary objective was not to preserve an empty shell of a company but rather to rescue the company with the whole or a substantial part of its business intact.[25] The government was equally clear[26]

10–29

---

[20] See below, para.10–30.

[21] See above, para.10–21.

[22] [1990] B.C.L.C. 397.

[23] That is, a specially formed subsidiary of the company in administration to whom the whole or a substantial part of the company's business and assets are transferred but not the liabilities. Usually the hive-down company is then sold and the purchase price paid to the company in administration as sole beneficial owner of the shares. The hive-down procedure is of long standing and originated in administrative receivership (see generally Lightman and Moss, *Law of Receivers and Administrators of Companies* (3rd ed.), paras 9–058 *et seq.*). However, it is now less common with the disappearance of some of the advantages it once provided under the transfer of undertakings legislation.

[24] See the extract from the speech of Lord McIntosh, above, para.10–26.

[25] *Hansard*, H.L. Deb. 29 July 2002, col. 766, *per* Lord McIntosh and H.L. Deb. 21 October 2002, cols 1100–1105.

[26] *ibid.*, col. 768.

that where in the opinion of the administrator it was not reasonably practicable to preserve both the company and the business then the first objective became inapplicable and one moved to the second objective:

"achieving a better result for the company's creditors as a whole than would be likely if the company were wound up (without first going into administration)."

This leaves the administrator free to pursue, in conjunction with the creditors, any course of action calculated to put the creditors in a better position than on an immediate winding-up, for example, a hive-down, a sale of the assets or a CVA. This second objective is likely to be the most common under the new regime, as it was under the old.

(3) Realising property in order to make a distribution to one or more secured or preferential creditors

10–30   There are two qualifications. First, this objective is available only where the administrator thinks that it is not reasonably practicable to attain either of the prior-ranking objectives. Secondly, in performing his functions with this objective he must not unnecessarily harm the interests of creditors of the company as a whole. In this respect he has less freedom than the administrative receiver possessed, because the latter, while under a duty to use reasonable endeavours to obtain the best price, was free to determine the timing of any realisations and could thus proceed to an early sale even if delay would have resulted in enhancement of the value of the security and would not have prejudiced his debenture holder.[27] Now he has to avoid unnecessary harm to the general body of creditors. "Harm" is considered to be the equivalent of "prejudice". He is still entitled to subordinate the interests of the general body of creditors to those of secured and preferential creditors, since para.3(2) of Sch.B1 makes it clear that his duty to the general creditors is subject to the pursuit of the third objective. But he must avoid causing harm which is not necessary for the protection of the creditors for whom his realisations are intended. This imposes on him the duty to consider all aspects of the administration, including the timing of realisations. It is also a signal that the existence of security substantially in excess of the debt owed to the secured creditor or creditors does not entitle him to be lax in managing the business and realising the assets.

---

[27] See above, para.9–48.

5. ADMINISTRATION COMPARED WITH OTHER INSOLVENCY PROCEDURES

Administration compared with liquidation

Administration is in many ways different in concept and operation from liquidation. The primary objective of administration is not to bury the company forthwith but to restore it to profitable trading where possible and, in the event that liquidation becomes unavoidable (as is usually the case) to deal with the business or assets in such a way as to produce better dividends for creditors than if the company had gone into winding-up from the outset. However, the introduction by the Enterprise Act 2002 of a power to make a distribution to ordinary unsecured creditors with the permission of the court[28] has brought in its train the application of several rules previously confined to winding-up, for example, the rules on set-off,[29] the priority of preferential debts and *pari passu* distribution where the administrator obtains permission from the court to make a distribution to ordinary unsecured creditors.[30] Even under the previous regime the statutory provisions for the avoidance or adjustment of transactions applied to administration as well as to liquidation.[31] But there remain important differences:

10–31

(1) The administrator has full management powers; the liquidator may carry on business only for the beneficial winding up of the company[32] and rarely does so.

(2) The remedies of secured creditors and suppliers under reservation of title are frozen by an administration order but are unaffected by winding-up.

(3) The assets of the company remain its property and do not become subject to a "statutory trust" in favour of creditors as they do on liquidation.[33]

---

[28] Under item 13 of Sch.1 to the Insolvency Act 1986 the administrator already had power to make a distribution without the permission of the court where necessary or incidental to the performance of his functions or likely to assist achievement of the purpose of administration, though it would only be in special circumstances that any such condition would be satisfied. For examples, see *Re UCT (UK) Ltd* [2001] 1 B.C.L.C. 443; *Re WBSL Realisations 1992 Ltd* [1995] 2 B.C.L.C. 576.

[29] Set-off in administration is governed by r.2.85 of the Insolvency Rules 1986, set-off in liquidation by r.4.90. Changes have been made to bring the two rules into alignment. See above, para.8–16.

[30] See above, para.7–03 and below, para.10–81.

[31] Companies Act 1985, s.395(1). Insolvency Act 1986, ss.238–245. Prior to the changes made by the Enterprise Act 2002 insolvency set-off, the priority status of preferential debts and the *pari passu* principle of distribution among ordinary creditors did not apply to administration, since the administrator could not normally make a distribution.

[32] See above, para.5–03, n.40.

[33] See above, para.3–07.

(4) The expenses of liquidation rank behind claims secured by a floating charge; the expenses of administration rank ahead of such claims.[34]

(5) An administrator, unlike a liquidator, has no power to disclaim onerous property under s.178(3) of the Insolvency Act.[35]

(6) Only a liquidator can institute proceedings for misfeasance,[36] fraudulent trading[37] or wrongful trading,[38] except as regards proceedings against an administrator or former administrator which are initiated by a person listed in para.75(2)(a) of Sch.B1.

(7) In a liquidation, the convenor of a creditors' meeting may require the attendance of directors and employees;[39] in an administration the duty is merely to provide the administrator with information and to attend on him at such times as he may reasonably require.[40] Directors are thus much less exposed in an administration.

(8) The appointment of a liquidator is primarily a matter for the creditors, whereas the appointment of an administrator is usually left to the directors, though their decision may be influenced by major creditors.

It will be apparent that administration has several advantages over liquidation in helping to secure the statutory objective for which administration is available.[41] First, the liquidator can continue trading only for the purposes of beneficial winding up,[42] whereas an administrator can trade freely and dispose of the business or its assets on a going concern basis. Secondly, the freeze on enforcement of rights of secured creditors and suppliers under retention of title greatly facilitates the continuance of trading by the company as a going concern, and the value of a company's assets on a going concern basis is usually substantially higher than on a break-up basis. Thirdly, the freeze also makes it much easier to organise an arrangement with creditors than is the case on a winding up. There is a further point of which insolvency practitioners are keenly aware. In a compulsory liquidation (though no longer in a voluntary liquidation) all funds have to be deposited in the Insolvency Services Account, which imposes a high *ad valorem* charge. These disadvantages are avoided by the use of administration in parallel with a CVA.[43]

---

[34] See above, para.7–40.
[35] See above, para.6–21.
[36] Insolvency Act 1986, s.212.
[37] *ibid.*, s.213.
[38] *ibid.*, s.214.
[39] Insolvency Rules 1986, r.4.58(4).
[40] Insolvency Act 1986, s.235(2).
[41] As to these see above, para.10–28.
[42] Insolvency Act 1986, Sch.4, Part II, para.5.
[43] For a case where these factors influenced the decision as to the choice of insolvency process, see *Re TBL Realisation plc, Oakley-Smith v Greenberg* [2004] B.C.C. 81, discussed below, para.10–27. Until recently the Account also paid a lower than commercial rate of interest, but this has now changed.

Administration compared with administrative receivership

It will be recalled that administration is a procedure designed to provide for **10–32** the benefit of the general body of creditors the external management which administrative receivership provides by contract for the benefit of the debenture holder. The management powers of the administrator are co-extensive with those of the administrative receiver, but the powers of the former are given and exercised primarily on behalf of unsecured creditors. There are at least three other differences between the two regimes:

(1)   The administrator is not personally liable on contracts which he enters into or on contracts of employment which he adopts. In place of the personal liability of the kind imposed on receivers[44] the Act provides for claims under such contracts to rank in priority to the administrator's remuneration and expenses.[45]

(2)   Whereas the appointment of a receiver crystallises a floating charge, this is probably not the case when an administrator is appointed unless the charge so provides.[46]

(3)   As stated earlier, where the administrator is pursuing the objective of the kind previously pursued by the administrative receiver he owes a duty not to cause harm unnecessarily to the general body of creditors, and this imposes on him the duty to have regard to the interests of creditors when timing realisations,[47] a duty not imposed on administrative receivers.[48]

Formerly, the making of an administration order was not an event which determined the existence and amount of preferential debts except for the purpose of a meeting under s.4 of the Act to consider a CVA or where winding-up followed immediately upon the discharge of the administration order.[49] That has now changed. Except as otherwise provided by s387 of the Insolvency Act the relevant date in relation to a company in administration is the date on which it enters administration.[50]

---

[44] Insolvency Act 1986, s.44(1)(b). See above, paras 9–49 *et seq.*
[45] *ibid.*, Sch.B1, para.99(4), (5).
[46] See Roy Goode, *Legal Problems of Credit and Security* (3rd ed.), para.4–38.
[47] The duty was owed even before the change in the legislation (*Re Charnley Davies Ltd (No. 2)* [1990] B.C.L.C. 760.
[48] *Silven Properties Ltd v Royal Bank of Scotland plc* [2004] 1 B.C.L.C. 359.
[49] Insolvency Act 1986, s.387 as originally enacted.
[50] *ibid.*, s.387(3A).

Administration compared with CVA or scheme of arrangement

10–33   We have already noted that administration is not in itself a reorganisation procedure and that its outcome may or may not be a CVA or a scheme of arrangement. There are other important differences between the administration regime and that applicable to a CVA.

(1) No moratorium in a CVA

10–34   For a projected reorganisation to have maximum prospects of success it is necessary for the procedure which initiates it to attract a statutory moratorium in order to prevent individual creditors from taking separate enforcement action in their own interests, thereby potentially strangling the reorganisation initiative at birth. Yet except in the case of small eligible companies, whose directors, where intending to make a proposal for a CVA, may take steps to obtain a moratorium,[51] neither the initiation of a CVA nor the making of an application under s.425 triggers a moratorium. In both cases, with the exception just mentioned, individual creditors remain free to enforce their rights as they choose without regard to the views of the majority of creditors until a CVA is concluded or a s.425 order made. It is only where the CVA proposal or s.425 application is made in relation to a company already in administration or where a s.425 application is preceded by a winding-up petition[52] that the benefit of a moratorium is obtained. The lack of a statutory moratorium is one of the most serious deficiencies in the CVA procedure but proposals to introduce it into the regime have met with no success except in relation to small eligible companies,[53] for which the CVA rules are so stringent and so convoluted that few insolvency practitioners would view this route to a moratorium with enthusiasm. So the prevailing view is that a CVA should be initiated within the framework of an administration unless there are compelling reasons for avoiding administration.[54]

(2) Actual or impending insolvency not a prerequisite for a CVA

10–35   The company or its directors cannot appoint an administrator or apply for an administration order unless the company is insolvent or insolvency is imminent; there is no such pre-condition of a CVA or an order under s.425.

---

[51] See below, para.10–115.
[52] See Insolvency Act 1986, s.126.
[53] See below, para.10–115.
[54] See above, para.10–13.

(3) The company's participation in the process

In administration, the proposals for achieving the purpose or purposes of **10–36** the administration order are prepared and submitted by the administrator, not by the company, and only the creditors are involved in their approval; in a CVA or s.425 arrangement the scheme is formulated by the directors, and in a CVA the members also participate in the decision-making process. Indeed, a CVA cannot be concluded without an order of the court unless the separate meetings of creditors and members approve the arrangements in identical terms.[55]

(4) Management

Administration involves external management; in a CVA, although a **10–37** supervisor is appointed to oversee the implementation of the plan, his powers are confined by the terms of the CVA and the day-to-day management of the company is usually allowed to remain in the hands of its directors if it is not in administration.

(5) Dissenting and non-participating creditors

Finally, the rules determining when dissenting or non-participating credi- **10–38** tors are bound are not the same for a CVA as for the approval of proposals in an administration. In a CVA the arrangement binds only those who were entitled to vote at the meeting approving the arrangement or would have been so entitled if they had had notice of the meeting.[56] By contrast a resolution passed at a meeting of creditors to approve a proposal by the administrator in an administration, other than a proposal which is itself for a CVA, binds all creditors.[57] Moreover, a CVA must be approved by a majority in excess of three quarters in value of the creditors present in person or by proxy and voting on the resolution,[58] whereas a resolution on a proposal by the administrator other than for a CVA requires only a bare majority of those present and voting in person or by proxy, persons connected with the company being excluded.[59]

---

[55] Insolvency Act 1986, s.4A.
[56] *ibid.*, s.5(2)(b).
[57] The Insolvency Rules do not say this directly, they merely refer to the passing of the resolution.
[58] Insolvency Rules 1986, r.1.19(1). However, the voting on the resolution must be determined after excluding votes to be left out of account and votes of persons connected with the company (r.1.19(4)).
[59] *ibid.*, r.2.43(1),(2).

6. THE APPOINTMENT PROCEDURE IN OUTLINE

Administration without a court order

10–39   An administrator may be appointed out of court by the company,[60] the directors[61] or the holder of a qualifying floating charge.[62] The administrator must be qualified to act as an insolvency practitioner in relation to the company.[63] Neither the company nor the directors may appoint an administrator:

(1)   without first giving at least five business days' written notice to any person entitled to appoint an administrative receiver (thereby enabling such person to prevent an administration[64]) or to any person who is or may be entitled to appoint an administrator under para.14 of Sch.B1 to the Insolvency Act 1986 as holder of a qualifying floating charge,[65] or

(2)   obtaining the consent in writing[66] of each person to whom such notice has been given.[67]

(1) Appointment by the holder of a qualifying floating charge

10–40   The effect of the above provisions is that the holder of a qualifying floating charge[68] is the master of out-of-court appointments, which can be made by the chargee itself[69] and cannot be made by the company or the directors

---

[60] By resolution passed at a meeting of shareholders

[61] By majority decision (Insolvency Act 1986, Sch.B1, para.105), though it is thought this is subject to the provisions of the company's memorandum and articles of association.

[62] *ibid.*, Sch.B1, paras 14, 22. For the meaning of "qualifying floating charge" see above, para.10–10. Note that while the fact that the charge purports to provide for the appointment of an administrative receiver does not preclude the chargee from appointing an administrator (see para.14(2)(c)), the purported appointment of an administrative receiver rather than an administrator will be ineffective unless it can be interpreted by the court as intended to refer to an administrator.

[63] See Insolvency Act 1986, Sch.B1, para.6. The requirement to be qualified not only generally but "in relation to the company" means that the proper performance of his functions must be secured by a bond, either generally or in relation to the particular company concerned.

[64] Insolvency Act 1986, Sch.B1, para.25(c).

[65] *ibid.*, Sch.B1, para.26(1).

[66] Reference to a thing in writing includes a reference to a thing in electronic form (Sch.B1, para.111(1)).

[67] *ibid.*, Sch.B1, para.28(1)(b).

[68] A creditor who is not the holder of a qualifying floating charge can secure the appointment of an administrator only by application to the court under *ibid.*, Sch.B1, para.12(1).

[69] Assuming, of course, that the power to appoint an administrator has become exercisable under the terms of the charge (see above, para.10–12). But the chargee must first give at least two business days' written notice to the holder of any prior qualifying floating charge unless the latter has given his consent in writing to the making of the appointment (*ibid.*, Sch.B1, para.15(1)). Where the holder of a qualifying floating charge wishes to obtain an interim moratorium the notice must be in form 2.5B. See below as to the filing of a copy of the notice with the court. This notice should not be confused with the notice of appointment filed under Sch.B1, para.18, which is required to be in form 2.6B.

except on prior notice to the chargee or with the chargee's consent.[70] Moreover, whereas the company or its directors cannot appoint an administrator where a petition for winding-up has been presented or an administration application has been made and the petition or application has not been disposed of,[71] no such restriction applies to an appointment by the holder of a qualifying floating charge, who can also apply for an administration order even if the company is in compulsory winding-up.[72] Finally the holder of a qualifying floating charge who makes an out-of-court appointment is given the facility of filing a notice of appointment with the court outside court business hours.[73]

The holder of a qualifying floating charge must give at least two business days' written notice to the holder of any prior qualifying floating charge[74] or obtain his written consent to the appointment.[75] The purpose of this requirement is to give the holder of the prior charge an opportunity to appoint an administrator itself. But it is not necessary that the latter should consent, this is simply an alternative to its being given notice. That is in accordance with the general law relating to secured transactions inasmuch as a junior secured creditor does not need the consent of a senior secured creditor to enforce his security, whether by sale or otherwise, for anything he does takes effect subject to the rights of the senior creditor unless the latter is paid off.[76]

The holder of a qualifying floating charge who appoints the administrator must file with the court a notice of appointment incorporating the requisite statutory declaration,[77] and, if wishing to obtain the benefit of an interim moratorium under paras 44(2), (5) and 42 of Sch.B1 must at the same time file a copy of the notice of intention to appoint given to prior chargees under para.15.[78] There must also be filed the additional documents specified in r.2.16 of the Insolvency Rules. Under para.19 of Sch.B1 the appointment does not take effect until all the prescribed documents have been filed. In consequence the fact that at the time the administrator was appointed, in the sense of being designated by the debenture holder, the

---

[70] *ibid.*, Sch.B1, para.28(1).

[71] *ibid.*, Sch.B1, para.25.

[72] *ibid.*, Sch.B1, para.37(2).

[73] This is done by faxing it in form 2.7B to a designated telephone number provided by the Court Service (Insolvency Rules 1986, r.2.19(1), (3)). This has the same effect as a filing under r.2.16, which is subject to r.19 (r.2.16(6)). Under r.2.19(5) the appointment takes effect from the date and time of the fax transmission.

[74] By which is meant prior in time or having priority by virtue of an agreement to which the holder of the floating charge was a party (Insolvency Act 1986, Sch.B1, para.15(2)).

[75] *ibid.*, Sch.B1, para.15(1).

[76] See Roy Goode, *Legal Problems of Credit and Security* (3rd ed.), para.5–34.

[77] The notice must be in form 2.6B.

[78] Insolvency Rules 1986, r.2.15, The notice must be in form 2.5B. If there is no prior chargee, and thus no one to whom notice need be sent, the interim moratorium provisions do not apply. This is because the holder of the qualifying floating charge has no need of an interim moratorium; all he has to do is to file the notice of appointment.

power of appointment had not become exercisable because no demand for payment had been made, does not affect the validity of the appointment if demand is made by the time the appointment takes effect under para.19; there is no distinction between the appointment being "made" and its taking effect.[79] So it is not until all the prescribed documents have been filed that the conditions necessary for the exercise of the right to appoint an administrator have to be satisfied. Moreover, if the company acquiesces in what would otherwise be an invalid appointment and the administrator acts in reliance on that acquiescence the company is estopped from disputing the validity of his appointment.[80]

(2) Appointment by the company or the directors

10–41   The ability of the company or the directors to appoint an administrator is hedged around with restrictions. Such an appointment may not be made:

(a) unless the company is or is likely to become unable to pay its debts within the meaning of s.123 of the Insolvency Act[81];

(b) during the period of 12 months beginning with the date on which a prior appointment made by or on the application of the company or the directors ceases to have effect[82];

(c) if a petition for the winding-up of the company has been presented and not yet disposed of[83];

(d) if the company is in winding-up, whether voluntary or compulsory[84];

(e) if an administration application has been made and not yet disposed of[85];

(f) if an administrative receiver is in office[86]; or

(g) unless the person who makes the appointment has complied with the requirements of paras 26 and 27 of Sch.B1 and the period of notice

---

[79] *Fliptex Ltd v Hogg* [2004] B.C.C. 870.
[80] *ibid.*
[81] See above, paras 4–04 *et seq.*, as to s.123, and para.10–14, as to the curiously oblique way in which the requirement of actual or impending insolvency features in the legislation as regards out-of-court appointments by the company or its directors.
[82] Insolvency Act 1986, Sch.B1, para.23.
[83] *ibid.*, Sch.B1, para.25(a).
[84] *ibid.*, Sch.B1, para.8.
[85] *ibid.*, Sch.B1, para.25(b).
[86] *ibid.*, Sch.B1, para.25(c). However, if the security by virtue of which the receiver was appointed is vulnerable under sections 238–240 or 245 of the Insolvency Act were an administration order to be made, the court retains the power to make the order (Sch.B1, para.39).

specified in para.26(1) has expired or each person to whom notice has been given under para.26(1) has consented in writing to the making of the appointment.[87]

The procedure is laid down in Chapter 4 of Part II of the Insolvency Rules 1986 and largely mirrors that applicable to appointments by the holder of a qualifying floating charge. Where directors wish to propose a CVA incorporating proposals that will continue to leave day-to-day management in their hands and also to have the benefit of a moratorium, there is every incentive for them to take steps early before any holder of a qualifying charge has become entitled to enforce the charge and appoint an administrator of their choice who will become the supervisor of the CVA. An alternative, where they are dealing with a relatively small number of large creditors with whom they do not anticipate any serious difficulty in coming to an arrangement, is to move directly to a CVA without putting the company into administration.

Administration by court order

Though out-of-court administration is likely to be the norm, there will still be cases in which it is either expedient to apply for an administration order or necessary to do so because administration is sought by a person not eligible to make an out-of-court appointment[88] or because such an appointment is barred by other provisions.[89]   **10-42**

(1) Conditions to be satisfied

The court may make an administration order in relation to a company only if satisfied: **10–43**

(a) that the company is or is likely to become unable to pay its debts, and

(b) that the administration order is reasonably likely to achieve the purpose of administration.[90]

However, the first condition is dispensed with where the application is by the holder of a qualifying floating charge so long as the court is satisfied

---

[87] *ibid.*, Sch.B1, para.28(1).
[88] See above, para.10–39.
[89] In particular, Insolvency Act 1986, Sch.B1, para.17 (see above, para.9–26) and para.25 (see above, para.10–39).
[90] *ibid.*, Sch.B1, para.11. By "the purpose of administration" is meant an objective specified in Sch.B1, para.3 (Sch.B1, para.111(1)).

that the applicant could make an appointment under para.14.[91] "Unable to pay its debts" has the meaning given by s.123 of the Insolvency Act.[92] The meaning of present inability to pay debts has been considered in detail in an earlier chapter.[93] The requirement that the court should be "satisfied" that the company is "likely" to become unable to pay its debts follows the wording of the original statutory provisions. This has been held to require that the future insolvency is more likely than not and it is not sufficient that there is a real prospect of the company going into liquidation.[94] As regards the likelihood of the administration achieving the intended purpose, there has been a change in the language from "considers the making of an order would be likely to achieve one or more of the purposes mentioned below," for which it sufficed that there was a real prospect of the purpose or purposes being achieved,[95] to "satisfied that the administration order is reasonably likely to achieve the purpose of administration". The question is whether it alters the threshold that has to be crossed before an order has been made. This is not altogether easy because the new formulation pulls in opposite directions, "satisfied" being considered a more stringent requirement than "considers",[96] while "reasonably likely", in contradistinction to "likely" in the preceding sub-paragraph, suggests a slightly lower threshold. It is thought on balance that there was no intention to change the policy of the earlier legislation and it suffices that there is a real prospect of achieving the purpose of the administration.

(2) Who may apply

10–44   An administration application[97] may be made only by:

(a) the company,

(b) the directors of the company,

(c) one or more creditors of the company,[98]

(d) the justices' chief executive for a magistrates' court in the exercise of the power conferred by s.87A of the Magistrates' Courts Act 1980 (fine imposed on company),

---

[91] *ibid.*, Sch.B1, para.35(2)(a).

[92] *ibid.*, Sch.B1, para.111(1).

[93] Above, paras 4–13 *et seq.*

[94] *Re Colt Telecom plc* [2002] All E.R. (D) 347.

[95] *Re Harris Simons Construction Ltd* [1989] 1 W.L.R. 368.

[96] *ibid.*, *per* Hoffmann J. at 204.

[97] Formerly this was by way of petition.

[98] "Creditor" includes a contingent creditor and a prospective creditor (para.12(4)). See above, paras 4–20 *et seq.* A person claiming to be a creditor whose debt is disputed in good faith and on reasonable grounds is not a creditor for that purpose (*Re Simoco Digital UK Ltd, Thunderball Industries LLC v Digital UK Ltd* [2004] 1 B.C.L.C. 541). This follows the principle adopted in relation to *locus standi* for the presentation of a winding-up petition.

(e) a combination of the persons listed in paragraphs (a) to (d),[99] or

(f) the supervisor of a voluntary arrangement.[1]

Under the former regime almost all petitions were presented by the company or its directors; very few were presented by creditors. This is likely to be the case as regards administration applications under the new regime. The application may be withdrawn only with the permission of the court.[2]

As we have seen, the holder of a qualifying floating charge enjoys a number of privileges,[3] several of which relate to court-appointed administration.

The procedure for an administration application is laid down in Chapter 2 of Part II of the Insolvency Rules 1986. At the hearing, when any of the persons listed in r.2.12 may appear or be represented, the court may make the administration order sought, dismiss the application, adjourn the hearing conditionally or unconditionally, make an interim order, treat the application as a winding-up petition and make any order which the court could make under s.125 of the Insolvency Act 1986, and/or make any other order the court thinks appropriate.[4] The appointment of the administrator[5] takes effect at a time appointed by the order or, where no time is appointed, when the order is made.[6]

7. EFFECT OF ADMINISTRATION

Prior to the new regime introduced by the Enterprise Act 2002, the presentation of a petition for an administration order froze enforcement of the rights of secured and unsecured creditors, except with leave of the court, and prevented the company from going into voluntary or compulsory winding up.[7] The only enforcement steps that were not frozen were the presentation of a winding-up petition, the appointment of an administrative receiver and the carrying out of his functions.[8] Once an administration order had been made the freeze became almost total, since during the currency of the administration the same constraints applied as on presentation of the petition and in addition no administrative receiver could be appointed or remain in post, and any winding-up petition had to be

10–45

---

[99] Insolvency Act 1986, Sch.B1, para.12(1).
[1] *ibid.*, s.7(4)(b) as applied by Sch.B1, para.12(5).
[2] *ibid.*, Sch.B1, para.12(3).
[3] Above, para.10–09.
[4] Insolvency Act 1986, Sch.B1, para.13(1).
[5] And accordingly the commencement of the administration. See *ibid.*, Sch.B1, para.1(2)(b).
[6] *ibid.*, Sch.B1, para.13(2).
[7] *ibid.*, s.10(3). See below, para.10–47.
[8] *ibid.*, s.10(2).

dismissed.[9] Similar rules apply under the new regime but have been adapted and extended to cover out-of-court appointments.

This freezing of creditors' rights is peculiar to administration and is crucial to its viability. It means that the administrator can get on with the business of restoring the company to profitability or otherwise managing its affairs for the benefit of the creditors as a whole without having constantly to fend off enforcement steps by individual creditors; in some cases it provides an inducement to the holders of a floating charge not to appoint a receiver even where they are still entitled to do so; and it helps to ensure that negotiations for a voluntary arrangement are not scuppered by the precipitate action of a particular creditor wishing to jump the queue.

Vacation of office by administrative receiver

10–46 A further consequence of the administration order is that any administrative receiver must vacate office.[10] Upon so doing the receiver is given a charge on any property of the company in his custody or under his control for his remuneration, expenses and indemnity entitlement, in priority to his debenture holder's security,[11] and is released from any responsibility for payment of preferential debts.[12]

Moratoria

10–47 Under the Insolvency Act there may be four types of moratoria:

(i)   A moratorium for the period the company is in administration.[13]

(ii) An interim moratorium pending:
(a) the disposal of an application for an administration order; or
(b) the coming into effect of an out-of-court appointment of an administrator.[14]

(iii) A moratorium in favour of a small eligible company, being a company which is not undergoing any other insolvency process, pending a meeting to consider a CVA.[15]

(iv) A moratorium under an approved CVA.

---

[9] *ibid.*, s.11.
[10] *ibid.*, Sch.B1, para.41(1). A receiver of part of the property need vacate office only if so required by the administrator (Sch.B1, para.41(2)).
[11] *ibid.*, Sch.B1, paras 41(3), (4).
[12] *ibid.*, Sch.B1, para.41(4)(b).
[13] *ibid.*, Sch.B1, paras 42, 43.
[14] *ibid.*, Sch.B1, para.44.
[15] *ibid.*, s.1A and Sch.A1.

In addition, an informal workout typically has standstill provisions pending agreement on a restructuring plan.[16]

The first two kinds of moratoria featured in much the same form under the earlier statutory provisions embodied in ss.10 and 11 of the Insolvency Act 1986, so that case law on those provisions is relevant to the construction of the new provisions. These deal first with the moratorium that arises in administration and secondly with the interim moratorium that may be procured before the appointment of the administrator takes effect. Under the new regime, as under the earlier statutory provisions, most of the constraints are common to the two moratoria, and to this extent the case law and analysis relating to what is now called an interim moratorium[17] are relevant to the moratorium arising on the appointment of the administrator and will thus be referred to in that context. The moratorium for small eligible companies is subject to the complex provisions of Sch.A1 to the Insolvency Act and is mentioned only briefly later.[18] A moratorium is an almost universal feature of a CVA, though its effect is confined to those bound by the CVA.[19]

Breach of moratorium

An enforcement measure taken in violation of the statutory moratorium is actionable in damages for breach of statutory duty.[20]   **10–48**

(i) Moratorium during period of administration

There is a general moratorium on the enforcement of remedies when a   **10–49**
company is in administration, whether the administration is out of court or on an administration order, without the consent of the administrator or the permission of the court.[21] In such a case the restrictions set out below apply. But they are merely procedural in their effect; they do not destroy rights, they merely restrict their enforcement. So the inability of the owner of

---

[16] See below, para.10–135.

[17] In the heading to para.44 of Sch. B1.

[18] See below, para.10–115.

[19] See below, para.10–129.

[20] This was common ground in *Euro Commercial Leasing Ltd v Cartwright & Lewis* [1995] 2 B.C.L.C. 618, where, however, it was held that the breach was purely technical and no damage had resulted.

[21] Insolvency Act 1986, Sch.B1, paras 42, 43. In granting permission the court may impose a condition or requirement in connection with the transaction (Sch.B1, para.43(7)). Neither the administrator nor the court can dispense with the bar on winding-up (Sch.B1, para.42) or the appointment of an administrative receiver (Sch.B1, para.43(6A)). However, this does not prevent conversion of the administration into a CVL under para.83 or interfere with the right of the administrator to petition to wind up the company under r.4.7(7) of the Insolvency Rules 1986.

goods supplied to the company on hire-purchase to enforce its right to repossess them does not affect his substantive law right to immediate possession so as to enable him to maintain conversion against a person interfering with that right.[22]

Schedule B1 to the Insolvency Act 1986 provides for two categories of moratorium during the period in which a company is in administration: a moratorium on insolvency proceedings and a moratorium on other legal process.[23]

No winding-up

10–50 A winding-up petition must be dismissed on the making of an administration order and must be suspended while the company is in administration following an appointment of an administrator by the holder of a qualifying floating charge.[24] No resolution may be passed for the winding-up of the company,[25] nor may any winding-up order be made except under s.24A (public interest) or s.367 of the Financial Services and Markets Act 2000 (petition by Financial Services Authority).[26]

No appointment of administrative receiver

10–51 During the moratorium no administrative receiver may be appointed.[27]

No enforcement of security

10–52 No step may be taken to enforce security over the company's property except:

    (a) with the consent of the administrator, or

    (b) with the permission of the court.[28]

---

[22] *Barclays Mercantile Business Finance Ltd v Sibec Developments Ltd* [1993] B.C.L.C. 1077.
[23] See below.
[24] Insolvency Act 1986, Sch.B1, para.23(1). There is no comparable provision relating to an appointment by the company or directors under Sch.B1, para.22, since in contrast to a chargee under a qualifying floating charge they may not appoint an administrator during the pendency of a winding-up petition (Sch.B1, para.25(a)).
[25] *ibid.*, Sch.B1, para.42(1), (2). However, the administration may be converted into a company voluntary winding-up (para.83) or a compulsory winding-up on the petition of the creditor (Insolvency Rules 1986, r.4.7(7)).
[26] *ibid.*, Sch.B1, paras 42(1)–(4).
[27] *ibid.*, Sch.B1, para.43(6A).
[28] *ibid.*, Sch.B1, para.43(2). This restriction does not apply to a market charge (Companies Act 1989, s.175(1)), a money market charge (Financial Markets and Insolvency (Money Market) Regulations 1995, reg.21(2)(a)) or a collateral security charge (Financial Markets and Insolvency (Settlement Finality) Regulations 1999, reg.19(1)).

Under the previous statutory provisions these apparently straightforward provisions gave rise to a good deal of case law. At the level of interpretation words and phrases that caused difficulty in what was formerly s.11(3)(c) include "steps . . . to enforce", "security" and "property". Beyond these questions of interpretation the courts had to address the treatment of liens and rights of detention and felt constrained to lay down guidelines as to the grant or refusal of leave to proceed with remedial steps. All these issues arose in one form or another in *Bristol Airport plc v Powdrill*,[29] in which the facts were as follows:

Paramount Airways went into administration owing substantial debts, including landing fees and fuel charges owed to Bristol Airport in respect of aircraft which Paramount held under a sub-lease. During the course of the administration Bristol Airport applied to the court for leave to detain two of Paramount's aircraft under s.88 of the Civil Aviation Act 1982. Thereupon Birmingham Airport, without obtaining leave, parked a lorry loaded with concrete in front of another aircraft operated by Paramount and served the captain with a lien notice. That airport then applied for leave to detain the aircraft. At the time of these events the administration was substantially advanced and a proposed sale of the business on terms beneficial to the general body of creditors had been approved in principle by the creditors but could not be implemented if the aircraft were detained. On the substantive hearing of the applications the administrator asserted that the exercise of the lien came either within s.11(3)(c) as enforcement of a security or within s.11(3)(d) as "other proceedings" or the levy of a distress, and that leave should not be given. For the airports it was argued (a) that the aircraft were not Paramount's "property", since they were merely held under a sub-lease; (b) that the statutory right of detention was not a "lien or other security" but a statutory right possessing distinctive features; (c) that if the right of detention were a lien, its exercise was not "a step taken to enforce" a security but an act by which the security was created or perfected; (d) that the detention did not constitute "other proceedings" or the levy of a distress.

Harman J. rejected all four arguments and refused to give leave to detain the aircraft on the ground that this would have the effect of giving the airports an advantage over other creditors and would prevent a sale of the business and that the airports, having taken advantage of the administration proceedings, ought not to be allowed to detain the aircraft. This decision was affirmed by the Court of Appeal.

---

[29] [1990] Ch. 744, affirming the decision of Harman J. in [1990] B.C.C. 130 *sub nom. Re Paramount Airways Ltd.*

We shall revert to this case in examining each of the individual elements in para.43(2) of Sch.B1.

(1) "security"

10–53   Security is defined as "any mortgage, charge, lien, or other security".[30] The nature of mortgages, charges and liens is well-known.[31] A mortgage is a consensual transfer of ownership by way of security. A charge is an incumbrance, a right vested in one person to look to the proceeds of another's property for satisfaction of a debt due. It may be created by agreement or by law. A lien is a right to retain possession of another's property pending payment of sums due to the person in possession, the latter having acquired possession otherwise than for the purpose of security. It too may be created by agreement or by law.

What is meant by "other security"? Clearly this includes a pledge, the only remaining form of consensual security known to English law.[32] It also extends to non-consensual charges, liens and rights of detention, for example, the statutory right under s.88 of the Civil Aviation Act 1982 to detain an aircraft for payment of airport charges[33] or the statutory right of retention of an unpaid seller under the Sale of Goods Act 1979.[34] There had previously been a division of judicial opinion as to whether a landlord's right of re-entry under a lease fell within the phrase "other security". The balance of authority had swung sharply against this,[35] but the insertion of a separate provision dealing specifically with a landlord's right of entry[36] forecloses this issue. The same applies to the provision precluding repossession under a hire-purchase agreement.[37] We may therefore conclude that "security" is used in its strict sense to denote a mortgage, a pledge or a consensual or non-consensual charge, lien or other right of detention or retention, and nothing beyond these.

(2) "No step may be taken to enforce "

10–54   It should be observed that the phrase used in para.43(2) of Sch.B1 to the Insolvency Act is not "no security shall be enforced" but "no step may be taken to enforce security . . ." This suggests that steps preparatory to the

---

[30] Insolvency Act 1986, s.248(b).
[31] For detailed descriptions see Roy Goode, *Legal Problems of Credit and Security* (3rd ed.), Chap.1; and *Commercial Law* (3rd ed.), Chap.22.
[32] See Roy Goode, *Legal Problems of Credit and Security* (3rd ed.), para.1–42, and *Re Cosslett (Contractors) Ltd* [1998] Ch. 495, *per* Millett L.J. at 508.
[33] *Bristol Airport plc v Powdrill* [1990] Ch. 744.
[34] Sale of Goods Act 1979, s.41.
[35] The authorities were reviewed by Neuberger J. in *Re Lomax Leisure Ltd* [2000] B.C.C. 352.
[36] Insolvency Act 1986, Sch.B1, para.43(4).
[37] *ibid.*, Sch.B1, para.43(3).

actual act of enforcement may fall within the prohibition. What is not clear is what constitutes the taking of steps to enforce a security. The appointment of an administrative receiver would be one such case but is the subject of a separate prohibition with which neither the administrator nor the court can dispense.[38] On the other hand, the appointment of a receiver who is not an administrative receiver would fall within the present restriction as a step to enforce security over the company's property. It has been held that the mere assertion of a lien or right of detention constitutes enforcement for the purpose of what is now para.43(2).[39]

There are other cases in which there has been no clear ruling. Suppose, for example, that a loan is made to the company which is repayable on demand and that the loan is secured by a debenture which allows the debenture holder to appoint an administrative receiver or to take possession of or sell the mortgaged property if payment of any money secured by the debenture is not made on demand. Does the making of a demand constitute the taking of a step to enforce the security? The point was mooted but not answered by Millett J. in *Re Olympia & York Canary Wharf Ltd*[40] and again in *Barclays Mercantile Business Finance Ltd v Sibec Developments Ltd*,[41] where he regarded the point as "a difficult one" but unnecessary for his decision since the proceedings were against the administrators, not the company. It seems clear that "step" is not confined to legal proceedings or process, for these are specifically dealt with in para.43(6) of Sch.B1, but embraces any act of enforcement, such as the act of repossession, the act of sale, etc. Does it also extend to preparatory acts, and if so, must these be acts which are specifically referable to enforcement or does it suffice that they are acts which in themselves are not so referable but lay the foundation for enforcement? It is thought that "steps to enforce" is narrower than steps towards enforcement and denotes acts which in some degree interfere with the company's enjoyment of its property or of property in its possession or inhibit the administrator's use of such property in the conduct of the business. The underlying purpose of para.43 is to preclude the taking of steps which might impair the administrator's ability to manage the company, use its property and carry through the purpose or purposes for which the administration order was made free from interference by creditors.[42] The assertion of a lien or right of detention is plainly a factor which inhibits the administrator's use of the property.[43] So too is a threat to enforce a consensual security interest. Similarly, where a debenture provides for security over, say, the company's

---

[38] *ibid.*, Sch.B1, para.43(6A). See below, para.10–65.
[39] *Bristol Airport plc v Powdrill* [1990] Ch. 744; *Euro Commercial Leasing v Cartwright & Lewis* [1995] 2 B.C.L.C. 618.
[40] [1993] B.C.L.C. 453 at 454.
[41] [1992] 1 W.L.R. 1253 at 1259.
[42] See *Bristol Airport plc v Powdrill*, above, *per* Sir Nicolas Browne-Wilkinson V.C. at 758.
[43] See above, para.10–53.

book debts, a demand for payment addressed to the company's debtors by the debenture holder or his receiver would, it is thought, constitute a step to enforce the security, for it may inhibit the ability of the administrator to collect in the debts himself and represents an interference in his management of the company's assets.

10–55   By contrast, preparatory steps which do not have this effect are outside the mischief against which para.43 is aimed. Accordingly the service of a demand on the company for payment or of a notice terminating a contract or making time of performance of the essence is not, it is thought, a step to enforce a security, even if exclusively referable to an intention to do so rather than simply to trigger a payment obligation on the part of the company or a surety, since such a demand or notice has no impact whatsoever on the company's enjoyment of its property or the administrator's management of it. Again, the service of a notice crystallising a floating charge is not a step to enforce security, since its effect is simply to convert the charge into a fixed charge, and the mere holding of a fixed charge is not itself a step to enforce the charge.

It follows from what has been said above that a mortgagee or chargee of book debts or other receivables who without the consent of the administrator or leave of the court collects or demands payment from the account debtors is taking steps to enforce security over the company's property in breach of the prohibition. The position is otherwise where the collection or demand is by a person who has bought the debts or other receivables for he is the owner of them, not merely a secured creditor, and they are no longer the property of the company. So a factoring company which has purchased receivables under a factoring agreement with the debtor company remains entitled to collect the debts from the account debtors.

The inclusion of liens in the statutory prohibition creates no difficulty in the case of equitable liens, such as the lien of the unpaid vendor of land, for these do not depend on possession and are enforceable by sale.[44] But the prohibition does raise a problem for the holder of a possessory lien, whose only right under the lien, in the absence of an agreement or statutory provision to the contrary, is to retain possession of the goods over which the lien is asserted and whose lien is lost once possession has been surrendered.[45] How, then, can the lienee preserve his lien without detaining the goods after demand by the administrator for their surrender? The conundrum was neatly solved in *Bristol Airport plc v Powdrill*,[46] where Woolf L.J. drew an analogy with the tort of conversion. He pointed out[47] that a person in possession of goods is not guilty of conversion or other unlawful interference with the goods merely because he does not hand them over

---

[44] See 28 Halsbury's Laws (4th ed., 1997 reissue), paras 754 *et seq.*
[45] *Op. cit.*, paras 546, 550.
[46] [1990] Ch. 756.
[47] [1990] 2 W.L.R. 1362 at 1382.

immediately he receives a demand from the person entitled to possession. He is entitled to reasonable time to verify the other person's right to possession. Similarly, a person entitled to a lien is not to be regarded as taking steps to enforce it unless he makes an unqualified refusal to hand it over. This is not the case where he invites the administrator to consent to the exercise of the lien and indicates that in the absence of such consent he will apply to the court promptly for leave and does so. His continued possession meanwhile is not an unlawful enforcement of the lien, nor does it constitute a contempt of court. Moreover, one would in general expect the administrator to give his consent pending an application to the court. But if the lienee simply refuses to hand over the goods and puts no proposals to the administrator the court will order delivery up to the administrator.[48] What usually happens in practice is that the lienee releases the goods from the lien on condition that the security interest attaches to the proceeds of sale.[49]

(3) "enforce"

In the context of an administration moratorium, as opposed to an interim moratorium, it would have been more accurate if the prohibition had been on the realisation of security rather than its enforcement, for the prohibition does not apply where the administrator consents to the step that is being taken, and if consent is given there is no "enforcement". The word "enforce" has greater significance in the context of the interim moratorium.[50]

10–56

(4) "security over the company's property"

"Property" is defined as including "money, goods, things in action, land and every description of property wherever situated and also obligations and every description of interest, whether present or future or vested or contingent, arising out of, or incidental to, property".[51] In the words of Sir Nicolas Browne-Wilkinson V.C. in *Bristol Airport plc v Powdrill*, "It is hard to think of a wider definition of property".[52] Nevertheless it was argued in that case that aircraft held by the company on lease did not constitute property and that the company's rights were purely contractual. At first

10–57

---

[48] *Re Sabre International Products Ltd* [1991] B.C.L.C. 470.
[49] The nature of the interest will usually change from lien to charge, because a lien cannot be taken over intangibles. See Roy Goode, *Legal Problems of Credit and Security*, para.1–67.
[50] See below, para.10–69.
[51] Insolvency Act 1986, s.436.
[52] [1990] Ch. 744 at 759. See also above, para.6–03, in relation to what constitutes an asset of the company.

instance, Harman J. had held that a chattel in respect of which the company had what were strictly contractual rights was part of its property.[53] On appeal the Vice-Chancellor reached the same result by a different route, holding that since each aircraft had unique features peculiar to itself, a court would order specific performance of a contract to lease an aircraft, and it followed from this that the "lessee" had an equitable interest in it.[54] However, neither explanation seems wholly satisfactory. Purely contractual rights are, of course, a species of property—the statutory definition expressly includes choses in action—but in the case in question the security was asserted over a physical asset, an aircraft, not over the contractual rights in it. No doubt it was for this reason that the Vice-Chancellor sought to establish the existence of an *in rem* right to the aircraft. But his solution is difficult to reconcile with the fundamental distinction between land and chattels. A lease of land confers an estate on the lessee, so that an agreement for a lease does indeed create an equitable estate. But the doctrine of estates does not apply to chattels. An agreement for a lease of chattels is merely an agreement to give possession, and English law does not recognise any concept of equitable possession.[55] Such an agreement confers no *in rem* rights on the intended lessee at all; its effect is purely contractual. On taking delivery the lessee acquires a limited legal interest,[56] but this derives from his possession, not from the agreement.[57] Accordingly, it is both simpler and more accurate to treat the lessee's *in rem* rights as derived from its possession of the aircraft under the leasing agreement, a possession which conferred on it a limited legal interest.

No repossession of goods under a hire-purchase agreement

10–58 A further effect of the administration is that no steps may be taken to repossess goods in the company's possession under any hire-purchase agreement, except with the consent of the administrator or the permission of the court.[58] Again, we encounter definitional issues.

(1) "Hire-purchase agreement"

10–59 "Hire-purchase agreement"[59] includes a conditional sale agreement,[60] a chattel leasing agreement[61] and a retention of title agreement.[62] Section 251 of the Insolvency Act defines a retention of title agreement as:

---

[53] *Sub nom. Re Paramount Airways Ltd* [1990] B.C.C. 130 at 136.
[54] [1990] Ch. 744 at 759.
[55] See Roy Goode, *Commercial Law* (3rd ed.). p.39, n.63 and pp.41, 627.
[56] *ibid.*, pp.33, 46–47.
[57] *ibid.*, pp.34–35.
[58] Insolvency Act 1986, Sch.B1, para.43(3). For the administrator's right to use the goods while the remedy of repossession is suspended, see below, para.10–96.
[59] As defined by the Consumer Credit Act 1974, s.189(1) (Insolvency Act 1986, s.436).
[60] As so defined (*ibid.*).
[61] That is, an agreement for the bailment of goods which is capable of subsisting for more than three months (Insolvency Act 1986, s.251).
[62] Insolvency Act 1986, Sch.B1, para.111(1).

"an agreement for the sale of goods to a company, being an agreement—

(a) which does not constitute a charge on the goods sold, but
(b) under which, if the seller is not paid and the company is wound up, the seller will have priority over all other creditors of the company as respects the goods and any property representing the goods."

This definition is distinctly odd and almost certainly unnecessary. Limb (a) appears to be concerned to exclude agreements which in form are sale and repurchase or sale and hire-purchase/lease-back agreements but which in substance are mortgages or charges,[63] but if this is the case it is otiose, since if an instrument is in law a mortgage or charge it cannot be a sale agreement and in any event security is already covered by para.43(2). Limb (b) overlaps the definition of conditional sale agreement and does so in an unsatisfactory manner, because its reference to priority "over all other creditors as respects the goods and any other property representing the goods" seeks to ascribe to a sale agreement a legal effect which it does not necessarily have, since whether a seller has priority depends on legal priority rules. There may, for example, be a person with a stronger title to the goods themselves, whilst if any retention of title clause has been extended to cover proceeds this extension will in most cases create a charge over book debts which will be void if not registered under s.395 of the Companies Act 1985,[64] and even where this is not the case a subsequent assignment of the proceeds to a factor who gives notice of assignment to the account debtors will usually give the factor priority.[65] It is hard to think of a retention of title agreement which does not fall within the definition of conditional sale agreement.[66]

---

[63] See Roy Goode, *Commercial Law* (3rd ed.), pp.605 *et seq.*
[64] Goode, *op. cit.*, p.608.
[65] *Op. cit.*, p.752.
[66] One might add that the way in which the definitions have been distributed leaves much to be desired. One of the drafting features of the Consumer Credit Act 1974, which could usefully have been adopted in the insolvency legislation, is that it gathers together in a single section, s.189(1), all the definitions, whether given in that section or by way of cross-reference to definitions elsewhere. So to find whether a term is a defined term it is necessary to look only at s.189(1). By contrast, the Insolvency Act has interpretation provisions for the first group of Parts, a separate set of interpretation provisions for the second group of Parts and a third set for expressions used generally and for two other terms, not to mention definitional cross-references to other legislation. Take, for example, the reference to "hire-purchase agreement" in para.43(1) of Sch. B1 to the Insolvency Act 1986. To find the meaning of this one might suppose one starts with s.436 of the Act, which does not itself define the term but routes one to the definition in s.189(1) of the Consumer Credit Act 1974. That, however, is a false trail, because it turns out that that in para.43(1) of Sch.B1 the draftsman is using the phrase "hire-purchase agreement" not in its normal sense as defined by the Consumer Credit Act but as a shorthand embracing a conditional sale agreement, a chattel leasing agreement and a retention of title agreement (para.111(1)). To find the definition of "conditional sale agreement" one goes back to s.436 and thence once again to

(2) "in the company's possession"

10–60   In *Re Atlantic Computer Systems plc*[67] the Court of Appeal had to consider whether a lessee of equipment which it had sub-let and which was in the physical possession of the sub-lessee was nevertheless to be considered in possession of the equipment itself for the purpose of the statutory provisions. The court had no difficulty in concluding that it was, and that repossession from the sub-lessee would constitute repossession from the lessee so as to require the leave of the court. In prohibiting repossession of goods in the possession of a company in administration, s.11(3)(c) of the Act[68] was concerned with relations between the lessor and the company. As between the lessor and the company the latter was in possession of the goods, and it did not matter whether the goods remained on the company's premises or were entrusted to others for repair or were sub-let by the company as part of its trade to others.[69]

(3) "under a hire-purchase agreement"

10–61   We have seen earlier that "hire-purchase agreement" has an extended meaning. In *Re David Meek Plant Ltd*[70] the question arose whether goods could still be considered in the possession of a company "under a hire-purchase agreement" after the agreement had been terminated. It was held to be sufficient that the possession of the goods was attributable to, or derived its legal origin at some time from, a hire-purchase agreement; it was not necessary that the agreement was still subsisting. This is plainly correct.

No exercise of a right of forfeiture by re-entry

10–62   A landlord may not exercise a right of forfeiture by peaceable re-entry[71] in relation to premises let to the company except with the consent of the administrator or the permission of the court.[72] This provision, which was not contained in the original legislation, was inserted to resolve doubts as to whether a right of forfeiture was a security.[73] It is thought that the word

---

s.189(1) of the Consumer Credit Act. For the final step, discovery of the meanings of "chattel leasing agreement" and "retention of title agreement," it is necessary to turn to s.251 of the Insolvency Act. Surely our legislative drafting can be better than this!

[67] [1992] Ch. 505.
[68] See now Insolvency Act 1986, Sch.B1, paras 43(2),(3).
[69] [1992] Ch. 505 *per* Nicholls L.J. at 532.
[70] [1994] 1 B.C.L.C. 680.
[71] Forfeiture by legal proceedings is separately barred under para.43(6). See below.
[72] Insolvency Act 1986, Sch.B1, para.43(4).
[73] See above, para.10–53.

"premises" is used in its legal rather than its popular sense so as to include not only buildings and land with buildings but also land on its own.[74] Where the lease provides that it can be forfeited by notice in stated events there is nothing to preclude the landlord from terminating the lease in this way, for this is not a forfeiture by re-entry. The landlord cannot, however, proceed to enforce the forfeiture by action or re-entry without the consent of the administrator or the permission of the court.

Repossession and re-entry to which the restrictions do not apply

The restriction on repossession or peaceable re-entry has no application to   **10–63** a proprietary claim which does not constitute a security interest and does not depend on retention of title under a supply agreement but is based, for example, on the fact that the company is wrongfully in possession or holds the property as the claimant's agent with a duty to surrender it. But if peaceful repossession or re-entry is not possible it will be necessary to have the permission of the court or the consent of the administrator to bring proceedings.[75]

No legal process

No legal process (including legal proceedings, execution and distress) may   **10–64** be instituted or continued against the company or property of the company except with the consent of the administrator or the permission of the court.[76] This clarifies but also expands the previous restriction, where the preponderance of judicial opinion had been that it did not cover distress.[77] The original provisions contained in s.11 of the Insolvency Act stated that no "other" proceedings could be taken, and this led the Scottish Court of Session to conclude, in *Air Ecosse Ltd v Civil Aviation Authority*,[78] that "other proceedings" had to be construed *ejusdem generis* with the preceding provisions and thus as limited to proceedings by a creditor of the company which were in some way related to a debt due from the company. That view has not gained acceptance in England, where it has been held that "legal process" covers not only civil proceedings in a court of law but criminal proceedings[79] and any other proceedings of a judicial or quasi-judicial

---

[74] See, for example, *Bracey v Read* [1963] Ch. 88.
[75] See below, para.10–64.
[76] Insolvency Act 1986, Sch.B1, para.43(6).
[77] *Re Olympia & York Canary Wharf Ltd* [1993] B.C.C. 154, in which Millett J. declined to follow the decision of Harman J. on this point in *Exchange Travel Agency Ltd v Triton Property Trust plc* [1991] B.C.L.C. 396; *McMullen & Sons Ltd v Cerrone* [1994] B.C.L.C. 156, a decision on s.252 of the Insolvency Act.
[78] 1987 S.L.T. 751.
[79] *Re Rhondda Waste Disposal Ltd* [2001] Ch. 57.

nature, including proceedings before an employment appeal tribunal,[80] arbitration proceedings[81] proceedings for revocation of a patent,[82] and an application for an adjudication under s.108 of the Housing Grants, Construction and Regeneration Act 1996.[83] Presumably also an English court would take the view that an application to the Civil Aviation Authority by the competitor of an airline to revoke the airline's air transport licence under the Civil Aviation Act 1982 would also constitute a legal process,[84] and so, by the same token, would proceedings by the Director General of Fair Trading to revoke a licence granted under the Consumer Credit Act 1974. However, an application for leave to register a charge out of time is not a proceeding "against the company or property of the company", for it could equally well be made by the company, and the court would not compel the absurdity of an application for leave to make an application for leave to register out of time.[85] Again, the service of a contractual notice, such as a notice making time of the essence or terminating a contract for a repudiatory breach, does not constitute a legal process.[86]

No appointment of an administrative receiver

10–65   While a company is in administration no administrative receiver may be appointed.[87] The position thus differs from that applicable for an interim moratorium.[88] At first sight this provision seems unnecessary, since it would be covered by the more general restriction on the taking of steps to enforce security over the company's property.[89] However, the appointment of an administrative receiver must be treated as a distinct category since the bar is absolute; there is no provision for an appointment with the consent of the administrator or the permission of the court, for the obvious reason that such an appointment would prevent the administrator from fulfilling his functions. The prohibition does not apply to other kinds of receiver. The appointment of these is covered by the prohibition of steps to enforce security[90] but may be made with the consent of the administrator or the permission of the court. There may, for example, be cases where a creditor

---

[80] *Carr v British International Helicopters Ltd* [1994] 2 B.C.L.C. 474.

[81] *Re Paramount Airways Ltd* [1990] Ch. 744, *per* Sir Nicolas Browne-Wilkinson V.C. at 765; *Carr v British International Helicopters Ltd* [1994] 2 B.C.L.C. 474, *per* Lord Coulsfield at 482.

[82] *Biosource Technologies Inc v Axis Genetics plc* [2000] 1 B.C.L.C. 286, where it was also held that the restrictions on enforcement were not confined to proceedings by creditors.

[83] *A. Straume (UK) Ltd v Bradlor Developments Ltd* [2000] B.C.C. 333.

[84] By contrast with the decision of the Scottish Court of Session in *Air Ecosse Ltd v Civil Aviation Authority* 1987 S.L.T. 751.

[85] *Re Barrow Borough Transport Ltd* [1990] Ch. 227.

[86] *Re Olympia & York Canary Wharf Ltd*, above n.77.

[87] Insolvency Act 1986, Sch.B1, para.43(6A).

[88] See below, para.10–68.

[89] Insolvency Act 1986, Sch.B1, para.43(2). See above, para.10.52.

[90] *ibid.*, Sch.B1, para.43(2). See above, para.10–52.

can show a legitimate interest in the appointment of a receiver over a particular asset or class of assets outweighing the interest of the general body of the creditors. That could not be the case on the appointment of an administrative receiver, for since by definition he is receiver of the whole or substantially the whole of the company's property[91] his appointment would completely stultify the administrator's functions.

Self-help remedies unaffected by the moratorium

While there is a general prohibition on the institution of proceedings **10–66** without the consent of the administrator or the permission of the court,[92] the only self-help remedies falling within para.43 of Sch.B1 are those mentioned earlier, namely the taking of steps to enforce a security or to repossess goods in the company's possession under a hire-purchase agreement, the exercise of a right to forfeit a lease by peaceable re-entry, and the levying of a distress. The moratorium therefore does not cover exercise of a right of set-off or combination of accounts, a right to terminate or rescind a contract, accelerate monetary liability under a contract or give any other contractual notice.

It is not uncommon for contracts with a company to contain a provision terminating the contract, or empowering the other party to terminate it, on the company going into administration or an application being made for an administration order. This has caused concern among insolvency practitioners, who consider that such clauses are detrimental to the administration procedure and should be rendered void as contrary to the public interest. But if contractual provisions for the termination of a contract on winding-up are valid[93] it is hard to see that similar provisions relating to administration should be treated differently.

(ii) Interim moratorium pending entry of the company into administration

Whether a company enters into administration by an out-of-court appoint- **10–67** ment of an administrator or by court order, there will inevitably be some delay between the time the process leading to an administration is initiated and the time the administration begins except where, in the case of out-of-court appointment, there is no one to whom notice has to be given under para.26 of Sch.B1. The original statutory provisions, embodied in s.10 of the Insolvency Act, imposed a moratorium between the time a petition for

---

[91] *ibid.*, s.29(2).
[92] See paras 10–49 *et seq.*
[93] A matter discussed above, para.7–11.

an administration order was presented and the time the order was made or the petition dismissed. The new provisions are to similar effect[94] but they are extended to cover out-of-court administration. Where no notice is required under para.26 the appointor can proceed immediately to file a notice of appointment, so that in such a case no interim moratorium is necessary or available.

Moratorium pending disposal of administration application

10–68   Where an administration application has been made and has not yet been granted or dismissed or has been granted but has not yet taken effect[95] the interim moratorium imposed by paras 42 and 43 (ignoring any reference to the consent of the administrator) comes into play until the application is dismissed or the order takes effect,[96] whereupon the moratorium provisions already discussed, which for brevity will be described as "the full moratorium", become applicable directly under the provisions of those paragraphs. The scope of the interim moratorium is somewhat narrower than that of the full moratorium in two respects, reflecting the favoured position of the holder of a qualifying floating charge. First, if there is an administrative receiver of the company when the administration application is made, the provisions of paras 42 and 43 do not begin to apply until the person by or on behalf of whom the receiver was appointed consents to the making of the administration order.[97] So the administration application does not preclude the appointment of an administrative receiver, and indeed to make the position crystal clear para.44(6) expressly so provides. Secondly, the making of the application does not prevent or require the permission of the court for the appointment of an administrator by the holder of a qualifying floating charge or the appointment of an administrative receiver (where still permitted) or the carrying out by him (whenever appointed) of his functions.[98] This must by necessary implication cover all acts preparatory to the appointment of the receiver, for otherwise the dispensation given by para.44(6) of Sch.B1 would be rendered nugatory.

Since paras 42–44 are concerned only with the situation arising between the administration application and its disposal, during which time no administrator is yet in post, it is necessary to say a few words about the

---

[94] Though the petition has been replaced by an application and where an order is made the relevant time is when it takes effect, not when it is made. See below, para.10–71.

[95] This is a reference to the fact that the appointment of an administrator, and thus the commencement of the administration (Insolvency Act 1986, Sch.B1, para.1(2)(b)), takes effect at a time appointed by the order or where no time is appointed then when the order is made (Sch.B1, para.13(2)). Hence the court may fix a future time for the appointment to come into effect.

[96] *ibid.*, Sch.B1, para.44(5).

[97] *ibid.*, Sch.B1, para.44(6).

[98] *ibid.*, Sch.B1, para.44(7).

effect of the company's acquiescence in acts by the solvent party to exercise his rights.

(1) Enforcement of security

In relation to security it is only the taking of steps to *enforce* the security that is prohibited, from which it would seem to follow that the secured creditor remains free to take possession of the security or to realise it if he obtains the company's consent, given through its duly authorised officer or, if the company is under interim management pursuant to an order under para.13 of Sch.B1 to the Act, the interim manager.

10–69

(2) "repossess"

In contrast to the provisions relating to security, the restriction on repossession of goods held under a hire-purchase agreement is not expressed to be confined to *enforcement* of a right to repossess and at first sight appears to prevent even a repossession effected with the consent of the company. But it is thought that the restriction is intended to be limited to enforcement measures. There is no rational policy reason for distinguishing the exercise of title-retention rights from the exercise of security rights, and if the company, being still under its own management pending the hearing of the petition, wishes to surrender the goods, it seems pointless to involve the owner in the expense of an application to the court. It may be that the draftsman, in defining hire-purchase agreement and conditional sale agreement by reference to the Consumer Credit Act 1974, considered the word "repossess" to have the same meaning as "recover possession" in s.90(2) of that Act, but s.173(3) of the Consumer Credit Act makes it clear that repossession with consent of the debtor given at the time is lawful.

10–70

In either case, given the underlying purpose of the interim moratorium, which is to preserve the company's assets pending completion of steps to put the company into administration, the court is likely to look carefully at the reality of the company's consent where it is not under interim management, and a "consent" obtained under threat of other action, such as the presentation of a winding-up petition or the appointment of a receiver, may well be disregarded as not being a true consent.

Moratorium pending coming into effect of out-of-court appointment

The interim moratorium also comes into operation, and with the same effect, where a notice of intention to appoint an administrator has been filed by the holder of a qualifying floating charge or by the company or its directors. In the case of a notice filed by the holder of the charge the

10–71

moratorium lasts until the appointment of the administrator takes effect or the period of five business days beginning with the date of filing expires without an administrator having been appointed.[99] In the case of a notice filed by the company or its directors the moratorium continues until the appointment of the administrator takes effect or the period of ten business days beginning with the date of filing expires without an administrator having been appointed.[1]

As pointed out earlier, neither the administration application nor any resulting administration order affects substantive rights; its impact is on the exercise of remedies.[2] Similarly, filing of the notice of intention to appoint by the holder of a qualifying floating charge or by the company or the directors, leaves the directors' management powers unimpaired.[3] Further, in contrast to the position where a winding up petition is presented,[4] dispositions of the company's property made after the filing of an administration application do not require to be validated by the court.[5]

(iii) Interim moratorium pending proposal for a CVA for a small eligible company

10–72　This is considered later in the discussion of CVAs.[6]

(iv) The approach of the court to the exercise of discretion

The grant of leave during an interim moratorium

10–73　All the decisions on the grant of leave to enforce remedies under the old legislation concerned s.11(3) of the Insolvency Act, dealing with moratoria arising on the making of an administration order.[7] The relevant considerations are discussed below. What is not clear is the extent to which the same considerations apply on an application for leave made prior to administration and whether a further distinction is to be made between out-of-court

---

[99] Once the administrator has been appointed the full moratorium applies.
[1] Insolvency Act 1986, Sch.B1, paras 44(4), 28(2).
[2] See above, para.10–49.
[3] But once the application has come before the court (which it may on an abridged notice) it may make an interim order which could, among other things, restrict the exercise of a power of the directors and make provision conferring a discretion on a person qualified to act as an insolvency practitioner in relation to the company (Insolvency Act 1986, Sch.B1, para.13(3)). Under this power the court could appoint an interim manager.
[4] See Insolvency Act 1986, s.127, and below.
[5] But see n.3, above.
[6] Below, para.10–115.
[7] This is now to be found in para.43 of Sch.B1, which applies whether the administration is by court order or out-of-court.

appointments that have not yet taken effect and undisposed of administration applications. It is evident that in all cases the onus is on the applicant for leave to make out a case. But given that no administrator is yet in the saddle and that the information available to the court is likely to be less detailed than when the company has gone into administration it is thought that the court will be more reluctant to grant leave to enforce than when an administrator has taken office, particularly since most appointments will be out of court and the interval between the filing of a notice of intention to appoint and the appointment becoming effective will in many cases be relatively short, so that the court may consider that on balance the delay imposed on the creditor by refusing leave is outweighed by the desirability of allowing the administrator, when in post, an opportunity to consider to what extent the interests of the general body of creditors will be adversely affected by the grant of leave. For this purpose there seems no reason to distinguish prospective out-of-court appointments from prospective appointments by the court.

The grant of leave when the company is in administration

In deciding whether to grant leave under para.43 of Sch.B1 to take steps to enforce security, etc. and if so, on what terms, the court will have in mind the list of guidelines helpfully, if reluctantly, supplied by Nicholls L.J. in *Re Atlantic Computer Systems plc*.[8]

10–74

> "(1) It is in every case for the person who seeks leave to make out a case for him to be given leave.
> (2) The prohibition in section 11(3)(*c*) and (*d*)[9] is intended to assist the company, under the management of the administrator, to achieve the purpose for which the administration order was made. If granting leave to a lessor of land or the hirer of goods (a "lessor") to exercise his proprietary rights and repossess his land or goods is unlikely to impede the achievement of that purpose, leave should normally be given.
> (3) In other cases when a lessor seeks possession the court has to carry out a balancing exercise, balancing the legitimate interests of the lessor and the legitimate interests of the other creditors of the company: see *per* Peter Gibson J. in *Royal Trust Bank v Buchler* [1989] B.C.L.C. 130, 135. The metaphor employed here, for want of a better, is that of scales and weights. Lord Wilberforce adverted to the limitations of this metaphor in *Science Research Council v Nassáe* [1980] A.C. 1028, 1067. It must be kept

---

[8] [1992] Ch. 505 at 542–544.
[9] See now Sch.B1, para.43.

in mind that the exercise under section 11 is not a mechanical one; each case calls for an exercise in judicial judgment, in which the court seeks to give effect to the purpose of the statutory provisions, having regard to the parties' interests and all the circumstances of the case. As already noted, the purpose of the prohibition is to enable or assist the company to achieve the object for which the administration order was made. The purpose of the power to give leave is to enable the court to relax the prohibition where it would be inequitable for the prohibition to apply.

(4) In carrying out the balancing exercise great importance, or weight, is normally to be given to the proprietary interests of the lessor. Sir Nicolas Browne-Wilkinson V.-C. observed in *Bristol Airport Plc v Powdrill* [1990] Ch. 744, 767D-E that, so far as possible, the administration procedure should not be used to prejudice those who were secured creditors when the administration order was made in lieu of a winding up order. The same is true regarding the proprietary interests of a lessor. The underlying principle here is that an administration for the benefit of unsecured creditors should not be conducted at the expense of those who have proprietary rights which they are seeking to exercise, save to the extent that this may be unavoidable and even then this will usually be acceptable only to a strictly limited extent.

(5) Thus it will normally be a sufficient ground for the grant of leave if significant loss would be caused to the lessor by a refusal. For this purpose loss comprises any kind of financial loss, direct or indirect, including loss by reason of delay, and may extend to loss which is not financial. But if substantially greater loss would be caused to others by the grant of leave, or loss which is out of all proportion to the benefit which leave would confer on the lessor, that may outweigh the loss to the lessor caused by a refusal. Our formulation was criticised in the course of the argument, and we certainly do not claim for it the status of a rule in those terms. At present we say only that it appears to us the nearest we can get to a formulation of what Parliament had in mind.

(6) In assessing these respective losses the court will have regard to matters such as: the financial position of the company, its ability to pay the rental arrears and the continuing rentals, the administrator's proposals, the period for which the administration order has already been in force and is expected to remain in force, the effect on the administration if leave were given, the effect on the applicant if leave were refused, the end result sought to be achieved by the administration, the prospects of that result being achieved, and the history of the administration so far.

(7) In considering these matters it will often be necessary to assess how probable the suggested consequences are. Thus if loss to the applicant is virtually certain if leave is refused, and loss to others a remote possibility if leave is granted, that will be a powerful factor in favour of granting leave.

(8) This is not an exhaustive list. For example, the conduct of the parties may also be a material consideration in a particular case, as it was in the *Bristol Airport* case. There leave was refused on the ground that the applicants had accepted benefits under the administration, and had only sought to enforce their security at a later stage: indeed, they had only acquired their security as a result of the operations of the administrators. It behoves a lessor to make his position clear to the administrator at the outset of the administration and, if it should become necessary, to apply to the court promptly.

(9) The above considerations may be relevant not only to the decision whether leave should be granted or refused, but also to a decision to impose terms if leave is granted.

(10) The above considerations will also apply to a decision on whether to impose terms as a condition for refusing leave. Section 11(3)(c) and (d) makes no provision for terms being imposed if leave is refused, but the court has power to achieve that result. It may do so directly, by giving directions to the administrator: for instance, under section 17, or in response to an application by the administrator under section 14(3), or in exercise of its control over an administrator as an officer of the court. Or it may do so indirectly, by ordering that the applicant shall have leave unless the administrator is prepared to take this or that step in the conduct of the administration. Cases where leave is refused but terms are imposed can be expected to arise frequently. For example, the permanent loss to a lessor flowing from his inability to recover his property will normally be small if the administrator is required to pay the current rent. In most cases this should be possible, since if the administration order has been rightly made the business should generally be sufficiently viable to hold down current outgoings. Such a term may therefore be a normal term to impose.

(11) The above observations are directed at a case such as the present where a lessor of land or the owner of goods is seeking to repossess his land or goods because of non-payment of rentals. A broadly similar approach will be applicable on many applications to enforce a security: for instance, an application by a mortgagee for possession of land. On such applications an important consideration will often be whether the applicant is fully secured. If he is, delay in enforcement is likely to be less prejudicial than in cases where his security is insufficient.

(12) In some cases there will be a dispute over the existence, validity or nature of the security which the applicant is seeking leave to enforce. It is not for the court on the leave application to seek to adjudicate upon that issue, unless (as in the present case, on the fixed or floating charge point) the issue raises a short point of law which it is convenient to determine without further ado. Otherwise the court needs to be satisfied only that the applicant has a seriously arguable case."

All these factors arose in the context of applications for leave after the making of an administration order, which was the only form of administration under the old regime. There seems no reason why the same considerations should not be considered applicable to an out-of-court administration.

8. STATUS, POWERS AND AGENCY OF THE ADMINISTRATOR

Administrator compared with administrative receiver

10–75   There are close similarities between the functions of the administrator and those of the administrative receiver. The administrator has similar management functions and all the powers of the receiver,[10] together with certain powers which the receiver does not possess, in particular the power to remove and appoint directors and to call any meeting of the members or creditors of the company.[11] Like the receiver, the administrator is deemed to act as agent of the company in exercising his powers.[12] It follows that the powers he exercises as such agent cannot exceed those conferred on the company itself by its memorandum of association.[13] There are, however, important differences between the two posts. First, the administrator is appointed to protect the interests of the company and the general body of creditors, not a particular secured creditor. Secondly, whether appointed out of court or by the court he is an officer of the court.[14] Thirdly he is not personally liable on contracts he enters into or on employment contracts he adopts. Instead, the liabilities arising under such contracts[15] are charged on

---

[10] Insolvency Act 1986, Sch.B1, paras 59(1), 60, and Sch.1.
[11] Insolvency Act 1986, Sch.B1, para.61.
[12] *ibid.*, Sch.B1, para.69, and see below, para.10–84. In contrast to s.44(1)(a), dealing with receivers, Sch.B1, para.69 makes no reference to the termination of the administrator's agency on winding up. This is because there cannot be a winding up during the currency of an administration order.
[13] *Re Home Treat Ltd* [1991] B.C.L.C. 705. An administrator who exceeds those powers may be able to claim relief under s.727 of the Companies Act 1985 where he has acted honestly and reasonably and ought fairly to be excused *(ibid.)*.
[14] Insolvency Act 1986, Sch.B1, para.5.
[15] See *ibid.*, Sch.B1, paras 99(5), (6), and above, paras 10–93, 10–94.

and payable out of any property of the company in his custody or under his control in priority to his remuneration and expenses.[16] Finally, he enjoys the benefit of the statutory moratorium on enforcement of creditors' rights and remedies, a benefit not available to a receiver.

Powers of the administrator

The administrator enjoys a wide range of powers. Many of these relate to the general conduct of the administration. There are then separate provisions relating to the power to dispose of property[17] and to make distributions.[18] The former deal respectively with the disposition of property subject to a floating charge, property subject to other forms of security and property subject to a hire-purchase agreement, which for this purpose includes a conditional sale agreement, a chattel leasing agreement and a retention of title agreement.[19]   **10–76**

(1) Conduct of the administration generally

The administrator may: **10–77**

(1)   do anything necessary or expedient for the management of the affairs, business and property of the company[20];

(2)   without prejudice to the generality of the above, exercise the powers specified in Sch.1 to the Insolvency Act (which are the powers also conferred on an administrative receiver)[21];

(3)   remove a director of the company and appoint a director of the company, whether to fill a vacancy or otherwise[22];

(4)   call a meeting of members or creditors of the company[23];

(5)   apply to the court for directions in connection with his functions[24];

(6)   make a distribution to secured and preferential creditors and, with the permission of the court, to unsecured creditors.[25]

---

[16] *ibid.*, Sch.B1, para.99(4).
[17] *ibid.*, Sch.B1, paras 70–72.
[18] *ibid.*, Sch.B1, para.65.
[19] *ibid.*, Sch.B1, para.111(1).
[20] *ibid.*, Sch.B1, para.59(1).
[21] *ibid.*, Sch.B1, para.60.
[22] *ibid.*, Sch.B1, para.61.
[23] *ibid.*, Sch.B1, para.62.
[24] *ibid.*, Sch.B1, para.63.
[25] *ibid.*, Sch.B1, para.65.

If the court gives directions to the administrator in connection with any aspect of his management of the company's affairs[26]1 the administrator must comply with them but subject to this he is required to manage the company's affairs in accordance with any proposals approved at the initial creditors' meeting and revision of such proposals.[27] The administrator may dispose of assets prior to the creditors' meeting if he considers it expedient to do so, but if time allows he should wherever possible put a proposal for such disposal to the creditors. If he is in doubt he can apply to the court, who in a proper case will sanction the disposal, but the court will also be mindful that the effect of its order will be to make the creditors' meeting a complete *brutum fulmen* and may therefore decide that it is for the administrator to exercise his own judgment and assume the risk.[28]

(2) Power to dispose of property subject to a floating charge

10–78 In addition to the powers just enumerated the administrator may dispose of or take action relating to property which is subject to a floating charge[29] as if it were not subject to the charge.[30] Where property is disposed of in reliance on this power the holder of the floating charge has the same priority in respect of acquired property as he had in respect of the property disposed of.[31] By "acquired property" is meant property of the company which directly or indirectly represents the property disposed of.[32] In other words, the priority previously enjoyed in relation to the property disposed of carries through to its products or proceeds.

(3) Power to dispose of property subject to other security

10–79 The administrator may, with the permission of the court,[33] dispose of property subject to a security other than a floating charge as if it were not subject to the security,[34] the court's power to grant permission being

---

[26] This wording puts it beyond doubt that the administrator does not require leave of the court to dispose of the company's assets. See *Re Transbus International Ltd* [2004] 2 B.C.L.C. 550. The point was unclear in the previous wording (which required the administrator to manage the business "in accordance with any directions given by the court"), but was interpreted in the same sense by the court (*Re T. & D. Industries plc* [2000] 1 W.L.R. 646).

[27] Insolvency Act 1986, Sch.B1, para.68(2), (1).

[28] *Re T. & D. Industries plc* [2000] 1 W.L.R. 646, in which the authorities are reviewed; *Re Consumer & Industrial Press Ltd (No.2)* (1987) 4 B.C.C. 72, where Peter Gibson J. declined to make the order requested on the ground that it would frustrate the purpose of the creditors' meeting. In later cases, including *Re T. & D. Industries*, the courts have been more sympathetic to the position of the administrator in seeking leave.

[29] "Floating charge" means a charge which as created was a floating charge (Insolvency Act 1986, s.251), so that the administrator's power of disposal free from the charge is not affected by the fact that it has crystallised.

[30] Insolvency Act 1986, Sch.B1, para.70(1).

[31] *ibid.*, Sch.B1, para.70(2).

[32] *ibid.*, Sch.B1, para.70(3).

[33] There is obviously no need to obtain leave if the chargee or title-reserving owner consents.

[34] Insolvency Act 1986, Sch.B1, para.71(1).

exercisable only on the application of the administrator and only where it is satisfied that the disposal would be likely to promote the purpose of administration in respect of the company.[35] Any such order is subject to the same conditions for the protection of secured or retention of title creditors as has been previously mentioned[36] in relation to administrative receivers.[37] Since the investigation of individual claims by those asserting reservation of title rights is arduous and time-consuming, there is considerable advantage in obtaining a global order for leave to sell assets subject to reservation of title, leaving the validity of individual claims to be examined afterwards.

(4) Power to dispose of goods held under a hire-purchase agreement

The court may by order enable the administrator to dispose of goods in the possession of the company under a hire-purchase agreement[38] as if the rights of the owner under the agreement were vested in the company in the same circumstances and subject to the same conditions as on the disposal of property subject to fixed charge.[39]

10–80

(5) Power to make a distribution

Under the old regime the administrator's powers did not as a general rule include the distribution of assets or dividends to creditors even with their consent,[40] except pursuant to an approved voluntary arrangement under Part I of the Insolvency Act or a compromise or sanction under s.425 of the Companies Act 1985.[41] Even the powers of the court were circumscribed, though in exceptional cases the administrator could obtain the approval of the court to the exercise of his powers under item 13 of Sch.1 to the Act to make a payment by way of distribution to preferential and ordinary unsecured creditors.[42] Now the position is much easier. The administrator can make a distribution to secured and preferential creditors without leave and the court is given a general discretion, previously lacking, to permit a distribution to unsecured creditors.[43] However, where the company is to

10–81

---

[35] *ibid.*, Sch.B1, para.71(2).
[36] See para.9–45 above. The requirement that the net proceeds of sale of a fixed security be applied towards discharging the sums secured covers not only the principal outstanding but interest and costs which the secured creditor is entitled to add to his security (*Morris & Atkinson v 3i plc and the Development Commission* July 27, 1988, Knox J.).
[37] Insolvency Act 1986, s.43(3).
[38] See above n.36.
[39] Insolvency Act 1986, Sch.B1, para.72.
[40] *Re St. Ives Windings Ltd* (1987) 3 B.C.C. 634.
[41] *ibid.*, *per* Harman J., expressing a provisional view only.
[42] *Re John Slack Ltd* [1995] B.C.C. 1116; *Re WBSL 1992 Realisations Ltd* [1995] B.C.C. 1118.
[43] Insolvency Act 1986, Sch.B1, para.65. See above, para.10–77.

continue trading it will almost always be easier and less expensive to arrange distributions through a CVA.[44] This avoids the cost attendant on applications to the court, with all the information that will be required and the problem of securing the consent of creditors, which is much more easily organised within a CVA. Moreover, the latter is very flexible, and so long as the rights of enforcement of secured creditors and the priority of preferential creditors are not adversely affected without their consent, almost anything can be agreed within a CVA. Among the matters that can be included in a CVA that would not usually be appropriate for a distribution order are compromises, dispute resolution mechanisms such as arbitration or expert determination and the setting of time limits for claims. Alternatively, but usually less conveniently, a distribution can be made pursuant to a compromise or arrangement under s.425 of the Companies Act 1985.

Where he does make a distribution the administrator must not pay debts secured by a floating charge without first satisfying the claims of preferential creditors[45] and setting aside the prescribed part for ordinary unsecured creditors[46] but this requirement may be disapplied by the CVA or the compromise or arrangement.[47] Since in making distributions to creditors the administrator is performing a function similar to that of a liquidator, the same machinery for proofs, quantification of claims and declaration of dividends, together with a rule for *pari passu* distribution, is now provided by the Insolvency Rules 1986.[48]

Displacement of directors' powers

10–82   The powers conferred on the company or its officers by the Insolvency Act, the Companies Act 1985 or the memorandum or articles of association are not exercisable, except with the administrator's consent,[49] so far as they could be exercised in such a way as to interfere with his exercise of his powers.[50] The practical effect of this provision is similar to the effect of administrative receivership, in that the directors are almost entirely divested of their powers, for the question is not whether the intended exercise of their powers will or might interfere with the administrator's exercise of his own powers but whether they *could* be exercised in such a way. The directors have a duty to co-operate with the administrator,[51] and

---

[44] Where the business is to end or be disposed of, it may be easier to put the company into a creditors' voluntary winding-up. See below, para.10–104.

[45] Insolvency Act 1986, s.175, as applied by Sch.B1, para.65(2).

[46] *ibid.*, s.176A. See above, para.6–31.

[47] *ibid.*, s.176A(4).

[48] Insolvency Rules 1986, Part 2, Chapter 10.

[49] Which may be either general or specific.

[50] Insolvency Act 1986, Sch.B1, para.64. As to the power to remove directors, see above, para.10–77.

[51] *ibid.*, s.235.

breach of this duty renders them liable to disqualification.[52] A director can at present be required to answer questions put to him by the administrator even if his answers are self-incriminating,[53] but these can no longer be used in subsequent criminal proceedings.[54] This follows a ruling by the European Court of Human Rights that to require self-incrimination is a breach of the European Convention on Human Rights.[55] On the other hand, incriminating material in documentary or other evidence which is independently obtainable may be given in evidence in subsequent criminal proceedings even though it is located as the result of compelled testimony.[56]

Protection of third parties

A person dealing with an administrator in good faith and for value need not inquire whether the administrator is acting within his powers.[57] In view of the width of those powers a third party will not usually find it necessary to invoke the statutory protection. Possible cases where he might are where the administrator disposes of property subject to a fixed security without leave of the court or without complying with the conditions on which leave is granted or where he concludes a contract or makes a transfer which is not in accordance with the proposals approved by the creditors.

10–83

The administrator as agent

In exercising his powers the administrator acts as the company's agent.[58] But as in the case of an administrative receiver the agency is only notional, so that it is not competent to the company to terminate it; the administrator is not subject to the control of the company or directors but on the contrary controls the company, a point reinforced by para.64(2) of Sch.B1 to the Insolvency Act and by his power under para.61 to appoint and remove directors; and his fiduciary and other duties to the company are subordinate to his statutory duties as administrator.

10–84

Payments by the administrator

Though it is not within the normal powers of an administrator to make distributions to ordinary unsecured creditors except with the permission of the court[59] or as part of an approved arrangement,[60] he may make a

10–85

---

[52] Company Directors Disqualification Act 1986, ss.6, 9, and Sch.1, para.10(g).
[53] *Bishopsgate Investments Ltd v Maxwell* [1993] Ch. 1.
[54] Youth Justice and Criminal Evidence Act 1999, s.59 and Sch.3, para.7(3)(a). But they may still be used to disqualify a director (*ibid.*, para.8(3)(a)(i)).
[55] *Saunders v United Kingdom* (1997) 23 E.H.R.R. 313.
[56] *Attorney-General's Reference (No.7 of 2000)* [2001] 1 W.L.R. 1879.
[57] Insolvency Act 1986, Sch.B1, para.59(3).
[58] *ibid.*, Sch.B1, para.69. As to the administrator's liabilities see below, paras 10–93 *et seq.*
[59] See below, para.10–86.
[60] See above, para.10–81.

payment otherwise than in accordance with para.65 (that is, otherwise than by way of a distribution) or with item 13 of Sch.1 if he thinks it likely to assist achievement of the purpose of the administration.[61] Item 13 confers a more restricted power to make any payment which is necessary or incidental to the performance of his functions, and this may justify a "duress" payment to prevent termination of a contract or forfeiture of a lease or even, in exceptional cases, an application to the court to authorise a distribution to creditors.[62] A utility supplier is entitled, as the condition of continuing supply, to require the administrator personally to guarantee payment but is not entitled to impose a condition that charges outstanding at the date of the administration are paid.[63]

Business documents

10–86 While a company is in administration, every business document issued by or on behalf of the company must state (a) the name of the administrator and (b) that the affairs and the property of the company are being managed by him.[64] By "business document" is meant an invoice, an order for goods or services and a business letter.[65] If without reasonable excuse the administrator, an officer of the company or the company itself authorises or permits a contravention of such requirement, that person commits an offence.[66] Since a company in administration is not a free agent, it is hard to see how it could authorise or permit anything! Interestingly, though the administrator's failure to state that the company is in administration could mislead a supplier of goods or services the Act does not make the administrator personally liable on the contract.[67] In practice the supplier will usually be adequately protected by the fact that he enjoys a super-priority.[68]

Administrator's remuneration and expenses

10–87 The provisions governing the administrator's expenses and remuneration are contained in para.99 of Sch.B1, which rather strangely is confined to cases where he has ceased to be the administrator. However, the courts have rejected any implication that the administrator has to wait until after

---

[61] Insolvency Act 1986, Sch.B1, para.66.
[62] See below, para.10–86.
[63] Insolvency Act 1986, s.233(2).
[64] *ibid.*, Sch.B1, para.45(1).
[65] *ibid.*, para.45(3).
[66] *ibid.*, para.45(2).
[67] The administrator is not otherwise liable on contracts he enters into as agent of the company. See below, para.10–93.
[68] *ibid.*, para.99(4). See below, para.10–93.

his appointment has ended before recouping his remuneration and expenses and have held that he is entitled to recover these as the administration proceeds, the statutory provisions being read as dealing only with expenses and remuneration not previously recovered.[69] In recovering his expenses and remuneration the administrator is not entitled to resort to assets that are not the property of the company and his rights are subordinate to those of a holder of a fixed mortgage or charge but take priority over claims secured by a floating charge, which are also subject to the setting aside of the prescribed part. The ranking of the administrator's entitlement to expenses and remuneration from assets of the company not subject to a fixed security is thus as follows.

(1) Sums payable in respect of a debt or liability arising under a contract made by the administrator or a predecessor, or a contract of employment adopted by the administrator or a predecessor, before cessation of his appointment.[70]

(2) The administrator's remuneration and expenses,[71] which as between themselves rank in the order set out in r.2.67(1) of the Insolvency Rules.[72]

(3) The prescribed part which the administrator is required to set aside for ordinary unsecured creditors from assets subject to a floating charge, if created on or after September 15, 2003, and remaining after preferential debts have been paid.[73]

(4) Sums payable to the chargee under the floating charge.

9. DUTIES AND LIABILITIES OF THE ADMINISTRATOR

No common law duty of care to unsecured creditors

In the absence of some special relationship an administrator owes no general common law duty of care to unsecured creditors any more than a director of a company owes a duty of care to its shareholders.[74] The

10–88

---

[69] *Re Atlantic Computer Systems plc* [1992] Ch. 505; *Re Salmet International Ltd* [2001] B.C.C. 796.

[70] Insolvency Act 1986, Sch.B1, para.99(4), (5).

[71] *ibid.*, Sch.B1, para.99(3), (4).

[72] From which it will be seen that in a list of nine items the administrator's remuneration ranks last but one. The moral, of course, is to accept an appointment as administrator only where the assets remaining after payment of the contractual claims having priority under Sch.B1, para.99(4) and the expenses listed in the Insolvency Rules, r.2.67, are likely to be amply sufficient to cover the administrator's remuneration.

[73] Insolvency Act 1986, s.176A(2), so far as not disapplied under s.176A(3), (4) or (5). See above, para.6–31.

[74] *Kyrris v Oldham* [2004] 1 B.C.L.C. 305.

interests of the creditors are mediated through the administrator's duties to the company.

Duties owed to the company

10–89 Under para.3(2) of Sch.B1 to the Insolvency Act 1986 the administrator must perform his functions in the interests of the company's creditors as a whole. An administrator guilty of misapplication of the company's property or of misfeasance or breach of a fiduciary or other duty to the company in the conduct of the administration could formerly have been the subject of summary proceedings under s.212 of the Insolvency Act 1986 if the company was in winding-up. But in relation to administrators this section no longer applies and has been replaced by para.75 of Sch.B1, which is to similar effect except that it is no longer necessary for the company to be in winding-up. In addition, under para.74 of Sch.B1 a creditor or member of the company may apply to the court claiming that:

(a) the administrator is acting or has acted so as unfairly to harm the interests of the applicant (whether alone or in common with some or all other members or creditors), or

(b) the administrator proposes to act in a way which would unfairly harm the interests of the applicant (whether alone or in common with some or all other members of creditors).

It is neither necessary nor sufficient to the grant of relief under para.74 that the administrator has acted unlawfully or in breach of some legal duty to the applicant. For those breaches other remedies are available. What has to be shown is unfairness or threatened unfairness to the applicant in a manner which prejudices his interests.[75]

In fulfilling his functions the administrator must give thought to all relevant considerations and his decisions must be properly informed.[76] If he does this, the court will not seek to substitute its own judgment for the considered commercial judgment of the administrator. However, the administrator must not neglect to take account of the role of the creditors and any creditors' committee, and is well advised to consult them on major issues where time permits.

Taking control of the company's property

10–90 On his appointment the administrator must take custody or control of all the property to which he thinks the company is entitled.[77] The phrase "thinks the company is entitled" implies that the administrator is to be

---

[75] *Re Charnley Davies (No.2)* [1990] B.C.L.C. 760, based on the former s.27 of the Act, which referred to conduct "prejudicial" to the petitioner. ". . . unfairly to harm", the phrase used in Sch.B1, para.74, is intended to be a more homely way of saying the same thing.

[76] For a useful development of the fiduciary's obligations in this regard see Mokal, *op., cit.,* pp.237 *et seq.*

[77] Insolvency Act 1986, Sch.B1, para.67.

immune from liability if he takes control of property later found to belong to a third party, and the immunity is made express by s.234(4)(a) of the Act, though obviously it endures only for so long as the company remains actually or apparently entitled to the property. The administrator's powers in relation to the collecting in of property are similar to those of a liquidator, and he may bring proceedings in conversion against a person who takes possession of the company's property pursuant to a charge which is void for want of registration under s.395 of the Companies Act 1985 and may invoke the summary remedy provided by s.234 of the Insolvency Act 1986 to recover the property in question.[78]

Carrying on the business

Before the approval of his proposals by the creditors the administrator must manage the affairs, business and property of the company in accordance with such directions, if any, as may be given by the court, and after such approval, in accordance with those proposals.[79] If the company does not have adequate working capital the administrator may need to negotiate with the bank to obtain this. The administrator ought not, in general, to dispose of substantial assets until his proposals have been considered by the creditors, but in cases of urgency he may do so where this is in the interests of creditors and, depending on the circumstances, the court may be willing to protect him by an order expressly authorising the disposition.[80] In carrying on the business the administrator owes the company a duty of care and fiduciary duties of good faith, subordination of personal interests, and the like, but only so far as consistent with his statutory duties.

10–91

Making applications to the court

The administrator has a general power to apply to the court for directions,[81] and may at any time apply for his appointment to cease to have effect from a specified time.[82] He is obliged to make such an application if it appears to him that the purpose of administration cannot be achieved or the company should not have entered administration or if he is required to make an application by a creditors' meeting or, in the case of a court administration, he thinks its purpose has been sufficiently achieved in relation to the

10–92

---

[78] *Smith v Bridgend County Borough Council* [2002] 1 A.C. 336.
[79] See above, para.10–77.
[80] See above, para.10–77.
[81] Insolvency Act 1986, Sch.B1, para.63. The court may in addition give directions under para.63 within the limits permitted by sub-para.(3).
[82] *ibid.*, Sch.B1, para.79(1).

company.[83] In the case of an out-of-court appointment, if the administrator thinks the purpose of the administration has been so achieved he can simply file a notice with the court and the registrar of companies, upon which his appointment ceases to have effect.[84]

Position of the administrator in relation to new contracts

10–93 In considering liabilities arising under new contracts it is necessary to distinguish contracts entered into by the administrator personally from those entered into by the company through the administrator. If for the benefit of the administration the administrator enters into a contract in his own name—which could happen because that is the only basis upon which the other party is willing to deal—he is personally liable on the contract but has a right to be indemnified by the company. The administrator incurs no personal liability on new contracts which he enters into as agent for the company except where he agrees to assume such liability. Accordingly it is only the company which incurs a liability on such contracts. In this respect the administrator is much less vulnerable than the administrative receiver, who is personally liable on contracts entered into by him, whether in his own name or in the name of the company.[85] By para.99(4) of Sch.B1 to the Insolvency Act, any sums payable in respect of debts or liabilities incurred while he was administrator under contracts entered into by him or a predecessor of his in the carrying out of his or the predecessor's functions are charged on any property of the company which is in his possession or under his control, and he has a duty to ensure that these are paid in priority to his own remuneration and expenses,[86] which are themselves charged on and payable out of the company's property and are payable in priority to claims secured by a floating charge[87] but not by a fixed charge. Apart from the administrator's own remuneration the charge on the company's property under para.99(4) is given only to secure contractual liabilities incurred by or in the name of the company, not liabilities incurred by the administrator personally.

A recent addition to r.2.67 has clarified the relationship between para.99(3) and r.2.67 of the Insolvency Rules, which prescribes the priority of the expenses of the administration.[88] Rule 2.67(4)[89] provides that for the purposes of para.99(3) the former administrator's remuneration and

---

[83] *ibid.*, Sch.B1, para.79(2), (3).
[84] *ibid.*, Sch.B1, para.80.
[85] *ibid.*, s.44(1)(b); and see above, paras 9–49 *et seq.*
[86] *ibid.*, Sch.B1, para.99(4).
[87] *ibid.*, Sch.B1, para.99(3).
[88] In so doing it has also resolved the question raised in *Re Allders Department Stores Ltd* [2005] 2 All E.R. (D) 122.
[89] Added by the Insolvency (Amendment) Rules 2005 (SI 2005/527), r.8.

expenses comprise all the items set out in r.2.67(1). The effect is that all such items are charged on the company's property in priority to any floating charge and as between themselves are to be paid in the order prescribed by r.2.67(1) unless varied by the court under r.2.67(3), but all of them are subordinate to the charge under para.99(4) covering contractual liabilities incurred by the company after it has entered administration. This gives the claims of post-administration creditors a super-priority which ranks them above the expenses of the administration. Redundancy payments and payments for unfair dismissal are not within para.99, nor do they constitute "necessary disbursements" within r.2.67(1)(f).[90]

If the administrator fails or declines to procure the company's performance of a contract the company incurs a liability to the other party in damages but the administrator would not, though if he acts in wanton disregard of the company's interests, due account being taken of his overriding statutory duties, he may be liable to the company for any legal liability and other loss it incurs. He may also be restrained by injunction from acting in this way.[91]

Position of the administrator in relation to existing contracts

(1) Contracts in general

The entry of the company into administration does not terminate contracts entered into by the company except where the contract in question so provides.[92] Moreover, the administrator incurs no personal liability either for sums accruing due post-administration under continuing contracts or for sums accrued due prior to the commencement of the administration. However, if the administrator adopts the contract for the benefit of the administration then the *Lundy Granite* principle applicable in winding-up[93] would seem to apply here too, so as to make post-adoption liabilities an expense of the administration within para.2.67(1)(a) of the Insolvency Rules ranking at the head of the list but subordinate to the claims of post-administration creditors under para.99(4). Further, contrary to what had previously been thought,[94] this would not be a matter of discretion but of the application of r.2.67.[95]

10–94

---

[90] *Re Allders Department Stores Ltd*, above. The same is true of protective awards and claims for payment in lieu of notice. See *Re Ferrotech*, unreported, August 9, 2005, CA, reversing the decision of Peter Smith J. in *Krasner v McMath* [2005] EWHC 1682 (Ch.), July 27, 2005.

[91] *Astor Chemicals Ltd v Synthetic Technology Ltd* [1990] B.C.C. 97.

[92] As is not uncommon.

[93] Namely that where the liquidator procures the company to continue in occupation of leased premises for the benefit of the winding-up the rent is payable as an expense of the liquidation in priority to other claims. See above, paras 7–23, 7–25.

[94] *Re Atlantic Computer Systems plc* [1992] Ch. 505 *per* Sir Donald Nicholls V.C. at 523.

[95] *Re Toshoku Finance UK plc* [2002] 1 W.L.R. 671, a decision of the House of Lords on expenses of a liquidation.

Administration is not a bar to the termination of the contract by the other party,[96] so that if the administrator wishes to avoid termination he will usually need to discharge accruing liabilities as they fall due and may also have to pay arrears accrued prior to the company's entry into administration. Such payments are expressly authorized by para.66 of Sch.B1.

(2) Rent under leases of premises or equipment

10–95   If follows that the administrator is entitled, without incurring personal liability for either accrued or accruing sums, to procure or allow the company to continue to occupy premises held on lease and to use equipment held on lease, conditional sale or hire-purchase, so long as the lease or agreement is current. The lessor of premises cannot sue for rent or other payments, levy distress or exercise a right of forfeiture by peaceful re-entry without the consent of the administrator or the permission of the court,[97] nor can the owner of equipment supplied on hire-purchase[98] take any step to repossess it without such consent or permission.[99] Here again, the *Lundy Granite* principle would seem to apply so as to entitle the lessor to recover rentals as they fall due where the premises are occupied for the beneficial conduct of the administration,[1] and the administrator may in any event feel constrained to continue payments under the lease in order to avoid the risk of forfeiture or an application by the lessor or other creditor for leave to enforce its rights or alternatively for relief under para.74(1)(b) of Sch.B1 on the ground of unfair harm to the lessor.

Liability in conversion

10–96   Where goods are held under a hire-purchase agreement[2] the administrator is entitled to retain and use it for the proper purpose of the administration, in which case the rentals become an expense of the administration and are payable in full as they become due. But the administrator is not entitled to keep and use the goods otherwise than for the proper purpose of the administration, so that if he retains possession of the goods where he has no intention of using the goods for the purpose of the administration or that purpose cannot be achieved and he refuses to deliver up the goods to

---

[96] See above, para.10–66.
[97] Insolvency Act 1986, Sch.B1, para.43(4).
[98] As to the meaning of "hire-purchase", see above, para.10–59.
[99] Insolvency Act 1986, Sch.B1, para.43(3).
[1] See above, para.10–94.
[2] For the extended meaning of "hire-purchase agreement" in this context, see above, para.10–59.

the owner or uses them for a purpose other than the administration he liable in conversion.[3] The moratorium does not mean that the owner lacks the immediate right to possession necessary to found a claim for conversion; it is merely the remedy that is suspended.[4] But it is not necessary to obtain leave to bring proceedings for conversion; the more appropriate way of dealing with the matter is to apply to the court in the administration for compensation for the administrator's wrongful detention or use and for an order for return of the goods.[5]

10. THE ADMINISTRATOR'S PROPOSALS

Requirements relating to proposals

Having armed himself with the requisite information from the statement of affairs and other sources the administrator must then prepare a statement setting out proposals for achieving the purpose of administration[6] and send a copy to the registrar of companies and every creditor and member of whose address he is aware.[7] This must be done as soon as is reasonably practicable after the company has entered administration, with a maximum time limit that has been shortened from a maximum of three months to a maximum of eight weeks[8] subject to extension.[9] This is part of a general tightening up of the rules on time in order to accelerate the administration process. The statement of proposals must be accompanied by an invitation to attend the initial creditors' meeting at which these are to be considered,[10] and the date set for this meeting must be as soon as reasonably practicable after the company enters administration and in any event within the period of ten weeks beginning with the date on which the company enters administration.[11] Both time limits may be varied by the court on an

10–97

---

[3] *Barclays Mercantile Business Finance Ltd v Sibec Ltd* [1992] 1 W.L.R. 1253.
[4] *ibid.*
[5] *ibid.*
[6] And, where applicable, explain in the statement why he thinks that the objective mentioned in para.3(1)(a) or (b) of Sch.B1 cannot be achieved. The statement must contain the particulars prescribed by r.2.33 of the Insolvency Rules 1986.
[7] *ibid.*, Sch.B1, para.49(4).
[8] *ibid.*, Sch.B1, para.49(5)(a), (b).
[9] *ibid.*, paras 107, 108.
[10] *ibid.*, Sch.B1, para.51(1).
[11] *ibid.*, Sch.B1, para.51(2). The meeting cannot be held where the statement of proposals states that the administrator thinks that the company has sufficient property to enable each creditor to be paid in full or has insufficient property to enable a distribution to be made to unsecured creditors other than by virtue of s.176A(2)(a) (which relates to the prescribed part—see above, para.6–31) or neither of the first two objectives of para.3 of Sch.B1 can be achieved. But creditors of the company whose debts amount to at least 10% of the total may require the administrator to summon an initial creditors' meeting (*ibid.*, Sch.B1, para.52).

application of the administrator[12] or by up to 28 days with the consent of the creditors.[13] At the meeting the administrator must present his proposals to the creditors, who may approve them without modification or approve them with modification to which the administrator consents.[14] The creditors may not modify the proposals without the consent of the administrator. The proposals may include a proposal for a CVA under Part I of the Insolvency Act 1986 or a compromise or arrangement under s.425 of the Companies Act 1985,[15] but may not include any action which affects the right of a secured creditor to enforce his security or would result in a preferential debt of the company losing its priority to non-preferential debts or would result in one preferential creditor being paid a smaller proportion of his debt than another,[16] except in either case where the creditor consents or the proposal is for a CVA or for a compromise or arrangement under s.425 of the Companies Act 1985.[1] The administrator may propose a revision to the proposals and must then submit the revised proposals to a creditors' meeting summoned by him if he thinks the proposed revision is substantial.[18]

Consultation with creditors

10–98   In advance of the creditors' meeting the administrator is well advised to consult with major creditors over any significant action he proposes to take, e.g. sale of a substantial asset or the conclusion of a compromise on behalf of the company.

The creditors' meeting and decision on the proposals

10–99   In presenting the proposals to creditors the administrator should bear in mind any need for confidentiality *vis-à-vis* third parties, *e.g.* as to the identity of a prospective purchaser and the price to be paid. It is standard practice for members of a creditors' committee to be required to execute confidentiality agreements when they are appointed. In addition, steps need to be taken to ensure that bondholders do not make use of price-sensitive information in trading their bonds. The creditors may approve the proposals without modification or may modify them, but each modification

---

[12] ibid , Sch.B1, para.107.
[13] *ibid.*, para.108.
[14] *ibid.*, Sch.B1, para.53(1).
[15] *ibid.*, Sch.B1, para.49(3). As to CVAs, see below, paras 10–106 *et seq.*
[16] *ibid.*, Sch.B1, para.73(1).
[17] The exclusion of proposals in a CVA appears to have no significance other than the avoidance of duplication, since s.4 of the Act precludes both a proposal which affects the enforcement rights of a secured creditor (a provision expressly reserved by s.73(2)(b)) and one which alters the priority, etc., of a preferential creditor.
[18] *ibid.*, Sch.B1, para.54.

requires the administrator's consent.[19] If a scheme of arrangement provided for in the proposals and approved by the creditors proves fruitless and the proposals do not specify what is to happen in that eventuality, the court may sanction a substitute scheme, since this is filling a gap rather than overriding a positive decision by the creditors.[20] Where the proposals are for a CVA they may nominate the administrator himself as the intended supervisor.[21]

Voting

The majority required to pass a resolution to approve proposals put forward by the administrator depends on whether or not the proposal is for a CVA. This has been discussed earlier.[22] Votes are calculated according to the amount of the creditor's claim as at the date on which the company entered administration, less any payments that have been made to him after that date in respect of his claim and any adjustment by way of set-off in accordance with r.2.85 as if that rule were applied on the date that the votes are counted.[23]

10–100

11. TERMINATION OF THE APPOINTMENT AND THE ADMINISTRATION

Cessation of office

An administrator ceases to hold office on death,[24] on resignation in conformity with the Insolvency Rules,[25] on removal by the court,[26] on substitution of another administrator[27] or on his appointment ceasing to have effect under other provisions,[28] of which the most significant is the provision that the appointment of an administrator comes to an end automatically after the period of one year beginning with the date on which it takes effect unless the administrator's term of office is extended by the court[29] or by consent of the creditors.[30] In addition, the administrator is

10–101

---

[19] *ibid.*, para.53(1)(b).
[20] *Re Smallman Construction Ltd* (1988) 4 B.C.C. 784, Knox J.
[21] See below, para.10–133.
[22] Above, para.10–38. See further para.10–120, below, as to voting on a proposed CVA.
[23] Insolvency Rules 1986, r.2.38(4). As to voting by a secured creditor, see r.2.40.
[24] Insolvency Act 1986, Sch.B1, para.99(1).
[25] *ibid.*, Sch.B1, para.87; Insolvency Rules 1986, rr.2.119-2.121.
[26] *ibid.*, Sch.B1, para.88.
[27] Under *ibid.*, Sch.B1, para.96 or 97.
[28] See *ibid.*, Sch.B1, paras 76, 79(1), 80(3), 81(1), 82(3), 83(6)(a), 84(4). The grounds for cessation of office are also set out in general form in para.99(1).
[29] *ibid.*, Sch.B1, para.76(2)(a).
[30] *ibid.*, Sch.B1, paras 76(2)(b), 78.

required to vacate office if he ceases to be qualified to act as an insolvency practitioner in relation to the company.[31] A new procedure introduced by the Enterprise Act 2002 for bringing administration to an end is an application by a creditor for the administrator's appointment to cease to have effect on the ground of improper motive on the part of the applicant for the administration order, in the case of a court appointment, or of the person appointing the administrator, in the case of an out-of-court appointment.[32] The court has a wide discretion as to the orders it can make.[33]

Effect of administrator's ceasing to hold office

10–102   It is necessary to distinguish cases where an administrator vacates office by reason of resignation, death, removal by order of the court or disqualification from acting as an insolvency practitioner in relation to the company from cases where the administrator's appointment ceases to have effect.[34] None of the events in the first of these categories affects the continuance of the administration,[35] it merely necessitates the appointment of a new administrator. By contrast, when the appointment of an administrator ceases to have effect the administration comes to an end.[36]

12. EXITS FROM ADMINISTRATION

10–103   Under the new regime there is a greater range of exits from administration than was formerly the case. These include a CVA under Part I of the Insolvency Act,[37] a compromise or arrangement under s.425 of the Companies Act 1985,[38] a distribution within the administration with the permission of the court,[39] a creditors' voluntary winding-up,[40] a compulsory winding-up[41] and a dissolution of the company without first going into winding-up.[42] This last is appropriate where there are no assets to distribute. In other cases, the most likely outcome of administration is a

---

[31] *ibid.*, Sch.B1, para.89(1). It would seem that his period of office ends automatically on his becoming disqualified. Note that the administrator is required to vacate office if he ceases to be qualified "in relation to the company", which means that he must continue not only to be qualified generally but also to be appropriately bonded in relation to the company (*ibid.*, s.390(3)).

[32] *ibid.*, Sch.B1, para.81(1), (2).

[33] *ibid.*, para.81(3).

[34] See the provisions referred to in n.295 above.

[35] Insolvency Act 1986, Sch.B1, para.1(2)(d).

[36] *ibid.*, Sch.B1, para.1(2)(c).

[37] *ibid.*, Sch.B1, para.49(3)(a).

[38] *ibid.*, Sch.B1, para.49(3)(b).

[39] *ibid.*, Sch.B1, para.65(3).

[40] *ibid.*, Sch.B1, para.83.

[41] *ibid.*, Sch.B1, para.79(4)(d).

[42] *ibid.*, Sch.B1, para.84.

creditors' voluntary liquidation. A new factor to be considered in the decision on exit routes is the Pensions Act 2004 and its provisions for assumption by the Pension Protection Fund Board of responsibility for failed pension schemes following an insolvency event[43] and compensation from the pension protection fund for members of such schemes.[44]

13. ADMINISTRATION FOLLOWED BY LIQUIDATION AND VICE VERSA

Relevant date for computation of preferential debts

The advent of administration may have an effect on the relevant date for determining preferential claims both on a subsequent winding up and, under the new regime, in the administration itself where a distribution is to be made.[45] Of particular importance to the computation of preferential claims is the definition of "relevant date", which features in several paragraphs of Sch.6 to the Insolvency Act 1986 and is defined in s.387. In the case of an administration followed immediately by a winding-up, s.387 as originally drawn distinguished between a compulsory and a voluntary winding-up, stating that in the case of a compulsory winding-up the relevant date was the commencement of the administration, whereas in the case of a voluntary winding-up it was the date of passing of the resolution for voluntary winding-up, which could have the effect of extinguishing the eligibility of certain debts for preferential status because of expiry of the period to which the preferential claim was limited.[46] Section 387 has now been amended[47] so as to provide that in both cases the relevant date is the date on which the company entered administration.[48] **10–104**

To attract these provisions, and also to ensure that the date of the onset of insolvency for the purpose of ss.238 and 239 of the Insolvency Act is the date of entry into administration rather than the date of the voluntary winding-up,[49] it is important to avoid a gap between the ending of the administration and the commencement of the winding-up by making arrangements to ensure that a resolution for voluntary winding-up is passed or a winding-up petition presented immediately after the cessation of the

---

[43] Pensions Act 2004, s.127.

[44] *ibid.*, s.162 and Sch.7.

[45] It will be recalled that the administrator may now make a distribution to preferential creditors without having to obtain the permission of the court.

[46] This is well explained by Andrew Keay and Peter Walton, *Insolvency Law: Corporate and Personal*, pp.122–123.

[47] By the Insolvency Act 1986 (Amendment) (No.2) Regulations 2002 (SI 2002/1240).

[48] Insolvency Act 1986, s.387(3)(a), (ba).

[49] See *ibid.*, s.240(3)(d).

administration. Under the former regime this presented difficult technical problems. The resolution could not be passed while the administration was still on foot,[50] nor could the passing of the resolution be made conditional on the cessation of administration.[51] Now, however, the company can move straight from administration to a creditors' voluntary winding-up where the administrator thinks that the total amount each secured creditor is likely[52] to receive has been paid to him or set aside for him and that a distribution will be made to unsecured creditors of the company, if there are any.[53] The process is quite simple. The administrator sends a notice to the registrar of companies that para.83 of Sch.B1 applies and files a copy with the court and sends a copy to each creditor of whose claim and address he is aware and the registrar registers the notice. Upon such registration the appointment of the administrator ceases to have effect and the company is wound up on the day of such registration as if a resolution for voluntary winding-up had been passed, the liquidator being the person nominated by the creditors in the prescribed manner or, if none, the administrator.[54] This procedure has been held to be available even if the administrator was appointed by the court, and there is no need for him to apply to the court for his discharge under para.79 of Sch.B1.[55]

Where a compulsory winding-up precedes the administration,[56] there are two relevant dates for determining the preferential debts, the first being the date of the winding-up order[57] and the second the date on which the company enters administration.[58]

Administrators usually advise a voluntary winding-up, rather than a compulsory winding-up, in order to avoid the payment of fees to the Department of Trade and Industry for the Official Receiver's services and what are considered by many to be the inadequate service and high fees for the operation of the Insolvency Services Account into and from which all payments must be made in a compulsory liquidation. But the mode of winding-up influences the relevant date for preferential debts, as stated above, and this is a factor to be taken into account.

---

[50] *ibid.*, Sch.B1, para.42(2).

[51] *Re Norditrack (UK) Ltd* [2000] 1 B.C.L.C. 467.

[52] A slightly odd word to use where the secured creditor has actually received payment. Perhaps "due" would have been better.

[53] Insolvency Act 1986, Sch.B1, para.83(1).

[54] *ibid.*, Sch.B1, para.83(3)–(7).

[55] *Re Ballast plc* [2005] 1 All E.R. 630.

[56] Which can now occur as the result of an administration order made on an administration application by the holder of a qualifying floating charge or the liquidator, in which event the court must discharge the winding-up order (Insolvency Act 1986, Sch.B1, para.37).

[57] Insolvency Act 1986, s.387(3)(b). However, if (a) the company had previously been in voluntary winding-up, the relevant date is the date of the winding-up resolution (s.387(3)(c)) or (b) a provisional liquidator had been appointed, the relevant date is the appointment (or first appointment) of a provisional liquidator (s.387(3)(b)).

[58] *ibid.*, s.387(3).

14. VARIATION OR RESCISSION OF THE ADMINISTRATION ORDER

Rule 7.47 of the Insolvency Rules 1986 provides as follows: **10–105**

"Every court having jurisdiction under the Act to wind up companies may review, rescind or vary an order made by it in the exercise of that jurisdiction."

It has been held that this rule empowers the court to review, rescind or vary an administration order.[59] The procedure is governed by the CPR.[60]

15. COMPANY VOLUNTARY ARRANGEMENTS AND REORGANISATIONS

The nature of the CVA[61]

A CVA made by a company[62] with its creditors and members under Part I   **10–106**
of the Insolvency Act 1986 is a composition in satisfaction of the company's debts[63] or a scheme of arrangement of its affairs,[64] the composition or scheme resulting from acceptance of a proposal by the directors to the company and its creditors.[65] Except as otherwise provided by the terms of the CVA or where the company is in administration (in which case the administrator has charge of its affairs) the directors remain in control of the company and continue to have power to carry on the business and to realise assets. A CVA may be made whether or not the company is insolvent or likely to become insolvent.[66]

---

[59] *Cornhill Insurance plc v Cornhill Financial Services Ltd* [1992] B.C.C. 818, applying the reasoning in *Re Tasbian Ltd (No.2)* [1990] B.C.C. 322.

[60] Insolvency Rules 1986, r.7.51. The CPR are the Civil Procedure Rules 1998, which replaced most of the Rules of the Supreme Court.

[61] For contrasts with administration, see above, paras 10–20, 10–33 *et seq.*

[62] The effect of art.3 of the EC Insolvency Regulation (1346/2000/EC) had been held to extend the power to make administration orders, and by the same token CVAs, to legal persons other than companies, and was utilised rather imaginatively to enable the Dean and Chapter of Bradford Cathedral to enter into a CVA, the court applying *Re The Salvage Association* [2003] 2 B.C.L.C. 333 (see Philip Mudd and Caroline Whittington, "Cathedral Saved by CVA" (2005) 21 IL & P 10). This enterprising ecclesiastic feat can no longer be undertaken, since under the Insolvency Act (Amendment) Regulations 2005 (SI 2005/879) only companies as defined by s.735(1) of the Companies Act 1985 will be able to avail themselves of a CVA or an administration.

[63] That is, an agreement by creditors to accept less then the amount due to them in discharge of their claims. See above, para.1–25.

[64] Insolvency Act 1986, s.1.

[65] See generally Edward Bailey, *Voluntary Arrangements*; Andrew Keay and Peter Walton, *Insolvency Law: Corporate and Personal*, Chap.8.

[66] See Insolvency Act 1986, s.1(1). Rule 1.6(1)(a) of the Insolvency Rules 1986 suggests the contrary but cannot, it is thought, be intended to introduce the requirement of an existing or impending insolvency by a side wind and is to be interpreted as confined to cases where the company is in fact insolvent or threatened with insolvency.

CVAs typically involve either a sale of assets and a distribution of the proceeds to creditors, which is usually a relatively short-term procedure, or a continuance of trading under which the company makes periodic payments from its trading income to the supervisor of the CVA for distribution in accordance with its terms, a process which may continue for a considerable time. A distribution CVA is likely to be used only in special circumstances (e.g. because of tax considerations), since it is normally easier to place the company into a creditors' voluntary winding-up, thus avoiding the likely need to apply to the court to extend the administration period. So the CVA is used mainly as a vehicle for trading, and though it rarely succeeds in preserving the business for the company itself it may facilitate a disposal of it on more favourable terms than would otherwise have been the case.

The wording of s.5(2)(b), discussed below,[67] has led the courts to characterise the relationship between the parties to a CVA as essentially contractual in nature[68] and its scope and effect are determined by its terms. It follows that the court has no power to give directions to amend a concluded CVA.[69] Whether the CVA operates as an accord or a release so as to discharge a co-debtor or surety not a party to the arrangement depends solely on the terms of the arrangement.[70] So too does the question whether the CVA imposes a stay on proceedings by a creditor who is bound by it.[71]

Relationship of CVA to other types of arrangement

(1) Composition

10–107   A CVA may itself include a composition but this is not a necessary component of a CVA.[72]

(2) Scheme of arrangement

10–108   Though s.1(1) refers to a "scheme of arrangement," this phrase is normally used to denote a scheme made under s.425 of the Companies Act 1985. The procedure for a scheme of arrangement under s.425 and the effect of such a scheme differ materially from a CVA.[73]

---

[67] See para.10–124.
[68] *Re TBL Realisations plc, Oakley-Smith v Greenberg* [2004] B.C.C. 81; *Whitehead v Household Mortgage Corp* [2003] 1 All E.R. 319; *Johnson v Davies* [1999] Ch. 117; *Re Halson Packaging Ltd* [1997] B.C.C. 993. All these cases were decisions on the comparable wording in s.260(2) of the Act relating to individual voluntary arrangements.
[69] *Re Alpa Lighting Ltd* [1997] B.P.I.R. 341.
[70] *Johnson v Davies*, above, n.68.
[71] See below, para.10–129.
[72] *March Estates plc v Gunmark Ltd* [1996] 1 B.C.L.C. 1.
[73] See above, para.1–26, and below, para.10–134.

(3) Restructuring ("workout")

A restructuring, or workout, is a contractual arrangement or reorganisation **10–109**
negotiated among creditors outside any formal insolvency proceeding.[74]

The CVA and administration or winding-up

A CVA may be concluded without any prior or subsequent insolvency **10–110**
proceeding or it may precede or follow a winding-up or administration. It
may also run in parallel with a winding-up[75] and with an administration,[76]
which has the advantage of attracting the statutory moratorium. For this
reason most CVAs are conducted within the framework of administration.[77]
Where a CVA is made when the company is not in administration or
winding-up the effect of a subsequent administration or winding-up
depends on the terms of the CVA itself. It may or may not bring an end to
the CVA as such, depending on the circumstances,[78] but even if it does the
trusts created by the CVA remain in force for the benefit of the CVA
creditors except so far as the terms of the CVA otherwise provide.[79]

(1) CVA within administration

Where, as will usually be the case, a CVA is concluded while the company **10–111**
is in administration, the normal procedure is for the administrator to
continue to manage the company and to pass over assets and/or trading
surpluses to the supervisor of the CVA for distribution among creditors.
Usually the supervisor is the administrator himself, who thus acts in two
capacities. As supervisor he is responsible for the implementation of the
CVA where this proves capable of being achieved.

---

[74] See below, para.10–135.
[75] Insolvency Act 1986, s.1(3).
[76] *ibid*. However, the appointment of an administrator automatically ceases to have effect after
one year beginning with the date is takes effect unless extended by the court (Insolvency Act
1986, Sch.B1, para.76).
[77] Further factors are that (a) in a distribution CVA within administration the set-off rules
embodied in r.2.85 of the Insolvency Rules 1986 apply, whereas outside administration set-
off is governed by the general law, and (b) the priority of new creditors in an administration
does not apply in a CVA outside administration.
[78] *Welsby v Brelec Installations Ltd* [2000] 2 B.C.L.C. 576; *Re Maple bal Services Ltd* [2000]
B.C.C. 93.
[79] *Re N.T. Gallagher & Son Ltd* [2002] 2 B.C.L.C. 133. For a detailed survey of the relevant
authorities see Andrew R. Keay, *McPherson's Law of Company Liquidation*, para.7.92. See
further below, para.10–130, as to the trusts created by a CVA over funds coming into he
hands of the supervisor.

(2) CVA followed or preceded by administration

10–112 A CVA may itself provide for administration as the exit route once the purposes of the CVA have been fulfilled, and the supervisor has power to apply for an administration order.[80] The situation in which a CVA is most likely to be followed by administration is where there are assets outside the scope of the CVA in relation to which the purpose of the administration may be achieved. Where the administration comes first and a CVA is concluded within the administration[81] then if the CVA covers all the company's assets it will usually provide for the appointment of the administrator to cease to have effect, for the administrator will no longer have any functions to perform in his capacity as administrator, though he may assume the role of supervisor of the CVA. Again, however, there may be cases where the CVA does not cover the whole of the assets, in which case the administrator, if able to achieve the purpose with the assets outside the CVA, will continue in office to that end.

(3) Liquidation

10–113 A CVA may precede liquidation and provide for it as the exit route, with distribution of assets according to the rules applicable on winding-up, and, the supervisor may petition for winding-up.[82] Alternatively the liquidation may come first, and the liquidator may propose a CVA[83] with himself or another person as supervisor. The liquidator may wish to do this, for example, where he considers that it would be advantageous for the business of the company to be carried on but he lacks the necessary powers.[84]

Outline of procedure leading to a CVA

(1) Preliminary steps

10–114 A reading of s.1(1) of the Insolvency Act and rr.1.2 to 1.5 of the Insolvency Rules would suggest that a CVA is initiated by a proposal by the directors to the company and its creditors, followed by delivery to the intended nominee[85] of the proposal and a statement of the company's affairs.

---

[80] Insolvency Act 1986, s.7(4)(b).
[81] Less likely with the automatic expiry of the administrator's appointment after one year. The administrator may make a proposal for a CVA (Insolvency Act 1986, s.1(3)(b)) and propose either himself or another nominee as supervisor.
[82] *ibid.*, s.7(4)(b).
[83] *ibid.*, s.1(3)(b).
[84] A liquidator may carry on the business of the company only so far as may be necessary for its beneficial winding-up (*ibid.* Sch.4, para.5).
[85] *i.e.* the person whom the directors intend to nominate as supervisor of the CVA. When such person accepts the nomination he becomes the nominee; when he is appointed to administer the arrangement and this takes effect he becomes the supervisor.

However, there are important preliminary measures to be taken. A threshold question is whether a CVA is in fact the best option for the company. Before initiating a CVA, prudent directors will take the advice of a qualified insolvency practitioner (usually the intended nominee) and examine other alternatives. They will in any event need to have a fall-back position in case they are not able to secure the support of their creditors. The intended nominee will require sufficient information about the company's financial position—including details of its business, its assets and liabilities, and cash flow—to enable him to advise. Assuming that a decision is taken to seek to negotiate a CVA the next step is to organise a standstill on the pursuit of individual claims by the major creditors or alternatively put the company into administration or, in the case of a small eligible company, initiate the formal moratorium which is now available,[86] and to arrange for the continuance of day-to-day funding by the company's bank. The proposal itself has to contain a considerable number of prescribed particulars,[87] and its formulation may be expected to take a little time, during which it is important to keep the creditors informed and interim financial support maintained.

In some cases it is possible to organise in advance arrangements for sale of the business when the company goes into a CVA. Such pre-packaging arrangements ("prepacks") speed the CVA process and reduce much of the risk, though it does not always follows that they result in the best price being obtained.

(2) Who may propose a CVA

If the company is not in administration or liquidation a CVA may be proposed by the directors.[88] Where the company is in administration the proposal must be made by the administrator and where it is in liquidation, by the liquidator.[89] Neither creditors nor members have the power to make a proposal. A CVA proposed in the context of an administration or liquidation has the advantage of the statutory moratorium which applies automatically upon the company entering administration[90] or liquidation,[91] whereas a CVA proposed by the directors does not attract a statutory moratorium except in the case of a small eligible company[92] and then only

10–115

---

[86] See para.10–115.
[87] See below.
[88] Insolvency Act 1986, s.1(1).
[89] *ibid.*, s.1(3).
[90] See above, paras 10–49 *et seq.*
[91] Insolvency Act 1986, s.130(2). See above, para.5–03.
[92] An eligible company is one which (a) in the year ending with the date of filing of the documents required for a moratorium or in the financial year of the company ending last before that date met the qualifying conditions, that is, satisfied two or more of the requirements for a small company specified for the time being in s.247(3) of the Companies Act 1985, and (b) is not excluded from being eligible because it is already subject to a voluntary arrangement or insolvency proceeding or by virtue of paras 2(2), (3), 3(4) or 4A–4C of Sch.A1 to the Insolvency Act 1986. See Sch.1A, paras 2–4.

when the directors file the requisite documents, including a statement that the company is eligible for a moratorium.[93]

(3) Proposal by the directors

10–116 Though the Insolvency Rules require the directors' proposal to be prepared for and delivered to the intended nominee,[94] in practice he will already have been put in the picture, as indicated above, and the proposal will usually have been formulated in consultation with him. The proposal must provide a short explanation why, in the opinion of the directors, a CVA is desirable and why the company's creditors may be expected to concur in it.[95] The procedure is in all cases governed by Chapters 2, 5, 7 and 8 of Part I of the Insolvency Rules 1986. Additionally for a CVA proposed by the directors the provisions of Chapter 2 (and if a moratorium is proposed, Chapter 9) apply; and where the company is in liquidation or administration, then if the nominee is the liquidator or administrator Chapter 3 applies, otherwise Chapter 4 (Chapter 6 was repealed). The content of the proposal must conform to r.1.3(2) of the Insolvency Rules, which requires the name, address and qualification of the person proposed as supervisor and the inclusion of a long list of other matters designed to enable the court, assisted by a report from the nominee, to form a view as to whether the proposed arrangement is both viable and fair to the different categories of creditor (secured, preferential, ordinary unsecured) and whether the arrangements to be put in place for the management of the CVA are satisfactory.[96] The proposals will thus contain not only details that will feature as terms of the CVA itself but all other relevant information, including any agreement on the part of a debenture holder to release its security.

The assets covered by the CVA are not necessarily the same as those detailed as belonging to the company. The CVA may exclude some assets of the company, in order, for example, to leave something for its members as an inducement to them to support the proposal. In the case of a trading CVA the trading assets may be left with the company, which will make periodic payments to the supervisor of the CVA from trading income. The arrangement may also include property belonging to a third party, for example, new funds to be injected by the company's bank or its shareholders. Similarly, there may be liabilities which will be excluded from the CVA.[97]

---

[93] *ibid.*, Sch.A1, para.7.
[94] Insolvency Rules 1986, r.1.4(2).
[95] *ibid.*, r.1.3(1).
[96] See also the R3 Statement of Insolvency Practice 3, Appendix.
[97] For typical provisions of a CVA, see below, para.10–122.

(4) Notice to the intended nominee

The directors must give the nominee written notice of their proposal, **10–117** together with a copy of the proposal itself.[98] If the intended nominee agrees to act he must have a copy of the notice indorsed to the effect that it has been received by him on a specified date, which marks the commencement of the period allowed him for submission of his report to the court.[99] Within seven days after delivery of their proposal to the intended nominee, or within such longer period as he may allow, the directors must deliver to him a statement of the company's affairs setting out the prescribed particulars and made up to a date not earlier than two weeks, before the above notice.[1] The nominee may call on the directors to provide him with any further information he requires to prepare his report,[2] and must give him access to the company's accounts and records.[3]

(5) Nominee's report

Within 28 days of the date specified in the nominee's indorsed receipt, or **10–118** such longer period as the court may allow, the nominee must submit a report stating whether in his opinion meetings of the company and its creditors should be summoned to consider the proposal and, if so, when and where.[4]

(6) Meetings of company and creditors

Where the nominee's report states that meetings should be summoned he **10–119** must proceed to do this unless the court otherwise orders.[5] The meetings, which will normally be chaired by the nominee, must then decide whether to approve the proposed arrangement, with or without modification.[6] However, no modification must be approved which affects the right of a secured creditor to enforce his security, or the priority of a preferential creditor or his entitlement to the same proportional payment as any other preferential creditor, except with the concurrence of the creditor concerned.[7]

Voting

Entitlement to vote is significant for at least three reasons. First, a creditor **10–120** entitled to vote may use his vote to influence the decision whether to approve or reject the CVA. Secondly, a creditor entitled to vote is bound by

---

[98] Insolvency Act 1986, s.2(3); Insolvency Rules 1986, r.1.4(1), (2).
[99] *ibid.*, r.1.4(3).
[1] *ibid.*, r.1.5.
[2] *ibid.*, r.1.6.
[3] *ibid.*, r.1.6(3).
[4] Insolvency Act 1986, s.2(2).
[5] *ibid.*, s.3.
[6] *ibid.*, s.4(1).
[7] *ibid.*, s.4(3), (4).

the CVA even if he did not receive notice of the meeting[8] or, having received notice of the meeting, he chooses not to attend or to vote by proxy.[9] Thirdly, a creditor not entitled to vote is not bound by a CVA,[10] though it may have an effect on his ability to obtain any leave that may be necessary to enforce his claim.[11] A creditor with several claims may be entitled to vote in respect of some of them but not others, in which case he will be bound by the CVA only as to the former.

The general rule is that every creditor[12] who has notice of the creditors' meeting is entitled to vote at the meeting or any adjournment of it.[13] However, there is one exception.[14] The chairman of the creditors' meeting has a discretion to admit or reject a creditor's claim, wholly or in part, for the purposes of his entitlement to vote.[15] The chairman may wish to reject a claim because it is too uncertain or speculative to accept for voting even as a contingent claim, or because it is by a creditor who has no interest in the outcome of the CVA, as where his claim is fully secured and he wishes to rest on his security or where it is subordinated and all the available assets will be exhausted in meeting the claims of ordinary creditors[16] or is a claim which falls outside the CVA altogether.

What is the position where a creditor's claim is for an unliquidated or otherwise unascertained amount? Previously the rule was that if the chairman refused to place a minimum value on the claim the creditor could not vote at all. The new rule is that a creditor may vote in respect of such a debt and for the purpose of voting (but not otherwise) it is to be valued at £1 unless the chairman agrees to place a higher value on it.[17]

The chairman's decision on any of these matters is subject to appeal to the court by any creditor or member of the company[18]; and if the chairman is in doubt whether a claim should be admitted or rejected he is to mark it

---

[8] The rule was formerly different. See below, para.10–124.

[9] *Beverley Group plc v McClue* [1995] 2 B.C.L.C. 40; *Re Cancol Ltd* [1996] 1 B.C.L.C. 100.

[10] Insolvency Act 1986, s.5(2)(b); and see below, para.10–127.

[11] See below, para.10–127.

[12] This includes a future or contingent creditor *(Re Cancol Ltd* [1995] B.C.L.C. 1133).

[13] Insolvency Rules 1986, r.1.17(1).

[14] There was formerly a second, namely where the debt was for an unliquidated amount or of an unascertained value and the chairman refused to place an estimated minimum value on it for the purpose of voting. That has now changed, though the minimum value is nominal, so that the change is not one of substance. See below.

[15] Insolvency Rules 1986, r.1.17A(2).

[16] See *Re British and Commonwealth Holdings plc (No.3)* [1992] B.C.L.C. 322. The question of lack of an economic interest also arises in determining whether particular creditors or creditors of a particular class have a *locus standi* to take part in and vote on a proposed scheme of arrangement under s.425 of the Companies Act 1985. See *Re MyTravel Group plc* [2004] 4 All E.R. (D) 385; *Re Tea Corporation* [1904] 1 Ch. 12, where bondholders whose claims were subordinated were held to have no economic interest in the CVA because they would receive nothing if the company went into winding-up.

[17] Insolvency Rules 1986, r.1.17(3).

[18] Insolvency Rules 1986, r.1.17A(3). If on appeal the chairman's decision is reversed or varied, or if votes are declared invalid, the court may order another meeting to be summoned, or make such order as it thinks just (r.1.17A(5)).

as objected and allow votes to be cast in respect of it, subject to those votes being subsequently declared invalid if the objection to the claim is sustained.[19] Subject to the outcome of any appeal to the court the effect of the chairman's rejection of a claim is that the creditor whose claim is rejected is not entitled to vote and is therefore not bound by the CVA.[20]

Under r.1.19(3) votes in respect of certain claims, in particular, secured claims, are to be left out of account. It has been held that this is purely for the purpose of determining the number of votes in considering whether the requisite majority has been achieved for the approval of the CVA, and that far from treating creditors of the excluded claims as not entitled to vote r.1.19(3) is premised on the assumption that they have a right to vote but the vote is not to be counted.[21] Such creditors are therefore bound by the CVA.

Approval of a CVA

Approval of a CVA requires: **10–121**

(1)   at the creditors' meeting, a majority in excess of three-quarters in value of the creditors present in person or by proxy and voting on the resolution,[22] and

(2)   at the members' meeting, voting for the CVA by more than one-half in value of the members present in person or by proxy, value being determined by the number of votes conferred on each member by the company's articles.[23]

The decision has effect if, in accordance with the rules, it has been taken by both meetings or by the creditors' meeting alone, but in the latter case the decision is subject to an order of the court made on an application under s.4A(6).[24] As stated earlier, a proposal may not be approved if it would affect the right of a secured creditor to enforce his security or the priority of a preferential creditor or his pari passu ranking with other preferential creditors.[25] But there is nothing to stop ordinary unsecured creditors from being separately paid from funds supplied by a third party, even if this

---

[19] *ibid.*, r.17A(4).
[20] See below, para.10–124.
[21] *Re Bradley-Hole* [1995] 2 B.C.L.C. 163.
[22] Insolvency Rules 1986, r.1.19(1). In determining whether the proposals have been approved by the requisite majority there must be excluded votes in respect of the claims mentioned in r.1.19(3). See below.
[23] *ibid.*, r.1.20(1).
[24] Insolvency Act 1986, s.4A(2)(b) says "subject to any order made under subsection (4)" but this is clearly a slip as that subsection deals only with the application for the order.
[25] Insolvency Act 1986, s.4(3), (4).

results in their receiving more in the pound than preferential creditors, provided that the funds supplied are not in reduction of a sum to which the company would otherwise have become entitled.[26]

Reorganisation under a CVA

10–122　Most CVAs do not in fact involve reorganisation of the company and focus on preservation of the business with a view to its sale as a going concern and/or disposal of particular assets, followed by a distribution of realisations by way of dividend, after which the company usually goes into winding-up. However, it may also be possible to restructure the company and its indebtedness with a view to restoring it to profitable trading. A typical reorganisation plan is likely to involve a combination of two or more of the following: a moratorium (where not already in operation under an administration order); the cessation or disposal of part of the company's business; the injection of new funds for the carrying on of the business or the completion of outstanding projects; the release of certain claims and securities for them and the composition of other claims; a reordering of priorities by advancing the ranking of particular debts or by subordinating debts which would otherwise have had priority or ranked *pari passu*; the conversion of debt into equity, so that creditors become shareholders[27]; the injection of additional share capital; and the creation of a new corporate structure, as by forming a new parent company into which assets and liabilities can be transferred and in which creditors take shares,[28] or the hiving down of the business into a specially formed subsidiary. It may also be found desirable for a creditor or group of creditors to take over a part of the company's loan indebtedness to other creditors with a view to reducing the number of creditors involved in the negotiations and replacing an unsympathetic creditor with one who is prepared to join with others in working towards a solution[29]; and it may be possible to improve the company's liquidity by securing the whole or part of its loan assets. A further alternative is for the shares to be acquired by a new funder whose

---

[26] *IRC v Wimbledon Football Club Ltd* [2005] 1 B.C.L.C. 66. See above, para.10–24.

[27] This may provide creditors with greater recovery opportunities than on a winding-up, whilst from the viewpoint of the directors any risk of liability for wrongful trading is removed at a stroke, and members have some prospect of retaining at least a partial stake in the enterprise. For a fuller description of the advantages and disadvantages see Philip R. Wood, *Principles of International Insolvency*, paras 20–7 *et seq.*

[28] See, for example, the arrangement in *Fidelity Investments International plc v MyTravel Group plc* [2004] All E.R. (D) 385 and on appeal [2004] All E.R. (D) 221, a scheme under s.425 of the Companies Act 1985 put forward as an alternative to a scheme involving the conversion of bondholders' debt to equity, which the bondholders had opposed.

[29] Some of the problems involved in the sale of debts due from companies in financial difficulty ("distressed debt") are examined in the Financial Law Panel's Discussion Paper *Legal Uncertainties in the Secondary Debt Market* (January 1997).

injection of funds is to facilitate the compromise of claims and is conditional upon approval of a CVA on terms acceptable to the funder.

The CVA derives from collective decisions by creditors and members, not from an order of the court, and cannot by itself deal with matters beyond their decision-making powers. So a plan involving a reduction in share capital will, except so far as authorised by the Companies Act 1985,[30] require the consent of all creditors and the sanction of the court under s.137 of the Act; and where, in disposing of the company's undertaking, it is proposed to transfer the liabilities as well as the assets, so as to substitute the transferee for the company as the party liable, application should be made for the sanctioning of a scheme of arrangement under s.425 of the Companies Act and for a transfer order under s.427.

Some typical provisions in a CVA relating to creditors' rights

In addition to setting out the assets and liabilities of the company by reference to the directors' statement of affairs, together with arrangements for the management of the CVA, any plans for continued trading by the company and any provisions for its reorganisation, a CVA will have to deal with a range of matters relevant to creditors' rights. These include the following: **10–123**

- Assets and liabilities included and excluded from the CVA.

- The application of any additional assets that the company may acquire.

- The treatment of secured and preferential claims.[31]

- The admission to the CVA of creditors who would have been entitled to vote if they had received notice of the creditors' meeting and of creditors whose claims are disputed by the supervisor but later determined or compromised.

- The proof and ranking of creditors' claims in much the same way as for a winding-up.

- The management of the business (which may be left in the hands of the directors, subject to overall control by the supervisor and, where appropriate, a creditors' committee).

- Details of any assets to be transferred to or held on trust for the supervisor by the company.

---

[30] *e.g.* for private companies (Companies Act 1985, s.155).
[31] The rights of secured and preferential creditors must be respected (Insolvency Act 1986, s.4(3), (4)). Whether secured creditors are brought within the CVA is a matter for agreement between them and the other CVA creditors.

- Any restrictions on the powers of the directors, for example, a prohibition on the payment of dividends to shareholders or on the payment of remuneration to the directors themselves otherwise than as agreed with the supervisor.

- The imposition of a moratorium on the CVA creditors[32] so long as the CVA is current and, where so agreed, the release of the company from all creditors' claims except their entitlements under the CVA itself or a composition of their claims by payment of dividends in the CVA.[33]

- The amount and frequency of payments by the company to the supervisor and the distribution of dividend to moratorium creditors after deduction of the supervisor's remuneration and expenses.

- The convening of a meeting of creditors to reconsider the CVA if the claims of creditors not known at the time of its conclusion exceed a stated percentage of the known debts or would reduce the dividend payable to the moratorium creditors by more than a stated percentage.

- The duration of the CVA.

- Provision for what is to happen in the event of failure of the CVA. For example, the CVA may provide that if the company fails to comply with its terms the supervisor may or shall issue a certificate of non-compliance, following which the CVA creditors cease to be bound by the CVA and, if the company is not in administration or subject to some other statutory moratorium, may pursue their ordinary remedies, including presentation of a petition for the winding-up of the company and proof as a creditor in the winding-up.

- Where it is envisaged that there may be a surplus after meeting all claims, payment of the surplus to the company.

Effect of CVA

(i) Parties bound by the CVA

10–124   Once the decision to approve the CVA has become effective the CVA:

---

[32] In general, all creditors who would be entitled to prove in a winding-up other than preferential creditors, secured creditors and creditors whose claims were not accepted for voting and are not admitted to the CVA subsequently by agreement or court order. If and so long as the company is in administration there is a general moratorium under Insolvency Act 1986, Sch.B1, para.43.

[33] In the absence of provision for a release or composition of the CVA creditors' claims they are entitled, if the company goes into liquidation after the ending of the CVA, to prove in the liquidation for the balance of the amounts due to them after giving credit for dividends received or to be received under the CVA (*Re N.T. Gallagher & Son Ltd, Shierson v Tomlinson* [2002] B.C.C. 867). Where the CVA does provide for a composition or release on the basis of the assets then known, consideration should be given to a provision preserving the right of CVA creditors to prove in the winding up of the company for the outstanding balance of their claims in relation to assets coming into the company's hands after fulfillment of the CVA.

"(a) takes effect as if made by the company at the creditors' meeting, and

(b) binds every person who in accordance with the rules—

    (i) was entitled to vote at the meeting (whether he was represented at it or not), or

    (ii) would have been so entitled if he had had notice of it,

as if he were a party to the voluntary arrangement."

Dissenting creditors and creditors whose votes are required to be left out of account under r.1.19(3), are thus bound by a decision taken by the requisite majority. Previously a creditor was not bound if he did not have notice of the meeting, which could easily happen because the nominee was unaware of him or because he had moved and the nominee did not know his new address. This meant that potentially substantial numbers of creditors were not bound by the CVA, a fact which tended to undermine confidence in its efficacy and lead to a decision to use the more cumbersome s.425 route. Under the new rule even unknown creditors and creditors not receiving notice of the meeting because it was sent to the wrong address become bound,[34] so that the problem previously alluded to is much less acute than it was.

However, the fact that unknown creditors are bound does not solve all the difficulties, for they may have substantial claims which, had they been known, would have materially affected the terms of the CVA. This possibility can be taken into account in the terms of the CVA itself, as was done quite neatly in the CVA in *Re TBL Realisations Ltd*.[35]

(ii) Position of CVA creditors

Creditors bound by the CVA must adhere to its terms in the same way as **10–125** under any other contract. Under the typical CVA creditors give up their rights against the company in return for payments by the company to the supervisor from trading income, the transfer of assets if so agreed and the payment of dividend distributions as provided by the CVA. Pending due fulfillment of the CVA the rights of the CVA creditors are suspended under a moratorium provision. If the CVA is carried through to completion

---

[34] But they are also, of course, entitled to benefit from the CVA on establishing their claims under it. Alternatively they can take the position that they are not bound by the CVA, though this does not necessarily result in their being in a more favourable position. See below, para.10–127.

[35] *Re TBL Realisations Ltd, Oakley-Smith v Greenberg* [2004] B.C.C. 81, where the CVA permitted the supervisors to allow creditors outside the CVA to participate in it if they agreed to be bound and their claims would not in the aggregate reduce the dividend to participants by more than 10%, but otherwise the supervisors were to convene a meeting to consider alternative proposals. For a detailed discussion of this case, see below, para.10–127.

then unless the terms otherwise provide those creditors have no further remedies against the company even if it goes into liquidation with additional assets. It is therefore important for the CVA to make provision for the application of such assets.

(iii) Parties not bound by the CVA

10–126   A person is not bound by a CVA if he was neither entitled to vote nor someone who would have been entitled to vote if he had received notice of the meeting.[36] We have seen that a decision by the chairman of the creditors' meeting rejecting a creditor's claim is subject to an appeal to the court.[37] But the creditor concerned is not obliged to appeal the decision and if he does not do so he is not bound by the CVA.[38] The effect of this is a little more complex than it might appear.

(iv) Position of creditor not bound by CVA

10–127   A creditor whose claim has been rejected retains his substantive rights in respect of it. Where the company is not in administration or otherwise subject to a statutory moratorium the non-CVA creditor is free to pursue his remedies under the general law, as by instituting proceedings to obtain a judgment and then issuing execution or by putting the company into winding-up. In other cases he must obtain the permission of the court to enforce his rights, and in deciding what order to make the court must have regard to the interests of other creditors, including the moratorium creditors.

We have seen that where the company is in administration and the creditor is a secured creditor or is the owner of goods supplied to the company under a conditional sale, hire-purchase or leasing agreement, permission will normally be given where a refusal of permission would cause loss to the creditor substantially greater than would be caused to the general body of creditors by the grant of leave.[39] This reflects the principle that on a winding-up proprietary rights remain untouched, so that the grant of permission does not result in any diminution of the estate. The position is otherwise in the case of an unsecured creditor, because if he is allowed to pursue his claim to judgment and then enforce the judgment by execution

---

[36] The right to vote is confined by r.1.17(1) of the Insolvency Rules 1986 to creditors having notice of the creditors' meeting. See further above, para.10–124.

[37] Insolvency Rules 1986, r.1.17A(3). The appeal must be made within the time limit laid down by r.1.17A(6).

[38] *Re TBL Realisationa plc, Oakley-Smith v Greenberg* [2004] B.C.C. 81; *R.A. Securities Ltd v Mercantile Credit Co Ltd* [1994] 2 B.C.L.C. 721.

[39] See above, para.10–74.

he will avoid the application of the *pari passu* principle that would be triggered by the subsequent winding-up of the company and would thus be advantaged at the expense of the general body of creditors. That is not conclusive but it is a powerful factor to be taken into account in any decision on the grant of leave. A good illustration, though not free from difficulty as to the basis of the decision, is the ruling of the Court of Appeal in *Re TBL Realisations Ltd*, where it was held that creditors whose claims were rejected could not be treated more favourably than if the claim had been accepted or the company wound up and would therefore be adequately protected by an order ensuring that they received a payment equal to what they would have received on a *pari passu* distribution among CVA creditors, or alternatively upon winding-up, if their claims had been accepted.[40] In that case the facts were as follows:

> The joint administrators of TBL Realisations Ltd. proposed a CVA. Members of the Greenberg family, who had previously instituted proceedings for substantial damages for negligence against the company pursuant to permission given by the court, sought to vote by proxy at the meeting of creditors convened to approve the CVA. On legal advice the chairman, who was one of the joint administrators, rejected the Greenbergs' claim for voting purposes, declining to put a minimum value on the claim, which was unliquidated, with the result that they could not vote, though had they been allowed to do so they would have supported the CVA. They then applied for an injunction requiring the administrators to retain outside the CVA sufficient assets to meet their claim if it was successful. The joint administrators, having intimated to the Greenbergs that they would agree to their participation in the CVA, applied to the court for directions,. The deputy High Court judge, Mr David Donaldson QC, held that since the Greenbergs' claim had been disallowed for voting purposes they were not bound by the CVA and there was therefore no reason to limit any injunction to the amount they would have received on a *pari passu* distribution under the CVA. In lieu of an order he accepted an undertaking from the administrators to retain out of the CVA the full amount of the Greenbergs' claim pending any further order. Later a compromise was reached whereby judgment was entered in their favour by consent for US$ 575,000 and costs.

> In subsequent proceedings Pumfrey J. held that the court should approach the matter as if the Greenbergs had applied for leave to enforce the judgment debt by execution. On this basis the issue had to be approached as a matter of exercise of the court's discretion and the need to balance the interests of the claimants against those of other creditors,

---

[40] *Re TBL Realisations plc, Oakley-Smith v Greenberg*, above.

that the Greenbergs had intended to support the CVA, that the error made in rejecting their claim was without consequence and they had suffered no additional prejudice and that to permit them to execute for the full amount of the judgment was inconsistent with the purpose of the administration. The judge pointed out that the Greenbergs, as well as other creditors, would in fact receive slightly more under a CVA than on a winding-up, because the CVA route avoided the need to use the Insolvency Services Account. The judge accordingly released the administrators from their undertaking and directed payment to the Greenbergs of the amount they would have received as participants in the CVA.

The Court of Appeal upheld the decision, adding a direction that the balance of the funds held by the administrators after paying the above sum be transferred to the supervisors.[41] Chadwick L.J., who gave the leading judgment, concluded that since the only alternative to administration was winding-up, which the Greenbergs were entitled to pursue if the administration ended, they were entitled to be treated no less favourably than they would be (a) under the CVA or (b) on an immediate discharge of the administration order followed by a winding-up, whichever was the more advantageous to them. Chadwick L.J. demonstrated mathematically that they would always be better off under the CVA than on the liquidation.[42] However, he departed from the reasoning of the trial judge as to the basis of the court's approach and accepted the submission of the administrators that the issue should be determined not on the basis of what the court in its discretion would have done if the application had been for leave to enforce a judgment but rather on the ground that there was no principled basis on which they could be required to hold a sum outside the CVA greater than the Greenbergs' *pari passu* entitlement.

10–128 It is clear that the court was influenced by what it saw as the lack of merit of the Greenberg's opposition to the judge's order.

"Their opposition can be seen as an opportunistic attempt to take advantage of the mistake [of the chairman in rejecting their claim] . . . an attempt by which they sought to obtain more favourable treatment than that which they would have been willing (or obliged) to accept if they had been permitted to vote . . ."

---

[41] Who were in fact the administrators themselves, who would thus retain the funds but hold them in a different capacity.

[42] He rejected the argument that the Greenbergs would be the only creditors on two grounds, first, that discharge of the administration before completion of the CVA would result in a certificate of non-compliance by the supervisors entitling the CVA creditors to prove in the winding-up, and (b) that would be the case even without such a certificate. The latter is questionable in the light of the provision in the CVA that payments under it would operate in full discharge of the company's liabilities to the CVA creditors.

The court signified its displeasure by ordering the Greenbergs to pay a substantial proportion of the costs of the administrators' application. The description of their claim as "opportunistic" seems a little harsh when they had made every effort to have their claim accepted, its rejection was not due to any fault on their part and its effect was to preclude them from participating in the meeting, albeit they would have supported the proposed arrangement. More significantly, the decision has been criticised on the ground that, while holding that the Greenbergs were not bound by the CVA, the court went on to rule that they could not be more favourably treated than if they were bound by it, and that what the court could and should have done was to provide for the full amount of the Greenbergs' judgment debt to be retained outside the CVA and let the CVA run its course, when payments to the CVA creditors would be in full and final settlement, leaving the Greenbergs as the sole creditors in any subsequent liquidation.[43] However, this presupposes that a creditor who is not a party to the CVA is on that account entitled to have a sum equal to the amount of his claim (so far as established or agreed) withdrawn from the assets covered by the CVA so as to be available to meet his claim. In consequence, if there were no other creditors outside the CVA and if, as is common, the CVA creditors had agreed to accept payment of dividends in satisfaction of all claims against the company, the creditor outside the CVA would, sooner or later,[44] receive payment in full as the sole remaining creditor, thereby gaining a preference over the CVA creditors. Neither principle nor policy compels such an outcome. Where the CVA empowers the supervisor to accept a claim from a creditor not previously within the CVA and the creditor agrees to participate in the CVA there is no problem. Where the creditor, having been offered the opportunity to do so, declines to participate in the CVA the solution adopted by the court, namely to order withdrawal from the CVA of a sum equal to what the creditor would have received if he had been a participant, seems eminently fair. The mere fact that creditors have entered into a CVA does not preclude their interests from receiving consideration when the court undertakes its balancing task in deciding whether a creditor should be given leave to pursue proceedings or to enforce a judgment.

(iv) No moratorium unless so provided by CVA

It is important to bear in mind that whereas the entry of a company into administration produces an automatic stay of proceedings against it, a CVA has this effect only if its terms so provide. In the absence of such a   **10–129**

---

[43] Look Chan Ho and Rizwaan Jameel Mokal, "Interplay of CVA administration and liquidation—(Part I)", (2003) 25 Co. Law. 3.

[44] Depending on whether it was necessary for him, after completion of the CVA, to put the company into liquidation—a rather pointless procedure, since if he were to be the only liquidation creditor the sum in question might just as well be paid to him without more ado after fulfillment of the CVA, though not, of course, before, because if it came to an end prematurely the CVA creditors would retain a right to prove in the winding-up.

provision even a creditor bound by the CVA is free to pursue his claims by action, and this despite the fact that he may have an alternative remedy in the shape of an application to the court under s.7(3) of the Insolvency Act.[45] Accordingly if the risk of such actions is to be avoided the CVA should make it clear that while it is current no creditor bound by it shall pursue his claim outside the CVA.

(v) Trust of the assets

10–130 It is established law that sums paid and property transferred to the supervisor pursuant to the CVA are held on trust for the CVA creditors[46] and that unless otherwise provided by the terms of the CVA the trust is not affected by the subsequent winding-up of the company, so that the assets cannot be reached by creditors who are outside the CVA.[47] Whether the proposals for the CVA or the terms of the CVA itself create a trust in favour of the CVA creditors even before the transfer to the supervisor depends on its terms. If no trust is expressed or implied from the express terms of these documents then the CVA operates simply as a contract, with the result that the company retains ownership of its property and funds until these are handed over to the supervisor. However, if the proposals or the terms of the CVA declare a trust in favour of the CVA creditors, either in those terms or by referring to the pursuit of proceedings or the collection of some other asset for the benefit of the CVA creditors, then on the proposals taking effect, with any modifications, pursuant to the CVA the assets in question become trust property.[48] Similarly if the company agrees to transfer to the supervisor identified or identifiable assets for the purposes of the CVA that may suffice to create a trust in favour of the CVA creditors.[49] This would be consistent with the rule of equity that an agreement for a transfer is to be treated as a transfer in accordance with the maxim that equity treats as done that which ought to be done.

Who can take advantage of a CVA

10–131 Not surprisingly, the courts have held that only parties bound by a CVA are entitled to take advantage of its provisions.[50] But the terms of a CVA will usually contain provisions empowering or requiring the supervisor to allow

---

[45] *Alman v Approach Housing Ltd* [2002] B.C.C. 723. As to small eligible companies, see para.10–115.

[46] If the company, instead of transferring property to the supervisor, makes a declaration of trust in his favour then he is a sub-trustee.

[47] *Re TBL Realisations plc, Oakley-Smith v Greenberg* [2004] B.C.C. 81.

[48] *Re N.T. Gallagher & Son Ltd, Shierson v Tomlinson* [2002] B.C.C. 867.

[49] *Re TBL Realisations plc, Oakley-Smith v Greenberg* [2004] B.C.C. 81.

[50] *R.A. Securities Ltd v Mercantile Credit Co Ltd* [1995] 3 All E.R. 581; *Johnson v Davies* [1997] 1 All E.R. 921.

creditors who have failed to submit their claims the opportunity to participate in the CVA, though not so as to disturb prior distributions.

Challenge to CVA

A person entitled to vote at a meeting of creditors or members, or the nominee under the CVA or the liquidator or administrator of the company if it is in winding-up or administration, may challenge the CVA on the ground of unfair prejudice or of material irregularity, at or in, relation to either of the meetings.[51] Where the court is satisfied as to the ground or grounds of the challenge it may revoke or suspend the approvals given by the meeting or meetings and/or direct the summoning of further meetings; and where the court is satisfied that the person making the original proposal does not intend to submit a revised proposal it must revoke the direction and revoke or suspend any approval given at the previous meetings.[52]

10–132

The role of the insolvency practitioner

It will be apparent from what has been said earlier that the insolvency practitioner involved with the preparation and management of a CVA is likely to wear a number of different hats.[53] Initially he will advise on the viability of a CVA and the form it should take and prepare or assist in the preparation of the proposal. In that capacity he owes the usual duties of care in contract and tort owed by a professional adviser.[54] Then, if he is offered and accepts an invitation to do so, he becomes the nominee and will act as chairman of the meetings of members and creditors. As nominee and chairman he is fulfilling statutory functions and in principle ought not to incur any liability in private law. The remedy of a party who feels aggrieved by the acts or omissions of the insolvency practitioner while acting as nominee or chairman is to apply to the court under s.6 of the Insolvency Act.[55] Once the CVA has taken effect the nominee becomes the supervisor. As such he is an officer of the court and subject to its control. Since the Insolvency Act provides the means by which his conduct can be reviewed by the court, which can give appropriate directions, an aggrieved party is not entitled to pursue a private law action.[56]

10–133

---

[51] Insolvency Act 1986, s.6(1), (2).
[52] *ibid.*, s.6(4).
[53] See generally Edward Bailey, *Voluntary Arrangements*, para.4.17, for a good discussion of this topic.
[54] *Prosser v Castle Sanderson* [2003] B.C.C .440. See also *Pitt v Mond* [2001] B.P.I.R. 624.
[55] Or, in the case of a CVA by a small eligible company, Sch.A1, para.39(3).
[56] *King v Anthony* [1998] 2 B.C.L.C. 517.

We have not yet quite exhausted the possible capacities of the insolvency practitioner, for if the company is in administration it is likely that the administrator will initiate the proposal for a CVA and, if this is approved, will become the supervisor. He will now be wearing two hats simultaneously and it is important to distinguish his two capacities. As administrator he is responsible for the management of the company, subject to any powers given to him in his capacity of supervisor, and as administrator he makes payments to and holds property for himself in the capacity of supervisor. It is at that point that a trust of the payments and property comes into being for the benefit of the CVA creditors unless this has been created earlier under the proposal or the CVA itself.[57] As supervisor he is responsible for the implementation of the CVA, the collection of payments from the company or its administrator (who could be a different person), the distribution of dividends and the oversight of compliance by the company with the terms of the CVA, reporting any breaches to the creditors and where necessary issuing a certificate of non-compliance that may have the effect of releasing the CVA creditors from the moratorium. It is even possible for him to acquire a fifth hat. If the company is put into liquidation he could become the liquidator. Certainly today's insolvency practitioners cannot complain of lack of variety!

Scheme of arrangement under section 425[58]

10–134   Reference has already been made to schemes of arrangement under s.425,[59] which provide an alternative to CVAs. Like a CVA, a scheme of arrangement under s.425 may be made even if the company is not insolvent or likely to become insolvent. The procedure is more complex and cumbersome and may take a good deal longer, and since the proposal for a scheme, like the proposal for a CVA, does not attract a moratorium there is scope for disaffected creditors to take individual action in the same way as for a CVA outside administration. In practice that difficulty is often overcome by entering administration or by filing a winding-up petition, obtaining a stay of proceedings against the company under s.126 of the Insolvency Act 1986 and procuring approval of the scheme by application to the court by the liquidator. A scheme of arrangement under s.425 has the advantage of binding all creditors or, in the case of a scheme for a class, all members of the class.[60] Moreover, in confirming the scheme the court can also approve any requisite reconstruction, such as the reduction of capital or the transfer of assets and liabilities.[61]

---

[57] See above, para.10–130.
[58] See *British Company Law and Practice* (looseleaf), paras 67-050 *et seq.*
[59] See above, para.1–26.
[60] Insolvency Act 1986, s.425(2); and see Prentice, Oditah and Segal, above, para.10–01, n.1, at p.494.
[61] See above, para.1–26.

There are three phases to a scheme under s.425.[62] First, there is an application to the court under s.425(1) for an order that a meeting or meetings of the creditors or different classes of creditor be summoned. The relevant classes must be correctly identified if the court is to have jurisdiction to sanction the scheme at a later stage. Then proposals must be put to the meeting or meetings and approved by the requisite majority. Finally, the approved scheme must be submitted to the court for its sanction.

Restructurings (workouts)

For large multi-banked companies it may be possible to bypass formal **10–135** insolvency procedures, at least in the first instance, and organise a rescue on a contractual basis, following the guidelines embodied in the London Approach and the INSOL Principles.[63] The preparations for a restructuring, or workout, typically involve a number of stages. First, there is an informal moratorium for an agreed standstill period in order to enable the company to provide information and for the creditors to evaluate it and consider proposals to address the company's financial difficulties. It is important to involve in the process all bank and other financial institution creditors as well as representatives of bondholders (who are now more actively engaged in restructurings as a result of the increased use of bonds as a method of financing) and any major trade suppliers whose participation is needed to facilitate the rescue. The participating creditors agree to co-operate with each other and refrain from steps designed to improve their position *vis-à-vis* other participating creditors, while the company undertakes to refrain from acts that would prejudice the position of the participating creditors. It is normal to appoint a lead bank and to establish one or more committees representative of the main classes of creditor. The lead bank co-ordinates information and action among the participating banks and appoints accountants to investigate the company's financial position and to evaluate information obtained.

It is not always the case that banks retain their claims; sometimes they may decide to sell these or a sub-participation in them to distressed debt traders at a substantial discount, a practice which can cause difficulties in that the purchasers of distressed debt may be less willing to give up or suspend their rights and the confidentiality of information may be threatened.

---

[62] See the judgment of Chadwick L.J. in *Re BTR plc* [2000] 1 B.C.L.C. 740 at 742, and his restatement in *Fidelity Investments International plc v MyTravel Group plc* [2004] EWCA Civ. 1734.

[63] For an illuminating discussion see Nick Segal, "Rehabilitation and Approaches Other Than Formal Insolvency Procedures" in *Banks and Remedies* (ed. Ross Cranston), Chap.8.

When the relevant information has been obtained the participants and the company can then move to the second stage, the preparation and consideration of proposals. Meanwhile it is necessary to keep the company trading, for which purpose it may be necessary to procure additional funding. This is one of the major hurdles to be overcome and usually entails a funding agreement by which the funder obtains a much higher rate of interest on the new funds than it did on those originally advanced, as well as substantial arrangement fees and an agreement for priority of its claim for the new money advanced.

If the negotiations are successful they will result in a support agreement between the banks and the company and a separate agreement between the banks themselves governing the decision-making process in the restructuring. The terms of the restructuring vary greatly from one plan to another, ranging from disposal of the business or assets and winding-up of the company to a major reorganisation and from debt deferment to conversion of debt into equity or a compromise in which creditors waive part of their claims.[64] Moreover, once the principal terms of an informal restructuring have been agreed with the principal creditors a formal scheme of arrangement is put in place under s.425 of the Companies Act 1985 in order to bind dissentient creditors.[65]

---

[64] See above, para.10–122, discussing reorganisation in the context of a CVA. For an example of restructuring of a group of companies so that they ceased to be insolvent and could then be taken out of administration, see *Re Olympia & York Canary Wharf Ltd (No.4)* [1994] 1 B.C.L.C. 702.

[65] An example is the restructuring of Marconi.

Chapter 11

The Avoidance of Transactions on Winding-up or Administration

Where a company goes into winding-up or administration, unperformed **11–01** obligations of the company to a creditor cannot in general be enforced without the consent of the office-holder,[1] but payments, transfers or other benefits already made or conferred by the company are in principle undisturbed. This is a corollary of the rule previously enunciated[2] that only those assets which belong to the, company at the time of the insolvency proceeding[3] are available for the claims of the general body of creditors. But the liquidator or administrator[4] can invoke any ground of avoidance available to the company at common law,[5] and any restitutionary remedy open to the company to reverse unjust enrichment,[6] and in the case of misfeasance by the officers of the company he is given a summary remedy.[7] Again, the voluntary disposition of a company's assets by way of gift or sale at a gross undervalue may be *ultra vires* under company law as outside its objects[8] or as an unauthorised reduction of capital.[9] These various grounds

---

[1] *i.e.* the liquidator or administrator.
[2] Above, paras 3–03, 6–34 *et seq.*
[3] The exact cut-off point varies according to the proceeding involved.
[4] Most of the avoidance provisions apply equally to winding-up and administration, and in the text that follows "winding-up" and "liquidator" should be taken to include administration and the administrator unless otherwise indicated. There is one ground of avoidance which is not dependent on the company being in winding-up or administration, namely that the transaction is one defrauding creditors (Insolvency Act 1986, s.423), but it is convenient to include it in the present chapter.
[4] Insolvency Act 1986, s.127.
[5] For example, misrepresentation.
[6] For example, rescission of a contract and recovery of benefits received by the solvent party.
[7] Insolvency Act 1986, s.212.
[8] See *Aveling Barford Ltd v Perion Ltd* (1989) 5 B.C.C. 677 and cases there cited.
[9] Contrary to the rule in *Trevor v Whitworth* (1887) 12 App. Cas. 409. See now Companies Act 1985, ss.135-181, and John Armour, "Avoidance of Transactions as a 'Fraud on Creditors' at Common Law" in *Vulnerable Transactions in Corporate Insolvency* (ed. John Armour and Howard Bennett) at 281 *et seq.*

of avoidance owe nothing to insolvency law; they merely reflect the preservation of the company's pre-liquidation entitlements and limits on its powers. They are not discussed further.

However, the principle of equity among creditors that underlies the *pari passu* rule of insolvency law will in certain conditions require the adjustment of concluded transactions which but for the winding-up of the company would have remained binding on the company, and the return to the company of payments made or property transferred under the transactions or the reversal of their effect.

1. THE DIVERSE NATURE OF THE AVOIDANCE PROVISIONS

Some Remedies pre-post order.

11–02 The mode of adjustment of these vulnerable transactions takes a variety of forms. In some cases the transaction will be rendered void, either wholly or against designated categories of third party, automatically upon winding-up under statutory provisions which are self-executing. Thus in a compulsory winding-up dispositions of the company's property made after presentation of the winding-up petition are wholly void unless authorised or validated by the court,[10] and a floating charge given by an insolvent company otherwise than for specified forms of new value becomes wholly invalid if the company goes into winding-up or administration within a specified period,[11] whilst a charge given by the company which should have been registered[12] but was not is void against the liquidator and creditors but not against other classes of third party, such as purchasers.[13] In other cases the transaction itself remains valid but the liquidator is given the right to apply for an order reversing its effect. For example, while it is common to speak of the avoidance of a preference or transaction at an undervalue, the act of preference or transfer is not avoided as such but its effects may be reversed by whatever method the court thinks fit[14] including the (re)vesting of the property transferred.[15] However, nothing will happen unless the liquidator makes an application to the court. A third category is that of the extortionate credit transaction, which is neither invalid nor necessarily wholly reversible but may be set aside, wholly or in part, or simply varied, as the justice of the case requires.[16] Again, the statutory provisions are not self-executing; they have to be invoked by the office-holder.

For brevity all these forms of adjustment will be referred to as "avoidance" in the ensuing pages, but it should be constantly borne in mind that

---

[10] Insolvency Act 1986, s.127.
[11] *ibid.*, s.245.
[12] Under s.395 of the Companies Act 1985.
[13] *ibid.*, s.395(1).
[14] *ibid.*, ss.238, 239, 241.
[15] *ibid.*, s.241(l)(a).
[16] *ibid.*, s.244.

this term is shorthand for a widely differing range of effects and reliefs. In particular, where payments or transfers of property made by the company are void, they are deemed to remain assets of the company in its own right so as to be susceptible to capture by a floating charge or a fixed charge over after-acquired property of the same description, whereas recoveries resulting from a court order after application by the liquidator are considered to be held for the creditors and not for the company itself and are therefore not captured by a prior security.[17]

2. THE POLICIES UNDERLYING THE AVOIDANCE PROVISIONS

The conditions of avoidance vary according to the particular ground of avoidance involved but are for the most part dictated by a common policy, namely to protect the general body of creditors against a diminution of the assets available to them by a transaction which confers an unfair or improper advantage on the other party. All but two of the grounds of avoidance known to insolvency law[18] involve the unjust enrichment of a particular party at the expense of other creditors, whether they are preferential creditors or ordinary unsecured creditors.[19] Once this crucial point is grasped much of the legislative structure falls into place. The unjust enrichment may affect other creditors in one of two ways. It may reduce the company's net asset value, as where it involves a transfer of the company's property to another party (whether or not a creditor) at a wholly inadequate price or a purchase of property by the company at an inflated price; or it may, without disturbing the company's net asset position, involve payment or transfer to a particular creditor in satisfaction or reduction of his debt, thereby giving him a preference over other creditors in disregard of the priority position of preferential creditors or, if there remains enough to pay them in full, then in breach of the *pari passu* principle of distribution among ordinary unsecured creditors. The avoidance provisions may thus be seen as necessary to ensure equality of distribution, at least among classes of creditors. Whether the defendant is or should be entitled to avail himself of defences and cross-claims that would be available in answer to claims of unjust enrichment at common law is a question we shall discuss later in this chapter.[20]

It will be apparent from what is said above that the phrase "unjust enrichment" is here used in a restricted sense to denote the conferment on

11–03

---

[17] See below, paras 11–138 *et seq.*

[18] The two exceptions are failure to register a registrable charge and the making of a post-petition disposition of the company's property without the authorisation of the court.

[19] In *Hollicourt (Contracts) Ltd v Bank of Ireland* [2001] Ch. 555 it was common ground that a claim under s.127 of the Insolvency Act 1986 is restitutionary in character. See the judgment of Mummery L.J. at para.22.

[20] Below, para.11–67.

the other party of an unfair or improper benefit to the prejudice of its existing *creditors*. Damage to the members of the company is not our present concern. If the directors improperly apply the company's assets they can be called to account by the members. If the company is solvent it is the prerogative of the members to ratify the improper acts of the directors, for only the members themselves are injured. The position is otherwise where the company is insolvent, for then it is the creditors who have the primary interest in the proper application of the company's assets, though this can usually be asserted only when the company is in winding-up or administration.[21]

There is a subsidiary policy underlying the avoidance provisions, namely the protection of an insolvent company's business from dismemberment through the improper disposition of its assets.

11–04   A third policy is sometimes invoked as the rationale of the rule against preferences, namely deterrence of future creditors from gaining an unfair advantage. But it is hard to see why a creditor should be deterred from taking the benefit of a preference when if he is lucky the company will survive the preference period, the liquidator might anyway take no steps to recover the preference and even if he does the worst that happens is that the creditor will have to give up the benefit he received.[22]

Despite references to the first two of these two policies in a number of cases it cannot be said that the underlying rationale of the statutory provisions has been very clearly articulated either by the legislature or by the courts. The point has been trenchantly made by a leading scholar, Professor Andrew Keay, with reference to that country's insolvency laws:

> "Over the years avoidance provisions have regularly come under the scrutiny of the courts. Yet, there is little evidence of the courts seeking to ascertain the rationale for the existence of these provisions. It is submitted that the existence of such provisions is not a matter which excites any debate in Australia. There has been hardly any consideration of the underlying basis for the decisions; in fact there are few cases in which the reason for the inclusion of avoidance provisions in corporation or bankruptcy legislation has been mentioned."[23]

The same is true of the avoidance provisions of the United Kingdom Insolvency Act. Invocation of the policy of protecting the general body of creditors does not explain why it is necessary to avoid unregistered charges, post-petition dispositions of the company's assets for full value and in the

---

[21] See below, para.11–06.

[22] See to similar effect Vern Countryman, "The Concept of a Voidable Preference in Bankruptcy", 38 Vand. L. Rev. 713, 747 (1985); David Gray Carlson, "Security Interests in the Crucible of Voidable Preference" U. Ill. L. Rev. 211, 215 (1995).

[23] Andrew Keay, "In Pursuit of the Rationale Behind the Avoidance of Pre-Liquidation Transactions" (1996) 18 Sydney Law Rev. 55.

ordinary course of business, or floating charges given by an insolvent company for new value in the form of land, debts or intellectual property rights. Nor does reference to the *pari passu* principle tells us why it is all right for a particular creditor to gain a preference by threatening or bullying the company into making a payment but not all right if the company makes the payment voluntarily to a creditor who receives it in good faith, or why, indeed, the desire or intention of either party should be relevant rather than the mere fact that one creditor has been given an advantage over the others in the run-up to liquidation. For this one has to resort to the historical origins of the preference rule.[24] Again, the reason why some kinds of transaction are rendered completely and automatically invalid while others are merely subject to adjustment in the discretion of the court on application by the liquidator has never been articulated; nor has it been explained why the period for which a company has to survive before an initially vulnerable transaction in favour of a party unconnected with the company becomes immune from attack is 6 months for a preference, 12 months for a floating charge, 2 years for a transaction at an undervalue, 3 years for an extortionate credit bargain and no time limit at all for a transaction defrauding creditors.

The fact is that every ground of avoidance in the Insolvency Act is derived from earlier legislation and each ground has been individually modified at different times but without any attempt to rework the avoidance provisions into a coherent whole. A brief evaluation of the provisions is offered at the end of the present chapter.[25]

3. THE MINIMUM CONDITIONS FOR AVOIDANCE

The four conditions

In general at least four conditions must be satisfied before a transaction **11–05** entered into by the company can be upset under insolvency law.[26]

(1) The company must be in winding-up or administration.

(2) The transaction must have resulted in a diminution in the assets available to the general body of creditors.

---

[24] See below, para.11–69.
[25] Below, para.11–142.
[26] I shall not discuss grounds for avoidance under the general law, *e.g.* for misrepresentation. These can, of course, be invoked by a liquidator or administrator in the name of the company and, as stated above, raise no questions of insolvency law as such. For the special exemptions applicable to market contracts, market charges and certain other types of contract, see below, para.11–141.

(3)   The company must have been unable to pay its debts at the time of or in consequence of the transaction.

(4)   The transaction must have been entered into within a specified time before the onset of insolvency,[27] the time varying according to the circumstances.

As stated, these conditions, each of which is examined below, represent the minimum prerequisites for avoidance in most cases. It does not follow that where they are fulfilled the transaction will inevitably be vulnerable; usually some further elements have to be considered. Moreover, there are certain exceptional cases in which a transaction may be avoided even where one or more of the above conditions is not satisfied. These will be noted as we proceed.

Company in winding-up or administration

11–06   As I have pointed out earlier,[28] the fact that a company is insolvent does not by itself attract legal consequences. The ability of creditors of an insolvent company to obtain redress for an improper diminution of its assets in favour of another party depends in general[29] upon the company being in winding-up or administration. Why should this be so? Why should not unsecured creditors be free to attack a transaction even before the advent of a formal insolvency proceeding? There are several answers to these questions.[30] First, so long as the company is conducting its business in a lawful manner there is no justification for allowing interference by unsecured creditors in its affairs. They have no interest in the company's assets and therefore no right to complain of the way in which the company chooses to dispose of those assets. Secondly, the creditor of a company not in winding-up or administration has a more direct method of obtaining payment, namely by instituting proceedings, taking judgment and enforcing it by one or more of the available forms of execution, which include seizure and sale of the company's property and attachment of debts due to it. It is only if these measures fail, or are considered pointless because of insufficiency of the company's assets, that recourse to avoidance proceedings becomes necessary. Thirdly, different creditors may have different views as to avoidance proceedings. No single creditor or group of creditors can demand protection for himself or itself alone.[31] If, therefore a transaction is

---

[27] As defined by the Insolvency Act 1986, s.240(3).

[28] See above, para.9–01.

[29] The exceptional case is the avoidance of transactions defrauding of creditors. See below, para.11–06.

[30] See also R.M. Goode, "Is the Law Too Favourable to Secured Creditors" (1983–84) 8 Can. Bus. L.J. 53 at 71–73.

[31] For the exceptional case, see below, paras 11–134 *et seq.*

to be set aside it must be for the benefit of the general body of unsecured creditors. But the protection of unsecured creditors as a class requires legal machinery by which they can be brought together and given a *locus standi* and an office-holder to represent their interests. This machinery is provided by a formal collective insolvency proceeding in the shape of winding-up or administration, the interests of the class being asserted by the liquidator or administrator.

The Insolvency Act 1986 contains one ground of avoidance not dependent on winding-up or administration, namely entry into a transaction at an undervalue in order to place assets outside the reach of an existing or potential creditor.[32] Since such a provision is available to protect a particular deprived creditor, not merely creditors at large, it does not necessarily involve any collective proceeding.

Diminution of assets available for the general body of creditors

As noted earlier, a diminution in the assets available to the general body of   **11–07**
creditors may occur in one of two ways: by a reduction in the net assets of the company itself or by a preference, that is, a payment or transfer in favour of one particular creditor at the expense of the others.

Where a company receives full value for a payment or transfer, other than a payment or transfer in discharge or reduction of a debt, creditors will rarely have cause for complaint, for there is no diminution in the company's asset worth, merely the conversion of an asset from one form into another, nor is there a preference of another creditor. The position is otherwise where the effect of the transaction is to reduce the company's net assets, as where it buys an asset at an inflated price, sells an asset for substantially less than its value, grants a tenancy which, though at a full market rent, reduces the capital value of the property let, enters in to a burdensome contract or releases a debtor from liability.[33] The absence or inadequacy of new value is by far the most important factor in the various statutory provisions rendering transactions vulnerable on liquidation or administration. Indeed, of the eight grounds of avoidance discussed in this chapter only two are capable of applying despite the furnishing of full value, namely non-registration of a registrable charge[34] and failure to obtain leave of the court to make a disposition of the company's assets after presentation of a winding-up petition.[35] I shall discuss the rationale of these two exceptions a little later.[36]

---

[32] Insolvency Act 1986, s.423. See below, para.11–134.

[33] Taking security for a previously unsecured debt does not in itself reduce the company's net assets, it merely subjects a particular asset to a particular liability, and if the security is realised and the proceeds applied in discharge of the debt both the asset (except as to any surplus) and the liability disappear from the balance sheet. See below, para.11–37.

[34] See para.11–120.

[35] See below, paras 11–124 *et seq.*

[36] See below, paras 11–121, 11–124 *et seq.*

Insolvency at time of transaction

11–08 Even where the transaction does diminish the company's assets it will not normally be vulnerable to attack on winding-up or liquidation unless the company was unable to pay its debts[37] at the time of the transaction or became unable to do so in consequence of the transaction. In other words, the transaction must be one which prejudices those who are creditors[38] at the time the transaction is concluded. If, after entering into the transaction, the company is still able to pay its debts as they fall due, creditors are not prejudiced by a diminution in the company's assets and only the members of the company have a *locus standi* to complain of its entry into a disadvantageous transaction.[39] But insolvency at the time of or in consequence of the transaction is not a prerequisite of avoidance of an unregistered charge,[40] an extortionate credit transaction,[41] a transaction defrauding creditors[42] or a floating charge given otherwise than for a specified form of new value in favour of a person connected with the company.[43] The first three of these exceptions are perfectly logical. As mentioned earlier, want of registration and the making of a post-petition disposition without court approval are the only grounds of avoidance having nothing to do with diminution of assets, so that the company's ability to pay its debts at the time registration should have been effected is irrelevant. The provisions relating to extortionate credit bargains are designed to avoid the inclusion of exorbitant rates of interest in proofs of debt,[44] and again the question of the company's ability to pay its debts at the time of the transaction is irrelevant for this purpose. The avoidance of transactions in fraud of creditors, being designed primarily for the protection of particular creditors, is likewise unconnected to a state of insolvency at the time of the transaction. Less clear is the reason for the exception as regards floating charges, though it is possible to find an explanation for this.[45]

---

[37] Within the meaning of s.123 of the Insolvency Act 1986. See above, paras 4–03 et seq.

[38] Whether their claims are existing, contingent or prospective. See above, paras 9–20 *et seq*.

[39] This point is further discussed below, para.455, where it will be seen that there are dicta suggesting that directors may owe a duty to future creditors. But this is in the context of a breach of duty owed by the directors to the company itself and has no application to the avoidance provisions of the Insolvency Act.

[40] Companies Act 1985, s.395(1). See below, para.11–120.

[41] *ibid.*, s.244. See below, para.11–105.

[42] *ibid.*, s.423. See below, para.11.134.

[43] *ibid.*, s.245. See below, para.11–108. Section 127 of the Insolvency Act, dealing with post-petition dispositions of the company's property not authorised by the court, is not expressed to require insolvency of the company at the time of the disposition but in practice this will almost invariably be the case, for an order on the petition, unless made exclusively on the "just and equitable ground", presupposes that the company is unable to pay its debts.

[44] Insolvency Law Review Committee, *Insolvency Law and Practice*, para.1381. However, they have a wider impact than this, since they empower the court to set aside the whole or part of any obligation created by the transaction and to order repayment of any sum paid by the company. See below, para.11–107.

[45] See below, para.11–108.

Advent of liquidation or administration within specified time

Even where all three features described above are present, the transaction **11–09** will usually cease to be vulnerable if winding-up or administration does not supervene within a specified period[46] after the transaction was concluded. The transaction thus becomes cleansed by the passage of time, a sensible rule, for it is unfair to a contracting party (and indeed contrary to well settled principles of property law and limitation of actions) that a party should be indefinitely exposed to a liability to restore that which he lawfully received. Moreover, the link between cause and effect, between the offending transaction and its impact on creditors, becomes ever more tenuous with the passage of time. If no creditor takes steps to wind up the company or put it into administration within the specified period, creditors have no cause to complain of the disappearance of a ground of avoidance. But there are two exceptional cases. The failure to register a charge is not pardoned by the lapse of time, for the obvious reason that it is a continuing breach with continuing adverse consequences for innocent third parties; and avoidance of a transaction in fraud of creditors is not subject to a time limit, which no doubt reflects not only the fact that the statutory provision has a long history but also that the transaction involves the intentional removal of an asset for the purpose of defeating a creditor and is thus a species of fraud.

4. OTHER RELEVANT CONSIDERATIONS

I have said that the four conditions mentioned earlier are minimum **11–10** prerequisites for avoidance and that other factors may be material in determining whether a transaction is vulnerable under the Insolvency Act. In particular, the application of the statutory provisions may depend on whether the other party to the transaction was a person connected with the company[47]; whether in the case of a preference the company was influenced by a desire to give a preference; whether, in the case of a charge, it was created as a fixed charge or as a floating charge; and whether the transaction was made in good faith and for the purpose of carrying on the company's business. There is also a question whether, given the fact that the avoidance provisions are rooted in the concept of unjust enrichment, restitutionary defences and cross-claims, such as change of position and counter-restitution, are available.

5. THE GROUNDS FOR AVOIDANCE: A SUMMARY

A transaction may be avoided or adjusted under insolvency law or its effect **11–11** reversed on no fewer than eight distinct grounds, *viz.* as a transaction which is:

---

[46] Ranging from six months to three years, according to the nature of the case.
[47] Within the meaning of s.249 of the Insolvency Act 1986.

(1)   in contravention of the principle of *pari passu* distribution;

(2)   a transaction at an undervalue;

(3)   a preference;

(4)   an extortionate credit transaction;

(5)   a floating charge given otherwise than for specified forms of new value;

(6)   a registrable but unregistered charge;

(7)   a disposition of the company's property made without leave of the court after presentation of a winding-up petition;

(8)   a transaction in fraud of creditors.

The first of these has already, been examined in detail in an earlier chapter[48]; I shall examine each of the others in turn.

6. TRANSACTIONS AT AN UNDERVALUE[49]

(i) Overview

The basic provision

11–12   Where a company in administration or liquidation has at a relevant time entered into a transaction with any person at an undervalue and the statutory defence referred to below is not available, the office-holder may apply to the court to order restoration of the status quo, with consequential relief.[50]

As we shall see below, there is a possibility of overlap between the provisions relating to transactions at an undervalue and those relating to preferences. Some transactions at an undervalue within s.238 of the Insolvency Act will also be vulnerable as preferences under s.239. Where this is so, the office-holder is likely to rely primarily on s.238, which is wider in scope and reaches back longer in time.[51]

What constitutes a transaction at an undervalue

11–13   A company enters into a transaction with a person at an undervalue if it:

---

[48] See above, paras 7–02 *et seq.*

[49] For a penetrating analysis, see John Armour, "Transactions at an Undervalue", in *Vulnerable Transactions in Corporate Insolvency* (ed. Armour and Bennett) 37.

[50] Insolvency Act 1986, ss.238, 240, 241. "Relevant time" is defined in s.240. See below, para.11–38, text and n.6.

[51] Two years in all cases, in contrast with preferences in favour of a person not connected with the company, where the period is six months.

(1)   makes a gift to that person; or

(2)   otherwise enters into a transaction with that person on terms that provide for the company to receive no consideration; or

(3)   enters into a transaction with that person for a consideration the value of which is significantly less than the value, in money or money's worth, of the consideration provided by the company.[52]

"Transaction" is defined as including a gift, agreement or arrangement, and references to entering into, a transaction are to be construed accordingly.[53]

Examples of transactions at an undervalue

The company enters into a transaction at an undervalue where it: **11–14**

(1)   makes a gift of property;

(2)   undertakes a burden (*e.g.* binds itself to supply goods or services) for no consideration (this would usually require a deed);

(3)   purchases an asset for significantly more, or sells an asset for significantly less, than its value;

(4)   takes an asset on lease or hire at a rent significantly above the rental value of the asset or lets it out on lease or hire at a rent significantly below its rental value;

(5)   agrees to pay for services a sum significantly more, or to charge for services a sum significantly less, than their value;

(6)   allows an asset to be retained by the other party in satisfaction of a claim against the company which is significantly less than the value of the asset or takes an asset in satisfaction of a claim which is significantly more than the value of the asset;

(7)   accepts in satisfaction of a debt a sum significantly less than the recoverable value of the debt; or

(8)   gives a guarantee or indemnity and receives by way of benefit significantly less than the value of the benefit conferred by the guarantee or takes a guarantee or indemnity against a benefit which is significantly less in value than that of the guarantee.

In all these cases the company either receives nothing for what it supplies or pays too much or receives too little to ensure equality of exchange, and

---

[52] Insolvency Act 1986, s.238(4).
[53] *ibid.*, s.436.

the transaction will be vulnerable under s.238 unless the statutory defence under s.238(5) is available. The same applies to the distribution of a declared dividend at a time when the company is insolvent, and this could also be attached as a preference.[54] Most of the examples given are straightforward and require no explanation. However, it will be necessary to say something about gifts, transactions for no consideration, the benefits to be considered in valuing the consideration, and the treatment of guarantees, and to explain the omission from the list of security given by the company for a previously unsecured loan.

It will be obvious that where a transaction is attacked on the ground of significant inequality of exchange difficult questions of valuation may arise which are similar in kind to those previously discussed in relation to the test of insolvency.[55] As will be seen, what matters is the true value of a benefit received or given up, which is not necessarily its stated or face value.

Conditions to be satisfied under section 238

11–15 The court cannot make an order under s.238 unless the following seven conditions are satisfied:

(1) The company is in liquidation or administration

(2) Application for the order is made by the liquidator or administrator

(3) A transaction was concluded

(4) The company was a party to the transaction

(5) The transaction was at an undervalue

(6) The transaction was entered into at a relevant time

(7) The company was unable to pay its debts at the time of or in consequence of entering into the transaction.

Even where all these elements are present the court may be precluded from making any order by reason of s.238(5) of the Act. Under s.241 the court has wide powers both as to the orders it can make to reverse the effect of the transaction and as to the persons against whom an order can be made but the particular defendant may be protected by s.241(3) of the Act. It is also necessary to consider whether a restitutionary defence or cross-claim is available based on principles of unjust enrichment.

Onus of proof

11–16 In general, the onus lies on the office-holder to show that the above seven conditions are satisfied and on the defendant to make out a defence under s.238(5) or 241(3). But in the case of a transaction entered into by the

---

[54] See below, para.11–76, n.67.
[55] Above, paras 4–06 *et seq.*

company with a person connected with the company[56] condition (7) is presumed to be satisfied unless the contrary is shown,[57] and there is a presumption against good faith as regards such a person in the circumstances set out in s.241(2A).[58]

(ii) The elements in detail

Company is in liquidation or administration

The statutory provisions do not apply unless the company is in liquidation **11–17** or administration. The reasons for this have already been discussed.[59]

Application is made by the liquidator or administrator

The requirement that the application for an order be made by the relevant **11–18** office-holder reflects two considerations. First, the remedy is not automatic, it has to be sought. This is because the application of the statutory provisions depends on a careful examination of the facts and does not lend itself to an automatic trigger. Second, the remedy also is necessarily discretionary, since the circumstances may vary widely from case to case, and since it is designed for the protection of the creditors generally in an insolvency proceeding it would be inappropriate to allow application to be made by anyone other than the liquidator or administrator as the representative of the creditors' interests. So it is not open to a creditor or group of creditors or to a member or group of members to invoke the statutory provisions, though what they are entitled to do, if they believe that the liquidator or administrator is neglecting to pursue a remedy which ought to be pursued, is to apply to the court,[60] though the court will be slow to substitute its own judgment for that of the office-holder.

"Transaction"

The word "transaction" has a very wide meaning. It is not confined to **11–19** contracts but extends to gifts and other arrangements which are not based on contract, and where there is a contract, "transaction" may cover not only that contract but any linked transaction, even though involving a different

---

[56] See below, para.11–38, n.6.
[57] Insolvency Act 1986, s.240(2).
[58] See below, para.11–42.
[59] Above, para.11–06.
[60] Under the Insolvency Act 1986, ss.167(3), 168(5), 212(1) (liquidator) or Sch.B1, para.74 (administrator).

party.[61] In Australia it has been established in a series of cases that "transaction" is wide enough to include a series of steps over a period involving several parties and not always contractual consequences; a unilateral act[62] ; and arrangements giving rise to an estoppel.[63] But apart from gift there has to be some element of dealing, this being implicit in the word "transaction" itself and being reinforced by the references in s.238 to (a) the "entry into" a transaction, (b) "with a person" and (c) "on terms that provide".[64]

The company as party to the transaction

11–20 Section 238 applies only where it is the company that enters into the transaction at an undervalue. So a transaction is not within the ambit of the section unless the company is a party to it. The first step is thus to identify the relevant transaction. So, in a case involving s.423 of the Act, when debtors to a bank decided to place farming assets out of its reach by forming a company of which they were the sole directors and shareholders, selling the assets to the company at a proper value and then procuring the grant to it of a 20-year agricultural tenancy, the relevant transactions were the sale and the tenancy agreement, not the incorporation of the company and the issue of shares in it, so that the impact of the sale and the grant of the tenancy on the value of the shares in the company was irrelevant.[65]

The transaction having been identified, the next question is to determine whether the company was a party to it. While s.238 bites only on transactions to which the company is a party, it is not necessary that all parts of the transaction should involve the same counterparty; the section is

---

[61] See *Phillips v Brewin Dolphin Bell Lawrie Ltd* [2001] 1 W.L.R. 143, discussed in more detail below, para.4–30; *Re Taylor Sinclair (Capital) Ltd, Knights v Seymour Pierce Ellis Ltd* [2001] 2 B.C.L.C. 176; *Department for Environment, Food and Rural Affairs v Feakins* [2004] EWHC 2735, Hart J., decided before the House of Lords ruling in *Brewin Dolphin* but consistent with it.

[62] For example, a gift (expressly provided by the section) or a declaration of trust, as in *Ramlort Ltd v Reid* [2004] B.P.I.R. 985.

[63] *Australian Kitchen Industries Pty Ltd v Albarran* (2005) 51 A.C.S.R. 604, a decision of the New South Wales Supreme Court, in which Barrett J. cited, among other authorities, *Re Emanuel (No. 14) Pty Ltd, Macks v Blacklaw & Shadforth Pty Ltd* (1997) 14 A.L.R. 281 and *Somerset Marine Inc v New Cap Reinsurance Corp.* [2003] NS.W.C.A. 38.

[64] *Re Taylor Sinclair (Capital) Ltd, Knights v Seymour Pierce Ellis Ltd* [2001] 2 B.C.L.C. 176, *per* Mr Robert Englehart Q.C. (sitting as a Deputy High Court Judge). See further John Armour, above, n.49 at 55 *et seq.*

[65] *National Westminster Bank plc v Jones* [2002] 1 B.C.L.C. 55. The statement by Lord Scott in *Phillips v Brewin Dolphin Bell Lawrie Ltd* [2001] 1 W.L.R. 143 at para.20 that "the issue in the present case is not, in my opinion, to identify the section 238(4) 'transaction'; the issue is to identify the section 238(4) 'consideration'" is not, it is thought, intended to deny the importance of identifying the relevant transaction but is simply a consequence of his conclusion that in the case before the House of Lords the various linked contracts all formed part of the transaction, so that the real question to be considered *in that case* was what constituted the consideration.

capable of applying to a composite transaction in which there is a contract between the company and A and a separate but linked contract between the company and B. Indeed, a contract to which the company is not a party at all may nevertheless constitute part of a transaction entered into by the company where this is the common understanding of the parties and the company.[66] Where the company is in administrative receivership and the receiver sells property within the security in the name of the company, rather than having it sold by his debenture holder as mortgagee, that constitutes a sale by the company and if it is at an undervalue it falls within s.238. That is not simply because the receiver is the deemed agent of the company unless and until it goes into liquidation[67] but because the sale is indeed by the company itself acting through the receiver as its directing mind and will in just the same way as if the sale had been authorised by the directors prior to the receivership.[68] The position is otherwise where the debenture holder sells as mortgagee, for even if the receiver executes the conveyance on behalf of the debenture holder it is the latter, not the company, which is the party to the sale.[69] If the sale is at undervalue the remedy is not a claim under s.238 against the purchaser but a claim in equity against the mortgagee under the general law for breach of the mortgagee's duty to take reasonable care to obtain the best price. If the company is in liquidation at the time of the sale the sale can be effected only by and in the name of the debenture holder, for the receiver's status as deemed agent of the company ends with its liquidation. An administrator is in a different position, for he has no property interest himself and invariably acts as the company's agent,[70] so that any disposition he makes is a disposition by the company.

Gifts

A gift is a transfer of an asset for no consideration. The fact that the gift is by deed is irrelevant, for though it is sometimes said that a deed imports consideration this does not alter the character of the transaction as a gift.   **11–21**

At first sight it seems obvious that a gift by a company which goes into liquidation or administration within the requisite two-year period should be a candidate for restoration by the donee, for surely a company has no business giving away its assets. In practice the matter is less clear cut. Most companies make payments during the course of a trading year for which

---

[66] As in *Phillips v Brewin Dolphin Bell Laurie Ltd* [2001] 1 W.L.R. 143, where part of the transaction was held to be a covenant by the company's parent to pay rent to a person from whom the company had purchased shares.

[67] Insolvency Act 1986, s.44(1)(a).

[68] *Demite Ltd v Protec Health Ltd* [1998] B.C.C. 638.

[69] *Re Brabon, Treharne v Brabon* [2001] B.C.L.C. 11, a decision on s.339 of the Act.

[70] See above, para.10–75.

they receive no consideration but which are recognised as legitimate forms of expenditure and as likely to benefit the paying company in some indirect or intangible way. Two cases in particular deserve mention, namely gratuitous payments to employees and payments to charity. It should be borne in mind that while both kinds of payment are perfectly normal and in principle, lawful within certain limits,[71] different considerations apply where the company is insolvent,[72] for it is not entitled to be so free with its money at the expense of creditors.

(1) Gratuitous payments to employees

11–22   Payments are frequently made to employees to which they have no legal entitlement under the terms of their contract of employment. They include bonuses for work done or profit targets met, Christmas and other gratuities, and golden handshakes and other terminal payments. To what extent are such payments recoverable as transactions at an undervalue in the event of the employer company going into winding-up or administration? In many cases, of course, the size of the payment to any one employee would be too small to warrant the expense of proceedings, and in the case of a company continuing to trade while under administration the administrator would no doubt be reluctant to risk disturbance to industrial relations by seeking recoupment. But where the company is no longer trading and the size of the payment is substantial—as it may well be in the case of a golden handshake to a retiring senior executive—the office-holder may well consider it appropriate to try to recover the payment.

Given the breadth of meaning of "transaction"[73] it is hard to resist the conclusion that such payments constitute transactions at an undervalue. Uncovenanted bonuses to employees are no doubt considered as emoluments rather than as gifts in normal parlance but are undoubtedly given for no consideration, however effective they may be as inducements to the work force to work even harder in the future. But such bonuses may be justifiable under s.238(5) as bona fide payments for the purpose of carrying on the company's business that could reasonably be expected to benefit the company, either because they provide positive encouragement to the workforce and enhance industrial relations or because they stave off threatened industrial action or produce a settlement. Golden handshakes and other terminal payments made without obligation to do so are much

---

[71] As to payments to employees made redundant on cessation or transfer of a business, see Companies Act 1985, s.719. By s.187 of the Insolvency Act 1986 any such payments decided on by the company before liquidation may be made by the liquidator, but only after the company's liabilities have been fully satisfied.

[72] As stated above, s.238 does not apply unless the company was insolvent at the time of the transaction in question.

[73] See above, para.11–19.

harder to justify, since they can hardly be said to be made for the purpose of carrying on the company's business, nor *prima facie* can they be of benefit to an insolvent company. Whether the court would consider, in the case of a company in administration which is continuing to trade, that the goodwill created by its tangible appreciation of the services rendered by retiring employees satisfies the requirements of s.238(5) must be a matter of doubt; and if the company has ceased trading or is about to do so then even this rather flimsy basis for the payment disappears.

(2) Payments to charity

This may seem a rather remote case to raise but I do so in order to make the point that there is no general defence of receipt in good faith. Of course, a company which knows itself to be insolvent is unlikely to make a significant payment to charity; but it is by no means uncommon for the management of a company to believe that the business is sound when in truth, as the result of concealed defalcations or losses through incompetence, the company is insolvent. If in this situation a payment is made to charity, can the liquidator or administrator recover it as a transaction at an undervalue? In principle, yes, if the other conditions of s.238 are satisfied. It is no defence that the charity received the money in good faith,[74] nor even that it has spent it and unalterably changed its position. But it is for the court to decide what order, if any, to make in the exercise of its powers under s.238, and there seems no reason why the court should not be able to take all the circumstances into account, including the status and good faith of the recipient.

11–23

Transactions under which the company receives no consideration

(1) "Consideration"

"Consideration" is not defined but would appear to have the normal meaning ascribed to it by the law of contract. It is thus to be contrasted with objective value. Consideration is the *quid pro quo* for a promise. It denotes that which a party exacts as the price of his promise. This could include detriment suffered by the other party if that was what the promisor wanted and was thus part of the bargain.[75] If he requires nothing in

11–24

---

[74] Section 241(2) of the Insolvency Act 1986, which restricts the orders the court can make, is limited to recipients for value.

[75] The mere suffering of unbargained-for detriment does not constitute consideration in general contract law, though it might in appropriate cases give rise to an estoppel. In *Agricultural Mortgage Corp Ltd v Woodward* [1994] B.C.C. 688 the Court of Appeal left open the question whether unbargained-for detriment which is of no benefit to the promisor is to be taken into account in valuing the consideration received by the promisor for the purpose of s.238 of the Insolvency Act 1986. It is submitted that it does not, for what s.238 is concerned with is inequality of exchange, and where the promisee suffers detriment for which the promisor did not bargain and in which he has no necessary interest this has nothing to do with the assessment of the benefit the promisor receives.

exchange, then his promise is given without consideration. But if he exacts a counter-undertaking or the performance of a designated act this constitutes consideration for his promise whether or not the counter-presentation has any objective value, for contract law does not concern itself with the adequacy of consideration. Accordingly anything which is valid consideration in law constitutes consideration for the purpose of s.238(4)(a). That this is the meaning of consideration is evident from the phrase "enters into a transaction . . . on terms that provide for the company to receive no consideration," which shows that the relevant question for the purpose of s.238(4)(a) is what the parties agreed, not whether the *quid pro quo* exacted had any intrinsic value. This is reinforced by the wording of s.238(4)(b), which specifically refers to the *value in money or money's worth* of the consideration and requires the *value* of the consideration provided to the company to be compared with the *value* of the consideration provided by it. So a guarantee given in consideration of an advance to a third party is not a gift or other no-consideration transaction within s.238(4)(a) but a transaction within s.238(4)(b), even if the objective value of the advance to the surety is nil. However, in that case if the value of the guarantee is significant the transaction will be one at an undervalue. As in general contract law, past consideration does not suffice. In the context of the statutory provisions consideration obviously means consideration moving from the company in liquidation or administration to the other party, or from the other party to the company, not consideration moving from or to a third party. So if G Ltd gives a guarantee to C in consideration of an advance by C to G Ltd's parent, D plc, and G Ltd then goes into winding-up, then while the consideration for the guarantee is the advance by C to D plc the value of that consideration for the purpose of s.238 is its value to the surety, G Ltd, not its value to D plc.[76]

(2) Distinction between gifts and other no-consideration transactions

11–25   A gift by definition involves a transfer of an asset for no consideration. However, as s.238(4)(a) implies, there are other types of transaction which are unsupported by consideration but are not gifts because they do not involve the transfer of an asset. These include unperfected gift-promises (normally binding only if by deed or by way of proprietary estoppel), voluntary releases of a debt and voluntary acceptance of part-payment in satisfaction of a debt.

---

[76] See below, para.11–36.

Valuing benefits received or given up

(1) The approach to the valuation

Prima facie the value of an asset is not less than the amount that a **11–26** reasonably well-informed purchaser is prepared, in arms-length negotiations, to pay for it.[77] Where there is a market for assets of the type in question then in general the figure to be taken is the market value.[78] This is normally to be determined by expert evidence. The fact that the parties took reasonable steps to obtain an accurate valuation is not in itself the determining factor, for the valuation may have ignored relevant factors or taken into account factors that should not have been considered or may simply have been based on a mistaken view as to the attributes of what was being sold.[79]

Even where there is no mistake as to the quality of the subject-matter, there may be significant differences among competent experts as to the value of an asset. In such a case the court has to weigh the expert testimony and do the best it can to determine the appropriate figure or alternatively the appropriate range of figures within which the value must lie. In the former case the transaction will be a sale at an undervalue if at a price significantly below the amount so determined, even if that price was supported by one of the valuers; in the latter case the transaction should be upheld if the price falls anywhere within the range selected[80] but if significantly below the lowest figure of that range it should be held a transaction at an undervalue.

(2) From whose viewpoint?

The question to be determined in each case is whether the value of the **11–27** consideration given by the company significantly exceeds the value received by the company. This has to be assessed from the viewpoint of the company, not the other party.[81] So while an asset of the company may be disposed of for full value the sale may nevertheless be a transaction at an undervalue if its effect is to reduce the value of the remaining assets held by the company and this effect was part of the bargain. In other words, the consideration provided by the company is considered to include any bargained-for detriment it suffers to its remaining assets or business, *e.g.* because of a "ransom" power it confers on the other party.[82] Conversely,

---

[77] *Phillips v Brewin Dolphin Bell Lawrie Ltd* [2001] 1 W.L.R. 143, *per* Lord Scott at para.30.
[78] *Re Brabon, Treharne v Brabon* [2001] B.C.L.C. 11, *per* Jonathan Parker L.J. at 38.
[79] *ibid.*, at 38–41.
[80] *Ramlort Ltd v Reid* [2004] B.P.I.R. 985. See below, para.11–31.
[81] *Re M.C. Bacon Ltd (No.2)* [1990] B.C.L.C. 324, *per* Millett J. at 340.
[82] *Agricultural Mortgage Corp plc v Woodward* [1994] B.C.C. 688. But not, it is thought, unbargained-for detriment.

the fact that an asset has a special value to the purchaser—for example, for where it is a painting which completes his collection—is to be ignored in determining whether the company has parted with it at an undervalue; what has to be compared (leaving aside questions of detriment) is the consideration received by the company and the market value of the asset rather than its ransom value.

(3) Values to be based on the totality of the transaction

11–28   In valuing the consideration on either side for the purpose of determining whether there is a significant inequality of exchange—for which purpose both values must be measurable in money or money's worth[83]—it is necessary to look at the whole of the transaction and the totality of the benefits the party dealing with the company will receive, not merely the market value in isolation from other factors. This is well illustrated by the decision of the Court of Appeal in *Agricultural Mortgage Corp plc v Woodward*.[84]

> The first defendant had borrowed money from the plaintiff and given in security a charge by way of legal mortgage of his farm. Shortly before expiry of the deadline set by the plaintiff for payment of arrears outstanding under the mortgage the first defendant granted the second defendant a tenancy of the mortgaged property at a rent which all parties to the proceedings accepted was the full market rent. However, the tenancy was a protected agricultural tenancy under the Agricultural Holdings Act 1986 and the transaction was in fact entered into by the first and second defendants with the intention of giving the second defendant security of tenure. The effect was to reduce the value of the mortgaged land from its vacant possession value of over £1 million to a value of less than £500,000, and to put the second defendant in a "ransom position" in negotiating a surrender value with the plaintiff.
>
> *Held:* the fact that the second defendant was paying a full market rent did not prevent the transaction from being a transaction at an undervalue, for its effect was that the first defendant suffered a substantial diminution in the value of his land while the second defendant gained the benefit of security of tenure in the family home, the preservation of the farm business from its previous creditors and an ability to negotiate a large surrender value, so that the true value of the consideration she received was significantly greater than that received by the first defendant.

---

[83] *Re M.C. Bacon Ltd*, above, n.72.

[84] Above, n.82. The case involved s.423 of the Insolvency Act 1986 (transactions defrauding creditors), not s.238, but s.423 imports the requirement of s.238 that the transaction be at an undervalue.

A similar decision was reached in interlocutory proceedings in *Barclays Bank plc v Eustice.*[85]

What the decision in *Agricultural Mortgage Corp plc v Woodward* shows is that in each case it is necessary to look at the reality of the benefit received, not merely the stated consideration. The same applies in valuing what is given up in exchange.

Example

Shortly before going into liquidation Alpha plc agreed to accept £50,000   **11–29**
from Beta Ltd in settlement of a debt of £100,000 owing by Beta to Alpha. At the time of the agreement Beta was itself in serious financial difficulty and other creditors were pressing. There was therefore a risk that Beta might go into liquidation and that Alpha would receive only a small dividend, if anything, in the winding-up. The value of what Alpha gave up in exchange for what it received should be measured as the likely recoverable value of the debt, not its face value. On this basis the settlement was not a transaction at an undervalue.

(4) The use of hindsight to value benefits

The benefits given and received by the company must be valued as at the   **11–30**
time of the transaction. Where one of those values is uncertain the court may have regard to subsequent events in order to test the accuracy of the value ascribed to the benefit in question at the time of the transaction. The decision of the House of Lords in *Phillips v Brewin Dolphin Bell Lawrie Ltd*[86] provides a good example of this as well as of what constitutes the transaction for the purpose of the valuation exercise.

AJB agreed to sell its business to Brewer Dolphin for £1.25 million. To that end AJB transferred its business and assets to its wholly owned subsidiary BSL for £1 and then sold its shares in BSL to Brewer Dolphin in consideration of (i) the assumption by Brewer Dolphin of AJB's liability to its employees for redundancy payments, later discharged at a net cost of £325,000, (ii) a covenant by Brewer Dolphin's parent, PCG, to pay rent of £312,500 to AJB for five years under a sub-lease of computer equipment, against which was to be set a loan of £312,500 by PCG to AJB. The sub-lease was in breach of covenant, the head lease was terminated for default and PCG repudiated its liability under the sub-lease. The value of the business sold by AJB was assessed by the trial judge at £1,050,000. Later AJB went into insolvent liquidation and

---

[85] [1995] B.C.C. 978.
[86] [2001] 1 W.L.R. 143.

shortly afterwards into administrative receivership. The liquidator and administrative receiver (the same person) applied for an order under s.240 on the ground that the sale to Brewer Dolphin was a transaction at an undervalue within s.238.

The trial judge upheld this contention and ordered Brewer Dolphin to pay a sum which he considered to represent the undervalue. An appeal and cross-appeal to the Court of Appeal were dismissed, though on grounds different from those of the trial judge as to what constituted the transaction. The House of Lords affirmed the decision of the Court of Appeal while differing both from the trial judge and the Court of Appeal as to the reasoning and varying the order of the former by allowing a credit which he had refused.

In delivering the Opinion of the House Lord Scott made the following points:

(1) The linked agreements together constituted the transaction. Accordingly the issue before the court was not the transaction but the consideration. It was irrelevant who provided this. Accordingly the covenant by PCG to pay rent under the sub-lease formed part of the consideration received by AJB and had to be valued.

(2) The sub-lease was in breach of the sub-lessor's covenant under the head lease, and the court was entitled to look at subsequent events— in particular, the termination of the head lease for default by AJB and the consequent termination of the sub-lease by PCG for repudiatory breach—in order to value PCG's covenant at the time it entered into the sub-lease, and those events made it clear that the value was nil.

(3) However, Brewer Dolphin was entitled to be given credit for the amount of its loan and interest.

11–31 Lord Scott's speech has generated much debate on the use of hindsight to determine a value at the time of the transaction. But it seems clear that Lord Scott was not in truth applying a hindsight test; rather he was relying on evidence of subsequent events to show that from the outset the covenant under the sub-lease was so precarious and its value so speculative that even at the time it was entered into a bank or finance house with knowledge of the surrounding circumstances would not have attributed any value to the sub-lease covenant.[87] In this connection it is helpful to recall the distinction drawn by the accountancy profession between adjusting and non-adjusting events in determining whether a balance sheet value should be corrected by reference to subsequent facts.[88] In the present context an adjusting event is

---

[87] See para.26.
[88] See above, para.4–37.

one which helps to establish the value of consideration at the transaction date, while a non-adjusting event is one which simply reduces or increases such value at the time the event occurs. It is obvious that a mere decline in the value of consideration by reason of an event after the transaction date is of no relevance whatsoever in determining whether the transaction was at an undervalue. But *Brewer Dolphin* did not concern a non-adjusting event; Lord Scott relied on the post-transaction termination of the sub-lease as validating what would anyway have been the perception at the time of the sub-lease of the nil value of the sub-lessee's covenant. In accountancy terms the termination was an adjusting event.

To be contrasted with this is the case of *Ramlort Ltd v Reid*.[89]

T, a heavy drinker, took out a unit-linked life policy providing for a sum assured of £180,000. T owned two companies which together owed £185,000 to Ramlort Ltd. T, though not legally liable for the debts, regarded himself as morally bound to see that they were paid. To that end he arranged for the sum assured to be increased to £185,000 and, while seriously ill and awaiting a liver transplant, executed a declaration of trust of the policy in favour of Ramlort in consideration of two cheques issued by Ramlort totalling £3,000. At that time the policy had a surrender value of £71. Two months later T had a liver transplant and the following day he died. The judicial factor challenged the declaration of trust as a transaction at an undervalue. The medical evidence showed that at the time the declaration of trust was executed T was gravely ill and without a transplant his illness would be terminal, while if the transplant were to be carried out he might survive, though the mortality risk was not measurable. The greater the risk of T's death, the higher the value of the policy. There was a conflict of evidence as to the value of the policy. On one view it was no more than the surrender value, on another it was a value substantially higher than £33,000. The trial judge rejected the former view as unrealistic but concluded that it was not possible to assign a precise value to the policy, which would appear to be within the range £25,000-£35,000 but with an absolute minimum of £10,000, the figure he determined to be the outgoing value He pointed out that the fact that there might not be a market for an asset did not mean it had no value, an example being shares in a private company. Neither valuer relied on the fact of T's death as a factor in his valuation and the judge did not apply the hindsight principle. The Court of Appeal, upholding the decision apart from allowing a credit for the two cheques, also found it unnecessary to apply hindsight to the valuation.[90]

---

[89] [2004] B.P.I.R. 985, affirming the decision of Judge Norris Q.C. *sub. nom. Re Thoars (dec'd)* [2003] B.P.I.R. 1444.

[90] The court also held, in agreement with the trial judge, that there was nothing to preclude the court from taking a range of possible values rather than a precise figure.

Other examples where hindsight would be inappropriate are the valuation of a lottery ticket by reference to its proving to be the winning ticket; the valuation of a policy covering a young and healthy life assured by reference to his accidental and premature death; and the valuation of residential property by reference to a subsequent increase in its market value.[91] In all these cases the subsequent event is not one which helps to establish the value at the transaction date for it has no relation to what a willing purchaser might be prepared to pay for the asset in question; it is simply an event which changes the situation.

(5) Value of property sold subject to a security interest

11–32 Where property of the company is sold subject to a security interest previously given by the company its value is the value of the equity of redemption, for to the extent of the security interest the property is not that of the company at all.[92]

Guarantees[93]

11–33 Particular difficulties are raised by guarantees.[94] Company A in a group of companies gives a guarantee to secure advances already made or intended to be made by X Bank to Company B, another member of the group—usually Company A's parent, subsidiary or co-subsidiary. If Company A goes into winding-up or administration, in what circumstances, if any, will the issue of the guarantee be considered a transaction at an undervalue?

The first question is whether a guarantee is within s.238 at all. Undoubtedly it is a transaction within the meaning of s.436. The difficulty in applying s.238 lies in the fact that whereas most transactions involve the transfer of property, the provision of services or the payment of money by the company and the receipt of money or property in exchange, the issue of a guarantee by the company merely involves it in a contingent liability which may never crystallise and the *quid pro quo* is the making of an advance to a third party, the principal debtor. So in contrast to the usual case a guarantee does not at the time of its issue involve any form of transfer either from or to the company and, indeed, it may never pay anything or receive anything as a result of the transaction. But these are

---

[91] These were among the examples given on the trial of a preliminary issue by Sir Andrew Morritt V.C. in *Re Thoars (dec'd)* [2003] 1 B.C.L.C. 499.

[92] *Re Brabon, Treharne v Brabon* [2001] 1 B.C.L.C. 11, a decision on s.339(3)(c) of the Insolvency Act.

[93] See also Roy Goode, *Legal Problems of Credit and Security* (3rd ed.), 207.

[94] The same considerations apply to indemnities, and for brevity the term "guarantee" will be used to cover both forms of transaction.

matters which go merely to the valuation of benefit and burden, they do not affect the applicability of s.238 to contracts of guarantee.

As stated earlier, a guarantee is not a gift or no-consideration transaction, even though the advance to which it relates is made to the principal debtor, not to the surety. The consideration is the making of the advance,[95] since this is the act exacted by the surety as the price of his guarantee. So the fact that the money goes to the principal debtor does not of itself render the guarantee a transaction at an undervalue. The crucial question is whether there is a broad equality of exchange, that is, whether the benefit conferred on the creditor by the issue of the guarantee is significantly greater than the value to the surety of the advance to the principal debtor. It is clear that the relevant time for measuring these respective values is the date the guarantee is given, not the date when the principal debtor defaults or the guarantee is called or payment is made under it. But as will be seen, this involves an assessment at the date of the guarantee of what is likely to happen when payment becomes due.

(1) Measuring the value to the creditor

The value of a guarantee to the creditor varies inversely with the financial **11–34** strength of the principal debtor. If the principal debtor is financially strong the creditor's dependence on the guarantee, and thus its value to him, is correspondingly reduced and may, indeed, be so small that it can be disregarded altogether. By contrast, if the principal debtor is already insolvent and the guarantee is furnished to secure a last-ditch injection of funds in the hope of reviving the principal debtor's fortunes, the risk of the guarantee being called is high and its value to the creditor may approach the full amount of the guaranteed debt. The mere fact that the principal debtor is solvent at the time of the guarantee does not by itself mean that it is of no value, for the guarantee relates to the future and what has to be measured when it is given is the likelihood of its being called when repayment falls due. A company may be technically solvent at the time of the guarantee and yet beset with so many impending troubles that its future insolvency can be predicted with a high degree of assurance.

To what extent is the value of a guarantee to the creditor reduced by the fact that he already holds security, whether from the company itself or from third parties? The answer to this question is not entirely straightforward. Let us start with security taken from the debtor company itself, such as a mortgage or charge of its property. The existence of such security reduces

---

[95] Alternatively the creditor's promise to make the advance. But in general creditors prefer not to commit themselves to the surety in a bilateral contract; they prefer either to make the advance, generating a unilateral contract of guarantee, or (if they change their mind) to decline to do so, in which case the guarantee does not come into force.

the creditor's need for the guarantee and therefore its value to him, which may be no more than the supportive value of a belt to a man already wearing braces. So at first sight such security should be brought into the equation as a factor which reduces the likelihood that the guarantee will be called. The technical objection to this approach is that the creditor is not obliged to use the security taken from the principal debtor as his first port of call in a storm. If the principal debtor defaults the creditor is free to pursue all or any of his remedies against all or any of the parties liable to him. He may thus, if he chooses, defer proceedings against the principal debtor and move directly against the surety. The effect of his election is that the guarantee becomes the primary support, the braces, whilst the security taken from the principal debtor is left to perform the subsidiary role of the belt, to which resort is made only if the braces prove inadequate. Does this mean that security taken from the principal debtor should be ignored in valuing the benefit of the guarantee to the creditor? Instinctively we would recoil from such a conclusion and rightly so. What matters at bottom is not the immediate but the ultimate source of satisfaction of the creditor's claim. Where lies the true incidence of liability? If the surety pays he has a right to be subrogated to securities held by the creditor[96] and thus to take over any mortgage or charge on the company's property to secure recoupment of his payment. This remedy of subrogation is given to ensure that the burden falling upon a surety is not at the end of the day dictated by the choice of the creditor, to look to him alone and exempt others from payment.[97] So even if the creditor collects payment from the surety his claim is ultimately satisfied from security given by the principal debtor so far as resort to this by the surety is necessary for his recoupment. Our first thought therefore turns out to be correct: in valuing the benefit of the guarantee to the creditor account must be taken not only of the principal debtor's financial strength but of any real security taken from the principal debtor by the creditor.

11–35   Next we have to consider the relevance of security taken from other third parties. The creditor may already hold another guarantee, which may be a purely personal guarantee by another surety, a guarantee reinforced by real security from the surety or a guarantee limited to real security. This complicates life a little in that where there are two or more sureties they bear the burden rateably in proportion to the amounts for which they are respectively liable under their guarantees, so that if one of them discharges the debt in full his right of subrogation to securities taken from the principal debtor and from his co-sureties is limited to what is needed to recoup him for the amount by which his payment, exceeds his own due

---

[96] This right is given both in equity (*Craythorne v Swinburne* (1807) 14 Ves. 160; *Forbes v Jackson* (1882) 19 Ch.D. 615) and at law under s.5 of the Mercantile Law Amendment Act 1856.

[97] *Craythorne v Swinburne*, above, at 162; Story, *Equity Jurisprudence* (1st English ed.), 315.

contribution.[98] The result is that in valuing the benefit to the creditor of the guarantee given by the company in winding-up or administration there must be deducted the value of the creditor's rights against co-sureties[99] up to the amount they are liable to contribute but not beyond.

In valuing the benefit of a guarantee to the creditor for the purpose of s.238 no account should be taken of the possibility that the surety itself may default in performance of its obligations under the guarantee. What has to be measured is the value of the consideration, not the likelihood of its being executed. In essence, the question is whether the company giving the guarantee is committing itself to parting with a benefit significantly greater than that which it will receive. The principle is the same as that applicable to straight supply transactions. If, for example, a company which has run out of funds agrees to buy goods for £10,000, the question whether it has thereby entered into a transaction at an undervalue is determined by asking whether the goods are worth a sum approaching that figure, not by comparing the value of the goods with the amount the creditor is likely to recover from the company when it defaults in payment of the price. The same applies to the valuation of a guarantee. If the position were otherwise s.138 could hardly ever apply to guarantees, for *ex hypothesi* the company giving the guarantee is already unable to pay its debts.[1]

From what has been said above it will have become obvious that valuation of a guarantee is in many cases a matter of judgement rather than of science and that a broad brush approach is needed. I would suggest as a working guide that for the purpose of s.238 of the Insolvency Act the value of a guarantee to a creditor is the amount (if any) for which, at the time of the guarantee, a prudent creditor with full knowledge of the debtor's affairs would make provision in his accounts for default, after taking into account what he could reasonably expect to recover from securities taken from the principal debtor and from co-sureties in respect of their proportionate share of the suretyship liabilities. Alternatively, looked at from the viewpoint of the surety, it is the amount for which a prudent surety with full knowledge of the debtor's affairs would make provision in his accounts after allowing for the value of securities taken from the principal debtor and contributions from co-sureties.

(2) Measuring the value to the surety

The other side of the equation is, of course, the value of the consideration received by the surety, that is, the value to the surety of the advance provided to the principal debtor. A member of a group of companies—in

11–36

---

[98] For a detailed treatment of the right of contribution among sureties see O'Donovan and Phillips, *The Modern Contract of Guarantee* (English ed., 2003), paras 12.116 *et seq.*, with detailed examples of calculations at paras 12.217 *et seq.*

[99] Which involves measuring their financial strength and the value of securities they have given to support their guarantees.

[1] This being a condition of the application of s.238. See ss.238(2), 240(2).

our example Company A—can in many cases reasonably expect that the infusion of funds into another member of the group (Company B) will benefit the group as a whole, including Company A. Valuing the benefit, however, is likely to be a matter of considerable difficulty. In some cases there will be no value at all, as where Company B is already on the rocks and the giving of the guarantee for a temporary advance is merely staving off disaster. In such cases Company A's guarantee is given solely for the benefit of Company B and will almost certainly constitute a transaction at an undervalue; indeed, the directors of Company B may well be in breach of duty to the company in authorising the issue of the guarantee in the first place, for their loyalties are owed in law solely to their company, not to the group as a whole. But where Company B's business is basically sound and the infusion of funds will enable it to expand its activities, and increase its profitability, for the benefit of the group as a whole, at least some value may be ascribable to the consideration given by Company A for its guarantee. This may (indeed usually will) be less than the amount of the advance to Company B but as long as it is not significantly below the ultimate burden likely to fall on Company A as the result of furnishing the guarantee this will not be a transaction at an undervalue.

In practice it is unlikely that a guarantee will be impeached as a transaction at an undervalue except where it is clearly of no benefit to the surety company. There are serious problems of valuation on both sides of the equation and the onus is on the office-holder who is impeaching the transaction to prove that the guarantee is a transaction at an undervalue. Hence the difficulties of valuation lie primarily on him rather than on the creditor.

Giving of security for a past debt not a transaction at an undervalue

11–37   Suppose that a company gives its bank security for a previously unsecured loan and then goes into liquidation. Is the furnishing of security for past consideration a transaction at an undervalue? No, because it does not reduce the net assets of the company but merely attaches an existing liability to an existing asset, leaving the net balance sheet figures unchanged. This was so held by Millett J. in *Re M.C. Bacon Ltd.*[2] Likewise, the realisation of the security has no impact on the net asset position, for while the asset given in security disappears from the balance sheet so also does the liability which it secured. A simple example will demonstrate the point. Suppose that A Ltd borrows £100,000 unsecured, uses it to buy stock and later gives a charge over its factory to secure the loan. Prior to the giving of the security A Ltd's balance sheet, assuming that no part of the

---

[2] [1990] B.C.C. 78.

stock has yet been sold, the factory has a value (at cost) of £500,000 and that there are no other assets or liabilities, would look like this:

Assets		£500,000
Factory (at cost)		
Stock (at cost)		£100,000
		£600,000
Less liabilities		
Bank loan	£100,000	
Trade creditors	£ 50,000	£150,000
Net assets		£450,000

When the charge is given it will be recorded by way of a note to the accounts (or alternatively the loan will be shown in the balance sheet as a secured loan) but the figures remain unchanged. Now suppose that on default by the company the factory is sold for £500,000 and the debt of £100,000 repaid from the proceeds, the balance of £400,000 being paid into the company's bank account. The balance sheet will now look like this:

Assets	
Cash at bank	£400,000
Stock (at cost)	£100,000
	£500,000
Less liabilities	
Trade creditors	£ 50,000
Net assets	£450,000

We can see that there has been no depletion of the value of the company's assets through realisation of the security, for the payment of £100,000 from the proceeds is exactly matched by the disappearance of the bank loan from the liabilities. So the effect of giving security for a previously unsecured loan is not to reduce the company's assets but simply to allocate the asset given in security to a particular creditor instead of leaving it available for creditors generally. The proper ground of attack, then, is not that the transaction is at an undervalue but that it is a preference. As Millett J. pointed out,[3] all that the company loses in giving the security is the ability to apply the proceeds of the charged assets otherwise than in satisfaction of the charged debt, and "that is not something capable of valuation in

---

[3] *ibid.*, at 92.

monetary terms and is not customarily disposed of for value."[4] This comment should not be misunderstood. The point Millett J. was making was not the difficulty of valuing a detriment but the fact that detriment by itself is irrelevant, for the crucial question is whether it was incurred as part of the bargained-for consideration so as to confer on the other party a benefit capable of being valued. In *Agricultural Mortgage Corp plc v Woodward*[5] the fact that one party suffered a detriment by reason of a reduction in value of his property through the grant of a tenancy was not in itself material; what mattered was that the grant of the tenancy gave the tenant a protected status which placed her in a position to hold the landlord and the mortgagee to ransom in negotiating a surrender value, and the conferment of that benefit formed part of the bargained-for consideration. By contrast, the loss of a mortgagor's ability to apply the proceeds of a mortgaged asset otherwise than in satisfaction of the debt confers no additional benefit on the mortgagee for which he would expect to pay; on the contrary, it is the very remedy which the mortgage is designed to provide. One might add that, by the same token, the fact that the grant of a mortgage over an asset inhibits the company's ability to obtain credit from other sources is equally irrelevant, not simply because it is incapable of valuation but because it is not something which confers a bargained-for benefit on the mortgagee.

The position is otherwise, of course, where the company gives security for the indebtedness of a third party, for in that situation realisation of the security does not result in the discharge of any debt owed by the company, which accordingly suffers a loss of the charged asset.

The "relevant time"

11–38   Under s.238(2) of the Insolvency Act 1986 the office-holder is not entitled to apply for an order to reverse the effect of a transaction at an undervalue unless the transaction was entered into at "a relevant time". This is defined by s.240(1) as:

(1)   at a time within the period of 2 years ending with the onset of insolvency, but only if at that time the company was unable to pay its debts within the meaning of s.123 of the Act or became so in consequence of the transaction[6]; or

---

[4] *ibid.*
[5] [1994] B.C.C. 688. See above, para.11–27.
[6] Such inability to pay debts is presumed to be satisfied unless the contrary is shown, in relation to any transaction at an undervalue entered into by a person connected with the company (s.240(2)), that is, a person who is a director, a shadow director, an associate of such a director or shadow director or an associate of the company as defined by s.435 of the Act (s.249). For the meaning of "onset of insolvency", see s.240(3).

(2) at a time between the making of an administration application in respect of the company and the making of an administration order on that application; or

(3) at a time between the filing with the court of a notice of intention to appoint an administration under paras 14 or 22 of Sch.B1 and the making of an appointment under that paragraph.

The general statutory defence[7]

Under s.238(5) of the Insolvency Act the court may not make an order   **11–39**
under s.238 in respect of a transaction at an undervalue if it is satisfied:

(a) that the company which entered into the transaction did so in good faith and for the purpose of carrying on its business, and

(b) that at the time it did so there were reasonable grounds for believing that the transaction would benefit the company.

This useful defence, which it is for those resisting an order to establish,[8] will protect a range of bona fide business transactions that might otherwise be vulnerable, including a transaction weighted in favour of the other party because he was in a stronger negotiating position and a disadvantageous transaction reasonably considered necessary to avoid or terminate litigation or to prevent the termination of a valuable contract or the loss of important intellectual property rights.

(1) Good faith

The requirement of good faith must, it is thought, be related to the purpose   **11–40**
of s.238, and is not a requirement of honesty in a general sense. So limb (a) of s.238(5) should be considered satisfied if those involved on behalf of the company genuinely thought the transaction would promote its interests, even if they acted dishonestly in the transaction itself, *e.g.* by buying goods on behalf of the company knowing it would be unable to pay for them or by knowingly misrepresenting the condition or quality of goods they were selling for the company. Transactions entered into by the company in the course of closing down its business would, it is thought, be considered to be "for the purpose of carrying on its business" within the above statutory provision.[9]

---

[7] Possible restitutionary defences and cross-clams are considered below, para.11–67.

[8] *Re Barton Manufacturing Co Ltd* [1999] B.C.L.C. 740.

[9] See *Re Sarflax Ltd* [1979] Ch. 592, a decision on the meaning of "carrying on a business" in s.332(1) of the Companies Act 1948, in which Oliver J. held that the phrase was not confined to the active carrying on of the trade but encompassed the collection of assets and the distribution of their proceeds in discharge of liabilities in the course of closing down the business.

It should be noted that it is the company that must act in good faith; the good faith of the other party is irrelevant. This reflects the historical origins of preferences and transfers in fraud of creditors where the focus was on the intent of the debtor to defeat the statutory provision governing distribution on bankruptcy.[10] It does, however, run counter to the general principle of English law that it is the party seeking relief who must show good faith. It seems objectionable that a company, acting through its liquidator, should be able to invoke its own bad faith and its own state of insolvency to undo the effects of a transaction with another party who acted in good faith and was unaware either that the company was acting in bad faith or that it was insolvent.[11]

(2) Benefit to the company

11–41   Limb (b) requires the existence of reasonable grounds for believing that the transaction would benefit the company. Whether the transaction in fact benefits the company is not the question, though there may be a temptation to apply hindsight. Nor does limb (b) require that the company should in fact have believed it would benefit from the transaction; the test is an objective one—"reasonable grounds for believing"—though if the company did not believe the transaction would be of benefit it may be hard pressed to establish that it acted in good faith as required by limb (a).

The protection of innocent third parties

11–42   A separate statutory defence is provided by s.241(2) of the Act in favour of bona fide transferees and recipients of benefit *otherwise than from the company* in good faith, for value and without notice. This defence, which is not available to the company's counterparty to the transaction at an undervalue, will be examined in the context of orders the court can make under s.238.[12]

The general power of the court

11–43   On an application by the office-holder for an order under s.238 the court is required to make such order as it thinks fit for restoring the position to what it would have been if the company had not entered into the

---

[10] See above, para.1–05.

[11] For a discussion of the question whether s.238 might infringe art.1 of the First Protocol to the Human Rights Convention, set out in Sch.1 to the Human Rights Act 1998, see Janet Ulph and Tom Allen, "Transactions at an Undervalue, Purchasers and the Impact of the Human Rights Act 1998" [2004] J.B.L. 1.

[12] See below, para.11–65.

transaction.[13] Despite the word "shall" the expression "think fit" has the effect that it is entirely within the court's discretion whether to make an order under s238.[14] An order can be made only if the company is in administration or winding-up and only on an application by the office-holder. A creditor has no *locus standi* to apply for an order. Whether an order is a made and if so the type of order are entirely within the discretion of the court; the office-holder is not entitled as of right to have a transaction at an undervalue set aside or to obtain a particular form of relief. Even where the court is satisfied that the company entered into a transaction at an undervalue it will not make an order under s.238 where the company would have found itself in an even worse position if the transaction had not been carried out.[15] The order the court is required to make is to restore the company to the position in which it would have been if it had not entered into the transaction at all; the court is not permitted to reconstruct the position to what it would have been if the company had entered into a different transaction.[16] In deciding what order to make the court does not start with any presumption in favour of monetary compensation as opposed to setting aside the transaction and revesting the asset transferred or, indeed, any other *a priori* assumption.[17]

In the typical case the company will have purchased an asset at significantly more than its value or sold an asset at significantly less than its value. The former case can be dealt with by an order for repayment of the excess to the company and the latter by an order for payment of an additional sum to make up the price to the full value of the asset sold or alternatively an order for retransfer of the asset to the company and repayment by it of the price received. But such an order will not normally be sufficient by itself to restore the position to what it would have been if the company had not entered into the transaction, for account must also be taken of any additional income or profits it would have been likely to earn if the transaction had not taken place.[18] The defendant will as a rule be entitled to counter-restitution of benefits received by the company, for example, repayment of the price it received for the property which is to be retransferred to it, compensation for the value added by any improvements made by the defendant,[19] reimbursement of the cost of performing obligations undertaken by the company, *e.g.* to meet the redundancy costs of

---

[13] Insolvency Act 198.6, s.238(3).

[14] *Re Paramount Airways Ltd* [1993] Ch. 223, *per* Sir Donald Nicholls V.C. at 239.

[15] *Re MDA Investment Management Ltd, Whalley v Doney* [2004] 1 B.C.L.C. 217. In that case the judge found that at the time of the transaction the company was on the verge of collapse and failure to enter into the transaction would have made its position still worse.

[16] *ibid.*

[17] *Ramlort Ltd v Reid* [2004] B.P.I.R. 985, *per* Jonathan Parker L.J. at para.125, approving the observation of Judge Havelock-Allan Q.C. in *Walker v W.A. Personnel Ltd* [2002] B.P.I.R. 621.

[18] See the examples given below, paras 11–46 *et seq.* and the discussion of restitutionary principles at para.11–67.

[19] See *Weisgard v Pilkington* [1995] B.C.C. 1108.

employees, and repayment of a loan made by the defendant to the company as part of the total transaction.[20] In the case of an order for retransfer of property to the company counter-restitution will involve repayments by the company as a condition of the transfer. Where the order against the defendant is for payment of money, counter-restitution will take the form of a deduction from the amount repayable to the company.[21] The relevance of general principles of the law of unjust enrichment is considered later.[22]

The general power conferred by s.238(3) to restore the company to the status quo is unfettered. The court is thus able to make various orders of a kind rather surprisingly omitted from the list of its specific powers under s.241(1).[23]

Specific powers

11–44 Without prejudice to the generality of the power conferred on the court by s238(3) the court may (subject to s.241(2)) make any of the seven types of order specified in s.241(1) of the Act. The list is interesting not only for what it contains but for several significant omissions. The particular remedies given to the company through an application by the office-holder are orders *in personam* directing property to be vested (or revested) in the company or money to be paid to the company and orders for the release or discharge of any security given by the company. There is no provision in s.241(1) for a transaction at an undervalue, whether it be a contract or a conveyance, to be invalidated or set aside, nor is there provision for an order discharging the company from liability under a contract,[24] *e.g.* for the excess of its commitment over the value of the consideration for the commitment. The underlying concept is that the original transaction was and remains valid but that its adverse effects are to be reversed by a conveyance (or reconveyance) or payment of a sum of money and the discharge of any security where appropriate.[25] Similarly, there is no express reference to the power of the court to impose conditions in any order it makes, *e.g.* that when property is retransferred to the company it is to repay the price originally received. Instead, there is a curiously limited power to allow proof in the winding-up "for debts or other liabilities which arose from, or were released or discharged (in whole or in part) under or by, the transaction,"[26] which hardly meets the case.[27]

---

[20] *Phillips v Brewin Dolphin Bell Laurie Ltd* [2001] 1 W.L.R. 143.
[21] See *ibid.*
[22] See below, para.11–67.
[23] See below.
[24] Other than a security.
[25] See further below, para.11–140.
[26] Insolvency Act 1986, s.241(l)(g), discussed below, para.11–63.
[27] See below, para.11–63.

However, since s.241(1) is without prejudice to the generality of the court's powers under s.238, which predicates restoration of both parties to the position existing prior to the transaction, there seems no reason why the court should not in a proper case deal with a transaction at an undervalue by setting it aside and releasing the company, wholly or in part, from any liability incurred under it, and by making it a condition of vesting of property in the company that it is to repay any money or the value of any other benefit it received under the transaction. The susceptibility of the transaction to avoidance by the court in exercise of its powers under s.238 would, it is thought, constitute an equity binding on the defendant's liquidator or trustee in bankruptcy if the defendant were in, or were to go into, winding-up or bankruptcy.[28] The effect of s.241(1) is thus to make the transaction voidable,[29] though it has to be borne in mind that "voidable" in this context means liable to avoidance at the discretion of the court rather than as of right.

The various orders listed in s.241(1) fall into the following groups.

(1) Orders vesting property in the company

First, the court may require any property transferred as part of the   **11–45** transaction at an undervalue to be vested in the company. The generality of this provision should be noted. It is not confined to cases where the property was originally vested in the company but extends to transfers by a third party at the direction of the company, as where the company agreed to buy from the third party and sub-sell to the ultimate transferee or agreed that a debt owed to the company by the third party should be discharged wholly or in part by the transfer of an asset from the third party to the transferee. Further, an order for transfer may be made not only against the original transferee (if he still has the property) but against the successor in title in whom it is currently vested. This, indeed, is made clear by the opening words of subs.(2) of s.241.[30] Again, if an order is made against a party who becomes bankrupt or goes into liquidation before complying with it, the court can direct the conveyance to be executed by the trustee or liquidator.

Secondly, the court may require any property to be vested in the company if it represents in any person's hands the application either of the proceeds of sale of property transferred as part of the transaction, at an undervalue or of money so transferred.[31] Again, an order may be made against any holder of the property, whether or not the original transferee.

---

[28] See below, para.11–51.
[29] The view also taken by Simone Degeling, below, para.11–67.
[30] However, the court is precluded by subs.(2) of that section from making any order which would prejudice the rights of a bona fide purchaser for value without notice. See below, para.11–65.
[31] See examples 3 and 4 below.

Where the company received consideration for the original transfer it would obviously be wrong to direct a retransfer of the property (or the transfer of other property acquired by the transferee with the proceeds of the original property) to the company without taking account of that consideration. So although s.241 contains no express reference to the imposing of conditions of an order under that section it seems clear from the generality of s.238(3) that the court, when directing retransfer of property to the company, has power to impose a condition that the company shall repay the sum it received for the property or such part of that sum as will ensure that the company is in no better position than if it had not entered into the transaction.

A few examples will help to illustrate the above.

Example 1

11–46   The company sells to A for £100,000 property worth £250,000. The court can order A to reconvey the property to the company but account must be taken of the £100,000 originally paid. The order for retransfer could incorporate a condition that by way of counter-restitution the company repay the whole of the £100,000 originally received, with interest, but this would not necessarily suffice to restore the status quo, for in the intervening period the company has been deprived of £150,000 of value which, if it had not entered into the transaction, might have been put to income-producing use. So it might be appropriate to deduct from the amount to be repaid by way of counter-restitution the income that the company could have expected to receive from the property if it had not been sold less the interest on the consideration it received.

Example 2

11–47   The company sells to A for £100,000 property worth £250,000. A makes a gift of the property to his wife, B. An order can be made requiring B to convey the property to the company. Under the general power conferred by s.238(3) the court could also specify as a condition of its order that the company make a repayment to B as in example 1.

Example 3

11–48   The company sells Blackacre to A for £100,000. Blackacre is then worth £250,000. A subsequently resells Blackacre to B for £300,000 and uses the proceeds to buy Whiteacre for £350,000. The court can order A to convey Whiteacre to the company but as in example 1 account must be taken of the £100,000 originally received by the company. The court could as an alternative order B to convey Blackacre back to the company but not if B had acquired Blackacre in good faith and without notice of the relevant circumstances.[32]

---

[32] See Insolvency Act 1986, s.241(2) and below, para.11–65.

Example 4

The company makes a payment of £100,000 to A for which there is no   **11–49**
consideration. A uses the money to buy Blackacre. The court can order A
to convey Blackacre to the company.

Example 5

The company sells its business and factory premises to A for £1 in   **11–50**
consideration of A's assuming responsibility for redundancy payments
due to the company's employees and discharging the company's obligations to its bankers. The business and premises are worth £1 million. A
settles the redundancy claims for £249,999 and the bank's claim for
£200,000. Some months later A lends the company £100,000. A also
spends £150,000 improving the factory premises. The company then goes
into insolvent liquidation. The court could order A to retransfer the
business and factory premises to the company but could be expected to
require the company, as a condition of the retransfer, to repay the
£450,000 expended by A pursuant to the agreement and to pay for the
value added by the improvements (which is not necessarily the amount of
£150,000 spent).[33] Repayment of the loan would not be a condition, this
being an independent transaction not attracting a right of counter-
restitution, and A would be left to prove for it in the winding-up.
However, the court might instead take the view that it was unsatisfactory
to dislocate the business by ordering it to be retransferred and also that it
would be unfair to A to make an order which would preclude it from
exercising a right of insolvency set-off.[34] Accordingly the court might
conclude that a better solution would be to allow A to retain the business
and factory premises and to pay the amount of the undervalue (£1
million less £450,000, *i.e.* £550,000) and interest, against which A would
then be able to set off his cross-claim for repayment of the loan of
£100,000 and interest.

It will be seen from the above examples that the court may order the
vesting in the company of (1) the property originally transferred or (2)
other property acquired with the proceeds of the original property or (3)
property acquired with money paid by the company. However, in case (2) it
must be shown that the new property was acquired with the proceeds of the
original property and in case (3) that the property was acquired with the
money originally paid by the company. It may not always be easy to
establish the necessary nexus between the property of which recovery is

---

[33] See *Weisgard v Pilkington* [1995] B.C.C. 1108, a decision on a preference, but the principle is
the same.
[34] This is because a money claim cannot be set off against an obligation to retransfer property.
See above, para.8–27.

sought and the property or money originally transferred or paid by the company. To return to example 3, suppose that on selling Blackacre A paid the £300,000 into his bank account, that this already had a credit balance of £400,000, and that A draws £350,000 out of his account to pay for Whiteacre. Is Whiteacre to be considered purchased with the proceeds of Blackacre, the £400,000 already in the account or a mixture of the two? If A were a trustee being pursued by the company for breach of trust there would be no great difficulty in applying equitable tracing rules to arrive at a solution, using whatever presumptions were considered appropriate, *e.g.* the rule in *Clayton's Case* that what is first in the account is the first to go out or the presumption that a trustee does not intend to commit a breach of trust and should therefore be assumed to have resorted to his own moneys before raiding the trust funds. But A is not a trustee and the purpose of s.238 is not to require A to hand over property acquired or profits made with trust moneys but simply to ensure that the company is no worse off than it would have been if it had never entered into the transaction in the first place. So there is no point in engaging in an elaborate tracing exercise; all the court need do is to order A to pay such sum as will recompense the company for the value lost, if necessary directing that payment be secured by a charge on Whiteacre.[35]

11–51   Section 241 does not prescribe the machinery by which property is to be vested or revested in the company and this is regulated by the general law. In the case of land the court may simply make an order *in personam* directing the estate owner to convey the land to the company. In most cases this will suffice. If the person against whom the order is made becomes bankrupt or goes into liquidation before executing the conveyance there seems no reason why the court cannot order the conveyance to be executed by the trustee in bankruptcy or liquidator, for the susceptibility of the transaction to reversal under ss.238 and 241 would appear to constitute an equity binding on the trustee or liquidator. Alternatively the court, when making the order, may reinforce it by making a declaration that the party against whom it is made is to hold the land as trustee,[36] and by using that declaration as a springboard for a vesting order under s.44 of the Trustee Act 1925.

(2) Orders for the release or discharge of security given by the company

11–52   The court may release or discharge (in whole or in part) any security given by the company. So if a mortgage secures obligations under a contract or conveyance which is held to be a transaction at an undervalue, the court

---

[35] For which a separate power is conferred by s.241(1)(f). See below, para.11–59.
[36] Trustee Act 1925, s.48.

may order the mortgage to be discharged. As stated earlier, the contract or conveyance itself is not set aside; the court simply reverses its effect by ordering a reconveyance or the payment of such sum as will redress the balance.

(3) Orders to repay the value of benefits received

The court may make an order requiring any person to pay, in respect of benefits received by him from the company, such sums to the office-holder as the court may direct.[37] A payment order can be made in respect of any kind of benefit received from the company, whether money or otherwise. So where property has been transferred at an undervalue the court may, in lieu of ordering retransfer of the property, direct the transferee to repay to the company the shortfall in the consideration he gave and also (to ensure the company is placed in no worse position than if it had not entered into the transaction) interest on the shortfall or other compensation for loss suffered as the result of being deprived of it. Again, the recipient of the benefit need not, it seems, have received it directly from the company.

11–53

Example 6

The company sells to A for £100,000 property worth £250,000. The court can direct A to repay £150,000 and interest on that sum for the period between the time of the transfer and the time of payment in compliance with the order.

11–54

Example 7

The company sells to A for £100,000 property worth £250,000. A makes a gift of the property to his wife, B. An order as in example 5 can be made against either A or B or, indeed, against both A and B.

11–55

(4) Orders reviving the obligations of a surety

The court may make an order providing for any surety, or guarantor[38] whose obligations to any person were released or discharged (in whole or in part) under the transaction to be under such new or revived obligations to that person as the court thinks fit. Such person will usually be the company itself, though it could be the transferee or a third party. Revival of the obligation in effect restores the suretyship, wholly or in part. But the court may alternatively impose a new obligation on the erstwhile surety and this

11–56

---

[37] As to the application of recoveries, see below, para.11–140.
[38] In English law usage the terms "surety" and "guarantor" are synonymous.

need not be restricted to a suretyship obligation but could be a primary and independent obligation running parallel to that of the principal debtor.

Example 8

11–57 The company makes an advance of £50,000 to A which is guaranteed by B. A repays £20,000 but makes no further repayments. Subsequently the company's managing director, a close friend of A, arranges for the outstanding balance of the debt to be written off and for A to be released from liability, despite the fact that he is well able to pay. In consequence B is also discharged from liability.[39] The release of A constitutes a transaction at an undervalue. Soon afterwards an administration order is made against the company. On the application of the administrator the court may order A to pay the balance of the debt, with interest, and may further order that B's obligations as surety are to be revived or alternatively that he is to come under a new and independent liability for payment as a principal jointly and severally with A.

Example 9

11–58 The company agrees to buy the business and undertaking of A Ltd, which is wholly owned by the buying company's managing director. The price agreed is £10 million, though on a realistic valuation the business is worth no more than £2 million. As a condition of the sale A Ltd releases the buying company's parent, B plc, from its liability as guarantor of a loan of £500,000 previously made by A Ltd to the buying company. Soon after completion of the sale the buying company goes into liquidation. On the application of the liquidator the court may set aside the sale, in exercise of its general powers under s.238(3), or make an order under s.241(1) for repayment of the excess value paid to A Ltd. The effect of either kind of order is to destroy the basis upon which B plc was discharged from liability under its guarantee, and in these circumstances the court may consider it just to direct B's obligations to A Ltd revive, in order to produce a full restoration of the parties to their status quo.

(5) Orders securing obligations imposed by the orders

11–59 An order may provide for security to be provided for the discharge of any obligation imposed by or arising under the order, for such an obligation to be charged on any property and for the security or charge to have the same priority as a security or charge released or discharged (in whole or in part) under the transaction. Thus where the original security was a first charge and before it was released the company had given a second charge over the

---

[39] Since a surety's obligation is coterminous with that of the principal debtor.

same property to another creditor the court can direct the new security to have the priority over the second charge, thus displacing its promotion to first charge resulting from the release of the original security. Assuming that the second chargee did not make any further advances after release of the original charge, such an order leaves him no worse off than he was before the original charge was released. But the court cannot make an order which will prejudice rights acquired in good faith and for value.[40] So if in reliance on the release of the original security the second chargee makes a further advance the court cannot give the new charge priority over the second charge as regards that further advance. Similarly, if the company, without having granted a second charge, releases the original security and then gives a mortgage to another creditor to secure an advance by that creditor acting in good faith and without notice, the court cannot make an order which will displace the priority of that creditor as first mortgagee.

Example 10

The company sells to A for £100,000 property worth £250,000 and soon **11–60** afterwards goes into liquidation. On the application of the liquidator the court can order the payment by A of the shortfall of £150,000, with interest, and can direct that all or any of A's assets stand charged to secure compliance with the order.

Example 11

The company makes an advance of £50,000 to A which is guaranteed by **11–61** B. The guarantee is secured by a charge on B's house Blackacre. A then arranges an overdraft facility with C Bank and gives C Bank a second charge on Blackacre to secure existing and future indebtedness. C Bank advances money on the security of its second charge. Subsequently the company's managing director, a close friend of A, arranges for the company to release A from his guarantee for no consideration and to discharge the charge. This is a transaction at an undervalue. The court may direct B's obligations as surety to be revived and secured by a charge on Blackacre having the same priority over C Bank's charge as that enjoyed by the original security.

Example 12

The facts are as in example 10 except that after A's release and the **11–62** discharge of his mortgage and before the company goes into liquidation A borrows a further £20,000 from C Bank and also borrows £30,000 from D, secured by a charge on Blackacre, D advancing his money in good

---

[40] Insolvency Act 1986, s.241(2). See below, para.11–65.

faith and without notice. The court may direct B's obligations as surety to be revived and secured by a charge on Blackacre having priority over C Bank's charge as to advances made by C Bank prior to the release of the original security given by A, but the new charge must be made subordinate to C Bank's charge as regards the further advance of £20,000 and must also be made subordinate to the charge in favour of D.

(6) Orders permitting proof of debt by a person affected by the order

11–63   The order may provide for the extent to which any person whose property is vested by the order in the company, or on whom obligations are imposed by the order, is to be able to prove in the winding-up of the company for debts or other liabilities which arose from or were released or discharged (in whole or in part) under or by the transaction. This provision, though applicable to transactions at an undervalue as well as to preferences, is directed mainly to the latter. In the case of transactions at an undervalue the justice of the case will usually require a condition of repayment by the company (through its liquidator or administrator) of any sum received in exchange for property ordered to be reconveyed to the company.

Example 13

11–64   The company sells to A for £100,000 property worth £250,000 and soon after goes into liquidation. The court can order restoration of the property to the company but if it does so it should normally make it a condition of the order that the company repays the original purchase price of £100,000 with interest at the appropriate rate.[41] Alternatively the court can order A to pay the company £150,000, being the excess value he received, but allow him to prove in the liquidation for the same amount.

Orders affecting third parties

11–65   Reference has already been made to the power of the court under s.241 of the Act to make an order under s.238 affecting the property of, or imposing an obligation on, any person, whether or not he is the person with whom the transaction at an undervalue was entered into. But by s.241(2) such an order:

(a)   must not prejudice any interest in property which was acquired from a person other than the company and was acquired in good faith and

---

[41] See *Phillips v Brewin Dolphin Bell Lawrie Ltd* [2001] 1 W.L.R. 143; *Ramlort Ltd v Reid* [2004] B.P.I.R. 985.

for value, or prejudice any interest deriving from such an interest, and

(b) must not require a person who received a benefit from the trans-action in good faith and for value to pay a sum to the office-holder except where that person was a party to the transaction.

It is worth emphasising that this is a rule for the protection of third parties, not the company's counterparty to the transaction at an undervalue.

Prior to its amendment by the Insolvency (No.2) Act 1994, s.241(2) required not merely that the third party should have acquired the asset in good faith and for value but also that he should have taken it "without notice of the relevant circumstances". For this purpose "relevant circum-stances" were defined, in relation to transactions at an undervalue, as "(a) the circumstances by virtue of which an order under section 238 . . . could be made in respect of the transaction if the company were to go into liquidation, or an administration order were made in relation to the company, within a particular period after the transaction is entered into . . and (b) if that period has expired, the fact that the company has gone into liquidation or that such an order has been made." Two problems arose from this provision. First, the definition of "relevant circumstances" was couched in such general terms as to make it unclear whether the third party was required to be without notice of any element in s.238, including the state of insolvency of the company, or merely of the fact that it had entered into a transaction at an undervalue. Secondly, a purchaser from a donee of property was placed in a difficulty where he knew that his vendor was a donee, as might happen particularly in the case of unregistered land, where the consideration or absence of consideration would be shown on search certificates unless the vendor took the precaution of removing it. Such a purchaser would have to rely on a declaration of solvency by his vendor.

Section 241 has now been substantially altered to give greater protection to the bona fide purchaser for value. In the first place, there is now a presumption of good faith. In keeping with the characteristically oblique style of Westminster drafting, s.241 does not express this in positive terms. Instead, it provides that, unless the contrary is shown, a person is presumed to have acquired the interest or benefit otherwise than in good faith where he had notice of the relevant surrounding circumstances and of the relevant proceedings or was connected with[42] or an associate of[43] either the company itself or the person with whom it entered into the transaction at an undervalue.[44] "The relevant surrounding circumstances" is defined more narrowly than its predecessor, and in relation to transactions at an

---

[42] See Insolvency Act 1986, s.249.
[43] See *ibid.*, s.435.
[44] Insolvency Act 1986, s.241(2A).

undervalue the only relevant circumstance is the fact that the company in question entered into the transaction at an undervalue. Even this reformulation is ambiguous. Is the third party on notice merely because he was aware of the transaction and (even if he did not know it) the transaction was in fact at an undervalue? Or must he also be on notice that the transaction was at an undervalue? It seems clear that the latter interpretation is that intended, for a third party can hardly be said to be acting in bad faith if he has no notice of the crucial fact rendering the transaction vulnerable. There is no direct definition of "the relevant proceedings"; what these are is to be gleaned from the provisions of s.241(3A)–(3C) laying down when a person is to be considered to have notice of relevant proceedings. This depends on whether s.238 applies by virtue of an administration order, a liquidation immediately upon discharge of an administration order or a liquidation at any other time. In the first case what is required is that the third party has notice either of the presentation of the petition on which the administration order is made or of the fact that the order has been made. In the second case what is required is either notice of one of the above facts or notice of the fact that the company has gone into liquidation. In the third case, the effect of the statutory provisions is that in a compulsory winding-up the third party should have notice either of the winding-up order or of the presentation of the petition on which the winding-up order is made and that in a voluntary winding-up the company has gone into liquidation, *i.e.* by the passing of a resolution for voluntary winding-up.

It should be noted that if a third party acquires his interest in good faith and for value, the protection he thereby acquires enures for the benefit of his successors in title, whether or not they were aware of the relevant surrounding circumstances. This principle of "sheltering", embodied in the phrase "or prejudice any interest deriving from such an interest", is well-established in English law[45] and reflects the fact that a person who acquires a good title must be free to dispose of to whomever he wishes, otherwise the marketability of his property is impaired.[46]

Summary of protection for third parties

11–66   We are now in a position to summarise the statutory provisions for the protection of innocent third parties. Where the company has entered into a transaction by which it transfers property to another at an undervalue and a third party acquires an interest in that property, the third party is protected from an order under s.238 if, but only if, he acquired his interest in good faith and for value. There is a rebuttable presumption of *want* of good faith

---

[45] See Roy Goode, *Commercial Law* (3rd ed.), p.55.
[46] *ibid.*

in any of the following cases,[47] that is, where the third party, at the time of acquiring his interest:

(1)   has notice of the fact that the transaction under which the company disposed of the property was a transaction at an undervalue; or

(2)   is connected with, or was an associate of, the company or its transferee; or

(3)   has notice of the fact that the company has gone into administration or liquidation or that any petition on which an administration order or winding-up order was made has been presented.

"Notice" is broader than knowledge and covers not only facts of which a party is aware but facts which he could have discovered by proper enquiry. Thus a person might be considered to have notice of a winding-up petition by reason of its advertisement and of a winding-up order by reason of its publication in the London Gazette.

The application of principles of unjust enrichment?

Given that the policy underlying most of the avoidance provisions, includ-   **11–67**
ing those relating to transactions at an undervalue, is to reverse unjust enrichment, a question for consideration is whether, and to what extent, the court should apply the principles of unjust enrichment developed by the common law in deciding how its discretion should be exercised. This question is discussed in some detail by Dr Simone Degeling in a most instructive paper,[48] in which she points out that there are two symmetrical unjust enrichment claims, that of the liquidator to recover the asset transferred or its value and that of the transferee by way of counter-restitution of payments he has made and the value added by improvements to the asset, and that while the latter claim may be invoked to reduce the former the two claims are analytically distinct in that each has to satisfy the criteria for unjust enrichment.

The concept of unjust enrichment embodies two distinct remedial notions. One is the restoration of property or money received by the defendant at the expense of the claimant; the other is disgorgement of gains improperly made by the defendant as the result of a wrong done to the claimant not involving a subtraction from the claimant's estate, as where directors of a company use their position to obtain for themselves benefits which, if obtained at all, should have been procured for their company.

---

[47] And thus a rebuttable presumption of good faith where none of these cases is applicable.
[48] "Restitution for Vulnerable Transactions", in *Vulnerable Transactions in Corporate Insolvency* (ed. John Armour and Howard Bennett), Chap.9.

Only the former is embodied in the concept of a transaction at an undervalue, for what the court has to do is to restore the company to the position in which it would have been if the transaction had not been concluded, not to give it additional benefits derived by the defendant from his wrongdoing. These would have to be recovered in a common law action for disgorgement of the gains improperly made.

A crucial question is whether the defence of change of position, which is well established in the law of unjust enrichment, is available as an answer to a claim under s.238. Dr Simone Degeling takes the view that it is.[49] This receives some support from *Rose v AIB Group (UK) plc*,[50] in which Mr Nicholas Warren Q.C., sitting as a deputy High Court judge, held in relation to a claim under s.127 of the Insolvency Act that a defence of change of position could not be entirely ruled out as a defence,[51] though on the facts of that case he held it to be inapplicable. In reaching this conclusion he relied on the fact that whereas ss.238 and 239 prescribe remedies that the court can award, s.127 does not but leaves the remedy to the general law. Even so, the conclusion is debatable.[52] But whatever the position in relation to s.127, the better view is that change of position is not a defence to a claim by the liquidator under s.238, for what is involved is not private litigation between two solvent parties but a statutory claim for the benefit of creditors as a whole for the restoration of value improperly lost by the company, and where the Act sets out the powers of the court to reverse the effect of a transaction at an undervalue it is not legitimate to invoke the common law defence of change of position to bypass the statutory scheme.[53] This conclusion, that the overriding consideration is restoration of value to the company in the interests of the creditors generally, so that general principles of the law of restitution do not apply, is reinforced by two further considerations. First, contrary to the general principle of the common law, the creditor's good faith does not provide a defence to a claim under s.238, while the company's lack of good faith entitles its liquidator to invoke the section. Secondly, the defence of bona fide purchase, which is one of the other defences to a restitutionary claim, is not available under the Act, since as we have seen s.241 is confined to third parties and does not protect the party who dealt with the company. This clearly demonstrates that the overriding concern is to ensure that asset value is not lost in the run-up to liquidation, even if this causes hardship to a wholly innocent counterparty. Acts of reliance by the creditor on the validity of the transaction should therefore be regarded as *res inter alios*

---

[49] Above, n.48, paras 9.92, 9.93 and 9.100.
[50] [2003] 1 W.L.R. 2791; [2003] 2 B.C.L.C. 374 *sub. nom. Re Tain Construction Ltd, Rose v AIB Group (UK) plc.*
[51] *ibid.*, para.41.
[52] See below, para.11–133.
[53] See Duncan Sheehan, [2004] C.L.J. 41.

acta and irrelevant to the s.238 claim except so far as they found a right to counter-restitution (*e.g.* for the value of improvements to the transferred property), in which case they can be invoked for that purpose, not to support a defence of change of position. For the same reason change of position ought not, it is thought, to be a factor to be taken into account by the court in the exercise of its discretion. s.238(5) and 241(2) provide the only defences to a claim otherwise made out and the purpose of the discretion is not to allow the court to take account of hardship to the transferee but simply to ensure that where there has been a transaction at an undervalue the remedy is tailored to the purpose specified in s.238(3), namely "restoring the position to what it would have been if the company had not entered into that transaction." This same provision takes care of the case where the defendant has added value to property ordered to be retransferred, as by making improvements to it. It is unnecessary to resort to rights of counter-restitution in the general law, since s.238(3) makes it clear that the intention is to restore the company to its *status quo*, not to put it into a better position than it was before, so that a necessary condition of any retransfer is the payment to the creditor of a sum equal to the value added. Alternatively the court can make an order for payment of the value the property would have had without the improvements.

Recovery or disclaimer?

It may happen that a transaction at an undervalue imposes continuing obligations on the debtor company which would enable it to disclaim the transaction as onerous property in regard to the future obligations. The office holder may then have to elect between remedies. If the transaction is reversed as a transaction at an undervalue then, depending on the order made by the court, there may be nothing to disclaim. On the other hand, exercise of a right of disclaimer as to future obligations may have the result of reversing the imbalance in value in the original transaction, so that while it remains the case that the transaction was at an undervalue at the time it was entered into no relief, or only reduced relief, is necessary to restore the company to its former position.

11–68

7. PREFERENCES

(i) Overview

The pre-1986 law

English bankruptcy law has long had provisions enabling the court to set aside payments and transfers made in the run-up to bankruptcy in favour of a particular creditor which were designed to prefer him over other

11–69

creditors. Fraudulent preferences, as they were known, were struck down by the courts on policy grounds long before legislation was enacted to deal with them. Prior to the Insolvency Act 1985 the law relating to fraudulent preferences was set out in s.44 of the Bankruptcy Act 1914,[54] which was made applicable to companies by s.320 of the Companies Act 1948. The term "fraudulent preference" was not in fact used in s.44; what the section in fact provided in essence was that every disposition of property or payment, every obligation incurred, and every judicial proceeding taken or suffered by a person unable to pay his debts with a view to giving a creditor or a surety preference over the other creditors was to be deemed fraudulent and void against the trustee in bankruptcy if the transferor, etc., became bankrupt within six months. It was not in fact necessary to show a fraudulent intent; all that was required was that the debtor should make a voluntary transfer, payment, etc. with the dominant intention of favouring a particular creditor or surety at the expense of other creditors. The debtor was not considered to act voluntarily if he made the transfer or payment under pressure from the creditor, *e.g.* a threat of legal proceedings which genuinely influenced the debtor.

Bearing in mind that the object of rules as to preference is to prevent a creditor from gaining an unfair advantage by concluding a transaction with the company during the twilight period which precedes winding-up or administration[55] it may seem odd that avoidance of a preference should be made to depend on the intention of the company to give a preference, rather than on the fact of the creditor receiving one.[56] Indeed, there is no such requirement under Australian or United States law, where it suffices that the transaction improves the creditor's position during the twilight period. The focus on the intent (now the desire) of the debtor stems from the historical origins of fraudulent preference as an act intended to give one creditor an advantage at the expense of the general body of creditors.[57] The Cork Committee considered whether to recommend that English law be brought into line but the majority view came out against this on the ground that without an intention to prefer the element of impropriety on which the existing statutory provisions were based was missing and that

---

[54] As amended by s.115(3) of the Companies Act 1947.

[55] For an excellent treatment of legal policy relating to preferences, described from the perspective of United States law but in many ways equally applicable to English law, see Professor Jackson's elegant study *The Logic and Limits of Bankruptcy Law*, Chap.6. See also D.D. Prentice, "Some Observations on the Law Relating To Preferences", in *Making Commercial Law* (ed. Ross Cranston), 439 *et seq.*

[56] One of the more curious features of s.44 of the Bankruptcy Act 1914 was that it did not say in terms that the transaction had to have the effect of giving the creditor a preference; it referred merely to the fact of payment, transfer, etc. and the intention of the debtor to prefer the creditor. So on a literal construction a payment or transfer which, though intended to favour the creditor, did not in fact do so was voidable.

[57] Similarly with what are transactions at an undervalue. See *Alderson v Temple* (1768) 4 Burr. 2235, 98 E.R. 165, and above, para.11–40.

creditors who were active in the pursuit of payment should be allowed to retain the fruits of their diligence, particularly since they may well have used these to pay their own creditors.[58] The argument is unpersuasive. The whole purpose of the *pari passu* principle is to ensure that once a company becomes insolvent no individual creditor should be allowed to steal a march on his competitors. Diligence should not be a factor at this stage. Indeed, a rule which allows the creditor who exerts greatest pressure on the debtor company the best chance of resisting a preference claim scarcely reflects a principled approach to the question of equitable distribution in insolvency.[59]

The policies underlying the preference rules have been discussed in this context as in relation to transactions at an undervalue,[60] where it was seen that deterrence is not a credible objective and that the real policy is to preserve equality of distribution during the run-up to winding-up or administration. There is, however, an important difference between the two in that transactions at an undervalue necessarily result in a diminution in the company's net asset position whereas preferences do not, since the payment or transfer in favour of the preferred creditor produces a corresponding reduction in the company's liabilities, leaving its net asset position unchanged. So the rules as to preferences are not aimed at protecting the company's assets, only in ensuring that one creditor is not given an unfair advantage over others.

The changes effected by the Insolvency Act

The Insolvency Act 1986, re-enacting the Insolvency Act 1985, introduced **11–70** the following changes:

(1) References to "fraud" have been dropped. This is not a change of substance.

(2) Though the vulnerable transaction is still referred to as a preference, this is defined in terms which refer not to a preference of the creditor over other creditors but to placing him in a better position on liquidation than he would have had if the transaction had not been concluded. In fact, this comes to the same thing as a preference, but at least the factual improvement of the creditor's position is now expressly stated as an essential element.

---

[58] Insolvency Law Review Committee *Insolvency Law and Practice* (Cmnd. 8558, 1982), paras 1254 *et seq.*

[59] See the strong criticisms by R.C.C. Cuming, "Transactions at Undervalue and Preferences under the Bankruptcy and Insolvency Act: Rethinking Outdated Approaches" (2002) 37 Can. Bus. L.J. 5.

[60] See above, paras 11–03 *et seq.*

(3) In place of the old "dominant intention to prefer" the statutory provisions prescribe a less stringent requirement that in giving the preference the company was influenced by a desire to produce the effect referred to in s.239(4)(b).

(4) The time limit for avoidance is extended from six months to two years in the case of a preference in favour of a person connected with the company.

The basic provision

11–71   Where an administration order has been made against a company or it goes into liquidation and the company has at a relevant time given a preference to any person, the court may, on an application by the office-holder, make such order as it thinks fit for restoring the position to what it would have been if the company had not given that preference and give consequential relief.[61]

Conditions to be satisfied under section 239

11–72   The court cannot make an order under s.239 unless the following seven conditions are satisfied:

(1) The company is in liquidation or administration.

(2) Application for the order is made by the liquidator or administrator.

(3) A preference was given to a creditor, a surety or a guarantor.

(4) The preference was given or suffered by the company.

(5) In giving the preference the company was influenced by a desire to improve the position of the person preferred

(6) The preference was given at a relevant time.

(7) The company was unable to pay its debts within the meaning of s.123 of the Insolvency Act either at the time of or in consequence of entering into the transaction.[62]

Thus there must be a factual preference, a desire to prefer and the giving of the preference at a relevant time.[63] Conditions (1), (2) and (6) have been

---

[61] Insolvency Act 1986 ss.239(1)-(3), 238(1), 240, 241. See above, paras 11–65 *et seq.*

[62] *ibid., s.*240(2). In contrast to the position in regard to transactions at an undervalue, there is no presumption of inability to pay debts in the case of a preference in favour of a person connected with the company.

[63] Adrian Walters, "Preferences", in *Vulnerable Transactions in Corporate Insolvency* (ed. Armour and Bennett) 123 at 126.

discussed earlier in relation to transactions at an undervalue. However, the concept of "relevant time" raises additional considerations in relation to preferences which it is necessary to examine. Condition (7) was fully explored in Chapter 4.

Defences

Even where all the above conditions are satisfied a defence may be available under s.241(2). For reasons already given, there would appear to be no scope for the application of general principles of unjust enrichment and no need for any general law right of counter-restitution.[64] **11–73**

Onus of proof

In general, the onus lies on the office-holder to establish that all the conditions necessary for the making of an order under s.239 have been satisfied, including the fact that the company was influenced by a desire to give a preference. But there is a rebuttable presumption of such desire where the preference is in favour of a person connected with the company otherwise than by reason only of being its employee.[65] On the other hand, in contrast to the position in regard to transactions at an undervalue, there is no presumption of inability to pay debts in the case of a preference in favour of a person connected with the company. **11–74**

(ii) The elements of a preference

What constitutes a preference

By s.239(4) a company gives a preference to a person if: **11–75**

(a) that person is one of the company's creditors or a surety or guarantor for any of the company's debts or other liabilities, and

(b) the company does anything or suffers anything to be done which (in either case) has the effect of putting that person into a position which, in the event of the company going into insolvent liquidation,

---

[64] See above, para.11–67.

[65] Insolvency Act 1986, s.239(6). For a case where a director of the debtor company was also managing director of the creditor and effectively took decisions for both companies, see *Re Transworld Trading Ltd, TFS Cargo Services Ltd v Saunders* [1999] B.P.I.R. 628, where the judge declined to accept a picture of "poor Mr. Kirby as managing director of TFS exerting legitimate pressure upon himself as director of TWT."

will be better than the position he would have been in if that thing had not been done.

The basic features of factual preference[66] are (1) an improvement of the creditor's position (2) at the expense of other creditors.

Examples of preference of creditor

11–76   A preference of a creditor typically takes one of three forms, namely a payment to the creditor[67] or to a third party by direction of the creditor,[68] the provision of security (or additional security) for past advances, and the transfer of debts or other assets in reduction or discharge of the company's liability.[69] But any other act or thing which improves the creditor's position relative to what it would be in an immediately ensuing liquidation suffices as a preference,[70] for example:

(1)   a transaction entered into with the creditor at an undervalue[71];

(2)   an agreement for set-off going beyond what would be allowed the creditor under the rules governing insolvency set-off[72];

(3)   the conferment on the creditor of a right of set-off against a debt already owing to the company by the creditor;

(4)   voluntary submission of the debtor company to an unjustified or excessive judgment;

---

[66] See below, para.11–80.

[67] This could include the distribution of a declared dividend to controlling shareholders if the company was insolvent at the time and the shareholders could not, as persons connected with the company (see Insolvency Act 1986, ss.249(b), 435(7), (10)) rebut the presumption of a desire to prefer them (see *ibid.*, s.239(6)). Where shareholders have to repay the dividend received they will rank as deferred creditors, for the amount of the dividend *(ibid.,* s.74(2)(f)).

[68] See *Re Exchange Travel (Holdings) Ltd* [1996] B.C.C. 933, *per* Rattee J. at 948.

[69] An agreement that security shall be given only on demand by the creditor or the occurrence of some other uncertain event is not a present security but a mere contract. If the creditor subsequently demands security or the other stated contingency occurs and security is furnished, this will be regarded as given for past value (except to the extent of any new value furnished) and if given within the preference period (six months or two years, as the case may be) will be caught by s.239 if the other conditions of application are satisfied. See *Re Jackson & Bassford Ltd* [19061 2 Ch. 467 and Roy Goode, *Legal Problems of Credit and Security*, paras 1–76, 2–15.

[70] Assuming satisfaction of the other conditions for the application of s.239.

[71] In practice, s.238 would usually be relied on, since it is wider in scope and covers in every case a period of two years prior to winding-up or administration.

[72] The fact that such an agreement is of no effect on liquidation, being displaced by the insolvency set-off rules, does not make this example purely theoretical, for in the first place s.238 may be triggered by an administration rather than a liquidation and in the second place the point of time at which the efficacy of the set-off agreement has to be tested is not the date of actual liquidation but the date of the hypothetical liquidation, which as stated above would seem to be immediately after the act asserted to constitute the preference.

(5)   allowing payment to the creditor by a third party who has a right to be recouped by the company;

(6)   performance of a contract in favour of a creditor who had already made payment in advance when performances were also due under other contracts to other creditors in a similar position, as where a seller of goods collects payment from a number of buyers but only makes delivery to a few selected buyers.

Preference rules confined to creditors, sureties and guarantors

Since the rules as to preference are designed to preserve the sanctity of the *pari passu* principle by which creditors in a winding-up share rateably in the assets available for distribution, the rules as to preference are confined to, creditors of and sureties and guarantors for the company,[73] for only a creditor, a surety or a guarantor can prove in a winding-up.[74]   **11–77**

"Creditor"

Though the term "creditor" includes, for other purposes, future, prospective and contingent creditors as well as creditors to whom debts are currently payable the preference provisions are necessarily confined to existing creditors, for it is only they who by definition will have received a payment or transfer without giving new value. It is true that a future creditor could be paid in advance of performance, but that is not a preference, since he remains liable to perform and thereby give value.   **11–78**

"Surety"; "guarantor"

These terms are examined later in the discussion of a preference in favour of a surety or guarantor.[75]   **11–79**

Improvement of the creditor's position as the criterion of a preference

In determining whether a creditor has been preferred the acid test is whether what is done would have the effect of disturbing the statutory   **11–80**

---

[73] Insolvency Act 1986, s.239(4)(a); *Re Beacon Leisure Ltd* [1991] B.C.C. 213. As to the preference of sureties, see paras 11–97 *et seq*. See also above n.67.

[74] A surety can prove when he has discharged the debt or that part of it for which he agreed to be responsible.

[75] See below, paras 11–97 *et seq*.

order of priorities in an insolvent liquidation[76] by placing the creditor or surety in a more favourable position than he would otherwise have had. The mere fact that the thing is done or suffered in pursuance of a court order does not, without more, prevent it from constituting a preference.[77] This re-enacts previous law in enabling the court to look behind collusive judgments.[78]

I have remarked earlier that the former legislation contained no express requirement that the creditor should in fact have received a preference; all that had to be established was that a payment, transfer, etc., was made with a view of giving the creditor or a surety a preference over the other creditors, a provision interpreted by the courts as requiring that the company's dominant intention should be to give such a preference. Section 239(4)(b) of the Insolvency Act 1986, in defining a preference, says nothing about preferring a creditor over other creditors; the test is whether what was done has the effect of putting the creditor in a better position upon winding-up than he would have been in if it had not been done. But this comes to the same thing. If the effect of a payment or transfer made or suffered by the company is to make the creditor better off on winding-up than he would otherwise have been, this can only be at the expense of other creditors. So the new test of improvement is merely another way of describing a preference, and perhaps a more satisfactory way, since it underlines the separately stated requirement that the company be insolvent at the time of the payment or transfer in question or become insolvent because of it.[79] Obviously a payment or transfer made by a company which remains solvent after making it does not improve the creditor's position, for he would in any event have been paid in full if the company had gone into winding-up.

(1) No preference to the extent of new value

11–81 The payment, transfer or other act under attack must relate to a past indebtedness, for to the extent that the creditor gives new value he gains no advantage[80] and even if he happens to be a creditor already in respect of some prior transaction he does not receive the payment, transfer, etc., in his capacity as such but derives it from the independent new transaction concluded for value.

---

[76] "Insolvent liquidation" is not defined for the purpose of this section but presumably has the same meaning as in ss.214(6) and 216(7), namely liquidation at a time when the company's assets are insufficient for the payment of its debts and other liabilities and the expenses of the winding-up.

[77] Insolvency Act 1986, s.239(7).

[78] For an example, see *Re Menastar Finance Ltd* [2003] 1 B.C.L.C. 338.

[79] See para.11–72.

[80] See below, para.11–82.

Example 14

C grants D Ltd an overdraft facility. Subsequently C makes a fixed loan   **11–82**
of £300,000 to D Ltd for the purchase of capital equipment, the loan
being secured by a charge on the company's factory premises. At that
time the company's account is overdrawn by £20,000. The grant of the
charge does not constitute a preference for it was given not in respect of
the existing indebtedness of £20,000 but to secure a new advance. The
charge was therefore not taken by C in the capacity of an existing
creditor.[81]

Since a preference involves a payment, transfer or other act which,
assuming the company were to go into insolvent liquidation immediately
thereafter,[82] would put the creditor in a better position than if the payment
or transfer had not been made or the other act performed, the preference
provisions cannot apply to the extent that the creditor gives new value, for
he does not take out a penny more than he puts in. So a creditor who takes
security for a contemporaneous or subsequent advance does not obtain a
preference, since the diminution in assets created by the security is matched
by the infusion of new funds. Again, a simultaneous exchange of goods and
money on a sale transaction cannot involve a preference, whether the
company be the buyer or the seller.

(2) Security in after-acquired property

The concept of new value is of particular importance in relation to a charge   **11–83**
taken over after-acquired property to secure contemporaneous or future
advances, for each newly acquired asset, having been bargained for as
security at the outset, is considered given in security for new value, a point I
have developed elsewhere.[83]

Some problems concerning new value

The concept of new value is easy to understand but sometimes hard to   **11–84**
apply. Let us consider, first, the single transaction involving the provision of
services for payment, and second, a course of dealing between the parties
reflected in the operation of a running account.

(1) Simultaneous exchange

In relation to the single transaction, we have seen that a simultaneous   **11–85**
exchange gives rise to no preference problem. What is not clear is the
degree of simultaneity the court will expect in order to treat a payment or

---

[81] *See Robertson v Grigg* (1932) 47 C.L.R. 257.
[82] See below. As to whether post-liquidation assets fall within the scope of an after-acquired
property clause, see above, paras 6–25 *et seq.*
[83] Roy Goode, *Legal Problems of Credit and Security* (3rd ed.), para.2–13.

transfer as being for new value. Suppose, for example, that a solicitor deals with the purchase of land for a client company, renders his bill after completion and then receives payment. Has he thereby improved his position? Or can he contend that he collected his charges so closely after the provision of his services that these should be considered to constitute new value? A commonsense approach indicates that it suffices that payment is made within a time normal for a transaction not intended to involve the extension of credit. In any event, in the ordinary way the making of the payment will be pursuant to that intention and not from a desire to improving the position of the solicitor *vis-à-vis* other creditors.

(2) Mutual dealings on running account

11–86 Now let us turn to the position where there is a continuous flow of dealings between parties. Must each payment be treated in isolation to see whether it would have given the creditor an advantage if the company were to go into winding-up immediately thereafter? How far can credit be given for contra items? The Act itself gives no guidance. It is unfortunate that it contains no general exemption of transactions entered into bona fide by the creditor in the ordinary course of business. What is relevant is not the creditor's good faith but the question whether the company was influenced by a desire to confer an advantage on him, which as we shall see is a necessary prerequisite to any order under s.239 or 241. In practice, the two are likely to go together. Where the creditor receives a payment in good faith it will almost invariably be the case that the company makes the payment as a normal part of its business or to protect its own interests (*e.g.* for the purpose of ensuring the continuance of supplies), not to favour the creditor to whom payment is made.

In the typical case there is a running account between the parties to record mutual dealings. Suppose that a company whose account with its bank is overdrawn pays a cheque into the account, thus reducing the overdraft. If the company were at that time insolvent the payment in would constitute a preference and would be vulnerable to attack if made with intent to prefer the bank. But suppose a few days later the bank honoured a further drawing. Would it be liable to repay the preference without being given credit for the fresh advance? Such a result would seem unfair in the extreme, giving a windfall to the general body of creditors. Could the fresh drawing be treated as a reversal of the preferential payment? This is one way out of the dilemma. The court makes no order because the bank has already put right the wrong. Another way of approaching the matter is to say that "where a payment is not in pursuance of an isolated transaction but is bound up with a series of transactions, it is the effect of the total transactions, of all the connected items, that has to be looked at".[84] This

---

[84] *Ferrier v Civil Aviation Authority* (1995) 127 A.L.R. 472; M. & R *Jones Shopfitting Co Pty Ltd v National Bank of Australasia Ltd* (1983) 7 A.C.L.R. 445, citing *Re Weiss* [1970] A.L.R. 654, in which all the earlier Australian authorities are reviewed.

approach by the Australian courts[85] has much to commend it, for even if a payment into the account was intended to be preferential, a connected payment out should be treated as negating the preference *pro tanto* for it restores the loss of assets which is the rationale of the preference provisions. However, the preference will not be undone to the extent that the new drawing is secured by a fresh and valid security.[86]

Moreover, the fact that there is a series of mutual dealings, with debits and credits on both sides, will usually suffice to negate an intention to prefer, for it suggests either that a payment into the account was made in the expectation that further drawings would be allowed or that the bank allowed a further drawing on the understanding that it would be covered by a further payment into the account. In either case there is no intention to prefer or, indeed, a true preference at all. Indeed, it has been said that the real question is not whether the labelling of the account as a running account but rather the intention that payments into the account will generate future supplies of goods, services or credit. Accordingly it is not necessary that payments into the account should go in reduction of the ultimate debit balance; even payments made to discharge specific debit items will qualify for the application of the principle if the intention is that they should form part of a continuing relationship involving the extension of further credit. The leading authority is the decision of the High Court of Australia in *Airservices Australia v Ferrier*,[87] in which there were mutual dealings between the parties, sums paid were applied in discharge of particular debts but the debit balance substantially increased over the period of the mutual dealings. It was held by Dawson, Gaudron and McHugh JJ. (Brennan C.J. and Toohey J. dissenting) that none of the payments except the last (which was not a trigger for new credit) was a preference. The principle was stated by the majority in the following terms:

"Since the decision of this Court in *Richardson v Commercial Banking Co of Sydney Ltd*, the term 'running account' has achieved almost talismanic significance in determining when the ultimate, rather than the immediate and isolated, effect of a payment is to be examined for the purpose of a determination under s.122 of the Bankruptcy Act. However, the significance of a running account lies in the inferences that can be drawn from the facts that answer the description of a 'running account' rather than the label itself. A running account between traders is merely another name for an active account running from day to day, as opposed to an

---

[85] Which has since been adopted by the legislature in s.588FA(2) of the federal Corporation Law Reform Act 1992 (generally known as the Corporations Law), pursuant to the recommendations of the Harmer Report (Australian Law Reform Commission, *General Insolvency Inquiry*), para.655.

[86] *cf.* the US Bankruptcy Code, s.547(c)(4). If the overdraft had been previously secured there would not be a preference at all. See below, para.11–91.

[87] (1996) 185 C.L.R. 483.

account where further debits are not contemplated. The essential feature of a running account is that it predicates a continuing relationship of debtor and creditor with an expectation that further debits and credits will be recorded. Ordinarily, a payment, although often matching an earlier debit, is credited against the balance owing in the account. Thus, a running account is contrasted with an account where the expectation is that the next entry will be a credit entry that will close the account by recording the payment of the debt or by transferring the debt to the Bad or Doubtful Debt A/c.

If the record of the dealings of the parties fits the description of a 'running account', that record will usually provide a solid ground for concluding that they conducted their dealings on the basis that they had a continuing business relationship and that goods or services would be provided and paid for on the credit terms ordinarily applicable in the creditor's business. When that is so, a court will usually be able to conclude that the parties mutually assumed that from a business point of view each particular payment was connected with the subsequent pro-vision of goods or services in that account. Sometimes, however, the transactions recorded in the account may be so sporadic that a court cannot conclude that there was the requisite connection between a payment and the future supply of goods even though the account was kept 'in the ordinary form of a running account in which debits and credits are recorded chronologically and in which payments are not shown as attributable to any particular deliveries but are brought generally into credit'. Thus, it is not the label 'running account' but the conclusion that the payments in the account were connected with the future supply of goods or services that is relevant, because it is that connection which indicates a continuing relationship of debtor and creditor. It is this conclusion which makes it necessary to consider the ultimate and not the immediate effect of individual payments."[88]

Improvement in creditor's position must be at expense of other creditors

11–87   Since s.239 is aimed at transactions which disturb the statutory order of distribution, it follows that to be a preference within s.239 the payment or transfer must be one by which the creditor is put in a better position *at the expense of other creditors*. Accordingly it is not a preference for the company to pay a secured creditor a sum not exceeding the value of the security, for this leaves the position of other creditors unaffected.[89] By the same token a payment or transfer is not a preference if made to the creditor by a third

---

[88] *ibid.*, at 504–505 (footnotes omitted).
[89] See below, para.11–91.

party except to the extent to which the ultimate burden falls on the company's assets that would otherwise have been available to all its creditors, as where the third party is entitled to recoupment from the company and that right is secured. There is, however, the difficult decision of the High Court of Australia in *G & M Aldridge Pty Ltd v Walsh*[90]:

> A bank took a fixed charge over certain assets of a company, TLL, and a floating charge over the remaining assets, which included a sum standing to the credit of an account with the bank by another company as agent for TLL. The amount owed to the bank exceeded the value of the security, so that no part of the assets given in security would remain for unsecured creditors. The bank's charge crystallised. Nevertheless it continued to allow drawings on the account, including payments to certain creditors which TLL's liquidator sought to recover as preferences. Neither the Court of Appeal nor the High found it necessary to deal with the contention that the bank had waived its security or was otherwise estopped from enforcing it. Nevertheless the High Court rejected the contention that the payments had come not from moneys available to the company but moneys that could have been taken by the bank under its charge and upheld the decisions of the courts below allowing recovery as a preference under s.588FA of the Corporations Law.

It is clear that the court was strongly influenced by the bank's conduct in allowing the company to continue operating the account despite the crystallised charge, and perhaps the perception that since it had shown no signs of enforcing its charge the moneys were in fact available to the company. What is difficult is the court's disagreement with the reasoning of Brennan C.J. in *Sheahan Carrier Air Conditioning Pty Ltd*[91] to the effect that if a fund is fully charged to a secured creditor who consents to payment out of the fund to another creditor that creditor gains no preference at the expense of other creditors, to whom no part of the fund would have been available anyway. Rejecting this proposition the High Court held that the question was not whether the payment was "at the expense of other creditors" but whether it gave the recipient a preference, priority or advantage. However, s.588FA(1)(b) does require that the transaction under attack as a preference should result in the creditor receiving a benefit *from the company*, and it would seem to follow from the decision of the High Court that this is to be construed literally as including payments and transfers passing *through* the company under a transaction to which it is a party even if the company itself has no beneficial interest in the subject-matter of the payment or transfer. The decision may, however, have turned on its own rather special facts and does not, it is thought, reflect the

---

[90] (2003) C.L.R. 662.
[91] (1999) 161 A.L.R. 1 at 12.

position under the differently worded provisions of s.239 of the Insolvency Act 1986. If a third party chooses to pay a particular creditor without this resulting in any diminution in the company's assets the creditor's position is undoubtedly improved but the payment is not within the mischief at which the preference provisions are aimed. There would be no doubt about that if the third party made the payment direct to the creditor without involving the company. Why should it make any difference if the payment comes from a fund held by the company but impressed with a trust or charge in favour of the third party to secure an amount exceeding the value of the fund? Assuming that the burden of the payment does not ultimately fall on the company's assets, the payment is not in any real sense made by the company at all; it is merely the vehicle for the transmission of the third party's funds.[92] Again, the mere fact that the payment is made at the request of the company or event that it is a party to the transaction under which the payment is made by another, does not by itself engage the company's assets so as to give rise to a preference.

11–88   The position is otherwise, of course, where the third party is entitled to be indemnified by the company and the indemnity is secured by a charge on an asset which exceeds in value what is owed to the chargee, so that if the security has not been released and remains intact the payment operates to reduce the value of the company's equity of redemption. The third party's payment to the creditor is then a preference, because the ultimate effect of the transaction is that payment is being made by the company itself from the asset given in security. The same situation arises where the third party, though not secured in the technical sense, has a right of set-off or combination in respect of a separate account of the company which is in credit, for this right is an equity to which the account is subject and its exercise reduces *pro tanto* the amount of the credit balance. But if the right of indemnity is wholly unsecured there is no preference, merely the substitution of one creditor for another. So if a creditor is paid from the company's overdrawn account, increasing its overdraft still further, then if the overdraft is not secured or covered by a right of set-off or combination against an account in credit there is no preference, for the bank simply replaces the original creditor and there is no depletion of the company's assets.

There has been much discussion of direct payment clauses in construction contracts empowering the building owner, on the insolvency of the main contractor, to make payment direct to sub-contractors of sums due to them from the main contractor. The validity of such clauses has been discussed earlier in the context of the *pari passu* principle,[93] but the question also arises whether a direct payment is a preference of the sub-contractor at the expense of the main contractor's creditors. Again, in the

---

[92] See to similar effect Adrian Walters, (2003) 119 L.Q.R. 28.
[93] See above, para.7–16.

absence of a trust or equitable assignment in favour of the sub-contractor,[94] a direct payment to the latter is vulnerable as a preference if influenced by the requisite desire to improve his position.[95]

Payment or transfer need not be by company

Although, as stated above, the payment or transfer must ultimately come from the company's assets in order to constitute a preference, it is not necessary for the company itself to make the preferential payment or transfer; it suffices that the company "suffers" the payment or transfer to be made.[96] "Suffer" means permit or allow in circumstances where the company has control of the payment or transfer in the sense that its permission is needed to make it and can be refused,[97] and *a fortiori* if the company can require the payment or transfer to be made it suffers it to be made.[98]

11–89

The hypothetical liquidation

Preference is tested by reference to a hypothetical, not an actual, liquidation. It is not necessary that the company shall in fact have gone into liquidation, for the preference provisions apply equally in administration. If the company enters administration the question of preference still has to be tested by asking whether the effect of the payment, transfer or other act would be to put the creditor in a better position if winding-up were to supervene than he would otherwise have had. It would seem that for this purpose liquidation should be assumed to have taken place immediately after the payment, transfer or other act in question,[99] and with reference to creditors then existing, so that subsequent events (*e.g.* the accrual of new preferential debts) should be ignored, a point which may assist a creditor who is collecting payment under a floating charge.[1]

11–90

Payments to secured creditors

In general, payment to a secured creditor in reduction or discharge of the debt is not a preference, for the effect of the payment is to reduce or extinguish the security interest and thus *pro tanto* to increase the company's

11–91

---

[94] See above, para.6–11.
[95] See para.11–94.
[96] Insolvency Act 1986, s.239(4)(b).
[97] *Sefton v Tophams Ltd* [1967] 1 A.C. 50; *Earl of Leicester v Wells-next-the-sea Urban District Council* [1973] Ch. 110; *Berton v Alliance Economic Investment Co Ltd* [1922] 1 K.B. 742.
[98] *Earl of Leicester v Wells-next-the-sea Urban District Council* , n.97 above, *per* Plowman J. at 124 in a decision on "permit".
[99] The date of any actual liquidation is irrelevant as a temporal point for determining improvement of the creditor's position.
[1] Though not, as a rule, a secured creditor. See below, para.11–91.

equity in the previously charged assets and make them available to other creditors. Accordingly the payment produces no change in the value of the assets available for the general body of creditors. Moreover, if the company were to refrain from making the payment that would not help the other creditors, for the secured creditor would still be entitled to enforce his security, assuming the giving of it had not itself been by way of preference. Thus it has been held in Australia that a bank which in good faith and in the ordinary course of business collects a cheque for a customer and credits the proceeds to the customer's overdrawn account does not receive a preference, for the bank had a lien on the cheque to secure the overdraft and thus a security interest in the proceeds, so that the application of these in reduction of the overdraft does not alter the customer's asset position.[2]

However, there are at least four situations in which payment to a secured creditor may constitute a preference. The first is where the amount of the payment exceeds the value of the security; in that event the payment is vulnerable to the extent of the excess. The second is where the security is one which, if winding-up had occurred immediately after the payment, would have been rendered void, *e.g.* for want of registration, for on that hypothesis the payment reduces the net value of the company's assets.[3] The third is where the payment is made to the holder of a floating charge and at the time of the payment there were insufficient free assets to pay the preferential creditors then existing, for upon a winding-up immediately after the payment these would have had priority over the holder of the floating charge,[4] who thus derives an advantage from the payment made to him. But since (if the view expressed above is correct) the notional liquidation must be assumed to have commenced immediately after the payment to the floating chargee, only preferential debts then in existence are relevant, and the chargee will not be considered tunsecuredo have improved his position merely because new preferential debts come into existence at a later date. The fourth case is where payment is made to the holder of a floating charge and discharges the security, so that the general creditors lose the benefit of the prescribed part, which, on the hypothesised winding-up, would have had to be surrendered to the liquidator to form a fund available to unsecured creditors.[5]

---

[2] *National Australian Bank v KDI Construction Services Pty Ltd* (1988) 12 A.C.L.R. 683. The position would be otherwise, of course, if the cheque were given to the bank not simply for collection but with a view to giving it an advantage it would not otherwise have enjoyed, for then the giving of the lien over the cheque to the bank will itself constitute a preference.
[3] Where the security would not have been void but merely liable to be discharged, *e.g.* under s.241(1)(c), the court must presumably decide whether it is likely that an order under s.241(l)(c), or an order producing a similar effect, would have been made.
[4] Insolvency Act 1986, s.175(2)(b).
[5] Insolvency Act 1986, s176A. See above, paras 6–31 *et seq.*

Exercise of right of set-off

No question of preference can arise where the creditor collects payment by exercise of a right of set-off, for this does not require the consent of the company at all, let alone a desire on its part to improve the creditor's position.[6] Payment by the company into an overdrawn account with its bank is likewise not capable of being a preference where the payment does not exceed the amount of a credit balance held by the company on another account to which the bank could have resorted by way of combination of accounts if the payment in question had not been made, for the effect of the payment is *pro tanto* to reduce the available amount of set-off against the account in credit, so that the position of other creditors is unaffected. Where the company has a contractual right to set off against one customer's credit balance amount due from another customer, exercise of that right is not a preference of the first customer, for it is for the company's benefit, not that of the first customer.[7]

11–92

What does not constitute a preference

It will have been apparent from what is said above that the following transactions *(inter alia)* do not involve the giving of a preference.

11–93

(1)   Payment to a validly secured creditor of a sum not significantly exceeding the value of his security, having regard to any preferential debts then in existence ranking in priority to the security.

(2)   Payment to avoid loss of an asset (*e.g.* property or equipment held on lease) or of a right (*e.g.* under a contract) having a value not less than the amount of the payment.

(3)   The exchange of an asset of the company for one of at least equal value.

(4)   The grant of security for a contemporaneous or subsequent advance or other new value.

(5)   Payment or transfer of property to a person who is not a creditor of the company.

(6)   Payment to the creditor by a third party which does not involve any call on the company's assets.

---

[6] However, a party who has received a preference cannot avoid repayment by exercising a right of set-off. See above, para.8–25.
[7] *Re Exchange Travel (Holdings) Ltd*, above.

(iii) The company's desire to prefer

"Influenced by a desire"

11–94   As stated earlier,[8] under the old law a preference was not voidable unless the company's dominant intention in making the payment, transfer, etc., to the creditor was to prefer him to the other creditors. The Insolvency Act 1986, re-enacting the provisions of the Insolvency Act 1985, formulates the criterion rather differently. As before, the mere fact of preference does not suffice to make the court's power's exercisable. What has to be shown in addition is that in giving the preference the company was influenced in deciding to give it by a desire to produce in relation to the preferred party the effect of putting him in a better position than he would have been in if the payment, transfer, etc. had not been made.[9]

Since preference itself is defined in terms of improvement of the creditor's position rather than in terms of preferring him to other creditors, no reference is made to an intention to prefer. Instead the question is whether the company was influenced by a desire to improve the creditor's position compared with what it would have been on an immediate winding-up. Three questions arise. First, what is "desire"? Is it the same as intent? Or motive? Secondly, does "influenced by" require the desire to prefer should be the sole factor, the dominant factor or some lesser degree of influence in the decision to make the payment or transfer? Thirdly, what is the relevant time at which to test the desire: the time the debenture is given or the time when the decision to give it is made? The root decision on all three questions is that of Millett J. in *Re M.C. Bacon Ltd.*[10] In that case the company had run up a substantial unsecured overdraft with its bank, which was prepared to continue its support but stipulated that in view of the serious position in which the company found itself an essential condition of this was the provision of a first mortgage debenture over the company's assets. Three months after executing the debenture the company went into liquidation. The liquidator attacked the debenture as a transaction at an undervalue and a preference. As noted earlier, the first of these two grounds failed on the basis that the giving, of security did not reduce the assets.[11] Millett J. proceeded to deal with the allegation of preference in the following terms:

"Section 44(1) has been replaced and its language has been entirely recast. Every single word of significance, whether in the form of statutory

---

[8] Above, para.11–69.
[9] Insolvency Act 1986, s.239(5). For the position relating to preference of a surety, see below, para.11–97.
[10] [1990] B.C.C. 78.
[11] See above.

definition or in its judicial exposition, has been jettisoned. 'View', 'dominant', 'intention' and even 'to prefer' have all been discarded. These are replaced by 'influenced', 'desire' and 'to produce in relation to that person the effect mentioned in subsection (4)(b)'.'

I therefore emphatically protest against the citation of cases decided under the old law. They cannot be of assistance when the language of the statute has been so completely and deliberately changed.

This is a completely different test. It involves at least two radical departures from the old law. It is no longer necessary to establish a *dominant* intention to prefer. It is sufficient that the decision is *influenced* by the requisite desire. That is the first change. The second is that it is no longer sufficient to establish an *intention* to prefer. There must be a *desire* to produce the effect mentioned in the subsection.

This second change is made necessary by the first, for without it it would be virtually impossible to uphold the validity of a security taken in exchange for the injection of fresh funds into a company in financial difficulties. A man is taken to intend the necessary consequences of his actions, so that an intention to grant a security to a creditor necessarily involves an intention to prefer that creditor in the event of insolvency. The need to establish that such intention was dominant was essential under the old law to prevent perfectly proper transactions from being struck down. With the abolition of that requirement intention could not remain the relevant test. Desire has been substituted. That is a very different matter. Intention is objective, desire is subjective. A man can choose the lesser of two evils without desiring either.

. . . A man is not to be taken as *desiring* all the necessary consequence of his actions. Some consequences may be of advantage to him and be desired by him; others may not affect him and be matters of indifference to him; while still others may be positively disadvantageous to him and not be desired by him, but be regarded by him as the unavoidable price of obtaining the desired advantage. It will still be possible to provide assistance to a company in financial difficulties provided that the company is actuated only by proper commercial considerations. Under the new regime a transaction will not be set aside as a voidable preference unless the company positively wished to improve the creditor's position in the event of its own insolvent liquidation.

There is, of course, no need for there to be direct evidence of the requisite desire. Its existence may be inferred from the circumstances of the case just as the dominant intention could be inferred under the old law. But the mere presence of the requisite desire will not be sufficient by itself. It must have influenced the decision to enter into the transaction. It was submitted on behalf of the bank that it must have been the factor which 'tipped the scales.' I disagree. That is not what subsection (5) says; it requires only that the desire should have influenced the decision. That requirement is satisfied if it was one of the factors which operated on the minds of those who made the decision. It need not have been the only factor or even the decisive one. In my judgment it is not necessary to prove that, if the requisite desire had not been present, the company would not have entered into the transaction. That would be too high a test.

It was also submitted that the relevant time was when the debenture was created. That cannot be right. The relevant time was the time when the decision to grant it was made."[12]

11–95   Millett J. went on to hold that the company was not motivated by a desire to improve the bank's position as creditor in the event of the company's liquidation, and that accordingly the allegation of preference had not been, made out. In a subsequent case[13] the subjective nature of desire was emphasised and it was held that a payment made by the company in winding-up to its bank was not a preference where the payment was motivated by commercial considerations such as the need to obtain finance from other sources. This raises the question how a company forms a desire. Plainly this can only be done through a human agent, who must, it is thought, be a director, general manager or other person of sufficient authority in the company that he can be said to represent its mind and will or a person acting on his instructions, as opposed to a junior employee who in paying a creditor simply fulfils a routine function.

Banks are in a somewhat special position as creditors because one of their functions is to collect cheques for customers and credit the proceeds to the customers' accounts. If an insolvent customer whose account is overdrawn pays in cheques for collection this has the effect of improving the bank's position, for it acquires a lien on the cheque and thus a security interest in the proceeds. The payment in of the cheque is thus a preference but s239 will not apply unless the office-holder can show that in doing this the customer was influenced by a desire to improve the bank's position rather than because the normal method of collecting cheques is to give them to one's bank for collection. The office-holder may not always find it easy to show this, particularly where the company has only one bank account, for if it is taxed with being influenced by a desire to give a preference its response is likely to be: "What else should we have done with the cheques?"

Good faith of creditor irrelevant

11–96   As in the case of transactions at an undervalue,[14] the party whose desire is relevant is the company. The defence of good faith is not open to the preferred creditor or preferred surety, a point made clear by s.241(2)(b).

---

[12] *ibid.*, at 87–88.
[13] *Re Fairway Magazines Ltd* [1992] B.C.C. 924.
[14] See above, para.11–40.

(iv) Preference of a surety or guarantor

Preference of a surety

In applying the statutory provisions to preference of a surety[15] (we shall come to the term "guarantor" in a moment) the Insolvency Act follows the old law, though as we shall the powers of the court in relation to a preferred surety are more extensive than they were generally considered to be under the Bankruptcy Act 1914.   **11–97**

(1) The fact of preference

Where the debtor company makes a payment to its creditor in discharge or reduction of a guaranteed debt, the payment benefits not only the creditor but the surety: the creditor because it extinguishes or reduces his claim, and the surety because it discharges or reduces his secondary liability. If the surety is fully solvent, can the creditor argue that his position has not been improved by the debtor company's payment because he would have been paid in full anyway by the surety? No, because the payment has reduced the company's assets and obviated the need to proceed against the surety.[16]   **11–98**

(2) The desire

In making a payment the company may be influenced by a desire to improve the position of the creditor, the surety or both the creditor and the surety.[17] The question whether there is the requisite desire must be asked in respect of each person to whom a preference has been given.[18] A desire to prefer the creditor does not of itself indicate an intent to prefer the surety; conversely, the company may intend to prefer the surety without being in any way influenced by a desire to assist the creditor.[19] The typical case is where a company's account has been guaranteed by the directors, who at a time when the company is insolvent arrange for it to repay the bank, not   **11–99**

---

[15] A person may be a surety for this purpose if has merely charged his property as security for the principal debtor's indebtedness without assuming any personal liability (*Re Conley* [1938] 2 All E.R. 127).

[16] See Walters, above, n.63, at 149, n.116.

[17] But in this last case it remains the fact that there is only one payment, not two, so that if an order is made against both the creditor and the surety it cannot provide in total for payment of a sum greater than is necessary to restore the amount of the preference.

[18] *Re Agriplant Services Ltd* [1997] B.C.L.C. 598, where it was held that the desire was to improve the position both of the debtor company and of the surety. As to what is the relevant time in proceedings against a surety, see below, para.11–101.

[19] Though this would not preclude the court from directing repayment by the creditor as under the previous law. See below.

out of any desire to improve the bank's position but to obtain a release from their own liability to the bank. This is a preference of the sureties because the repayment operates not merely to affect the relations between the bank and the sureties but to avoid a situation in which the sureties, having paid the bank under their guarantee, are left to prove in the winding-up in competition with other creditors for their indemnity entitlement. Discharge of the sureties therefore improves their position relative to what it would have been on a winding-up. As will be seen, the working out of the statutory provisions in relation to sureties is not free from complications.

(3) "Surety"; "guarantor"

11–100   The terms "surety" and "guarantor" are nowadays used interchangeably to denote a person who undertakes payment or other performance of an obligation owed to a creditor if the debtor defaults. The obligation is thus both secondary, in that the surety's liability is dependent on default by the principal debtor, and accessory in that it is coterminous with the principal oblgiation and enforceable only to the extent that the principal obligation is enforceable. However, the word "guarantee" has acquired a distinctive meaning in the context of demand guarantees (also called performance bonds), which are undertakings by a bank in favour of a designated beneficiary to pay an amount, or maximum amount, to the beneficiary on presentation of a written demand and other specified documents.[20] The purpose of the guarantee is to provide an assurance of performance by the counterparty to a transaction with the beneficiary. For example, the employer under a construction contract may require the successful bidder for the contract to procure the issue of a demand guarantee by a bank covering the contractor's performance of its obligations. As between the contractor and the employer the guarantee is intended to be called only in the event of the contractor's default, but the guarantee itself is conditioned only on the presentation of stated documents.[21] Thus the bank's obligation is a primary obligation which has to be performed whether or not there has been default in performance of the underlying contract. The question arises whether this type of guarantee also falls within the preference rules. There are good reasons for thinking that it does. In the first place, if s.239 were confined to suretyship guarantees the addition of the words "or guarantor" would be redundant. More significantly, the issuer of the demand guarantee has the same right of indemnity against the contractor as it would have under a suretyship guarantee and is exposed to the same risk of the

---

[20] See Roy Goode, *Commercial Law* (3rd edn.), pp.1015 *et seq.*
[21] And, in the case of a guarantee governed by the ICC Uniform Rules for Demand Guarantees, a statement of breach in conformity with art.20 of the Rules.

contractor's insolvency, a risk reduced by the amount of the contractor's performance. In practice, however, it will rarely be the case that performance by the contractor is a preference at all, because it will not normally be given for payment already made by the employer under an executed contract but will for new value in the form of stage payments made by the employer as each stage of the work is completed, the contract thus being executory.[22]

(v) A relevant time

Only a preference given at a relevant time is caught by the statutory provisions.[23] The meaning of "relevant time" has been discussed earlier in relation to transactions at an undervalue.[24] There is, however, a difference in that the period for transactions at an undervalue is in all cases two years ending with the onset of insolvency, whereas in the case of a preference it is two years in the case of a preference in favour of a person connected with the company but is otherwise six months.[25] Where a guarantee has been given and there has been a preference both of the creditor and of the surety and only one of them is a person connected with the company it would seem that the six-month limit applies in relation to that person and cannot be circumvented by an order under s.241(1)(d).[26]

11–101

(vi) Powers of the court

General power of the court

On an application by the office-holder for an order under s.239 the court, if satisfied that the section applies, is required to make such order as it thinks fit for restoring the position to what it would have been if the company had not given the preference.[27]

11–102

Specific powers

These are the same as for transactions at an undervalue and are dealt with in the same section of the Act, namely s.241(1). I need not repeat the earlier discussion of the court's powers under that section, but a few additional comments on the position of the surety are appropriate.

11–103

---

[22] See above, para.11–81, as to the inapplicability of the preference provisions to payment or performance for new value. It would be possible to construct a preference situation, as where the contractor procures the issue of a demand guarantee in favour of A, receives part payment in advance, fails to do any work under his contract with the beneficiary as well as under contracts with B, C and D and then, when approaching insolvency, decides to give performance to A, a close friend, without doing any work for B, C or D. In that situation the performance is capable of being a preference of both A and the issuer of the guarantee.

[23] Insolvency Act 1986, s.239(2).

[24] Above, para.11–38.

[25] Insolvency Act 1986, s.240(1)(b).

[26] See below, para.11–103.

[27] Insolvency Act 1986, s.239(3). As to the application of recoveries, see below, para.11–140.

First, the court's powers in relation to sureties are considerably wider than under the previous law, which on the better view did not enable the court to make an order, for payment direct against the surety[28] or to direct the revival of his obligations to the creditor.[29] Secondly, a payment which was made solely to prefer the surety can nevertheless be ordered to be repaid by the creditor, as under the previous law, for it remains the case that he is the recipient of a preference and of a benefit within s.241(1)(d).[30] Thirdly, a payment made solely to prefer the creditor can be ordered to be repaid by the surety, except in the unlikely event that he qualifies for protection under s.241(2)(b) as a person receiving a benefit not only in good faith but for value.

Finally, the court now has power to order that where the effect of the preference was to discharge the obligation of the surety, wholly or in part, to the creditor or any other person the surety is to be under such new or revived obligation as the court thinks appropriate.[31] Under the previous law a creditor who received payment from the company might give the surety a discharge and release any security given by the surety, only to find himself on the receiving end of an order for repayment of the preference, so that he once again became a creditor of the company but without the benefit of the guarantee. To cover this eventuality every well-drawn guarantee now provides that no payment shall be effective to discharge the surety to the extent that the creditor has to repay it as a preference. Creditors should continue to include such a provision in their guarantees so as not to be dependent upon the making of an order in their favour, which is entirely within the discretion of the court.

One difficult question remains. In the case of a creditor or surety not connected with the company a preference is voidable only if the onset of insolvency occurs within six months; in the case of a creditor or surety connected with the company it is two years. Now suppose that a payment is made to the creditor nine months before the onset of insolvency and the creditor is not connected with the company whereas the surety is a director. If the decision to pay the creditor was influenced by a desire to prefer the surety, can an order be made against the creditor under s.241(1)(d) when he himself would no longer be susceptible to a claim as a preferred party? It is thought that the answer is no[32] and that the appropriate order is an order for payment direct against the surety, who on making the payment will be entitled to prove for its amount as creditor in the winding-up.

---

[28] *Re Lyons Ex p. Barclays Bank Ltd v Trustee* (1934) 152 L.T. 201, approved by Luxmoore J. in *Re Conley* [1938] 2 All E.R. 127, at p.139 and not following *Re G. Stanley & Co* [1925] Ch. 148.

[29] As to which see above, para.11–52.

[30] But see below as to the position where the creditor is not connected with the company and the payment was made more than six months before the onset of insolvency.

[31] Insolvency Act 1986, s.241(l)(e).

[32] *Contra* D.D. Prentice, "Some Observations on the Law Relating to Preferences", in *Making Commercial Law* (ed. Ross Cranston) 439 at 458–459.

Relationship between transactions at an undervalue and preferences

It has been seen that there is some overlap in the impact of the statutory **11–104** provisions relating to transactions at an undervalue and those concerning preferences. It may be helpful to identify more precisely the relationship between the two sets of provisions.

(1)   A key distinction is that the provisions relating to transactions at an undervalue are aimed at payments, transfers or other acts which diminish the assets of the company, whereas the provisions relating to preferences are concerned with transactions that unfairly favour one creditor at the expense of the others, whether or not they diminish the company's assets. In some cases a preference will also reduce the company's assets, but in most cases it will not. For example, payment of a debt which does not exceed the amount due is not a transaction at an undervalue as the net asset position is unchanged. The same is true where the company gives security for a previously unsecured loan.[33]

(2)   The provisions relating to transactions at an undervalue are concerned with the existence of a significant imbalance between a payment, transfer or other act and the consideration for which is made or done. If the bargain is fair, the provisions do not apply. By contrast the preference provisions are concerned not with the fairness of the original bargain but with the improvement of the creditor's position relative to other creditors on a winding-up notionally occurring immediately after the payment, transfer, etc., in question. So payment by an insolvent company of one creditor but not the others gives rise to a preference.

(3)   A preference will also be a transaction at an undervalue where the company makes a payment or transfer to its creditor which significantly exceeds in amount or value, the amount of the debt.

(4)   The rules as to preference are confined to payments, transfers, etc., in favour of an existing creditor, and thus do not apply to gifts, whereas the rules as to transactions at an undervalue are aimed primarily at transfers involving a gift element, whether in favour of a creditor or anyone else, and, indeed, will usually apply to creditors only as regards the grant of security for an existing indebtedness.

(5)   The two sets of statutory provisions have two characteristics in common. First, both transactions at an undervalue and preferences are determined without reference to the bona fides of the payee or

---

[33] See above, para.11–37.

479

transferee. Secondly, both sets of provisions embody a subjective element in that the company's good faith in an ingredient of the defence to a claim to upset a transaction made at an undervalue, whilst the avoidance of a preference requires the company to be influenced by a desire to prefer.

(6) For policy reasons which remain unclear, the backward reach of the provisions relating to transactions at an undervalue is two years in all cases, whereas for preferences the normal period is six months and the two-year period is confined to preferences in favour of a person connected with the company otherwise than solely as its employee.

8. EXTORTIONATE CREDIT TRANSACTIONS

Re-opening of extortionate credit transactions

11–105   Under s.244 of the Insolvency Act 1986 the court may set aside or vary a transaction for, or involving, the provision of credit to the company where the following conditions are satisfied:

(1)   The company is or has been a party to the transaction.[34]

(2)   The company is in liquidation or administration.[35]

(3)   The transaction is or was extortionate.

(4)   The transaction was entered into within the three years prior to the company going into liquidation or administration.

"Extortionate"

11–106   For the purposes of s.244 a transaction is extortionate if, having regard to the risk accepted by the person providing the credit:

(a)   the terms of it are or were such as to require grossly exorbitant payments to be made (whether unconditionally or in certain contingencies) in respect of the provision of the credit, or

(b)   it otherwise grossly contravenes ordinary principles of fair dealing.[36]

There is a rebuttable presumption that a transaction with respect to which an application is made under s.244 is extortionate.[37]

---

[34] Thus the court's powers are exercisable both in relation to settled transactions and to those that are still current.
[35] Insolvency Act 1986, s.244(1), applying s.238(1).
[36] *ibid.*, s.244(3).
[37] *ibid.*

The above provisions are modelled on ss.138(1), 139(1) and 171(7) of the Consumer Credit Act 1974, which I have analysed in detail elsewhere.[38] Suffice it to say that it does not suffice that the transaction was or is burdensome to the company or the terms of it severe. What has to be demonstrated is that they were extortionate within the statutory definition and this implies that they must be not merely unfair but oppressive, reflecting an imbalance in bargaining power of which the other party took improper advantage.[39]

Orders the court can make

An order under s.244 with respect to any transaction may contain such one or more of the following as the court thinks fit: **11–107**

(a) provision setting aside the whole or part of any obligation created by the transaction;

(b) provision otherwise varying the terms of the transaction or varying the terms on which any security for the purpose of the transaction is held;

(c) provision requiring any person who is or was a party to the transaction to pay to the office-holder any sums paid to that person, by virtue of the transaction, by the company;

(d) provision directing accounts to be taken between any persons.[40]

The court's powers are exercisable concurrently with any powers exercisable in relation to the transaction as a transaction at an undervalue.[41]

9. FLOATING CHARGES FOR PAST VALUE[42]

The previous law

There have long been statutory provisions invalidating floating charges given by an insolvent company otherwise than for new value. Prior to the Insolvency Act 1986 these were embodied in s.617 of the Companies Act **11–108**

---

[38] See *Goode: Consumer Credit Law and Practice*, Chap.47. The provisions relating to extortionate credit bargains have rarely been invoked with success, and cl.19 of the Consumer Credit Bill (2005) introduces new provisions, inserted into the Consumer Credit Act 1974 as ss.140A–140D, enabling the court to reopen credit agreements if it determines that the relationship between the creditor and the debtor arising out of the agreement is unfair to the debtor. However, the new provisions have no impact on s.244 of the Insolvency Act 1986.

[39] See *Wills v Wood* [1984] C.C.L.R. 7, (1984) 128 Sol. Jo. 222 and Goode, *op. cit.*, para.[2913].

[40] Insolvency Act 1986, s.244(4).

[41] *ibid.*, s.244(5).

[42] See Howard N. Bennett, "Late Floating Charges", in Armour and Bennett, *op. cit.* n.9, Chap.5.

1985, re-enacting s.322 of the Companies Act 1948. The purpose of these provisions, as of other avoidance provisions, was to prevent the conferment of an unfair advantage on an existing creditor at a time when liquidation was imminent. But they have always been confined to floating charges, no doubt reflecting a view that the all-embracing nature of the floating charge had such a potentially deleterious effect on other creditors that it should be subject to a special rule.[43] The broad effect of s.617 was that if a floating charge was given by a company that was insolvent immediately after its granting, the charge became invalid except to the amount of any cash paid to the company on or after and in consideration of the charge if the company went into liquidation within the ensuing 12 months.

Changes in the statutory provisions

11–109   Section 245 re-enacts the substance of s.617 of the Companies Act but with important changes:

(1)   A floating charge is now defined as a charge which as created was a floating charge.[44] But the new definition, though highly relevant to priorities *vis-à-vis* preferential debts,[45] is not significant for the purpose of s.245, since the avoidance provisions have always continued to apply even after crystallisation of the floating charge.

(2)   Under s.617 new value had to take the form of cash in order to exclude the section. Under s.245 virtually every normal form of new value suffices.[46]

(3)   The section applies to companies in administration as well as liquidation.

(4)   Where the charge is given in favour of a person connected with the company:
        (a) the period of 12 months is extended to two years; and
        (b) it is not necessary that the company shall have been insolvent at the time of or consequent upon the giving of the charge.

Presumably the application of s.245 to floating charges given to a connected person even where the company is still solvent after giving the charge

---

[43] The Cork Committee gave as the reason for special statutory treatment of floating charges the fact that it enabled the secured creditor to have his security reinforced by after-acquired property for which the debtor had not paid at the expense of the unpaid sellers. See *Insolvency Law and Practice*, para.1553.

[44] Insolvency Act 1986, s.251.

[45] See Roy Goode. *Legal Problems of Credit and Security* (3rd ed.), paras 5–65 *et seq*.

[46] See below, para.11–111.

reflects a view that a connected person, as an insider, is likely to have the opportunity to be aware of impending insolvency and to take steps to protect himself at the expense of other creditors.

Conditions necessary to attract section 245

A floating charge[47] is void under s.245 of the Insolvency Act if the following **11–110** conditions are satisfied:

(1) The company is in liquidation or administration.[48]

(2) The floating charge was created at a relevant time, that is:
    (a) in favour of a person connected with the company,[49] within the period of two years ending with the onset of insolvency,[50] or
    (b) in favour of a person not so connected, within the period of 12 months ending with the onset of insolvency; or
    (c) whether in favour of a connected or an unconnected person, between the presentation of a petition for an administration order and the making of an order on that petition.

(3) The charge was given otherwise than for what may conveniently be described as appropriate new value. For this purpose a charge is given for appropriate new value only to the extent that the consideration for it represents an amount not exceeding the aggregate of:
    (a) the value of so much of the consideration for the creation of the charge as consists of money paid,[51] or of goods or services supplied, to the company at the same time as, or after, the creation of the charge;
    (b) the value of so much of that consideration as consists of the discharge or reduction, at the same time as, or after, the creation of the charge, of any debt of the company[52];
    (c) the amount of such interest (if any) as is payable on an amount under (a) or (b) in pursuance of any agreement under which the money was paid, the goods or services supplied or the debt discharged or reduced.

---

[47] *i.e.* a charge which as created was a floating charge (Insolvency Act 1986, s.251), even if it has crystallised prior to the winding-up or administration. For the nature of a floating charge, see Goode, *Commercial Law* (3rd ed.), Chap.25 and *Legal Problems of Credit and Security*, Chap.IV. See also above, para.9–15.

[48] Insolvency Act 1986, s.245(1), applying s.238(1).

[49] In contrast to the provisions of ss.238 and 239 relating to transactions at an undervalue and preferences, there is no exclusion of a person connected with the company solely by reason of being its employee.

[50] As defined by s.245(5) of the Act.

[51] "Money paid" is not defined but would seem to encompass cash, cheques and other negotiable instruments (if honoured) and any other form of inter-bank transfer of funds, whether by credit transfer, direct debit or other means.

[52] Whether to a third party or to the company itself, *e.g.* by a refinancing in discharge of a prior loan to the company.

(4) Where the charge was given to a person not connected with the company, the company was then unable to pay its debts within the meaning of s.123 of the Act or became unable to do so in consequence of the charge.[53]

The expanded concept of new value

11–111 It will be seen that the provisions dealing with value are considerably more liberal, and indeed fairer, than under the earlier legislation, which treated cash as the only admissible form of new value and thus invalidated a floating charge given by an insolvent company to secure, for example, the price of goods supplied to the company, despite the fact that such a transaction involved no diminution whatsoever in the company's assets. Let us now take a closer look at the concept of new value under s.245 and see what is and is not covered. There are four essential requirements for value if the floating charge is to escape invalidity under s.245. First, it must be given in consideration for the creation of the charge. Secondly, it must be given at the same time as or after the creation of the charge. Thirdly, it must fall into one or more of the categories of value specified in s.245(2) of the Act. Fourthly, it must be furnished to the company itself or be applied in discharge or reduction of the company's indebtedness.

(1) Value as consideration for the charge

11–112 This is not new. The value must be given against the charge. So if an advance is initially made on an unsecured basis and then it is decided to take security for it, the advance will not qualify for new value however soon afterwards the charge is taken.

(2) Value must be contemporaneous or subsequent

11–113 Again, the statutory provisions are similar to those originally contained in s.322 of the Companies Act 1948, which required that the advance be made "at or after" the charge. Until recently there had been a curious line of authority, headed by the Court of Appeal decision in *Re Columbian Fireproofing Co Ltd*,[54] which appeared to consider an advance to be made at the time of the charge if it was made in consideration of the charge, notwithstanding a significant interval between the making of the advance

---

[53] Insolvency Act 1986, s.245(4). Again, there is no exception in favour of a person connected with the company solely by reason of being its employee.
[54] [1910] 1 Ch. 758.

and the giving of the charge,[55] particularly where the delay in taking the charge was considered excusable. However, in *Re Shoe Lace Ltd*[56] Hoffmann J., relying on a slight difference between the wording of s.245 of the 1986 Act and that of s.322 of the 1948 Act, felt able to dive over the decision in *Re Columbian Fireproofing Co Ltd* and to hold, as was clearly correct, that s.245 imposes two distinct requirements, that the advance is in consideration of the charge and that it is at or after the time the charge was taken, and that the latter requirement could not be said to have been met where the charge was taken nearly four months after the first advance it secured and eight days after the last such advance. His decision was upheld by the Court of Appeal[57] which, though ruling that there was little or no material difference in wording between s.245 and its predecessor, declined to follow *Re Columbian Fireproofing*. That case had purported to follow the decision in *Re Jackson & Bassford Ltd*[58] but had overlooked the vitally important distinction drawn in the latter case between a debenture executed after the advance in reliance on a promise to execute it which created a present equitable right and a debenture executed after a mere contingent agreement for security which created no such right.[59] In the former case a delay in execution of the formal debenture was immaterial, because the charge had already been created by the binding agreement and had thereupon became registrable; in the latter it had not and only came into existence when the debenture was executed.

Accordingly the position now reached is that the requirement of contemporaneity is satisfied where there is a binding agreement for a debenture creating an immediate equitable charge and made at or before the time of making of the advance, however long afterwards the formal debenture is executed pursuant to the agreement, but that in the absence of such an agreement the requirement of contemporaneity is not met "if the making of the advance precedes the formal execution of the debenture by any time whatsoever, unless the interval is so short that it can be regarded as de minimis—for example a 'coffee-break.'"[60]

(3) Kinds of permitted new value

The effect of s.245 is that the most common forms of new value—money, goods, services,[61] payment of debt—now suffice to preserve the validity of the floating charge. This extension in the concept of new value represents a

11–114

---

[55] In the *Columbian Fireproofing* case the interval was 11 days, in *Re F & E Stanton Ltd* [1929] 1 Ch. 180 it was eight weeks.

[56] [1992] B.C.C. 367.

[57] *Re Shoe Lace Ltd, Power v Sharp Investments Ltd* [1993] B.C.C. 609.

[58] [1906] 2 Ch. 467.

[59] See further as to this distinction Roy Goode, *Legal Problems of Credit and Security* (3rd ed.), paras 1–76, 2–15 and *Commercial Law* (3rd ed.), pp.662, 714.

[60] *Re Shoe Lace Ltd* [1993] B.C.C. 609, *per* Sir Christopher Slade at 619.

[61] Which in this context would, it is thought, include facilities.

compromise between the views of the hardliners who considered that the old restriction to cash should be retained and the proponents of the opposing view that any form of money's worth should suffice. The Cork Committee rather cautiously recommended the addition of goods to cash but the exclusion of services.[62] In the end services were added to the list. The result in broad terms is that admissible new value is restricted to those forms of benefit to the company which arise from day-to-day trading and finance and have a readily ascertainable value.[63] Excluded are a wide range of other assets, both tangible and intangible, including land and buildings, intellectual property rights, debts and other receivables and rights under contracts.

One of the forms of recognised new value is the supply of goods or services, and for this purpose their value is to be taken as the amount of money which at the time they were supplied could reasonably have been expected to be obtained for supplying the goods or services in the ordinary course of business and on the same terms (apart from the consideration) as those on which they were supplied to the company.[64] Another is "the value of so much of the consideration as consists of the discharge or reduction . . . of any debt of the company". No distinction is drawn between an advance made by the chargee to pay off or reduce a debt due from the company to a third party and an advance made to refinance an existing indebtedness of the company to the chargee itself. Does this enable an unsecured lender to transform its status into a secured lender for a contemporaneous advance by the simple device of refinancing the unsecured loan? If so, it would drive a coach and horses through the contemporaneity requirement, for all the lender would have to do would be to make a book-keeping entry recording that the new loan had been applied in discharge of the existing loan. The answer would seem to lie in the fact that what matters is not merely the *consideration* for the giving of the charge but the *value* of that consideration. If the creditor is not effectively parting with anything then no value is given, even though the refinancing constitutes good consideration in general contract law for the execution of the floating charge.[65] The position is otherwise, of course, where the charge is taken to secure payment to a third party of a debt owed by the company to the third party, for in that case the lender is parting with real money.

---

[62] *Insolvency Law and Practice*, para.1564.
[63] This is less true of services than of goods, which no doubt explains why the Cork Committee recommended that services be excluded.
[64] Insolvency Act 1986, s.245(6).
[65] See *Re GT Whyte & Co Ltd* [1983] B.C.L.C. 311.

(4) Benefit to company

In order to qualify as new value under s.245 the payment of money or the supply of goods or services must be made to the company itself, not to a third party, though payment to a third party in or towards satisfaction of a debt due from the company suffices.

    In order for money to be "paid ... to the company" it must in a real sense be available to the company for its own benefit and to do with what it likes. So payment by cheque in exchange for the company's cheque of the same amount is not payment to the company, nor is a refinancing or a payment which is to be matched by a payment out by the company to other parties or which goes round a circle of payees, in either case leaving the company no better off than it was before,[66] or a payment made by the lender directly into the company's overdrawn bank account[67] or by cheque to the company on terms that the cheque is to be paid into the company's overdrawn account.[68] However, while payment into the company's overdrawn bank account does not constitute a payment to the company within para.(a) of s.245(2), it does fall within para.(b) as a payment which discharges or reduces a debt of the company. This point appears to have been overlooked in *Re Fairway Magazines Ltd,*[69] where the applicant should have succeed on this ground.

11–115

What does not constitute new value

It can be said from the foregoing that the following do not constitute relevant value:

11–116

(1)   Money paid or goods or services supplied to the company prior to the creation of the charge (including for this purpose a binding agreement for the charge).

(2)   Money paid prior to the creation of the charge in discharge or reduction of the company's indebtedness to a third party.

(3)   Money paid or goods or services supplied to a third party (including a company which is a member of the same group as the chargor company), except where paid or supplied on or after the creation of the charge and in discharge or reduction of a debt owed to the third party by the company.

---

[66] *Re Destone Fabrics Ltd* [1941] Ch. 319.
[67] *Re Fairway Magazines Ltd* [1992] B.C.C. 924.
[68] *Re Orleans Motor Co Ltd* [1911] 2 Ch. 41.
[69] See above, n.67.

(4)   Money paid or goods or services supplied in discharge of a debt due from a third party (including a member of the same group), whether before or after the creation of the charge, except so far as the company was also liable in respect of the same debt and its liability was discharged or reduced by the payment or supply.

(5)   Money paid to the company in such manner or on such conditions that it is not truly available to be used by the company for its own benefit, as where the money refinances an existing unsecured debt owed to the chargee or is to be matched by payments out to third parties or a payment to the chargee itself.

Insolvency at time of charge

11–117   It is not necessary to show that the company was insolvent at the time of or in consequence of the charge in cases where the chargee was a person connected with the company. As previously mentioned, this reflects the fact that such a person, as an insider, is better placed than an independent creditor to be aware that a state of insolvency looms and to look after his own interests at the expense of other creditors.

Hardening of a floating charge

11–118   Where the company has a running account with the chargee and dealings on the account continue between them the rule in *Clayton's Case* may have the effect of "hardening" the charge. Under the rule in *Clayton's Case* there is a presumption that in the case of a current account items credited to the account are applied to the earliest indebtedness first. Accordingly where a floating charge is taken to secure a preexisting overdraft, sums are paid to the credit of the account and new drawings are then made, the effect of the rule is that the credits are applied to the pre-existing indebtedness, so that any new drawing constitutes new value, even if the resulting balance is the same as before. In effect, the turnover of money in the account converts old value into new.

Example 15

11–119   An insolvent company has a bank overdraft of £100,000 which is unsecured. The bank, which is concerned about the position, takes a floating charge over the company's factory premises to secure both past and future advances. Subsequently a cheque for £40,000 is paid into the account and a few days later the company draws a cheque for the same amount in favour of a supplier. The cheque for £40,000 is applied in discharge of the earliest indebtedness first, that is, the original £100,000, reducing the past indebtedness to £60,000, whilst the drawing in favour of the supplier represents new value by the bank, for which the floating charge is valid. Thus although the debit balance is still £100,000, the mix has changed, in that £40,000 of past value has been converted into new value through the operation of the rule in *Clayton's Case*.[70]

The Cork Committee regarded this result as objectionable and recommended a statutory provision that all payments into the account should be treated as discharging debit items incurred after the creation of the floating charge.[71] It is hard to see either the logic or the fairness of such a recommendation, for which no reasoning was advanced beyond the cryptic statement that the rule in *Clayton's Case* "defeats the object of the section.." This is simply not true. The statutory provisions are aimed at charges which, being given for past indebtedness, reduce the value of the estate. By allowing a new drawing, without obligation to do so, the bank is genuinely extending new value. It could have kept the benefit of the payment into the account without allowing any further drawings but chose not to do so. To the extent of those new drawings the company has received a benefit which is secured by the floating charge. The transaction is no way within the mischief against which the statutory provisions are aimed, and the government rightly decided not to implement the Committee's recommendation. The position would, of course, be otherwise if there were no genuine new value, for example, if the bank stipulated that it would not honour a new drawing unless this was covered by a contemporaneous payment into the account, so that there was a ritual exchange of cheques and the company never had recourse to the funds drawn since these had to be simultaneously repaid.

10. REGISTRABLE BUT UNREGISTERED CHARGES

Introduction

Under s.395 of the Companies Act 1985, where a charge created by a **11–120** company[72] is one to which the section applies it must be registered within 21 days after its creation,[73] failing which it will be void against a liquidator

---

[70] See *Re Yeovil Glove Co Ltd* [l965] Ch. 148, a decision on s.322 of the Companies Act 1948. However, the payment into the account might be vulnerable as a preference under s.239 of the Insolvency Act.

[71] *Insolvency Law and Practice*, paras 156–62.

[72] As opposed to a charge or security created by law, *e.g.* an unpaid vendor's equitable lien *(London and Cheshire Insurance Co Ltd v Laplagrene Properties Ltd* [1971] Ch. 499).

[73] Or such later time as may be allowed by the court on an application under s.404 of the Act for leave to register out of time. See generally Gerard McCormack, *Registration of Company Charges*.

or administrator[74] and any creditor of the company[75] and the sum secured by the charge will become immediately due and payable.[76] The charges to which s.395 applies are those listed in s.396.[77]

Rationale of the avoidance provisions

11–121   It is not at first sight obvious why non-registration should render a registrable charge void on winding-up or administration. The failure to register a charge does not cause any diminution in the company's assets— the usual ground for avoidance—which would have occurred earlier, on the making of the charge, and then only if it was taken to secure a past indebtedness. Subsequent secured creditors are protected by being given priority even without a winding-up or administration. Unsecured creditors have no rights or interest in the assets of the company and are prejudiced by want of registration only insofar as their decision to extend credit might have been different if they had known of the unregistered interest; yet the avoidance provisions apply even if there was no unsecured creditor who was both misled and influenced by the absence of registration. There is no anti-preference policy underlying the statutory provisions, for there are separate rules relating to preferences and in any event s.395 applies even if the charge was taken well outside the preference period.[78] The effect of avoidance is thus to give unsecured creditors who did not act in reliance on the want of registration an apparently unjustified windfall addition to the assets available for distribution.

Yet there are sound policy reasons for the avoidance of unregistered securities. In the first place, the avoidance rule reflects the law's dislike of the secret security interest, which leaves the debtor's property apparently

---

[74] This means void against the company acting by its liquidator or administrator. See *Smith (Administrator of Cosslett (Contractors) Ltd v Bridgend County Borough Council* [2002] 1 AC 336, in which the House of Lords reversed the rather startling decision of the Court of Appeal that an unregistered charge was void against an administrator but not against the company itself.

[75] *i.e.* secured creditors or creditors in a winding-up or administration.

[76] Companies Act 1985, s.395.

[77] Part IV of the Companies Act 1989 provided for repeal of the whole of the registration provisions of the Companies Act and their replacement by provisions which would not be dissimilar but which would introduce a number of important changes. However, both the drafting and the content of Part IV were widely considered to be seriously flawed and its provisions are unlikely ever to be brought into force, particularly in view of the more fundamental changes proposed by the Law Commission in its paper *Company Security Interests: a consultative report* (Law Com. Cons. Paper No. 176, 2004).

[78] A preference may, of course, arise as the result of deferment of the initial grant of the security interest in order to avoid registration, *e.g.* by making a contingent agreement for security (see above, para.11–76, n.69), but the act of preference in this case is not the want of registration (for nothing is registrable so long as the agreement is purely contingent) but the giving of the security at the time the contingency occurs, at which point it will constitute a security for a pre-existing indebtedness.

unencumbered and at common law was considered a fraud on the general creditors.[79] Secondly, the registration provisions help to curb the fabrication or antedating of security agreements on the eve of winding-up. Thirdly, though unsecured creditors have no existing interest in the company's assets outside winding-up, and thus no immediate *locus standi* to complain of want of registration, they have an inchoate interest, in that upon winding-up the whole of the company's property, so far as not utilised in discharging the expenses of the winding-up and the payment of preferential claims, becomes available for the general body of creditors, so that their rights become converted from purely personal rights into rights more closely analogous to that of beneficiaries under an active trust.[80] Fourthly, there may well be unsecured creditors who were misled by the want of registration into extending credit which they would not otherwise have granted. But it would be both expensive and impracticable to expect the liquidator (or administrator) to investigate each unsecured creditor's claim to see whether he did or did not act on the assumption that the unregistered charge did not exist. So a broad brush approach which in effect assumes detriment to unsecured creditors at large is justified. Finally, the registration provisions serve a general public notice function as well as being a perfection requirement, and the avoidance provision can be seen as an inducement, and a powerful inducement, to comply with the requirements of the law, reinforcing criminal sanctions for non-compliance. However, these policy considerations have been somewhat undermined by decisions holding (correctly in terms of legal analysis) that to the extent that the security has already been enforced or paid off prior to the winding-up or other invalidating event its avoidance has no effect.[81]

Registration out of time

The court may, on the application of the company or a person interested,[82] **11–122** extend the time for registration on such terms and conditions as seem to the court just and expedient.[83] Before making such an order the court must be satisfied that the failure to register was accidental or due to inadvertence or to some other sufficient cause, or is not of a nature to prejudice the position of creditors or shareholders of the company, or that on other grounds it is just and equitable to grant relief.[84] Where these conditions are satisfied leave is readily granted so long as the company is not in liquidation

---

[79] Hence the former reputed ownership doctrine, which no longer features in our insolvency law.
[80] See above, para.3–07.
[81] See below, para.11–123.
[82] Usually the application is made by the holder of the registrable charge.
[83] Companies Act 1985, s.404(2).
[84] *ibid.*, s.404(1).

and no winding-up is pending, but an order will almost invariably be expressed to be subject to the intervening rights of creditors acquiring an interest in the property, such as subsequent chargees[85]; and where liquidation is imminent the court may, instead of refusing an order for an extension, grant it subject to the right of the company to apply for discharge of the order within a given period after the commencement of the winding-up.[86] An order is liable to be refused where the creditor, instead of applying promptly for an extension of time and bringing all the facts before the court, seeks to deal with the matter by taking a new charge or series of charges.[87]

Non-registration does not invalidate the charge against the company

11–123   It should be borne in mind that registration is purely a perfection requirement designed to give notice to third parties; it is not a condition of validity of the charge, which remains fully enforceable against the company prior to winding-up or administration. It follows that if the company does go into liquidation or administration the consequent avoidance of the unregistered charge has no impact on the chargee to the extent that he has already realised his security or perfected it by seizure or judicial foreclosure or has otherwise obtained payment, for to that extent his security has been satisfied and there is nothing for him to enforce.[88]

11. DISPOSITIONS OF PROPERTY AFTER THE COMMENCEMENT OF COMPULSORY WINDING-UP

The statutory provisions

11–124   Section 127 of the Insolvency Act 1986, re-enacting s.522 of the Companies Act 1985, provides that in a winding-up by the court any disposition of the company's property[89] made after the commencement of the winding-up is void unless the court otherwise orders. In this context "the court" means the court dealing with an application under s.127 in the winding-up

---

[85] The standard form of order was first laid down by Clauson J. in *Re L.H. Charles & Co Ltd* [1935] W.N. 15, and has been followed with minor modifications ever since.

[86] See *McCormack, op. cit.*, pp.126 *et seq.*; Goode, *Commercial Law* (3rd ed.), p.668.

[87] *Re Telomatic Ltd* [1993] B.C.C. 404.

[88] *Re Row Dal Construction Pty Ltd* [1966] V.R. 249; *N.V. Slavenburg's Bank Ltd v Intercontinental Natural Resources Ltd* [1980] 1 All E.R. 955. See also *Mace Builders (Glasgow) Ltd v Lunn* [1985] 2 W.L.R. 465, a decision to similar effect on s.321 of the Companies Act 1948.

[89] And any transfer of shares or alteration in the status of the company's members; but these will not be discussed.

proceedings. The fact that the disposition has been made pursuant to an order made by another court for, other purposes does not save it from invalidation,[90] and it makes no difference whether that order was or was not by consent nor whether the effect of the order was itself to transfer an interest in equity to the transferee even before implementation of the order by execution of a formal conveyance.[91]

For the purposes of s.127 the winding-up is deemed to commence on the presentation of the petition on which the winding-up order was made, unless the company was already in voluntary liquidation at the time of the petition, in which case the winding-up is deemed to commence on the passing of the resolution for voluntary winding-up.[92]

The purpose of this "relation back" of the commencement of winding-up is to prevent a dissipation of the company's assets while the hearing of the petition is pending and to ensure that no payment or transfer is made which is preferential and would, thus infringe the principle of *pari passu* distribution.[93] If the section were limited in scope to the achievement of this purpose it would cause no great inconvenience, for it would then be providing no more than a logical extension of the preference period to the date of the winding-up order. Unhappily it is not so limited: it applies as much to bona fide business transactions as to preferences[94]; it nullifies transactions that increase the company's asset value no less than transactions which reduce that value. Indeed, it effectively paralyses the company's business, for without the leave of the court not so much as a stitch of cloth can be disposed of, not one penny spent even to acquire an asset worth a pound, and technically the company cannot even pay cash into its bank account. Hence the importance of the company's ability to obtain authority from the court which will enable it to continue trading pending the hearing of the petition.[95]

---

[90] *Re Flint* [1993] Ch. 319, a decision on comparable provisions in s.284 of the Insolvency Act relating to dispositions by an individual after presentation of a bankruptcy petition.

[91] *ibid.*

[92] Insolvency Act 1986, s,129.

[93] It is because s.127 takes care of post-petition dispositions in winding-up that s.240(l)(c) makes no reference to winding-up petitions and is confined to transactions at an undervalue and preferences between the presentation of an administration application and the making of the order on that application.

[94] Section 42(l)(a) of the Companies Act 1985, which in stated conditions precludes a company from relying against other persons on the making of a winding-up order, or the appointment of a liquidator in a voluntary liquidation, has no effect on the operation of s.127 of the Insolvency Act, for although that section cannot be invoked until the company is in compulsory winding-up its nullifying effect is confined to dispositions made between the presentation of the petition and the making of the winding-up order.

[95] See below, para.11–132. That s.127 is concerned to do no more than prevent a reduction in the assets of the company between winding-up petition and hearing is demonstrated by the fact that in ordering a bank or other recipient to repay moneys improperly received the court will penalise the payee no further than is necessary to restore to the fund of assets available for distribution the amount (if any) that has been lost (*Re Cray's Inn Construction Co Ltd* [1980] 1 All E.R. 814).

"Disposition"

11–125   The word "disposition" is not defined but must be given a wide meaning if the purpose of the section is to be achieved, particularly in view of the fact that there is no exemption in favour of transfers for full value. "Disposition" should therefore be considered to include not only any dealing in the company's tangible or intangible assets by sale, exchange, lease, charge, gift or loan, but also the conferment of a possessory or other lien on an asset[96] and any other act which, in reducing or extinguishing the company's rights in an asset, transfers value to another person. On this basis "disposition" includes an agreement by which the company surrenders a lease or gives up its contractual rights,[97] contractual set-off by which a debtor to the company is given and exercises the right to apply a cross-claim of his own against the company in diminution of his indebtedness and arguably even the extension of further credit to the company during the post-petition period which leads to the exercise of a right of equitable set-off against the company's credit balance.[98] Moreover, the section is not confined to voluntary dispositions by the company itself; it applies equally to dispositions taking effect under a court order[99] and, it is thought, post-petition payments to a creditor of the company under a garnishee order made against one of the company's debtors, the effect of which is *pro tanto* to extinguish an asset of the company, namely the debt due to it.

However, the reduction or extinction of the company's rights in an asset must be one which leads in a real, not merely a technical, sense to the transfer of value to another party, for as was pointed out by Street C.J. in an Australian decision. *Re Mal Bower's Macquarie Electrical Centre Pty Ltd,*[1] the word disposition connotes both a disponor and a disponee. So a company which does no more than collect in a debt is not disposing of an asset, even though the effect of the payment is to extinguish the chose in action represented by the debt, for value cannot in any real sense be said to move from the creditor to the debtor.

---

[96] *e.g.* by delivery of a car to a garage for repair or of a cheque to a bank for collection at a time when money is owing to the bank (see below).

[97] But exercise by the creditor of a unilateral right to terminate an agreement would not be a disposition.

[98] See generally Philip Wood, *English and International Set-Off*, paras 7–303 *et seq.* I agree with Mr Wood that exercise of a statutory right of set-off under the Insolvency Rules cannot be within the scope of s.127 (for if it were, the provisions of the rules making the time of taking of the accounts the cut-off point for determining mutuality would be rendered nugatory) and that the contrary decision at first instance in *Barclays Bank Ltd v TOSG Trust Fund Ltd* [1984] B.C.L.C. 1 is wrong.

[99] *Re Flint*, above, n.90.

[1] [1974] 1 N.S.W.L.R. 254 at 258. cited in *Re Barn Crown Ltd* [1994] 4 All E.R. 42 at 48. See below, para.11–128.

Only dispositions of the company's property are affected

Section 127 is confined to post-petition dispositions of the company's **11–126** property, which includes transfers of property beneficially owned by the company and taking effect by virtue of a court order.[2] Assets held by the company are not its property to the extent of any security interest it has given over them in favour of a creditor. So if a bank in good faith and the ordinary course of business collects a cheque for its customer and credits the proceeds to the customer's overdrawn account this does not constitute a disposition of the company's property, for the bank had a lien on the cheque and thus a security interest in the proceeds and the credit to the account merely produced a realisation of its security rights.[3] Similarly a sale by a mortgagee is outside the scope of s.127, whether the conveyance is by the mortgagee or by the company acting through its receiver.[4] Likewise the vesting of a company's property in a secured creditor or other party under an after-acquired property clause in the security or other instrument is outside s.127[5]; and completion of an unconditional contract for the sale of land by the company is not a disposition of the company's property, for in equity the land already belongs to the purchaser upon exchange of contracts.[6] But waiver of a condition in a conditional contract or affirmation of a contract voidable by the company might constitute a disposition within s.127.[7]

Payments into the company's bank account

The question whether a disposition is of the company's property raises **11–127** special problems in the case of payments into the company's bank account. It is necessary to treat separately the case where the account is in credit from the case where it is overdrawn.

(1) Account in credit

We may begin by distinguishing the payment of cash (notes and coins) into **11–128** the account from the payment in of a cheque. Where the company pays cash into its account, the payment constitutes a disposition of its property,

---

[2] *Re Flint*, above, n.90.
[3] *National Australian Bank v KDI Construction Services Pty Ltd* (1988) 12 A.C.L.R. 663; and see *Re Margaret Ply Ltd* (1984) 9 A.C.L.R. 269. But it is not clear why the delivery of the cheque to the bank, which gave rise to the lien in the first place, was not itself an unauthorised disposition. See further below, para.11–130.
[4] *Sowman v David Samuel Trust Ltd* [1978] 1 All E.R. 616.
[5] See Roy Goode, *Legal Problems of Credit and Security* (3rd ed.), para.2–14.
[6] *Re French's Wine Bar Ltd* (1987) 3 B.C.C. 173.
[7] *ibid.*

whether or not the account is in credit, for ownership of the notes and coins passes to the bank.[8] The company acquires a corresponding claim against the bank, which will be recorded by a credit of the payment to its account, so that the net effect of the transaction is simply to convert an asset of the company from one form, cash, into another, a claim on the bank. Hence in terms of its effect the breach will usually be a merely technical one, but the position would be quite otherwise if the bank were to become insolvent before the company had withdrawn the amount credited.

The situation is somewhat different in the case of a cheque.[9] Deposit of the cheque with the bank for the purpose of collection[10] is not in itself a disposition within s.127 where the company's account is in credit, for the bank collects purely as agent and has no interest of its own in the cheque. However, in the first edition of this book it was argued that the collection process itself involves the disposition of an asset of the company, for the bank surrenders the customer's cheque, which represents both a negotiable instrument and the embodiment of a claim against the drawer, in exchange for payment, so that one form of property belonging to the company is converted into another. In *Re Barn Crown Ltd*[11] H.H. Judge Rich Q.C. rejected this analysis as over-technical and not according with ordinary usage. This criticism is well-founded, for merely to collect a cheque as agent does not in itself do more than the company could have done by collecting payment from the debtor in cash.[12] Judge Rich accordingly took the view that no disposition of any kind was involved. In reaching this conclusion he drew on the judgment of McPherson J. in *Re Loteka Pty Ltd*[13] which concerned the effect of payment *from* a credit account and concluded that the collection of a cheque and payment of the proceeds *into* an account in credit could be analysed in the same way.

> "In collecting payment upon a cheque the bank credits the customer's account with the amount of the cheque. If the account is already in credit, no disposition of the property of the customer takes place in favour of the bank. The amount standing to the credit of the customer is increased in return for the surrender of the cheque, which becomes a voucher for payment. It is the drawer of the cheque whose property is disposed of. All that happens between the customer and the banker is an

---

[8] The same view is taken by Adrian Walters, "Void Dispositions in Compulsory Winding-Up", in *Vulnerable Transactions in Corporate Insolvency* (ed. Armour and Bennett), para.8.35.

[9] Or any other kind of instrument deposited for collection.

[10] A process which does not involve the receipt of cash by the collecting bank but merely a transfer of funds from the paying bank through the books of a third bank (the Bank of England, where the paying and collecting banks are clearing banks) with whom both banks hold an account.

[11] See above, n.1.

[12] See above.

[13] (1989) 7 A.C.L.C. 998.

adjustment of entries in the statement recording the accounts between them."[14]

But this, with respect, over-simplifies the problem and equates payment *into* an account in credit with payment *from* an account that is in credit, when in reality the two cases are entirely different.[15] Let us assume that the company is owed £1 million by a debtor of undoubted financial stability from whom it receives a cheque for this amount. We can agree that the company does not make a disposition of its property by arranging for the cheque to be collected through its bank as agent rather than directly. But what happens next is that, by virtue of the banker-customer relationship, the bank proceeds to borrow the collected proceeds and credit the company's amount with the sum so borrowed. That borrowing is not a mere matter of book entry; it involves the transfer of collected funds from company to bank in exchange for a promise of repayment.[16] That transfer it is submitted, is a disposition of the company's property in breach of s.127. In 99 cases out of 100 the breach is technical and the court can be expected to validate the transfer. The one hundredth case is where the bank closes its doors the day after collecting the cheque and soon afterwards goes into liquidation with only enough assets to pay unsecured creditors 10p in the pound. The company is now in the position where it has lent £1 million and will recover a mere £100,000 by way of dividend. The making of the loan is no longer a mere technical breach; its effect is to remove £1 million that would have been available to the company's creditors and make it available instead to the bank's creditors. The inescapable conclusion is that this constitutes a disposition of the company's property in breach of s.127. This receives support from the decision of Buckley L.J. in *Re Gray's Inn Construction Co Ltd.*[17]

> "In the present case the company's account with the bank was over-drawn, so that I need not consider what the position would have been if any cheque had been paid in when the account was in credit, but I doubt whether even in those circumstances it could properly be said that the

---

[14] [1994] 4 All E.R. 42 at 45.

[15] See below, para.11–130 as to the effect of payments out of an account.

[16] It is true that the fact that a bank collects a cheque "for" a customer does not mean that the bank's receipt (by credit to its account with the Bank of is the customer's receipt; the bank receives the proceeds of the cheque as part of its own moneys but with a duty to credit the customer's account with an equivalent amount (see Goode, *Commercial Law* (3rd ed.), pp.470–471, 540). Nevertheless it is well established that in crediting the account rather than paying the customer the cash equivalent of what it has received the bank is borrowing the money from the customer. See *Foley v Hill* (1848) 2 H.L. Cas. 28; *Joachimson v Swiss Bank Corp* [1921] 3 K.B. 110; and generally Michael Brindle and Raymond Cox, *Law of Bank Payments* (3rd ed.), paras 7–078 *et seq*. There is therefore a disposition in favour of the bank.

[17] [1980] 1 All E.R. 814 at 818.

payment in did not constitute a disposition of the amount of the cheque in favour of the bank."

As a final point, if the company had lent money to an ordinary borrower this would without doubt be a disposition of the company's property. Why should it make a difference that the borrower is the company's bank? In a decision of the Irish High Court in *Re Pat Ruth Ltd*[18] Costello J. held that all payments into the company's bank account were dispositions of its property for the purpose of the equivalent provision of the Irish legislation[19] and in *Re Industrial Services Company (Dublin) Ltd*[20] this was not contested. As indicated above, this will not matter in most cases, since the money paid into the account will be held by the bank and will be available as part of the company's assets. It is only if the bank is insolvent that the issue is a live one.[21]

(2) Account overdrawn

11–129   Where the company owes money to the bank, there can be no doubt of the position. Even where the delivery of the cheque for collection is not by itself a disposition it is clear that payment of the proceeds into the overdrawn account transfers funds from the company to the bank.[22] But in most cases the true analysis is that the disposition occurs earlier, by delivery of the cheque, which confers on the bank a lien for the company's indebtedness.[23] In this situation the crediting of the account does not give rise to any further disposition, for the bank is then exercising its rights as a secured creditor[24] and it is the delivery of the cheque to it in the first instance that constitutes the infringement of s.127. Payment of cheques into an overdrawn account may also constitute a preference of the bank.

Withdrawals from a bank account

11–130   Where a company withdraws money from a bank account which is in credit, then for the purpose of s.127 that is a disposition of the company's property to the extent of the pre-existing credit balance, for the value of its claim

---

[18] [1981] I.R.L.M. 51.

[19] Companies Act 1963, s.218.

[20] [2001] 2 I.R. 118.

[21] Walters, n.8 above, suggests (at paras 8.41–8.42) that the bank would remain liable under s.127, in the absence of a validation order, even if the company's claim on the bank had been reduced by subsequent drawings. However, to the extent that such drawings are to be regarded as coming from the sum paid into the account (applying the rule in *Clayton's Case* (1816) 1 Mer. 572) the bank will in effect have repaid the money to or at the direction of the company and thus negated the effect of the payment into the account.

[22] *Re Gray's Inn Construction Co Ltd*, above, n.95; *Re Tain Construction Ltd, Rose v AIB Group (UK) plc* [2003] 2 B.C.L.C. 374.

[23] *Re Keever* [1967] Ch. 182; *Barclays Bank Ltd . Astley Industrial Trust Ltd* [1970] 2 Q.B. 527. If the bank has already advanced money against the cheque it becomes a holder for value to the extent of the advance and to that extent collects on its own account.

[24] *National Australian Bank v KDI Construction Services Pty Ltd* (1988) 12 A.C.L.R. 663. See above, para.11–126.

against the bank is correspondingly reduced. It has, however, been held that where the company's money is paid into an account of a third party so as to become part of a mixed fund from which drawings are made in good faith, then while the payment into the account is a disposition of the company's money a withdrawal from it is not, even if the company could by appropriate proceedings have obtained a declaration of charge on the mixed fund.[25]

What is the position where the account is already in overdraft before the further withdrawal? Such was the, case in *Re Gray's Inn Construction Co Ltd,*[26] where, despite having notice both of the petition and of the winding-up order, the company's bank allowed the company to continue to operate its overdrawn account, receiving sums to the credit of the account and honouring further drawings on the account. The result was that in addition to what was held to be the unjustified payment of certain pre-liquidation debts to the bank and other creditors the company incurred a further trading loss. In invalidating some of the payments out of the account in discharge of pre-liquidation debts as well as payments into the account to the extent of the post-petition trading losses suffered by the company, the Court of Appeal entertained no doubt that the former payments were as much dispositions of the company's property as the latter. Indeed, counsel for the bank conceded the point. In my view he was wrong to do so, for the effect of the concession was that the court was led to regard the proposition as "indisputable"[27] without qualification and without any attempt to identify the property of the company which was the subject of the so-called disposition.

What is the effect of a withdrawal from a company's overdrawn account where that is the only relevant fact? The short answer is that it merely increases the company's liability to the bank. If there is one thing that is still clear in the increasingly complex financial scene generated by London's Big Bang it is that a liability is not an asset and that an increase in a liability is not by itself a disposition of an asset. Section 127 cannot apply unless there is a disposition of the company's property. What, then, was the item of property supposedly disposed of in the *Gray's Inn* case? Again, the short answer is: none. The payments out of the account were all in discharge of pre-liquidation debts for goods and services supplied[28] and (since the account was at all times in overdraft[29]) did not involve the application of a

---

[25] *Re J Leslie Engineers Co Ltd* [1976] 1 W.L.R. 292.

[26] See above, n.22.

[27] [1980] 1 All E.R. 814, per Buckley L.J. at 818.

[28] See the judgment of Buckley L.J. [1980] 1 All E.R. 814 at 823.

[29] *ibid.*, at 817. The details contained in the judgment are insufficient to enable the account to be reconstructed, and it is possible that some of the items drawn on a particular day were covered by a credit balance even if at the end of the day the account was still in overdraft. But to the extent (if any) that this was the case it is irrelevant to the question here under discussion, viz. whether payments not covered by a credit balance constitute a disposition of the company's property.

single asset of the company. Not one tiny tittle of a right in tangible or intangible property was affected one iota. Not one smidgen of interference with the *pari passu* principle resulted. All that happened was that the bank used its own moneys to meet the company's cheques for what were presumably payments to suppliers and other creditors in the normal course of business, so that in relation to such payments the bank became substituted as creditor for the persons to whom they were made, leaving the position of other credits entirely unchanged. The only other item invalidated was a payment into the account, which went to reduce the pre-liquidation overdraft and was clearly a disposition of the company's property, as stated earlier.

What I suggest went wrong in the *Gray's Inn* case was that the court had a picture of trading losses in respect of which the company's assets were reduced by outflows from the account, whereas the true position was that any reduction in the assets resulted from payments into the account in reduction of the overdraft and such individual intra-day drawings as may have been matched by a temporary credit balance.

My contention, then, is that s.127 can never apply solely by reason of the drawing on an overdrawn account. In *Coutts & Co v Stock*[30] Lightman J. entertained no doubt that an increase in the company's overdraft fell outside s.127. It does not, however, follow that use of an overdraft can never give rise to a disposition of the company's property. There appear to be at least three cases where it does. The first is where the bank holds security for future advances, for an increase in the overdraft automatically expands the quantum of the bank's security interest, and correspondingly reduces the company's equity in the charged assets, unless these were already charged to their full value at the time of the further drawing on the account. The second is where the company has a credit balance on another account and the effect of the further drawing is to increase the amount for which the bank has a right of set-off against the credit balance.[31] The third is where the further drawing is within the limit of an agreed overdraft which the bank is contractually committed to extending, for the effect of the drawing is to reduce the amount of the facility remaining available and thus the quantum of the chose in action vested in the company.[32]

---

[30] [2000] 1 W.L.R. 906.

[31] The judgment of Buckley L.J. does not indicate the purpose for which the payments were made but does contain the statement (at 817) that the bank made sure, so far as it was able to do so, that all cheques were drawn in the ordinary course of the company's business.

[32] See *R v Kohn* (1979) 69 Cr. App. R. 395, in which the Court of Appeal upheld the conviction of the director of a company for theft for improperly drawing cheques on the company's account, holding that he was guilty of a theft of debts due from the bank to the company to the extent that the cheques were covered by a credit balance or by the amount of the contractually agreed overdraft facility but not beyond. However, in *Coutts & Co v Stock*, n.30 above, Lightman J. held that the use and, indeed, partial or total exhaustion of the company's overdraft limit cannot constitute a disposition within s.127.

Consequences of unauthorised disposition

Section 127 provides that a post-petition disposition not sanctioned by the court is void. It says nothing about the method of recovery or the parties against whom recovery is available. This has to be determined by the general law.[33] There is no great difficulty where the disposition relates to tangible property such as land or goods. The transfer is simply of no effect and the transferee therefore has no title to it and can be ordered to return it. Again, where money is paid into the company's overdrawn account with its bank the payment is ineffective to confer rights on the bank, and the practical effect is that the bank is not entitled to debit the company's account with the sum paid in and can be ordered to re-credit the account or make repayment in some other way. But what is the position where a cheque is drawn by the company on an account in credit and paid by the bank? Is the amount of the payment recoverable from the bank, the payee or both? In *Hollicourt (Contracts) Ltd v Bank of Ireland*[34] the Court of Appeal, following a series of Australian decisions,[35] held that only the payee is liable. It was pointed out that the bank acts purely as an agent or intermediary of its customer, the company, and in making payment is simply carrying out its customer's instructions. The disposition is not the reduction in the company's credit balance as such but the transfer of funds to the payee, who is the only recipient of the disposition. Accordingly any claim for recovery of money paid under the void disposition must be against the payee, not the bank.

11–131

Authorisation by the court

The court may authorise any disposition that would otherwise be void. Such authorisation can be given in advance of the winding-up,[36] and this should be sought wherever possible, for otherwise the party dealing with the company runs the risk that the court will refuse to validate the transaction retrospectively. There may be cases where prior authorisation is impracticable, *e.g.* because time is of the essence or because the parties are unaware of the presentation of the petition. But in such cases, though the court may be sympathetic, there is no guarantee that the transaction will be validated. The principles upon which the court will act in dealing with applications for a validation order are discussed in some detail in *Re Gray's Inn Construction Co Ltd*,[37] *Re S & D Wright Ltd*[38] and *Denney v John Hudson & Co Ltd*.[39] From these three decisions the following can be extracted:

11–132

---

[33] *Re J Leslie Engineers Co Ltd* [1976] 1 W.L.R. 292, *per* Oliver J. at 298.
[34] [2001] Ch. 555.
[35] *Re Mal Bower's Macquarie Electrical Centre Pty Ltd (VIA)* 1 N.S.W.L.R. 254; *Re Loteka Pty Ltd* (1989) 1 A.C.L.R. 620; *Tasmanian Primary Distributors Pty Ltd v R.C. & M.B. Steinhardt Pty Ltd* (1994) 13 A.C.S.R. 92.
[36] *Re A.I. Levy (Holdings) Ltd* [1964] Ch. 19.
[37] [1980] 1 All E.R. 814.
[38] [1992] B.C.C. 503.
[39] [1992] B.C.L.C. 901.

(1)   The discretion of the court is at large.

(2)   The basic principle of *pari passu* distribution among creditors should generally be respected. The court will be reluctant to validate payments and transfers pursuant to pre-liquidation transactions where the effect would be to give a preference to a pre-liquidation creditor or would otherwise prejudice the interests of unsecured creditors.

(3)   But in appropriate cases such payments and transfers will be sanctioned, as where the payment of sums due to particular suppliers is necessary to ensure future supplies that will enable the company to continue trading and the court considers that the continuance of trading will be in the best interests of creditors. This is a sensible recognition of the fact, well known to administrative receivers and administrators, that it is often necessary to make certain involuntary, or "pressure", payments to particular creditors in order to protect the wider interests of the creditors as a whole.

(4)   Transactions which do not in any way diminish or dissipate the company's net assets, such as post-petition transactions for full value, will normally be validated, and *a fortiori* transactions which would increase, or have increased, the value of the company's assets or which would preserve or have preserved the assets from harm that would result in a paralysis of the company's business.[40]

(5)   Where the parties were unaware that a petition had been presented and the disposition was in good faith and in the ordinary course of business, that is a powerful factor in inducing the court to exercise its discretion to validate the transaction but is not sufficient by itself; it must also be shown that the transaction was one which was likely to be for the benefit of creditors generally.[41]

(6)   In deciding whether a post-petition payment made to obtain delivery of goods purchased before the presentation of the petition on terms of cash against delivery is of benefit to the company the court does not look simply at the benefit, if any, to be derived from the particular goods but also takes into account the fact that the payment will enable the company to obtain further supplies and thereby continue the business and earn revenue.

(7)   The court can authorise or validate not merely a particular disposition or contract but the general continuance of trading and for that purpose the continued operation of a bank account. The desirability

---

[40] Citing *Re Wiltshire Iron Co* (1868) L.R. 3 Ch. App. 443; *Re Park Ward & Co Ltd* [1926] Ch. 828, *Re Clifton Place Garage Ltd* [1970] 1 All E.R. 353 and *Re A.I Levy (Holdings) Ltd* [1964] Ch. 19.

[41] See also *Re Tain Construction Ltd*, above, n.22.

of the company continuing to trade is inherently more speculative than that of being allowed to adhere to a particular disposition and is likely to depend on whether the sale of the business as a going concern will probably be more beneficial than the realisation of the company's assets on a break-up basis.[42] Where the court does authorise the continuance of trading the proper course is to freeze the existing account and require all fresh dealings to be conducted through a new account.

It has also been held that the court has power to validate a transaction to a limited extent or for a limited purpose, so that where the company in liquidation had transferred property to another company which had then given a charge to a bank, the transaction could be validated to the extent of the charge to the bank.[43]

Defence of change of position?

In *Re Tain Construction Ltd*[44] Mr Nicholas Warren Q.C., sitting as a deputy High Court judge, held that the defence of change of position was arguably available as a defence to a claim under s.127 if the usual conditions were satisfied, since that section, unlike ss.238 and 239, did not prescribe any remedy for its breach but left this to the general law. However, this does not appear to take account of the wide power of the court to validate transactions, a power which it is arguable ought not to be fettered by defences available to restitutionary claims in the general law.

11–133

12. TRANSACTIONS DEFRAUDING CREDITORS

The statutory provisions

Where a transaction at an undervalue is entered into by the company for the purpose of putting assets beyond the reach of a person who is making or may at some time make a claim against the company or of otherwise prejudicing the interests of such a person in relation to the claim he is making or may make, the court may make an order restoring the status quo and protecting the interests of persons who are victims of the transaction.[45]

11–134

---

[42] This obviously depends to a considerable degree on whether there are reasonable prospects of the company moving into profitable trading and meanwhile having sufficient cash flow to carry on the business.

[43] *Re Dewrun Ltd, Royal Bank of Scotland v Bhardwaj* [2002] B.C.C. 57.

[44] Above, n.22.

[45] Insolvency Act 1986, s.423.

This section derives from the provisions of s172 of the Law of Property Act 1925 relating to fraudulent conveyances. The definition of a transaction at an undervalue in relation to companies is the same as under s.238(4) of the Insolvency Act, discussed earlier.[46]

Conditions for the making an order

11–135 An order can be made under s.423 only if the following conditions are satisfied:

(1) There has been a transaction at an undervalue.[47]

(2) It was made for the purpose of defeating the claims of an existing or putative creditor.

It is not necessary that the company shall be in winding-up or administration, nor is there any statutory time limit.

The fact that the transaction was not entered into from any dishonest motive and that the parties acted in reliance on legal advice is no answer to a claim under s.423; it suffices that it was intended to place the assets out of the reach of creditors or a particular creditor.[48] There is no need to show that such intention was the sole purpose of the transaction; it is enough that it was a dominant purpose,[49] though perhaps not necessarily *the predominant* purpose.[50] On the other hand it is not sufficient to show merely that the *result* of the transfer was to put assets beyond the reach of a creditor, for result is not to be equated with *purpose*.[51] So s.423 does not apply if the purpose of the transaction was not to place assets outside the reach of creditors but to gain a tax advantage.[52]

Who can apply for an order

11–136 Application for an order under s.423 can be made:

(1) by the liquidator or administrator of a company in winding-up or administration or by the official receiver;

---

[46] Above, paras 11–12 *et seq.*

[47] See in this connection *Agricultural Mortgage Corp plc v Woodward* [1994] B.C.C. 502, the facts of which have been given above, para.11–28.

[48] *Arbuthnot Leasing International Ltd v Havelet Leasing Ltd (No.2)* [1990] B.C.C. 636.

[49] *Chohan v Saggar* [1992] B.C.C. 306.

[50] See *Royscot Spa Leasing Ltd v Lovett* [1995] B.C.C. 502, *per* Sir Christopher Slade at 507.

[51] *ibid.*

[52] *Pinewood Joinery v Starelm Properties Ltd* [1994] B.C.C. 569.

(2)   with leave of the court, by a victim of the transaction;

(3)   where a victim of the transaction is bound by a voluntary arrangement, by the supervisor of the voluntary arrangement.[53]

Orders that can be made

These are set out in s.425 and correspond broadly to the orders that can be made under s.241 of the Act,[54] with the same restrictions for the protection of bona fide third parties as in s.241(2).[55]   **11–137**

13. APPLICATION OF RECOVERIES

In all these cases the question arises whether the recoveries[56] form part of the company's general assets so as to be or become subject to a prior security interest granted by the company (including a security interest arising under an after-acquired property clause in a fixed or floating charge) or whether instead they are to be treated as a distinct pool of assets not belonging to the company in its own right but received by the liquidator for the benefit of the general body of creditors and therefore outside the scope of the prior security interest.[57]   **11–138**

Recoveries in right of the company

This category comprises all cases where the company through its liquidator recovers the disposed of asset *in specie* because of the invalidity or avoidance of the disposition or can treat it as free from a security interest because of the nullity of the security interest.   **11–139**

Where the disposition is wholly void the effect is that the asset purportedly disposed of never ceased to be the property of the company and remains subject to a prior security interest. The recovery thus occurs automatically by force of law and, in contrast to other grounds of recovery, does not involve any action on the part of the liquidator or any use of the

---

[53] *ibid.*, s.424.
[54] See above, paras 11–44 *et seq.*
[55] *Chohan v Saggar* [1992] B.C.C. 750.
[56] This term is used for brevity to cover both the case where assets or their monetary value come back to the company and cases where an asset held by the company is freed from a security interest because of the invalidation of that interest.
[57] See generally D.D. Prentice, "Creditors' Interests and Directors' Duties" [1990] 10 O.J.L.S. 265; Fidelis Oditah, "Wrongful Trading" [1990] L.M.C.L.Q. 205 at 215-222, and *Legal Aspects of Receivables Financing*, 214–222.

company's resources. The invalidity may arise at common law, as where the disposition is effected pursuant to a contract which is void for want of *consensus ad idem*, or by statute, as where it is a disposition made after presentation of the winding-up petition and without leave of the court[58] or is a security interest invalidated for want of registration[59] or as a floating charge which falls foul of s.245 of the Insolvency Act.[60] In all these cases the effect of the invalidity is that the asset never ceased to be subject to the prior assignment or security interest. Invalidity at common law plainly has nothing to do with the particular interests of general creditors in a winding-up so that there is no basis for giving them a special status as regards recoveries. A post-petition disposition made without the approval of the court is likewise wholly void, so that the asset does, not escape from the prior security interest.[61] The invalidity of a charge simply expands the company's equity in the charged asset and does not affect existing security interests. A registrable but unregistered charge is void against the liquidator and creditors. For this purpose "creditors" includes subsequent secured creditors, whether or not the company is in winding-up, and the effect of the failure to register the prior charge is that a subsequent chargee is promoted. Similarly the invalidity of a floating charge under s.245 does not affect existing security interests except to free them from the floating charge if it would otherwise have had priority.

Recoveries for the benefit of creditors

11–140 All the statutory provisions referred to above[62] involved the invalidation of dispositions by the company, thus operating to preserve or restore prior security interests in the assets the subject of the ineffective disposition. By contrast, the provisions relating to transactions at an undervalue and preferences, though often loosely referred to as rendering the transactions voidable, are not true invalidating provisions. Nothing in ss.238 or 239 refers to avoidance of transactions at an undervalue or preferences, nor do the powers conferred on the court by s.241 include the power to rescind such transactions or preferences or declare them void. Instead, they enable the court to reverse the effect of the transaction at an undervalue or preference in whatever manner it considers fit. This includes the power to

---

[58] Insolvency Act 1986, s.127. See above, para.11–124.
[59] Under s.395 of the Companies Act 1985.
[60] Because it is taken otherwise than for a requisite form of new value from a company which goes into winding-up within a specified statutory period. See above, paras 11–108 *et seq.*
[61] *Merton v Hammond Suddards* [1996] 2 B.C.L.C. 470; *Bayley v National Australia Bank* (1995) 16 A.C.S.R. 38; *Campbell v Michael Mount PSB* (1995) 16 A.C.S.R. 296. The contrary view was adopted in a majority decision of the Full Court of the Victoria Supreme Court in *Re Fresjac Pty Ltd* (1995) 65 S.A.S.R. 334 (Debelle J. dissenting), but it is thought that the earlier cases reflect the position in English law.
[62] *i.e.* Companies Act 1985 ss.395–396; Insolvency Act 1986, ss.127, 245.

order any transferred property to be vested in the company, but such a power is purely remedial and does not impeach the validity of the transfer.

It might be thought, therefore, that it is the absence of revesting in the company as the result of the avoidance that debars the secured creditor from reaping the fruits of recoveries in the case of transactions at an undervalue and preference. That, indeed, was the conclusion reached in relation to preferences by the High Court of Australia in *N.A. Kratzmann Pty Ltd (in liquidation) v Tucker (No.2)*,[63] in which a distinction was drawn between the avoidance of a preference in the form of a transfer of specific property, which revested in the company *in specie* and was thus held to be captured by the prior security interest, and the avoidance of payment where there was no such revesting and the claim against the preferred creditor was a purely personal claim for repayment. However, such a distinction was never applied in English law,[64] where the avoidance of preference has long been established to enure for the benefit of the general body of creditors.[65] The true justification for treating recoveries in respect of preferences as held for the general body of creditors is that the legislation is remedial in character, embodying a policy decision to benefit the general body of creditors and not any individual creditor, and that the claim is accordingly, vested by statute in the liquidator, not in the company.[66] Moreover, the recovery does not arise by force of law but results from the activity of the liquidator in making application to the court and, to that end, the use of the company's resources, so that the position is analogous to that which obtains where the liquidator carries out a contract on behalf of the company.[67] A third ground advanced by Bennett J. in *Re Yagerphone Ltd*, is that assets recovered by way of preference are impressed with a trust in favour of the general body of creditors, an *obiter dictum* subsequently approved by Millett J. in *Re M.C. Bacon Ltd*.[68]

Similar considerations apply to recoveries by the liquidator in relation to transactions at an undervalue[69] and extortionate credit bargains.[70]

All these cases assume that what is recovered by the liquidator either was never the property of the chargee or ceased to be so prior to the winding-

---

[63] (1968) 123 C.L.R. 295.

[64] See Oditah, *Legal Aspects of Receivables Financing*, 220.

[65] *Re Yagerphone Ltd* [1935] Ch. 392; *Willmott v London Celluloid Co* (1886) 31 Ch.D. 425, affirmed (1886) 34 Ch.D. 147. Prior to the Insolvency Act 1985 no statutory provisions existed for the avoidance of transactions at an undervalue. In the case of an individual s.42 of the Bankruptcy Act 1914 provided for the avoidance of settlements made within the two years preceding the bankruptcy but there was no comparable rule in winding-up

[66] *Re M.C.Bacon Ltd (No.2)* [1990] B.C.C. 430; *Re Yagerphone Ltd* [1935] Ch. 392; *Willmott v London Celluloid Co*, above. See also *Re Oasis Merchandising Services Ltd* [1997] 1 All E.R. 1009, a decision on the application of the fruits of a contribution claim for wrongful trading under s.214 of the Insolvency Act.

[67] See above, paras 6–25 *et seq.*

[68] [1991] Ch. 127 at p.137. See also Oditah, *op. cit.*, p.219.

[69] Insolvency Act 1986, s.238.

[70] *ibid.*, s.244.

up as the result of the fact that the transfer in question overrode the charge. In such a case the chargee is not entitled to use the avoidance provisions to recover what he had lost or had never had. Where however, the charge was not overridden by the transfer and the property transferred is recovered, the charge continues to attach to the recovered property.[71]

14. EXEMPTIONS FOR MARKET AND RELATED CONTRACTS

11–141   The provisions of ss.238, 239 and 423 of the Insolvency Act 1986 do not apply to market contracts to which a recognised investment exchange or recognised clearing house is a party or to a disposition of property in pursuance of such a contract.[72]

15. CRITIQUE OF THE AVOIDANCE PROVISIONS

11–142   From the analysis given above it will be apparent that the avoidance provisions of the Insolvency Act 1986 are long overdue for reform. Though the broad underlying policies are reasonably clear, there is little coherence in the working out of those policies in the legislation, which remains bound by its historical antecedents. The rules as to transactions at an undervalue and preferences are predicated on the assumption that the purpose of the legislation is not to preserve the *pari passu* principle as such but to avoid voluntary transfers which are not made in good faith. Hence the legislation looks not to the fact of preference or loss of value but to the state of mind of those acting on behalf of the company in entering into the transaction under attack. This is in marked contrast to the position in other jurisdictions such as Australia and the United States, where the test of preference is an objective one. The Cork Committee was divided on the issue, a minority favouring the objective test, whilst the latter adhered to the position that a creditor who exerts pressure should be allowed to retain the fruits of his own diligence. If there is to be any real prospect of improving the position of unsecured creditors it is necessary to substitute an objective for a subjective test, while on the other hand allowing exemptions for transactions on reasonable commercial terms in the ordinary course of business. Moreover, the preference rules should apply to involuntary, as well as voluntary, dispositions, such as those made pursuant to a court

---

[71] For a development of this point see John Armour "Transactions at an Undervalue" in *Vulnerable Transactions in Corporate Insolvency* (ed. Armour and Bennett), paras 2.135 *et seq.*; Adrian Walters, "Preferences" (*op. cit.*), paras 4.102 *et seq.*

[72] Companies Act 1989, s.165.

order in contested proceedings. That would have the additional effect of avoiding the risk of unfairness to unsecured creditors that can result from the imposition of a remedial constructive trust or a constructive trust not based on the plaintiffs initial proprietary base.[73] A strong case can be made out for repealing s.127 of the Insolvency Act, which forces a company to apply to the court in order to be able to continue its business when a petition has been presented against it which may be well-founded but may equally be insupportable. There is no good reason for imposing a total statutory paralysis on a company merely because of a winding-up petition. It should be sufficient that leave of the court has to be obtained for any transaction not made in the ordinary course of business and on reasonable commercial terms. Finally, thought should be given to rationalising the widely differing periods within which a company must go into liquidation or administration if a transaction is to become void or liable to reversal. It is legitimate to distinguish between transactions in favour of a person connected with the company and other transactions, but apart from this a case needs to be made out to show why it is necessary to have a range of time factors running from six months at one end (preferences) to eternity at the other (transactions defrauding creditors). On the way, opportunities that were missed in the enactment of the Insolvency Act 1986 can be taken to remove the more detailed problems identified long ago in case law.

---

[73] See Roy Goode, "Property and Unjust Enrichment", in *Essays on the Law of Restitution* (ed. Andrew Burrows), at 240–244.

Chapter 12

Improper Trading and the Duties and Liabilities of Directors

English law has had a long tradition of indulgence towards directors of companies. Honesty and the observance of fiduciary obligations of good faith, including subordination of a director's own interests to those of his company, have always been required. But the level of prudence, care and skill expected of a director in the conduct of the company's business has generally been low, so that directors of failed companies who could not be demonstrated to have acted dishonestly were rarely held to account because their negligence or incompetence brought ruin of their company.

12–01

Over the past two decades there has been a marked change in the climate of opinion, indeed a sense of outrage that it had become all too easy for directors of a company to obtain credit, milk the company of its assets, drive it into insolvency and then, with brazen effrontery, set up a new "phoenix" company with a similar name engaged in the same type of business to take over the assets of the insolvent at a knock-down price and even offer to complete its unfulfilled engagements for an extra payment. Moreover, there was concern that the law, while addressing fraudulent trading, did little to promote reasonable standards of care and diligence in the conduct of business, particularly where companies had reached the point where insolvent liquidation was unavoidable.

The first fruits of public pressure for reform came with the enactment of the Insolvency Act 1976, which provided for the disqualification of a person who had acted as director of two companies one of which went into insolvent liquidation within five years of the other and whose conduct in the management of one of them made them unfit to be concerned in the management of a company.[1] Six years later came the Cork Report,[2] which

---

[1] The provisions were originally in s.9 of the Insolvency Act 1976, which was repealed and re-entered by s.300 of the Companies Act 1985 and is now to be found in more stringent form in s.6 of the Company Directors Disqualification Act 1986. See below, paras 12–58 *et seq*.

[2] Report of the Review Committee, *Insolvency Law and Practice* (Cmnd. 8558, 1982). The Chairman of the Committee was Sir Kenneth Cork.

drew attention to the inadequacies of the law relating to fraudulent trading and recommended the introduction of a new concept of wrongful trading which did not require a fraudulent intent,[3] and also a wider range of grounds for disqualifying delinquent directors.

This chapter is concerned with the liabilities of directors of a company which goes into insolvent liquidation where they have been guilty of improper trading, whether fraudulent or merely wrongful. As we shall see, contrary to popular belief it is neither a criminal offence nor a civil wrong for a company to continue trading while insolvent, so long as it does not incur new credit with no expectation that this will be repaid when due and the directors take all proper steps to minimise the potential loss to creditors after becoming aware (if it is indeed the case) that there is no reasonable prospect of the company avoiding insolvent liquidation.[4] The directors may properly take the view that it is in the interests of the company and its creditors for the company to trade out of its difficulties. *A fortiori* the directors do not incur any liability for fraudulent or wrongful trading when there is no evidence to show that they knew or ought to have known that there was no reasonable prospect of meeting creditors' claims.[5] But before I turn to the statutory provisions relating to improper trading it may be helpful to give a brief picture of the duties of directors generally.[6]

1. THE DUTIES OF DIRECTORS: SOME GENERAL OBSERVATIONS

To whom the duties are owed

12–02 The director of a company owes duties to the State under the criminal law, to the company of which he is director and, in certain conditions, must have regard to the interests of creditors, which are enforced through the company.

Who is treated as a director

12–03 At common law these duties are imposed both on *de jure* and on *de facto* directors. A *de jure* director is one who has been validly appointed in accordance with the requirements of the law, and this includes any person

---

[3] *ibid.*, Chap.44.

[4] *Secretary of State for Trade and Industry v Taylor* [1997] 1 W.L.R. 407, *per* Chadwick J. at 414.

[5] *Secretary of State for Trade and Industry v Creegan* [2004] B.C.C. 835.

[6] Many of the statutory liabilities of directors are imposed also on other officers of the company, but for brevity the term "directors" will be used to include officers where appropriate.

occupying the position of a director, by whatever name called.[7] A *de facto* director, or director *de son tort*, is one who acts as a director although not (or not validly) appointed as such.[8] The concept is not dissimilar to that of an executor *de son tort*, one who by intermeddling without authority in the administration of a deceased person's estate incurs the same responsibilities and liabilities as if he were a duly appointed executor. But a person is not a *de facto* director where there are directors in place and he performs acts which are referable to some other capacity, such as employee; to be a *de facto* director a person must either be the sole person conducting the management or someone who is on equal footing with the *de jure* or other *de facto* directors.[9] Another way of putting it is that the person concerned must undertake functions which can only be performed by a director.[10] Facts held to be evidence that a person was a *de facto* director include sharing responsibility for management[11]; having charge of or monitoring the company's trading[12]; controlling the company's bank account and deciding which creditors should be paid[13]; being held out by the company as a director and using the title of director.[14] It is necessary that the person concerned should have real influence over the affairs of the company but not necessarily over the whole field of its corporate activities.[15] Even if no one factor is sufficient to show that a person was a *de facto* or shadow director, the cumulative effect of all the factors may show this.[16]

To these two common law categories of director statute had now added a third, namely a shadow director, that is, a person in accordance with whose directions of instructions the directors of the company are accustomed to

---

[7] This is now enshrined in a number of enactments. See Companies Act 1985, s.741; Insolvency Act 1986, s.251; Company Directors Disqualification Act 1986, s.22(4).

[8] *Re Canadian Land Reclaiming and Colonising Co: Coventry and Dixon's Case* (1880) 14 Ch.D. 660). According to Millett J. in *Re Hydrodam (Corby) Ltd* [1994] B.C.C. 161 a *de facto* director must claim or purport to be a director or be held out as a director, but there seems no reason why this additional element is necessary and in subsequent cases it has been held sufficient that the person concerned acted as director though not holding himself out as such (*Re Richborough Furniture Ltd* [1996] B.C.C. 155; *Re Moorgate Metals Ltd* [1995] B.C.C. 143).

[9] *Re Richborough Furniture Ltd* above; *Secretary of State for Trade and Industry v Hickling* [1996] B.C.C. 678.

[10] *Re Hydrodam (Corby) Ltd* [1994] 2 B.C.L.C. 180, *per* Millet J. at 182.

[11] *Re Moorgate Metals Ltd* [1995] B.C.L.C. 698.

[12] *Re Tasbian Ltd (No.3)* [1992] B.C.C. 358; *Re a debtor (No.87 of 1993) (No.2)* [1996] B.C.L.C. 63.

[13] *Re Tasbian Ltd (No.3)*, above, n.12.

[14] *Secretary of State for Trade v Tjolle* [1998] 1 B.C.L.C. 333. For reviews of the authorities, see the judgments of Robery Walker L.J. in *Re Kaytech International plc, Secretary of State for Trade and Industry v Kaczer* [1999] 2 B.C.L.C. 351 at 420 *et seq.* and Sir Donald Rattee in *Secretary of State for Trade and Industry v Becker* [2003] 1 B.C.L.C. 555.

[15] *Re Lo-Line Electric Motors Ltd* [1988] Ch. 477, *per* Sir Nicolas Browne-Wilkinson at 489.

[16] *Re Tasbian Ltd (No.1)* [1991] B.C.C. 435, affirmed [1992] B.C.C. 358.

act.[17] The difference between a *de facto* director and a shadow director is that the former acts himself as if he were a director whereas the latter acts through the *de jure* or *de facto* directors.[18] It is possible to envisage circumstances in which a *de jure* or *de facto* director also fits the definition of shadow director. For example, the late Robert Maxwell was a *de jure* director of a number of public and private companies but it was also the case that his fellow directors would usually defer to him and carry out his instructions. But where a person is a *de jure* or *de facto* director no additional significance attaches *per se* to his status as shadow director. The view expressed by Millett J. that the categories of *de jure*, *de facto* director and shadow director are mutually exclusive,[19] though likely to be true in most cases, has not been endorsed in subsequent cases as being of universal application.[20]

A company may be a director *de jure* or *de facto*[21] or may be a shadow director. So it is possible, for example, for a company to be treated as the *de facto* director or shadow director of its subsidiary. But a parent company is not taken to be a director, or to be responsible on other grounds for the management of its subsidiary, merely because as parent it controls the composition of the board of directors of the subsidiary or because members of the parent board are also directors of the subsidiary or because the parent imposes on the subsidiary budgetary rules or operational guidelines within which the subsidiary is required to conduct its business or stipulates that certain decisions taken by the directors of the subsidiary exercising their own independent discretion and judgment require the approval of the parent.[22] More direct assumption of the day-to-day running of the business is required before the parent can be treated as a director of the subsidiary,

---

[17] Companies Act 1985, s.741(2); Insolvency Act 1986, s.251; Company Directors Disqualification Act 1986, s.22(5). A person is not deemed a shadow director by reason only that the directors act on advice given by him in a professional capacity (*ibid*), nor can a parent company be a shadow director for the purposes of ss.319–322 and 330–346 of the Companies Act 1985 (Companies Act 1985, s.741(3)).

[18] It has been said that he "lurks in the shadows" (*Re Lo-Line Electric Motors Ltd*, above, n.10, *per* Millett J. at 183), but it has since been held that this is not necessary and that a person can be a shadow director who quite openly acts through the *de jure* directors, as where he is controlling a shareholder resident abroad who acts through a local board of directors and takes no steps to hide the part he plays in the affairs of the company (*Secretary of State for Trade and Industry v Deverell* [2001] Ch. 340, *per* Morritt L.J. at para.36).

[19] See *Re Hydrodam (Corby) Ltd*, above, n.10.

[20] *Re Kaytech International plc* [1999] 2 B.C.L.C. 351; *Secretary of State for Trade and Industry v Becker* [2003] 1 B.C.L.C. 555, *per* Sir Donald Rattee at para.24.

[21] *Re Bulawayo Market & Offices Co Ltd* [1907] 2 Ch. 458.

[22] *Re Hydrodam (Corby) Ltd*, above. It should be noted that since the term "shadow director" is defined in s.251 of the Insolvency Act 1986, the provisions of that section applying s.741(3) of the Companies Act 1985 (under which a parent company is not a shadow director of its subsidiary merely because the directors of the subsidiary are accustomed to act in accordance with the parent's directions or instructions) do not apply for the purposes of the Insolvency Act 1986.

and assertions that a company is a *de facto* director of its subsidiary are infrequently made and rarely successful.[23]

The fact that Company B is a director of Company A does not by itself make the directors of Company B *de facto* or shadow directors of Company A.[24]

2. THE DUTIES OF DIRECTORS UNDER THE CRIMINAL LAW

A director must observe the criminal law in the performance of his functions. Criminal sanctions may be imposed for causing or procuring the company to commit an offence at common law (*e.g.* conspiracy to defraud) or for causing or procuring a company to commit a statutory offence. Examples of statutory offences are the following:

12–04

(1) A director guilty of fraudulent trading commits an offence.[25]

(2) A director who knowingly and wilfully authorises or permits a default by the company in the performance of its statutory duties under the Companies Act 1985 is liable to a fine or penalty as set out in Sch.24 to the Act.[26]

(3) Where a company commits an offence under the Financial Services and Markets Act 2000 and this is proved to have been committed with the consent or connivance of, or to be attributed to any neglect on the part of, an officer[27] he also is guilty of that offence.[28]

(4) A director who consents to or connives at an offence committed by a company under certain .provisions of the Theft Act 1968[29] is also guilty of that offence.[30]

(5) A director who with intent to deceive members or creditors of a company about its affairs publishes or concurs in publishing a

---

[23] English company law has not yet adapted to the concept of group trading. The group as such does not constitute a legal entity, though for certain tax purposes it may be treated as such. Each member of the group is a distinct legal person and the directors of a subsidiary are required to have regard solely to the interests of the subsidiary in running its business and not to those of the parent or of co-subsidiaries. For a comparative treatment see Frank Wooldridge, *Groups of Companies: The Law and Practice in Britain, France and Germany* (Institute of Advanced Legal Studies, London, 1981) and *Groups of Companies in European Laws* (ed. Klaus J. Hopt), which contains (*inter alia*) a perceptive treatment of groups of companies in English law by D.D. Prentice.

[24] *Re Hydrodam (Corby) Ltd,* above, n.22; *Norman v Theodore Goddard* [1992] B.C.L.C. 1028.

[25] Companies Act 1985, s.488.

[26] *ibid.,* s.730(5).

[27] Which includes a director (Financial Services and Markets Act 2000, s.400(5)).

[28] *ibid.,* s.400(1).

[29] *i.e.* ss.15 (obtaining property by deception), 16 (obtaining a pecuniary advantage) and 17 (false accounting).

[30] Theft Act 1968, s.18.

statement which to his knowledge is or may be misleading, false or deceptive in a material particular commits an offence.[31]

(6) A person who was a director or shadow director of a company going into insolvent liquidation and who without leave of the court becomes a director of, or involved in the management of or carrying on of a business by, another company under (a) a name by which the liquidating company was known in the period of 12 months ending with the day before it went into liquidation or (b) a name so similar in name as to suggest some association with the company in liquidation commits an offence,[32] and becomes personally responsible, jointly and severally with the company and others similarly liable, for all debts of the company incurred at a time when he was so involved.[33]

A person unfit to act as a director may be disqualified from so doing whether or not he has been guilty of a criminal offence.[34]

3. THE DUTIES OF DIRECTORS TO THE COMPANY[35]

Relevance to winding up or administration

12–05 The directors of a company owe the company various duties which are summarised below. The existence of these duties is particularly relevant on the winding-up or administration of the company in that the liquidator or administrator may bring proceedings in the name of the company for any breach of a director's duties to the company so far as the conduct constituting the breach has not been effectively ratified by its members. As we shall see, the ability of members to waive a breach or ratify improper conduct becomes severely circumscribed where the improper acts occur at a time when the company is insolvent.[36]

Executive and non-executive directors

12–06 An executive director, that is, one who is not merely a member of the board but a full-time employee engaged in day-to-day management of the company, owes two distinct sets of duties, those deriving from his status as

---

[31] *ibid.*, s.19.

[32] Insolvency Act 1986, s.216. This provision is aimed in particular at directors who establish "phoenix" companies.

[33] *ibid.*, s.217. However, since the applicant for leave has not necessarily been guilty of any misconduct himself his application should not be approached in the same way as an application for leave under s.17 of the Company Directors Disqualification Act 1986 *(Penrose v Official Receiver* [1996] 2 All E.R. 96).

[34] See paras 12–54 *et seq.* Acting while disqualified is itself a criminal offence. See para.12–72.

[35] See generally *Gower and Davies' Principles of Modern Company Law* (7th ed. 2004), Chap.16; *Gore-Browne on Companies*, Chap.15; *Boyle and Birds' Company Law* (5th ed. 2004), Chap.16.

[36] See below, para.12–14.

director and those imposed on him as an employee participating in day-to-day management, usually under the terms of a service contract. A non-executive director, an outsider brought on to the board by virtue of his general standing or business acumen and devoting only part of his time to the company's affairs (primarily by attending board meetings and reading the relevant papers), owes only the first set of duties. In setting the standard of duty the courts do not in general distinguish between executive and non-executive directors.[37] A director is not personally liable for negligent advice given by the company unless he assumed personal responsibility for it and that assumption was relied on by the claimant.[38]

The director's duties as director

A director owes three broad sets of duty to the company in his capacity as director: the duty to act within his powers, the duties of care and skill, and fiduciary duties of a kind similar to those owed by an agent to his principal and embodying in different forms the duty of loyalty. The standards are the same for executive and non-executive directors.[39] The duty will vary according to the size and business of the particular company and the experience or skills that the particular director holds himself out as possessing.[40] A non-executive director cannot be expected to have the detailed knowledge of the company's affairs required of an executive director, but even non-executive directors are required to take reasonable steps to guide and monitor the management of the company.[41]

12–07

(1) Duty to act within his powers

The directors of a company owe a duty to act both within the company's powers and within the powers conferred on them by the company's memorandum and articles or (so far as lawful) by the members of the company in general meeting. Where they act in excess of their powers then unless the resulting transaction is validly ratified by the members it is liable to be set aside if the other party did not act in good faith, and the directors will be liable for any loss sustained by the company even if they acted in good faith and without negligence.

12–08

---

[37] See *Dorchester Finance Co Ltd v Stebbing* [1988] B.C.L.C. 488; but see paras 12–07, 12–11, below. For the role of the non-executive director generally, see B.R. Cheffins *Company Law*, Chap.13.

[38] *Williams v Natural Life Health Foods Ltd* [1998] 1 W.L.R. 830.

[39] *Dorchester Finance Co Ltd v Stebbing,* above.

[40] *Daniels v Anderson* (1995) 16 A.C.S.R. 607.

[41] *Equitable Life Assurance Society v Bowley* [2004] 1 B.C.L.C. 180; *AWA Ltd v Daniels* (1992) 7 A.C.S.R. 759, affirmed on appeal *sub. nom. Daniels v Anderson,* above, n.40.

(2) Duty to exercisable reasonable care and skill

12–09   A director is required to exercise reasonable care, skill and diligence in the performance of his duties. This duty is owed both at common law and in equity but it is not a fiduciary duty.[42] However, the common law has tended to pitch the standard of care at a relatively low level. Thus it has been held that a director:

(a) need not be an expert in the type of business in which his company is engaged, so that is suffices if he used the care and skill of the non-professional reasonable man[43];

(b) is not required to give his whole time and attention to the affairs of the company[44];

(c) if a non-executive director, is entitled to rely on the executive directors and officers of the company, *e.g.* for the accuracy of financial statements presented[45];

(d) is entitled to rely on outside advice by a person whom he reasonably believes to be competent to give it, so long as he exercises his own judgment as to such advice.[46]

In *Dorchester Finance Co Ltd v Stebbing*[47] Foster J. accepted as accurate the three main submissions on the law made by counsel for the plaintiffs, namely that:

(a) a director is required to exhibit in performance of his duties such a degree of skill as may reasonably be expected from a person with his knowledge and experience;

(b) a director is required to take in the performance of his duties such care as an ordinary man might be expected on his own behalf;

(c) a director must exercise any power vested in him as such honestly, in good faith and in the interests of the company.

The duty of care, or due diligence, means that a director must not abdicate involvement or responsibility. He therefore risks liability if he neglects to attend board meetings and leaves all decisions to others, if he fails to apply

---

[42] *Bristol and West Building Society v Mothew* [1996] 4 All E.R. 698, *per* Millett L.J., citing with approval the judgment of Ipp J. in *Permanent Building Society v Wheeler* (1994) 14 A.C.S.R. 109 at 157–158.
[43] *Re City Equitable Fire Insurance Co* [1925] Ch. 407.
[44] *ibid.* This reflects the fact that a director is not as such an employee of the company.
[45] *ibid.*, *Dovey v Cory* [1901] A.C. 477. But see below, para.12–11, n.54.
[46] *Re Faure Electric Accumulator Co* (1888) 40 Ch.D. 141.
[47] [1988] B.C.L.C. 488. See also *Re Barings plc (No.5)* [2000] B.C.L.C. 523.

his judgment to the advice of outsiders or if he signs cheques without inquiry[48]or insurance proposal forms without reading them.[49] Moreover, it has been held that s.214(4) of the Insolvency Act 1986 relating to wrongful trading accurately reflects the standard of a director's duty of care, skill and diligence at common law, so as to require him to take the steps that would be taken by a reasonably diligent person having the general knowledge, skill and experience that may reasonably be expected of a person carrying out the same functions, as well as the general knowledge, skill and experience which the director in fact possesses.[50] Though this equation of the common law standard with that imposed by s.214(4) is not uncontroversial, there seems little doubt that it reflects the shift of opinion towards a standard which requires as a minimum the objective standard referred to above,[51] particularly in the light of the increasingly stringent disqualification provisions of the Company Directors Disqualification Act 1986.[52]

(3) Duty to observe fiduciary obligations

Directors must not only act within their powers and those of the company, they must exercise their powers in good faith in the interests of the company and the shareholders as a whole. In particular, they must not misappropriate the company's assets, nor must they usurp for their own advantage corporate opportunities which, if they pursue them at all, should be pursued for the benefit of their company, or otherwise subordinate the company's interests to their own or those of third parties or abuse their powers or position.[53]

12–10

The director's duties as an employee-manager

An executive director must, in addition to discharging his duties *qua* director, fulfil in his capacity as an employee participating in day-to-day management the express and implied terms of his service contract[54] and

12–11

---

[48] *Re City Equitable Fire Insurance Co*, above n.43; *Re Faure Electric Accumulator Co*, above n.46; and see *Re Majestic Recording Studios Ltd* (1988) 4 B.C.C. 519.

[49] *Re D'Jan of London Ltd* [1993] B.C.C. 646.

[50] *Re D'Jan of London Ltd* above.

[51] *Gower and Davies' Principles of Modern Company Law*, pp.434–435; *Gore-Browne on Companies*, para.15[17]. See also *Peoples Department Stories Inc v Wise* (2004) 24 D.L.R. (4th) 564, in which the Supreme Court of Canada noted (at para.61) that the standard of care of directors had traditionally been low and the Court had sought to raise it, and expressed the view that the argument that to do this might detract people from accepting directorships was unsupported by evidence and was specious.

[52] See below, para.12–50.

[53] For further details the reader is referred to the standard textbooks on company law.

[54] Which will usually involve his devoting his whole time and attention to the company's affairs.

apply to the performance of his duties that degree of knowledge, care and skill which is reasonably to be expected of a person holding his position. A person holding the post of chief executive or managing director will be expected to exercise the care, skill and knowledge appropriate to that office, though obviously the degree of skill and knowledge required will vary with the size and complexity of the company.

Proceedings by liquidator or administrator for breach of duty owed to the company

12–12   The liquidator or administrator of a company can institute proceedings in the name of the company for any breach of duty by a director in respect of which the company itself could have made a claim prior to the liquidation or administration. Alternatively, if the company is winding-up and has a claim for misappropriation of money or other property the liquidator (or the official receiver, a creditor or a contributory) may institute summary misfeasance proceedings against the director for an order in the winding-up for examination of the director and for repayment of the money, return of the property or payment of compensation to the company for the misfeasance[55] Claims for misfeasance may include not only loss to the company through misappropriation, or through improper payments such as unlawful distributions from capital[56] or wrongful preferences,[57] but also secret profits and other benefits obtained by directors in breach of their fiduciary duties, which are assumed to reflect loss to the company.[58] Misfeasance is not a

---

[55] Insolvency Act 1986, s.212. The misfeasance procedure is also available against a liquidator, administrator or administrative receiver (s.212(1)). The court has power to grant relief under s.727 of the Companies Act 1985 where satisfied that the director concerned acted honestly and reasonably, even if negligent. The postulate of a negligent director acting reasonably is a curious one; nevertheless the section makes it clear that conduct which is negligent at common law may be reasonable for the purpose of s.727 (*Re D'Jan of London Ltd* [1993] B.C.C. 646).

[56] See Companies Act 1985, s.263.

[57] *West Mercia Safetywear Ltd v Dodd* (1988) 4 B.C.C. 30.

[58] See Oditah, *Legal Aspects of Receivables Financing*, p.213 and *Re Derek Randall Enterprises Ltd* [1990] B.C.C. 749. In the latter case a director who had received for himself commission for which he should have accounted to the company subsequently gave the company's bank a guarantee in support of which he paid into a special blocked account with the bank a sum exceeding that which he had misappropriated. A majority of the Court of Appeal upheld the decision of Millett J. that the effect of the payment was to restore to the company the sum misappropriated, so that it no longer had any loss. Dillon L.J. dissented on the ground that the moneys paid in were represented as those of the director concerned and that they did not in reality benefit the company, for though they reduced the debt to the bank the director as surety was entitled to be subrogated *pro tanto* to the bank's claims. The difference of opinion in the Court of Appeal seems to have turned on whether the sum paid in was that which had been misappropriated or was the surety's own money. Millett J. and the majority in the Court of Appeal adopted the former view, and on this basis concluded that the director would not have been subrogated, since it was not his money that was used to support the guarantee and thereby reduce the overdraft. Accordingly the payment did in fact benefit the company.

distinct wrongdoing, simply a well-worn label, now redundant, to denote any breach of duty by directors causing loss to the company on the basis of which summary proceedings may be instituted in the Companies Court within the liquidation.[59]

However, a claim by the liquidator or administrator for misfeasance or other breach of duty owed to the company is purely derivative[60]; he can sue only in respect of claims vested in the company and has no rights of action in respect of claims vested in particular creditors or other third parties, *e.g.* for loss suffered by them through the company's fraud or misrepresentation induced by the director concerned.[61]Again, the liquidator does not sue in right of the general body of creditors, as he is considered to do in proceedings for contribution under s.214 of the Insolvency Act[62]; he sues in right of the company,[63] and while this may benefit the general body of creditors by increasing the amount available for distribution this is not necessarily the case, since any recoveries will in the first instance enure for the benefit of a prior assignee or chargee under a charge covering the money or property recovered.[64]

Relief from liability

Where a director or other officer of the company has been found liable for negligence, default, breach of duty or breach of trust, then if the court finds that he has acted honestly and reasonably, and that having regard to all the circumstances of the case (including those connected with his appointment) he ought fairly to be excused, the court may relieve him, either wholly or partly, from his liability on such terms as it thinks fit.[65] But if the conditions for the grant of relief are not satisfied, because the director has not acted honestly and reasonably, the court may still temper the wind to the shorn lamb by limiting the amount to be paid under s.212 to a sum below that which is necessary to remedy the misfeasance.[66]   **12–13**

Ratification by the members

Where the company is solvent and likely to remain so, it is open to its members to approve or ratify what would otherwise have been a breach of duty by the directors, in which case the liquidator has no cause of action, to   **12–14**

---

[59] See *Re Continental Assurance Co of London plc.* [2001] B.P.I.R. 733, *per* Park J. at para.[393], who also pointed out that though s.212 does not create any additional liabilities and obligations it does confer on the court a measure of discretion as to remedies going beyond what is available at common law.

[60] Albeit misfeasance proceedings have distinctive characteristics. See Fidelis Oditah, "Misfeasance proceedings against company directors," [1992] L.M.C.L.Q. 207 at p.210.

[61] *Re Ambrose Tin & Copper Mining Co* (1880) 14 Ch.D. 690.

[62] See below, para.6–39 and above, paras 12–40, 12–46.

[63] See further para.12–15 as to the position of creditors.

[64] See above, para.6–30, and below, para.12–15, text and n.78.

[65] Companies Act 1985, s.127.

[66] For a case where this was done, see *Re Loquitur Ltd, Inland Revenue Commissioners v Richmond* [2003] 2 B.C.L.C. 442.

pursue in the company's name,[67] in which case the liquidator has no cause of action to pursue in the company's name.[68] The situation is quite different where the transaction is likely to cause loss to creditors because the company is insolvent at the time of or inconsequence of the breach or (probably) likely to become so, for it is then the creditors, not the members, who have the primary interest in the proper application of the company's assets, so that a purported approval or ratification by the members of a breach of duty by the directors causing loss to the company will be ineffective.[69]

4. DUTIES TO CREDITORS AT COMMON LAW

12–15   In *Winkworth v Edward Baron Development Co Ltd*[70] Lord Templeman stated that a company owes a duty to future, as well as present, creditors to preserve its assets, but this dictum must, it is thought, be intended to be confined to cases where the company, though solvent at the time of the breach of duty complained of, is unlikely to remain so, and there is accordingly a risk to creditors.[71] Indeed, even in relation to existing creditors it is important to bear in mind that the duties are owed to them through the company, not directly, and their interests are protected by proceedings in the name of the company to which ratification of the breach of duty by the shareholders is no defence.[72]

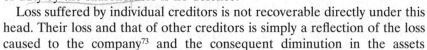

Loss suffered by individual creditors is not recoverable directly under this head. Their loss and that of other creditors is simply a reflection of the loss caused to the company[73] and the consequent diminution in the assets

---

[67] *Rolled Steel Products (Holdings) Ltd v British Steel Corp* [1986] Ch. 246; *Multinational Gas and Petrochemical Co v Multinational Gas and Petrochemical Services Ltd* [1983] Ch. 258. But the shareholders cannot effectively ratify acts which are a fraud on the company creditors or are otherwise unlawful. See *Avelin Barford Ltd v Perion Ltd* (1989) 5 B.C.C. 677; *Ridge Securities Ltd v I.R.C.* [1964] 1 W.L.R. 479; *Attorney-General's Reference (No. 2 of 1982)* [1984] 1 Q.B. 624; *Re Halt Garages (1964) Ltd* [1982] 3 All E.R. 1016.

[68] *Salomon v A. Salomon & Co Ltd* [1987] A.C. 22; *Multinational Gas and Petrochemical Co v Multinational Gas and Petrochemical Services Ltd*, above; *Rolled Steel Products (Holdings) Ltd v British Steel Corp*, above; *Brady v Brady* [1988] 2 All E.R. 617.

[69] *Walker v Wimborne* (1976) 50 A.L.J.R. 446; *Re Horlsey & Weight Ltd* [1982] Ch. 442; *Nicholson v Permakraft (NZ) Ltd* [1985] 1 N.Z.L.R. 242; *Kinsela & Am. v Russell Kinsela Pty Ltd* (1986) 10 A.C.L.R. 395. See generally David A. Wishart, "Models and Theories of Directors' Duties to Creditors" [1991] 14 N.Z.L.R. 323; D.D. Prentice, "Creditors' Interests and Directors' Duties" (1990) 10 O.J.L.S. 265.

[70] [1986] 1 W.L.R. 1512, at 1516.

[71] See *Brady v Brady*, above, n.68.

[72] *Sycotex Pty Ltd v Baseler* (1993) 13 A.C.S.R. 766, *per* Gummow J. at 785; D.D.Prentice, "Creditors' Interests and Directors' Duties", (1990) 10 O.J.L.S. 275.

[73] It thus parallels the principle of reflected loss which debars individual shareholders from asserting claims against a party causing loss to the company solely in their capacity of shareholders and on the basis of a diminution in the value of their shares. The breach is of a duty owed to the company, the loss is that of the company and only the company can sue for it. See *Johnson v Gore Wood & Co* [2002] 2 A.C. 1; *Perry v Day* [2005] B.C.C. 375; *Gardner v Parker* [2005] B.C.C. 46; *Shaker v Al-Bedrawi* [2003] Ch. 350.

available for distribution, and their protection lies in the principle of law which (the company being in or near insolvency at the time of or in consequence of the breach of duty) recognises their status as the real owners of the company and thus (a) requires directors to consider the impact of their actions on the interests of creditors ahead of, though not to the exclusion of, shareholders and (b) denies effect to a purported ratification by the shareholders of the conduct constituting the breach of duty. If creditors could sue directly, this would breach both the collective procedure of insolvency and the *pari passu* rule.[74] So the true principle is not that the directors owe duties to creditors as well as to the company but that when the company is insolvent or approaching insolvency the directors, in discharging their duty to act in the best interests of the company by maximising its value,[75] must have regard predominantly to the interests of creditors,[76] who now have the primary interest in the proper application of the company's assets. Thus while shareholders retain a residual interest that has to be taken into account, high-risk strategies which they might support when the company is in financial trouble in order to attract a high-potential payoff may have to go give way to the interests of creditors in seeing a safer course of action to protect the assets.[77] This point is of particular significance in relation to the application of sums recovered by the liquidator for breach of duty. Recoveries in right of the company form part of its general assets and are thus susceptible to capture under a prior assignment or charge over future property.[78] This is in contrast to recoveries under the statutory provisions designed for the benefit of the general body of creditors.[79]

---

[74] Prentice, *loc. cit.* See also the interesting article by Andrew Keay, "Directors' Duties to Creditors: Contractarian Concerns Relating to Efficiency and Over-Protection of Creditors" (2003) 66 M.L.R. 665, which notes the general acceptance of the principle that the duty is indirect and cannot be enforced by creditors but goes on to examine the nature and weight of creditors' interests from a law and economics standpoint.

[75] E.M. Iacobucci, "Director's Duties in Insolvency: What Is at Stake?" (2003) 39(3) Can. Bus. L.J. 398 at 400–401.

[76] See the authorities cited n.69 above and *Facia Footwear Ltd v Hinchcliffe* [1998] B.C.L.C. 218 at 228.

[77] *Peoples Department Stores Inc v Wise* (2004) 244 D.L.R. (4th) 564 at para.45. This decision, which also concerns the statutory duties of directors, has attracted widespread interest in Canada, and an entire issue of the Canadian Business Law Journal was devoted to a symposium on it. See [2005] Can. Bus. L.J. 167 For a detailed comment on the case after the decision of the Court of Appeal, see Jacob S. Ziegel, "Corporate Governance and Directors' Duties to Creditors: Two Contrasting Philosophies", *Annual Review of Insolvency Law 2003*, p.133.

[78] A view reluctantly reached by Vaughan Williams J. in *Re Anglo-Austrian Printing and Publishing Union* [1895] 2 Ch. 891.

[79] *i.e.* all the statutory provisions other than those which declare a transaction void. See above, para.11–140; below, para.12–46.

5. LIABILITY FOR FRAUDULENT TRADING

The statutory provisions

12–16   Reference has already been made to the criminal liability of directors and others for fraudulent trading,[80] which does not depend on the company being in winding-up.[81] Running in parallel with this is a civil liability. Under s.213 of the Insolvency Act 1986, if in the course of winding-up of a company it appears that any business of the company has been carried on with intent to defraud creditors of the company or creditors of any other person, or for any fraudulent purpose, the court may, on the application of the liquidator, declare that any persons who were knowingly parties to the fraudulent trading are to be liable to make such contributions (if any) to the company's assets as the court thinks proper.

The elements of liability

12–17   To establish liability under s.213 three elements are required:

(1)   that the business of the company has been carried on with intent to defraud creditors, or for some other fraudulent purpose;

(2)   that the defendant sought to be made liable participated in the carrying on of the business in that manner; and

(3)   that the defendant did so with knowledge that the transaction in which it was participating was intended to defraud creditors or was in some other way fraudulent.[82]

Persons who may be held liable

12–18   Liability, whether criminal or civil, is not confined to directors or others involved with the management of the company but is imposed on any person, including a complete outsider, who was knowingly party to the carrying on of the company's business with intend to defraud its creditors. Thus in *Re Gerald Cooper (Chemicals) Ltd*[83]:

---

[80] Under the Companies Act 1985, s.458. See above, para.12–04.

[81] *ibid.*

[82] *Re Bank of Credit and Commerce International SA, Morris v State Bank of India* [2003] B.C.C. 735, *per* Potter J. at para.11.

[83] [1978] 2 Ch. 262.

A company received from a customer advance payment of the price of goods which it knew it would not be able to deliver and utilised the sum received in repayment of a loan from the respondents, thereby disabling itself from either supplying the goods to the buyer or repaying the price. The respondents, having received repayment of their loan with knowledge of these facts, were held liable as parties to fraudulent trading although they had not themselves been involved in the management of the company.

However, a person cannot be a party to fraudulent trading unless the company itself was engaged in fraudulent trading.[84] A curious situation arose in *Morphitis v Bernasconi*,[85] where proceedings under s.213 were taken not only against the directors of the company but also against the company's solicitors, the sole basis of the claim being that the company through its solicitors deceived a creditor's solicitors into believing that a payment would be made when they knew it would not. The directors defended the claim while the solicitors paid £75,000 into court in settlement, this sum being accepted by the liquidator. The decision of the deputy judge that the deceit constituted fraudulent trading was reversed by the Court of Appeal, which held that the offence had not been made out. So had the solicitors not made the payment into court they would have escaped liability altogether.

Intent to defraud

The statutory provisions do not apply unless the business was carried on **12–19** with intent to defraud. This involves actual dishonesty, not merely blameworthiness.[86] In *Twinsectra Ltd v Yardley*,[87] which concerned a claim against a person for a person to be liable as an accessory to a breach of trust, the House of Lords held (Lord Millett dissenting) that it was not sufficient for the defendant's conduct to be dishonest by the ordinary standards of reasonable and honest people, it was also necessary that he should himself have been aware that by those standards he was acting dishonestly. If he was so aware he is guilty of dishonesty and cannot be allowed to shelter behind some private standard of honesty not shared by the community.[88]

The mere provision by a company of financial support for its subsidiary to enable it to trade as a going concern and in so doing incur debts does not

---

[84] *Re Augustus Barnett & Son Ltd* (1986) 2 B.C.C. 98,904.
[85] [2003] B.C.C. 540.
[86] *Re Patrick & Lyon Ltd* [1933] Ch. 786; *Re Augustus Barnett & Son Ltd* (1986) 2 B.C.C. 95,904; and see D.D. Prentice (1987) 103 L.Q.R. 11.
[87] [2002] 2 A.C. 164.
[88] *Aktieselskabet Dansk Skibsfinansiering v Brothers* [2001] 2 B.C.L.C. 324 at 334; *Royal Brunei Airlines Sdn Bhd v Tan* [1995] 2 A.C. 378.

constitute fraudulent trading.[89] In *Re White & Osmond (Parkstone) Ltd*[90] Buckley J. stated that there was nothing wrong in directors incurring credit at a time when, to their knowledge, the company was not able to meet its liabilities as they fell due. What was wrong was allowing a company to continue incurring debts when it was clear it would never be able to satisfy its creditors.

> ". . . there is nothing to say that directors who genuinely believe that the clouds will roll away and the sunshine of prosperity will shine upon them again and disperse the fog of their depression are not entitled to incur credit to help them get over the bad time."

But in *R. v Grantham*[91] this "clouds and sunshine" (or "silver lining") test was disapproved. The question, said the Court of Appeal, was not whether the directors thought the company would be able to pay its way at some indeterminate time in the future but whether they thought the company, in incurring further credit, could pay its debts as they fell due or shortly thereafter. If they realised there was no prospect of the company being able to do this they were guilty of fraudulent trading even if they had some expectation that ultimately all debts would be paid. In general it is fraudulent trading for a company to obtain new credit, knowing it will unable to repay it when due, in order to pay off existing creditors.[92] However, this may now need to be qualified in the light of the principle affirmed in *Twinsectra*, the effect of which, when applied to s.213, is that a director who genuinely believes that right-minded members of the community would see nothing wrong in continuing the company's business and paying off existing creditors with new credit which he knows the company will be unable to repay at about the time it falls due is not guilty of fraudulent trading. So for the purposes of s.213, robbing Peter to pay Paul is all right if you genuinely believe that it would not be regarded as dishonest by the standards of reasonable and honest people, though it would not suffice that such conduct met your own private standards of morality if you are aware that the community would regard such conduct as dishonest.

Section 213 is capable of applying even if there is only one defrauded creditor and even if he is defrauded by only one transaction, provided that the fraud was perpetrated in the course of carrying on a business.[93] But not

---

[89] *Re Augustus Barnett & Son Ltd*, above.

[90] A decision of Buckley J. in 1960 which is unreported but referred to in *R. v Grantham* [1984] 2 All E.R. 166.

[91] Above.

[92] To this extent the mere fact that the net deficiency is reduced by the continued trading, which would be a defence to an allegation of wrongful trading under s.214, provides no answer to a claim under s.213 for fraudulent trading. See further below, para.12–36.

[93] *Morphitis v Bernasconi* [2003] B.C.C. 540, applying *Re Gerald Cooper (Chemicals) Ltd*, above, n.83.

every deception of a creditor constitutes the carrying on of a business with intent to defraud creditors. So it has been said that:

> "the director of a company dealing in second-hand motor cars who willfully misrepresents the age and capability of a vehicle in stock is, no doubt, a fraudulent rascal but I do not think he can be said to be carrying on the company's business for a fraudulent purpose, although no doubt he carries out a particular business transaction in a fraudulent manner."[94]

It has also been held that the mere fact of preferring one particular creditor does not of itself constitute fraudulent trading.[95]

Who can apply for an order

Application for an order under s.212 can be made only by the liquidator.   **12–20**

Sanctions for fraudulent trading

The criminal sanction for wrongful trading is a fine and/or imprisonment[96];   **12–21**
the civil sanction is a contribution to the assets of the company, which will be discussed later in relation to wrongful trading. Suffice to say that the basis of contribution is restoration to the company of what it lost as the result of the defendant's wrongful conduct; the court cannot include a punitive element in determining the amount of contribution.[97]

6. LIABILITY FOR WRONGFUL TRADING

Genesis of the wrongful trading provisions

The burden of establishing fraud to the standard of proof required by the   **12–22**
criminal law in order to obtain either a conviction for the offence of fraudulent trading or a contribution order in the winding up of the company proved a serious deterrent to the institution of proceedings, and the statutory provisions became almost, though not quite, a dead letter. The Cork Committee concluded that whilst it was right that the law should

---

[94] *Re Murray-Watson Ltd*, (unreported, April 6, 1977), *per* Oliver J., cited by Templeman J. in *Re Gerald Cooper (Chemicals) Ltd* [1978] Ch. 262 at 267.
[95] *Re Sarflax Ltd* [1979] Ch. 592. However, a director who procures the preference is guilty of a misfeasance. See above, para.12–12.
[96] Companies Act 1985, s.458.
[97] *Morphitis v Bernasconi*, above, n.93.

require proof of dishonesty before a person could be convicted of an offence, different considerations applied to the provision of a civil remedy for those who suffered loss in consequence of the mismanagement of a company.[98] The Committee therefore recommended that the existing statutory provisions relating to contribution should be replaced by a new section which would enable contribution orders to be made for wrongful trading without proof of dishonesty and without requiring the criminal standard of proof. A company would engage in wrongful trading if it incurred liabilities with no reasonable prospect of meeting them; and a director would be made personally liable for the company's debts if, being party to the company's trading, he knew that it was wrongful.[99] In determining whether there was a reasonable prospect of the company meeting its liabilities and, if not, whether the director ought to have known this, the test would be objective, namely that of the ordinary, reasonable man.[1] Under these proposals trading when a business was heavily under-capitalised would often come within the concept of wrongful trading.[2]

What is now s.214 of the Insolvency Act 1986 seeks to capture the essential idea of the Committee's proposals, but in much broader terms. In particular, instead of adopting as the criterion of wrongful trading the incurring of new debt without any reasonable prospect of payment, s.214 focuses on the failure of a director, knowing there is no reasonable prospect of the company avoiding insolvent liquidation, to show that he has taken every step which he ought to have taken with a view to minimising loss to creditors. The primary sanction for wrongful trading, like the civil sanction for fraudulent trading, is an order requiring the delinquent director to contribute to the assets of the company.[3]

The statutory provisions

12–23   Section 214 provides as follows:

"**214 Wrongful trading**

(1) Subject to subsection (3) below, if in the course of the winding up of a company it appears that subsection (2) of this section applies in relation to a person who is or has been a director of the company, the court, on the application of the liquidator, may declare that that person is to be liable to make such contribution (if any) to the company's assets as the court thinks proper.

---

[98] *Insolvency Law and Practice*, paras 1776–1777.
[99] *ibid.*, para.1783.
[1] *ibid.*
[2] *ibid.*, para.1785.
[3] See below, para.12–44.

(2) This subsection applies in relation to a person if—

    (a) the company has gone into insolvent liquidation,

    (b) at some time before the commencement of the winding up of the company, that person knew or ought to have concluded that there was no reasonable prospect that the company would avoid going into insolvent liquidation, and

    (c) that person was a director of the company at that time;

but the court shall not make a declaration under this section in any case where the time mentioned in paragraph (b) above was before 28th April 1986.

(3) The court shall not make a declaration under this section with respect to any person if it is satisfied that after the condition specified in subsection (2)(b) was first satisfied in relation to him that person took every step with a view to minimising the potential loss to the company's creditors as (assuming him to have known that there was no reasonable prospect that the company would avoid going into insolvent liquidation) he ought to have taken.

(4) For the purposes of subsections (2) and (3), the facts which a director of a company ought to know or ascertain, the conclusions which he ought to reach and the steps which he ought to take are those which would be known or ascertained, or reached or taken, by a reasonably diligent person having both—

    (a) the general knowledge, skill and experience that may reasonably be expected of a person carrying out the same functions as are carried out by that director in relation to the company, and

    (b) the general knowledge, skill and experience that that director has.

(5) The reference in subsection (4) to the functions carried out in relation to a company by a director of the company includes any functions which he does not carry out but which have been entrusted to him.

(6) For the purposes of this section a company goes into insolvent liquidation if it goes into liquidation at a time when its assets are insufficient for the payment of its debts and other liabilities and the expenses of the winding up.

(7) In this section "director" includes a shadow director.

(8) This section is without prejudice to section 213."

Wrongful trading distinguished from fraudulent trading

There are several differences between wrongful trading and fraudulent **12–24** trading.

(1) It is not necessary to show fraud or dishonesty; what may loosely be described at this stage as a negligent disregard of the interests of creditors suffices. Dishonesty is an essential ingredient of fraudulent trading.

(2) Only a director[4] can be proceeded against for wrongful trading, since this is essentially a negligent failure of management, whereas any person knowingly a party to fraudulent trading by the company may be the subject of proceedings.

(3) The wrongful trading provisions are confined to culpable conduct after the time when the director concerned knew or ought to have known that there was no reasonable prospect of the company avoiding insolvent liquidation.[5] In the case of fraudulent trading the whole period of trading is potentially relevant.

(4) Proceedings for wrongful trading are purely civil, the only sanctions being an order requiring the director concerned to contribute to the company's assets and disqualification from being concerned in the management of a company.

(5) The provisions relating to fraudulent trading are directed primarily against the improper incurring of new debt where there is no reasonable prospect of this being paid. The wrongful trading provisions are designed for the protection of past as well as future creditors. There is thus a tension between the two sets of provisions, for it is not permissible to protect existing creditors at the expense of new creditors.[6] So directors who continue trading without increasing the net deficiency of assets are free from liability under s.214, if they achieve this result by using new credit to pay off existing creditors knowing that the new creditors will not be able to be paid when payment is due or shortly thereafter but will be guilty of fraudulent trading except where they genuinely believe that this would not be regarded as dishonest by reasonable and honest people.[7] In short, s.213 has paramountcy, and in determining whether the directors have taken every step they ought to have taken to minimise the potential loss to the company's creditors the court must take into account in their favour that they could not lawfully rob Peter (the new creditors) to pay Paul (the existing creditors) even if the result of so doing would have been to reduce the net deficiency as at the time of commencement of the winding-up to a figure lower than that existing

---

[4] As to the meaning of "director" in this context see below, para.12–27.
[5] So it is not wrongful trading to bring a company to the point of insolvency by negligent management.
[6] See above, para.12–19, as to incurring new debt.
[7] See above, para.12–19.

when they first ought to have concluded that there was no reasonable prospect of the company avoiding insolvent liquidation.

The ingredients of wrongful trading

Before a person can be held guilty of wrongful trading four conditions must be satisfied: **12–25**

(1)   The company has gone into insolvent liquidation.[8] The wrongful trading provisions are confined to liquidation; they cannot be invoked by an administrator or administrative receiver. A company goes into insolvent liquidation if it goes into liquidation at a time when its assets are insufficient for the payment of its debts and the expenses of the winding-up.[9] This is the balance sheet test described in an earlier chapter.[10] "Debts and liabilities" includes prospective and contingent debts. It is thought that whether the company is in fact insolvent according to this test is to be determined in the light of all facts known when the matter comes before the court, whether or not they were known at the time the company went into liquidation. The use of hindsight creates no problem in this situation, for what the court has to consider in an application under s.214 is whether there is a net deficiency of assets and, if so, whether and how the delinquent director should be required to contribute to the assets.

(2)   At some time, before the commencement of the winding up[11] a person knew or ought to have concluded that there was no reasonable prospect that the company would avoid going into insolvent liquidation.

(3)   That person was a director at that time.

(4)   The director fails to establish the statutory defence of taking every step he ought to have taken to minimise the potential loss to creditors.

The onus is one the liquidator to establish the first three elements and on the defendant to establish the defence.

Trading not an essential requirement

Although the marginal heading to s.214 refers to "wrongful trading" the text of s.214 makes no reference to trading at all. All that is required is a culpable failure to act properly with a view to minimising the potential loss **12–26**

[8] Insolvency Act 1986, s.214(2)(a).
[9] *ibid.*, s.214(6).
[10] Above, paras 4–24 *et seq.*
[11] And on or after April 28, 1986 (Insolvency Act 1986, s.214(2)).

to the company's creditors.[12] It is worth underlining the point made earlier that what attracts s.214 is not mismanagement which brings a company to the brink of insolvency[13] but a failure thereafter, when the writing is on the wall, to take proper steps for the protection of creditors. Accordingly a director can be involved in wrongful trading if he is guilty of an act or omission which is not a reasonable step in minimising potential loss to creditors, even if he procures the company to cease trading as soon as he realises that insolvent liquidation is inevitable. Indeed, the premature cessation of trading might constitute wrongful trading.[14] Non-trading activity capable of attracting liability includes the failure to collect in debts due to the company, the failure to preserve asserts, the payment of excessive remuneration to directors and entry into transactions at an undervalue after cessation of trading.

Who is a "director"

12–27 For the purpose of s.214 "director" not only covers a *de jure* director, whether executive or non-executive, but also includes a shadow director[15] and *de facto* director.[16] This exposes to potential liability various types of person who might not ordinarily be thought of as directors.

(1) Controlling shareholders

12–28 In appropriate cases a controlling shareholder (including a parent company and even, it is thought a government department responsible for a company in State ownership) could be susceptible to a claim for wrongful trading if interfering too regularly in the day-to-day management of the company, as could the controller of a company that is itself a director.

---

[12] See below, paras 12–36 *et seq.*
[13] Though such mismanagement might be a breach of the director's duty of care to the company for which the liquidator could take proceedings in the company's name.
[14] See below, para.12–39.
[15] Insolvency Act 1986, s.214(7). See above, para.12–03.
[16] *Re Hydrodam (Corby) Ltd* [1994] B.C.C. 161, *per* Millet J. at 162; *Re Richborough Furniture Ltd* [1996] B.C.C. 155. See above, para.12–03. For s.214 to apply it is not necessary that the defendant should still be a director at the time of the acts or omissions which are alleged to constitute wrongful trading. It suffices that he was a director at some time when he had what is referred to below as "deemed knowledge" of the company's impending liquidation. Hence resignation after the acquisition of such knowledge does not by itself relieve him of liability.

(2) Company doctors

There is no exemption for the company doctor who is brought in to extricate the company from its difficulties and who acts as a director or shadow director;[17] indeed, the company doctor's very expertise, or professed expertise, imposes on him a high standard of care if he is to avoid liability for wrongful trading.

12–29

(3) Lending banks

A bank exercising control for the protection of its loan and security—as opposed to merely giving professional advice[18]—is capable of being a shadow director.[19] So banks should be even more careful than previously to restrict themselves to advice and not seek to dictate what cheques should be paid, what parts of the business should be sold or what policies should be adopted by the board.

12–30

Who is not a "director"

(1) Professional advisers

A person is not a shadow director solely because the directors act on advice given by him in a professional capacity,[20] *e.g.* as solicitor, banker or accountant. But the professional adviser acting as such is excluded only from the definition of a shadow director. So a solicitor or other professional man who is on the board or who is a *de facto* director does not have exemption even if he restricts himself to the giving or professional advice. Indeed, such a restriction would be an abnegation of his duties as a director under general company law as well as under s.214.

12–31

(2) Administrative receivers

It is thought that an administrative receiver would not be a shadow director merely by virtue of his status as a deemed agent of the company[21] and the exercise of his functions as administrative receiver, for these involve

12–32

---

[17] *See ReTasbian Ltd (No.3)* [1992] B.C.C. 358, where it was not disputed that a company doctor was capable of being a *de facto* or shadow director for the purpose of disqualification proceedings and it was held that there was an arguable case on the facts.

[18] See below, para.12–31.

[19] See *Re A Company (No.005009 of 1987)* (1988) B.C.C. 424, where Knox J. refused to strike out a claim against the bank, ruling that the liquidator had raised a triable issue.

[20] Insolvency Act 1986, s.251.

[21] *ibid.*, s.44(1)(a).

managing the company in right of and for the primary benefit of the debenture holder, not of the members of the company. Nor would he be a shadow director, since far from instructing the directors in the exercise of their management functions he assumes those functions himself. However, an administrative receiver who hives down the business to a specially formed subsidiary over whose board he exercises control could be vulnerable as a shadow director.[22]

(3) Administrators

12–33   For the same reason an administrator would not as such be a shadow director, nor would he be a *de facto* director, his functions being exercised for the benefit of creditors, not members.

Pleading the facts relied on to establish *de facto* or shadow directorship

12–34   Where it is contended that a person acted as *de facto* or shadow director the facts relied on as establishing this contention must be properly pleaded. For this purpose the pleadings should be careful to distinguish facts relied on to show that a person acted as *de facto* director from those relied on to show that he was a shadow director, the two types of status being essentially different.[23]

Deemed knowledge of impending liquidation

12–35   In order for a director or former director to be susceptible to an order under s.214 it has to be shown that at some time while he was a director, being a time after April 28, 1986, he knew or ought to have concluded that there was no reasonable prospect that the company would avoid going into insolvent liquidation. For brevity I will refer to this as "deemed knowledge". It is submitted that the onus of showing deemed knowledge is on the office-holder, in contrast to the onus of proof in relation to the question whether proper steps were taken to minimise loss to creditors.[24] Determination of the time at which deemed knowledge is first acquired may be crucial, in that there can be no liability for wrongful trading in respect of acts or omissions before that time. For the purposes of s.214 insolvent liquidation means liquidation at a time when the company's assets

---

[22] Lightman and Moss, The *Law of Receivers and Administrators of Companies* (3rd ed.), para.7–064.
[23] *Re Hydrodam (Corby) Ltd* [1994] B.C.C. 161 at 163.
[24] See above, para.12–25.

are insufficient for the payment of its debts and other liabilities and the expenses of the winding-up.[25] So a director who, though aware that the company is unable to pay its debts as they fall due and will be forced into winding up, reasonably believes that on liquidation its assets will be sufficient to cover its liabilities and the expenses of winding-up incurs no liability under s.214. The reason why that section adopts the balance sheet test is, of course, that if it were to be satisfied there would be no ultimate loss to creditors and no need for a contribution to the assets of the company. It is not sufficient for the application of s.214 (though it is a necessary precondition of its application) that the company in fact fails the balance sheet test of solvency on winding-up; what has also to be shown is that the director concerned knew, or ought to have concluded that it would fail that test. Inevitably there will be a temptation to use hindsight, a temptation which should be resisted.[26]

In deciding what a director "ought to have concluded" the combined objective and subjective tests prescribed by s.214(4) must be applied.

The statutory defence

The court may not make a declaration under s.214 with respect to any **12–36** person if it is satisfied that after he first acquired deemed knowledge he took every step with a view to minimising the potential loss to creditors as (assuming him to have had that knowledge) he ought to have taken.[27] The onus is on the person concerned to show that he took the proper steps, not for the liquidator to prove that he did not. So the starting position is that liability is imposed once a person has acquired deemed knowledge while a director and the company thereafter goes into insolvent liquidation. But where it is alleged that the directors continued to cause the company to trade after it should have ceased trading, no question of contribution under s.214 can arise unless it is shown that on a net basis the company was worse off at the time of commencement of the winding-up than it was at the time the directors ought to have ceased trading. The fact that the company incurred new debt after it ceased trading is not in itself relevant to a contribution claim under s.214,[28] though it will be very material to a claim for fraudulent trading if the defendant directors avoided an increase in the net deficiency by incurring fresh credit at the expense of new creditors in order to pay off existing creditors and knew when they did so that there was no reasonable prospect of the company being able to pay its debts to the new creditors when these fell due or shortly thereafter.[29]

---

[25] Insolvency Act 1986, s.214(6).
[26] See below, para.12–37.
[27] Insolvency Acy 1986, s.214(3).
[28] *Re Continental Assurance Co of London plc* [2001] B.P.I.R. 733; *Re Marini Ltd, Liquidator of Marini Ltd v Dickenson* [2004] B.C.C. 172.
[29] See above, para.12–19.

The standard of knowledge and skill required

12–37   Section 214(4), (5), provides as follows:

> "4. For the purpose of subsections (2) and (3), the facts which a director of a company ought to know or ascertain, the conclusions which he ought to reach and the steps which he ought to take are those which would be known or ascertained, or reached or taken, by a reasonably diligent person having both—
>
> > (a) the general knowledge, skill and experience that may reasonably be expected of a person carrying out the same functions as are carried out by that director in relation to the company, and
> > (b) the general knowledge, skill and experience that that director has.
>
> 5. The reference in subsection (4) to the functions carried out in relation to a company by a director of the company includes any functions which he does not carry out but which have been entrusted to him."

Several points arise in relation to the above provisions:

(1)   The test of knowledge, skill and experience is a combination of the objective and the subjective. The minimum standard is what would have been ascertained, foreseen and done by a reasonably diligent person carrying out (or entrusted with) the same functions as those entrusted to the director concerned. A director who falls below this minimum standard cannot invoke the statutory defence even if he did his best. In deciding whether the minimum standard was observed regard must be had to the particular company and its business, so that "the general knowledge, skill and experience postulated will be much less extensive in a small company in a modest way of business, with simple accounting procedures and requirements, than it will be in a large company with sophisticated procedures."[30] But observance of the minimum standard is not necessarily sufficient. The director must also meet such higher standard as is appropriate to his own general knowledge, skill and experience. So while the minimum standard does not necessarily call for particular expertise or skill, only that of a reasonably diligent person, a real professional possessing a high degree of general knowledge, skill and experience must use it and act accordingly.

(2)   The test of proper mitigating behaviour—"every step"—seems very stringent but when read with "reasonably diligent person" may mean no more than "every reasonable step".

---

[30] *Re Produce Marketing Consortium Ltd* (1989) 5 B.C.C. 569, *per* Knox J. at 594.

(3)   While there is no immunity for non-executive directors as such, prima facie a non-executive director is not expected to possess the knowledge and skill of an executive director, still less to give his continuous time and attention to the affairs of the company.[31]

(4)   The knowledge and skill required of an executive director depends on the nature of the functions entrusted to him. Thus a director in charge of marketing and sales cannot be expected to possess the financial knowledge and skills of a finance director.

Finally, the court should not be too astute to find the directors at fault without taking account of the difficult choices that frequently confront them.

"An overall point which needs to be kept in mind throughout is that, whenever a company is in financial trouble and the directors have a difficult decision to make whether to close down and go into liquidation, or whether instead to trade on and hope to turn the corner, they can be in a real and unenviable dilemma. On the one hand, if they decide to trade on but things do not work out and the company, later rather sooner, goes into liquidation, they may find themselves in the situation of the respondents in this case—being sued for wrongful trading. On the other hand, if the directors decide to close down immediately and cause the company to go into an early liquidation, although they are not at risk of being sued for wrongful trading,[32] they are at risk of being criticised on other grounds. A decision to close down will almost certainly mean that the ensuing liquidation will be an insolvent one. Apart from anything else liquidations are expensive operations, and in addition debtors are commonly obstructive about paying their debts to a company which is in liquidation. Many creditors of the company from a time before the liquidation are likely to find that their debts do not get paid in full. They will complain bitterly that the directors shut down too soon; they will say that the directors ought to have had more courage and kept going. If they had done, so the complaining creditors will say, the company probably would have survived and all of its debts would have been paid. Ceasing to trade and liquidating too soon can be stigmatised as the cowards' way out."[33]

---

[31] See above, para.12–06.

[32] The basis of this statement is not clear. There seems no reason why ceasing to trade when the company, though insolvent, has a manifestly viable business could not constitute wrongful trading, though no doubt this situation would be unusual. See above, para.12–26.

[33] *Re Continental Assurance Co of London plc* [2001] B.P.I.R. 733, *per* Park J. at para.281.

No relief under section 727

12–38 It has been held that a director who engages in wrongful trading contrary to s.214 of the Insolvency Act 1986 cannot obtain relief under s.727 of the Companies Act 1985, since the subjective approach of s.727 is inconsistent with the objective duty imposed by s.214(4) of the 1986 Act.[34]

How to avoid liability for wrongful trading

12–39 What practical advice should be given to a director as to the steps he should take to minimise the risk of being found guilty of wrongful trading. Here is my list of 12 points for survival!

(1) Do not assume that the safest course is to stop trading. You have to take every step that can properly be expected of you to minimise loss to creditors. You can be faulted just as much for a premature cessation of trading as for continuing to trade while insolvent. This makes it essential to obtain competent outside advice as to whether to stop trading or continue.

(2) Consider carefully with your fellow directors whether the business is viable. If it is, insist on the preparation[35] of:
  (a) a business review;
  (b) a sensible and constructive programme to reduce expenditure, increase income, ensure an adequate cash flow and restore the company to profitable trading, disposing of unprofitable or marginal parts of the business and dismissing staff who are surplus to the company's needs or are not doing their job.

(3) Insist on frequent board meetings.

(4) Make sure that there is a proper distribution of responsibility within the company.

(5) Ensure that the accounts are being properly kept and up to date or if not, that prompt steps are being taken to do so, with outside help being brought in as and when necessary.

(6) See that the board regularly receives an updated budget and a full, accurate and up-to-date picture of the company's trading, financial and cash flow position.

---

[34] *Re Produce Marketing Consortium Ltd* [1989] B.C.L.C. 513.
[35] With any necessary professional help. See below.

(7)   Get the company to take appropriate outside professional advice on suitable remedial measures.

(8)   Keep major creditors regularly informed and enlist their support for the continued operation of the company where this is likely to be of benefit to the general body of creditors. In this connection it is just as important to have the support of major unsecured creditors as of secured creditors, for it is the former who are most likely to suffer loss and whose support makes it easier for you to show subsequently that you took every step available to you to minimise loss to creditors.

(9)   Ensure that you are kept fully in the picture and, so far as possible, that all directors agree on what needs to be done.

(10) Consider the advisability of putting the company into administration in order to give it breathing space and prevent action by individual creditors. Such appointment has the further advantage of ending your management responsibilities, though you still have a duty to co-operate with the office-holder.[36]

(11) Insist that all recommendations for remedial action made by the directors (and particularly by you), together with your dissent from any unwise actions or inactivity advocated by your fellow directors, are fully minuted or otherwise placed on record, *e.g.* by the circulation of a memorandum to the other directors.

(12) If you are in the minority and your recommendations are repeatedly rejected, so that the company is getting deeper into the mire, resign and record your reasons for doing so in a letter. But resignation is very much the last resort. A director who simply resigns without having taken every step he should have done to minimise loss to creditors will not escape liability. So don't resign before you have gone as far as you can in getting things put right.[37]

Wrongful trading and misfeasance

There is no direct relationship between the remedies of the liquidator for wrongful trading and for misfeasance; he is entitled to pursue either or both. But the choice of remedy may have significant effects on the   **12–40**

---

[36] Failure to do this is an offence (Insolvency Act 1986, s.235).
[37] See *Secretary of Slate for Trade and Industry v Arif* [1996] B.C.C. 586 and *Re C.S. Holidays Ltd* [1997] B.C.C. 172, cases on the position of a director for disqualification purposes where he has resigned after his recommendations went unheeded by the rest of the board. In *Secretary of State for Trade and Industry v Taylor* [1997] 1 W.L.R. 407 Chadwick J. rejected the contention that a director's failure to resign even after his views have gone unheeded was necessarily unfit to be concerned in the management of a company, though he did indicate (at 415) that a person who, having ceased to exert any influence over his colleagues, remained on the Board for no purpose other than to draw his director's fees or preserve his status might well be found so lacking in appreciation of his duties as to be unfit to be concerned in the management of a company.

creditors. As we have seen, misfeasance is a remedy actionable in right of the company and any money or property recovered forms part of its general assets and is therefore capable of being captured by a prior assignment or charge covering future property. By contrast, sums paid under a contribution order in respect of wrongful trading are held for the creditors generally, and though preferential creditors have a prior claim to them they do not fall within a prior assignment or charge since they are not assets of the company.[38] Three questions now arise. First, to what extent does a recovery for misfeasance under s.212 reduce the amount of the director's liability under s.214?[39] Secondly, to what extent does a recovery under s.214 reduce his liability under s.212? Thirdly, where recovery under one section does not affect the amount recoverable under the other but the director's assets are insufficient to meet both claims in full, how should the claims and recoveries be dealt with?

(1) Effect on section 214 claim of recovery under section 212

12–41 Recovery from a director under s.212 will, or course, *pro tanto* reduce the company's net indebtedness, but it does not follow from this that the director's separate liability for wrongful trading will fall by the same amount or, indeed, at all. In considering the effect of a s.212 recovery on the amount chargeable to a delinquent director under s.214 two factors have to be taken into account. The first is whether the loss caused by the misfeasance is also the loss, or part of the loss, embodied in the claim under s.214 or is entirely unconnected. It is clear that loss resulting from a misfeasance committed before the commencement of the director's duty under s.214 to take steps to minimise loss cannot form part of the s.214 claim, so that no duplication is involved in allowing full recovery under both sections. Where, on the other hand, the misfeasance occurred after the start of the director's duty under s.214, it will usually constitute a breach of that duty as well as a misfeasance under s.212. In this case the claims under ss.212 and 214 will be duplicated, and any recovery under s.212 will at the same time reduce the loss chargeable to the director under s.214.[40] The second factor is that a director's liability to contribute under s.214 cannot exceed the amount of the net deficiency in the company's assets available for creditors. To the extent that recovery for unconnected loss under s.212 reduces the net deficiency below the amount of the loss caused by the director's breach of s.214 his liability under that section will abate. Where

---

[38] *Re Oasis Merchandising Ltd* [1997] 1 All E.R. 1009. See below, para.12–46.
[39] The question was raised in *Re Purpoint Ltd* [1991] B.C.L.C. 491, where the application under s.214 was stood over. The outcome is not known.
[40] This was the case in *Re DKG Contractors Ltd* [1990] B.C.C. 903, where it was rightly held that recoveries under ss.212 and 239 were to be taken as *pro tanto* satisfying the order under s.214.

this is not the case the recovery under s.212 will not reduce the director's liability for unconnected loss under s.214. Two examples will make this clear.

Example 1

(a)	Amount recovered under s.212:	£100,000
(b)	Unconnected loss due to breach of s.214:	£ 75,000
(c)	Net deficiency of assets before s.212 recovery:	£150,000
(d)	Maximum liability under s.214 ((c)–(a)):	£ 50,000

In this example the loss caused by the director through his breach of s.214 (£75,000) is partially offset by the recovery under s.212, which reduces the net deficiency, and thus the director's maximum s.214 liability, to £50,000.

Example 2

(a)	Amount recovered under s.212:	£100,000
(b)	Unconnected loss due to breach of s.214:	£ 75,000
(c)	Net deficiency of assets before s.212 recovery:	£500,000
(d)	Maximum liability under s.214:	£ 75,000

In this example the net deficiency remaining after the recovery under s.212 (*i.e.* £500,000-£100,000 = £400,000) still exceeds the maximum contribution liability under s.214, which accordingly is not reduced by the s.212 recovery.

In summary, a s.212 recovery will reduce the director's maximum liability under s.214 only to the extent that (a) the s.212 claim also forms part of the loss for which the director is answerable under s.214 or (b) the s.212 recovery reduces the net deficiency to an amount below the loss attributable to the breach of s.214.

(2) Effect on section 212 claim of recovery under section 214

It will be clear from what has been said above that there cannot be a double **12–42** recovery for the same loss. To the extent that the misfeasance also constitutes a breach of s.214 the sum recovered under s.214 goes in reduction of any amount otherwise recoverable under s.212. Where, however, the two claims are entirely unconnected, as where the s.212 claim relates to a misappropriation of the company's property committed before the commencement of the director's duty under s.214, recovery under s.214 does not in any way reduce the amount recoverable under s.212. This is so even if the effect of the s.214 recovery is that there is no longer a deficiency of assets as regards creditors, for the members of the company still have an interest in the remedying of the misfeasance.[41]

---

[41] A contributory may, with leave of the court, take misfeasance proceedings under s.212 even where he will not benefit from any order made (Insolvency Act 1986, s.212(5)), but where he does have an interest his case for being given leave where the liquidator does not wish to pursue the claim himself is obviously much stronger. In practice, claims under the two sections would normally be made concurrently.

(3) Priorities

12–43   So far, we have assumed that where the claims under ss.212 and 214 are unconnected, the delinquent director has enough assets to meet in full the claims under both sections. Where this is not the case, the question arises which claim should be given priority. Members of the company will not, of course, have any interest in recoveries until creditors have been paid in full. The contest is potentially between the general body of creditors, for whose benefit recoveries under s.214 enure, and debenture holders asserting security rights over recoveries under s.212, which as we have seen form part of the assets of the company. No hard and fast rule can be laid down. Under both sections an order is discretionary and it is for the court to consider what best meets the justice of the case. In the absence of any special factors the most appropriate solution would seem to be to respect the debenture holder's rights as regards assets recovered in a proprietary claim and to divide the total sum awarded in respect of the director's personal liability between the two heads of claim in the proportion which each bears to the total.

7. CIVIL SANCTIONS FOR IMPROPER TRADING

The five sanctions

12–44   The civil sanctions for improper trading are the same for fraudulent trading as for wrongful trading. They are[42]:

(1)   A declaration by the court that the defendant is to be liable to make such contribution (if any) to the company's assets as the court thinks fit.[43]

(2)   Such further directions as the court thinks fit for giving effect to the declaration, including provision for the director's contribution to be charged on any debt or obligation due to him from the company[44] or

---

[42] Insolvency Act 1986, ss.213(2), 214(1), 215(2)–(4); Company Directors Disqualification Act 1986, ss.4(1)(a), 10. These provisions relate to fraudulent trading and wrongful trading. As to the personal liability of the director of a company trading under a prohibited name, see *ibid*, s.217, and above, para.12–04.

[43] This claim survives the death of the delinquent director and is payable out of his estate (*Re Sherborne Associates Ltd* [1995] B.C.C. 40).

[44] Insolvency Act 1986, s.215(2)(a). This form of security had at one time been thought conceptually impossible (*Re Charge Card Services Ltd* [1989] Ch. 497), but now considered by the House of Lords to be unobjectionable (*Re Bank of Credit and Commerce International S.A.* [1998] A.C. 214. Interestingly, neither the arguments advanced in the courts nor the judgments in successive decisions ever drew attention to s.215(2)(a). See further Roy Goode, *Legal Problems of Credit and Security* (3rd ed.), para.3–12.

on any mortgage or charge or any interest in a mortgage or charge on assets of the company held by or vested in him, or any person on his behalf, or any person claiming as assignee from or through the person liable or any person acting on his behalf who is not a bona fide assignee for value and without notice.

(3) Such further order from time to time as may be necessary for enforcing such charge.

(4) In the case of a director who is a creditor of the company, subordination of his debt, wholly or in part, to all other debts of the company and interest thereon.

(5) disqualification.[45]

The court's power under s.727 of the Companies Act 1985 to grant relief to a delinquent director is not exercisable in relation to claims for wrongful trading under s.214 of the Insolvency Act.[46]

The court's approach to contribution orders

In *Re Produce Marketing Consortium Ltd*[47] Knox J. provided an instructive analysis of the approach the court should adopt in deciding on the level of contribution a director should be ordered to pay in the event of a finding of wrongful trading. Two alternative views were canvassed before the learned judge. The first, contended for by counsel for the defendant directors, was that s.214 is both compensatory and penal. Insofar as it was compensatory the sum ordered to be paid should not exceed the loss to creditors caused by the wrongful trading complained of, insofar as it was penal it should reflect the degree of culpability of the director concerned, so that a director who had done nearly everything he should have done but not quite should be treated more leniently than a director who had done nothing to minimise loss to creditors. On this view the court should exercise its discretion so as to ensure that the sum ordered to be contributed did not exceed the lesser of the loss suffered by creditors from the wrongful trading and the sum that it would be appropriate to order as a punitive measure having regard to the director's efforts to put matters right. The alternative view was that s.215 is purely compensatory and that in principle directors found guilty of wrongful trading should be ordered to make good the loss thereby caused to creditors, without regard to the degree of their culpability. Knox J. concluded that the latter was in principle the correct

12–45

---

[45] See below, paras 12–58 *et seq.*
[46] *Re Produce Marketing Consortium Ltd* (1989) 5 B.C.C. 399.
[47] (1989) 5 B.C.C. 569.

test, though it would be wrong to exclude entirely from consideration the degree of the director's culpability, having regard to the wide discretion conferred on the court. In fixing the total contribution of the two directors at £75,000 Knox J. took into account a range of factors, including on the one side the fact that the case was one of failure to appreciate what should have been clear, rather than of deliberate wrong-doing, and on the other side the fact that there had been some positive untruths by the directors, solemn warnings by the auditor were ignored and the directors had reduced the indebtedness to the bank, which was a secured creditor, at the expense of unsecured creditors, and it was the latter who should benefit from the way in which the court's discretion was exercised.

Since the above decision it has been held by the Court of Appeal that even in the case of proceedings under s.213 for fraudulent trading no punitive element may be included in fixing the contribution payable by the defendant;[48] *a fortiori* no such element can be included in a contribution order under s.214.

Application of recoveries

12–46 Contribution orders under s.214 of the Insolvency Act are intended for the benefit of creditors generally and recoveries, though payable to the company through its liquidator, do not constitute an asset of the company.[49] Three consequences ensue from this principle. First, sums recovered under a contribution order do not go to enhance a prior assignment or security in favour of a debenture holder but form part of the general assets of the company to be applied in the statutory order of priority.[50] Secondly, the court has no power to order payment direct to creditors or to a particular class of creditor, and creditors whose debts were incurred before the wrongful trading have no greater entitlement than those whose debts were incurred subsequently.[51]Thirdly, since the liquidator's statutory power of sale[52] is confined to sale of "any of the company's property" and since the cause of action under s.214 and the fruits of such an action are not the property of the company, they are incapable of assignment by a liquidator, and any such assignment is void for champerty.[53]

When should a liquidator take proceedings for wrongful trading?

12–47 The mere fact that a liquidator believes wrongful trading to have taken place does not mean that he should necessarily institute proceedings under s.214. There are several factors he will wish to consider before embarking

---

[48] *Morphitis v Bernascon* [2003] B.C.C. 540. See above, para.12–21.
[49] *Re Oasis Merchandising Ltd* [1998] Ch. 170; *Re M.C. Bacon Ltd* [1991] Ch. 127.
[50] *ibid*.
[51] *Re Purpoint Ltd* [1991] B.C.L.C. 491.
[52] Under the Insolvency Act 1986, Sch.4, para.6.
[53] *Re Oasis Merchandising Services Ltd*, above, in which it was also held that the residual power contained in Sch.4, para.13, did not assist.

on the labour and expense of an application under that section. Firstly, how strong is the evidence and how easy will it be to prove wrongful trading? In some cases the evidence may be crystal clear, in other cases it may depend on uncertain inferences of fact based on incomplete documents and the possibly faulty recollection by witnesses of events long past. Secondly, is the loss attributable to the wrongful trading sufficiently substantial to make the proceedings worthwhile? Thirdly, what degree of culpability is involved? It is true that the principal function of a contribution order is not to act as a penal sanction but to compensate for loss;[54] even so, the court may feel disinclined to make a significant contribution order where the remedial steps taken by the director fall only marginally short of what s.214 requires. Fourthly, is the prospective defendant worth powder and shot? There is little point seeking a contribution order when the defendant has not means to meet it. Finally, what is the attitude of the creditors? The liquidator may be reluctant to institute proceedings if he cannot carry at least the major creditors with him, and they may be reluctant to throw good money after bad. All these are matters which the liquidator will wish to take into account before spending the creditors' money.

8. DISQUALIFICATION OF DIRECTORS: GENERAL CONSIDERATIONS

Introduction

The various statutory provisions relating to the disqualification of directors—an important sanction for improper trading and for other culpable behaviour—are now consolidated in the Company Directors Disqualification Act 1986, as amended by the Insolvency Act 2000 and the Enterprise Act 2002. The Act provides ten separate grounds for disqualification.[55] As regards seven of these, disqualification is in the discretion of the court. In two cases disqualification is mandatory, namely (1) under s.6 of the Act, where the court is satisfied that a person against whom disqualification proceedings is or has been a director of a company which has at any time become insolvent and his conduct as a director makes him unfit to be concerned in the management of a company, and (2) under s.9A of the Act, where the company of which he is a director commits a breach of competition law and the court considers that his conduct as a director

12–48

---

[54] *Re Produce Marketing Consortium Ltd*, above, n.46.
[55] The subject of disqualification goes well beyond the scope of insolvency law and is here treated in outline only and with a specific focus on disqualification arising from a company's insolvency. The leading textbook is Adrian Walters and Malcolm Davis-White, *Directors' Disqualification & Bankruptcy Restrictions* (2nd ed. 2005).

makes him unfit to be concerned in the management of a company. In the tenth case, failure to pay under a county court administration order, disqualification is automatic.[56] Disqualification under s.6 is by far the most common in practice and is the focus of the present chapter.

Policy considerations

12–49 The history of the disqualification provisions[57] reflects the concern of successive governments on the one hand to prevent abuse of the privilege of limited liability and to secure standards of responsible management and protect those dealing with companies and on the other to avoid steps so draconian that they would discourage entrepreneurial activity. Any business undertaking entails risk, and inevitably a number of businesses will be unsuccessful for a variety of reasons, ranging from managerial incompetence or fraud to under-capitalisation and loss of market share through competition. The insolvency of a company has therefore to be seen not as a failure of the market but on the contrary as a necessary consequence of market forces. It is therefore important not to set standards so high that people of ability and drive whose activities could contribute to the national economy are not deterred from forming companies or becoming directors of companies.[58]

The meaning of disqualification

12–50 An order for disqualification of a director means that the person disqualified must not without leave of the court:

(a) be a director of a company, or

(b) be a liquidator or administrator of a company, or

(c) be a receiver or manager of a person's property, or

(d) in any way, whether directly or indirectly, be concerned or take part in the promotion, formation or management of a company,

for a specified period beginning with the date of the order.[59]So disqualification makes it as unlawful without leave of the court to act as a *de facto* or a shadow director as it is to act as a director who is (apart from the order) duly appointed.

---

[56] Insolvency Act 1986, s.12.
[57] See Walters and Davis-White, *op. cit.*, paras 1–25 *et seq.*; *Re Pantmaenog Timber Co Ltd* [2004] 1 A.C. 158.
[58] For a full discussion, see Walters and Davis-White, *op. cit.*, paras 1–32 *et seq.*
[59] Company Directors Disqualification Act 1986, s.1.

Discretionary, mandatory and automatic disqualification

The grounds for disqualification fall into three groups: those on which   **12–51**
disqualification is within the discretion of the court; those on which the
court is obliged to make a disqualification order; and those where
disqualification is automatic and is not dependent on a court order. In cases
within the second (mandatory) category the court retains its discretion to
grant leave to carry on any of the activities referred to above despite the
disqualification,[60] though obviously an order giving leave ought not to be
made in such sweeping terms as to render the disqualification nugatory.
There is no power to limit the disqualification itself to a given class of
company, *e.g.* by disqualifying a person from acting as director of a public
company but not of a private company.[61]

It cannot be said that there is a uniform policy underlying the distinction
between discretionary and mandatory disqualification. One might have
thought that in every case the question should be whether the director's
conduct makes him unfit to be concerned in the management of a company,
yet that is not a pre-condition of disqualification under ss.2, 3, 4, 5 or 10[62];
only under ss.6 (insolvency) and 8 (investigation of the company) is
unfitness made a prerequisite of disqualification. This indicates that disqualification is not simply a means of removing from involvement in
corporate management those considered unfit for it but is also seen as an
inducement to those acting as directors to fulfil their statutory obligations, a
deterrent against wrongdoing and a punishment for serious misbehaviour.
Again, one might think that where the court is satisfied that the director
concerned is unfit to be concerned in the management of a company
disqualification should be mandatory, yet that is not the case as regards
disqualification proceedings under s.8[63] or s.10.[64] The courts themselves
have in several cases declined to disqualify a person held unfit to be
concerned in the management of the company, usually on the basis that his
conduct, though reprehensible, was not so serious as to justify such a heavy
sanction.

Who can be disqualified

The short title of the Act refers to disqualification from acting as a director,   **12–52**
not to the status of those who are being disqualified. In general a
disqualification order may therefore be made against any person, whether

---

[60] See para.12–71.
[61] *R. v Goodman* [1992] B.C.C. 625 at 627.
[62] Dealing respectively with conviction of an indictable offence, persistent breaches of
companies legislation, fraud in a winding-up, convictions for at least three summary
offences, and participation in wrongful trading.
[63] Disqualification after investigation of the company on behalf of the Secretary of State.
[64] Participation in wrongful trading.

or he is or has acted as a director, if he is guilty or one of the statutory grounds for disqualification. This is true of all the discretionary grounds. But the provisions for mandatory disqualification on the ground of unfitness are confined to those who are or have been directors of a company which has become insolvent.[65]

Period of disqualification

12–53 The maximum period of disqualification is either five years or 15 years, depending on the ground of disqualification. Where it is unfitness to act, the Act sets not only a maximum period of 15 years but a minimum period of two years[66]; in other cases there is no prescribed minimum.

Grounds for discretionary disqualification

12–54 There are seven grounds upon which the court has discretion to order disqualification.

(1) Conviction for an indictable offence (whether the conviction is on indictment or summarily) in connection with the promotion, formation, management or liquidation of a company, or with the receivership or management of a company's property.[67] Management is not confined to internal management but includes external activities, *e.g.* the fraudulent raising of finance,[68] and, indeed, any offence having some relevant factual connection with the management of the company.[69] Moreover, it is not necessary that the company's affairs be mismanaged; conducting the business competently but without legal authorisation is within the statutory provisions.[70]

(2) Persistent default in relation to the provisions of the companies legislation requiring any return, account or other document to be filed with, delivered or sent, or a notice of any matter to be given to the registrar of companies.[71] Persistent default is conclusively presumed

---

[65] Company Directors Disqualification Act 1986, s.6.
[66] *ibid.*, s.6(4).
[67] *ibid.*, s.2(1).
[68] *R. v Corbin* (1984) 6 Cr. App. R. (S) 17; *R. v Austen* (1985) 1 B.C.C. 99, 528.
[69] *R. v Goodman* [1992] B.C.C. 625 (conviction for insider trading under the Company Securities (Inside Dealing) Act 1985).
[70] *R. v Georgiou* (1988) 4 B.C.C. 322.
[71] Company Directors Disqualification Act 1986, s.3(1). By "companies legislation" is meant the Companies Act 1985, the Companies (Consequential Provisions) Act 1985, Parts I to VII and ss.411, 413, 414, 416 and 417 of the Insolvency Act 1985. Relevant sections of the Companies Act include ss.221, 222, 227, 288, 352, 363-365, 399 and 415. Relevant sections of the Insolvency Act include ss.15(7), 18(4), 21(2), 24(6), 27(6), 38(1), 43(5), 45(4), 89(3), 106(3), 192(1), 201(4), 203(5) and 205(6).

by showing that in the five years ending with the date of the application the person concerned has been adjudged guilty (whether or not on the same occasion) of three or more defaults in relation to the above provisions.[72] It has been held that "persistent" connotes some degree of continuance or repetition, whether by continuing or repeating the same default or by a series of different defaults.[73] Culpability, however, is not an essential ingredient, though obviously relevant to any decision whether to disqualify and the length of any disqualification.[74] The court can take all circumstances into account, including the damaging effect of a disqualification order on employees.[75]

(3) The offence of fraudulent trading (whether or not convicted[76]).

(4) Other fraud in relation to the company or breach of duty, as officer, liquidator, receiver or manager.[77]

(5) Summary conviction for failure to file returns, etc., where during the previous five years the person concerned has three or more default orders or convictions.[78]

(6) A finding of unfitness to be concerned in the management of a company, following a statutory investigation.[79]

(7) Participation in wrongful trading.[80]

Discretionary disqualification and contribution orders

In *R Holmes*[81] the Court of Appeal held that it was inconsistent to make an **12–55** order for compensation under s.35 of the Powers of Criminal Courts Act 1973 and at the same time to make a disqualification order, thereby depriving the defendant of the best means of earning the money with which to pay the compensation. However, it is thought that the court was addressing the facts of the particular case and cannot have intended to lay

---

[72] Company Directors Disqualification Act 1986, s.3(2). As to when a person is to be treated as adjudged guilty of a default, see s.3(3).
[73] *Re Arctic Engineering Ltd* (1985) 1 B.C.C. 99, 563.
[74] *ibid.*
[75] *ibid.*, where Hoffmann J. held there had been persistent default by a liquidator in filing returns but declined to make a disqualification order on the ground that the liquidator in question was neither dishonest nor incompetent and a disqualification order would have very serious consequences for him, his employees and his clients.
[76] Insolvency Act 1986, s.4(1)(a).
[77] *ibid.*, s.4(1)(b).
[78] *ibid.*, s.5.
[79] *ibid.*, s.8.
[80] *ibid.*, s.10.
[81] [1991] B.C.C. 394.

down a general rule of this kind, for the same considerations would apply to the disqualification of a director against whom a contribution order is made under s.214 of the Insolvency Act 1986 in respect of wrongful trading,[82] yet s.10(1) of the Company Directors Disqualification Act 1986 expressly provides for disqualification in addition to a contribution order.

Ground for mandatory disqualification order

12–56   There are two grounds on which disqualification is mandatory, namely unfitness to be concerned in the management of a company where the person concerned is or has been a director of a company that has at any time become insolvent[83] and breach of competition law on the part of a person whose conduct makes him unfit to be concerned in the management of a company.[84]

Automatic disqualification

12–57   A person is automatically disqualified from acting without leave of the court as director of, or directly or indirectly taking part in or being concerned in the promotion, formation or management of, a company, where he is an undischarged bankrupt[85] or where as a result or his default in payment under a county court administration order the court revokes that order.[86]

9. DISQUALIFICATION FOR UNFITNESS OF DIRECTOR OF INSOLVENT COMPANY

The statutory provisions

12–58   Under s.6 of the Company Directors Disqualification Act the court is obliged to impose a disqualification order where it is satisfied—

(a) that a person is or had been a director of a company which has at any time become insolvent (whether while he was a director or subsequently), and

(b) that his conduct as a director of the company (either taken alone or taken together with his conduct as a director of any other company

---

[82] See above, paras 12–44 *et seq.*
[83] Company Directors Disqualification Act 1986, s.6. See below.
[84] *ibid.*, s.9A.
[85] *ibid.*, s.11.
[86] *ibid.*, s.12.

or companies) makes him unfit to be concerned in the management of a company.

For the purpose of the above provisions:

(1) "director" includes a shadow director[87] and a *de facto* director;[88] and

(2) a company becomes insolvent if it goes into liquidation when its assets are insufficient to pay its debts and other liabilities and the expenses of the winding-up or if an administration order is made in relation to it or an administrative receiver of the company is appointed.[89]

Burden and standard of proof

The burden of proof is on the Secretary of State; the standard of proof is not the standard in criminal cases ("beyond reasonable doubt") but the civil standard, the balance of probabilities, a flexible standard which requires that the graver the allegation the heavier the burden of showing the truth of the matters alleged.[90]   **12–59**

Reporting requirements and their significance

In order for the Secretary of State to be able to act against directors considered to be unfit to be concerned in the management of a company the Secretary of State has to have adequate information about their misconduct which he can place before the court. To that end s.7(3) provides that where it appears to the office-holder[91] that the conditions of s.6(1) are satisfied as respects a person who is or has been a director of the company the office-holder is required forthwith to report the matter to the Secretary of State. Section 7 is buttressed by the Insolvent Companies (Reports on Conduct of Directors) Rules 1996,[92] which are confined to companies in voluntary winding-up but are in practice followed by the Official Receiver in a compulsory winding-up. The Rules require the office-holder to furnish to the Secretary of State reports and returns in a prescribed form.[93] Thus a liquidator will either send a report under s.7(3) of the Act[94] setting out   **12–60**

---

[87] *ibid.*, ss.6(3), 22(4).
[88] *Re Lo-Line Electric Motors Ltd* [1988] Ch. 477; and see above, para.12–03.
[89] Company Directors Disqualification Act 1986, s.6(2).
[90] *R. v Verby Print for Advertising Ltd* [1998] B.C.C. 652.
[91] The official receiver in a compulsory winding-up, the liquidator in a voluntary winding-up, the administrator in an administration and the administrative receiver in an administrative receivership (s.7(3)). See also para.12–74 as to reporting by officers of courts.
[92] SI 1996/1909, as amended.
[93] Commonly known as a "D" form, the forms being numbered D1, D2, etc.
[94] A "D1" report.

details of the conduct which in his view makes the director unfit for the purpose of s.6(1) or, if no such report has been submitted before the expiry of six months from the relevant date, a return[95] giving prescribed information about the company but stating that the liquidator has not become aware of any information which would require him to make a report under s.7(3) of the Act.

It will be evident that the success of the disqualification provisions to a considerable degree stands or falls by the effectiveness of the reporting requirements and procedures. A report on the Insolvency Services Agency produced by the National Audit Office in 1993,[96] while showing that directors of companies in compulsory liquidation were more likely to escape proceedings than directors of companies in voluntary liquidation (which might be thought to indicate that the Agency was under-resourced and/or relatively ineffective), also contained some disturbing figures about the incompleteness of reports, and in particular the failure to submit documentation and evidence sufficient to justify the institution of disqualification proceedings. Detailed research conducted by Professor Sally Wheeler[97] probed beneath the surface to examine the decision-making process.

"Firms organise their liquidation work into a work pack which then provides temporal triggers for submitting any official documents to the DTI, the Registrar of Companies and creditors. Disqualification is added into this system. It is dealt with by means of a standard form checklist which either the insolvency practitioner completes or the director completes and then the insolvency practitioner adds any information he may have. The standard forms ask for positive or negative answers to a series of questions the legislation invites the court to consider when hearing an application for disqualification. This information is then used to fill in the conduct report. The character of the decision that is reached is evident from the way in which the information is collected; it displays a procedural concern rather than a substantive evaluation."[98]

This is a phenomenon with which observers in other fields of regulation, both in this country and abroad, have become familiar, namely the preoccupation with the observance of procedures rather substance. The concern is whether the form has been filled in correctly rather than with the substantive facts which it reveals.[99]

---

[95] A "D2" return.

[96] *The Insolvency Executive Agency: Company Directors Disqualification* (HMSO, 1993).

[97] See Sally Wheeler, "Directors' disqualification: insolvency practitioners and the decision-making process," (1995) 15 *Legal Studies* 283.

[98] Wheeler, *loc. cit.*, at p.298.

[99] A well-known humorist, on arriving in a foreign country, had his attention drawn to the fact that he had failed to insert his occupation on the immigration form. He promptly complied, inserting the word "smuggler," and was then waved through by the immigration officer, the documentation now being in perfect order.

But there are indications that over the past few years the problem has been taken seriously. One manifestation of this is the steady increase in the number of disqualification proceedings and of reported decisions concerning disqualification.

Procedure

Under several of the above provisions of the Company, Directors Disqualification Act,[1] the court has power to order disqualification of its own motion. But disqualification on the ground of unfitness to act requires an application to that end by the Secretary of State or, in the case of a company in compulsory winding-up, the official receiver if so directed by the Secretary of State.[2] There is no time limit for making application except in cases under s.6, where the time limit is two years beginning with the day on which the company became insolvent, unless the court gives leave to bring proceedings late.[3] Not less than 10 days' notice of the intention to apply for a disqualification order must be given to the person against whom the order is sought,[4] but the Court of Appeal has held that this requirement is directory, not mandatory, so that failure to give the requisite notice is a procedural irregularity which does not vitiate the proceedings.[5] Proceedings on an application for a disqualification order are governed by the Insolvent Companies (Disqualification of Unfit Directors) Proceedings Rules 1987[6] and by the Disqualification Practice Direction.[7]

The court has no power to dispense with proceedings by means of a consent order. In every case the court has itself to be satisfied that there is sufficient evidence of unfitness to act as a director before it makes a disqualification order.[8] However, in *Re Carecraft Construction Ltd*[9] Ferris J. approved a summary procedure by which the parties to disqualification proceedings can avoid a full-scale hearing by placing before the court an agreed statement of facts concerning unfitness, coupled with some evidence of unfitness on which the court can act. This procedure became enshrined in the Disqualification Practice Direction,[10] under which parties desiring to make an application under the *Carecraft* procedure are required to inform

12–61

---

[1] In particular, ss.2, 4, 5 and 10, and possibly also s.3.
[2] *ibid.*, s.7(1).
[3] *ibid.*, s.7(2).
[4] *ibid.*, s.16(1).
[5] *Secretary of State for Trade and Industry v Langridge* [1991] Ch. 402, Nourse L.J. dissenting; [1991] B.C.C. 148 *sub. nom. Re Cedac Ltd, Secretary of State for Trade and Industry v Langridge.*
[6] SI 1987/2023, as amended.
[7] Practice Direction: Directors' Disqualification Proceedings [1999] B.C.C. 717.
[8] [1994] 1 W.L.R. 172.
[9] [1994] 1 W.L.R. 172.
[10] Above, n.7, r.13.

the court immediately, obtain a date for the hearing and, except in simple cases or where the court otherwise directs, submit a written statement containing in respect of each defendant any material facts which (for the purposes of the application) are either agreed or not opposed (by either party) and specify in writing the period of disqualification which the parties accept that the agreed or unopposed facts justify (*e.g.* 4 to 6 years) or bracket (*i.e.* 2 to 5 years; 6 to 10 years; 11 to 15 years) into which they will submit the case falls.[11] However, the *Carecraft* procedure has been largely superseded by the procedure for statutory undertakings given to the Secretary of State as described below.

Statutory undertakings

12–62 Useful though it has been, the *Carecraft* procedure involved time and expense which both parties and the courts considered burdensome and unnecessary. When the Secretary of State and the parties were content to agree on the terms of disqualification it seemed pointless to require them to go to the court for approval. It is true that the Secretary of State, in lieu of initiating or continuing disqualification proceedings, could accept an undertaking by the director concerned not to be concerned in the management of a company for a specified period, but in various respects such an undertaking was weaker than a disqualification order.[12] Accordingly s.6 of the Insolvency Act 2000 inserted a new s.7(2A) into the Company Directors Disqualification Act empowering the Secretary of State to accept a disqualification undertaking in lieu of applying for or proceeding with an application for a disqualification order. A disqualification undertaking is an undertaking that the person concerned:

(a) will not be a director of a company, act as receiver of a company's property or in any way, whether directly or indirectly, be concerned or take part in the promotion, formation or management of a company unless (in each case) he has the leave of the court, and

(b) will not act as an insolvency practitioner.[13]

The content of the undertaking thus corresponds exactly to that prescribed for a disqualification order by s.1 of the Act, and the maximum and minimum period of disqualification is likewise the same.[14] The Secretary of State is not obliged to require an agreed statement of the facts rendering the disqualified party unfit but in practice will not normally accept an

---

[11] Practice Direction, paras 13.1, 13.2.
[12] See Walters and Davis-White, *op. cit.*, para.9–12.
[13] Company Directors Disqualification Act 1986, s.1A, inserted by the Insolvency Act 2000, s.6.
[14] *ibid.*, s.1A(2).

undertaking without an admission of the key facts, recorded in a schedule annexed to the undertaking, and has been held entitled to insist on this condition.[15] The schedule takes the form of a summary of misconduct that, for the purposes solely of the CDDA and other purposes consequential to the giving of a disqualification undertaking, the disqualified person does not dispute.[16] The sanctions for breach of a disqualification undertaking are the same as those for breach of a disqualification order and such undertakings are registered in the same way as orders.[17]

Statutory undertakings have largely displaced disqualification orders. In the year 2003–2004, 84 per cent of the 1,367 disqualifications were by way of a director's undertaking.[18]

What conduct is relevant

Under s.6(1)(b) of the Company Directors Disqualification Act the court **12–63** must determine whether the director's conduct "either taken alone or together with his conduct as a director of any other company or companies" makes him unfit to be concerned in the management of a company. Thus the court can take into account not only conduct in relation to the insolvent company (the "lead company") but also that of any other company ("collateral company") of which the person concerned is or was director. It is not necessary that his conduct in the management of a collateral company should be the same as or similar to his conduct in the management of the lead company.[19] Though conduct in relation to other companies (whether or not themselves insolvent) may be taken into account, there must be some misconduct in relation to the insolvent company before s.6 can apply. Moreover, only misconduct *as director* (including conduct as a *de facto* or shadow director[20]) is relevant; conduct in some subordinate capacity is not within the scope of the section.[21] The court must have regard to the matters set out in Part I of the Schedule to the Company Directors Disqualification Act and, where the company has become insolvent, to the matters set. out in Part II of that Schedule.[22] But any misconduct as director, whether or not mentioned in the Schedule or

---

[15] *Re Blackspur Group plc (No.3), Secretary of State for Trade and Industry v Eastaway* [2002] 2 B.C.L.C. 263.

[16] For a form of this, see Walters and Davis-White, *op. cit.*, App.8.

[17] See below, para.12–74.

[18] Insolvency Service Annual Report and Accounts 2003–04.

[19] *Re Country Farm Inns Ltd, Secretary of State v Ivens* [1997] B.C.L.C. 174.

[20] Company Directors Disqualification Act 1986, ss.6(3), 22(4); *Re Richborough Furniture Ltd* [1996] 1 B.C.L.C. 507; *Re Moorgate Metals Ltd* [1995] 1 B.C.L.C. 503; *Re Lo-Line Electric Motors Ltd* [1988] Ch. 477.

[21] *Re Richborough Furniture Ltd* above; *Secretary of State for Trade* and *Industry v Hickling* [1996] B.C.C. 678.

[22] *ibid.*, s.9.

whether or not a breach of a specific provision of the Companies Act or the Insolvency Act, may be relevant.[23]

The competing policy considerations

12–64   Cases on the application of the disqualification provisions reveal a tension between two important principles, individual liberty and protection of the public. This tension was accurately identified by Sir Nicolas Browne-Wilkinson V.C. in *Re Lo-Line Electric Motors Ltd*[24]:

> "What is the proper approach to deciding whether someone is unfit to be a director? The approach adopted in all the cases to which I have been referred is broadly the same. The primary purpose of the section is not to punish the individual but to protect the public against the future conduct of companies by persons whose past records as directors of insolvent companies have shown them to be a danger to creditors and others. Therefore, the power is not fundamentally penal. But if the power to disqualify is exercised, disqualification does involve a substantial interference with the freedom of the individual. It follows that the rights of the individual must be fully protected."

This passage has been cited with approval in a number of subsequent cases.[25]

Criteria for determining unfitness

12–65   The degree of culpability that has to be established in order to render a person unfit to be concerned in the management of a company has been expressed in different ways by different judges. Thus in the *Lo-Line* case cited above the Vice-Chancellor continued:

> "Ordinary commercial misjudgment is in itself not sufficient to justify disqualification. In the normal case, the conduct complained of must display a lack of commercial probity, although I have no doubt that in an extreme case of gross negligence or total incompetence disqualification could be appropriate."[26]

---

[23] *Re Bath Glass Ltd* (1988) 4 B.C.C. 130; *Re Churchill Hotel (Plymouth) Ltd* [1988] B.C.L.C. 341.
[24] [1988] Ch. 477 at 485–486.
[25] See, for example, *Secretary of Stale for Trade and Industry v Langridge* [1991] Ch. 402; *sub. nom. Re Cedac Ltd Secretary of State for Trade and Industry v Langridge* [1991] B.C.L.C. 543; *Re Living Images Ltd* [1996] 1 B.C.L.C. 348.
[26] *ibid.*, at 486.

Similarly in *Re Bath Glass Ltd*[27] Peter Gibson J stated the test as follows:

"To reach a finding of unfitness the court must be satisfied that the director has been guilty of a serious failure or serious failures, whether deliberately or through incompetence, to perform those duties of directors which are attendant on the privilege of trading through companies with limited liability."

In several cases the degree of culpability required has been referred to in terms of commercial morality.

"There must, I think, be something about the case, some conduct which if not really dishonest is at any rate in breach of standards of commercial morality, or some really gross incompetence which persuades the court that it would be a danger to the public if he were to be allowed to continue to be involved in the management of companies, before a disqualification order is made."[28]

However, more recently the trend has been towards tightening up the standards of behaviour required and lowering the culpability threshold. In particular, the test of commercial morality has been described as "misleading (or at least unhelpful")[29] and greater emphasis has been placed on placing creditors' money at risk,[30] whether intentionally, recklessly or through incompetence or negligence in a marked degree, even if the incompetence is not "total".[31]

The courts have been divided on the question whether nonpayment of Crown debts carries a greater degree of culpability than failure to pay other types of debt. In *Re Dawson Print Group Ltd*[32] Hoffmann J considered that a failure to pay PAYE, national insurance contributions and value added tax was not of itself a breach of commercial morality. He pointed out that the Exchequer and the Customs and Excise, by appointing traders as tax collectors, assumed the attendant risk, for which they were to some extent compensated by the preference they had on insolvency. Hoffmann J. was equally unsympathetic to the argument that sums for which the insolvent company was accountable in respect of such collected taxes were in the nature of quasi-trust moneys. He agreed that in some cases that might be so

---

[27] (1988) 4 B.C.C. 130 at 133.
[28] *Re Dawson Print Group Ltd* (1987) 3 B.C.C. 322 (a decision on s.300 of the now repealed Companies Act 1985), *per* Hoffmann J. at 324, cited with approval by Sir Nicolas Browne-Wilkinson V.C. in *Re McNulty's Interchange* Ltd (1988) 4 B.C.C. 533; and see to similar effect *Re Douglas Construction Services Ltd* (1988) 4 B.C.C. 533.
[29] *Re Stanford Services Ltd* (1987) 3 B.C.C. 326, *per* Vinelott J. at 334.
[30] See, for example, *Re Stanford Services Ltd*, above; *Re Churchill Hotel (Plymouth) Ltd* [1988] B.C.L.C. 341.
[31] *Re Sevenoaks Stationers (Retail) Ltd* [1991] Ch. 164.
[32] Above, n.28.

but emphasised that there was no obligation on traders to keep such moneys in a separate account, as there might be if they were really trust moneys, and that they were simply debts due. A different view was taken in *Re Stanford Services Ltd*[33] by Vinelott J., who took the view that the Crown is an involuntary creditor and (perhaps more significantly) that a director owes a duty not merely to keep a full and up-to-date record of tax deducted and collected but a duty to account for it and not use such tax to finance his business. This latter approach was the one preferred by Peter Gibson J. in *Re Churchill Hotel (Plymouth) Ltd*[34] who shared the view of Vinelott J. that it was improper to fail to account for value added tax, PAYE, or national insurance, since this involves the misapplication of funds which are deducted from employees' salaries or collected from third parties for the purpose of onward transmission to the Inland Revenue and should not be used to finance current trading. But in *Re Sevenoaks Stationers Ltd*[35]Dillon L.J., giving the substantive judgment in the Court of Appeal, expressed entire approval of the views expressed by Hoffmann J. as set out above, adding that it was not necessarily more heinous to withhold payment of collected taxes than to fail to pay a supplier, who might be in a small way of business.[36] Accordingly it may now be taken as settled that what matters is not whether the debt is a Crown debt in respect of collected taxes or some other kind of debt but the circumstances in which the debt came to be outstanding, and in particular the decision of the company to pay only those creditors who press for payment.

A director does not escape the statutory provisions by shirking his responsibilities and leaving all decisions to be taken by others,[37] for the board has a collegiate or collective responsibility;[38] nor is he entitled to deny responsibility for false statements in the company's accounts, rely on his fellow directors or the company's auditors.[39]

Time as at which unfitness to be tested

12–66   Whether a director is unfit to be concerned in the management of a company is to be determined by reference to the facts known to the court at the time of the hearing.[40] The question of fitness or unfitness is purely for

---

[33] (1987) 3 B.C.C. 326.
[34] Above, n.30.
[35] *ibid.*
[36] No reference was made to the separate argument that the Crown is an involuntary creditor; but as noted in an earlier chapter, this is in reality true of many other creditors whose extension of credit is in form voluntary. See above, paras 148, 158.
[37] *Re Majestic Recording Studios Ltd* (1988) 4 B.C.C. 519.
[38] *Secretary of State for Trade and Industry v. Griffiths* [1998] 2 All E.R. 124.
[39] *Re Queen's Moat Houses plc (No.2)* [2005] B.C.L.C. 136.
[40] *Re Bath Glass Ltd* (1988) 4 B.C.C. 130, approved by the Court of Appeal in *Re Grayan Services Ltd* [1995] Ch. 241.

the trial judge and affidavits which purport to present expert evidence on the subject or to provide evidence of general reputation of the director where this has not been put in issue have been struck out[41] as irrelevant.[42]

Disqualification of unfit director is mandatory

Once it has been established that in a case within s.6 of the Company **12–67** Directors Disqualification Act a director is unfit to be concerned in the management of a company, the court is obliged to disqualify him for a period of at least two years. The court has no discretion in the matter and the fact that the director concerned is no longer a danger to the public is irrelevant, for the focus is on the offence, not on the offender.[43] On the other hand, this fact will be highly relevant in considering whether leave should be granted under s.17 of the Act.[44]

Disqualification applies in relation to all companies

A disqualification order or undertaking precludes the disqualified person **12–68** from being concerned in the management of any company, not merely the company in the management of which his misconduct occurred, and the court has no power to exclude specified companies from the scope of the order or to limit its application to specified companies. However, the disqualified person can apply for leave under s.17, though the courts have not always insisted on a formal application and have implicitly exercised jurisdiction under that section by excepting specified companies from the scope of the disqualification order.

Commencement of period of disqualification

Unless the court otherwise orders, any period of disqualification begins at **12–69** the end of the period of 21 days beginning with the date of the order.[45] The purpose of the 21-day deferment is to give the disqualified director a

---

[41] Under RSC Ord.41, r.6. Under the Civil Procedure Rules expert evidence may not be given at all without leave of the court (C.P.R. r.35.4(1)).

[42] *Secretary of State for Trade and Industry v Dawes* [1997] B.C.C. 121; *Re Oakfame Constructions Ltd* [1996] B.C.C. 67.

[43] *Re Grayan Building Services Ltd* [1995] Ch. 241.

[44] *ibid.* See below para.12–71.

[45] Company Directors Disqualification Act 1986, s.1(1). At the present time, as previously noted, the great majority of disqualifications have effect by virtue of the director's undertaking, not a court order, and the practice of the Insolvency Service is to accept an offer of an undertaking which provides that the period of disqualification is to commence 21 days after acceptance of the undertaking by the Secretary of State.

limited breathing space within which to reorganise his affairs, for example, by resigning all his directorships and handing over his management activities to others. The court cannot give credit for the period during which the disqualification proceedings were pending.[46]

Period of disqualification

12–70 The minimum period of disqualification is two years, the maximum 15 years.[47] In *Re Sevenoaks Stationers (Retail) Ltd*[48] Dillon L.J. endorsed the division of the potential period of 15 years into three brackets put forward by counsel for the Official Receiver at first instance, namely:

(i) the top bracket of over 10 years should be reserved for particularly serious cases, which might include cases where the director had already had a period of disqualification imposed on him before;

(ii) the minimum bracket of two to five years' disqualification was appropriate where, though disqualification was mandatory, the case was, relatively, not very serious; and

(iii) the middle bracket of from six to ten years should be used where the case, thought serious, did not merit the top bracket.

Factors which will incline the court towards a more serious view of a case include fraudulent trading, misappropriation of assets or other dishonesty, a reckless disregard of creditors' interests and persistent breaches of statutory obligations (*e.g.* in relation to the filing of accounts), knowingly trading under a prohibited name, and adopting the practice of setting up phoenix companies[49] as each company of which he was a director became insolvent.[50] The court is also entitled to have regard to the conduct of the director concerned in the disqualification proceedings themselves, and in particular to the falsity of evidence given in those proceedings[51] and the failure to co-operate with the official receiver.[52] Conversely the absence of dishonest conduct is a mitigating factor,[53] as is the fact that the director has

---

[46] *Secretary of State for Trade and Industry v Arif* [1996] B.C.C. 586.
[47] Company Directors Disqualification Act 1986, s.6(4).
[48] [1991] Ch. 164 at 174.
[49] See above, para.12–04.
[50] See, for example, *Secretary of State for Trade and Industry v McTighe* [1997] B.C.C. 224; *Re Living Images Ltd* [1996] B.C.C. 112; *R. v Moorgate Metals Ltd* [1995] B.C.L.C. 503; *Re Travel Mondial (U.K.) Ltd* [1991] B.C.C. 224; *R. v T. & D. Services (Timber Preservation and Damp Proofing Contractors) Ltd* [1990] B.C.C. 592.
[51] *Re Mooreate Metals Ltd*, above; *Re Godwin Warren Control Systems plc* [1992] B.C.C. 557.
[52] *Secretary of State for Trade and Industry v McTighe* [1997] B.C.C. 124.
[53] *Secretary of State for Trade and Industry v Arif* [1996] B.C.C. 586; *Re Hitco 2000 Ltd* [1995] B.C.C. 161.

himself risked and lost a substantial amount of his own money.[54] In most cases the minimum band of two to five years is that adopted.[55]

Leave to act while disqualified

The effect of a disqualification order is that the director concerned cannot **12–71** be a director of a company, or engage in any of the other activities specified in s.1(1) of the Company Directors Disqualification Act 1986, without leave of the court. The court's power to grant leave is largely unfettered[56] and is exercisable either at the time the order is made or subsequently,[57] so that in making the disqualification order the court can grant leave to the persons concerned to act in such capacities and within such limits as the court thinks fit to specify. This power has been exercised in several cases. Thus in *Re Majestic Recording Studios Ltd*[58] Mervyn Davies J., when disqualifying a director of several companies, gave him leave to continue to act as director of one of them only on condition that he had as a co-director an independent chartered accountant who was willing to act with him; and in *Re Lo-Line Electric Motors Ltd*[59] Browne-Wilkinson V.C., in disqualifying the director of four companies which had become insolvent, gave leave to him to remain director of the two family companies, in which it was necessary for him to play a managerial role, on condition that another party remained a director of both companies with voting control. An overriding criterion for the grant of leave is that there is no danger to the public,[60] and to that end the court may impose whatever conditions it considers appropriate.[61] It is also necessary to show that there is a need for the disqualified director to be allowed to act, *e.g.* that the health of the company in respect of which leave is sought depends upon his assumption of or involvement in its management.[62]

Sanctions for acting while disqualified

A person who, without leave of the court under s.17, acts in contravention **12–72** of a disqualification order is guilty of a criminal offence[63] and is personally liable for all the relevant debts of a company in the management of which he is involved.[64]

---

[54] *Re Cargo Agency Ltd* [1992] B.C.C. 388.
[55] Walters and Davis-White, *op. cit.*, para.5–1–1.
[56] It ought not, however, to give leave in terms so wide or general as to undermine the mandatory character of the minimum period of disqualification prescribed by the Act.
[57] It is obviously more satisfactory to give leave at the time the disqualification is imposed.
[58] (1988) 4 B.C.C. 519.
[59] [1988] Ch. 477.
[60] *Re Grayan Building Services Ltd* [1995] Ch. 241.
[61] See, for example, the conditions set out in the schedule to the order made in *Re Gibson Davies Chemists Ltd* [1994] B.C.C. 11, and the decisions referred to in n.58, and 59.
[62] *ibid.*
[63] Company Directors Disqualification Act 1986, s.13.
[64] *ibid.*, s.15. "Relevant debts" is defined in s.15(3).

Appeals

12-73   Though in general the Court of Appeal will be slow to interfere with the exercise of the trial judge's decision as to fitness or his discretion as to the period of disqualification, it will do so where it considers that the trial judge has erred in principle.[65]

Reporting of disqualifications orders and undertakings

12-74   Reference has already been made to the reporting duties of office holders.[66] In addition, court managers and chief executives of magistrates' courts are required to notify to Companies House in the prescribed form particulars of all disqualification orders made by their courts, any action by such courts in consequence of which such an order ceases to be in force, and permission to a disqualified person to act in a prohibited capacity notwithstanding a disqualification order. The Secretary of State, acting by the Registrar of Companies, is required to maintain a register of all order so made and of any undertakings given to the Secretary of State.[67]

---

[65] *Secretary of State for Trade and Industry v McTighe* [1997] B.C.C. 224; *Re Sevenoaks Stationers (Retail) Ltd* [1991] Ch. 164.

[66] Company (Disqualification Orders) Regulations 2001, SI 2001/967 (made under s.18(1) of the Company Directors Disqualification Act 1986), as amended by SI 2002/1834.

[67] Company Directors Disqualification Act 1986, s.18(2). The register is open to the public.

Chapter 13

The European Insolvency Regime

1. INTRODUCTION

The influence of European Community law on the insolvency law of the   **13–01**
United Kingdom has been steadily growing. Reference has already been
made to the legislative measures introduced pursuant to the settlement
finality directive[1] and the financial collateral directive[2] to safeguard transactions in the financial markets from invalidity under some of the avoidance provisions that would otherwise be applicable.[3] These directives
qualify certain aspects of substantive insolvency law, which in other respects
does not fall within the competence of the European Community and is
exclusively within the purview of Member States. By contrast, the Insolvency Regulation,[4] though containing a few peripheral substantive law
provisions, is essentially a conflict of laws regulation which deals with
jurisdiction to open insolvency proceedings, the applicable law, the effects
of insolvency proceedings and recognition across the European Union of
judgments by a court in a Member State having jurisdiction. The directives
governing the winding-up of credit institutions and insurance companies
draw heavily on the Insolvency Regulation, and are not discussed further.[5]

---

[1] European Parliament and Council Directive of 19 May 1998 on settlement finality in
payment and securities settlement systems, 98/26/EC (OJ L166, 11.06.1998, p.45).
[2] European Parliament and Council Directive of 19 March 2001 on the reorganisation and
winding-up of insurance undertakings, 2001/17/EC (OJ L110, 20.4.2001, p. 28).
[3] See above, paras 1–33, 1–34.
[4] Council Regulation (EC) No. 1346/2000 of 29 May 2000 on insolvency proceedings (OJ
L160, 30.6.2001, p.1).
[5] The last major bank failures were Barings and the Bank of Credit and Commerce
International SA. The collapse of the latter led to massive litigation both in England and
elsewhere. At the time of writing, the court is hearing proceedings in a claim by BCCI's
liquidators against the Bank of England for negligence in its supervision of the bank.

This chapter is devoted to key features of the Insolvency Regulation and its implementation in the United Kingdom.[6]

2. BACKGROUND TO THE INSOLVENCY REGULATION

The 1968 Brussels Convention and Brussels I

13–02   The 1968 Brussels Convention[7] introduced detailed provisions governing jurisdiction in proceedings brought within the European Community and the mutual recognition and enforcement of judgments of courts of Member States. However, the Convention excluded from its scope bankruptcy, proceedings relating to the winding-up of insolvent companies or other legal persons, judicial arrangements, compositions and analogous proceedings.[8] In *Gourdain v Nadler*[9] the European Court of Justice held that in order to be excluded from the Convention judicial decisions "must derive directly from the bankruptcy or winding-up and be closely connected with [the insolvency proceedings]".[10] In other words, they must be decisions in proceedings based on insolvency law. This would include proceedings under ss.213 and 214 of the Insolvency Act 1986 for fraudulent and wrongful trading respectively and proceedings for the avoidance of transactions under ss.238–245, but not, for example, an action by a liquidator in the ordinary courts to enforce a duty owed to the company by a third party under the general law of contract, tort or property,[11] an action to set aside a transaction in fraud of creditors under s.423 of the Insolvency Act,[12] proceedings for the approval of a scheme of arrangement under s.425 of the Companies Act 1985,[13] an action by the liquidator to recover a debt due to the company,[14] proceedings to hold a person who acts as director while

---

[6] For detailed analyses, see Miguel Virgós and Francisco Garcímartin, *The European Insolvency Regulation: Law and Practice*; Ian Fletcher, *Insolvency in Private International Law* (2nd ed.), Chap. 7; Gabriel Moss, Ian Fletcher and Susan Isaacs (eds.), *The EC Regulation on Insolvency Proceedings*; Virgós/Schmit Report on the Convention on Insolvency Proceedings, a report on the failed EC Convention on Insolvency Proceedings (see below); Paul J. Omar, *European Insolvency Law*. For a comparative treatment, see Jennifer Marshall (ed.) *European Cross-Border Insolvency* (looseleaf).

[7] Convention on jurisdiction and the enforcement of judgments in civil and commercial matters, implemented in the UK by the Civil Jurisdiction and Judgments Act 1982, but now operative only in relation to Denmark consequent on replacement of the Convention by the EC Jurisdiction and Judgments Regulation ("Brussels I"), which has direct effect but to which Denmark declined to be a party. See below, para.13–04.

[8] Art.1.

[9] Case 133/78, [1979] 1 ECR 733.

[10] *ibid.*, at 744.

[11] *Re Hayward deceased* [1997] Ch. 45.

[12] For this applies whether the company is solvent or insolvent.

[13] Which again is not dependent on the company's insolvency.

[14] *Re Hayward deceased* [1997] Ch. 45, *per* Rattee J. at 54D; *UBS AG v Omni Holdings AG* [[2000] 1 W.L.R. 916, *per* Rimer J. at 922. The mere fact that the proceedings have been triggered by the insolvency is not sufficient to oust the application of Brussels I and bring the case within the Insolvency Regulation (*UBS AG v Omni Holdings AG*, above).

disqualified personally liable for the company's debts,[15] or a claim against a director for breach of fiduciary or other duty.[16]

The Brussels Convention became converted into a Regulation[17] with effect from March 1, 2002 and closely follows the Convention. Like the Convention it does not apply to insolvency proceedings, though it is applicable to the winding-up of solvent companies.

The EC Convention

After some 30 years of work and the rejection of one draft after another the Member States of the European Community completed the text of a Convention on Insolvency Proceedings in September 1995, the Convention being opened for signature within six months. Within that time 14 Member States signed the convention; only the signature of the United Kingdom was not forthcoming,[18] with the result that the Convention lapsed. The Convention was designed to dovetail with the Brussels Convention so that anything excluded from the latter as being related to insolvency would fall within the Insolvency Convention.

13–03

The conversion of the EC Insolvency Convention into an EC Regulation

A few years after the failure of the Convention the project was revived in the form of a proposal for an EC Regulation, which took over most of the provisions of the Convention verbatim,[19] with an amendment to Art.5 to capture floating charges and various other amendments reflecting the

13–04

---

[15] Even where the disqualification was imposed in insolvency proceedings, the liability for acting whole disqualified results not from the insolvency as such but from s.15 of the Company Directors Disqualification Act 1986, which applies whatever the circumstances of the disqualification.

[16] *Grupo Torras SA v Sheikh Fahad Mohammed Al-Sabbah* [1995] 1 Lloyd's Rep. 374. Such a claim is excluded from the Rome Convention by Art. 1(2)(e) and is governed by the law of the place of the company's incorporation (*Base Metal Trading Ltd v Shamurin* [2005] B.C.C. 325). See also Ben Jones, "EU Regulation and Directors' Duties" [2005] 18 Insol. Int. 29.

[17] Council Regulation (EC) No. 44/2001 of December 22, 2000 (also known as "Brussels I").

[18] Two reasons have been ascribed to this: the hostility of John Major, then Prime Minister, because of the refusal of the European Commission to lift the ban on the export of British beef that had been imposed because of the BSE epidemic ("mad cow disease"), which led to a policy of non-co-operation in EC matters (H.C. Deb. 18 June 1996, col. 394), and the concern that the failure to empower the United Kingdom to exclude Gibraltar could impair the sovereignty of the United Kingdom over a colony for whose international relations the UK is responsible but to which Spain has continued to lay claim. For the history of the project, see Fletcher, *op. cit.*, paras 7.1 *et seq.*; Paul J. Omar, "Genesis of the European Initiative in Insolvency Law", (2003) 12 Int. Insol. Rev. 147.

[19] This has facilitated use of the Virgós/Schmit Report as a guide to the Regulation. The report has no official status, because the failure of the Convention meant that it was never formally endorsed, but it has strong persuasive value and continues to be widely cited.

different status of the instrument. The change from convention to regulation avoided the need for ratification by all Member States and also had the effect of conferring power on the European Court of Justice to interpret the instrument without the need for any express provision in it to that effect. The use of a regulation rather than a directive meant that the instrument has direct effect in Member States, thus not only dispensing with the need for implementation under national law but positively precluding Member States from any measure of implementation. The Regulation came into force on May 31, 2002. Following the admission of 10 new Member States and additions to the lists of proceedings in Annexes A, B and C to the Regulation, these were replaced by an amending regulation in April 2005.[20]

3. AN OVERVIEW OF THE REGULATION

Key features

13–05 In relation to insolvency proceedings within its scope[21] the EC Regulation on Insolvency Proceedings (hereafter "the Insolvency Regulation") has six key features:

(1) A dovetailing with Brussels I designed to leave no gaps between the two.[22]

(2) A principle of qualified unity embodied in rules for international jurisdiction in "main proceedings" which are based on the place where the debtor has its centre of main interests ("COMI") and which preclude the opening of insolvency proceedings in other Member States except those in which the debtor has an establishment and then only in relation to local assets.

(3) A principle of qualified universality by which the court of a Member State in which the main proceedings are opened has jurisdiction over all the debtor's assets on a worldwide basis, while allowing secondary insolvency proceedings in another Member State in whose territory the debtor has an establishment, restricted to winding-up and to assets within that territory.

---

[20] Council Regulation (EC) No. 603/2005 of 12 April 2005 amending the lists of insolvency proceedings, winding-up proceedings and liquidators in Annexes A, B and C to Regulation (EC) No. 1346/2000 on insolvency proceedings (OJ 20.4.2005, p.1).

[21] See below, paras 13–07 *et seq.* Only corporate insolvency proceedings are discussed in the present chapter, but it should be borne in mind that the Regulation also covers personal bankruptcy.

[22] Virgós and Garcimartín, *op. cit.*, para.77.

(4)   Subjection of insolvency proceedings and their effects to the law of the state in which such proceedings are opened, except for *in rem* rights and certain other rights established by some other applicable law.

(5)   A requirement that any judgment of a court of a Member State opening insolvency proceedings pursuant to the jurisdiction conferred upon it by the regulation be recognised and given effect in all other Member States.

(6)   Conferment on the liquidator in the main proceedings of a right to exercise in all other Member States the powers conferred on him by the law of the state of the opening of proceedings, coupled with a right to require the stay of secondary proceedings, subject to measures to guarantee the interests of creditors in the secondary proceedings.

The role of the recitals

Another distinctive feature of the Regulation is its set of 33 recitals, which **13–06** are designed to serve as an interpretative aid and for that purpose draw on the Virgós-Schmit Report. The less happy effect of such extensive reliance on recitals is that all too often they are made to carry the burden of answering questions which are not addressed in the text. So the meaning of "centre of main interests", which is fundamental to the rules on jurisdiction and thus to selection of the *lex concursus*, is not to be found in the body of the Regulation (which tells us where COMI is presumed to be but not what it is), only in the recitals, which are of only limited assistance.

4. SCOPE OF THE REGULATION

Introduction

The Regulation is concerned solely with insolvencies within the Com-   **13–07** munity. Accordingly it applies only where the debtor has its centre of main interests within the Community and insolvency proceedings are opened in a Member State. However, when these and other conditions listed below have been satisfied, the jurisdiction of the court in which main proceedings are opened extends to all the debtor's assets on a worldwide basis, though obviously recognition and enforcement of the liquidator's powers in a non-EU state are subject to the law of the state concerned and the jurisdiction of its courts. Since the Regulation is concerned only with relations between EU states it is careful to limit its rules governing *in rem* rights, reservation of title, and the like, to assets situated within the territory of a Member State. But the same conflict rules will apply to determine such rights as regards assets situated in a non-Member State.

Proceedings within and outside the Regulation

13–08   The Regulation applies only if the following six conditions are satisfied:

(1) Insolvency proceedings are opened

13–09   "Insolvency proceedings" means the collective proceedings referred to in Art.1(1) and listed in Annex A.[23] The Regulation does not define insolvency, and it is left to national law to determine whether proceedings of a kind listed in Annex A are insolvency proceedings. Thus in England a creditors' voluntary winding-up falls within the Regulation, a members' voluntary winding-up does not,[24] nor does a winding-up on a petition presented by the Secretary of State on public interest grounds under s.124A of the Insolvency Act 1986,[25] even though both types of proceeding are among those listed in Annex A. Conversely, a proceeding which a Member State characterises as an insolvency proceeding but is not listed in the Regulation is outside its scope. In short, to be within the Regulation proceedings must fulfil the dual test of falling within Annex A and being characterised as insolvency proceedings under the relevant national law. What constitutes the opening of proceedings is discussed a little later.[26]

(2) The proceedings are collective insolvency proceedings

13–10   These are defined in Annex A, and divide primarily into winding-up proceedings, involving collection and realisation of assets and distribution of the proceeds, and proceedings designed to lead to reorganisation or restructuring of the debtor company. In relation to the United Kingdom, Annex A lists voluntary liquidation where confirmed by the court, compulsory liquidation,[27] administration (whether by court order or out of court[28]) and voluntary arrangements under insolvency legislation, that is, company voluntary arrangements under Part I of the Insolvency Act 1986 but not schemes of arrangement under s.425 of the Companies Act 1985, since these cover solvent as well as insolvent companies. Administrative or other receivership is outside the Regulation since it is not a collective insolvency proceeding.[29] The status of an order for the appointment of a

---

[23] Art.2(a). See below.

[24] This example is given in the Virgós-Schmit Report, para.49(b).

[25] *Re Marann Brooks CSV Ltd* [2003] B.P.I.R. 1159.

[26] Below, para.13–28.

[27] Winding-up under the supervision of the court is also listed, but was abolished many years ago. See above, para.1–24. However, it is still relevant to Gibraltar.

[28] This results from a change made to Annex A by including in administration appointments made by filing prescribed documents with the court.

[29] See above, para.1–23.

provisional liquidator is an intermediate one, being neither wholly within nor wholly outside the Regulation. Such an order is not within the list in Annex A and therefore does not constitute a form of collective insolvency proceeding for the purposes of the Regulation. On the other hand, a provisional liquidator is included in the list in Annex C and is therefore a liquidator within the definition in Art.2(b). However, he is not "the liquidator in the main proceedings", for these will not yet have been opened; he therefore has no *locus standi* to apply under Art.29 for the opening of secondary proceedings. So in order to enable him to have the assets safeguarded pending such opening he is empowered as "temporary administrator" to apply to the court of another Member State in which assets of the debtor are situated to request measures to secure and preserve any of those assets.[30]

We must now look a little more closely at the four types of collective insolvency proceeding listed in Annex A for the United Kingdom.

(a) Winding-up proceedings

Article 2(c) defines "winding-up proceedings" in the following terms: **13–11**

> "Winding-up proceedings" shall mean insolvency proceedings within the meaning of art. 2(a) involving realising the assets of the debtor, including where the proceedings have been closed by a composition or other measure terminating the insolvency or closed by reason of the insufficiency of the assets. Those proceedings are listed in Annex B."

Annex B, as revised in April 2005, covers creditors' voluntary winding-up, compulsory winding-up and winding-up through administration. This last is a reference to winding-up as an exit route from administration[31] and is limited to the winding-up itself. It does not apply to the administration itself preceding such winding-up. Accordingly "winding-up through administration" cannot be used as a vehicle to bring within the scope of secondary proceedings CVAs and schemes of arrangements carried out within the framework of administration. There is an apparent difficulty in applying the Regulation in that it is based on the concept of court proceedings, both in the jurisdiction rules in Arts.3 and 27 and in the recognition rules in Art.16. Article 2(d) defines "court" as meaning "the judicial body or any other competent body of a Member State empowered to open insolvency proceedings or to take decisions in the

---

[30] Art.38.

[31] Winding-up through administration is mentioned specifically because it is neither a compulsory winding-up on a petition or a creditors' voluntary winding-up but results, in the case of a compulsory winding-up, from a winding-up order made under the Insolvency Act 1986, Sch.B1, paras 79(4)(d) or 81(3)(d) and, in the case of a CVL, from the resolution for voluntary winding-up deemed to have been passed on registration of the administrators' notice under Sch.B1, para.83(6)(b).

course of such proceedings", while by Art.2(e) "judgment", in relation to the opening of insolvency proceedings or the appointment of a liquidator, includes the decision of any court empowered to open such proceedings or to appoint a liquidator.[32] On the face of it, therefore, despite Annex A the Regulation is capable of biting only on compulsory liquidation, since none of the other three insolvency proceedings listed is "opened" by a court. However, it is clear from recital (10) that on this aspect at least the Regulation is intended to be liberally construed:

> "(10) Insolvency proceedings do not necessarily involve the intervention of a judicial authority; the expression 'court' in this Regulation should be given a broad meaning and include a person or body empowered by national law to open insolvency proceedings."

The amended Annex, like the original, refers to creditors' voluntary winding-up "(with confirmation by the court)," which implies that such confirmation is an essential ingredient of a creditors' voluntary winding-up if it is to qualify as an insolvency proceeding within the Regulation.[33] The Insolvency Rules were amended to prescribe the procedure for such confirmation,[34] and they apply not only to a CVL effected by resolution of the members but also to one to which the company has moved from administration in accordance with para.83 of Sch.B1 to the Act.[35]

(b) Administration and CVAs

13–12   The view of the Insolvency Service is that this construction is wide enough to apply the word "court" to the holder of a qualifying floating charge appointing an administrator out of court and to creditors when approving a CVA.

In relation to out-of-court appointments of administrators this broad interpretation receives support from the inclusion in the amended Annex A of "administration, including appointments made by filing prescribed documents with the court."

---

[32] "Liquidator" is defined by Art.2(b) as meaning any person or body whose function is to administer or liquidate assets of the company of which the debtor has been divested or to supervise the administration of his affairs, such persons being listed in Annex C, which in the case of the UK covers a liquidator, a provisional liquidator, a supervisor of a voluntary arrangement, an administrator and an official receiver.

[33] For most purposes the opening of the insolvency proceedings is considered to take place on the passing of the resolution for winding-up, not on confirmation by the court. See below, para.13–29.

[34] Insolvency Rules 1986, rr.7.62, 7.63. An application under r.7.62 was granted by Mr Registrar Baister in relation to two oversea companies in *Re TXU Finance Co BV* [2005] B.P.I.R. 209, where it was held that the Regulation applied to a voluntary winding-up and that while an unregistered company, including an oversea company, could not normally be put into voluntary winding-up, s.221(4) of the Insolvency Act 1986, as amended, allowed this to be done in accordance with the Insolvency Regulation, and jurisdiction did indeed flow from the Regulation.

[35] Insolvency Rules 1986, r.7.62(8).

As to CVAs, which do not involve the court at all except where an application is made under s.4A of the Insolvency Act,[36] it might appear hard to see how the conclusion of a CVA could be regarded as the opening of insolvency proceedings or how the participating creditors and members could collectively constitute "the court", particularly since a members' resolution putting the company into a CVL is not by itself sufficient and requires confirmation by the court. But CVAs are included in the list of insolvency proceedings in Annex A, while the supervisor of a CVA features in the list of liquidators in Annex C, and these inclusions would be deprived of all meaning if the coming into force of a CVA were not to be treated as the opening of insolvency proceedings by a "court" consisting of the parties to the CVA.[37] In *Re Salvage Association Ltd*[38] Blackburne J. held that the parties to a CVA did indeed constitute a "court" for the purposes of the Regulation. By contrast, purely consensual restructurings (workouts) fall outside the Regulation.

(3) The proceedings entail the partial or total divestment of a debtor and the appointment of a liquidator

Only those collective proceedings which entail the partial or total divestment of a debtor and the appointment of a liquidator are within the Regulation.[39] This excludes proceedings based on the concept of a "debtor in possession" as exemplified by Chapter 11 of the US Bankruptcy Code.　**13–13**

(4) The proceedings are opened in a Member State

The Regulation obviously cannot control proceedings opened in a jurisdiction outside the European Union.　**13–14**

(5) The debtor has its COMI in a Member State at the time of opening of the insolvency proceedings

This central requirement is stated in those terms only in recital (14), not in the text, but it clearly follows from the wording of Art.3, which is limited to such proceedings. That the relevant time is that of the opening of the proceedings is supported by the commentators,[40] and there is now an　**13–15**

---

[36] See above, para.10–121.
[37] See to the same effect Moss, Fletcher and Isaacs, *op. cit.* above, n.6, paras 8.18–8.20.
[38] [2004] 1 W.L.R. 174.
[39] Art.1(1).
[40] "This is the only reference date that avoids the incentives for forum shopping that the Insolvency Regulation expressly tries to eliminate . . ." (Virgós and Garcimartín, *op. cit.*, para.68). As to what constitutes the opening of the proceedings, see below, paras 13–28 *et seq.*

English decision to that effect.[41] If the COMI is in a Member State the fact that the debtor company was incorporated in a non-Member State is irrelevant; the Regulation still applies.[42]

(6) The debtor is not an institution excluded from the Regulation

13–16   Finally, there are excluded from the Regulation insolvency proceedings concerning insurance undertakings, credit institutions, investment undertakings which provide services involving the holding of funds or securities for third parties, and collective investment undertakings.[43] These are taken out of the scope of the Regulation because "they are subject to special arrangements and, to some extent, the national supervisory authorities have extremely wide-ranging powers of intervention".[44] In addition, they are regulated by EC directives, two of which relate specifically to the winding-up of credit institutions and insurance undertakings.[45]

5. JURISDICTION GENERALLY

Jurisdiction under national law

13–17   It is important to note that the Regulation does not confer jurisdiction on a national court which it would not have under its own law. Whether the conditions necessary to open insolvency proceedings in a Member State are satisfied is in the first instance to be determined by the law of that state. Where those conditions are satisfied it is then necessary to proceed to the next stage and see whether the courts of the Member State have jurisdiction under the Regulation. If they do not, they cannot entertain the case; if they do, they must entertain it.[46] So the Regulation is not an alternative

---

[41] *Shierson v Vlieland-Boddy* [2005] EWCA Civ. 974 (bankruptcy). As to when proceedings are deemed to be opened, see below, paras 13–28 *et seq*.

[42] *Re BRAC Rent-A-Car International Inc* [2003] 1 W.L.R. 1421 (COMI in the UK; held, the court had jurisdiction even though the company was incorporated in the USA); *Re Ci4net.com Inc* [2005] B.C.C. 277 (two companies incorporated in Jersey and the USA, respectively, held to have their COMI in England).

[43] Art.1(2). By "collective investment undertakings" is meant those that are duly authorised-in the UK, by the Financial Services Authority. Unauthorised collective investment undertakings are covered by the Regulation (*Financial Services Authority v Dobb White & Co* [2004] B.P.I.R. 479).

[44] Recital (9).

[45] See above, n.2.

[46] See below, para.13–22. For an excellent overview, see Bob Wessels, "International jurisdiction to open insolvency proceedings in Europe, in particular against (groups of) companies", published by the International Insolvency Institute and available on *www.iiiglobal.org*.

source of jurisdiction but an additional jurisdictional hurdle to be surmounted.

Classification of proceedings

The Regulation divides insolvency proceedings into two groups, main **13–18** proceedings and territorial proceedings. Main proceedings are those brought in the Member State within the territory of which the debtor's COMI is situated. Territorial proceedings are those brought in another Member State in which the debtor possesses an establishment. No insolvency proceedings may be instituted in a Member State which is neither that in which the debtors's COMI is situated[47] nor one in which he has an establishment.

Territorial proceedings sub-divide into secondary proceedings, which are those brought after the opening of main proceedings in another Member State, and proceedings opened in another Member State prior to the opening of the main proceedings, which the Virgós-Schmit Report conveniently labels "independent proceedings."[48] Once main proceedings have been opened, the *quondam* independent proceedings become secondary proceedings,[49] but with distinctive effects.[50] The distinction between main proceedings and territorial proceedings is significant in at least two ways. Main proceedings extend to all the debtor's assets except to the extent to which assets situated in another Member State are available to local creditors in territorial proceedings, these being confined to local assets. Main proceedings have primacy within the European Union and the liquidator in those proceedings has overall control and is entitled to have his position recognised and given effect in all Member States, whereas territorial proceedings and the liquidator who administers them fulfil a subordinate function. There are also important differences between secondary proceedings and independent proceedings. The former are confined to winding-up,[51] the latter may be any collective insolvency proceedings within the Regulation. So if, in a case where the debtor has an establishment in the UK but its COMI is situated outside the UK, it is thought desirable to have an administration and/or CVA in England, it is essential to open proceedings here before any proceedings have been opened in another

---

[47] See below, para.13–36.
[48] Para.25.
[49] *ibid.*
[50] For example, if initiated as reorganisation proceedings they are not automatically converted into winding-up proceedings, so that until converted (*e.g.* following a request by the liquidator in the main proceedings under Art.37) they can continue as reorganisation proceedings. Further, Arts.31–35 apply to them only so far as the progress of those proceedings permits.
[51] Insolvency Regulation, para.3(3). But this now includes winding-up through administration. See above, para.13–11.

Member State. However, independent proceedings can be opened only if one of the two conditions specified in Art.3(4) is satisfied.[52] Though independent proceedings involving a reorganisation are automatically converted into secondary proceedings where main proceedings are subsequently opened in another Member State, this does not automatically convert them into winding-up proceedings.[53]

Unity and universality

13–19   The ideal within a common market would be to vest jurisdiction in insolvency proceedings exclusively in the courts of a single state ("unity") and to subject the totality of the debtor's assets to that one insolvency jurisdiction ("universality"). The principles of unity and universality are embodied in the Regulation in that main proceedings can be opened only in one state, the state in which the debtor's COMI is situated, the jurisdiction of the courts of that state has to be recognised in all other Member States and the main proceedings encompass all the debtor's assets on a worldwide basis.[54] But the Regulation accepts that, as with cross-border insolvencies at international level,[55] this purity of concept is in practice unattainable, and to seek to impose it would cause severe problems.

> "This Regulation acknowledges the fact that as a result of widely differing substantive laws it is not practical to introduce insolvency proceedings with universal scope in the entire Community. The application without exception of the law of the State of opening of the insolvency proceedings would, against this background, frequently lead to difficulties. This applies, for example, to the widely differing laws on security interests to be found in the Community. Furthermore, the preferential rights enjoyed by some creditors in the insolvency proceedings are, in some cases, completely different."[56]

Accordingly the Regulation adopts the principle of qualified unity and qualified universality.

---

[52] See below, para.13–20.
[53] See the Virgós-Schmit Report. para.86.
[54] Virgós-Schmit Report, para.73. The Insolvency Rules 1986 have useful provisions requiring affidavits in support of administration applications and winding-up petitions to state (i) whether in the opinion of the person making the application the EC Regulation will apply and (ii) if so, whether the proceedings will be main proceedings or territorial proceedings (rr.2.4(4), 4.12(8), the latter being added by the Insolvency (Amendment) Rules 2005, SI 2005/527, r.20).
[55] See below, para.14–05.
[56] Insolvency Regulation, recital (11).

(1) Qualified unity

While giving primacy to the main proceedings opened in the Member State **13–20** where the debtor has its COMI the Regulation recognises that wherever the debtor has an establishment in the territory of a Member State which is not that in which it has its COMI, local creditors should be entitled to institute winding-up proceedings (but not any other types of proceeding) and to have recourse to local assets (though in neither case to the exclusion of creditors situated in other Member States) and that in relation to those assets the ranking of claims and other rules of insolvency should be governed by the local *lex concursus*. So exclusive jurisdiction is not given to the courts of any one Member State, nor is there necessarily a single *lex concursus*. It is theoretically possible to have territorial proceedings which are never followed by main proceedings, and, of course, there may be as many territorial proceedings as there are territories within which the debtor has an establishment, so long as in each case the conditions of Art.3(4) are satisfied.

Only one set of main proceedings may be opened in the territory covered by the Regulation.[57] By this is meant that it is not possible for main proceedings to be opened in a Member State while there are current main proceedings in another Member State. But once main proceedings in one Member State have been closed or discontinued, there is no longer a barrier to new main proceedings being opened in another Member State, though this is likely to be infrequent. Moreover, the concept of unity of the insolvency operates only at the international level within the Community. There is nothing in the Regulation to preclude multiple main proceedings within the same jurisdiction. These may be successive, as where administration is followed by a CVL, or may run in parallel, as where a CVA is concluded within an administration or is uncompleted when winding-up supervenes but remains operative as to the assets comprised in it.[58]

(2) Qualified universality

Although main proceedings encompass the whole of the debtor's assets **13–21** worldwide, yet where territorial proceedings have been opened the local assets must first be applied to the settlement of claims of creditors (local or otherwise) in the territorial proceedings, only those assets (if any) remaining after payment of such claims in full being handed over to the liquidator

---

[57] Virgós-Schmit Report, para.73; Virgós and Garcimartín, *op. cit.*, para.70; Ian Fletcher, *op. cit.*, para.7.50.

[58] See above, para.13–19 and *Oakley v Ultra Design Ltd* [2005] All E.R. (D) 380, where Lloyd J. concluded (at para.34) that there was no reason why there should not be concurrent main proceedings within the UK (in that case, a compulsory liquidation and a CVA, which continued to operate after the company had gone into liquidation), though he found it unnecessary to deal with the relationship between them.

in the main proceedings. Further, the Regulation can only control the opening of proceedings within the European Union. There is nothing to prevent a creditor from bringing such proceedings in a non-Member State which has jurisdiction under its own jurisdictional rules. It thus a little unfortunate that Art.3 is headed "International jurisdiction" instead of the more accurate "Community jurisdiction", signifying jurisdiction at the level of Community law as opposed to jurisdiction within a Member State, this being the exclusive prerogative of the national law of that state,[59] which can thus declare attempted insolvency proceedings inadmissible[60] even where the courts of the state concerned would have jurisdiction under the regulation.[61] However, in order to ensure that courts in England have jurisdiction in relation to entities that fall within the Regulation the definition of "company" has been extended, for the purpose of the provisions relating to CVAs and administration, to embrace not only a company within s.735(1) of the Companies Act 1985 but also a company incorporated in an EEA state other than the UK and a company not incorporated in an EEA state but having its centre of main interests in a Member State other than Denmark, "centre of main interests" having the same meaning as in the EC Regulation.[62]

No power to invoke *forum non conveniens*

13–22   One effect of the exclusivity of the jurisdiction conferred by the Insolvency Regulation, whether it be the exclusivity of main proceedings or that applicable to local assets in a Member State where the debtor has an establishment, is that a court seised of a case cannot decline jurisdiction on the ground of *forum non conveniens*, for if it were allowed to do this there would be no court elsewhere within the European Union able to open main proceedings or to open territorial proceedings in respect of assets situated within the territory of the state whose court had refused jurisdiction.

The relationship between different proceedings

13–23   Under the Regulation it is possible to have main proceedings in the jurisdiction in which the debtor has its COMI and territorial proceedings in every jurisdiction in which it has an establishment. The relationship

---

[59] *ibid.*, recital (15) and Art.4(2).

[60] *e.g.* where, in winding-up proceedings in England, the petitioner lacks *locus standi*. See above, para.5–07.

[61] As Dr Burkard Göpfert has pointed out, the concept of international jurisdiction has its origin in the terminology of private international law. Whether at the level of international law the courts of a particular state have jurisdiction in a matter regulated by an international instrument is determined by that instrument; whether the jurisdiction so conferred is exercisable within a state is determined by that state's own law. See Göpfert, "International Jurisdiction in European Insolvencies", an article published by the International Insolvency Institute and accessible on www.iiiglobal.org.

[62] Insolvency Act 1986, ss.1 and 436 and Sch.B1 para.111, as amended by the Insolvency Act 1986 (Amendment) Regulations 2005, SI 2005/879.

between the different proceedings has been well expressed by a leading American scholar when analysing the EU Convention:

"In the EU Convention system, no court acts in a role 'ancillary' to another. Instead, assets and claims in a given jurisdiction are either in a universalist or a territorialist position. If no local proceeding is opened, then the liquidator in the main proceedings has considerable power to seize assets and remove them for distribution in the main proceedings. The local creditors will be expected to file there. The result is universalist to that extent. On the other hand, if a local proceeding is opened, then assets and claims will be administered almost entirely in that proceeding. The administration in that case will be almost entirely territorial, unless resolved by a cooperative rescue plan accepted locally." [footnotes omitted][63]

The same writer draws attention to the benefits resulting from the "universal cross-filing" system embodied in what is now the Regulation, by which the liquidator in each proceeding is required to lodge claims on behalf of creditors in all other proceedings. Whilst the ranking of claims in each winding-up is governed by the *lex concursus* applicable to that winding-up, yet to the extent that in any linked proceedings non-local creditors are given the same priority as local creditors the universal cross-filing system would produce substantially the same outcomes as a universalist system.[64]

The principle of recognition and respect within the Community

A fundamental principle underlying the Regulation, and one that is essential to its proper functioning, is that a judgment of a court of a Member State opening insolvency proceedings is to be respected and enforced in subsequent proceedings in all other Member States. In the language of recital (22): **13–24**

"Recognition of judgments delivered by the courts of the Member States should be based on the principle of mutual trust. To that end, grounds for non-recognition should be reduced to a minimum. This is also the basis on which any dispute should be resolved where the courts of two Member States both claim competence to open the main insolvency proceedings."

This is reinforced by the text of the Regulation, in Arts.16, 17 and 25:

---

[63] Jay Lawrence Westbrook, "Universal Participation in Transnational Bankruptcies", in *Making Commercial Law* (ed. Ross Cranston) 419 at 423.
[64] *ibid.*, at 427.

"Article 16
Principle
1.   Any judgment opening proceedings handed down by a court of a Member State which has jurisdiction pursuant to Article 3 shall be recognised in all the other Member States from the time that it becomes effective in the State of the opening of the proceedings.

Article 17
Effects of recognition
1.   The judgment opening the proceedings referred to in Article 3(1) shall, with no further formalities, produce the same effects in any other Member State as under this[65] law of the State of the opening of the proceedings, unless this Regulation provides otherwise and as long as no proceedings referred to in Article 3(2) are opened in that other Member State.
2.   The effects of the proceedings referred to in Article 3(2) may not be challenged in other Member States . . .

Article 25
Recognition and enforceability of other judgments
1.   Judgments handed down by a court whose judgment concerning the opening of proceedings is recognised in accordance with Article 16 and which concern the course and closure of insolvency proceedings, and compositions approved by that court shall also be recognised with no further formalities. Such judgments shall be enforced in accordance with Articles 31 to 51, with the exception of Article 34(2), of the Brussels Convention on Jurisdiction and the Enforcement of Judgments in Civil and Commercial Matters, as amended by the Conventions of Accession to this Convention.

The first subparagraph shall also apply to judgments deriving directly from the insolvency proceedings and which are closely linked with them, even if they were handed down by another court.

The first subparagraph shall also apply to judgments relating to preservation measures taken after the request for the opening of insolvency proceedings.
2.   The recognition and enforcement of judgments other than those referred to in paragraph 1 shall be governed by the Convention referred to in paragraph 1, provided that that Convention is applicable.
3.   The Member States shall not be obliged to recognise or enforce a judgment referred to in paragraph 1 which might result in a limitation of personal freedom or postal secrecy."

The principle of recognition and respect has several facets. In the first place, save in exceptional circumstances it is improper for a court in

---

[65] The word "this" is a slip and should be "the".

one Member State to enquire into the basis on which the court of another Member State assumed jurisdiction to open insolvency proceedings. For example, once main proceedings have been opened in France an English court must in principle recognise the effectiveness of these automatically and without further formality or enquiry and cannot examine the legal or factual basis upon which the French court assumed jurisdiction. So while an English court might take the view that on the facts the debtor's COMI was England, not France, it must respect the finding of the French court on this issue. This rule of recognition is not at first sight consistent with the wording of Art.16(1), which in terms requires only that recognition be given to a judgment handed down by a court of a Member State *which has jurisdiction pursuant to Article 3*. This might be thought to imply that the court of another Member State may examine the question whether that condition has been satisfied. But such an interpretation would completely undermine the principle of respect for judgments within the European Union and generate the very uncertainty and multiplicity of proceedings which the Regulation is designed to avoid. Article 3 must therefore be read purposively as precluding the court of a Member State from entertaining main proceedings when the court of another Member State *has assumed* jurisdiction under Art.3. It was on that ground that the Court of Appeal of Versailles reversed the decision of the Commercial Court of Cergy-Pontoise in the French *Daisy-Tek* proceedings, holding that it was a violation of the Regulation for the Commercial Court to treat an earlier administration order by the English High Court as of no effect.[66] Hence the correct procedure for a party wishing to challenge the basis of the first decision, *e.g.* on the ground that the debtor's COMI was not in fact situated in the Member State in which the proceedings were opened, is to use the appellate process in that state to seek to overturn the decision, not to institute separate proceedings in another Member State and invite the court in that state to disregard the earlier judgment. It is always open to the highest court of the jurisdiction in which the proceedings were opened to make a reference to the European Court of Justice for a preliminary ruling on the interpretation of the Regulation.[67]

Secondly, the rule of recognition applies not only where the court of the **13–25** first state has assumed jurisdiction but also where it has declined it.[68] This is less clear in that Art.16 requires recognition only of a judgment opening proceedings, not of a judgment declining jurisdiction to do so. Yet even here the principle of mutual respect must be allowed to operate, for if, for

---

[66] See below, paras 13–36 *et seq*. As to the effect of an application to open proceedings made in one Member State on the power of a court in another Member State to open proceedings in that state, see below, para.13–34.

[67] EC Treaty, art.68(2). This is in contrast to the position in relation to other aspects of EC law, where the highest court *must* make a reference and lower courts *may* do so (EC Treaty, art.234).

[68] Virgós and Garcimartín, *op. cit.*, para.70.

example, a court in Spain declined jurisdiction on the ground that the debtor's COMI was not situated in Spain but courts in other Member States disagreed, the result would be to preclude main proceedings from being opened anywhere. So a court in the second state must respect the basis of refusal of jurisdiction in the first state even if this means accepting that the debtor's COMI is in the second state when the court of that state would otherwise have taken a different view and declined jurisdiction. Where that court makes an order in ignorance of the earlier proceedings, its own proceedings should be converted into territorial proceedings.[69]

Thirdly, a judgment of a court opening proceedings must be given the same effect in the courts of other Member States as it has in the state in which the proceedings are opened. Article 4 contains a list of matters governed by the *lex concursus*[70] but this list is non-exhaustive. The principle of Community-wide effect of a judgment of a court in a Member State opening insolvency proceedings is a general one and would appear to include rules under the law of that state determining as from what time the proceedings are to be considered opened.[71]

Fourthly, judgments handed down by the court whose judgment opening the insolvency proceedings is recognised in accordance with Art.16 and which concern the course and closure of insolvency proceedings, and compositions approved by that court, must also be recognised in other Member States without further formalities. However, the sovereignty of other states must also be recognised, so that enforcement measures in such other states must first have authorisation (*exequatur*) from the court or other competent authority of the state concerned.

Exceptions to the rule of recognition

13–26   In exceptional cases the court of a Member State may be entitled to disregard an judgment of a court of another Member State. Where, for example, the court of the other state has assumed jurisdiction despite an express finding that the debtor's COMI is not situated within that state it must, it is thought, be open to a court entertaining subsequent proceedings elsewhere to disregard the earlier decision as *ultra vires* the Regulation on its face. A further exception is provided by Art.26:

> "A Member State may refuse to recognise insolvency proceedings opened in another Member State or to enforce a judgment handed down in the context of such proceedings where the effects of such recognition or enforcement would be manifestly contrary to that State's public policy,

---

[69] *ibid.*
[70] See below, paras 13–49 *et seq.*
[71] See further below, para.13–28.

in particular its fundamental principles or the constitutional rights and liberties of the individual."

An example is where an interested party was not given notice of the insolvency proceedings or was otherwise prevented from participating in them. It was on this ground that in the *Eurofood* case[72] the High Court in Ireland declined to recognise the decision of the Civil and Criminal Court of Parma, Italy, placing Parmalat SpA in extraordinary administration. The facts as set out in the judgment of Kelly J. were decidedly unusual.

On December 24 2003 Parmalat SpA, the parent company of an Irish company, Eurofood, was placed in extraordinary administration by the Italian Ministry of Productive Activities, following a new Italian law providing for extraordinary administration, and Signor Enrico Bondi was appointed extraordinary administrator. The insolvency of the company and the administration and appointment were confirmed by the Civil and Criminal Court of Parma on December 27. On January 27, 2004 a petition for the winding-up of Eurofood was presented to the High Court in Ireland and on the same day Mr Pearse Farrell was appointed provisional liquidator by Langham J. On January 30 he notified Signor Bondi of his appointment. On February 9 Signor Bondi was appointed extraordinary administrator of Eurofood by the Italian Ministry despite his knowledge of the appointment of a provisional liquidator by the Irish Court nearly two weeks earlier. On February 13 the provisional liquidator was served with notice of a hearing to take place before the Parma court on February 17 with a view to that court declaring Eurofood's insolvency. He was not supplied with the petition or any supporting documents then or thereafter in response to repeated requests. Despite a direction by the court that all interested parties be given notice, no notice was given to major creditors. The provisional liquidator sought to argue that main proceedings had already been opened in Ireland. The advice received by Signor Bondi and placed before the Parma court was that the appointment of the provisional liquidator did not amount to the opening of main proceedings or the determination of the debtor's COMI. The Parma court admitted Eurofood into insolvency and also held that its COMI was in Italy rather than Ireland.

Kelly J. made a winding-up order in the Irish proceedings on March 23 holding that Eurofood's COMI was in Ireland. The company's registered office was in Ireland, raising a presumption under Art.3(1) that Ireland was the COMI. The creditors' perception was that they were dealing with a company located in Ireland and (as was the case) subject to its fiscal and regulatory provisions. The only connection with Italy was that the

---

[72] *Re Eurofood IFSC Ltd* [2004] B.C.C. 383.

company was a subsidiary of an Italian company. Kelly J. concluded that the Parma court lacked jurisdiction to open main proceedings because (contrary to the advice placed before that court) the presentation of the winding-up petition and the appointment of a provisional liquidator on January 27 brought about the opening of main proceedings. The winding-up took effect from the time of presentation of the winding-up petition, pursuant to s.220(2) of the Companies Act 1963. It followed that the decision of the Parma court was not entitled to recognition. An additional ground for refusal of recognition was the denial of the opportunity to creditors to be heard in the Parma proceedings, and this entitled the Irish court to invoke the public policy exception in Art. 26.

13–27 The ruling that the appointment of a provisional liquidator constituted the opening of main proceedings was, with respect, incorrect, because such an appointment does not feature in the list of insolvency proceedings in Appendix A in relation to Ireland. The winding-up order would, indeed, have effect under Irish law as from the time of presentation of the petition, but that order had not been made at the time the case came before the Parma court. Accordingly at that time no main insolvency proceedings had been opened. The case should therefore have been decided not on the basis that such proceedings had been opened but rather on the footing that because of presentation of the winding-up petition the Parma court should not have proceeded with its own hearing until after the petition had been heard.

On Signor Bondi's appeal to the Irish Supreme Court,[73] which was solely on the issue of refusal to recognise the Parma court's decision, the Supreme Court noted that Signore Bondi had at no time given any explanation for his failure to provide the provisional liquidator with essential documents for the Parma hearing and that even on the appeal his counsel had been instructed to offer no explanation to the Supreme Court for the "extraordinary behaviour" of Signor Bondi, which the court criticised in the strongest terms. It was an intrinsic element of the principle of mutual trust that parties to proceedings receive a fair hearing, which had not happened in Parma. Kelly J. was therefore correct in holding that it would be contrary to the public policy of Irish law to recognise the judgment of the Parma court. Nevertheless the court felt bound to refer the question to the European Court of Justice for a preliminary ruling. This is expected in the near future. But the question of the effect of a winding-up petition or of an application to open any other insolvency proceedings has yet to be authoritatively determined.[74]

---

[73] [2005] Eu. L.R. 148.
[74] See below, para.13–34.

What constitutes the opening of proceedings

It may be important to determine what constitutes the opening of proceedings and thus the time at which they are deemed to have been opened. That is the time as at which the COMI has to be determined for the purpose of the jurisdictional rules, and in the case of main proceedings it establishes which court of competent jurisdiction is to be considered first in the field so as to have the exclusive right to recognition in other Member States. As we shall see, the date when the debts were incurred is irrelevant. Article 2(f) provides that:

13–28

"'the time of the opening of proceedings' means the time at which the judgment opening proceedings becomes effective, whether it is a final judgment or not."

As we have seen, "judgment" has to be given an extended meaning, covering not only winding-up and administration orders but creditors' voluntary liquidations, out-of-court administrations and CVAs. One might have thought it would be easy to determine the date of opening of these various proceedings but in various respects the position is far from clear, and it is necessary to take each type of proceeding in turn.

(1) Creditors' voluntary winding-up

The requirement that the proceedings be confirmed by the court[75] raises the question whether the relevant time is the time the confirming order is made or the time the resolution is passed. The history of this provision shows the intention to take the time of the resolution as the relevant time except for the purpose of allowing the liquidator to exercise his powers in another Member State.[76] The proceedings are opened on the passing of the resolution by the members for voluntary winding-up by reason of insolvency.

13–29

(2) Compulsory winding-up

The position here is complicated by the retrospective character of a winding-up order. Where the winding-up follows a CVL it is deemed to commence at the time of passing of the resolution for voluntary winding-up; where the winding-up order is made on an application for an administration order, the commencement is the time of the winding-up

13–30

---

[75] See above, para.13–11.
[76] Virgós-Schmit Report, paras 52, 68.

order; in other cases it is the date of presentation of the winding-up petition.[77] The question then arises whether in the first and third case the proceedings should be considered opened on the making of the winding-up order or on the passing of the resolution or (if there was no prior CVL) the presentation of the winding-up petition. Reference has already been made to the decision of the Irish High Court in *Re Eurofood IFSC Ltd*,[78] in which Kelly J. held that under the equivalent provisions of s.220(2) of the Irish Companies Act 1963 the winding-up likewise took effect as at the time of presentation of the winding-up petition, and this was to be treated as the time of opening of the insolvency proceedings for the purpose of the Insolvency Regulation. That conclusion receives support from Art.2(f)[79] and from the Virgós-Schmit Report.[80] It is disputed by some authorities[81] on the ground that other provisions of the Regulation clearly distinguish between the opening of proceedings and a request for the opening of proceedings.[82] But these provisions are dealing with the stage preceding the judgment when there is nothing except the request; they do not bear on the retrospective effect of a judgment once this has been handed down. Moreover, it is not in every Member State or in every type of insolvency proceeding that retrospective effect is given to the judgment.

(3) Administration

13–31 The proceedings are opened upon the administration taking effect,[83] whether out-of-court or by court order.

(4) CVA

13–32 In the case of a CVA, the proceedings are opened upon its taking effect.[84]

Effect of a request to open proceedings

13–33 While it is clear that a judgment opening insolvency proceedings in one Member State must be respected in all other Member States there is a singular lack of clarity as to the effect of a request to open proceedings.

---

[77] Insolvency Act 1986, s.129.

[78] [2004] B.C.C. 383.

[79] Which defines the time of the opening of the proceedings as the time at which the judgment opening the proceedings becomes effective, whether it is a final judgment or not, leaving it to the *lex concursus* to determine the time as at which the proceedings are to be treated as opened.

[80] "'The time of the opening of the proceedings' is deemed to be the time when the decision begins to be effective under the law of the State of the opening of the proceedings" (para.68). Similarly the tentative view of the majority of the Court of Appeal in *Shierson v Vlieland-Boddy* [2005] EWCA 974 was that the relevant time was the service of the petition. See further para.13–36.

[81] E.g. Moss, Fletcher and Isaacs, *op. cit.*, para.8.52; Dicey & Morris, *Conflict of Laws*, fourth supplement to the 13th ed., paras S30–157.

[82] See, for example, Arts.3(4), 29.

[83] See above, paras 13–10, 13–12.

[84] See above, para.13–12.

The various references to such a request[85] shed little light on its status. It seems clear that the request cannot itself constitute the opening of insolvency proceedings, though an ensuing judgment may, under the *lex concursus*, have effect as from the date of the request.[86] On the other hand, to allow a creditor who has notice of such a request to institute proceedings in another forum with a view to establishing main proceedings in that forum first would be to encourage the self-same forum shopping which the Regulation is designed to avoid. Similarly, allowing the debtor to move its COMI to another Member State between the time of the request and the time of judgment in order to frustrate proceedings that have been initiated in the first Member State would facilitate evasion of the Regulation, and the change of COMI could perhaps be disregarded on that ground, though this result is more easily achieved where a judgment opening proceedings in a Member State has effect from the time of the request, under the law of that State.[87] The principle of Community respect should thus extend to the initiation of the process by which collective insolvency proceedings will later be opened. So if in one Member State an application is made for a winding-up order, courts in other Member States should refrain from opening insolvency proceedings in their own jurisdiction until the winding-up proceedings have been determined. If a winding-up order is made this will establish the main proceedings, and any proceedings elsewhere will be territorial proceedings. If, on the other hand, the application is dismissed, this leaves it open to the courts of another Member State to open proceedings themselves if the jurisdictional requirements of the Regulation are satisfied. This deferment to proceedings pending in another Member State not only reflects the spirit of the Regulation but can properly be founded on the principle *lis pendens*[88] or, where the facts justify it, on the principle of estoppel by which the debtor company cannot be heard to say that its COMI is located at a place other than that at which the company

---

[85] See, for example, recital (16) in regard to provisional and protective measures; recital (17) and Art.3(4)(b) in regard to limiting to local creditors the right to make a request to open independent proceedings; recital (18), (19) and (25) and Art.29 as to the right of the liquidator of main proceedings to request the opening of secondary proceedings, and Art.37 as to his right to apply for the conversion of territorial proceedings.

[86] As in the case of a compulsory winding-up under s.29 of the Insolvency Act 1986.

[87] See further para.13–36. Under some conflict of laws rules, in particular those of French law, the change would be disregarded as a *fraude à la loi*, that is, a change in the location of the connecting factor made deliberately with a view to escaping from the otherwise applicable law. See Bernard Audit, *Droit International Privé* (2nd ed.), paras 230 *et seq*. In *Shierson v Vlieland-Boddy* [2004] All E.R. (D) 420, the contention that the debtor (in that case an individual who was made bankrupt) should not be allowed to evade the court's jurisdiction by changing his COMI was rejected, but in that case the move took place several months before presentation of the bankruptcy petition. The German Supreme Court has referred to the European Court of Justice the question whether the relevant time is the opening of the insolvency proceedings: BGH 27.11.2003—IX ZR 418/03, Zeitschrift fr Wirtschaftsrecht 2004, 94. The ECJ file number is C-1/04. I am indebted to Professor Herbert Kronke for this information.

[88] Virgós and Garcimartín, *op. cit.*, para.70.

held it out as located. Where the court in the later proceedings is unaware
of the request to open the earlier proceedings and opens its own insolvency
proceedings, and subsequently an order is made in the earlier proceedings,
the appropriate course in the later proceedings would seem to be to convert
them into secondary proceedings.

6. MAIN PROCEEDINGS AND DETERMINATION OF THE DEBTOR'S COMI

Effect of opening of main proceedings

13–34   Once main proceedings have been opened in a Member State, all other
proceedings in another Member State are secondary proceedings[89] which
can only be winding-up proceedings and are restricted to local assets.[90] Any
judgment opened in the main proceedings must be recognised throughout
the European Union from the time it becomes effective in the state of
opening of the proceedings,[91] and produces the same effects in other
Member States as under the law of the state of opening of the proceedings,
without further formality.[92] It is therefore not necessary to obtain any
exequatur in such other states in order to produce the effects in question.
The effects in question include the rules governing the matters listed in
Article 4 except so far as displaced by the exceptions in Arts.5 *et seq.* as
previously discussed. Such effects thus cover such matters as an automatic
stay of proceedings, the determination of the assets forming the debtor's
estate, the bringing of all assets under the control of the liquidator in the
main proceedings except for those subject to territorial proceedings and
located within the territory concerned, and the avoidance of transactions
under the rules of the *lex concursus*. So the *lex concursus*, so far as not
displaced, applies automatically throughout the European Union. The
liquidator may exercise in another Member State all the powers conferred
on him by the *lex concursus*, and may remove assets the debtor's assets, but
with three qualifications. He may not exercise his powers in the other
Member State if other insolvency proceedings have been opened there or if
any preservation measure to the contrary has been taken there. He must
respect any *in rem* and retention of title rights of third parties under Arts.5
and 7, subject to the avoidance provisions of the *lex concursus* under
Art.4(2)(m). Finally he must comply with the local law and must not

---

[89] Insolvency Regulation, art.3(3). See above, para.13–18.
[90] See below, para.13–40. Note that winding-up here includes winding-up through administration. See above, para.13–11.
[91] Art.16(1).
[92] Art.17(1). But this does not apply as regards a Member State in which territorial proceedings are opened (*ibid.*).

exercise coercive measures or the right to rule on legal proceedings or disputes.[93] The liquidator in the main proceedings may also apply in another Member State to open secondary proceedings.[94]

Redefinition of "property"

In order to conform to the Regulation, the definition of "property" in s.436 of the Insolvency Act 1986[95] has been modified as regards insolvency proceedings in England so as to limit the reference to property in the application of the Act to property which may be dealt with in the proceedings.[96] This means that where main proceedings have been opened in another Member State the jurisdiction of the English courts in relation to territorial proceedings opened there is confined to assets within the jurisdiction and that where main proceedings have been opened in England, then although in principle these cover the whole of the debtor company's estate on a worldwide basis this is subject to (1) the control by courts of another Member State in which territorial proceedings have been opened over assets situated in that state and (2) the *in rem* and other rights of third parties protected by the exclusions from Art.4 specified in Arts 5 *et seq.*

13–35

Ascertainment of the COMI

As we have seen, main proceedings can be instituted only in the Member State in the territory of which the debtor's COMI is situated. In addition, the situation of the debtor's claim against a third party is in the territory in which the third party has his COMI.[97] Astonishingly the text of the Regulation does not define the COMI or give any guidance as to its meaning. For that we have to rely on recital (13), which states that the 'centre of main interests'

13–36

"... should correspond to the place where the debtor conducts the administration of his interests on a regular basis and is therefore ascertainable by third parties."

All we know from the text of the Regulation is that in the case of a company or legal person, the place of the registered office is to be presumed as its COMI in the absence of proof to the contrary.[98] This

---

[93] Art.18(1), (3).
[94] Art.29.
[95] See above, paras 6–03 *et seq.*
[96] Insolvency Act 1986, s.436A.
[97] Art.2(g). The situation of assets is particularly relevant to the applicability of Arts.5 and 7. See below, paras 13–53 *et seq.*
[98] Art.3(1).

default rule has the merit of certainty but in practice is likely to be a very unreliable guide. Where the debtor conducts the administration of its interests on a regular basis will often have nothing to do with the location of its registered office. The presumption is therefore a weak one and readily displaced. The Virgós-Schmit Report (which as stated earlier was a report on the EC Convention, not the Regulation) elaborated on the rationale of the "centre of main interests" concept in the following terms:

"The concept of 'centre of main interests' must be interpreted as the place where the debtor conducts the administration of his interests on a regular basis and is therefore ascertainable by third parties.

The rationale of this rule is not difficult to explain. Insolvency is a foreseeable risk. It is therefore important that international jurisdiction . . . be based on a place known to the debtor's potential creditors. This enables the legal risks which would have to be assumed in the case of insolvency to be calculated.

By using the term 'interests', the intention was to encompass not only commercial, industrial or professional activities, but also general economic activities, so as to include the actions of private individuals (*e.g.* consumers). The expression 'main' serves as a criterion for the cases where these interests included activities of different types which are run from different centres."[99]

The second paragraph of the above passage has been criticised as implying that the relevant time for determining the debtor's COMI is the time the debts are incurred, when it is clear from the Regulation that it is the time when the judgment to open the proceedings becomes effective, which in English law is possibly the date of service of the petition.[1] There is force in this criticism, for it is hard to see how knowledge of the debtor's COMI (and thus of the potentially applicable insolvency regime) at the time of extending credit can enable the creditor to assess the risk when the debtor may move its COMI to another Member State the very next day and may incur fresh debt to creditors in the new State, raising the question which creditors are to be considered the relevant ones.[2] But the rationale for the COMI concept holds good in the many cases in which the situation of the COMI remains unchanged. The time factor cannot be controlled but the

---

[99] Report, para.75.

[1] *Shierson v Vlieland-Boddy* [2005] EWCA 974, a case in which the debtor had incurred debts when his COMI was in England but had shifted his COMI to Spain by the time of opening of the insolvency proceedings. The Court of Appeal held that he was entitled to do this and that there was therefore no jurisdiction to open main proceedings in England.

[2] The advantage of taking the date of service of the proceedings as the relevant date is that if the foreign court subsequently refuses to entertain main proceedings by reason of *lis alibi pendens* (see para.13-33) the English court could proceed to make a winding-up order with retrospective effect, thus negating the impact of a post-petition change of COMI.

place of the COMI is that which creditors generally would consider the most relevant.

Almost all the reported case law in England has focused on jurisdictional questions raised by the COMI issue, and in almost every case the court has concluded that it has jurisdiction because the company's COMI was situated here even though its registered office was elsewhere. Strikingly, two of the decisions that have attracted much attention here and overseas emanate from the High Court sitting at Leeds. The first of these was the *Daisy-Tek* case,[3] which had an impact going well beyond the shores of the British Isles. The facts were as follows:

Daisy-Tek ISA Ltd. was a subsidiary of a US company, Daisy-Tek International Corporation, which had filed for reorganisation under Chapter 11. Daisy-Tek ISA itself had a subsidiary, ISA International plc ("International") and through International was also the holding company of a number of other companies incorporated in England, France and Germany. Creditors of Daisy-Tek ISA and its direct and indirect subsidiaries applied for administration orders against them.

HH Judge McGonigal said in his judgment that in identifying the centre of the debtor's main interests the court had to consider both the scale of the interests administered at a particular place and their importance and then consider the scale and importance of its interests administered at any other place which might be regarded as its centre of main interests, whether as a result of the presumption in Article 3(1) or otherwise. The fact that the centre of the debtor's main interests had to be 'ascertainable by third parties' was very important. The evidence showed that the administration of their businesses was conducted from Bradford, where customers were serviced and contracts were concluded, and all the businesses were controlled from Bradford. Further, a large majority of potential trade and finance creditors knew that Bradford was the place where many of the important functions of the companies were carried out, and these were the most important 'third parties' referred to in recital (13) of the Regulation as those who should be able to ascertain the debtor's centre of main interests. He therefore held that he had jurisdiction to make such orders not only against the English companies but also against those incorporated in France and Germany.

The battle then moved to France, where the Commercial Court of Cergy-Pontoise, though informed of the decision of the English High Court, held that this was "without effect" in relation to the relevant French subsidiary, since each company within the Daisy-Tek group was a separate legal entity, there was no legal concept of a "group" and the English court could not

13–37

---

[3] *Re Daisytek-ISA Ltd* [2003] B.C.C. 562.

assume jurisdiction by denying the separate legal existence of the French company. The court thereupon made its own administration order against that subsidiary and later dismissed an application by the UK administrators to have its judgment set aside. The decision was reversed by the Court of Appeal of Versailles,[4] which in a clear and concisely reasoned judgment held that it was untrue to argue that the High Court's decision had been based on the notion of a corporate group, and that on the contrary the High Court had concluded that the company's centre of main interests was in Bradford. Accordingly the Insolvency Regulation required French courts to respect the order made by the High Court, which produced the same legal effects in France as under English law, the Commercial Court of Pontoise had no jurisdiction to put the company into administration and its order was in violation of the Regulation.[5]

A similar sequence of events occurred in relation to the German subsidiaries. The court of first instance at Düsseldorf, initially unaware of the English administration order, made its own order, so that there were two main insolvency proceedings, contrary to what is permitted by the Regulation. When the court learned of the English order it held that it was of no effect in relation to the German subsidiaries, but on appeal it was ordered that in relation to one of the German companies the proceedings be converted into secondary proceedings in recognition of the primacy of the English order.[6]

The situation of the debtor's COMI is a question of fact and degree. Among the factors the court will take into account in deciding whether the presumption in favour of the location of the registered office has been displaced are the following: the place where the company's business is managed and operated and its contracts concluded[7]; the location of any regulatory authorities[8]; the place where board meetings are held[9]; the place where the accounts are prepared and audited[10]; the location of customers, suppliers and loan creditors[11]; the place from which information technology and support and corporate identity and branding are run[12]; and the place where the chief executive spends most of his time in the running of the business.[13] None of these factors is necessarily decisive on its own, and

---

[4] 24th Chamber, September 4, 2003, case no. 03/05038. An English translation of the decision is reported *sub. Nom. Klempka v ISA Daisytek SA* [2003] B.C.C. 984.

[5] The question of respect for orders of the court which is the first to open proceedings is discussed below, para.13–45.

[6] For an English description of the course of the proceedings in Germany, see Fletcher, *op. cit.*, paras 7.71, 7.73.

[7] *Re Eurofood IFSC Ltd* [2004] B.C.C. 383; *Re AIM Underwriting Agencies (Ireland) Ltd* [2005] I.L.Pr. 22.

[8] *Re Eurofood IFSC Ltd* [2004] B.C.C. 383.

[9] *ibid.*

[10] *ibid.*

[11] *Re Daisy-Tek ISA Ltd* [2004] B.P.I.R. 30; *Re 3T Telecom Ltd* [2005] All E.R. (D) 91.

[12] *ibid.*

[13] *ibid.*

usually two or more of them are to be found in combination. The court has to weigh up all the facts and decide where the company's centre of gravity is situated. What is clear is that the COMI must have a reasonable degree of permanence; the concept of the location of the business shifting as its director moved from one country to another does not sit easily with the policy of the Regulation.[14] The central idea is captured by the phrase "command and control",[15] and in the difficult case where trading is mainly conducted in and from the territory of one Member State but control is exercised in and from headquarters in another it would seem that preference should be given to the latter in determining the COMI of the debtor.

Creditor control of the COMI

It would usually be difficult even for the main creditor to stipulate where the debtor's COMI should be located, since this is a business decision which should be left to the debtor. On the other hand, there would be nothing unreasonable in a stipulation that the COMI was not to be changed without a specified period of prior notice to the creditor and even that the debtor should be required to obtain the creditor's consent, such consent not to be unreasonably withheld. But a mere contractual stipulation, even if backed by a default remedy such as acceleration of the indebtedness, would have relatively limited force. Only a substantially secured creditor has the power to exercise the control required. Lenders usually seek both a representation as to the existing location of the COMI and an undertaking not to move it without consent. Borrowers are reluctant to make an unqualified representation as to the location of the COMI on the ground that this is a question of law as well as of fact, involving difficult definitional issues, and seek to restrict any representation to factual matters, such as where board meetings are held or the directors are based.

13–38

Powers of the liquidator

The liquidator in the main proceedings has extensive powers. He may exercise in other Member States all the powers conferred upon him by the *lex concursus*,[16] request notice of the judgment opening the main proceedings to be published in any other Member State[17] and registered in any land register,[18] may request the opening of secondary proceedings[19] or a stay of

13–39

---

[14] *Re Ci4net.com Inc.* [2005] B.C.C. 277.
[15] Fletcher, *op. cit.*, para.7.75.
[16] Art.18(1).
[17] Art.21(1).
[18] Art.22(1).
[19] Art.29.

secondary proceedings that have been opened,[20] propose a rescue plan, composition or comparable measure in the secondary proceedings[21] and request the conversion of proceedings opened in another Member State into winding-up proceedings if this proves to be in the interests of the creditors in the main proceedings.[22]

7. TERRITORIAL PROCEEDINGS

Types of territorial proceedings

13–40   Territorial proceedings are so called because they are confined to assets within the territory in which the proceedings are opened and thus do not enjoy the universal application of main proceedings. Where they are secondary proceedings they can only take the form of winding-up, for the obvious reason that their sole purpose is to realise local assets, and since they are restricted to such assets a reorganisation of the company as a whole would be impracticable and, moreover, would limit the efficacy of a reorganisation in the main proceedings. Territorial proceedings are independent if they are opened before any main proceedings have been opened; otherwise they are secondary proceedings.

The scope of the provision in Art.3(2) that territorial proceedings are restricted to local assets is not entirely clear. It is obvious that the proceedings have no effect on assets situated in another Member State. But what of proceedings that do not relate to the company's assets at all, for example, proceedings under s.113 of the Insolvency Act 1986 relating to fraudulent trading or s.114 relating to wrongful trading? There seems no reason why, in territorial winding-up proceedings in England, the court should not have power to make contribution orders against directors under those sections, since these do not relate to the company's existing assets, nor, as we have seen, are recoveries to be considered assets of the company. Again, disqualification proceedings against a director under s.6 of the Act do not appear to be precluded by Art.3(2).

Conditions in which territorial proceedings may be opened

(1) Jurisdiction at international and national level

13–41   As with main proceedings, the power to entertain territorial proceedings must satisfy a twofold test. It must meet the criteria for international jurisdiction laid down by the Regulation; and it must satisfy any additional

---

[20] Art.33.
[21] Art.34(1).
[22] Art.37. Secondary proceedings are by their nature limited to winding-up (Art.3(3)). See below, para.13–40.

jurisdictional requirements imposed by the national law of the state concerned.

(2) The need for an establishment

Territorial proceedings may be instituted only in a Member State in which the debtor has an establishment.[23] The time at which this condition has to be satisfied is on the hearing of the request to open the proceedings. "Establishment" is defined as:

13–42

> "any place of operations where the debtor carries out a non-transitory economic activity with human means and goods."[24]

The economic activity need not be central to the company's operations; it suffices that there is a place of business which is not purely temporary (though it need not be permanent), which is operated by staff who are either employees of the company or others for whose acts it is responsible and which is engaged in economic activity. The key elements have been described as the conduct of commercial, industrial or professional activities manifested externally, some form of organisational presence (a branch, an office, a factory, a workshop), and a degree of stability and iteration.[25]
The word "goods" has rightly been described as "unfortunate"[26] and belies the intention, which is to cover not only goods but intangible property, services and facilities, and Art.2(h) should be construed in that light. It has been held that the location in England of the premises business premises of a subsidiary of the debtor company does not by itself constitute an establishment of the company,[27] though if the premises are occupied by a branch rather than a subsidiary that will ordinarily suffice.

(3) Further conditions for independent proceedings

Independent proceedings (those instituted before the opening of main proceedings) can be instituted only where:

13–43

(a) main insolvency proceedings cannot be opened because of the conditions laid down by the law of the Member State in which the debtor has its COMI; or

---

[23] Art.3(2).
[24] Art.2(h).
[25] Virgós-Schmit Report, para.71; Virgós and Garcimartín, *op. cit.*, paras 298 *et seq.*
[26] Moss, Fletcher and Isaacs, *op. cit.*, para.8.63.
[27] *Telia AB v Hillcourt (Docklands) Ltd* [2003] B.C.C. 856.

(b) the opening of the independent proceedings is requested by a creditor who has his domicile, habitual residence or registered office in the Member State within the territory of which the establishment is situated, or whose claim arises from the operation of that establishment.

Point (a) refers in particular to national laws which prohibit the opening of insolvency proceedings against companies providing public services, and finds its echo in the definition of "insolvency-related event" in the Aircraft Equipment Protocol to the 2001 Cape Town Convention on International Interests in Mobile Equipment.[28]

No barrier to multiple territorial proceedings

13–44   The principle of unity does not apply to territorial proceedings. There can be as many of these as there are establishments of the debtor in different Member States. No conflict can arise, because each territorial proceeding is limited to the local assets.

Community respect

13–45   The principle of Community respect applies as much to secondary proceedings as it does to attempted second main proceedings. The court which is asked to open the secondary proceedings cannot question the basis upon which the court in the state of the debtor's COMI reached its decision, and accordingly may not go behind the findings of the court in which the main proceedings were opened as to the situation of the debtor's COMI or as to the fact of the debtor's insolvency. However, in the UK the only type of insolvency proceeding which requires the court to be satisfied of an existing state of insolvency is winding-up. There is no such requirement for a CVA or an out-of-court administration by the holder of a qualifying floating charge; and even where the administrator is appointed by the company, the directors or the court it suffices that the company is likely to become insolvent. It follows that where main proceedings are opened in England which do not involve a finding of insolvency it is open to the court of another Member State in secondary proceedings to determine for itself whether the company is insolvent. Such a finding in one secondary insolvency proceeding must then be respected in other Member States in which secondary proceedings are subsequently requested.

---

[28] Protocol to the Convention on International Interests in Mobile Equipment on Matters Specific to Aircraft Equipment, art.I(m). Paragraph 11 of the Official Commentary to the Convention and Protocol gives as an example the fact that in certain systems airlines are not eligible for insolvency proceedings.

Claims in secondary proceedings

Though secondary proceedings are limited to local assets, they are not **13–46** limited to local creditors. Creditors in the main proceedings may also, through the liquidator, prove in the secondary proceedings, and *vice versa*.[29] The local assets must first be applied in discharge of the claims of creditors in the secondary proceedings. If there is a surplus, this is handed over to the liquidator in the main proceedings.[30] But this can arise only if creditors in the main proceedings have not proved in the secondary proceedings.[31]

Creditors have a particular incentive to pursue secondary proceedings where the *lex concursus* governing their claims gives them better rights than they would enjoy under the law governing the main proceedings. For example, French law gives employees greater rights than English law on the insolvency of the employer, so that where main proceedings are opened in England against a French company, then, in terms of the range of claims ranking for preferential status, employees of the company will fare better in secondary proceedings in France than they would in main proceedings in England.[32]

Effects of territorial proceedings

These are more limited than the effect of main proceedings. Whereas a **13–47** judgment opening main proceedings has the same effects in any other Member State as in the state in which the proceedings were opened,[33] the position as regards territorial proceedings is merely that their effects (which are confined to local assets) may not be challenged in other Member

---

[29] Art.32.
[30] Art.35.
[31] Virgós-Schmit Report, paras 236–237.
[32] This was the position in administration proceedings in the Birmingham District Registry of the High Court against eight companies within the Rover group, including a French company, where HH Judge Norris QC, in a judgment handed down on May 11, 2005, held that, though the claims of French employees were governed by English insolvency law, the administrators nevertheless had power under para.66 of Sch.B1 to the Insolvency Act 1986 to pay employees of the French company what they would have received in secondary proceedings in France where this was likely to achieve the purpose of the administration. Had the administrators applied for an order to that effect it would have been granted on the ground that if such payments were not made there would be pressure to open secondary proceedings in France and thus lead to the uncoordinated destruction of the individual businesses in those proceedings and undermine the co-ordination of the insolvency process by the joint administrators within the main proceedings. An interesting feature of the judgment is the inclusion of a Schedule summarising the administrators' powers by reference to Sch.B1 for the assistance of practitioners in other Member States who are accustomed to seeing the powers of office holders set out in the order appointing them and may be reluctant simply to accept a statement of such powers from the solicitors representing the administrators. The judgment is available on the EIR Database at *www.eir-database.com*.
[33] Art.17(1).

States,[34] but restrictions imposed on creditors' rights, such as a stay or discharge, cannot produce those effects *vis-à-vis* assets situated within the territory of another Member State except as regards creditors who have given their consent.[35]

8. THE APPLICABLE LAW UNDER ARTICLE 4

General principles

13–48   Article 4(1) of the Regulation provides that the law applicable to insolvency proceedings and their effect is that of the Member State within the territory of which such proceedings are opened, referred to as the 'State of the opening of proceedings'. By Art.4(2) this law (the *lex concursus*) determines the conditions for the opening of the proceedings, their conduct and their closure, and in particular the various matters listed in sub-paragraphs (a) to (m) of Art.4(2). Each proceeding, whether main or territorial, is governed by its own *lex concursus*.[36] The list is non-exhaustive but covers most of the matters one would expect to find governed by the *lex concursus* in national insolvency law. However, as we shall see, the reach of the *lex concursus* is not as wide as it seems. Its operation is confined to insolvency effects, and even the description of *in rem* rights contained in Art.5(2) is not intended to define such rights, which are a matter of the applicable law, but rather to set certain boundaries to the range of rights that will be admitted to the status of rights *in rem* for the purposes of the Regulation.

Relationship between *lex concursus* and law governing pre-insolvency entitlements

13–49   Most insolvency laws start from the position that pre-insolvency entitlements—in particular, contract rights, ownership and security interests—are to be respected.[37] But those rights may be modified by insolvency law in various ways, for example, by subordinating certain rights which would have priority under the general law outside insolvency or by making void or voidable transactions concluded in the run-up to the opening of insolvency proceedings which are considered unfair to the general creditors, such as transactions at an undervalue, preferences and

---

[34] Art.17(2).
[35] *ibid*.
[36] A point reinforced by Art.38 in relation to secondary proceedings. The same applies to independent proceedings.
[37] In England that position is not expressly stated in the Insolvency Act 1986, it is assumed.

transactions in fraud of creditors. In the insolvency proceedings, therefore, the conflict rules of the state of opening of the proceedings are applied as the *lex fori* to ascertain the law governing a person's pre-insolvency entitlements (*lex causae*), the *lex causae* is applied to establish the existence and content of those entitlements and it is then for the *lex concursus* of the state concerned to determine to what extent, if at all, those entitlements are modified or nullified by the insolvency in the implementation of insolvency policy. Any reference in the Regulation to law of a Member State governing a particular issue is a reference to the internal law of that state, excluding its conflict of laws rules; in other words, as in most modern conventions, the concept of *renvoi* has no role to play.[38]

The same approach is adopted by the Regulation except that, in order to ensure that the *lex concursus* does not go beyond the legitimate bounds of insolvency law in its interference with pre-insolvency entitlements, it has a series of provisions excluding the application of the *lex concursus* as such to particular rights in order to protect legitimate expectations and the certainty of transactions in other Member States.[39] These provisions, contained in Arts.5 to 15, are themselves of four kinds. Into the first category fall rights *in rem* and reservation of title. In relation to these Arts.5 and 7 provide that the opening of the insolvency proceedings is not to affect such rights in relation to assets situated within the territory of another Member State at the time of opening of the proceedings. This is not in itself a conflict rule; it says nothing about the law to be applied to determine the existence and content of the rights in question, though in the case of an issue arising in the insolvency proceedings themselves it will be the law applicable under the conflict rules of the insolvency jurisdiction as the *lex fori*. By contrast, provisions in the second category, namely Arts.6, 8–11, 14 and 15, each lay down a positive conflict rule to determine the law applicable to the right in question. The third category contains only one provision, Art.12, under which Community patents and trade marks may be included only in main proceedings. The fourth category also contains only one provision, Art.13, which disapplies Art.4(2)(m)[40] in relation to detrimental acts governed by the law of a Member State which does not allow any means of challenging that act.

The list

Article 4(2) provides as follows:

13–50

"The law of the State of the opening of proceedings shall determine the conditions for the opening of those proceedings, their conduct and their closure. It shall determine in particular:

---

[38] This is nowhere stated as considered implicit in the Regulation. See the Virgós-Schmit Report, para.87.
[39] Recital (24).
[40] See below.

   (a) against which debtors insolvency proceedings may be brought on account of their capacity;

   (b) the assets which form part of the estate and the treatment of assets acquired by or devolving on the debtor after the opening of the insolvency proceedings;

   (c) the respective powers of the debtor and the liquidator;

   (d) the conditions under which set-offs may be invoked;

   (e) the effects of insolvency proceedings on current contracts to which the debtor is party;

   (f) the effects of the insolvency proceedings on proceedings brought by individual creditors, with the exception of lawsuits pending;

   (g) the claims which are to be lodged against the debtor's estate and the treatment of claims arising after the opening of insolvency proceedings;

   (h) the rules governing the lodging, verification and admission of claims;

   (i) the rules governing the distribution of proceeds from the realisation of assets, the ranking of claims and the rights of creditors who have obtained partial satisfaction after the opening of insolvency proceedings by virtue of a right in rem or through a set-off;

   (j) the conditions for and the effects of closure of insolvency proceedings, in particular by composition;

   (k) creditors' rights after the closure of insolvency proceedings;

   (l) who is to bear the costs and expenses incurred in the insolvency proceedings;

  (m) the rules relating to the voidness, voidability or unenforceability of legal acts detrimental to all the creditors."

All the items in this list, which is non-exhaustive and does not cut down the generality of the first sentence of Art.4(2), find their counterparts in UK insolvency law and for the most part they require no comment. There are, however, five points to be noted.

(1)   When sub-paragraph (b) refers to the assets which form part of the estate, that does not mean that pre-insolvency entitlements acquired under other law are ignored. On the contrary, insolvency law starts from the position that pre-insolvency entitlements are to be respected, and if those were created under other law, as where at the time of their creation the asset was situated in a Member State other than that in which the insolvency proceedings have been opened, then in principle that law governs the starting position in relation to the asset in question[41] and it is unnecessary to rely on the exceptions in Arts.5–

---

[41] For the application of this principle in relation to UK insolvency law, see above, para.13–49. That the same principle applies equally to Art.4 of the Regulation is very clearly stated by Virgó and Garcimartín, *op. cit.*, para.119.

15. But assets acquired by the debtor company under other law may be swollen by inclusion in the estate of additional assets under the rules of the *lex concursus*, for example, rules by which the estate includes after-acquired property or rules by which transfers and payments made by the debtor on the eve of insolvency are avoided.[42] In short, Art.4 is concerned only with *insolvency* effects, not with effects under the general law.

(2) While sub-paragraph (d) subjects rights of set-off to the *lex concursus*, this is subject to preservation of the right of a creditor under Art.6 to demand set-off under the law applicable to the insolvent debtor's claim.[43] This is a departure from English law rules of insolvency set-off, which displace all other forms of set-off not exercised prior to the commencement of the winding-up.

(3) Sub-paragraph (i), relating to the ranking of claims, is concerned solely with insolvency effects; it does not mean that priorities established under the general law prior to the insolvency proceedings are to be ignored, merely that in certain cases they may be modified or disapplied by rules of the *lex concursus*. For example, where English law is the *lex concursus* a secured creditor will generally have priority over an unsecured creditor, while priority as between secured creditors will usually be determined by the relevant priority rules under the general law, but under the Insolvency Act 1986 a floating charge will be subordinate to the claims of preferential creditors (that is, employees) and will be subject to surrender of the prescribed part, and a registrable charge not registered within the time prescribed by s.395 of the Companies Act 1985 will be void against the liquidator and creditors. The starting point, however, is to determine priorities by reference to the *lex causae*, thus in many cases making it unnecessary to invoke the exceptions in Arts.5–15, which appear in the regulation solely for the purpose of preventing the application of over-inclusive rules of the *lex concursus*. The insolvency rules governing the ranking of claims then operate to modify the pre-insolvency priority established under the *lex causae* except so far as those rules are displaced by one or more of the exceptions in Arts.5–15.

(4) The application of the avoidance rules in Art.4(2)(m) is cut down by Art.13, which is designed to prevent the application of rules of avoidance of two or more legal systems by putting a bar on the

---

[42] In personal bankruptcy, to which the Regulation also applies, the estate may not only be expanded but restricted by insolvency law. For example, in England the bankrupt's estate does not include damages the bankrupt recovers for defamation or necessary tools, books, vehicles and other forms of equipment necessary for his personal use in his employment, business or vocation.

[43] Art.6(1). See below, para.13–60.

application of Art.4(2)(m) where under the law governing the act to which Art.4(2)(m) would otherwise apply the act in question is not open to challenge.[44]

(5) The reference in Art.4(2)(m) to acts detrimental to "all" the creditors should not be taken literally, for there are always likely to be creditors unaffected by the acts in question, including secured creditors. Art.4(2)(m) should thus be read as referring to acts detrimental to the creditors collectively, that is, the general body of creditors.

9. EXCLUSIONS FROM ARTICLE 4

13–51 We can now turn to the cases in which Art.4 is either qualified or displaced by a rule designed to ensure that the *lex concursus* gives due respect to various important rights established by the *lex causae* and does not seek to carry the insolvency effects beyond their allotted sphere.

Third parties' rights *in rem*

13–52 Article 5 deals with the rights of third parties *in rem*. Its purpose is to safeguard such rights from the effect of the opening of insolvency proceedings, and it is therefore of considerable importance.

> **"Article 5**
> **Third parties' rights in rem**
> 1. The opening of insolvency proceedings shall not affect the rights in rem of creditors or third parties in respect of tangible or intangible, moveable or immoveable assets—both specific assets and collections of indefinite assets as a whole which change from time to time—belonging to the debtor which are situated within the territory of another Member State at the time of the opening of proceedings.
>
> 2. The rights referred to in paragraph 1 shall in particular mean:
>
> (a) the right to dispose of assets or have them disposed of and to obtain satisfaction from the proceeds of or income from those assets, in particular by virtue of a lien or a mortgage;
>
> (b) the exclusive right to have a claim met, in particular a right guaranteed by a lien in respect of the claim or by assignment of the claim by way of a guarantee;

---

[44] See below, para.13–66.

(c) the right to demand the assets from, and/or to require restitution by, anyone having possession or use of them contrary to the wishes of the party so entitled;

(d) a right in rem to the beneficial use of assets.

3. The right, recorded in a public register and enforceable against third parties, under which a right in rem within the meaning of paragraph 1 may be obtained, shall be considered a right in rem.

4. Paragraph 1 shall not preclude actions for voidness, voidability or unenforceability as referred to in Article 4(2)(m)."

This Article raises four questions. First, to whose assets does the Article relate? Second, what is a right *in rem*, and to what extent does it differ from the concept of a right *in rem* in English law? Third, where is an asset situated? Fourth, what is the effect of para.1 of the Article (as qualified by para.4) where it applies?

Whose assets?

Article 5 is confined to assets "belonging to the debtor" and situated within the territory of another Member State at the time of opening of the proceedings. The phrase "belonging to" does not necessary involve ownership by the debtor; entitlement to a limited interest, for example, a security interest or a right of possession under a lease, suffices. Though under Art.4(2)(b) the assets which form part of the debtor's estate are determined by the *lex concursus*, this takes as its starting point the pre-insolvency entitlements of third parties[45] and is qualified by Arts 5–15. Where the debtor has no interest of any kind in the asset under the *lex causae* and the asset is not brought into the estate as part of the effects of the *lex concursus* (*e.g.* under its provisions for the avoidance of past transactions) the insolvency proceedings do not affect it, and it becomes unnecessary to turn to Art.5. Conversely, the protection given to *in rem* rights by Art.5 does not preclude actions for avoidance or unenforceability of transactions as being detrimental to all the creditors,[46] such as rules relating to the avoidance of preferences and transactions at an undervalue, these being matters within the exclusive province of the *lex concursus*.[47]

13–53

Under what law is a right characterised as a right *in rem*?

At first sight one would think that Art.5(2) provided a definition of right *in rem*. However, we learn from the Virgós-Schmit Report that this is not the intention. What is a right *in rem* is governed primarily by the applicable

13–45

---

[45] See above, para.13–49.
[46] Art.5(4).
[47] Art.4(m). However, this in turn is subject to the defence under Art.13 that the act in question would not be open to challenge under applicable law. See below, para.13–66.

national law, typically the *lex situs* (*lex rei sitae*) of the right in question.[48] The function of Art.5(2) is not to supplant national law (except to a limited extent under Art.5(3)[49]) but rather to accord it recognition within certain parameters. In consequence:

(1)   a right not recognised by the applicable law as a right *in rem* will not be so recognised for the purposes of the Convention even if it possesses one or all of the characteristics set out in Art.5(2);

(2)   a right recognised by the applicable law as a right *in rem* will be so recognised for the purposes of the Convention so long as it possesses one of the characteristics set out in Art.5(2);

(3)   a right lacking any of those characteristics is not a right *in rem* for the purposes of the Regulation even if it would be classified as a right *in rem* under the applicable law.[50]

The object of Art.5(2) is thus to give its blessing to the *in rem* character of rights under national law where these fall within one of the cases mentioned in Art.5(2) but to avoid the application of an over-expansive concept of rights *in rem* in national law, given that the effect of characterisation of a right as a right *in rem* is to give it priority over rights that would otherwise be conferred by the *lex concursus*. So we must begin with what constitutes a right *in rem* under English law and then see how far this fits into the conception of a right *in rem* under Art.5(2).

Rights *in rem* under English law

13–55   Under English law a right *in rem* is an interest *in* an asset, tangible or intangible, as opposed to a personal right *to* an asset.[51] So ownership,[52] possession (*e.g.* under a lease) and a security interest are rights *in rem*, and these include equitable interests arising under a trust, an equitable mortgage, a fixed or floating charge or an agreement for the transfer of identified or identifiable existing or future property, other than a contract for the sale of goods. By contrast, a purely personal right to the delivery or transfer of an asset is not a right *in rem*. Examples are the buyer's right to delivery of goods under a contract of sale before the property in the goods

---

[48] There is, of course, an element of circularity here, for the very reference to a *situs* connotes the existence of an asset.

[49] See below, para.13–56.

[50] Virgós-Schmit Report, paras 100–104. See also the more expansive discussion in Virgós and Garcimartín, *op. cit.*, 138–157.

[51] See Roy Goode, *Commercial Law* (3rd ed.), pp.25 *et seq.*

[52] But as stated earlier the debtor must have at least some interest in the asset under the *lex concursus* in order to be covered by the insolvency proceedings at all.

has passed,[53] the right to call for the transfer of shares to a given value but not identified and the right to payment of money. *A fortiori* rights which are purely personal, in that they do not relate to an asset at all, are not rights *in rem*. Thus equities, such as a right to rescind a contract for misrepresentation or a right of set-off, are not rights *in rem* but rights to undo or qualify another's person's entitlement.[54]

In considering whether a right is a right *in rem* or a personal right it is necessary to have regard to the particular relationship under consideration. For example, a contract right is not a right *in rem* as between the parties to a contract or as between the assignee of one party and the other contracting party. So a creditor's right to payment under a loan agreement is a purely personal right, and the same is true of his assignee's rights against the debtor. By contrast in the relationship between creditor and assignee the right to pay by the debtor is a right *in rem*, for on the insolvency of the creditor-assignor the debt can be claimed by the assignor against the assignor's general creditors.

Rights *in rem* under Art. 5(2) and (3)

The Virgós-Schmit Report[55] identifies two characteristics of a right *in rem* **13–56** as set out in Art.5(2).The first is its direct and immediate relationship with the asset it covers; the second is the enforceability of that right against others.[56] The concept that a right *in rem* is to be distinguished from a right *in personam* by virtue of its enforceability against third parties, for example, by recovery of the asset from a subsequent purchaser, by the prevention of recourse to the asset by unsecured creditors or, in the case of successive security interests, by according the first in time priority over later interests, is well established in legal systems. The position where the right is enforceable against third parties only on registration is covered by Art.5(3), discussed below.

Article 5(2) itself states that a right *in rem* may be established not only with regard to specific assets but also with regard to collections of indefinite assets as a whole, so that security rights such as the floating charge over all assets or a designated class of assets are characterised as rights *in rem* for the purposes of the Regulation. But a right cannot be a right *in rem* if it does not relate to an asset at all, though what constitutes an asset is a matter of the applicable law.[57] There are various rights that may qualify as rights *in rem* but for the purpose of Art.5 full and unqualified ownership is

---

[53] Goode, *op. cit.*, pp.216–217.
[54] Goode, *op. cit.*, p.27.
[55] Para.103.
[56] Though not necessarily against *all* others, for there may be a competing interest enjoying a higher priority under the applicable law.
[57] For the concept of an asset in English insolvency law, see above, paras 6–03 *et seq.*

not one of them, because if the debtor has no interest in the asset at all it falls outside the scope of the insolvency proceedings. However, a limited interest suffices.

The wording of Art. 5(3) is somewhat curious, and it is here set out again:

> "The right, recorded in a public register and enforceable against third parties, under which a right in rem within the meaning of paragraph 1 may be obtained, shall be considered a right in rem."

Despite the ever-helpful Virgós-Schmit Report,[58] it is not easy to make sense of this opaquely drafted sub-paragraph. Assuming Art.5(3) is to be read in accordance with normal syntax, the phrase "under which" relates back to "The right", so that if one omits the text within the parenthetical commas the sub-paragraph becomes:

> "The right . . . under which a right in rem within the meaning of paragraph 1 may be obtained [,] shall be considered a right in rem."

Accordingly the elements that attract Art.5(3) are (a) the existence of a right which is not as such a right *in rem* but (b) from which a right *in rem* may be derived and (c) which itself may be made enforceable against third parties by registration even before giving birth to the intended right *in rem*. The effect of the Regulation is to treat the registered right as itself a right *in rem* whether or not it would be so regarded in national law. This covers both (a) the case where under the relevant national law registration is not merely a perfection requirement that has to be met in order to be effective against third parties but is a constitutive element of the creation of the right itself as a right *in rem*,[59] and (b) the case where the right is of such a kind that, though rendered enforceable against third parties by registration, it is not in itself a right *in rem* under the applicable national law but simply a right from which a right *in rem* may be derived. In the first case there is no need to depend on Art.5(3) for the desired effect is produced by national law; in the second, Art.5(3) operates independently of national law in characterising the registered right as a right *in rem*. Were it not for the rule of equity that an agreement for transfer is to be treated as a transfer, a good example in English law would have been a contract for the sale of land or the grant of an option to purchase land. Registration of the contract preserves the priority of the prospective legal title against subsequent purchasers but such title stems from the conveyance, not the contract. It is

---

[58] Para.101.

[59] For example, in some European legal systems a security interest is not even considered created so as to be effective as between the parties until it has been registered n a public register.

thus a right *in rem* derived from a right which , but for the rule of equity in question, would not itself be a right *in rem*, merely a contractual entitlement to call for a conveyance. This example does not in fact work for English law, because an agreement for sale of land and the grant of an option to buy land are both considered to create proprietary rights.[60] Indeed, it is not easy to think of a case of registered right "under which a right in rem may be obtained" where the registered right is not itself a right *in rem*.

An entirely separate question, which is not addressed in Art.5(3) but is left to the applicable law, is the position in regard to a right which is characterised by the applicable law as a right *in rem* but is enforceable against third parties only on registration and has not been registered at the time of opening of the insolvency proceedings. This is considered below.

Article 5(2) is sufficiently flexible to accommodate significant differences in national laws of Member States. For example, under English law a lessee of goods has possession, which is a right *in rem*, under French law he is a mere *détenteur* and thus enjoys a purely personal right. On the other hand, as shown above, not every right to demand an asset from the person in possession, contrary to his wishes, is a right *in rem* under English law, and if characterised as a personal right would fall outside Art.5(1) even though of a class described in Art.5(2).

It can be asserted with some confidence that while some rights of a kind listed in Art.5(2) would not be regarded as rights *in rem* under English law, all rights that are so regarded fall within the parameters of Art.5(2) and thus enjoy the benefits conferred by Art.5(1).

Situation of the asset

In order for Art.5(1) to apply so as to preserve the *in rem* rights of a third party it is necessary that the asset of the debtor be situated within the territory of a Member State. It has rightly been pointed out that this presupposes the existence of the *in rem* rights in the first place, a threshold question to be determined by the conflict of laws rules of the forum, which will normally apply the *lex situs* as ascertained by such conflict rules.[61] Article 2(g) has no application to this threshold question. But given the existence of the *in rem* rights under the applicable provision, Art. 2(g) tells us that "the Member State in which assets are situated"[62] means, in the case of:

13–57

- tangible property, the Member State within the territory of which the property is situated,

---

[60] Kevin Gray and Susan Francis Gray, *Elements of Land Law* (4th ed.), paras 9.23, 9.81.
[61] Virgós and Garcimartín, *op. cit.*, para.160.
[62] Though given in quotation marks, this phrase does not in fact in exactly this form anywhere in the Regulation.

– property and rights ownership of or entitlement to which must be entered in a public register, the Member State under the authority of which the register is kept,

– claims, the Member State within the territory of which the third party required to meet them has the centre of his main interests, as determined in Article 3(1).

"Tangible property", referred to in the first indent, includes goods, documents of title to goods, negotiable instruments and negotiable securities, all of which are susceptible to transfer by physical delivery. The second indent covers rights the entitlement to which must be entered in a public register. Under English law these include interests in land, ships and aircraft and charges registrable under s.395 of the Companies Act 1985. The third indent relates to claims, including debts due to the insolvent company. There are three problems with Art.2(g), all of which can be resolved by reference to the twin concepts underpinning Art.2(g), namely the place of *control* of the asset by the third party and the place where the third party's rights are *visible*. These concepts of control and visibility help to explain the relationship between overlapping indents and between overlapping rights within a single indent.

13–58   (1)   In relation to tangible property Art.2(g) does not address the situation where the underlying tangible asset is in one Member State and the document which embodies title to the asset is in another. So if, for example, goods are stored in a warehouse in England, the warehouseman issues a negotiable warehouse warrant which is delivered to a buyer in Switzerland, a non-EU state, and main insolvency proceedings are opened in France, does Art.5 apply because the goods are in England or is it excluded because the warrant is in Switzerland? The answer here lies in the concept of control.[63] The physical location of the goods in England should be regarded as irrelevant when control over them is held in Switzerland. Accordingly Art.5 does not apply and the pre-insolvency entitlement to the goods is governed by the law applicable under French conflict of laws rules.[64]

(2)   Article 2(g) fails to make clear (a) whether this is confined to registration as a condition of creation of the right or applies also to perfection of a right[65] validly created without registration, or (b) the relationship between rights covered by the second indent and those covered by the first and third indents. The Virgós-Schmit Report gives ships and aircraft as examples of assets within the second indent.

---

[63] Virgós and Garcimartín, *op. cit.*, para.160.
[64] See below.
[65] In the sense of making it enforceable against third parties.

Whatever the position under the laws of other Member States, it is certainly not the case under English law that the acquisition of rights in ships or aircraft is dependent on registration, which merely goes to the strength of the acquirer's property right.[66] The same is true of a further example, registered securities, which can be transferred in equity without the name of the transferee being entered on the register. Many other systems prescribe registration as a perfection requirement, not a condition of validity.[67] It can therefore be assumed that the second indent includes rights which require registration only to make them enforceable against third parties and is not confined to rights which can be created only by registration. This accords with the second concept underpinning Art.2(g), namely visibility.

(3)   The three categories listed in Art.2(g) are presented as if they were mutually exclusive, which, of course, is not the case. Ships and aircraft are forms of tangible property within the first indent but ownership and security rights in them are in many cases required to be perfected by registration in a public register. The position under UK law is complicated by the fact that in the case of a ship or aircraft there is both a nationality registration, so that the ship or aircraft becomes a UK-registered ship or aircraft, and a mortgage register, added to which registration of a mortgage is itself required in two different registers, the register of ship or aircraft mortgages and the register maintained by the companies registry. Fortunately all these registers are located within the UK, so that the problem is theoretical. The concept of visibility of the third party's rights indicates that the factor which determines the situation of a ship or aircraft is not its physical location at any time but the state under the authority of which the relevant register is maintained. It would have been helpful if Art.2(g) had made it clear that the first indent does not apply to tangible assets within the second indent. There is a similar overlap between the third indent, which relates to claims, and the first and second indents. Under the third indent claims are considered to be situated in the territory where the company's debtor has its COMI. This accords with a general principle of the conflict of laws governing the location of a debt. But claims cover not only ordinary debts but also (1) rights under negotiable instruments and negotiable securities within the first indent, and (2) rights to registered securities within the second indent. The twin concepts of control and visibility show that claims arising under negotiable instruments and negotiable instruments are covered by the first indent to the exclusion of the third indent and that claims

---

[66] For a detailed discussion, see Alison Clarke, "Ship Mortgages", in Norman Palmer and Ewan McKendrick (eds.), *Interests in Goods* (2nd ed.), Chap.26.

[67] For example, under French law a transfer of land is effected by agreement, and registration is required only to make the transfer effective against third parties.

in respect of registered securities held direct from the issuer are covered by the second indent[68] to the exclusion of the third indent, while claims in respect of securities held indirectly through a securities account with an intermediary are covered by the third indent, since these are not recorded in a public register.[69] We can thus deduce the following hierarchical order in which Art.2(g) is to be applied. The primary rule is to be found in the second indent. Anything within this indent is outside the others. The secondary rule is to be found in the first indent. Anything within this indent is outside the third indent. So the hierarchy, in descending order, is: second indent, first indent, third indent.

The effect of Article 5(1)

13–59   It is worth reiterating that Art.5 does not come into play at all unless the *lex concursus* has already determined that the asset in question is an asset of the estate in the sense that the debtor has at least some interest in it, whether ownership or a limited interest. If that determination has been made or the existence of the interest is not in dispute, it is then necessary to turn to Art.5(1) to ascertain the position in regard to those claiming an interest in the asset. There are several points to note about Art.5(1).

(1)   The asset in question is not excluded from the debtor's estate, for under the principle of universality the insolvency proceedings pick up all assets in which the debtor has an interest; the sole effect is that such interests take effect subject to whatever interest is vested in the third party. So where the debtor is the owner of an asset worth £100,000 but prior to the opening of the insolvency proceedings and at a time when the asset was situated in another Member State, the debtor gave it in security for a loan which, with interest, amounts to £40,000, the asset forms part of the estate but (assuming the security interest to be valid and enforceable under the applicable law) it is subject to that interest, the estate benefiting from the £60,000 equity in the asset if it is sold, the liquidator himself having the right to sell

---

[68] *i.e.* they are located in the state under the authority of which the share register is kept.

[69] Virgós-Schmit Report, para.69. A different position is taken by Virgós and Garcimartín, who allocate directly held registered securities to the third category so as to be situated within the account debtor's COMI, while treating securities held through an account with an intermediary as within the second category and located in the state under the authority of which the public register is kept (*op. cit.*, paras 311, 313). But this seems the wrong way round. It is the title to directly held registered securities which is recorded in a public register; an entitlement to securities held through an account with an intermediary is not recorded in any public register, solely in the account itself, to which only the account holder and those authorised by the account holder have access, so that the entitlement falls within the third category, claims.

so long as the security interest is discharged from the proceeds. The converse case where the third party is the owner and the debtor's interest is a security or other limited interest needs no comment, for in this situation it is the third party's entitlement that takes effect subject to the debtor's interest.

(2)   Article 5(1) does not lay down a conflicts rule, it merely says that the opening of insolvency proceedings is not to affect the rights of creditors or third parties in respect of assets belonging to the debtor which are situated within the territory of another Member State at the time of opening of the proceedings, so that neither the substantive law of the insolvency nor its procedural restrictions on the enforcement of rights *in rem* apply. Article 5(1) does not say which law is to determine those rights. It is left to the conflict of laws rules of the forum to determine what law applies and it is that law which decides whether the claimant has an *in rem* right and, if so, its nature and content. If the issue arises in the insolvency proceedings themselves, then the applicable law will be determined by the *lex concursus* as the *lex fori,* and this will necessarily be the case as regards secondary proceedings, which are confined to local assets.[70] The time of opening of the insolvency proceedings is fixed as the relevant time because that is usually the point at which the existence of pre-insolvency entitlements has to be established under national laws. The situation of the assets at the time of opening of the insolvency proceedings is relevant solely for the purpose of attracting Art.5(1) and is not necessarily indicative of the applicable law, a matter to be determined by the *lex fori*. However, the widely adopted conflicts rule in relation to assets is the *lex situs,*[71] and assuming this is the rule adopted by the *lex fori* (whether the forum is the insolvency state or some other state) it will be applied to the assets situated within the territory of a Member State when the insolvency proceedings are opened. Where, prior to the opening of the insolvency proceedings, an asset has moved from one Member State to another, it is the law of the second state (or in the case of multiple moves, the last state) that has to be applied. If by the law of that state a person has acquired an overriding title displacing that acquired by another under an earlier *lex situs* it becomes unnecessary for the court to look back to the effects of earlier law. If on the other hand the title of the claimant in the last state is dependent on the earlier title of his transferor established under the law of a prior state then that earlier law will be applied, but only because that is the effect of the later law.

---

[70] Art.27.
[71] That is, the general law of the place where the asset is situated, not its insolvency rules.

(3)   Although Art.5(1) is in terms confined to assets situated in another Member State, it does not follow that Art.4(1) governs rights to assets situated in a non-Member State. Article 5(1) is silent on this, not because the purpose was to raise an inference that Art.4(1) applied but because it was not considered appropriate for an EC regulation to purport to lay down rules for assets situated outside the European Union. For such assets the position is very much the same in that the *in rem* rights will be governed by the law determined by the conflict rules of the forum, whether this be the insolvency state or some other state, subject to any insolvency effects of the *lex concursus*.

Set-off

(i) The general rule

13–60   The opening of insolvency proceedings does not affect the right of creditors to demand the set-off of their claims against the claims of the debtor where such a set-off is permitted by the law applicable to the insolvent debtor's claim.[72] This would seem to be the case whether the applicable law is that of another Member State or of a state outside the European Union.[73] Where set-off is permitted under the *lex concursus* it is unnecessary to go further. Where the *lex concursus* does not permit set-off, Art.6(1) requires reference to be made to the law applicable to the debtor's claim, including its rules on set-off in insolvency. This involves a two-stage process. First, the forum applies its own conflict rules to determine the *lex causae* applicable to the debtor's claim. This having been identified, the rules of the *lex causae* applicable to insolvency set-off must then be applied even if no insolvency proceedings are on foot in the state to whose *lex causae* reference is made. In other words, insolvency set-off which is barred by the *lex concursus* must be accepted if it would have been permitted by the insolvency rules of the *lex causae* had insolvency proceedings been opened in the jurisdiction in question. Of course, in jurisdictions where insolvency law has no special rules of set-off and merely respects set-off available under the general law, it is that law which is to be applied, and in the case of contractual set-off the applicable law will be determined in accordance with the Rome Convention and usually will be the law chosen by the parties to the set-off agreement. However, that is not the case as regards insolvency proceedings

---

[72] Art.5. Note that it is the claim of the insolvent company, not the cross-claim of its debtor, that determines the applicable law.

[73] In the case of contractual set-off this is beyond doubt, since under Art.2 of the Rome Convention any law selected by the Convention applies even if it is not the law of a Member State. The law applicable to other forms of set-off depends on their character and in particular on whether under the *lex fori* they are characterised as procedural or substantive in their effect.

opened in England, since the rules of insolvency set-off apply automatically and displace other forms of set-off, including contractual set-off, so that the set-off rules of the general law, including those relating to contractual set-off, have no application.

Under English conflict of laws rules (which will apply only in proceedings in England) a claim arising in contract is governed by the rules laid down in the 1980 Rome Convention,[74] which normally give effect to an express choice of law by the parties, while the law applicable to a claim in tort is usually determined by Part III of the Private International Law (Miscellaneous Provisions) Act 1995,[75] the general rule being that the applicable law is that of the state in which the events constituting the tort occurred,[76] and a claim in unjust enrichment (restitution) is governed by the law of the state where the unjust enrichment occurs.[77] Where the *lex causae* is English law, its rules of insolvency set-off, which are automatic and displace set-off rules applicable outside insolvency,[78] must then be applied if more favourable than those of the *lex concursus*.

Article 6(1), like Art.5(1), does not preclude actions for voidness, etc., under Art.4(2)(m), for the obvious reason that if the transaction under which one of the claims arises is avoided there ceases to be a set-off situation. But Art.4(2)(m) cannot be used to apply the *lex concursus* to invalidate set-off as such, *e.g.* as being contrary to the *pari passu* principle, for that is covered not by sub-para.(m) of Art.4(2) but by sub-para.(d), which, if adverse to set-off, is disapplied by Art.6(2).

(ii) The financial markets

Reference has been made earlier to EC directives requiring the laws of Member States to ensure that close-out and netting agreements in the financial markets are not rendered subject to avoidance by insolvency law.[79] This is reinforced by Art.9, relating to payment systems.[80]   **13–61**

Reservation of title

(1) Effect where purchaser becomes insolvent

The opening of insolvency proceedings against the purchaser of an asset   **13–62**
does not affect the seller's rights based on a reservation of title where at the time of opening of the proceedings the asset is situated in the territory of

---

[74] EEC Convention on the law applicable to contractual obligations, implemented in the UK by the Contracts (Applicable Law) Act 1990. See Cheshire and North's *Private International Law* (13th ed.) pp.535 *et seq.*; Dicey and Morris, *op. cit.*, Chaps. 32 and 33 and 4th Supplement.
[75] Cheshire and North, *op. cit.*, Chap. 19; Dicey and Morris, *op. cit.*, Chap.35.
[76] Private International Law (Miscellaneous Provisions) Act 1995, s.11.
[77] Cheshire and North, *op. cit.*, Chap.20; Dicey and Morris, *op. cit.*, Chap.34.
[78] See above, paras 8–19 *et seq.*
[79] See above, paras 1–32, 13–01.
[80] See below, para.13–65.

another Member State.[81] It is, of course, necessary that the reservation of title shall have been validly created in the first place under the applicable law determined by the conflict of laws rules of the forum[82] and shall have continued in force under that or any succeeding applicable law[83] up to the time of opening of the proceedings. If that is not the case, Art.7 does not come into consideration. The impact of the opening of the insolvency proceedings upon a reservation of title valid under the applicable law immediately before such opening is determined by that law, which is not specified by Art.7 but will normally be the law of the *situs* of the asset at that time. The effect is that the seller's right to invoke his reservation of title is governed by either the *lex concursus* or the applicable law, whichever is the more favourable. So if the *lex concursus* renders a reservation of title void if not registered prior to the opening of the insolvency proceedings but the applicable law does not, the seller is entitled to rely on the reservation of title, and the same applies in the converse case where the reservation of title is valid under the *lex concursus* but void under the applicable law.

Article 7 is generally considered to be restricted to simple reservation of title and not to cover the extended reservation of title by which, upon the buyer's resale, the seller's rights are carried over to the proceeds of sale of the goods, though insofar as these constitute rights *in rem* under the applicable law[84] they may be protected by Art.5.[85]

(2) Effect where seller becomes insolvent

13–63　Where it is the seller who becomes insolvent, the opening of insolvency proceedings against him after delivery of the asset does not constitute grounds for rescinding or terminating the sale and does not prevent the purchaser from acquiring title if the asset sold is situated within the territory of another Member State.[86] Again, this is without prejudice to the rule as to avoidance in Art.4(2)(m).

Contracts relating to immovable property

13–64　In contrast to some of the earlier Articles, Art.8 lays down a positive and exclusive conflicts rule. The effect of the opening of insolvency proceedings on the right to acquire or make use of immovable property is governed

---

[81] Art.7.
[82] Which will normally apply the law of the situation of the asset at the time of the sale agreement.
[83] For example, a change of law resulting from a dealing in a new *situs* or re-perfection requirements imposed by the law of the new *situs*.
[84] Which is not normally the case in English law if the seller's reservation of title has not been registered under s.395 of the Companies Act 1985 as a charge on book debts. See Roy Goode, *Commercial Law*, p.608.
[85] Virgós and Garcimartín, *op. cit.*, para.172.
[86] Art.7(2).

solely by the *lex situs*. Under English law a contract of sale or of lease is treated in equity as a sale or lease and thus creates a right *in rem* which falls within Art.5 as well as Art.8 and in principle is unaffected by the opening of insolvency proceedings, subject to avoidance provisions relating to transactions at an undervalue, preferences and the like.[87]

Payment systems and financial markets

The effects of insolvency proceedings on the rights and obligations of parties to a payment or settlement system or to a financial market are governed solely by the law of a Member State applicable to that system or market.[88] One consequence of this is to add emphasis to the fact that rights and obligations protected from insolvency laws by national laws implementing the EC directives on settlement finality and financial collateral arrangements[89] remain unaffected by the insolvency laws of another Member State in which insolvency proceedings are opened. That would follow anyway from the paramountcy of the directives as as *leges speciales*,[90] and it is reinforced by Art.13, referred to below. Article 9(1) is without prejudice to Art.5, so that the law applicable to payments systems and financial markets does not displace *in rem* rights arising under other law and preserved by Art.5, for example, rights arising where financial collateral is given as security. Article 9(1) does not preclude actions for voidness, etc. but in contrast to earlier Articles, which preserve the application of Art.4(2)(m), Art.9(2) applies the avoidance rules of the relevant payment system or financial market.

13–65

Other issues

The impact of insolvency proceedings on employment contracts is governed solely by the law of the Member State applicable to the contract,[91] as determined by Arts.6 and 7 of the Rome Convention. The insolvency effects on the rights of the debtor in immovable property, a ship or an aircraft subject to registration in a public register are determined by the law of the state under which the register is kept.[92] The drafting of this Article is

13–66

---

[87] See above, Chap.11.
[88] Art.9(1). Where the system or market is not governed by the law of Member State, the rights and obligations of the parties are governed by the law determined by the conflict of laws rules of the forum, which in most cases can be expected to lead to the same result.
[89] See above, para.1–32.
[90] For a detailed discussion, see Virgós and Garcimartín, *op. cit.*, paras 211 *et seq.*
[91] Art.10. Under Art.2 of the Rome Convention the same applies if the applicable law is not that of a Member State.
[92] Art.11. Under Art.14 dispositions of such assets for consideration after the opening of the insolvency proceedings are governed by the *lex situs* in the case of an immovable or the *lex registri* in the case of a ship or aircraft.

not very felicitous. If read literally it could be taken to mean that the *lex registri* displaces in their entirety Arts.4, 5 and 8. That is not the intention. Article 11 is confined to the effects, if any, of the *lex registri*. Under English law, for example, registration is not at present a condition of the creation of a right in an immovable, only a prerequisite of its priority *vis-à-vis* subsequent interests.[93] So as *lex registri* it would have nothing to say about insolvency effects on the debtor, and the case would be governed not by Art.11 but by Art.5 and, in the case of a contract of sale or lease, Art.8. Where the *lex registri* does come into play, for example, in regulating the priority of a registered interest as against a subsequently registered or unregistered interest, Art.4 nevertheless has effect for other purposes, for example, in determining whether a transaction is void as a preference.

Article 13 imposes an important limitation of the avoidance rules of the *lex concursus* as provided by Art.4(2)(m). These are disapplied where the person benefiting from the act detrimental to all the creditors provides proof that the act is subject to the law of a Member State other than the state of the opening of proceedings and that law does not allow any means of challenging that act in the relevant case. For example, in the case of the United Kingdom statutory provisions have been introduced implementing the EC settlement finality and financial collateral directives designed to remove from attack under insolvency law netting and close-out arrangements and contractual arrangements to similar effect relating to financial collateral.[94] Article 15 provides that the effect of insolvency proceedings on a lawsuit pending concerning an asset or a right of which the debtor has been divested shall be governed solely by the law of the Member State in which that lawsuit is pending. It is thus for that law to determine whether the proceedings are to be suspended or may be allowed to continue.[95]

10. CO-ORDINATION OF PARALLEL PROCEEDINGS[96]

13–67   One of the important objectives of the Insolvency Regulation is to ensure the co-ordination of parallel insolvency proceedings in different Member States involving the same or related debtors. This objective sought to be

---

[93] This will change with the introduction of electronic conveyancing, when creation will coincide with registration. See Gray and Gray, *op. cit.*, paras 8.245, 12.69.

[94] Financial Collateral Arrangements (No.2) Regulations 2003, SI 2003/3226; Financial Markets and Services (Settlement Finality) Regulations 2001, SI 2001/1349. There is considerable overlap between Art.13 and Art.9 in this field. The rule in Art.13 precluding challenge to an act unless it meets the double test of liablility to avoidance not only under the *lex concursus* but also under the applicable law has not passed without criticism. See Michael Veder, *Cross-Border Insolvency Proceedings and Security Rights*, p.315, and literature there cited.

[95] See Virgós and Garcimartín, *op. cit.*, paras 252 *et seq.*

[96] For a detailed discussion, see Virgós and Garcimartín, *op. cit.*, Chap.10.

achieved in a number of ways. First, there is the principle of Community-wide recognition and effects to which reference has already been made. Next, the liquidators in the different insolvency proceedings have a duty to exchange information and co-operate with each other.[97] Then there is the provision, known in England as the hotchpot rule, that while every creditor may prove in all proceedings, whether main proceedings or territorial proceedings, a creditor who receives a dividend in one proceeding cannot share in distributions in other proceedings until the creditors in those proceedings have obtained an equivalent dividend.[98] The liquidator in each proceeding must lodge in other proceedings claims already lodged in the proceedings for which they were appointed, the liquidator in secondary proceedings being entitled to participate in other proceedings on the same basis as a creditor.[99] As mentioned earlier, the liquidator in main proceedings has extensive powers to intervene in other proceedings.[1]

In the simplest case, co-ordination measures relate to the same debtor. More difficult is the case where different but related debtors become insolvent, as on the collapse of a multinational enterprise consisting of a group of companies each operating in a different jurisdiction, for example, Enron, Parmalat and Rover. The Regulation treats each company as a separate legal entity and does not cater for a group of companies as such. So where it is desired to take an integrated approach to the winding-up or reorganisation of a corporate group it is essential that the different liquidators co-ordinate their approaches and that the different courts do what they can to support such co-ordination.[2]

---

[97] Art.31.
[98] Art.20(2).
[99] Art.32.
[1] See above, para.13–34.
[2] A good example in the UK relates to the Rover group, referred to above, para.13–46. See further Wessels, above, n.46, at pp.18 *et seq.* and para.14–27.

Chapter 14

International Insolvency[1]

1. THE PROBLEMS OF INTERNATIONAL INSOLVENCY

Hitherto we have devoted attention to purely domestic liquidations, that is, **14–01**
those which have no foreign element requiring particular consideration. But
companies incorporated in England may have foreign creditors and may
have assets or places of business in other countries. Conversely foreign
companies may incur debts, and have assets and places of business, in
England. Several major collapses have become *causes célèbres*, not least
because business failures were concealed by massive frauds. Maxwell
Communications Corporation, founded by the late Robert Maxwell, had
incurred most of its debts in England, where under Maxwell's direction it
looted pension funds, siphoning these off into Maxwell's private companies,
and conducted various fraudulent transactions, whereas 80% of its assets
were situated in the United States. Proceedings were brought in both
countries and led to a remarkable co-operation between the courts in

---

[1] A substantial volume of writing has grown up around this subject in recent years. The
leading English text is Ian F. Fletcher, *Insolvency in Private International Law: National and
International Approaches* (2nd ed.). Valuable insights are also provided by the insolvency
contributions to M.G. Bridge and R.H. Stevens (eds.), *Cross-border security and insolvency*
and by Fletcher, "The quest for a global insolvency law: a challenge for our time" [2002]
Current Legal Problems 427. American scholars have been particularly active in this field.
See in particular Jay Lawrence Westbrook, "A Global Solution to Multinational Default",
98 Mich. L. Rev. 2276 (2000) and "Theory and Pragmatism in Global Insolvencies: Choice
of Law and Choice of Forum" , 65 Am. Bankr. L.J. 457(1991) ; Lynn M. LoPucki, "The
Case for Cooperative Territoriality in International Bankruptcy", 98 Mich. L. Rev. 2216
(1999–2000) and "Co-Operation in International Bankruptcy: A Post-Universalist
Approach", 84 Cornell L. Rev. 696 (1998–1999). Earlier, though still relevant, literature
published in the U.K. but also containing valuable contributions from overseas scholars
includes Philip R. Wood, *Principles of International Insolvency*, Philip St. J. Smart, *Cross-
Border Insolvency* (2nd ed.); Jacob S. Ziegel (ed.), *Current Developments in International and
Comparative Corporate Insolvency Law*, Part B; David Brown, *Corporate Rescue*, Part III;
Harry Rajak (ed.), *Insolvency Law*, Part IV. Additional references will be found at different
points in this chapter.

London and New York.[2] The Bank of Credit and Commerce International S.A. was incorporated in Luxembourg but had 47 offices or branches in different countries. A winding-up order was made in Luxembourg and was followed shortly after by a similar order in England, the English winding-up proceedings being ancillary to those opened in Luxembourg. Proceedings were also instituted in the United States. BCCI's parent company, Bank of Credit and Commerce International (Overseas) Ltd, incorporated in the Cayman Islands, had 63 offices or branches in 28 countries. The group was found to be involved not only in fraudulent transactions but in a wide range of seriously unlawful activities, including establishing links with drug cartels and terrorist organisations. Depositors were said to have been defrauded of US$10 billion. Fortunately much of the money has been recovered by the liquidators as the result of proceedings in several jurisdictions. Currently the High Court is hearing a large claim by the liquidators of BCCI against the Bank of England for failing in its duty as regulator.

Such large failures, particularly where involving fraud, commonly lead not only to action by regulators in withdrawing authorisations to carry on business but also to concurrent insolvency proceedings in different jurisdictions as well as a multiplicity of law suits around the world as office holders ("office holders") seek to recover assets and pursue claims with a view to restoring lost value to the insolvent companies. The foreign elements involved in these cases raise special considerations which in some cases can be extremely complex. The first task of office holders is to safeguard the assets that remain. Where these are dispersed among different countries it is important to synchronise the various actions so that applications to the court in one jurisdiction do not lead to the disappearance of assets in others. However, the ability to do this depends to a considerable extent on the local law and on the willingness of local courts to assist with measures that facilitate an integrated approach with effects going beyond the borders of their own countries. Where the insolvent enterprises have been carrying on a regulated business activity, such as banking, there is a similar need for co-operation among the various regulators, who are faced not only with the task of establishing the facts but also with sensitive timing issues, in that premature action may bring about the collapse of a company that might otherwise be saved.

The hallmarks of internationality

14–02 An international insolvency is typically characterised by one or more of the following features: the debtor's business is conducted in different countries; the creditors are situated in different countries; the assets are located in

---

[2] See below, para.14–27.

different countries; there are parallel proceedings in different countries. The first of these requires a few words of explanation. A company may operate in different countries either through local subsidiaries or through branches or offices. In the former case the company and each of its subsidiaries are separate legal entities and in principle each insolvent company within the group has to be the subject of separate insolvency proceedings, though the relevant court or courts may approve pooling arrangements agreed by the different office holders either in order to maximise realisations for the corporate group as a whole or because the assets and liabilities of the companies concerned have become so inter-mingled that it is not practicable to disentangle them.[3] By contrast, branches and offices are not in general separate legal entities, simply part of the insolvent company and administered as such. But the distinction between corporate entities and branches and offices is not always to clear cut. In several jurisdictions, including the United States, every branch of a bank is treated as a separate legal entity for insolvency purposes, though this is not the position under English law.[4]

Issues in international insolvency

The central practical question confronting office holders in a cross-border   **14–03** insolvency is how to marshal the assets and co-ordinate the winding-up or reorganisation of the enterprise as a whole to the best advantage of creditors. Among the legal issues which may arise in an international, or cross-border, insolvency[5] are: whether an English court has jurisdiction over

---

[3] In *Re Bank of Credit and Commerce International S.A.* [1994] 1 W.L.R. 708, the judgment of Dillon L.J. records (at 711) that because of the manner in which the affairs of BCCI, incorporated in Luxembourg, and its associated company, Bank of Credit and Commerce International (Overseas) Ltd, incorporated in the Cayman Islands, had been conducted, a pooling agreement had been entered into and approved by the courts in England, the Cayman Islands and Luxembourg under which all realisations remaining and deduction of costs and preferential claims would form a single fund to be divided rateably among the general creditors of both companies.

[4] The general law does, however, recognise the separate character of branches for some purposes, for example, through the rule that a customer cannot draw on an account with one branch for an amount exceeding his credit balance or credit line with that branch even though he has deposits with other branches sufficient to cover the drawing.

[5] The terms "international insolvency" and "cross-border insolvency" have no defined meaning but are generally taken to refer to insolvencies which arise from cross-border trading or which involve the application, or possible application, of the insolvency laws of two or more jurisdictions. See Carl Felsenfeld, *A Treatise on the Law of International Insolvency* 1–5. The second edition of the work adopted the phrase "cross-border insolvency," but this now suffers the drawback that it does not distinguish insolvencies falling within a regional regime, such as the EU Regulation on insolvency proceedings, examined in Chap.13, from insolvencies having effects at the international level. Hence the replacement of "cross-border" with "international". It should nevertheless be borne in mind that much of the literature dealing with international insolvencies continues to refer to cross-border insolvency.

a foreign company and, if so, whether it may decline jurisdiction; whether an English winding-up extends to foreign assets; whether foreign creditors are entitled to equal treatment with English creditors in an English winding-up; the extent to which foreign insolvency proceedings preclude proceedings in England by English creditors against assets in England; the extent to which an English court will recognise foreign liquidation proceedings and the status of foreign office-holders and will be able and willing to give its assistance to foreign parties and foreign courts in relation to assets or person susceptible to the jurisdiction of the English court; the law applicable to the substance and procedure of a winding-up; and the manner in which assets and claims should be dealt with where there are concurrent insolvency proceedings in two or more jurisdictions, including the conditions on which a creditor who has received a dividend in one liquidation should be allowed to prove in another liquidation in a different country.

Countries differ in their approach to these problems. We may, however, detect certain common principles, notably the collective nature of the insolvency proceedings, *pari passu* distribution, the avoidance or deferment of liquidation where rescue, reorganisation or arrangements with creditors are likely to improve prospects for creditors; the principle of respect for pre-insolvency entitlements, such as the priority of secured creditors; the conferment of preferential status on certain unsecured creditors, notably for unpaid wages and taxes[6]; rules for the avoidance of transactions concluded in the run-up to liquidation or administration which are detrimental to the general body of creditors; and the absence of discrimination against foreign creditors, though in some jurisdictions this is dependent on reciprocity.

The rival approaches to jurisdictional issues

14–04   The battle lines are drawn when it comes to jurisdictional issues. Two sets of opposing principles are of particular significance. They are unity versus plurality and universality versus territoriality.[7]

The principle of unity ascribes exclusive jurisdiction over winding-up to the courts of the state of the company's incorporation,[8] to which all other

---

[6] But taxes are no longer preferential debts in the UK. See above, para.7–27.

[7] Which is not exhaustive. Deserving of particular mention is Professor Robert Rasmussen's contractual approach under which it would be pen to each company, at the time of incorporation, to select the legal regime to which it wished to be subject. Professor Rasmussen has extended this idea, initially developed in relation to the choice of insolvency regime within a single jurisdiction (see above, para.2–08), to allow choice of jurisdiction and applicable law at the international level. See Robert K. Rasmussen, "A New Approach to Transnational Insolvencies", 19 Mich. J. Int'l L. 1 (1997).

[8] There are variants on this, such as the principal place of business or the centre of the debtor's main interests, but the underlying idea is the same, namely the state with which the company has its closes juridical connection.

courts defer. The opposing principle of plurality admits of concurrent proceedings in different jurisdictions,[9] based on some connecting factor such as assets, a place of business or creditors within the jurisdiction.

The universality/territoriality classification relates to the question whether an insolvency proceeding opened in one jurisdiction should encompass all assets on a worldwide basis or should be confined to assets within the jurisdiction in question. This, of course, is linked to the unity/plurality issue, for if jurisdiction is confined to local assets there will necessarily be a plurality of proceedings where the debtor has assets in different jurisdictions. However, the converse is not necessarily true, for in parallel proceedings in different states the insolvency laws of each may claim jurisdiction over assets worldwide. Both issues have generated intense debate and have led to international as well as regional initiatives. Taken in combination, they can be described as the universalist approach on one side, encompassing the concept both of a single law and of a single jurisdiction covering all assets, and a territorialist approach, in which the jurisdiction of the courts of a given state is confined to those portions of the company and its assets that lie within the territory of that state.

Both approaches have their strengths and weaknesses. For the territorialist, the universalist approach is anathema. The opposition to it has been succinctly expressed by an American scholar in the following terms:

"Scholars of international bankruptcy are caught in the grip of a failed idea: universalism. Generations of scholars have advanced the universalist mantra: i.e., that the assets and liabilities of a multinational firm in bankruptcy should be administered by one court applying one nation's bankruptcy laws on a worldwide basis. Until recently, this advancement of universalism occurred largely without challenge. Even with recent challenges, however, universalism dominates the debate, as scholars attempt to debunk its claimed efficiency advantages.

This debate over universalism is misguided because, simply put, universalism will not work. In this Article, I argue that universalism is politically implausible and likely impossible. No nation has adopted it, and it is unlikely that any will. States will be reluctant to commit to enforcing the decisions of foreign courts applying foreign bankruptcy laws against local parties. In addition, even assuming states exist that would be interested in universalism, structural problems will preclude the achievement of workable universalist cooperation. I rely on elementary game theory and international relations theory to show that even states that prefer universalism will find themselves in a prisoners' dilemma with no ready solution. Impediments to cooperation will afflict even bilateral universalist ambitions, with multilateral universalism all the more

---

[9] For the advantages and disadvantages of a single forum, see *Wood, op. cit.*, para.13–4.

unlikely. Because the claimed superior efficiency of universalism implicitly depends on its widespread adoption—if not ubiquity—this implausibility of multilateral universalism is particularly damning to the universalist cause. Universalism should be shelved, and the terms of the scholarly debate should shift to more plausible goals."[10]

Others, too, have deprecated the emphasis on unity and universality.[11] Professor Lynn LoPucki is one of the leading protagonists to deploy the arguments against the universalist approach. These are that (1) the connecting factor favoured by universalists, namely the debtor's "home country" or the place where it has its centre of main interests, is too indeterminate and subject to strategic manipulation, (2) to impose foreign law and foreign courts on wholly domestic relationships is both confusing to local creditors and detrimental to the rights and priorities they had acquired under their own law and could reasonable expect to be preserved; (3) no workable rule can be devised for determining the extent to which the home country is to have jurisdiction over corporate groups.[12] Equally powerful arguments in favour of the universalist approach have been advanced by Professor Jay Westbrook, who makes the point that it is not possible to maximise value or ensure equality for creditors unless there is a unified regime for the assembly and realisation of the debtor's assets and a common pool to be applied under a common distribution scheme, and that reorganisation is even more dependent for its efficacy on the existence of a single regime under which it can be conducted.[13] Moreover, because of the relative inflexibility of local insolvency laws real co-operation in a territorial system is necessarily very limited and "recoveries will turn on the fortuitous or manipulated location of assets and the results will be highly unpredictable ex ante".[14]

The convergence of the universalist and territorialist approaches in practice

14–05   Over time, there has been a gradual convergence of the two approaches. It is generally accepted that to route everything to a single forum, however theoretically desirable in terms of avoiding concurrent insolvency proceedings, is not realistic, for assets are always subject to the sovereign control of the state in which they are situated and in no jurisdiction are courts willing to give up all control over local assets where there are local creditors. So

---

[10] Frederick Tung, "Is International Bankruptcy Possible?" 23 Mich. J. Int'l Law 31 (2001).
[11] See, for example, Jacob S. Ziegel, "Ships at Sea, International Insolvencies, and Divided Courts" [1998] 50 CBR (3d) 310.
[12] "The Case for Cooperative Territoriality in International Bankruptcy", above, n.1.
[13] "A Global Solution to Multinational Default", above, n.1.
[14] *ibid.*, at 2302.

the principle everywhere adopted is that of plurality, which admits of concurrent proceedings in different jurisdictions. On the other side, it is accepted that to allow a multiplicity of disconnected territorial proceedings, each confined to local assets, is inimical to the goal of maximising returns to creditors and is a serious obstacle to any plan for reorganisation, which requires an integrated approach. To this one might add that the difficulty of identifying a company's centre of main interests (COMI), though not to be dismissed, ought not to be overstated either. The location of the COMI in a Member State of the European Union is a condition of the application of the European Insolvency Regulation, and though it has given rise to litigation in a number of countries it is fair to say that in most cases the court had little difficulty in identifying the debtor's COMI.[15]

As to assets covered by a winding-up procedure, no country adopts a wholly universalist approach. The laws of some states adopt a principle of territoriality by which insolvency proceedings opened there are confined to local assets. More commonly, states adopt the principle of universality for their own proceedings but do not feel obliged to accept it for proceedings opened elsewhere. A potential conflict arises where there are concurrent liquidation proceedings in two different states and under the laws of both the debtor's estates embraces all its assets on a worldwide basis. In practice, such conflicts, if not wholly avoided, have been alleviated by the willingness of courts of one jurisdiction to recognise that the main liquidation is based elsewhere (typically in the state where the debtor company is incorporated or alternatively where it has its COMI) and that their own winding-up proceedings are ancillary to the main proceedings and should be used in aid of the latter, with the consequence that the ancillary liquidation will in practice be confined to local assets, which at some point will be transferred, together with a list of creditors in the ancillary liquidation, to the liquidator in the main proceedings, subject always to the court in which the ancillary proceedings were opened being satisfied that creditors in its own jurisdiction will be fairly treated in the main liquidation.[16]

Current theories

The two principal theories that emerge from this convergence[17] have been described as the co-operative territorialist approach, favoured by LoPucki, and the modified universalist approach, advocated by Westbrook. The co-operative territorial approach leaves each state with full territorial sovereignty and depends on various kinds of co-operation among states.[18] The

14–06

---

[15] See above, paras 13–36 *et seq.*

[16] See below, para.14–07.

[17] The contractualist theory elegantly propounded by Rasmussen remains a theory and has not been adopted in practice.

[18] LoPucki, "Cooperation in International Bankruptcy: A Post-Universalist Approach", 84 Cornell L. Rev. 696, 750 (1998–1999).

modified universalist approach takes as its starting point the principles of unity and universality, including a single set of internationally agreed priority rules, with overall control being vested in the court of the debtor's home country and courts of other states acting in an ancillary role to provide assistance to the foreign court while at the same time ensuring that if assets are surrendered to the main jurisdiction local creditors will be fairly treated. Thus while co-operation may play a significant role, the system is not dependent on it, because it is geared to the concept of global management.

The modern approach to international insolvency

14–07   The current trend, as exemplified by the UNCITRAL Model Law on insolvency proceedings and the EU Insolvency Regulation, which applies in 24 of the 25 Member States of the European Union,[19] is clearly in favour of a modified universalist approach, albeit with rather more territorial elements than may have been envisaged by the proponents of that approach. The key universalist elements are: (1) the concept of main proceedings in the state where the debtor has its COMI or equivalent, (2) the application of the *lex concursus* of that state to govern the effects of the opening of those proceedings; (3) recognition in other states of the judgments of the court by which the proceedings were opened and of the application of the *lex concursus*; (4) overall control of the insolvency process by the liquidator in the main proceedings; (5) treatment of all the debtor's assets worldwide as constituting the estate administered by that liquidator; (6) the provision of assistance by local courts in the recovery of assets and pursuit of claims by the office holder in the main proceedings, and access of office holders to foreign courts. But some leeway is also given to the concept of territoriality to accommodate the legitimate expectations of local creditors in relation to local assets. Thus the opening of territorial proceedings is permitted in a state where the debtor has an establishment or assets[20] though having its COMI elsewhere, but the proceedings are limited to local assets,[21] and will be governed by the local *lex concursus*, whose priority rules will continue to apply. So local creditors will preserve their rights and priorities under local law, while foreign creditors will be able to participate in the insolvency proceedings on an equal footing but on the basis of local law, not the law by which their rights would otherwise be governed.

---

[19] Denmark opted out of the Regulation.

[20] The EU Regulation requires an establishment (Art.3(2)), the Model Law requires assets only, but *foreign* non-main proceedings are by definition confined to those where the debtor has an establishment in the state where they are opened (Art.2(c)).

[21] And in the case of the Regulation, to winding-up proceedings.

The principle of non-discrimination

Hand in hand with the concepts of unity and universality goes the concept **14–08** of non-discrimination against foreign creditors. If all the company's assets, in whatever part of the world, are to be subsumed within a single liquidation, then claims of foreign creditors must be admitted on the same basis as those of local creditors. This principle is well brought out in an opinion on United States bankruptcy law given for the assistance of the English court in *Felixstowe Dock and Railway Co v U S Lines Inc*[22] by Judge Howard C. Buscnman of the US District Court for the Southern District of New York:

"The intended scope of bankruptcy and reorganization jurisdiction extends beyond the border of the United States . . . The nature of the jurisdiction is in rem. The res, the estate of the debtor created by the commencement of a bankruptcy or reoganization case, is viewed as a single entity to be dealt with in a single proceeding. The broad scope of bankruptcy jurisdiction under United States law is intended to permit similarly situated creditors, regardless of where they are located, to be treated equally in a bankruptcy or reorganization case. Discrimination on the basis of citizenship is not permitted. All creditors are given the opportunity to file claims against the state and their recovery is not limited to the assets in their own country."

The position is the same under English insolvency law.[23]

The treatment of corporate groups

One of the more difficult issues in international insolvency is the treatment **14–09** of corporate groups. In England, as in most other jurisdictions, a group of companies is not as such a legal entity. Each company within the group must be treated separately. It may be that some companies within the group are insolvent while others are in a healthy financial state. There may be cross-lending, cross-guarantees and cross-securities within the group. In many cases the interests of the various groups of creditors will best be served by an integrated approach to the group as a whole. Where all members of the group are within the European Union and are managed from one place which constitutes the common COMI, the EC Insolvency Regulation ensures that even though there are separate proceedings for each insolvent company these will be governed by the same law and will be

---

[22] [1989] Q.B. 360. An extract from the opinion is set out in the judgment of Hirst J. at 368.
[23] *Re Bank of Credit and Commerce International S.A. (No. 11)* [1996] B.C.C. 980, *per* Sir Richard Scott V.C. at 986.

susceptible to the appointment of a common office holder or joint administrators. This does, of course, assume that a judgment opened in main proceedings in one Member State will be recognised in others. So far, with a few hiccups on the way, the experience has been good. In *Daisytek* the French Cour de Cassation upheld the status of the administration proceedings opened in England as main proceedings,[24] while in the insolvency of the MG Rover Group the Nanterre Commercial Court accorded similar recognition to administration proceedings in England in which orders were made against various members of the group, including a French subsidiary.[25] In cases outside the scope of EU law the concept of ancillary proceedings and judicial assistance may help to cut through difficulties caused by the separate legal identities of members of a corporate group. English courts have been ready to recognise that their role is ancillary to that of a court elsewhere in which proceedings have been opened and to provide assistance under s.426 of the Insolvency Act 1986,[26] while courts in the United States have performed a similar service under s.304 of the Bankruptcy Code, which has been widely utilised by foreign representatives but is now to be replaced by the new Chap.15 of the Bankruptcy Code, incorporating the UNCITRAL Model Law on Cross-Border Insolvency.[27]

Independently of any statutory underpinning, much can be achieved by co-operation among the different office holders and the willingness of courts in their respective jurisdictions to assist the co-operative process in relation to a group of companies.[28] Even so, the problems of corporate groups are formidable. These exist at two levels, the substantive law and the insolvency administration. The substantive law issue concerns the extent to which one company in a group may be held liable for the debts and liabilities of another. This is a matter for the applicable law, which may have various legal techniques at its disposal, including agency, piercing the corporate veil and holding one company liable for losses caused by mismanagement of the other. The subject is briefly discussed in the useful UNCITRAL *Legislative Guide on Insolvency Law*[29] in the context of domestic law. Arrangements for an integrated approach to a group of insolvent companies are not easy to achieve, depending as they do on a combination of flexible laws, collaboration between office holders and the co-operation of the different courts involved.[30] Pooling of assets and

---

[24] See above, para.13–36.
[25] See above, para.13–46.
[26] See below, para.14–20.
[27] See below, para.14–29.
[28] For a good recent example, see 14–27.
[29] Published in 2005.
[30] This needs to be carefully handled so as to secure that the co-operative process is both transparent and fair. The American Law Institute has performed a signal service in its *Transnational Insolvency Project, Principles of Cooperation in Transnational Insolvency Cases among the Members of the North American Free Trade Agreement*, Appendix 2, *Guidelines Applicable to Court-to-Court Communications in Cross-Border Cases* (May 2000).

liabilities provides another solution but under English law this is infrequent and is generally confined to situations in which the assets and liabilities of the different companies are so intermingled that there is no sensible alternative to consolidation.[31] Professor LoPucki regards the problem of corporate groups as reinforcing the case for a territorial approach.[32] Professor Westbrook ripostes that this assumes a tidy division of corporate activity in which each company within the group operates exclusively within its own territory and has assets and liabilities only within that territory,[33] whereas in practice assets and operations are not territorially confined and each company may have assets, liabilities and business activities outside the borders of its own state. It is clear that problems will arise whichever approach is adopted.

The position under English law

English law shares with a number of other states the principle of univer-   **14–10**
sality as regards its own insolvency proceedings, coupled with a reluctance to accept that principle as regards insolvency proceedings opened elsewhere. However, English courts are very ready to accept, in appropriate cases, that their role is ancillary to that of the foreign court and to provide assistance to that court, particularly in regard to the removal of assets by the foreign liquidator. The UK is expected to adopt the UNCITRAL Model Law and bring it into force on April 1, 2006.

2. THE INSOLVENCY JURISDICTION OF ENGLISH COURTS: CASES OUTSIDE THE EC INSOLVENCY REGULATION

In determining the insolvency jurisdiction of English courts it is necessary   **14–11**
to distinguish cases outside the EC Regulation on Insolvency Proceedings, which are governed solely by the English jurisdictional rules discussed below, from those within the Regulation, which may exclude or limit jurisdiction that would otherwise be exercisable, a question discussed in section 4.

---

[31] See n.3, above.
[32] Lynn M. LoPucki, "Cooperation in International Bankruptcy: A Post-Universalist Approach", 84 Cornell L. Rev. 696, 751 (1998–1999).
[33] A charge vigorously denied by LoPucki, "The Case for Cooperative Territoriality in International Bankruptcy", 98 Mich. L. Rev. 2216, 2233 (1999–2000).

The application of English conflict of laws rules

14–12   The jurisdiction of English courts in insolvency proceedings is governed by the Insolvency Act 1986 and by English conflict of laws rules developed by the courts. Brussels I[34] does not apply to the winding-up of insolvent companies, judicial arrangements, compositions and analogous proceedings.[35]

Winding-up

14–13   The winding-up provisions of the Companies Act 1985 distinguish three principal classes of company, namely (a) a company registered in England and Wales under the Companies Act 1985, (b) a company registered in another part of the United Kingdom, (c) an unregistered company, that is, an association or company not registered in any part of the United Kingdom,[36] including an oversea company[37] and a foreign company which has not established a place of business in Great Britain. The court's jurisdiction to wind up a company under the Insolvency Act 1986 depends upon the category into which it falls. There is jurisdiction to wind up any company registered under the Companies Act, whether or not it has assets in this country or, indeed, any assets at all.[38] A company registered in another part of the United Kingdom can be wound-up in England only in limited conditions.[39] Under ss.220 and 221 of the Insolvency Act the court also has jurisdiction to wind up an unregistered company, including an oversea or other foreign company, even if it has not established a place of business in Great Britain[40] and even if it has been dissolved or has otherwise ceased to exist under the law of its incorporation[41] or is being wound up abroad.[42] The grounds for winding-up are:

---

[34] The popular name for Council Regulation (EC) No. 44/2001 on the recognition and enforcement of judgments in civil and commercial matters (OJ L12 16.1.2001, p.1), as amended and corrected, which replaced the Convention on Jurisdiction and Enforcement of Judgments in Civil and Commercial Matters 1968, and which as a regulation has direct effect, no UK implementing measure being either necessary or permitted.

[35] Art.1(2)(b). It does; however, to the winding-up of solvent companies, in relation to which the court of the Member State where the company has its seat has exclusive jurisdiction (Art.22(2)).

[36] Companies A ct 1985, s.220(1).

[37] That is, a company incorporated elsewhere than in Great Britain and establishing a place of business in Great Britain (Companies Act 1985, s.744).

[38] Insolvency Act 1986, s.117(1). See above, para.5–14.

[39] See Companies Act 1985, s.221(2) as to an unregistered company with a principal place of business in Northern Ireland, and generally Dicey and Morris. *Conflict of Laws* (12th ed.), Rule 158.

[40] But it will then not be an oversea company. See n.37 above.

[41] Insolvency Act 1986, s.225, enacting a principle already established at common law. Such dissolution is in fact a ground of winding-up. See below.

[42] *Re Commercial Bank of South Australia* (1886) 33 Ch.D. 174. An unregistered company cannot be put into voluntary winding-up except in cases governed by the EC Regulation on insolvency proceedings. See above, para.13–11.

> "(a) if the company is dissolved, or has ceased to carry on business, or is carrying on business only for the purpose of winding up its affairs;
>
> (b) if the company is unable to pay its debts;
>
> (c) if the court is of opinion that it is just and equitable that the company should be wound up."

But the court has a discretion whether to make winding-up order and will do so only in accordance with settled principles. The overarching requirement is that there should be a sufficient connection with England. At one time this was very strictly applied, so that it was considered necessary to show that the company either had a place of business in England when the petition was presented or had previously had a place of business in England.[43] Later this was held unnecessary so long as the company had assets in England[44] and persons in England claiming to be creditors.[45] By a further extension it was ruled unnecessary for the company itself to hold assets in England so long as there was a right of recovery from another source which would be available to creditors.[46] Finally, even the requirement of assets or recoverable funds was dispensed with. It was held that even if the foreign company had no assets in England the court could exercise its jurisdiction to wind up the company whenever (1) there was a sufficient connection with England, (2) there was a reasonable possibility of benefit to those presenting the winding-up petition, and (3) one or more persons interested in the distribution of assets was a person or persons over whom the court could exercise jurisdiction.[47] But it has also been said that:

> "the courts of this country should hesitate very long before subjecting foreign companies with no assets here to the winding-up procedures of this country. Of course if a foreign company does have assets in this country, the assets may need to be distributed among creditors, and a

---

[43] *Re Lloyd Generale Italiano* (1885) 29 Ch.D. 219.

[44] For this purpose potential claims under ss.213 or 214 of the Insolvency Act 1986 are not considered to be assets *(Re A Company (No.00359 of 1987))* [1988] Ch. 210.

[45] *Re Compania Merabello San Nicholas SA* [1973] Ch. 75.

[46] *Re Eloc Electro-Optiek and Communicatie B. V.* [1982] Ch. 43 (employees with right of recovery from the redundancy fund under s.122 of the Employment Protection (Consolidation) Act 1978).

[47] *Stocznia Gdanska SA v Latreefers Inc. (No.2)* [2001] 2 B.C.L.C. 1116; *Re Real Estate Development Co* [1991] B.C.L.C. 210, *per* Knox J. at 217. See also *Re Azoff-Don Commercial Bank* [1954] Ch. 315 (which held that the petitioners need not be within the jurisdiction so long as they were sufficiently connected to it, as by having worked here); *Re A Company (No.00359 of 1987)* [1988] Ch. 210 (where it was pointed out that if the presence of assets were a requirement the court could be deprived of jurisdiction by the simple expedient of removing the assets). For cases where the connection to England was held insufficient see *Banco National de Cuba v Cosmos Trading Corp* [2000] 1 B.C.L.C. 813; *Re Titan International Inc* [1998] 1 B.C.L.C. 102; *R. Compania Merabello San Nicholas SA*, above; *Re Wallace Smith & Co Ltd* [1992] B.C.L.C. 791.

winding-up order here, sometimes ancillary to a principal winding up in the place of incorporation of the foreign company, may be necessary. But a winding-up order here, while the foreign company continues to trade in its country of incorporation and elsewhere in the world, is in my view thoroughly undesirable. I would not say a winding-up order in those circumstances could never be right, but I do say that exceptional circumstances and exceptional justification would be necessary. After all, if we presume to make a winding-up order in respect of a foreign company which is continuing to trade in its place of incorporation and elsewhere in the world, where will our winding-up order be recognised? What effect will it have? These questions are difficult to answer and, absent some international convention regarding the winding up of foreign companies, I think no satisfactory answer can be given.

It is, moreover, somewhat of a weakness in our own winding-up law that it is not possible to have a winding up of a foreign company limited to its activities and assets in this jurisdiction. It has been held on a number of occasions, and is clear law, that once a winding-up order is made in this jurisdiction it purports to have worldwide effect. Hence the problems that arise if the order is made in respect of a foreign company that is continuing to trade."[48]

14–14   In the subsequent decision in *Stocznia Gdanska SA v Latreefers Inc. (No.2)*[49] the Court of Appeal held that this dictum should be followed unless good reason to the contrary was shown. So even the existence of the three elements referred to above as essential to the exercise of the court's discretion will not usually suffice if the company has no assets in England and is continuing to trade in its country of incorporation.

In all these decisions the court found it unnecessary to decide whether the existence of the three elements went to jurisdiction or merely to the exercise of the court's discretion. That point arose fairly and squarely for decision in *Re Drax Holdings Ltd*,[50] where Lawrence Collins J. had to consider whether he had jurisdiction to sanction a scheme of arrangement for a foreign company under s.425 of the Companies Act 1985. Since under ss.425(6) and 735A of the Act "company" meant any company liable to be wound up under that Act or under the Insolvency Act 1986, and since the factors relevant to winding-up did not necessarily apply to a scheme of arrangement, the effect of holding that the three elements went to jurisdiction would be to deprive the court of power to approve a scheme if the second or third element was lacking even if there was a sufficient connection with England and the second and third elements were not

---

[48] *Banco Nacional de Cuba v Cosmos Trading Corp* [2000] 1 B.C.L.C. 813, *per* Sir Richard Scott V.C. at 819–820.
[49] Above, n.47.
[50] [2004] 1 W.L.R. 1049.

relevant to a scheme of arrangement. He therefore held that while the "sufficient connection" test had to be satisfied in all cases the second and third elements went to discretion, not to jurisdiction, and since there was a sufficient connection with England and there were factors showing that it would be legitimate and appropriate for the discretion to be exercised in favour of sanctioning the scheme an order to that effect would be made.

In *Re Harrods (Buenos Aires) Ltd*[51] it was held that, the jurisdiction being discretionary, the court may invoke the doctrine of *forum non conveniens* to dismiss a winding-up petition. However, in that case the petition was not on the ground of insolvency. Though it has been said that the court should consider whether another jurisdiction is more appropriate for winding-up on the ground of insolvency,[52] it is thought that *forum non conveniens* will rarely apply to an insolvent liquidation, for the concept of an English liquidation running in parallel with and ancillary to a main liquidation elsewhere is well established,[53] so that if the petitioner establishes a sufficient interest in the outcome of winding-up proceedings in England and the other requirements necessary for a sufficient connection with England there will normally be no good reason to apply *forum non conveniens.*[54]

If a winding-up order is made against a foreign company it will extend to all the company's assets, both here and abroad.[55]

Administration

In the ordinary way there is no jurisdiction to make an administration order **14–15** against a foreign company.[56] This is because there is no definition of "company" for the purposes of the provisions of the Insolvency Act 1986 relating to administration, so that by s.251 of that Act it is necessary to

---

[51] [1992] Ch. 72.

[52] *Re A Company 24 (No.00359 of 1987)* [1988] Ch. 210, *per* Peter Gibson J. at 226.

[53] See below, paras 14–20, 14–26.

[54] See generally Kate Dawson, "The Doctrine of *Forum Non Conveniens* and the Winding Up of Insolvent Foreign Companies" [2005] J.B.L. 28.

[55] *Re Azoff-Don Commercial Bank*, above *per* Wynn-Parry J. at 333; *Re Bank of Credit and Commerce International S.A. (No.2)* [1992] B.C.L.C. 570, *per* Sir Nicolas Browne-Wilkinson V.C. at 577.

[56] There is no decision directly on the point but it has been assumed or conceded in a number of cases. See. for example, *Re Dallhold Estates (U.K.) Pty Ltd* [1992] B.C.C. 394; *Felixstowe Dock and Railway Co v U.S. Lines Inc* [1989] Q.B. 360. However, in *Re International Bulk Commodities Ltd* [1992] B.C.C. 463, Mummery J. held that the contractual nature of administrative receivership meant that a person appointed a receiver of an oversea company (in that case, a Liberian company) could qualify as an administrative receiver, since s.735(1) of the Companies Act applied only "unless the contrary intention appears" (s.735(4)), and that was the case as regards administrative receivership. Mummery J. considered that dicta concerning the inapplicability of administration to an unregistered company, on which he himself did not wish to express a view, it did not necessarily follow that the same applied to administrative receivership.

apply the definition in s.735 of the Companies Act 1985, which defines "company" as a company formed and registered under that Act, or an existing company. It must follow that a foreign company cannot enter an out-of-court administration either. However, it had been held that an administration order can be made against a foreign company where so requested by a foreign court under s.426 of the Insolvency Act.[57]

Statutory scheme of arrangement; CVA

14–16   It has already been mentioned that s.425 of the Companies Act 1985 applies to any company liable to be wound up under that Act or the Insolvency Act 1986, so that there is jurisdiction to approve a scheme of arrangement under that section as regards a foreign company.[58] By contrast, there is no special definition of "company" applicable to CVAs under Part I of the Insolvency Act, which accordingly has no application to a foreign company.

3. THE INSOLVENCY JURISDICTION OF ENGLISH COURTS: CASES WITHIN THE EC INSOLVENCY REGULATION

14–17   The above analysis has dealt with the jurisdiction of the English courts to open insolvency proceedings in cases where the EU Insolvency Regulation does not apply. The position is quite different in cases within the Regulation. Main proceedings cannot be opened in the UK unless the debtor company's COMI is here, and even then the control of assets situated in another EU state is subject to any territorial proceedings opened in that state. Territorial proceedings can be opened in the UK only where the debtor has an establishment here, and they are restricted to local assets and, if secondary proceedings, to winding-up.[59] Hence the provision in s.436A of the Insolvency Act 1986 that in the application of the Act to proceedings by virtue of Art.3 of the Regulation a reference to property is a reference to property which may be dealt with in the proceedings.

4. THE APPLICABLE LAW

Law applicable to winding-up

14–18   The Rome Convention on the law applicable to contractual obligations does not apply to winding-up proceedings.[60] Under English common law conflict of laws rules the applicable law governing winding-up is the *lex*

---

[57] *Re Dallhold Estates (U.K.) Pty Ltd*, above. As to s.426, see below.

[58] See above, para.14–13.

[59] See generally Chap.13. Although an unregistered company cannot normally be put into voluntary winding-up, it can where jurisdiction is given by the Insolvency Regulation. See above, paras 14–13 n.42, 13–11.

[60] Art.1(2)(e).

concursus (or *lex fori concursus*).[61] Where there are concurrent proceedings in England and a foreign country, an English court will apply English law to the winding-up in England.[62] The *lex concursus* governs all matters relating to the winding-up and its effects, whether substantive or procedural, including the assets comprising the estate, the proof and ranking of claims, the admissibility of set-off and. the avoidance of preferences and other transactions.[63] There is, however, much confusion as to the relationship between the *lex concursus* and the law governing the creation of security interests and other real rights in assets in the possession of the debtor company. Let us suppose that Debtco gives security over tangible movables situated in Urbania and subsequently goes into liquidation in Ruritania. What is meant by the statement that the validity and ranking of the security interest in the liquidation are governed by Ruritanian law? Does it mean that Urbanian law governing the creation and effects of the security interest is to be disregarded? The confusion arises because of a failure to distinguish the role of insolvency law from that of the law governing pre-liquidation entitlements. The distinction is well brought out in the Virgós-Schmit Report on the European Bankruptcy Convention in a passage that is equally applicable to the international insolvency.[64]

"The law of the State of the opening of the proceedings *(lex fori concursus)* determines all the effects of the insolvency, both procedural and substantial, on the persons and relations concerned. The substantial effects referred to are those which are typical of insolvency law. That is to say, effects which are necessary for the insolvency proceedings to fulfil its goals. To this extent, it displaces (unless the Convention sets out otherwise) the law normally applicable to the act concerned. That happens for instance when Art.4 makes applicable the law of the State of the opening to declare the voidness or voidability of any contract that may be detrimental to creditors."[65]

We have already seen that English law, like that of many other jurisdictions, starts from the position that pre-liquidation entitlements are to be

---

[61] *Re Suidair International Airways Ltd* [1951] Ch. 165, *per* Wynn-Parry J. at 173.

[62] See below, para.14–25 *et seq*, as to concurrent proceedings.

[63] Textbooks on the conflict of laws focus on jurisdiction and recognition and are curiously silent about the applicable law in winding-up. It seems that this phenomenon is not confined to English texts. See Westbrook and Trautman, "Conflict of Laws Issues in International Insolvencies" in *Current Developments in International and Comparative Corporate Insolvency Law* (ed. Jacob S. Ziegel), Chap.27 at p.657: "The most basic confusion in the traditional approach is conceptual, between choice of law and choice of forum. Each court confronted with a general default must make two threshold decisions: the identification of a national body of law that will govern the financial consequences of the default, and selection of public institutions in one or more countries that will manage the process. The need for two distinct choices—choice of law and choice of forum—is not often articulated."

[64] See above, para.13–49.

[65] *ibid.*, para.59. See to similar effect the UNCITRAL *Legislative Guide on Insolvency Law*, paras 81 *et seq*.

respected. These having been established, it is then for insolvency law to determine to what extent those rights are to be disturbed or set aside in order to fulfil the objectives of insolvency law, in particular, those of fairness and equitable distribution among creditors. The same is true of cross-border insolvencies. In our example, the Ruritanian bankruptcy court can be expected to look in the first instance to Urbanian law as the *lex situs* to determine whether the asserted security interest was validly created. If it was not, then *cadit quaestio*. But if it was, it is then for Ruritanian law to determine whether the security offends in some way against the policies and rules of Ruritanian insolvency law, for example, because it was a preference or a fraud on the general body of creditors or because it failed to comply with the registration requirements of Ruritanian law so far as applicable to security interests created under a foreign law. Similarly, where English law is the *lex concursus*, the English insolvency court will apply French law as the *lex situs* to determine the initial validity of a security interest created over assets in France, but if the security interest is held to have been validly created under French law, its efficacy in an English winding-up must then be tested by reference to English insolvency law, so that it may, for example be set aside under the Insolvency Act 1986 as a transaction at an undervalue[66] or a preference[67] if the facts establish this. Of course, it is always open to the insolvency law to defer to the *lex causae* on particular issues. An example is to be found in Art.13 of the EC Insolvency Regulation.[68]

5. FOREIGN LIQUIDATIONS AND ENGLISH COURTS

Recognition of foreign winding-up or dissolution

14–19   An English court will recognise the effect of a winding-up or dissolution of a foreign company under the law of its incorporation. This common law principle[69] is now enshrined in s.426(5) of the Insolvency Act.[70] Similarly, the court will recognise the status of a foreign liquidator[71] and, in principle, his right to be given control of English assets[72] and any title vested in him by the foreign law.[73] However, the court will not give up its right, in

---

[66] Insolvency Act 1986, s.238.
[67] *ibid.*
[68] See above, para.13–66 and the UNCITRAL *Legislative Guide* (above, n.65), paras 89–90.
[69] *Lazard Bros v Midland Bank Ltd* [1933] A.C. 289.
[70] See below, para.14–27.
[71] *Bank of Ethiopia v National Bank of Egypt* [1937] Ch. 513.
[72] *Felixstowe Dock and Railway Co v United States Lines Inc* [1989] Q.B. 360.
[73] Dicey and Morris, *Conflict of Laws* (12th ed.), Rule 169. This relates to bankruptcy but there seems no reason in principle to treat winding-up differently where the effect under the foreign law (contrary to English law) is to vest the property in the foreign liquidator.

concurrent winding-up proceedings in England, to control the conduct of its own liquidation.[74] Moreover, the court cannot give effect to or recognise an order of a foreign court or any act of an office-holder appointed under such an order where the making of the order, or doing of the act would be prohibited under Part VII of the Companies Act 1989,[75] for example, in relation to market contracts or the default rules of a recognised investment exchange or recognised clearing house.[76]

The rules on recognition of foreign proceedings and the status of foreign liquidators, and on available relief consequent on such recognition, will be substantially enhanced with the enactment of the UNCITRAL Model Law on Cross-Border Insolvency Proceedings.[77]

Assistance to foreign parties and foreign courts

A corollary of the principle of recognition of foreign winding-up orders and **14–20** the status of foreign liquidators is that an English court will give such assistance to a foreign office-holder as is compatible with the application of English insolvency law.[78] This applies not only where there are no concurrent winding-up proceedings in England but also where such proceedings are ancillary to a main liquidation in the foreign country.[79] This common law principle is now reinforced, albeit in much more restricted fashion, by s.426(4) and (5) of the Insolvency Act[80]:

> "(4) The courts having jurisdiction in relation to insolvency law in any part of the United Kingdom shall assist the courts having the corresponding jurisdiction in any other part of the United Kingdom or any relevant country or territory.
>
> (5) For the purposes of subsection (4) a request made to a court in any part of the United Kingdom by a court in any other part of the United Kingdom or in a relevant country or territory is authority for the court to which the request is made to apply, in relation to any matters specified in the request, the insolvency law which is applicable by either court in relation to comparable matters within its jurisdiction.
>
> In exercising its discretion under this subsection, a court shall have regard in particular to the rules of private international law."

---

[74] *Re English, Scottish and Australian Chartered Bank* [1893] 3 Ch. 385, *per* Vaughan Williams J. at 394. See below, para.14–26.

[75] Companies Act 1989, s.183(2).

[76] *ibid.* ss.158, 159. See above, paras 1–29, 1–32.

[77] See below, paras 14–29 *et seq.*

[78] For a full discussion, see Fletcher, *op. cit.*, Chap. 4.

[79] See below, paras 14–26 *et seq.*

[80] See also, in relation to evidence, the Evidence (Proceedings in Other Jurisdictions) Act 1975.

(1) The insolvency law to be applied

14–21   "Insolvency law" is defined, (1) in relation to England and Wales, specified provisions of the Insolvency Act 1986 and the Company Directors Disqualification Act 1986, but this has been held not to confine the court to those provisions so as to preclude the exercise of its general equitable jurisdiction, for example, to grant a worldwide stay of actions or proceedings by the defendants to a claim,[81] (2) in relation to any relevant country or territory, so much of its law as corresponds to English law.[82] "Relevant country or territory" means any of the Channel Islands or Isle of Man or any country or territory designated for the purpose of s.426 by the Secretary of State by order made by statutory instrument.[83] Only three such orders have been made,[84] and almost all the designated countries are Commonwealth countries.

It will be noted that s.426 involves a request for assistance from the foreign court; it does not cover requests from a foreign office-holder, which must be dealt with under the wider principles established at common law. That will change when the UNCITRAL Model Law on Cross-Border Insolvency Proceedings is adopted.[85]

Section 426(5) gives the English court a discretion whether to apply English law (whether substantive or procedural[86]) or the law of the requesting court, and it is in the exercise of this discretion that the court is required by the last sentence of the subsection to have regard to rules of private international law, by which is meant English conflict of laws rules. This "obscure and ill-thought out provision"[87] has given rise to differences of judicial as to whether the discretion in question is given to the requesting court or the requested court. In the most recent case on the subject the view has been expressed that the requested court should take the foreign elements into account in deciding what law to apply.[88] Thus where these point to the application of the foreign law this may influence the court in deciding to apply that law rather than English law, though the court would seem to retain a discretion as to which law to apply and to disregard the English conflicts rule in an appropriate case.[89]

The discretion to apply English law enables the English court in effect to make orders which could not have been made under the law of the

---

[81] *Hughes v Hannover Ruckversicherungs-Aktiengesellschaft* [1997] 1 B.C.L.C. 497.

[82] Insolvency Act 1986, s.426(10).

[83] Insolvency Act 1986, s.426(11).

[84] See the Co-operation of Insolvency Courts (Designation of Relevant Countries and Territories) Order 1986 (SI 1986/2123), the Co-operation of Insolvency Courts (Designation of Relevant Countries) Order 1996 (SI 1996/253), and the Co-operation of Insolvency Courts (Designation of Relevant Country) Order 1998 (SI 1998/2766).

[85] See below, para.14–29.

[86] *Re Bank of Credit and Commerce International S.A.* [1993] B.C.C. 787.

[87] *Re Television Trade Rentals Ltd* [2002] B.P.I.R. 859, *per* Lawrence Collins J. at para.17.

[88] *Ibid.*

[89] See Dicey and Morris, *op. cit.*, pp.1142–1143.

requesting court and to make such orders despite the fact that the foreign office-holder would have no *locus standi* to make application for them in English winding-up proceedings. Thus in *Re Bank of Credit and Commerce International S. A. (No.9)*[90] Rattee J. acceded to a request by the Grand Court of the Cayman Islands to make orders under ss.212, 213, 214 and 238 of the Insolvency Act against the Bank of Credit and Commerce International S.A., a company incorporated in Luxembourg, on the ground of its participation and/or assistance in the fraudulent activities of the senior management of the BCCI group, which included the Bank of Credit and Commerce International (Overseas) Ltd, a company incorporated in the Cayman Islands.[91] The remarkable effect of s.426 is to expose directors of a foreign company to potential liabilities under English law for activities perfectly lawful under the law of the company's incorporation. It is true, as Rattee J. pointed out, that this could happen only where the courts of both jurisdictions exercised their respective discretions to that effect. Even so, the potential translation of provisions of the United Kingdom Insolvency Act into foreign liquidations is striking.

Where the decision is made to apply the insolvency legislation of the other country, so far as corresponding to the provisions of the UK Insolvency Act, then it should be applied in accordance with the principles and practice by which that jurisdiction is exercised by the courts of that country, not in accordance with the rules established under English law in relation to the comparable provisions of the Insolvency Act, which cease to have any relevance once the foreign law has been chosen.[92] Thus although an English court will not assist in the enforcement of an order which is oppressive, the mere fact that it would be considered oppressive by English law in relation to the relevant provision of an English statute, such as s.236 of the Insolvency Act 1986 dealing with orders for examination of officers of the company, does not mean that it is to be considered oppressive for the purposes of the overseas legislation, which may have its own forms of protection against oppression.[93]

(2) Assistance a matter of discretion

There was an apparent division of judicial opinion as to whether the phrase "shall assist" in s.426(4) makes it mandatory for an English court to give assistance. In *Re Dallhold Estates (UK)Pty Ltd*[94] Chadwick J. held that this was the effect of the subsection, and that the only discretion lay with the

14–22

---

[90] [1993] B.C.C. 787.
[91] The order was subsequently varied by the Court of Appeal, but only as regards a different aspect.
[92] *England v Smith* [2001] Ch. 419.
[93] *ibid.*
[94] [1992] B.C.C. 394.

requesting court as to whether or not to make a request, there being no discretion in the requested court. In *Re Bank of Credit and Commerce International S.A. (No.9)*[95] Rattee J. expressed disagreement with that part of the judgment of Chadwick J., and held that the requested court has a discretion whether to apply its own law or that of the requesting court and how it should give such assistance.[96] But the difference of view is more apparent than real, for in a later passage in his judgment Chadwick J. had said, in reference to s.426(4):

> "Those are mandatory words. It appears to me that their effect is such that, if the conditions set out in para. (b) and (c) of section 8(1) of the 1986 Act are satisfied, then this court ought to make an administration order—and so give the assistance required—*unless there are powerful reasons to the contrary*" [emphasis added].[97]

In the subsequent decision in *Re Focus Insurance Co Ltd*[98] Sir Richard Scott V.C. declined to make an order for the assistance of foreign liquidators in the recovery of English assets in an English bankruptcy where the liquidators were the petitioning creditors in the bankruptcy and the relief sought could be obtained in the bankruptcy proceedings by the trustee in bankruptcy. More recently still the same judge held that assistance could not be given under s.426 where its effect would be to disapply the English statutory insolvency scheme, in that case the statutory set-off prescribed by r.4.90 of the Insolvency Rules 1996.[99] Finally, the Court of Appeal has confirmed that the court continues to enjoy a discretion to grant or reject a request for judicial assistance and rejected the notion that the only permissible ground of refusal is public policy, holding that the court must in every case fulfil its duty to do justice in accordance with law.[1]

(3) Forms of assistance

14–23   An English court may provide any form of assistance comparable to the relief that could be given in insolvency proceedings in England, whether under the provisions of the Insolvency Act or pursuant to the court's

---

[95] [1993] B.C.C. 787.

[96] *ibid.*, at 801.

[97] See further *Re Focus Insurance Co Ltd* [1996] B.C.C. 659.

[98] [1996] B.C.C. 659.

[99] *The Bank of Credit and Commerce International SA (No. II)* [1997] 1 B.C.L C. 80. See above, para.8–16. A further ground for the decision was that r.4.90 was not only mandatory but self-executing, so that to the extent of the set-off there would be no credit balance to be included in the assets transferred to the foreign liquidator in the main liquidation.

[1] *Hughes v Hannover Ruckversicherunngs-Aktiengesellschaft* [1997] 1 B.C.L.C. 497. In that case the court refused the request, made by the Supreme Court of Bermuda, on the ground that there had been a substantial change of circumstances since the signature of the letter of request by the Chief Justice of Bermuda and that there was no indication in the evidence whether the Supreme Court had reconsidered the matter in the light of the change of circumstances.

general equitable jurisdiction. Available forms of assistance include an order for examination of an officer of the company under s.236 of the Insolvency Act,[2] an injunction to restrain the commencement or continuance of actions against the debtor company, whether in England or elsewhere,[3] a declaration recognising the right and title of a foreign liquidator, provisional liquidator or other foreign representative,[4] the appointment of a receiver,[5] the making of an administration order,[6] and orders under ss.212, 213, 214 and 238 of the Insolvency Act.[7] Where the court does not feel able to grant the particular form of assistance requested it should consider whether it can properly assist in some other way in accordance with any of the available systems of law.[8]

Staying English proceedings where foreign insolvency proceedings

An English winding-up order automatically stays proceedings in England[9] but the same is not true of an order in foreign proceedings.[10] The court has a discretion to order a stay of English proceedings where there is a foreign liquidation or other insolvency process, but will only exercise this where it considers it appropriate to do so.[11] In particular, it will not normally restrain a secured creditor from enforcing his security or otherwise inhibit the *in rem* effect on an asset of a judgment of a foreign court of competent jurisdiction.[12] The court, in exercise of its *in personam* jurisdiction, may grant an order restraining an English creditor from pursuing proceedings abroad, *e.g.* by trying to attach foreign assets,[13] and this is so whether or not it has proved as a creditor in an English winding-up.[14] *and* has entertained, though not always granted, requests by other courts to give assistance under s.426 of the Insolvency Act 1986 by granting an injunction restraining foreign proceedings.[15] But where the English proceedings are ancillary to a

14–24

---

[2] *England v Smith* [2001] Ch. 419; *Re Trading Partners Ltd.* [2002] 1 B.C.L.C. 655.
[3] *Hughes v Hannover Ruckversicherungs-Aktiengesellschaft*, above, n.1.
[4] *ibid.*
[5] *Re a Debtor, Ex p. Viscount of the Royal Court of Jersey* [1980] 3 All E.R. 665; *Re Osborn, Ex p. Trustee* [1931–32] B. & C.R. 189.
[6] *Re Dallhold Estates (UK) Pty Ltd* [1992] B.C.L.C. 621.
[7] *Re Bank of Credit and Commerce International S.A. (No.9)* [1993] B.C.C. 787.
[8] *ibid.*
[9] Insolvency Act 1986, s.130(2). See above, para.5–16. The stay is not automatic in the case of voluntary winding-up.
[10] *Re Vocalion (Foreign) Ltd* [1932] 2 Ch. 196.
[11] *Felixstowe Dock and Railway Co v United States Line Inc* [1989] Q.B. 360.
[12] *Minna Craig Steamship Co v Chartered Mercantile Bank of India, London and China* [1897] 1 Q.B. 460.
[13] *Re Oriental Inland Steam Co* (1874) LR 9 Ch. App. 557.
[14] *Re Central Sugar Factories of Brazil, Flack's Case* [1894] 1 Ch. 369.
[15] See above, paraa.14–23. This cannot be done where the creditor is outside the jurisdiction of the English court, which in such cases must seek the assistance of the courts of the state in which the creditor is located.

main liquidation abroad a court in England will not normally grant an injunction to restrain proceedings in the foreign liquidation, taking the view that it is for the foreign court to decide whether the action should be allowed to proceed.[16]

6. CONCURRENT INSOLVENCY PROCEEDINGS

14–25 We have seen that the principle of unity of the insolvency is not adopted in practice except in very modified form. It is common to have concurrent insolvency proceedings in different jurisdictions. In some cases the proceedings in one court are ancillary to those of another,[17] but it is perfectly possible to have concurrent proceedings neither of which are ancillary proceedings; indeed, where one of the two states is a non-EU states and neither state has adopted the UNCITRAL Model Law there is nothing to stop the courts in both states from claiming jurisdiction over all the debtor's assets on a worldwide basis, so that in effect there are two main proceedings.[18] There is nothing to preclude the creditor from lodging a proof of debt in both sets of proceedings, but under the hotchpot rule applied in English law a creditor who has received a dividend in the foreign proceedings must bring in, for the purpose of dividend, the sum which he has received abroad.[19] This does not mean that he has to hand over the dividend he has received to the English liquidator, merely that he cannot receive a dividend in the English liquidation until the dividends he would have received in that liquidation equal his foreign dividend, so that other creditors in the English liquidation will have received a dividend at the same rate as that received in the foreign liquidation by the creditor in question.[20] But the hotchpot rule applies only to payments received from the company's assets and does not require the amount of realisations of security held by the creditor to be brought into account.[21]

The concept of ancillary proceedings

14–26 Reference has already been made to the concept of a main liquidation in one country and an ancillary liquidation in another. This concept is well established in English law, so that where a foreign company is being wound

---

[16] *Re Maxwell Communications Corp plc (No.2)* [1992] B.C.C. 757.
[17] See below, para.14–26.
[18] This is not possible in cases within the EU Insolvency Regulation (see above, para.13–19) or the UNCITRAL Model Law (see below, para.14–30).
[19] *Banco de Portugal v Waddell* (1880) 5 App. Cas. 161.
[20] *ibid.*, *per* Lord Blackburn at 175; *Ex p. Wilson, re Douglas* (1872) L.R. 7 Ch. App. 490.
[21] *Cleaver v Delta American Reinsurance Co* [2001] 2 A.C. 328.

up under the law of its incorporation winding-up proceedings in England will be regarded as ancillary to the foreign winding-up.[22]Its effect is that while the English court will apply rules of English insolvency law to the resolution of any issues in the English liquidation, it will direct the English assets, together with a list of creditors, to be transferred to the foreign liquidator, who will be best placed to declare the dividend and to distribute the assets among creditors.[23]

Surmounting the problems of concurrent insolvent proceedings

(1) Judicial co-operation

It has long been recognised that the institution of concurrent insolvency proceedings in courts of different countries may raise complex questions, particularly where the insolvency law of both countries adopts the principle of universality, with the potential for conflicts between the laws of the two jurisdictions and the orders of their respective courts. That these problems have not proved insurmountable is largely due to the spirit of co-operation and mutual assistance prevailing among the judges and to legislation such as that embodied in s.426 of the Insolvency Act which has just been examined.

    One of the most remarkable examples of judicial co-operation was triggered by the collapse of the Maxwell group of companies following the death of the business tycoon Robert Maxwell, a collapse resulting in major litigation in many different jurisdictions. Maxwell Communications Corp plc ("MCC") was an English holding company with a large number of subsidiaries scattered around the world. MCC filed under Chapter 11 of the US Bankruptcy Code and soon afterwards obtained an administration order in England. The peculiar feature of the case was that both sets of proceedings were primary proceedings, so that each court had jurisdiction over the assets of the company on a worldwide basis. The English proceedings were controlled by Hoffmann J., the US proceedings by Judge Tina L. Brozman, a judge of the Bankruptcy Court for the Southern District of New York. The English administrators were anxious to be heard in the US proceedings, and Judge Brozman fully recognised them as parties in interest but was anxious to create a mechanism that would facilitate co-operation and avoid conflict. To that end she appointed an examiner. The examiner and the joint administrators then collaborated with a view to harmonising the two sets of proceedings for the benefit of all creditors and eventually agreed on a Protocol to govern their respective roles and powers.

14–27

---

[22] See *Re Bank of Credit and Commerce International S.A. (No.11)* [1996] B.C.C. 980, where the relevant authorities are examined.
[23] *ibid.*

Both courts then responded positively to the invitation to approve the Protocol, each court agreeing that it would to the necessary degree defer its jurisdiction to that of the other. The examiner and the administrators then settled upon a reorganisation plan under Chapter 11 and a scheme of arrangement under s.425 of the Companies Act 1985. Simultaneously Judge Brozman approved the plan under Chapter 11 and Hoffmann J. the scheme of arrangement under s.425. The combination of the plan and the scheme produced the single distribution mechanism upon which the success of the whole operation so crucially depended, differences in the two sets of governing laws being resolved by accommodations on all sides. The result was to save substantial sums for the creditors in both jurisdictions.[24] Thus began the practice by which protocols are agreed between the office-holders in the different jurisdictions and approved by their respective courts.[25] Common provisions in such protocols include: a statement confirming the sovereignty and independence of the two courts involved and recording that each of the two office holders is subject only to the jurisdiction of its own court; a recognition by each court of the proceedings opened by the other and of any stays granted; the status of the two office-holders and the right of each to be heard as a foreign representative in the other proceedings; a direction to the office-holder in each court, while respecting this sovereignty and independence of the two courts, to co-operate with the other in connection with the management of the parallel insolvencies and to harmonise and co-ordinate their activities; a provision for similar co-operation between the two courts with a view to establishing methods of communication, with or without counsel, co-ordinating rulings and conducting joint hearings via a telephone link; an identification of the various cross-border issues to be addressed (*e.g.* reorganisation, treatment of claims, realisation of assets); a provision for mutual disclosure of relevant documents and for notice to all interested parties of any court motions; provision for the venue of applications for relief, which will depend on the nature of the relief sought and whether it relates to property within the

---

[24] For a detailed description of the case, with a reproduction of the agreed order and Protocol, see Evan D. Flaschen and Ronald J. Silverman "The Role of the Examiner as Facilitator and Harmonizer in the Maxwell Communication Corporation International Insolvency" in Ziegel (ed.), *op.cit.*, Chap. 25. See also Christopher K. Grierson, "Issues in Concurrent Insolvency Jurisdiction: English perspectives" (*ibid.*, Chap.24) describing this and other cases involving judicial co-operation, and *Re Bank of Credit and Commerce International S.A. (No. 2)* [1992] B.C.C. 715; *Re Maxwell Communications Corp. plc (No.2)* [1992] B.C.C. 757, *sub. nom. Barclays Bank Ltd v Homan* [1993] B.C.L.C. 680.

[25] These are described by Flaschen and Silverman, "Maxwell Communication Corporation plc: The Importance of Comity and Cooperation in Resolving International Insolvencies" in American Bar Association, *Multinational Commercial Insolvency*, and "Cross-Border Insolvency Cooperation Protocols" 33 Texas Int. L.J. 587 (1998); Leonard Hoffmann (now Lord Hoffmann), Cross-Border Insolvency: A British Perspective" 64 Fordham L. Rev. 2507 (1996). "Principles and Practice of Cross-Border Insolvency Cooperation Protocols" presented at a symposium on International Bankruptcy Law: Comparative and Transnational Approaches" held at the University of Texas at Austin in March 1997.

jurisdiction of one of the courts; and a direction to the two office-holders to submit to their respective courts reorganisation plans in substantially the same form.[26]

(2) International conventions

While judicial co-operation has worked successfully in a number of cases, **14–28** judges are bound by their national laws and have only limited room for manoeuvre. There has long been a perceived need for an international convention to govern cross-border insolvency. No such convention currently exists. There have been two regional conventions, the Istanbul Convention of 1990 on Certain International Aspects of Bankruptcy prepared by the Council of Europe and the second the EC Convention on Insolvency Proceedings of 1995. As recorded in the previous chapter the EC Convention fell away for want of signature by the United Kingdom and was replaced by the EC Insolvency Regulation, which closely follows the EC Convention and renders the Istanbul Convention otiose.[27] In the absence of an international convention UNCITRAL prepared its Model Law on Cross-Border Insolvency, which is now gaining increasingly widespread acceptance and is discussed in section 6 below, as well as a more recent guide to the preparation of domestic legislation on insolvency[28] which includes a recommendation for the adoption of the Model Law and which may itself facilitate the convergence of national laws.

---

[26] For an up-to-date picture of the protocol system as it has featured in parallel proceedings in Canada and the US and Israel, see Edward A. Sellers, "Coordinating U.S./Canadian Restructurings and Insolvencies", a paper presented at the Canadian-American Symposium on Cross-Border Insolvency, Toronto, February 11, 2005 and accessible on the Global Insolvency website. Of particular interest, in addition to the *Maxwell* protocol, are the protocols agreed in *Systech Retail Systems Corp. et al*, involving orders of the Canadian and US courts; and incorporating the American Law Institute Guidelines Applicable to Court-to-Court Communications in Cross-Border Cases; the *Inverworld* group, involving co-operation between the US, Cayman Islands and English courts; the *Everfresh* group and the *Solv-Ex* group, each involving orders of the Canadian and US courts; and the *Nakash* case, involving orders of the courts of Canada and Israel.

[27] Among other earlier initiatives to facilitate the administration of cross-border insolvencies may be mentioned the Model International Insolvency Co-operation Act ("MIICA"), prepared by Committee "J" of the International Bar Association and approved by the IBA; the IBA Cross-Border Insolvency Concordat and, at regional level, the American Law Institute Transnational Insolvency Project to examine the national and cross-border insolvency laws of the parties to the North American Free Trade Agreement. This major project has resulted in the publication of four volumes, the first devoted to principles of cooperation among the NAFTA countries and the others to international statements of US, Canadian and Mexican bankruptcy law respectively.

[28] *Legislative Guide on Insolvency Law.*

7. THE UNCITRAL MODEL LAW ON CROSS-BORDER INSOLVENCY[29]

14–29   The UNCITRAL Model Law on Cross-Border Insolvency is the product of collaboration between the United Nations Commission on International Trade Law and INSOL International,[30] which held a series of joint international meetings to examine prospects for the harmonisation of rules on cross-border insolvency.[31] Adopted in 1997, the Model Law is designed to provide a harmonised approach to the treatment of cross-border insolvency in national legal systems and to facilitate co-operation between courts and office holders involved in the same insolvency in different jurisdictions and provide for the mutual recognition of judgments and direct access of foreign representatives to the courts of the enacting state.[32] It is being adopted by a growing number of states,[33] and the United Kingdom plans to enact it by subordinate legislation on April 1, 2006 pursuant to s.14 of the Insolvency Act 2000.

Nature of the Model Law

14–30   A model law is simply that: a law which in itself has no binding force and which states are free to reject, adopt in its entirety or expand or modify at will. Different states use a model law in different ways. Some enact it virtually as it stands; some adopt the bulk of the provisions but introduce their own additions and amendments, either to suit local conditions or because—sometimes rather rashly—they assume they can improve on the drafting or the substance; and some look to the model law simply for ideas for their own legislation drafted for their own purposes. This last was the approach adopted in the field of commercial arbitration by the UK Arbitration Act 1996, which did not enact the UNCITRAL Model Law on international commercial arbitration but drew significantly on many of its basic concepts. These different approaches inevitably tend to weaken the

---

[29] See Fletcher, *op. cit.*, Chap.8 for the most detailed and up-to-date analysis of the Model Law in the UK.

[30] The International Association of Insolvency Practitioners.

[31] See in particular Report on UNCITRAL-INSOL Colloquium on Cross-Border Insolvency, 1994, UNCITRAL, 27th Sess., at 2, U.N. Doc. A/CN.9/398(1994), also reproduced in [1995] 4 *International Insolvency Review, Special Conference Issue*, and the subsequent Report on the 4th UNCITRAL-INSOL Judicial Colloquium on Cross-Border Insolvency, 2001, UNCITRAL, 35th Sess., at 8, U.N. Doc. A/CN.9/518 (2002).

[32] See *UNCITRAL Model Law on Cross-Border Insolvency with Guide to Enactment*.

[33] To date it has been adopted by Eritrea, Japan, Mexico, Poland, Romania, South Africa, within Serbia and Montegro, Montenegro, British Virgin Islkands, and, most recently, the United States, whose Bankruptcy Abuse Prevention and Consumer Protection Act 2005, signed into law by the President on April 20 2005, has incorporated the Model Law into a new Chapter 15 of its Bankruptcy Code. This will replace s.304 of the Bankruptcy Code.

harmonisation the model law is intended to achieve and make it difficult to give meaning to the statement that a given number of states have adopted a particular model law. Nevertheless the UNCITRAL Model Law seems set for a significant degree of successful adoption. The UK plans to implement the UNCITRAL Model Law on Cross-Border Insolvency substantially as drafted, with certain additions to reflect the different types of insolvency procedure and different categories of office-holder prescribed by UK legislation.

The Model Law, while obviously having important effects on the grant of relief, is a purely procedural law. It contains no rules of substantive law, whether relating to insolvency or otherwise, or any conflict of laws rules, all these being within the exclusive province of national laws and national courts. In this respect it differs markedly from the EC Insolvency Regulation. So where a foreign representative or foreign creditor brings proceedings in the enacting state to avoid a transaction as being, for example, a transaction at an undervalue or a preference, it is for the court in the enacting state to determine, first, whether the relief sought is one that would be available to an office holder appointed under its own insolvency law[34] and, secondly, under its own conflict rules what law governs the power of avoidance. Moreover, there is only one rule limiting jurisdiction, namely that after recognition of a foreign main proceeding, a proceeding under th insolvency laws of the enacting state may be commenced only in if the debtor has assets in that state and must be restricted to local assets.[35] With this exception the courts of the enacting state are free to apply their own jurisdiction rules.

Sphere of application

Article 1 defines the sphere of application of the Model Law in the following terms: **14–31**

"1. This Law applies where:
   (*a*) Assistance is sought in this State by a foreign court or a foreign representative in connection with a foreign proceeding; or
   (*b*) Assistance is sought in a foreign State in connection with a proceeding under *[identify laws of the enacting State relating to insolvency]*; or
   (*c*) A foreign proceeding and a proceeding under *[identify laws of the enacting State relating to insolvency]* in respect of the same debtor are taking place concurrently; or

---

[34] Which is a prerequisite for the grant of any form of relief not listed in Art. 21(1)(a)–(f). See Art.21(1)(g).
[35] Art.28.

> (d) Creditors or other interested persons in a foreign State have an interest in requesting the commencement of, or participating in, a proceeding under *[identify laws of the enacting State relating to insolvency]*.
>
> 2. This Law does not apply to a proceeding concerning *[designate any types of entities, such as banks or insurance companies, that are subject to a special insolvency regime in this State and that this State wishes to exclude from this Law]*."

With this must be read the definitions in Art.2:

"For the purposes of this Law:

> (a) "Foreign proceeding" means a collective judicial or administrative proceeding in a foreign State, including an interim proceeding, pursuant to a law relating to insolvency in which proceeding the assets and affairs of the debtor are subject to control or supervision by a foreign court, for the purpose of reorganization or liquidation;
>
> (b) "Foreign main proceeding" means a foreign proceeding taking place in the State where the debtor has the centre of its main interests;
>
> (c) "Foreign non-main proceeding" means a foreign proceeding, other than a foreign main proceeding, taking place in a State where the debtor has an establishment within the meaning of subparagraph (f) of this article;
>
> (d) "Foreign representative" means a person or body, including one appointed on an interim basis, authorized in a foreign proceeding to administer the reorganization or the liquidation of the debtor's assets or affairs or to act as a representative of the foreign proceeding;
>
> (e) "Foreign court" means a judicial or other authority competent to control or supervise a foreign proceeding;
>
> (f) "Establishment" means any place of operations where the debtor carries out a non-transitory economic activity with human means and goods or services."

So the Model Law is engaged where there are insolvency proceedings in one state and assistance is sought in another state or there are concurrent insolvency proceedings in two or more states or a creditor in one state seeks to commence or participate in insolvency proceedings in another state. The provisions have always to be read from the perspective of the state that has adopted the Model Law ("the enacting state"). A proceeding in the other state is a "foreign proceeding" as defined in Art.2. That state may or may not have enacted the Model Law but this is irrelevant where assistance is sought from the courts of the enacting state or foreign creditors desire to initiate or participate in proceedings in the enacting state except where, in adopting the Model Law, the enacting state has imposed a condition of reciprocity. On the other hand courts and creditors in the enacting state are obviously not entitled to invoke the Model Law in a foreign state that has not adopted it. Most of the provisions of the Model Law do not apply at all unless there is a foreign proceeding. However, this is not true as regards the rights of foreign creditors[36] to institute or partipate in insolvency proceedings in the enacting state to the same extent as local creditors[37] and, where they are known, to be individually notified of insolvency proceedings in the enacting state whenever local creditors would be so notified.[38] Such rights are not dependent on the opening of foreign proceedings.

Some definitional aspects

(1) "Foreign proceeding"

The definition of "foreign proceeding" makes it clear that the Model Law is **14–32** confined to collective proceedings in a state pursuant to its insolvency law as identified in the enacting statute. In the UK the Model Law will be adopted as regards companies in relation to administration, voluntary arrangements and liquidations, other than companies excluded from its scope because of special legislation. Administrative receivership will not be included as it is not a collective insolvency proceeding. Art.2 contains definitions of foreign main proceedings and foreign non-main proceedings. These correspond to the main proceedings and territorial proceedings under the EC Insolvency Regulation,[39] a foreign main proceeding meaning one taking place in the state where the debtor has its centre of main interests[40] and a foreign non-main proceeding meaning a proceeding, other than a main proceeding, taking place in a state where the debtor has an established, that is, any place of operations where the debtor carries out a non-transitory economic activity with human means and goods or services.[41] Unfortunately the classification is less clear than under the Insolvency Regulation, where insolvency proceedings are either main proceedings or territorial proceedings. That is not the case under the Model Law, where the definition of "foreign proceedings" makes no reference to main or non-main proceedings and thus is wide enough to cover proceedings opened in

---

[36] The phrase "foreign creditors" is not defined but would appear to denote creditors not having a place of business in the enacting state.
[37] Art.13. See below, para.14–38.
[38] Art.14. See below, para.14–38.
[39] Above, para.13–18.
[40] In proceedings for recognition there is a presumption that the debtor's registered office is its COMI (Art.16(2)); but as noted in relation to the equivalent provision in the EC Insolvency Regulation this presumption is readily rebutted. See above, paras 13–26 *et seq.*
[41] The definition of "establishment" tracks that contained in Art.2(h) the Insolvency Regulation except that "or services" has been added after "goods."

a state where the debtor has neither its centre of main interests nor an establishment. One such case is where foreign main proceedings have been recognised in the enacting state and the debtor, though not having an establishment in that state, has assets there.[42] But even the absence of this element does not preclude proceedings from constituting foreign proceedings within Art.2. It is unfortunate that the Model Law does not more clearly define the status of foreign proceedings in a state in which the debtor does not have its centre of main interests, an establishment or assets. We shall return to this question in a moment.

(2) "Foreign representative"

14–33 This means a person or body, including one appointed on an interim basis, authorised in a foreign proceeding to administer the reorganisation or the liquidation of the debtor's assets or affairs or to act as a representative of the foreign proceeding. The status of the foreign representative in a UK court is determined by the law of the foreign state under which he was appointed. Where it is a UK appointee who in relation to a company wishes to be recognised as a foreign representative in proceedings in another state that has enacted the Model Law, he could be the Official Receiver, a liquidator, a provisional liquidator, an administrator or the supervisor of a voluntary arrangement.

The status of foreign proceedings that are neither main nor non-main

14–34 We have previously seen that the classification of foreign proceedings as main or non-main is not exhaustive, because the definition of foreign proceedings does not require them to be either main or non-main. It has to be said that the position of foreign proceedings that are neither main nor non-main, because they are opened in a jurisdiction where the debtor has neither its COMI nor an establishment, is unclear from the text of the rules and is not clarified by the Guide. The Model Law does not contain any rules governing the jurisdiction to open foreign proceedings; that is exclusively a matter for the foreign law. So on the face of it, except as otherwise indicated, the provisions of the Model Law apply to all foreign proceedings, even if neither main nor non-main. That is borne out by Art.28, which postulates the opening of foreign main proceedings in state A and the opening of proceedings under Art.28 in state B where the debtor has assets but not necessarily an establishment. Of course, in the courts of state B these would not be foreign proceedings at all, but they would be so

---

[42] Art.28.

considered in state C as an enacting state if proceedings were opened there and would have to be treated as neither main nor non-main foreign proceedings.

The question then is: are there indeed provisions of the Model Law which apply to foreign proceedings that are neither main nor non-main proceedings, and if so, which? On a natural construction, provisions so applicable include access of foreign representatives and creditors to courts in the enacting state,[43] application by a foreign representative for recognition of the foreign proceeding,[44] recognition of a foreign proceeding,[45] urgent relief pending a decision of an application for recognition,[46] and proceedings under Art.28, if the debtor has no establishment there, when viewed from the perspective of a court in a third state that is an enacting state. However, Art.17(2) requires the foreign proceeding to be recognised as a main proceeding if taking place in the state where the debtor has its COMI and as a non-main proceeding if the debtor has an establishment in the foreign state,[47] this being relevant to the forms of relief available, and at least one commentator has construed Art.17(2) as limiting recognition to main and non-main proceedings.[48] This construction does some violence to Art.17(1), which in specifying the conditions under which recognition is mandatory does not include any such limitation, but it seems more in accord with the general thrust and purpose of the Model Law. If this be correct, the Model Law must be construed as if its provisions for access of a foreign representative or creditor to courts in the enacting state, recognition of foreign proceedings in the enacting state and the grant of provisional and final relief in that state, are limited to cases in which the foreign proceedings are either main or non-main, and thus cannot be invoked in relation to foreign proceedings opened in a state where the debtor had neither its COMI nor an establishment.

Rights given by the Model Law

It is not possible within the compass of this chapter to refer to all the provisions of the Model Law. The principal rights given by the Model Law are the following:

14–35

---

[43] Articles 9, 11–13.

[44] Art.15.

[45] Art.17.

[46] Art.19.

[47] By implication this must mean an establishment but not the debtor's COMI. It would have been better drafting to have referred back to the definitions in Art.2(b) and (c).

[48] Jenny Clift, "UNITED NATIONS COMMISSION ON INTERNATIONAL TRADE LAW (UNCITRAL): The UNCITRAL Model Law on Cross-Border Insolvency—A Legislative Framework to Facilitate Coordination and Cooperation in Cross-Border Insolvency", 12 Tulane J. Int'l and Comp. Law 307 (2004). This seems to receive some support from Fletcher, *op. cit.*, who at para.8–32 remarks somewhat cryptically that in such cases "the Model law provides no further assistance or advantages to the foreign representative beyond the bare recognition of the fact that his appointment has taken place under the law of the foreign State in question", adding that further assistance is dependent on the law and practice of the recognising state independently of the provisions of the Model Law.

(1) Foreign representative's rights of direct access and intervention

14–36   A foreign representative is entitled to apply directly to a court in the enacting state.[49] Consequently he has no need to obtain a licence or other authorisation from a regulator of the enacting state before making an application to the court, nor is he obliged to make such an application through a local insolvency practitioner. An application by the foreign representative does not subject him or the foreign assets and affairs of the debtor to the jurisdiction of the courts of the enacting state for any purpose other than the application.[50] But this does not render him immune from jurisdiction on other grounds. This right of access is buttressed by the separate right to intervene in any proceedings in which the debtor is a party.[51] Again, this provision goes only to standing; the foreign representative cannot intervene unless the ordinary requirements for intervention provided by the law of the enacting state are fulfilled.

(2) Foreign representative's right to commence an insolvency proceeding in the enacting state

14–37   Under Art.11 the foreign representative has the right to apply to commence a proceeding under the insolvency laws of that state if the conditions for commencing such a proceeding are otherwise met. This right relates purely to the foreign representative's *locus standi.* So if, for example, he were to apply for a winding-up order Art.11 ensures that he has standing to do so but he still has to show the existence of one of the statutory grounds on which a winding-up order may be made. In order to make the application the foreign representative must, of course, have been authorised in a foreign proceeding to administer the reorganisation or the liquidation of the debtor or to act as a representative of the foreign proceeding, this being inherent in the definition of foreign representative.[52] It is not, however, necessary for the foreign proceeding to have received recognition from a court in the enacting state, for urgent steps might be necessary in order to preserve the assets.[53]

(3) Foreign creditors' rights of access and notification

14–38   Under Art.13(1) foreign creditors are given the same rights regarding commencement of and participation in a proceeding as creditors in the enacting state. Article 13(1) is not confined to cases where foreign

---

[49] Art.9.
[50] Art.10.
[51] Art.24.
[52] Art.2(d).
[53] *Guide to Enactment*, para.99.

proceedings have been opened. Article 13(2) then goes on to say that Art.13(1) does not affect the ranking of claims except that the claims of foreign creditors must not be ranked lower than those of general non-preferential creditors unless an equivalent local claim would be so ranked. This is a curiously placed provision in that it deals with a subject-matter entirely different from that covered by Art.13(1). Even in a state which treats foreign creditors differently from local creditors there is no conceivable reason why a right of access should be in any way relevant to the ranking of claims. Article 13(2) would have been better formulated as an entirely separate provision dealing with the ranking of claims.

Article 14 entitles foreign creditors, where known, to be individually notified of insolvency proceedings in the enacting whenever under its law such notification would be goven to local creditors.

(4) Application for recognition of a foreign proceeding

A foreign representative may apply to the court for recognition of the foreign proceeding in which he has been appointed,[54] the application to be accompanied by the documents specified in Art.15(2) and (3).
14–39

(5) Recognition of a foreign proceeding

Whereas under the EC Insolvency Regulation an insolvency proceeding opened in one Member State is entitled to automatic recognition under another, the Model Law requires an application to be made to a court in the enacting state. Under Art.17(1) a foreign proceeding, as defined by Art.2(a), must be recognised on the application of a foreign representative, as defined by Art.2(d), if the application is accompanied by the documents specified in Art.15(2) and has been submitted to the appropriate court designated by the law of the enacting state under Art.4. These are the only requirements specified in Art.17(1). Nevertheless, as stated earlier, the effect of Art.17(2) appears to be that recognition will only be given if a further condition is satisfied, namely that the foreign proceeding is a main or non-main proceeding, so that there is no entitlement to recognition under the Model Law[55] if the foreign proceedings were opened in a state where the debtor does not have either its COMI or an establishment. Subject to fulfilment of these requirements the foreign proceeding is entitled to recognition and it is not open to the courts of the enacting state to question the basis on which the foreign court reached its decision, for
14–40

---

[54] Art.15(1).
[55] There is, of course, nothing to preclude recognition under applicable domestic law rules. See above, para.14–19.

example by applying its own analysis to determine whether the debtor company is insolvent. The finding of insolvency by the foreign court is conclusive in proceedings for recognition in the enacting state unless the public policy exception in Art. 6 applies.[56]

There is a sole exception to the entitlement to recognition. The court may refuse to make an order if the grant of recognition would be manifestly contrary to the public policy of the state.[57] So far as English law is concerned, "public policy" should be understood in this context as meaning public policy as applied in an international context,[58] so that recognition should not be refused merely because of some rule of public policy applicable to domestic transactions but should be based on facts that would make it incompatible with fundamental concepts of justice to accord recognition. An example would be where the order commencing the foreign proceeding was made in breach of principles of natural justice, as where the debtor company was not given notice of the proceedings or was denied the opportunity to present its case. The word "manifestly" is designed to send a signal courts to adopt a restrictive approach to the public policy exception and is now standard in private law conventions.[59]

(6) Automatic stay

14–41   Recognition of a foreign main proceeding produces effects which are automatic, in contrast to the position under Art.21, where relief has to be applied for. The automatic effects under Art.20 consist of a stay on the commencement or continuance of individual actions or individual proceedings concerning the debtor's assets, rights, obligations or liabilities and on execution against the debtor's assets, and suspension of the right to dispose of the debtor's assets. The automatic stay does not, however, apply to cases falling within any of the exceptions provided by the local law,[60] for example, the right of retention of title sellers to recover their property and the right of secured creditors to enforce their security.

(7) Relief at the request of the foreign representative

14–42   Under Art.21 relief may be granted as appropriate at the request of the foreign representative where necessary to protect the assets of the debtor or the interests of the creditors and not already effected automatically under

---

[56] The position is otherwise where what is in question is the status of insolvency under the law of the enacting state for the purpose of proceedings opened there. See below, para.14–45.

[57] Art.6.

[58] Para.88 of the *Guide* provides an encouragement to states to adopt an international approach to public policy, and this reflects English law.

[59] For a recent example, see Art.11(1) of the 2002 Hague Convention on the law applicable to certain rights in respect of securities held with an intermediary and the Explanatory Report by Professors Roy Goode, Hideki Kanda and Karl Kreuzer, assisted by Christophe Bernasconi, para.11–6.

[60] Art.20(2).

Art.20. Such request may be made whether the foreign proceedings are main or non-main proceedings. The forms of relief that may be given are:

(a) the stay of commencement or continuation of individual actions, and of individual proceedings concerning the debtor's assets, rights, obligations and liabilities, to the extent that they have not been stayed under Art.20(1)(a);

(b) the stay of execution against the debtor's assets to the extent that execution has not been stayed under Art.20(1)(b);

(c) the suspension of the right to dispose of the debtor's assets to the extent that this right has not already been stayed under Art.20(1)(c);

(d) the examination of witnesses, the taking of evidence or the delivery of information concerning the debtor's assets, affairs, rights, obligations or liabilities;

(e) the entrustment of the administration, realisation and distribution of all or part of the assets located in the enacting state to the foreign representative or another person designated by the court[61];

(f) the extension of provisional relief previously granted under Art.19(1); and

(g) the grant of any additional relief that may be available to the insolvency office holder under the laws of the enacting state.

Forms of relief under Art.21(a)(b) and (c) are confined to cases where the foreign proceedings are non-main proceedings, because in the case of main proceedings the effects will have been produced automatically under Art.20. By contrast with other forms of relief it is entirely within the discretion of the court in the enacting state whether to grant relief and, if so, what form or forms of relief; and in granting relief the court may impose such conditions as it considers appropriate.[62] The court must in all cases be satisfied that, in the case of authorised distributions, the interests of local creditors will be adequately protected[63] and that generally the interests of the creditors and other interested persons, including the debtor, are adequately protected.[64]

The foreign representative also has standing, upon recognition of the foreign proceeding under which he was appointed, to initiate proceedings for the avoidance of transactions detrimental to creditors,[65] which in

---

[61] This therefore includes the turnover of assets to the foreign representative.
[62] Art.22(2).
[63] Art.21(2).
[64] Art.22.
[65] Art.23.

England would include transactions at an undervalue, preferences, floating charges given otherwise than for specified forms of new value and transactions in fraud of creditors.[66] Such proceedings may be initiated by the foreign representative even though he is not the insolvency administrator appointed in the insolvency proceedings in the enacting state. But where the foreign main proceeding is a non-main proceeding the court must be satisfied that under the law of the enacting state an action relating to assets should be administered in the foreign main proceeding.[67]

(8) Co-operation with foreign courts and foreign representatives

14-43   Chapter IV of the Model Law is devoted to co-operation and direct communication between a court of the enacting state and foreign courts or foreign representatives. This is a central plank of the Model Law. The provisions of Chapter IV are designed to facilitate communications of all kinds, in particular (a) court-to-court communication without time-consuming formalities such as the issue of letters rogatory; (b) direct communication between a foreign representative and a court in the enacting state; (c) communication between a local insolvency administrator and foreign courts or foreign representatives. This follows the pattern previously established by the courts without any statutory underpinning through co-operative arrangements between the insolvency administrators in the different states and between their respective courts.[68] Co-operation may be implemented by any appropriate means, including the appointment of a person or body to act at the direction of the court, communication of information by any means considered by the court, coordination of the administration and supervision of the debtor's affairs, approval or implementation by courts of agreements concerning the co-ordination of proceedings and coordination of concurrent proceedings regarding the same debtor.[69]

(9) Concurrent proceedings

14-44   After recognition of a foreign main proceeding, a proceeding in the enacting state may be commenced only if the debtor has assets in that state.[70] Where there is a foreign proceeding and concurrently a proceeding in the enacting state, the court must seek co-operation and co-ordination

---

[66] See generally Chap.13.
[67] Art.23.
[68] See above, paras 14–27 *et seq.*
[69] Art.27.
[70] Art.28.

under the earlier provisions and any relief granted to the foreign representative under Arts.19 or 21 in relation to the foreign proceedings must be consistent with the proceeding in the enacting state and, if granted prior to the commencement of the proceedings in the enacting state, must be reviewed and modified or terminated to ensure such consistency.[71] The situation envisaged here is that in which two proceedings are brought in the court of the enacting state, a proceeding for recognition of the foreign proceeding (main or non-main) in which relief is applied for or granted and a subsequent proceeding in the enacting state. Relief applied for in the earlier proceedings must be granted only so far as consistent with the later proceedings and relief already granted in the earlier proceedings must be modified or terminated as necessary to be consistent with the later proceedings. The effect, in relation to relief sought in the enacting state, is to subordinate the foreign proceeding to the local proceeding. Article 30 contains a similar provision for the co-ordination of two or more foreign proceedings.

(10) Presumption of insolvency

In the absence of evidence to the contrary, recognition of a foreign main proceeding is, for the purpose of commencing a proceeding in the enacting state, proof that the debtor is insolvent. The presumption of insolvency resulting from recognition of the foreign proceedings is thus rebuttable. A finding in proceedings in the enacting state that the debtor is not insolvent does not involve challenging a finding of insolvency in the foreign proceedings *for the purposes of those proceedings*, which is not permitted; the position is simply that when it comes to proceedings in the enacting state its courts are free to decide for themselves whether, for the purposes of those proceedings, the debtor is insolvent.

14–45

(11) Hotchpot

Finally, Art.32 adopts the hotchpot rule previously referred to,[72] making it clear that this does not affect secured claims or rights *in rem*, which under English law, as we have seen, fall outside the hotchpot rule, this being confined to receipts by the creditor from assets of the debtor, not from realisation of the creditor's own property or security; nor does Art.32 affect the ranking of claims.

14–46

---

[71] Art.29.
[72] Above, para.14–25.

INDEX